THE
VEGAN
ARMENIAN
KITCHEN
COOKBOOK

Recipes and Stories from
Armenia and the Armenian Diaspora

Written by **LENA TASHJIAN**
Photography by **SIROON PARSEGHIAN**

Vegan Armenian Kitchen

First published 2019

www.veganarmeniankitchen.com

Text
© **Lena Tashjian 2019**
Photography and styling
© **Siroon Parseghian 2019**
Copy edit and index
Adrineh Der-Boghossian
Cover and book design
Maria Dermosessian

ISBN 9781645507338

Printed and bound in Canada

10 9 8 7 6 5 4 3 2 1

CONTENTS

INTRODUCTION

«Հիմա ի՞նչ պիտի ուտենք» ("What will we eat now?") is a question as a child I would always ask after the end of a meal. My family loves to jokingly remind me of this and recall times I would say it even when we were guests at a relative's home. Although on the surface my question appears simply to be a case of a greedy child hoping to get another piece of dessert, I like to think it was a testament to something else. Armenian cuisine, in both the Armenian diaspora and Armenia, is associated with a never-ending sense of abundance, generosity, and oftentimes a grandmother who takes it upon herself to lovingly (or forcefully) make sure that everyone is well-fed. When I decided to adopt a plant-based diet, I admit I felt I would miss out on this style of dining I enjoyed so much.

And rightfully so. At first glance, Armenian cuisine does seem to be a very meat-centric one. Starters, sides, and even drinks are made as additions to the anticipated centerpiece, which is a meat dish (aside from times of Lenten willpower). But look more closely and you will discover how much of the cuisine is comprised mainly of plant-based foods. Though they are relegated to side dishes, they are still present in abundance and variety. Many of these dishes play an integral role in Armenian cuisine, and with a few minor tweaks or complementary additions, they can easily be upgraded to—and shine—as mains. While the mainstream plant-based movement was focused solely on vegan-izing anything and everything, I found comfort in being able to enjoy most of the foods I grew up with and that meant something to me, just as they were.

Despite this, when I moved to Armenia, I again began to see the cuisine in a meat-centric light. Stating I was vegan, or later, vegetarian, was at best met with curiosity and at worst seen as incomprehensible. Ironically, the more I traveled outside the capital city, where I was often cautioned to expect a lack of understanding of a plant-based diet, the more I began to (slowly) discover traditional foods that were vegan by default. Realizing a lot of these foods were associated with fasting periods and Great Lent—serious business in Armenia, as it was the first country to adopt Christianity as a state religion—I acknowledged that my choice of terminology («խիստ բուսակեր» / "strict plant-eater") was not doing me any favors. A small switch in language (Lenten rather than vegan) made a world of difference and opened the floodgates to a seemingly endless array of options. Most of the dishes came from Lenten creativity, some came from times of scarcity, and others were based on using what was abundantly available in the area.

More than anything, I loved learning about the stories behind the dishes, where they originated from, and the reasoning behind the names. The love and warmth I saw reflected in the eyes of grandmothers talking about the food they knew so well, and what it meant to them to be able to make it for their children and grandchildren, further demonstrated the important connection cuisine provides to history—even when that history is a tragic one. As both my maternal and paternal grandparents were survivors of the 1915 Armenian Genocide, I understood early on that food has meaning, and it is political. My grandparents used their memories of food and cooking as a way to tell stories of the lands they were forcefully removed from and to preserve this unrecognized history, passing it down from generation to generation.

When the idea of creating this cookbook arose as Siroon and I, who had met eight years prior in Armenia, were catching up, it was within the framework of a *vegan* Armenian cookbook. As I began to draw out the recipe lists for the different sections, removing things, adding things, remembering things, and learning new things, the entire concept I had in mind began to slowly—and, at the time, frightfully, be chipped away. Before long, I

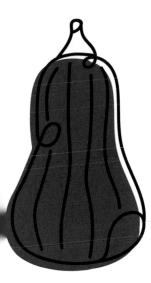

saw it as an Armenian cookbook, that *happened* to be vegan. Although there are a handful of vegan-ized, or I should say, Lenten-ized classics, the majority of the dishes are plant-based staples that have existed throughout history and have persevered through the simple act of storytelling.

In this context, this cookbook aims to showcase local and diasporan Armenian cuisine—traditional dishes, for the most part, just from a different perspective. The food still tells stories, is meant to unite people, and offers a source of connection to history.

To accomplish this goal, I am happy to work with Siroon, who, as a photographer, always focuses on bringing a different perspective to light, on showing a different side of a story. I still remember how on a mountaintop in Artsakh, while everyone took photos and felt content letting a majestic view do the work and speak for itself, Siroon made it her mission to portray the same view differently, as part of a larger narrative. She has transferred that same commitment and ingenuity to Armenian food, showcasing it through a unique and elevated lens. Her vision brings the cuisine to life, and her photos offer a harmonious balance between sentimentality of the traditional and necessity of the modern.

Vegan Armenian Kitchen is meant to serve as a resource for all things plant based within Armenian cuisine and to keep the recipes that so many grandparents painstakingly preserved in their memories alive and available. I had the privilege to learn many of these recipes from my own elders, from word of mouth, and from generous storytellers, and hope they continue to be created, shared, and enjoyed by everyone: vegan or not, Armenian or not.

At the very least, this cookbook serves as the answer to the ever-pressing «Հիմա ի՞նչ պիտի ուտենք» question!

HOW TO COOK WITH YOUR EYES
ԱՉՔԻ ՉԱՓ

The way my grandparents, mom, and aunts cooked always carried an element of mystery. They would never use recipes, measuring cups, or scales, but all seemed to instinctively know how to cook just about anything—no matter how complicated. While recipes were passed down to them and cherished, they rarely referred to them, and those recipes did tend to leave out some important details anyway, such as amounts. There were always unwritten rules in cooking they all knew and followed—some which made perfect sense, whereas others seemed to arise from folk wisdom, requiring an element of suspended belief. The food always spoke for itself, so believing was never that hard to do.

In most Armenian households, you will often hear the words *achki chap* when it comes to cooking. The concept, simple in theory, is to cook (or measure) everything with your eyes. It may seem like the antithesis of cooking with a recipe, but I believe it is a "tough love" way to encourage younger generations to *understand* food and cooking, rather than be weighed down by the specifics. It's a reminder that once you know the purpose behind a dish, using memory, intuition, or instinct, or a combination of all three, you will find a way to get the ingredients in front of you to where they need to be. Food has stories to tell, whether they are about family, history, necessity, or tradition, and *achki chap* promotes an important (and underrated) sense of mindfulness in cooking.

When my grandmother made large amounts of her famous *tolma* by hand, I never once saw her check notes, second-guess herself, or reach for a measuring cup. Watching her in her element was always a sight to see, and the idea of asking her for a recipe would have no doubt led her to say, «Դիտէ եւ սորվէ» ("Watch and learn!") as she would tell me about the dish and *why* it was made this specific way. She would famously end her explanations with «Ականջիդ օղ թող ըլլայ» ("Let it remain a piercing on your ears").

What is passed down from generation to generation tends to be this important concept rather than specific recipes. Once we understand the food—created sometimes out of tragedy, other times for celebration—it becomes part of us and can be recreated anytime, anywhere.

Although I was tempted to include those two famous words in at least a couple of the following recipes, I tried my best to anchor them with the necessary specifics as this *is* a cookbook, first and foremost.

I do hope that as you go through the recipes, however, you keep the magic of cooking *achki chapov* alive, and witness for yourself the genuine understanding of food that it encourages.

MEASURING GUIDE

CUPS

1 cup	**250 ml**
½ cup	**125 ml**
⅓ cup	**75 ml**
¼ cup	**60 ml**

SPOONS

1 tablespoon	**15 ml**
1 teaspoon	**5 ml**
½ teaspoon	**2.5 ml**
¼ teaspoon	**1.25 ml**
⅛ teaspoon	**0.625 ml**

VEGAN ARMENIAN ESSENTIALS

Before you begin your journey into vegan Armenian cooking, familiarize yourself with these kitchen staples and keep them on hand.

....

Որպէսզի մարդը ճանչնաս, անոր հետ բուռ մը աղ պետք է ուտես։
To know a person, you must eat a handful of salt with them.

SPICES

Coarse sea salt
Cinnamon
Cumin
Marash or Aleppo pepper
Urfa pepper

HERBS AND GREENS

Basil (purple or green)
Cilantro
Dill
Green onions
Mint
Parsley
Radish
Tarragon
Thyme

LEGUMES AND BEANS

Chickpeas
Green peas
Kidney beans (red and
    white)
Lentils (green, brown, and
    flat red)
Lima beans
Romano beans

GRAINS AND PASTAS

Flour
Orzo
Pearl barley
Peeled wheat
Quinoa
Semolina
Spelt
Vermicelli
White bulgur (fine and
    coarse)
White rice (short and long
    grain)

NUTS, SEEDS, AND DRIED FRUITS

Chia seeds
Currants
Dried apricots
Dried plums
Golden raisins
Pumpkin seeds
Sesame seeds (white and
    black)
Sunflower seeds
Tahini
Walnuts

SAVORY

Assorted pickles
Olive oil
Olives
Pepper (red and black)
Soy milk or coconut milk
    yogurt
Tomato paste

SWEET

Fruit jams
Molasses
Rose water
Simple syrup

EXTRAS

Black salt
Mahaleb
Mastic gum
Nutritional yeast
Turmeric

SAUCES
AND
EXTRAS

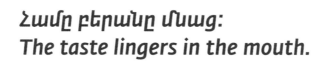

Համը բերանը մաց:
The taste lingers in the mouth.

Armenian food can stand on its own, its flavors and ingredients checking off all the bases. But once you are equipped with the staples of the Armenian pantry, you can try adding the spice mixes, infused oils, pastes, sauces and dressings, and syrups that elevate the already existent flavors found in Armenian cuisine.

CONTENTS

Armenian Herb Mix
Խառն համեմունք

The spice staples of the Armenian pantry join forces to provide an immediate flavor boost to just about any meal. I love sprinkling this on toast spread with tahini, over a stir-fry, and as a final touch to Vegetable Skewers (page 174).

1 tbsp cumin powder
½ tsp Marash pepper flakes
1 tsp Urfa pepper flakes
¼ tsp dried mint
½ tsp onion powder
½ tsp garlic powder
¼ tsp salt

Mix all spices together into a bowl and stir well. Transfer to an empty spice bottle and shake before each use.

Tip While you can add this spice mix during the cooking process, it tastes best on food that is already cooked.

Tatkhan
Թաթխան

As a result of the massive Armenian diaspora throughout the world, including a concentration in the Middle East, many Armenians grew up with a healthy dose of Middle Eastern classics such as hummus, tabouleh, and of course za'atar. I knew my obsession with za'atar in particular, an herb mix, signified something, and I was beyond fascinated to first learn about *tatkhan* when living in Armenia. Derived from the Armenian word *tatkhel* (to dip), it is a mix of herbs, spices, nuts, and seeds reminiscent of the one I grew up with and loved. Unfortunately, the recipe kindly given to me did not

withstand the test of time other than a few barely legible notes, but I remembered it originated from the Armenians of Musa Ler and Kharpert. Using the power of social media, I asked if anyone had family from either of these regions, providing an extremely vague description of the recipe to the many proud grandchildren of the people of Musa Ler and Kharpert who responded. One respondent, Lori Boghigian, whose grandmother Armenouhi Boghigian used to prepare *tatkhan*, shared her recipe with me. Below is Lori's family recipe, with a few additions from the recipe I originally had. Mixed with oil and served with freshly baked bread, you may find yourself unable to stop *tatkhel*-ing.

....

1 cup wheat berries
½ cup dry chickpeas
½ cup raw sunflower seeds, shelled
½ cup raw pumpkin seeds, shelled
½ cup sesame seeds
1 cup mixed nuts (walnuts, pistachios, almonds)
½ cup thyme
1 tbsp cumin seeds
1 tbsp Marash pepper (or to taste)
1 tbsp black pepper (or to taste)
1 tbsp salt (or to taste)
¼ cup watermelon seeds (optional)
¼ cup of savory (optional)

Roast each ingredient (except the peppers and salt) individually in a pan on medium-low heat, removing them from the heat just before they brown. If preferred, you can buy many of these ingredients already roasted to skip this step. After roasting them and once they have cooled, finely grind each ingredient separately. Combine all ingredients, as well as the salt, black pepper, Marash pepper, savory, and watermelon seeds (if using) and mix well, storing in an airtight jar. When ready to serve, shake well, spoon out the desired amount in a bowl and add enough olive oil to allow for easy dipping. Dip freshly baked bread and enjoy.

....

Suggestion Pair with fresh tomatoes, cucumbers, and mint for a great addition to any breakfast table!

Did you know? The kernel found in apricot pits are collected in Armenia and throughout the diaspora and eaten as snacks or enjoyed in recipes such as this one. Apricot kernels contain amygdalin, which our body converts to cyanide. The recipe for *tatkhan* traditionally includes apricot seed kernels, but I removed them from the recipe. If you choose to include them, make sure you do your research and be safe!

Tomato Paste
Լուիկի մածուկ
makes 2 cups

As tomatoes are a staple in Armenian cooking, it should come as no surprise that the end of the summer does not mean an end of the enjoyment of tomatoes—we are way too stubborn for that. My maternal grandmother spent a good portion of her summers drying out halved tomatoes in the sun all day to store and use throughout the winter, and use the rest of her bounty to make delicious tomato paste—a must in so many meals. Though tomato paste can be store-bought, making it at home means it is free of additives and preservatives and uses both the skin and seeds, making it less wasteful.

15 Roma (Italian plum) tomatoes
1 tsp salt

Chop the tomatoes by hand or with a food processor. Add to a pot and bring to a boil. Reduce the heat to medium, and about 15 minutes later, remove as much of the foam as possible. Add salt (adjusting according to taste). Cook for 30 to 45 more minutes, until the liquid has significantly reduced. Turn off the heat and allow paste to cool. Transfer to clean jar(s) and allow to cool before securing lid. Store in the fridge for up to one week or in a freezer-safe jar or bag in the freezer for up to one year.

Tip You can also follow this recipe to make tomato sauce. Simply add herbs or seasoning of your choice and halfway through the recommended cooking time, remove from heat so the sauce doesn't thicken into a paste.

Red Pepper Paste
Կարմիր պղպեղի մածուկ
makes 2 cups

The reasoning behind the red pepper version of tomato paste is the same: a desire to prolong the goodness of something seasonal throughout the year, especially for recipes made in the winter. Traditionally prepared with spicy red peppers, red pepper paste can be made milder by mixing in some sweet peppers.

15 red crimson peppers (can mix with red Cubanelle)
1 tsp salt

Core your peppers, deseeding them. Using a blender or food processor, blend or process your peppers into a paste. Add to a pot and bring to a boil. Reduce heat to medium, and about 15 minutes later, remove as much of the foam as possible. Add salt (adjusting according to taste). Cook for 30 to 45 more minutes, until the liquid has significantly reduced. Turn off the heat and allow paste to cool. Transfer to clean jar(s) and allow to cool before securing lid. Store in the fridge for up to one week or in a freezer-safe bag in the freezer for up to one year.

Red Pepper-Infused Oil
Կարմիր պղպեղով համեմուած բուսական իւղ

Infused oils are great to have on hand, as they provide an immediate flavor boost and a beautiful touch of color to the many soups in Armenian cuisine. They are also perfect for dipping freshly baked bread in, a definite (and colorful) upgrade when it comes to the common bread/oil appetizer.

6 tbsp oil
1 tsp Marash pepper (or paprika)

Warm oil in a small pot over medium heat, add pepper and swirl. Cook for one minute, then remove from heat. Allow to cool then pour into an airtight container as is or strain the oil from the pepper.

Mint-Infused Oil
Անանուխով համեմուած բուսական իւղ

Red pepper–infused oil may be more commonly used in Armenian cooking, but yogurt-based dishes, a classic of the cuisine, are just not the same without a swirl of this incredibly aromatic oil.

6 tbsp oil
¾ tsp dried mint

Warm oil in a small pot over medium heat, add dried mint, and swirl. Cook for one minute, then remove from heat. Allow to cool then pour into an airtight container as is or strain the oil from the flakes.

Simple Syrup
Պարզ շաքարաջուր

Some of the desserts in this cookbook require this simple syrup, also known as *tertanoush* or baklava syrup, as that is its main purpose. It's a good option to keep in the fridge as a simple sweetener instead of honey for teas, desserts, and even within *ghapama*, a stuffed pumpkin.

2 cups sugar
1 cup water
1 tbsp lemon juice
1½ tsp rose water
(optional)

Combine sugar and water in a saucepan and bring to a boil. No need to stir. Once the mixture is boiling, reduce heat to low-medium, and cook for 10 minutes. Stir in the lemon juice and cook for another 3 to 4 minutes before removing from heat and adding in the rose water (if using). Allow to cool completely, pour into an airtight container, and store in the fridge.

Garlic Yogurt
Սխտորով մածուն

The eternal inclusion of yogurt in savory foods in Armenian cuisine is highlighted with this recipe, which goes perfectly on *yeghints*, soups, stews, mains, and just about everything in between— drizzled lightly or generously.

1 cup Soy Milk or Coconut Milk Yogurt
1 garlic clove, grated or minced
1 to 2 tbsp lemon juice
Pinch of salt
Pinch of Marash or Urfa pepper (optional)

Whisk or stir yogurt until smooth. Add salt to taste and stir. Add the garlic, then the lemon juice, stir well, and taste. Add more salt, garlic, or lemon as preferred.

Tahini Sauce
Սուսամի (քունճութի) մածուկ

Armenians from historically different regions may share the same basic recipe, but depending on where they are from, they may prepare and even serve a dish very differently. I may be biased toward Marash cuisine, since my father's side of the family is from this region and my paternal grandmother was always my favorite cook, but I do believe the following tahini sauce speaks for itself. Traditionally served over Lenten pepper, eggplant, and zucchini *tolma*, this dish can easily be used as a dip or dressing for just about any meal.

3 tbsp tahini
2 tbsp lemon juice
¼ tsp cumin
1 garlic clove, minced or grated
2 tbsp water
Pinch of salt

Stir or whisk the tahini is a bowl well until smooth. Add the lemon juice, which will thicken it, then gradually add the water, until well blended. Add the garlic, cumin, and salt, and stir well. The sauce will thicken in the fridge. For a thinner consistency, add small amounts of water until desired consistency is reached.

Pomegranate Molasses
Նուռի մեղրակ
makes 1 cup

Armenian cuisine uses molasses from a variety of sources: grapes, dates, figs, and more. Pomegranate molasses is simply a versatile way to keep the beloved flavor of fresh pomegranates alive in every season. The use of the molasses extends beyond sweet dishes into savory ones as well, making it a great addition to every kitchen.

4 cups pomegranate juice
⅔ cup sugar
¼ cup lemon juice

Boil all igredients in a saucepan or pot over medium-high heat. As the mixture warms, stir to dissolve the sugar. Once the mixture comes to a boil, reduce heat to medium-low. Allow mixture to simmer for about an hour, stirring occasionally. After 30 minutes, if you notice the mixture has reduced significantly, you can lower the heat. At the one-hour mark, lightly dip a wooden spoon in the mixture, and then lift it, allowing the first few drops to fall back into the pot. The last drop should lag and drip off the spoon slowly. Alternatively, you can place about a teaspoon of the mixture on a flat plate and allow it to cool. The molasses is ready when you turn the plate sideways and the mixture gradually slides down. If the mixture is too thin, boil it for an additional 15 to 30 minutes. Once it is done, remove from heat and allow it to cool before pouring in a jar. It will thicken once completely cooled and kept in the fridge.

Կուտ կ'ուտէ երկինք կ'ելլէ

Eat seeds; rise to heaven.

Toasted Seeds
Ատացած կուտեր

There is an art to eating sunflower seeds, which is only evident when you witness professionals do it. The ability to crack open and eat the sunflower seed in one move is by far the most impressive, followed by those who put a few seeds in their mouths and shell them in an instant. Snacking on salted and roasted sunflower seeds is very common in both Armenia and the Armenian diaspora; in fact, a common sight is a group of men, standing or squatting, eating sunflower seeds, creating piles from the shells right below them as they chat or smoke. Pumpkin seeds are also very popular, usually collected fresh during fall and especially resulting from making ghapama. *In Armenia, I enjoyed a new seed mix: toasted and salted hemp seeds and wheat. Whichever seeds you choose, they all make perfect snacks, whether for the road, for an informal gathering, or when in squat-mode.*

Pumpkin Seeds
Դդումի կուտեր

1 cup raw pumpkin seeds (or as much as one pumpkin will yield)
Salt, to taste (optional)

If using seeds from a fresh pumpkin, remove as much pulp from the seeds as possible before placing them in a bowl, covering them with water, rinsing them thoroughly and draining the water/excess pulp. Place them on a towel and pat dry. Preheat the oven to 350ºF (180ºC). Place the pumpkin seeds in a bowl and add salt (if using), giving the mix a good stir. Spread the seeds in a layer on the baking sheet and bake for 20 to 25 minutes until they have completely dried and are crunchy.

Sunflower Seeds
Արեւածաղիկի կուտեր

1 cup raw
sunflower seeds
2 tbsp coarse sea salt
1½ cups water

Mix the salt and water in a bowl. Add the sunflower seeds and allow the mixture to sit for 6 to 8 hours, or overnight. Alternatively, heat the salt and water in a saucepan, add the sunflower seeds and bring the mixture to a boil, then simmer on medium-low for 15 minutes. Preheat the oven to 400ºF (200ºC). Drain the seeds, shaking off any excess water, and lay them on a baking sheet. Bake for 12 to 15 minutes, checking the seeds after 12 minutes.

Tip For a salt-free alternative, preheat the oven to 400ºF (200ºC), spread 1 cup of dry sunflower seeds on a baking sheet, and bake for 2 to 3 minutes. They can go from perfectly roasted to burned very quickly, so make sure to keep an eye on them!

Aghants
Աղանձ

1 cup wheat kernels
½ cup raw whole hemp
seeds (not hemp
hearts)
3 to 5 tbsp salt

Sort through the wheat kernels and hemp seeds and remove any debris or stones you find. In a bowl, combine 1½ cups water with a few heaping tablespoons of salt and stir to allow the salt to dissolve. Rinse the hemp seeds in a strainer and add them to the bowl, letting them soak in the salt water for a few hours. After the hemp seeds have soaked, rinse the wheat kernels in a strainer and drain the excess water. Warm a pan on medium heat, then add the wheat kernels, toasting until golden brown. Shake the pan or use a wooden spoon to move the wheat kernels around to ensure they are evenly toasted and don't burn. Once they are toasted thoroughly, place them in a bowl, leaving the stove on. Drain the hemp seeds, removing as much excess water as possible, and place them in the same pan, toasting them for a few minutes until they dry and begin to pop. Then add them to the same bowl with the wheat kernels and mix well. Allow to cool and enjoy.

Suggestion Some variations also add chickpeas and sesame seeds. Feel free to mix and match.

DRINKS

Երբ ջուր կը խմես, մի մոռնար աղբիւրը: When you drink water, never forget the source.

When you think of Armenian beverages, coffee (սուրճ) may be the first—and only—one that comes to mind. And for good reason: Armenians are definitely a coffee-loving people. Spend some time in Armenia, however, and you will quickly discover how just about any plant, herb, or fruit can be turned into a juice, tea, remedy, or even vodka.

Teas generally get the short end of the stick in the hierarchy of preferred hot beverages, but due to Armenia's long history of folk medicine and herbal remedies, teas are often presented (and respected) as a remedy for common ailments, with the added bonus that the herbs are abundantly available and accessible. Most often, the ingredients in tea are intentionally chosen, the herbs or dried fruits offering some sort of benefit to the drinker. In Armenia, you quickly learn that if you have an ailment, there's a tea (or teas) for that. Perhaps a shocking contradiction to some, alcohol is a close second to tea in terms of purported health benefits.

The art of making a toast (կենաց): every country and culture has its unique way of toasting, and Armenia is no exception. With shot glasses filled to the brim with Armenian moonshine (fruit-infused vodka) or cognac, guests are treated to a different toast with every newly poured glass, most often on the themes of health, wealth, and family. Toasts can also be personalized for an event (wedding) or individualized for the host or guests. Often, a toastmaster, who is responsible for keeping the toasts (and drinks) coming, is appointed. And the more alcohol that is consumed, the longer and more elaborate the toasts tend to become—a few words never cut it. A toast to parents and elders is usually made at the end, because no matter how much alcohol is consumed, older generations are *too* important to forget. If Armenian folk wisdom is true, most of the alcoholic drinks in this section offer some sort of health benefit, so you can always keep that in mind as you toast to another round!

CONTENTS

Armenian Coffee
Սուրճ
serves 2

Any time is a good time for Armenian coffee, or սուրճ. In the morning, as a midday post-lunch pick-me-up, with a cigarette, as a treat on a break from work, with dessert, and even after dinner for its supposed digestion benefits. Some even claim that unlike other coffee, Armenian coffee will not keep you up at night, justifying late-night cravings for its signature taste. While the last claim is definitely debatable, the process of making Armenian coffee and the traditions associated with it may be what keeps us all coming back for more.

Reading coffee grounds, or tasseography, is popularly associated with enjoying Armenian coffee. Almost all coffee drinkers, even the non-believers, will instinctively turn over their coffee cups once finished in the hopes that someone will read the cryptic coffee grounds, which can represent the past, present, and future. For a coffee cup to be read, all of the coffee must be consumed until there is nothing left but the grounds. You can always recognize the rookies when they look at you with coffee grounds all over their teeth, show you the inside of their almost-empty coffee cups, and ask, "Is this much okay?" Once the coffee has been consumed, the cup is turned upside down on the saucer, away from the drinker. It is left to dry and is then observed by an expert, usually self-appointed. Some read coffee cups in seconds without skipping a beat (often the older generations, who have done this for far too long), while some take their time, interpreting everything in detail, presenting it as a story. Listeners will make (or create) the connections immediately, sometimes even writing down every word for reflection later. Once the grounds are read, the coffee drinker is expected to "seal" their fortune by pressing their finger in the grinds three times. The resulting image can be considered an added bonus. Sometimes, the saucer is also turned sideways over the cup, draining any excess liquid and — surprise, the image that is formed is also read. While the magic of reading coffee grounds is based on the belief of the person whose fortune is being read, reading coffee grounds is an art that not everyone can (or wants to) do, making the older generations all the more eager to pass on this tradition and keep it alive.

There are different ways to prepare Armenian coffee, foam being the most important differentiating factor. When I was growing up, foam was revered and had to be portioned out equally for everyone the coffee was being served to. It was considered a mishap if the coffee was boiled too long, which would dissipate the foam. However, in Armenia, the opposite seems to hold true. Foam is seen as something to be boiled "out" of the coffee, to keep the coffee clean and light. Serving coffee with foam, no matter how little, is a sign of coffee improperly—or worse, carelessly—prepared. My advice to anyone planning to serve these cups of caffeine is to remove any guesswork out of the equation and ask guests directly what their preference is. When it comes to Armenians and their coffee, there is no such thing as taking it *too* seriously.

....

2 tsp ground Armenian coffee
⅔ cup water
Sugar (optional and to taste)

with foam
In a small pot, combine water and coffee and stir. Add sugar if using. Boil on high heat until the coffee rises and bubbles. Remove from heat. Pour equal amounts of foam into both cups, then fill with remaining liquid.

without foam
In a small pot, combine water and coffee and stir. Add sugar if using. Boil on high heat until the coffee begins to rise, then lower heat to maintain boiling. Once foam has dissipated, remove pot from heat and pour coffee into cups.

....

Did you know? Armenian merchants Pascal (Haroutiun) and Johannes Diodato (or Hovhannes Astvatsatour) are credited with opening some of the first cafes in Europe (Paris and Vienna, respectively). The name Haroutiun means "resurrection" and Astvatsatour means "God-given," which may shed some light on why coffee is so revered among Armenians.

Chicory Coffee
Եղերդի արմատով սուրճ
serves 2

Unlike coffee beans, chicory *does* grow in Armenia. Since too much of a good thing can be a bad thing, as with the copious amounts of coffee Armenians enjoy, chicory root coffee offers a caffeine-free (and locally grown) alternative to coffee.

2 tbsp roasted and ground chicory powder
4 cups water

Bring water to a simmer in a pot. Once water begins to simmer on medium-high heat, add chicory powder. When water begins to boil, turn off the heat and allow to steep for 5 minutes. Strain into mugs and add plant milk/creamer alternative and/or sweetener of choice!

Alternatively, use a coffeemaker, simply substituting coffee grounds with chicory powder.

TEAS

All of the following teas can be sweetened with simple syrup (page 19).

Mint Tea
Անանուխի թեյ
serves 2

Mint grows wild in Armenia, and when the season is right, you can take in its wonderful aroma outdoors, a memory I will never forget when I stood on a hilltop in Dilijan. Both fresh and dried mint are used, and since mint is known to help alleviate nausea and improve digestion, mint tea remains one of the most popular and beloved teas in the Armenian kitchen.

2 tsp dried mint or 15 leaves fresh mint
2 cups boiling water

Add the dried mint to a teapot and pour the boiling water over the dried mint and stir. Allow tea to steep covered for 5 minutes. Use a strainer to pour the tea.

If using fresh mint, twist the leaves to release their flavor and place them in a small pot. Pour the boiling water over the leaves on boil on medium heat for two minutes. Allow the tea to steep covered for 10 minutes. Use a strainer to pour the tea.

Enjoy hot, or allow to cool and add ice for a refreshing summer drink.

Thyme Tea
Ուրցի թեյ
serves 2

At the first sign of a cough or a sore throat, a glass of hot thyme tea is quickly suggested. A beautiful herb that is often collected and dried with its purple flowers in bloom, it is considered a remedy for a cold and touted as an immune system booster.

5 tsp dried thyme or 7 tsp fresh thyme leaves
2 cups boiling water

Place the dried thyme in a teapot, pour the boiling water over it, and stir. Allow tea to steep covered for 10 minutes. Use a strainer to pour the tea.

If using fresh, place the leaves in a small pot. Pour the boiling water over the leaves and boil for two minutes on medium heat. Allow tea to steep for 15 minutes. Use a strainer to pour the tea.

Enjoy hot, or allow to cool and add ice for a refreshing summer drink.

Rose Hip Tea
Մասուրի թեյ
serves 2

Rose hips are the edible pods of the rose plant and are used both fresh and dried. Once roses bloom in fall, rose hips are harvested, and you will see them sold in every market throughout Armenia—their beautiful bright red color is impossible to miss. Their season seems to be perfectly timed, since they are high in vitamin C, and we can all use some extra antioxidants just in time for the long and cold winter ahead.

2 tbsp crushed dried rose hip or ½ cup fresh rose hips
2 cups boiling water

Place the dried rose hips in a teapot and pour the boiling water over them. If using fresh, add to a pot with 2 cups of water, bring to a boil, reduce to medium, use a potato masher to flatten and crush the pods, and boil for 5 to 7 minutes. Steep (covered) for 10 minutes. When pouring tea into a cup, use a strainer to remove the pulp.

Pomegranate Peel Tea
Նուռի կեղևի թեյ

serves 1

Pomegranates are very symbolic in Armenian culture, and the fruit will be a recurring theme throughout this cookbook. This tea is made using not the ruby-esque arils found within the fruit, but rather, the peel. Prior to living in Armenia, I had no idea pomegranate peel was dried and boiled as a tea, offered as a remedy for stomach aches, and more commonly, used to alleviate menstrual cramps. Although it can be sweetened, the tea is not as bitter as you may think.

10 grams dried pomegranate peel
1 cup water

Place pomegranate peel in a pot, add water, and bring to a boil. Reduce to a low simmer and continue boiling for 15 minutes, covered. Enjoy warm.

Did you know? *You can learn more about herbal remedies and folk medicine in Armenia and in Armenian culture by visiting the Matenadaran Institute of Ancient Manuscripts in Yerevan, Armenia.*

Pomegranate Juice
Նուռի օշարակ
serves 1 or 2

Pomegranates are treasured in Armenian culture due to their rich symbolism: life, good fortune, fertility, and abundance. It is often said that each pomegranate contains 365 arils, one for each day of the year. A few traditions associated with this fruit include new business owners breaking one to bring good fortune to their business ("one fruit contains many seeds") and new brides breaking one open at their weddings to ensure they bear many children. A popular scene from the 2002 film *Ararat* depicts a character (played by the renowned late French-Armenian chansonnier Charles Aznavour) refusing to leave customs until he eats every aril of the pomegranate he packed to "bring luck in [his] stomach" after learning he cannot bring the fruit with him. For better or worse, pomegranate designs have become so widespread in Armenia, mostly to appease traveling diasporans looking to bring souvenirs home with them, that it is difficult to find items without their imagery proudly displayed.

Option 1
1 pomegranate

Cut open the pomegranate and carefully extract all of the arils, placing them in a blender. Blend until they are crushed. Pour the blended pomegranate arils into a container using a strainer, and use the back of a spoon to apply pressure on the strainer so that all the liquid is released. Enjoy immediately or transfer to bottle or jar and store in the fridge for up to three days.

Option 2
1 tbsp pomegranate molasses
1 cup water or soda water
Ice (optional)

Combine pomegranate molasses and water and stir well. Add ice and enjoy.

Suggestion: There are numerous hacks and how-to's associated with opening pomegranates. My best advice is to avoid wearing white (or any item of clothing you don't want stained) and to cut around the top of the pomegranate (the side with the "crown," or calyx), deep enough to be able to remove the crown when pulled firmly. Next, make four evenly spread cuts lengthwise and break open the fruit, holding the top end (where the crown was). Tackle each chunk of the fruit at a time, removing the arils in a bowl.

Sea Buckthorn Juice
Չիչխանի օշարակ

serves 1 or 2

The first time I saw sea buckthorn juice was on the way back to Yerevan from a day trip to Lake Sevan. Stand after makeshift stand along the road was dedicated to selling this vibrant orange liquid in reused plastic bottles, giving the drink an almost radioactive appearance. The bus driver stopped near one of the stands, and most of the passengers exited to stock up on these mysterious bottles. I soon learned that sea buckthorn juice has its season in Armenia and grows in abundance around Lake Sevan. Due primarily to the high levels of beta-carotene and vitamin C found in the fruit, the beverage is considered ideal for vitality and immunity. Though you can enjoy it however you like, a sweetener-free shot every morning for good health is how I will continue to consume this tart drink when I am in Armenia.

2 cups fresh sea buckthorn berries, washed with the stems removed
Water (optional)
Sweetener (optional)

Place the sea buckthorn berries in a blender and blend thoroughly. You can add water to dilute the juice and offset some of the sourness. Use a strainer to filter the liquid from the pulp, making sure to press down on the pulp with the back of a spoon to extract as much liquid as possible. Add sweetener if using. Enjoy immediately or transfer to a bottle or jar and store in fridge for two to three days.

Tahn
Թան
serves 2

Tahn is a delicious and refreshing drink made from tangy yogurt, water, and lots of salt. Considered a beverage perfect for the summer (perhaps due to the electrolytes), it is traditionally served in clay cups to keep cool. Fresh or dried mint or dill can be added for a little color and extra taste.

....

1 cup Soy Milk or Coconut Milk Yogurt (page 212)
1 cup water, or enough to reach desired consistency
¼ tsp sea salt
Pinch of dried mint (optional)
Ice cubes (optional)

Stir yogurt with a spoon or whisk until it is completely smooth and free of clumps. Add salt (remember that *tahn* is meant to be salty!) and mint (if using) and stir. Add water gradually, stirring well until desired consistency is reached. Pour into two cups, add ice cubes, and garnish each cup with fresh mint and cucumber.

....

Suggestion *You can use the water released from homemade or store-bought vegan yogurt in this recipe instead of (or in combination with) plain water.*

Suggestion *Try using a blender to blend the yogurt, water, salt, and mint for a few seconds to enjoy a frothy alternative!*

Pairing suggestion *Enjoy with freshly made* **Jingalov Hats** *(page 145)!*

Mulberry-Infused Vodka
Թութի օղի
serves 18 to 20

Vodka is made in Armenia from just about any fruit, including peach, apricot, cornelian cherry, and blackberry. But mulberry vodka, commonly referred to as the Armenian moonshine, reigns supreme. Homemade options in reused bottles are found at farmers markets throughout the country, and the refined versions are commercially available at major supermarkets. You will be hard-pressed to find any gathering, party, or celebration where toasts are being made without this popular (and *very* strong) drink. As with all prepared beverages in Armenia, mulberry vodka is believed to have beneficial health properties, often recommended to alleviate cold symptoms or to keep the body healthy. One shot may be all you need to stay clear of doctors, if you believe Armenian folk wisdom. The following is not the authentic recipe for mulberry vodka, but the next best thing: mulberry-infused vodka.

2 cups ripe mulberries, washed and patted dry
3 cups vodka (40% alcohol)

Place mulberries in a clean jar. Lightly mash them with a large utensil. Pour the vodka over the berries, making sure they are all completely covered. Place the jar in a dark room or cabinet for at least three days. On the third day, give the jar a good shake, and using a strainer, pour the vodka into a clean bottle or jar, and discard the fruit.

Suggestion *If you cannot find mulberries in your area, or prefer a sweeter alternative, use raspberries instead!*

Hot Brandy
Տաք գոնեակ
serves 1

Hot toddies are the inspiration behind this recipe since they are often treated as seasonal remedies to colds. During the winter in Armenia, brandy is often mixed in tea for the same reason. The best of both worlds is combined in this delicious, warming, and (arguably) cold-preventing drink!

¼ cup (2 oz) brandy
¾ cup hot water
   (optionally, black
   tea)
1 slice (wheel) of lemon
4 cloves
1 cinnamon stick
1 tsp pomegranate
   molasses

Bring the water to a boil. In a mug, add the brandy and pomegranate molasses. Mix thoroughly. Slice the lemon in half, slicing a lemon wheel from one of the halves. Insert four cloves in the flesh of the lemon and put it in the mug. Place the cinnamon stick in the mug. Add the hot water and give it a good stir for all the flavors to blend. Enjoy warm!

Holiday Drink
Տօնական խմիչք
serves 20 to 25

In some households, this Holiday Drink is a staple from New Year's Eve to Armenian Christmas (January 6). This recipe requires a bit of planning as it must be made in advance — 40 days, to be precise.

1L vodka
10 cups water
6 cups sugar
40 green walnuts
10 cloves
10 cinnamon sticks

Combine vodka, water, sugar, and walnuts in a large clean jar and keep it in a dark room or cupboard for 40 days. Using a strainer, pour the liquid in a pot and add the cinnamon and cloves. Bring mixture to a boil and simmer for five minutes. Remove from heat and let cool. Enjoy cold!

Pomegranate Sangria
Նուռի խմիչք (սանկրիա)
serves 6

Sangria may have no place in Armenia's history, but the art of winemaking does, as the earliest known winery was discovered near Areni village in 2007 by a team of archeologists, dating back 6,100 years. Today, you can taste the wide variety of delicious Armenian wines, including Van Ardi, at the widely popular Areni Wine Festival, which celebrates wine and the traditions associated with it every fall. Enjoy this sangria recipe, which combines the love of pomegranates with Van Ardi's Areni, Kakhet, and Haghtanak grape blend.

....

1 bottle (750 mL) Van Ardi's Classic Blend or a dry or semi-dry vegan red wine
2 cups pomegranate juice
⅓ cup brandy
2 tbsp pomegranate molasses
1 cup seasonal fruit: thinly sliced peaches, oranges, and/or pomegranate seeds (optional)
Fresh mint, to garnish (optional)
Ice, crushed or cubed

Pour the wine and pomegranate juice in a pitcher. In a separate glass, thoroughly mix the brandy and pomegranate molasses. Add this mixture to the pitcher and stir well. Add fruit (if including). When serving, add a generous amount of ice and garnish with mint leaves.

Armenian-Style Old Fashioned
Գոնեակ ընկոյզի անուշով
serves 1

Enjoy this Armenian take on the classic cocktail, with Tazah's Green Walnut Preserve, which is made in Armenia. Notes of clove and cinnamon from the walnut preserve pair perfectly with the rich flavor of Armenian brandy.

¼ cup (2 oz) brandy
1 tsp walnut preserve syrup and one preserved walnut from Tazah's Green Walnut Preserve or other walnut preserve
Mandarin or orange peel
Ice cube (optional)

Combine the walnut preserve syrup with a splash of water in a glass and stir. Add the brandy and stir well. Twist the mandarin or orange peel over the glass, releasing its juices into the drink. Place your preserved walnut in the glass, or pierce it with a toothpick and place over the glass. Garnish with the twisted mandarin or orange peel. Add ice if desired.

Armenian brandy, *also referred to as cognac, kanyak, or konyak struggled with its identity in its long history. Armenian brandy produced by Shustov & Sons (now the Yerevan Brandy Company) won the Grand Prix at the 1900 Paris Exposition, after French judges blind tasted it alongside local options. The award put Armenia's homegrown beloved beverage on the map, which was legally permitted to be sold under the name "cognac." However, the right to label the drink as such was eventually revoked by the European Union. Since then, the Armenian government has been trying — and failing — to have the decision overturned, attempting to do so as late as 2013. If a drink is not legally allowed to be sold as cognac, is it still cognac? Whatever you choose to call it, it provides a rich and deep base for the drinks on these pages.*

BREAKFAST

Անուշ ըլլայ:
May it be sweet.

Armenian breakfast is defined by two polar opposites: on weekends and holidays, it usually resembles a dinner-esque buffet: lots of options, lots of bread, and a nice (or overwhelming) mix of savory and sweet dishes to choose from. There are also many convenient on-the-go options available, most notably a simple wrap with lavash, salty cheese, and seasonal herbs, or the sweeter alternative of honey and butter also wrapped in lavash. While I did have some internal struggles including some of the following sweets in this section rather than in the dessert section where they may appear to be a more sensible fit, I've heard many times that a little something sweet (անուշ) in the morning will set your day to be all the sweeter, and I think we can all learn to treat ourselves a little more.

CONTENTS

Fruit Jam
Պտուղի անուշ

Jams are a great way to enjoy the goodness of every season throughout the year, and in a country known for its fruit, jams have a special place in almost every kitchen in Armenia—and throughout the Armenian diaspora. Jams saved me at traditional breakfasts in Armenia: while breakfast included many vegetarian options, such as eggs, cheese, yogurt, sour cream, butter, and honey, substantial vegan options were not always as easy to find. In Armenia, I learned to seek out vegan options at breakfast at every opportunity, mixing a delicious homemade apricot, peach, fig, sour cherry, and even pine cone jam with seeds or nuts, and spreading it generously on lavash or *matnakash* bread. The general rule of thumb to make this spread is to use half the amount of sugar to fruit (that is, 500 g sugar to 1 kg peach), and to use the ripest fruit possible. If the fruit is sour, increase the amount of sugar to 750 g to 1 kg.

....

1 kg peach
½ kg sugar
2 tbsp lemon juice

Halve the peaches and remove the pits. Weigh them to ensure they are 1 kg. Cube or finely chop.

Add the peaches to a large bowl, and pour the sugar on top, shaking the pot to ensure the sugar is distributed evenly. Allow fruit to sit overnight at room temperature. By this time, a lot of liquid will have been released. Pour the mixture into a pot and bring to a simmer on low-medium heat. Without stirring, allow jam to cook for 30 minutes. Then add the lemon juice and cook for an additional 3 to 5 minutes. To ensure jam is ready, take about 1 teaspoon of the liquid out and place it on a clean plate. Once it cools, turn the plate sideways, and if the mixture runs slowly, like a syrup, it is done. If it is still very runny, cook until you achieve syrup consistency.

Remove from heat. Once the jam is no longer boiling, use a potato masher to mash all of the fruit chunks into desired consistency. Allow to cool completely, then pour jam into clean jars or containers and place them in the fridge for up to six months.

....

Suggestion *If desired, peel the fruits before halving for a smoother consistency.*

Rose Jam
Վարդի անուշ

My great-grandmother was known for her delicious rose jam, a result of the rose garden she cared for meticulously. My mother always told me that preparation of the rose jam left the most wonderful aroma throughout the house, which would linger all through the night, making everyone dream about the rose jam they would be able to enjoy the following morning. Though a lack of rose gardens in my area means I tend to buy this specialty jam more than I make it, perhaps one day I will follow in my great-grandmother's footsteps and have a rose garden of my own, with a home that offers guests the true definition of sweet dreams.

1 kg edible rose petals
3 lemons
3 kg sugar
7 cups water

Rinse the rose petals well and then strain and pat them dry thoroughly. Place the dry rose petals in a container. Juice the lemons and pour the lemon juice over the rose petals. Massage the rose petals with the lemon juice until wilted. Remove the rose petals, squeezing them so the excess liquid remains in the container, and set them aside.

In a pot, bring the water to a boil, then reduce heat to medium and add the sugar, allowing it to dissolve completely, stirring occasionally, about 3 to 4 minutes. Add the rose petals to the pot, then pour in the lemon-rose juice. Gently mix and keep boiling the liquid for 30 to 40 minutes (the thicker the rose petals, the longer the cooking time). Occasionally stir the jam lightly on the surface, avoiding stirring too deeply. Take about 1 teaspoon of the liquid out and place it on a clean plate. Once it cools, turn the plate sideways, and if the mixture runs slowly, like a syrup, it is done. Turn off the heat. Take the pot and plunge it in a larger pot filled with cold water, making sure the water does not overflow into the pot with jam.

Allow jam to cool completely before pouring it into clean jars and storing the jars in the fridge for up to six months.

Khavidz
Խավից
serves 2 to 4

Khavidz is a porridge that is hearty and filling and can be prepared sweet or savory. In Armenia, especially in the villages, this porridge is traditionally prepared and served to women who just gave birth. The porridge is easy to consume, and is meant to provide strength and energy, and aid in the healing process for new mothers. My family uses this recipe but makes the porridge thicker by reducing the amount of water and spreading it on a tray to solidify and be served as a halva-like sweet—fit for breakfast or dessert. To make it savory, simply omit the sugar in the recipe below. While traditionally prepared for new mothers, this delicious, unique, and filling porridge can be enjoyed by everyone.

3 tbsp coconut oil or vegan butter, melted
6 tbsp flour
¼ cup sugar
2 cups hot water (more, if thinner consistency is preferred)
Pinch of salt
Cinnamon, for topping (optional)
Walnuts, for topping (optional)

Add the sugar to the hot water and set aside (you can add more water, if thinner consistency is preferred).
In a saucepan or pot, add the flour and toast it on low-medium heat until golden, approximately 10 minutes. Stir continuously so the flour doesn't burn. Remove the pot from heat (but do not turn off heat) and make a well so the flour is on the sides. Gradually add the oil, whisking it in thoroughly. Once oil has been incorporated, place the pot back on the heat, and slowly add the sugar water, constantly whisking the porridge until smooth consistency is reached, for 3 to 5 minutes. Add salt, stir, and remove from heat.

Portion out into bowls and top with cinnamon and walnuts (if using).

Tip You can replace the water with warmed plant milk for a creamier alternative!

Armenian Pancakes
Բիշի
serves 6 to 8

There are pancakes, and then there are Armenian pancakes. However, my discovery of *bishi* had little to do with Armenian cuisine. My father, as long as I can remember, has always been on a quest to find "fluffy pancakes full of bubbles" like the ones he used to enjoy growing up. No matter what recipe or restaurant we found promising such pancakes, after simply examining them he would confidently say—and confirm after the first bite—that they were "nothing like the ones back home." After searching many recipes from various cuisines, I stumbled upon *bishi*, or "Armenian pancakes," which I had never heard of. The photos resembled something that looked more like *loukoumades*, traditional Greek fried balls of dough covered in syrup, but the dish was clearly different and was referred to as breakfast pancakes. After a little research and asking around, I settled on a recipe that I vegan-ized (swapping in aquafaba for the eggs) and made it the traditional way, allowing the dough to rise all night, ready to become fuel (carbs) in the morning. I rebelled and opted for a shallow fry rather than the traditional deep fry, shocked at how much each of my modest spoons of dough were rising, creating the bubbles I had heard so much about. After allowing the pancakes to cool off, I again rebelled and instead of smothering them with simple syrup (page 19) and powdered sugar, I topped them with homemade apricot jam. To my pleasant surprise, my dad said these were the closest ones to the pancakes he grew up with, and that the inside texture was spot on. Though I used a different preparation method and different toppings, for me *bishi* is not only a delicious and indulgent breakfast, but also the closest answer to my dad's quest for the perfect pancakes. My mother also surprised me after trying them, telling me her grandmother used to prepare these as well, under a different name, topped with just sugar or homemade rose jam. I have simplified the recipe using active instant yeast to avoid waiting for the dough to rise overnight, and my only word of caution regarding this breakfast is to prepare it for a big gathering, as the "betcha can't eat just one" challenge is futile here.

1 tsp instant yeast
¾ cup warm water
1 tsp sugar
6 tbsp aquafaba
1¼ cup flour
½ tsp salt
1½ tsp baking soda
Oil, for frying
Powdered sugar and/or
    apricot jam, for
    topping (optional)

Mix the flour, salt, sugar, baking soda, and yeast in a bowl. Add the water and aquafaba and mix or whisk until dough is smooth and free of clumps. Cover and keep somewhere warm for 30 to 45 minutes.

Line a large flat plate with a paper towel (to absorb excess oil from the pancakes). Heat a generous amount of oil in a pan and drop a teaspoon of batter to see if it sizzles immediately. Reduce heat to medium and scoop desired size for pancakes out of the batter into the pan. Pancakes will begin to rise. Allow them to cook thoroughly on one side without burning. Flip them over and continue cooking until golden brown. Remove from heat and place on your paper towel—lined plate.

Once the pancakes have cooled, sprinkle on some powdered sugar or enjoy them with fruit or rose jam.

Tahini Bread
Սուսամի մածուկով
(թահինով) հաց
makes 16 cookies

Our freezer always contained tahini bread, usually as a result of trips to Armenian bakeries. Armenian Genocide survivors who fled to Lebanon brought this specialty with them, and it is therefore prevalent in the town of Bourj Hammoud, which is heavily populated by Armenians. Siroon, who grew up in Lebanon, recalls how she and her fiancé used to "follow the aroma" of this staple on the street, until they found the bakery that was baking it fresh. The dough is traditionally rolled out in a specific way, which, in my opinion, is reserved for expert bakers or those looking for a challenge (when it comes to working with dough, I fit in neither of these categories). Tahini bread, which is more like cookies than bread, is naturally free of any animal products, as it is a staple sweet at Lent. I wasn't always the biggest fan of these cookies growing up, usually eating them only out of a desire for something sweet, but after preparing them fresh, I finally learned to appreciate the harmonious balance of savory (tahini) and sweet (sugar) that they accomplish so well. While I have yet to try them freshly baked from a bakery in Bourj Hammoud, which word on the street (and Siroon) says is the best you'll ever have, homemade has definitely made me appreciate the appeal of these delicious flaky cookie-breads.

Bread
2½ tsp active dry yeast
¾ cup warm water
2½ cups all-purpose
  flour
1 tsp salt
½ tsp sugar
1 tbsp oil

Filling
1 cup tahini, stirred well
1 cup sugar
2 tsp cinnamon

Topping
Oil, for brushing
Remaining sugar and
  cinnamon
Sesame seeds (optional)

Make the bread Combine yeast, sugar, and warm water in a tall glass and allow it to sit for 10 minutes in a warm area, until it is frothy. In a bowl, mix together the flour and salt, create a well, and add the oil and the yeast-water mixture, combining well. Once combined, knead the dough until it assumes an elastic texture.

Lightly grease a bowl and coat the dough in oil, placing it in the bowl and allowing it to sit covered for about two hours (in the oven is a good option). After two hours, combine the sugar and cinnamon, and preheat oven to 400ºF (200ºC).

Add the filling Divide the dough into four equal parts, keeping three of them covered to avoid drying out. Roll out each piece of dough into circles as thin as you can with a rolling pin, and add enough tahini to generously coat the top of the dough, leaving about a one-inch border free of tahini. Add enough of the sugar-cinnamon mix to coat the entire tahini layer. Carefully roll the dough, as tightly and thinly as possible, or, if the traditional method is preferred, create a hole in the middle of the dough and carefully roll it outward, keeping it as tightly rolled as possible. Once the dough is rolled, using the palm of your hands, continue to roll the dough, to elongate it as much as possible. A little breakage here is okay and will provide color to the final result. Once you've lengthened your dough, cut into 4 equal pieces. Again, with your hands, roll them out as long as possible. Arrange the lengthened dough in a circular motion to mimic a snail shell and secure the end piece tightly at the bottom. Flatten out the dough with your palm or gently with a rolling pin.

Once the cookies are ready, brush them with oil, top with sesame seeds and the remaining sugar-cinnamon mix, and using a fork, pierce them all over to ensure they do not puff up. Bake for 12 to 15 minutes.

Tahini and Molasses
Սուսամի մածուկ
(թահին) եւ մեղրակ
serves 1 to 2

I always consider tahini and molasses to be the lesser known and underappreciated cousin of the more popular peanut butter and jam duo. This recipe was a staple weekend breakfast for my entire family, and some of my earliest childhood memories include my siblings and I sitting in a circle with my mom, waiting like eager baby birds for our turn to get the next bite of bread dipped into this delicious mix. My mom would always take a large flat plate, put the tahini on one side and the molasses on the other, and using a spoon or a piece of bread, she would swirl them together, creating a presentation that was almost too beautiful to eat. She would then dip pieces of lavash or pita bread in the mix, and we would enjoy it just like that, serving ourselves as we became older. My mother recalls that when she was a child, her father's duty was to buy the two ingredients, and her mother's, to mix them together. Tahini-molasses is such an ingrained part of my childhood that just looking at it floods me with so many happy memories and a sense of familiarity, and it will forever have a special place in my kitchen. We used grape molasses, but for a tangy alternative, I occasionally pair it with pomegranate molasses.

2 tbsp tahini
1 tbsp grape molasses
   or pomegranate
   molasses

On a flat plate, combine the tahini and molasses together. Enjoy by dipping freshly baked lavash (page 134) or pita bread in the mixture or spreading it on matnakash or toast.

Note Feel free to use any type of molasses you prefer: fig, date, mulberry, etc.!

Milk Pudding (*Gatnabour*)
Կաթնապուր
serves 8 to 10

Gatnabour means "milk soup," modified (understandably) to the more appealing "milk pudding." What *gatnabour* is not, however, is rice pudding. While it may seem like a strange detail to nitpick, so many recipes for this delicious, filling, and comforting breakfast (or dessert) tend to be far too generous with the rice and far too stingy with the milk, when it should be the opposite—the name forever serving as proof of that. This dish was traditionally made when there was a lot of milk that had to be used up, and the milk, or in our case, plant milk, is meant to be the star, thickening with the starch of the rice and cooking time, and providing texture, flavor, and creaminess. Rice, while it plays an important role, takes a back seat here, and I am happy to share a vegan-ized version of my family's recipe that follows this important principle. While *gatnabour* can be enjoyed as a sweet breakfast, it can be served also as a dessert—perfect for when you are expecting a lot of guests. If you are skeptical that milk, not rice, is what makes this breakfast so great, well, the proof is in the pudding.

2¼ cups water
½ cup short-grain white rice
6 cups unsweetened, unflavored plant milk
⅓ to ½ cup sugar, based on preference
1 tbsp rose water
Pinch of salt
Cinnamon, for sprinkling

Bring the water to a boil in a small pot or saucepan and add the rice, lowering heat to low-medium. Simmer until rice is fully cooked, approximately 15 minutes, stirring occasionally. Once the rice is cooked and most of the water has been absorbed, turn off the heat, cover the rice, and remove pot from heat.

In a different pot, heat the milk. Add a few spoonfuls of warmed milk to the rice and stir, then add all the rice to the pot with milk. Cook on low-medium heat for about 45 minutes, making sure to stir often. Add the sugar and a pinch of salt and continue to cook for an additional 15 minutes. Remove from heat, add the rose water, and stir. Empty pudding into a glass container or individual serving bowls (perfect for guests) and allow to cool completely. Once cooled, cover and place the pudding in the fridge for a few hours or overnight. Serve with cinnamon sprinkled on top.

Chia *Gatnabour*
Եղեսպակով կաթնապուր

serves 2

For a healthier and less time-consuming alternative, try this delicious *gatnabour*-inspired breakfast that uses the nutritional powerhouse that is chia seeds, which are grown in Armenia.

....

1½ cups unsweetened unflavored plant milk of choice

¼ cup Meline's Garden grown-in-Armenia or other chia seeds

1 tsp rose water

Pinch of salt

Cinnamon, for sprinkling

Crushed walnuts, for topping (optional)

Fresh fruit (including berries) or jam (optional)

Sweetener (optional)

In a bowl, combine the chia seeds and plant milk. Add the rose water and salt, and stir well. Add any choice of sweetener to taste (if using) and allow to sit for an hour or overnight in the fridge. Serve sprinkled with cinnamon and topped with crushed walnuts and fresh fruit or jam.

....

Suggestion For a creamier alternative, swap ½ cup of milk for ½ cup of Coconut Yogurt (page 214). Smooth out the yogurt, thin it out with the 1 cup of plant milk, and stir in the chia seeds, rose water, and salt!

Sweet Lavash
Անուշ լավաշ
serves 2 to 4

Sweet lavash, also referred to as *meghrov lavash* (lavash with honey), is a simple yet delicious breakfast wrap that hails from Zeytoun. In terms of flavor, it is reminiscent of Rolled *Tertanoush* (page 229), making me theorize that Sweet Lavash may have been a quick and easy fix when a craving for that signature phyllo-pastry dish hit. I veganized the traditional recipe by using homemade jam in place of the honey that is traditionally used.

1 sheet of lavash cut into four equal portions widthwise
⅓ to ½ cup Fruit Jam (page 58)
1 cup crushed walnuts
1 tsp cinnamon (optional)
Pinch of salt (optional)
Oil or vegan butter, for frying

Combine the walnuts, cinnamon, and salt (if using), stir well and add the jam. Evenly distribute and spread the mixture on the four pieces of lavash. Roll up each piece as you would a burrito or wrap (folding in the ends) until all the pieces are wrapped.

Warm the oil or vegan butter on medium heat. Fry the Sweet Lavash until golden and crispy on each side, about 1 to 2 minutes. Add more oil if needed.

Abukht Paste
Ապուխտի (չամանի) մածուկ

Vegans or vegetarians often say, somewhat smugly, that it is the plant-based spices that make meat or meat-based dishes taste good. In the case of *abukht*, I believe this claim wholeheartedly. *Abukht* is created by curing beef in an intense and flavorful spice paste that gives the sausage its signature taste—and long shelf life. The paste is said to have been created as far back as BC, when traveling Armenian trade merchants required something that would sustain them during their long travels, and cured beef, or *abukht*, was the solution. The Armenians of Gesarya (modern-day Kayseri) were particularly well known for their *abukht*, preparing it for the winter. Cut into very thin slices, *abukht* is often served as an appetizer on holiday tables or at breakfast on the weekend, as the intense aroma may linger on an individual for a day or two—not ideal in the workplace. The paste itself is what sets it apart from anything else, and you can enjoy the unique taste spread (thinly!) on lavash in a wrap or in bean stews for an instant flavor boost.

1 tsp allspice
1 tsp turmeric
½ tsp black pepper
1 tsp hot pepper
2 tsp cumin
4 tbsp fenugreek
3 tbsp garlic powder
1 tsp salt
2 tbsp paprika
Water, approximately
    ½ cup

Combine all spices into a bowl and mix well. Gradually add the water, until thickened to a paste.

*Pairing suggestion In addition to using this spice paste in wraps or bean stews, you can enjoy it in Bulgur **Yeghints** (page 201)!*

Zucchini Fritters
Դդմիկով ծրեխտակ (քոթլէթ)
makes 8 to 10 fritters

Something I always loved about zucchini fritters is that every Armenian I've met, regardless of where they are from, seems to know and love this staple dish. How it is served may differ—some are accustomed to enjoying it on its own, others by dipping it in garlic yogurt sauce—but it seems to be familiar to everyone. I was pleasantly surprised when at a work lunch in Armenia, these familiar fritters were presented, with a side of garlic yogurt. When I was informed that they were egg-free, I was again pleasantly surprised, as the recipe usually includes a few eggs to bind everything together. I asked what was used in place of eggs and was told nothing, as the flour and liquid released from the zucchini and onion bind everything together just fine. Enjoy these egg-free and egg replacer–free zucchini fritters for breakfast or lunch, or as a quick snack.

....

2 zucchinis, peeled
½ a small onion
¼ bunch parsley or dill, finely chopped
1 tsp baking powder
5 tbsp flour
Salt and black pepper, to taste
Oil, for frying
Squeeze of lemon (optional)

Grate your zucchini and onion into a bowl. Add the parsley or dill, baking powder, salt and pepper and mix thoroughly. Gradually add the flour, making sure to mix well. The batter will be very thin, but once all the flour is added, all the water should be absorbed. If there is water still in the bowl, add more flour as needed.

Add enough oil to coat one-third of the pan for frying. Heat the oil on high and test a teaspoon of the batter to see if it sizzles immediately. Lower the heat to medium and add tablespoonfuls of the mixture into the pan, keeping them somewhat flat. Cook for 1 to 2 minutes on each side, flipping three times so each side is cooked twice.

Remove from pan and place on a plate lined with a paper towel. Squeeze lemon on top.

....

Suggestion Enjoy dipped in Soy Milk or Coconut Milk Yogurt (page 212), Garlic Yogurt (page 20), or Tahini Sauce (page 20)!

Tofu Scramble with Green Beans and Tarragon
Կանաչ լուբիայով եւ թարխունով թոֆու
serves 4

Egg-based scrambles have always been centerpiece-worthy during weekend or holiday breakfast feasts. The scrambles were usually served in the pan they were cooked in to remain warm, and family members (or guests) would use pieces of lavash to scoop generous amounts, enjoyed with all the fixings of the breakfast table. Growing up, my siblings and I were accustomed to a delicious tomato-egg concoction, sometimes cooked with Armenian sausage or served with cured meat. In Armenia, I noticed a different version, which used green beans—usually the flat variety, but sometimes string beans. I had never seen green beans used in anything other than stews or main meals and was very intrigued. In the following vegan-ized recipe, I combine the best of both worlds: tomatoes, to provide a delicious and juicy base, and green beans, to add a pleasant crunch and nutritional upgrade.

1 package of firm or extra firm tofu (400 g), drained
1 large ripened tomato, chopped
1 cup green beans, flat or round
1 small onion, halved and sliced
½ to 1 tsp turmeric
Salt, black pepper, and red pepper, to taste
¼ cup nutritional yeast (optional)
1 tsp black salt (*kala namak*) (optional)
Oil, for sautéing

Heat enough oil to cover the bottom of the pan and cook the onions on medium heat until softened. Cut the end of the green beans and chop the beans into three parts. Add the green beans, salt, black pepper, and red pepper and cook for approximately 10 minutes, until the green beans have softened. Add the tomato and turmeric, cooking until the tomato has mostly softened and disintegrated.

Crumble in the tofu and incorporate well. After tofu has cooked (approximately 5 minutes), turn off heat and stir in the nutritional yeast and black salt, if using.

Armenian Breakfast Wrap
Նախաճաշի փաթաթան

serves 1 to 2

This recipe combines Lavash, *Abukht* Paste, and Tofu Scramble with Green Beans and Tarragon in a delicious, flavorful, and unique play on a breakfast burrito— Armenian-style!

....

½ **a sheet of Lavash (page 134)**
1 cup Tofu Scramble with Green Beans and Tarragon (page 77)
1 tbsp Abukht Paste (page 73)
Bunch of fresh tarragon leaves
Fresh vegetables: tomatoes, cucumbers, and bell peppers, sliced (optional)

Spread the *abukht* paste thinly in the middle of the lavash. Add the tofu scramble and fresh vegetables (if using) on top, and garnish with tarragon leaves. Roll the lavash tightly, cut in half (optional), and enjoy!

Green *Khash*
Կանաչ խաշ
serves 2

Whenever I heard someone talking about *khash*, it was described as either a sacred cultural tradition everyone must partake in or a foolproof hangover remedy. A hefty gelatinous stew, *khash* is understandably reserved for the wintertime, especially during the holidays. When I was living with a host family during my first winter in Armenia, my host mom told me I would witness how *khash* is made, which includes cleaning, preparing, and boiling cow's hooves for the entire night so it could be ready to serve in the morning. As I, thankfully, was assigned the lighter task of chopping vegetables for the many vegan and vegetarian options for the holiday table, I watched as my host mom and her cousins prepared the cow's hooves, and discussed (read: argued over) the best strategies to cook and serve *khash*. I quickly understood the importance of this dish, how it is meant to bring people together, and why the name literally translates to "boil." I was told that *khash* was initially considered "peasant food," as those preparing the meals for royalty would be left only with the unwanted scraps to sustain themselves. Instead of simply eating cow's feet, the peasants would boil them for hours, creating an extremely hearty stew, that would be consumed in the morning and keep workers full for hours, allowing them to work long days. As with many dishes, yesterday's "peasant food" became today's traditional cuisine, and *khash* is still boiled all night, served in the morning on weekends or during Christmas and New Year, and is meant to keep modern-day consumers full for hours—and, due to either the *khash* itself or the copious amounts of vodka served with it, sleepy and unproductive for the remainder of the day. The broth is also considered to be a great hangover remedy, perhaps due to its high sodium content or again, as a result of the vodka that accompanies it. While a vegan *khash* may seem like an oxymoron, this recipe keeps true to the original recipe's "boil" in the name, will keep you full, goes great with all the traditional sides, and due to either the suggested vodka accompaniment or the electrolyte content, may help cure a hangover too!

1 large or 2 medium potatoes
3 tsp vegetable broth powder (or 3 cups vegetable broth)
3 cups hot water (if using broth powder rather than broth)

Chop the potato or potatoes into large chunks, placing them in a small pot. Mix the vegetable broth powder into 1 cup of the hot water and stir well. Add to pot along with the remaining water. If using vegetable broth, add to the pot with potatoes. Bring to a boil, then reduce heat to medium and cook until potatoes are completely tender, about 10 to 15 minutes. Once potatoes are cooked, blend portions of the soup, making sure to leave a few large potato chunks. Pour into bowls.

Serve with minced garlic, pickles, lemon, Plate of Herbs (page 216), Lavash Crackers (page 135) and Mulberry-Infused Vodka (page 48).

SALADS

Ձեռքերուդ դալար:
Your hands evergreen.

Spend time in Armenia during the seasons of spring, summer, and fall and you will quickly understand the reasoning behind an abundance of diverse salads in Armenian cuisine. Salads are often made with fresh seasonal ingredients, giving each one its signature taste and timing. Salads are so much more than just sides and are seen as necessities for any given table or menu, due to both their nutritional qualities and the flavor they bring to the overall meal. From common ingredients like tomatoes and fresh herbs to somewhat unexpected ones like mountain sorrel and yogurt, salads range from light and seasonal to hearty, filling, and year-round.

C O N T E N T S

Summer Salad
Ամառային աղցան

serves 3 to 5

The moment tomato season begins, you can bet your last dram that every household in Armenia and the Armenian diaspora will be serving this classic tomato and cucumber salad, also referred to as "summer salad." It often feels as though a silent countdown has begun the moment the last snowfall of the year hits and the weather begins warming up. Tomatoes are no doubt the star of this salad, though I would argue fresh mint is a very close second. Beyond using perfectly ripened tomatoes (a must), I have learned through experts (my parents) that the order in which you prepare this salad also determines the quality of the final product.

1 small onion, finely chopped (or 3 green onions, chopped)

4 ripened medium tomatoes, chopped

2 to 3 medium cucumbers, peeled and chopped

5 to 10 fresh mint leaves, finely chopped (can use parsley or dill instead)

3 tbsp olive oil

3 tbsp lemon juice (or red wine vinegar)

Salt, to taste

Salt the onion and massage it well. Place in a bowl and add the tomatoes on top, followed by the cucumbers. Do not mix until salad is ready to be served. When ready to serve, add the mint, oil, and lemon juice, and stir gently. Add more salt if desired.

Tip The liquid that remains in the bowl once the salad is portioned out is considered precious by many. Pour it over the individual salad bowls, dip lavash into it, or drink it straight from the bowl!

Olive and Walnut Salad (Shepherd's Dinner)
Հովիւի Ճաշ
serves 4 to 6

Musa Ler, the site of a successful resistance movement during the Armenian Genocide, is rich in both history and cuisine. This salad is often referred to as the *Musalertsi* Shepherd's Dinner (dinner for a shepherd of Musa Ler), most likely because olives and walnuts, the main ingredients, are abundantly available and accessible throughout the mountainous region and the salad offers a convenient, filling, and nutritious meal for those working the land. Luckily, this dish, created perhaps out of utility, is delicious as well.

1½ **cups green olives, pitted, either whole or sliced**
½ **small onion, finely chopped**
½ **cup roughly crushed walnuts**
1 **tbsp Tazah or other pomegranate molasses or syrup, or ¼ cup fresh pomegranate seeds**
1 **tbsp tomato paste**
3 **tbsp olive oil**
2 **tbsp chopped parsley (optional)**

Mix the olives, onion, walnuts, parsley, and pomegranate molasses or syrup (or seeds, or both) together. Add the tomato paste and olive oil and mix very well. Set aside for 15 to 20 minutes to allow the flavors to combine.

Potato Salad
Գետնախնձորով աղցան

serves 6 to 8

I remember the first time I realized that "potato salad" could mean something very different depending on who you were talking to. Armenian potato salad may appear simple compared to its mayonnaise-filled counterparts, but I believe the simplicity of this recipe allows potatoes to shine as the main ingredient accentuated by a few trusty sidekicks. This delicious and filling salad will always be present as a side as it seems to be a universal favorite fit for any table and gathering.

7 Yukon Gold potatoes
Coarse sea salt, to taste
Red pepper, to taste (optional)
3 tbsp lemon juice
5 tbsp oil
3 to 5 green onions, halved and finely chopped
¼ bunch parsley, finely chopped

Boil the potatoes until soft, 12 to 15 minutes. Peel them while still warm and place them in a serving bowl or container. Halve them and keep the cut side facing up. Sprinkle coarse sea salt and red pepper (if using) over potatoes. Pour the lemon juice over them and allow the potatoes to sit for 1 to 2 minutes, to allow salt to seep in. Cube each potato into desired sizes. Pour over oil, onion, and parsley and gently stir everything until well blended. Adjust seasoning as needed.

BBQ Salad
Խորովածի աղցան
serves 4 to 6

When summer hits and the barbecues are fired up, you can expect to find this colorful and flavorful salad on the menu. Vegetables are conveniently roasted whole and then roughly chopped with very few ingredients added to keep the smoky flavor at the forefront.

1 large tomato
2 long, thin eggplants, or 1 large thick one
2 bell or Cubanelle peppers(or 1 spicy pepper, if desired)
1 medium onion, peeled
¼ bunch parsley, chopped
1 to 2 tbsp oil
Salt and black pepper, to taste

Preheat the barbecue by setting it to medium heat. Put the vegetables whole into a bowl and coat them lightly with oil. Place them on the grill and close the lid, cooking them for approximately 30 minutes, flipping them at least once halfway. Remove them once they are thoroughly cooked.

Once they have cooled to the touch, cut the vegetables into large chunks in a bowl. Halve the eggplants lengthwise, and scoop out the flesh, chop it up and add to bowl. Drizzle the oil and add the salt and black pepper and gently toss so they are mixed well. Sprinkle the parsley on top.

Suggestion If you do not have a barbecue, use the broil setting on an oven (on medium, if you can set the temperature) to cook the vegetables. Place the vegetables on a baking tray on the lowest rack and cook for 20 to 30 minutes, flipping them over at least once.

Pairing suggestion Enjoy with fresh lavash (page 134).

Chickpea Salad
Սիսեռով աղցան

serves 6 to 8

This chickpea salad may not be as well known as its lentil or bean counterparts, but it has never failed to please even the pickiest of eaters with its delicious medley of flavors. Great as a light lunch or as a tangy accompaniment to a savory main.

....

2 cups cooked chickpeas
1 small onion, finely sliced
⅓ cup chopped parsley, setting a small amount aside for garnish
½ tsp salt, or according to taste
½ tsp red pepper or paprika
½ tsp black pepper
1 tsp cumin
3 tbsp tahini
3 tbsp lemon juice

Combine chickpeas, onion, parsley, and spices in a bowl and mix. Add the tahini and lemon juice and mix well. Garnish with remaining parsley.

Green Lentil Salad
Ոսպով աղցան

serves 6 to 8

Green lentil salad always has a reserved spot as a side for Christmas dinner. It is healthy and filling, and can also be paired with lighter entrées to make the meal whole. In Armenia, smaller brown lentils are more popular and can easily be substituted in this recipe.

4 cups cooked green or
   brown lentils, drained
1 small onion, finely
   chopped
¼ to ½ bunch parsley,
   chopped
¼ tsp black pepper
½ tsp cumin
4 tbsp olive oil
2 tbsp lemon juice
1 tbsp red wine vinegar
Salt, to taste

Mix lentils, onion, and parsley in a bowl. Add the salt, spices, oil, lemon juice, and vinegar, and mix well.

Bean Salad
Լուբիայով աղցան
serves 6 to 8

White kidney bean salad is another great option for pairing with lighter entrées. Though the salad is filling, its flavor is light and refreshing, especially due to the fresh herbs used. As a result, the salad is often served during the summer.

3 cups cooked white
   kidney beans,
   drained
4 green onions, chopped
¼ to ½ bunch dill or
   parsley, finely
   chopped
1 large tomato, finely
   chopped
¼ tsp dried mint + fresh
   mint, to serve
   (optional)
3 tbsp olive oil
2 tbsp lemon juice or
   red wine vinegar
Salt, to taste
¼ tsp black pepper
¼ tsp paprika

Combine beans, green onions, tomato, and fresh herbs in a bowl and lightly mix. Add the spices, oil, and lemon juice or vinegar and mix well. Taste and adjust spices accordingly.

Eggplant Salad
Սմբուկով աղցան
serves 6 to 8

Armenians have a love affair with eggplant, even drying the vegetable to use throughout every season. Eggplant salad tends to be a staple during the summer, allowing the popular vegetable to shine as the main ingredient.

3 large eggplants
1 medium onion, finely chopped
2 garlic cloves, finely chopped
2 medium tomatoes, chopped
¼ to ½ bunch parsley, finely chopped
1 lemon, juiced
4 tbsp olive oil, plus extra for coating eggplants
¼ tsp paprika or red pepper
Salt, to taste

Preheat the oven at 400ºF (200ºC). Cut the eggplants in half lengthwise, brush the cut sides with oil, and salt them. Cook them cut side down for 30 minutes, then turn off the oven, leaving them inside for 5 more minutes. Remove and allow them to cool completely. Spoon out the flesh from each of the 6 halves and roughly chop it in large chunks and add to a bowl. Add the rest of the ingredients and mix well.

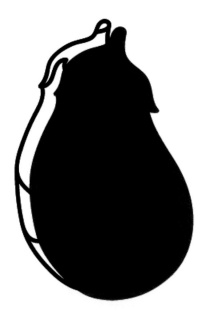

Eggplant *Khaviar*
Ամբուկով խավիար
serves 4 to 6

While I grew up enjoying eggplant salad, I discovered eggplant *khaviar* only while living in Armenia. It is made throughout the late summer, then preserved and jarred for use throughout all seasons. During hikes and camping trips, I found a jar of this flavorful and nutritious spread, accompanied by lavash and fresh cucumber, was perfect for a plant-based breakfast, snack, or lunch. In an indoor setting, however, this spread is best viewed and served as a salad, providing an incredible element of taste to any food lucky enough to be eaten alongside it.

5 thin eggplants
1 red pepper
2 jalapeños (optional)
1 medium onion, peeled
4 Roma (Italian plum) tomatoes
3 to 4 garlic cloves, peeled
Coarse sea salt, for sprinkling
1 tbsp tomato paste
1 tbsp red pepper paste
1 tbsp hot water
3 to 4 tbsp oil
Salt, black pepper, and red pepper, to taste
Chopped parsley (optional, for garnish)

Preheat the oven to 400ºF (200ºC). Lightly grease a baking tray.

Cut the eggplants, pepper, onion, and jalapeños (if using) in half. For a less spicy recipe, remove and discard the seeds of the jalapeños. Place the vegetables on the tray along with the whole tomatoes and garlic cloves. Sprinkle coarse sea salt over them. Bake the vegetables for 35 to 40 minutes until a knife is easily inserted in the eggplant. Once they are cooked and can be handled, peel the skin off the eggplants, tomatoes, pepper, and use a paper towel or wear gloves instead of your bare hands to peel the jalapeños as the capsaicin can cause your skin to burn. Finely chop the onion and jalapeños and add to a pan with the oil. Sauté on medium heat until onions are translucent. Dilute the tomato paste and pepper paste with hot water, then add this to the pan with the onions along with the salt, black pepper, and red pepper, and reduce the heat to low.

Stir and cook for another 2 minutes. Chop the eggplant, red pepper, tomatoes, and garlic, and add them to the pot, stirring well. Cook for another 10 to 15 minutes and with the back of a wooden spoon, break up any large pieces in the mixture. Allow to cool and serve with a drizzle of oil and chopped parsley.

Pairing suggestion Enjoy with fresh lavash (page 134)!

Mountain Sorrel Salad
Աւելուկի աղցան
serves 6 to 8

Before living in Armenia, I had no idea what mountain sorrel was, and by extension, I had never heard of or eaten this popular salad. The green itself is hard to go unnoticed, as the presentation of it alone in *shugas* (markets) and shops is worthy at least of a curious pause. Mountain sorrel is grown aplenty in Armenia and collected in the spring, woven into long braids and dried for use in the fall and winter. Although I was told it was commonly used in soups and salads, and the beauty of the dried mountain sorrel attracted me immediately, I really had no idea how to prepare this plant to use in recipes. This salad was a perfect opportunity to start my cooking adventures with mountain sorrel.

3 to 4 cups dried mountain sorrel
1 large onion
2 to 3 tbsp oil
Salt, black pepper, and red pepper, to taste
6 cups water
¼ cup crushed walnuts
Handful of pomegranate arils (optional)

Break up the sorrel into large chunks by hand or with scissors, removing the larger stems, and place in a pot, pouring hot water over it, enough to cover it completely. After stirring it rigorously, discard the water after a few minutes, repeating this step two to three times. In a pot, bring the 6 cups of water to a boil, adding salt. Add the sorrel, cooking it on medium heat, covered, until it softens, approximately 15 minutes.

Warm the oil in a pan and quarter the onion, slicing it thinly. Sauté until translucent and add the spices. Once the sorrel is cooked, remove it using a strainer and add it to the pan with the onions, cooking it for 5 to 7 minutes, adding more oil if necessary or desired.

Plate salad on a serving dish, and top with crushed walnuts and pomegranate arils (if using).

Bulgur Salad
Չավարով աղցան
serves 6 to 8

Bulgur salad is a delicious and flavorful salad. It was always in rotation in my family, especially since my grandmother was an expert at making it. She would prepare it in huge batches, fill up a large container, and tell us to eat half of it one day and the other half the next day. She referred to it as an oily salad, always reminding us to never skimp on the oil as it would make a difference in the final result. When recipe-testing this salad, I did try a few lighter versions, but my grandmother was right: don't skimp on the oil as it is an integral component of the deliciousness of this dish.

2 large onions, finely
    chopped
1 cup Tazah or other
    extra virgin olive oil
4 to 5 large ripe
    tomatoes, finely
    chopped
2 cups fine white bulgur
2 tbsp tomato paste
1 tbsp red pepper paste
Juice of one lemon
1 tsp salt
Black pepper, to taste
Red pepper, to taste
3 green onions,
    chopped, for garnish
⅓ bunch parsley,
    chopped, for garnish

In a pot, cook the onions on medium heat in the oil until they become translucent. Add the tomatoes and once they are thoroughly warmed, add the tomato paste and pepper paste, along with the spices and continue mixing. Taste and adjust spice levels according to preference. Cook tomatoes until they are completely soft and mostly dissolved, remove pot from heat, and allow mixture to cool. Once mixture has cooled, mix in bulgur, and allow it to sit for 20 minutes. Add the juice of one lemon and mix well. When ready to serve, spread the salad in a large serving dish and top with green onions and parsley

Pairing suggestion Enjoy rolled in romaine leaves or fresh grape leaves!

Yogurt and Cucumber Salad
Վարունգով ու մածունով աղցան
serves 4 to 6

This is a great example of a refreshing summer salad, using fresh yogurt that is commonly prepared during that season. There are two popular ways to make this dish: thinner to resemble a cold soup or thicker to be enjoyed as a dip-like salad. The following recipe falls into the latter category. If a thinner option is desired, simply add water until the ideal consistency is reached.

2 cups Soy Milk or Coconut Milk Yogurt (page 212)

3 medium cucumbers, peeled and chopped

2 garlic cloves, minced or grated

½ to 1 tsp dried mint

Salt, to taste

Stir or whisk the yogurt until completely smooth. Add the salt and mint, stirring well. Adjust salt and mint accordingly. Add the garlic and cucumbers, and stir. Serve with a drizzle of oil on top and garnish with fresh mint, if desired.

Beet Salad
Ճակնդեղի աղցան
serves 6 to 8

Beets are a popular ingredient in both Armenia and the Armenian diaspora. Besides beets being pickled in pickled vegetable medleys, providing a signature vibrant colour, and boiled in soups or roasted, beet leaves can be used in a specific type of potassium-rich *tolma*. Beet salad is another popular use of this common ingredient. Not only is the salad beautiful to have on the table due to the deep reddish-purple hue of the beets, but also the accompanying garlic and dill provide a great flavor boost.

6 medium apple-sized beets, washed with ends cut off
1 garlic clove, finely chopped
2 tbsp red wine vinegar
2 tbsp olive oil
¼ to ½ bunch dill, chopped
Salt, to taste

Preheat ovent to 375ºF (190ºC). Lightly drizzle olive oil over the beets, sprinkle them with salt, and bake in the oven for 45 minutes to 1 hour, until beets are easily pierced with a knife. Allow beets to cool, then peel them. Cut them in half, then slice into quarter-inch pieces. Place them in a bowl, add the remaining ingredients and mix well.

Watermelon Salad
Չմերուկի աղցան

serves 3 to 5

The combination of salty and sweet may be a take as old as time, but whenever I talk about enjoying watermelon with salty cheese and mint with people not familiar with this particular combination, I inevitably see perplexed faces. While this reaction may have led me to talk about it a little less, I didn't stop enjoying the classic sweet-and-salty duo of a thick watermelon wedge in one hand and a piece of salty cheese in another, with fresh mint to bring it all together. The following salad is a modern and veganized take that is just as refreshing, delicious, and "odd" as the original.

1 quarter of a large watermelon, chopped
Juice of half a lemon
5 (or more, if desired) green or Kalamata olives, pitted and sliced
6 to 8 leaves fresh mint, chopped

Combine all ingredients and lightly toss to avoid breaking up watermelon chunks.

Pairing suggestion Enjoy with fresh lavash (page 134)!

SOUPS AND STEWS

Եթէ սնուցիր, կշտացո'ւր: If you are feeding someone, satiate them.

Cravings for soup tend to signify a change of the seasons, a change that is understandably dreaded by most. The following soups and stews are perhaps a testament to the need for diverse (and creative) options, which may make the winters at least a *little* more bearable while offering much-needed sustenance and warmth. If you look for the silver lining in every situation, no matter how difficult, you could argue that the long and harsh winter laid the foundation for these delicious, comforting, and filling recipes, now enjoyed year-round. The following selection of soups and stews range from creamy to "brothy," hearty to light, savory to somewhat sweet, but one thing they all have in common is that they may just help you see winter in a new (and optimistic) light.

CONTENTS

Yogurt Soup (with *Klorchiks*)
Մածունով ապուր
serves 4 to 6

There is an Armenian saying: "What yogurt soups are to feasting days, lentil soups are to fasting days." As much as I love all kinds of lentil soup, yogurt soup is the definition of comfort food in my family. Since it is never meant to be boiling hot (when preparing or serving), it was always enjoyed year-round, rather than being delegated as "winter food." My mother is very appreciative of this soup because it was one of the few things all three of her children were equally very fond of and would request constantly. Luckily, this was another dish always in rotation in my grandmother's cooking, and she would prepare it in huge batches, calling my parents as soon as she finished to come pick it up for us. While it is not a difficult soup to make, it's important to warm the yogurt before adding it to the pot using the method described below and to never bring the soup (once the yogurt has been added) to a boil. Following these instructions will ensure a well-combined, creamy, and absolutely delicious and comforting soup.

For the klorchiks
¼ **cup fine white bulgur**
½ **cup semolina**
1 **small onion, finely chopped**
¼ **bunch parsley, finely chopped**
4 **tbsp water**
2 **tbsp oil**
Salt, black pepper, and paprika, to taste

Rinse and drain bulgur, eliminating as much water as possible, and set aside. Mix the semolina and spices together, then add the parsley, onion, and bulgur. Add the water and begin to mix the mixture with your hands. Add the oil and continue to mix well, kneading the dough. Let it sit for 10 minutes. Roll into balls smaller than the size of walnuts.

For the soup
**¼ cup short-grain white
    rice**
**2½ cups Soy Milk or
    Coconut Milk Yogurt
    (page 212)**
4 to 7 cups boiling water
Salt, to taste
**1 tbsp dried mint
    or a drizzle of Mint-
    Infused Oil**

Remove the yogurt from the fridge 1 to 2 hours before beginning the recipe, to ensure it reaches room temperature. In a large bowl, whisk yogurt so it is free of lumps. Set aside.

Add the rice and two cups of boiling water in a large pot on high heat. Once the rice is cooked (after approximately 15 minutes), add salt. Add more water, roughly two cups, and reduce the heat to medium. Once the rice is cooked, reduce the heat to medium. Add the *klorchiks* and more hot water if needed to ensure *klorchiks* are covered completely. Cook for 7 to 10 minutes, sampling a *klorchik* to make sure it is cooked. Turn off the heat and allow the soup to cool for 5 minutes (should not be boiling hot). Add a few large spoonfuls of the warm water from the pot to the bowl of yogurt, stirring thoroughly. Do this until the bowl of yogurt is warm. Gradually begin to add the warmed yogurt into the pot of soup, stirring well. Add salt, then the dried mint, or serve into bowls and add Mint-Infused Oil (page 19) to each individual bowl.

Tip Warm up any leftovers on low-medium heat, never allowing the soup to come to a boil.

Suggestion To save time, omit the klorchiks. This is perfect for a lighter option that still satisfies the craving for yogurt soup.

Pairing suggestion Enjoy with Lavash Crackers (page 135)!

Tahnabour (or Spas)
Թանապուր
serves 6 to 8

In the Armenian diaspora, yogurt soup reigns supreme, and in Armenia, a very similar version called *tahnabour* (or *spas*) is more common. The difference is the use of peeled wheat instead of rice, the absence of meatballs, as well as the addition of onion. This soup can be served cold during the summer or warm during the winter, and while peeled wheat is definitely the more popular choice, some variations do use rice or bulgur instead.

3 cups Soy Milk or Coconut Milk Yogurt (page 212), whisked so it is free of lumps
3 + 3 cups warm water
½ cup peeled wheat
1 tbsp flour
1 large onion, chopped
2 to 3 tbsp oil
Fresh chopped dill, mint, or cilantro, for serving
Salt, to taste

Six to 8 hours before (or overnight) you make the soup, rinse the peeled wheat, add it to a pot with just enough water to cover it, bring it to a boil, then turn off the heat and cover it.

Remove the yogurt from the fridge 1 to 2 hours before beginning the recipe, to ensure it reaches room temperature.

Add 3 cups of water to the pot with the wheat, bring to a boil, then reduce the heat to low, and cook, covered, until wheat is fully cooked, approximately 30 minutes.
In a separate pot, combine the yogurt and flour, whisking well to remove clumps. Turn the heat on low and gradually add 3 cups of warm water, stirring or whisking well. Salt to taste and continue cooking for 2 minutes.

Drain the wheat, adding it to the pot with the yogurt. Continue stirring on low heat until the soup warms fully, approximately 10 minutes.

In the meantime, in a pan, cook the onion in oil, sautéing it until translucent. Turn off the heat for the soup, add the onion, and mix well. Serve the soup warm or chilled with your choice of chopped fresh herbs on top. If serving warm, you can top individual bowls with a dollop of vegan butter.

Pairing suggestion *Enjoy with Olive and Walnut Bread (page 148)!*

Red Lentil Soup (Priest's Soup)
Ոսպով ապուր
serves 4 to 6

This recipe is proof that there is always beauty in simplicity. It is also known as *Vartabed Chorbah* (Priest's Soup), since it is an easy and delicious soup monks would (and could) prepare themselves. The creaminess of the red lentils—a result of their being cooked to perfection—brought to life by a small selection of additional ingredients explains the wide appeal and celebrity status of this soup, which I have made and enjoyed even on the hottest of summer days. Some variations call for the lentils to be blended at the end, but if the lentils are cooked fully, there is no need to blend. Despite the soup seeming plain, I hope you will try this recipe to understand for yourself why it is in constant rotation in almost every Armenian household.

3 cups red lentils
¼ cup short-grain white rice (or less)
1 medium onion
4 tbsp olive oil
7½ to 8½ cups water
Salt, to taste
Cumin, paprika, or hot red pepper, to taste
⅓ to ¼ cup chopped parsley
Few squeezes of lemon

Sort and rinse the lentils, removing any stones or other debris. The water should go from murky to completely clear. Lentils not cleaned well will affect the taste of the soup, so make sure to rinse them thoroughly! Set aside.

Finely chop the onion. Alternatively, peel it and add it to the soup whole when cooking the rice. Add the chopped onion to a pot on medium heat, add ½ cup of water, and cover until the water has been absorbed. Add the olive oil and fry the onions, making sure they do not brown. Add the rice and stir, adding 3 cups of hot water. Cook the rice completely, approximately 15 minutes. Once the rice has cooked, add the rinsed lentils and 3 cups of hot water. Add the salt and lower the heat. As the lentils cook, add 1 to 2 more cups of hot water. Continue to cook on low heat until the lentils are completely cooked. Add more salt if desired, and either add the spices and parsley now or top individual bowls with them. Squeeze in a generous amount of lemon juice before enjoying.

Tip If the leftover soup thickens too much in the fridge, simply add more hot water to thin it out when warming.

Pairing suggestion Enjoy with Potato Salad (page 91)!

Simple Green Lentil Soup
Կանաչ ոսպով ապուր
serves 2 to 4

This soup is traditionally eaten during Easter, specifically on լացուն գիշեր, literally "crying night," otherwise known as Holy Thursday, the day before Good Friday. It is meant to be a simple thick soup made with green lentils and salt, topped with olive oil and red wine vinegar. The soup is eaten in the evening before attending church as a way to reflect empathy and solidarity with Christ, who, after being crucified, was given vinegar or sour wine instead of water as a form of mockery and torment. While the story behind the soup definitely casts sadness on the recipe, when I was growing up, the church service on Holy Thursday was the one I looked most forward to. Consuming this soup with family was an important aspect of that night, and whether you are religious or not, the soup can be enjoyed by everyone.

1 cup green lentils
5 cups water
Coarse sea salt, to taste
Olive oil, for topping
Red wine vinegar, for
    topping
Fresh chopped parsley
    and green onion, for
    topping (optional)

Combine lentils and water in a pot and bring to a boil on high heat. Once soup boils, reduce heat to medium, and cook for 20 to 25 minutes, until lentils are cooked. Salt the soup to taste, turn off the heat, and keep pot covered. When serving, add about a tablespoon of red wine vinegar to each bowl, followed by a drizzle of olive oil.

Pairing suggestion Enjoy with fresh herbs or Beet Salad (page 104)!

Stinging Nettle and Potato Soup
Եղինջով ապուր
serves 3 to 5

Nettle may be commonly seen as a weed in North America, but in Armenia, along with its popular use in the kitchen, it is seen as a healing herb with many beneficial health properties. It is the dreaded stinging nettle that grows wild throughout Armenia, and as a result, collecting the leaves and preparing them to be cooked or dried does present a small challenge. I have found that using dish gloves when handling nettle (both in picking and washing or chopping) keeps my hands protected just fine, and once it's added to the pot, you are safe from any stinging effects. Alternatively, you can substitute spinach or another dark leafy green if nettle is unavailable (or too troublesome).

3 cups fresh nettle or spinach, rinsed well and roughly chopped
1 medium onion, finely chopped
2 small potatoes, cubed
2 garlic cloves, minced
½ cup green or brown lentils
3 tbsp oil
5 cups hot water
Salt and black pepper, to taste

Sauté onions in oil until translucent. Add potatoes and lentils and fry together for a few minutes. Add garlic and stir, then add the hot water, bringing to a boil. Reduce the heat to medium and cover the pot, cooking for 15 to 20 minutes until lentils and potatoes are fully cooked. Add the nettle or spinach, salt, and black pepper, and cook for an additional 5 minutes, covered.

Suggestion In Armenia, a lentil-free option that uses rice is also available. Feel free to swap out the lentils for 1/3 cup short-grain white rice instead.

Pairing suggestion Enjoy with Soy Milk or Coconut Milk Yogurt (page 212) or Garlic Yogurt (page 20)!

Mountain Sorrel Soup
Անելուկի ապուր
serves 5 to 7

Until I lived in Armenia, the main ingredient of this soup remained an intimidating mystery to me. Once I became more comfortable learning to cook with the wonder that is sorrel, I was provided with a recipe for this soup and also told that in addition to the flavor it brings to any meal, sorrel is also seen as a medicinal plant, used to alleviate a variety of digestive issues, especially when consumed as a soup. This soup, available in many restaurants, remains one of my go-to meals when I'm in Armenia, especially during the winter.

3 to 4 cups dried mountain sorrel
1 cup cooked red kidney beans
3 potatoes, cubed
1 large onion, chopped
3 large garlic cloves, minced
Salt, black pepper, and red pepper, to taste
3 to 5 tbsp oil
6 to 8 cups hot water

Break up the sorrel into large chunks by hand or with scissors, removing the larger stems, and place in a pot, pouring hot water over it, covering it completely. After stirring it rigorously, discard the water after a few minutes, repeating this step two to three times. Heat the oil in a large pot on medium heat. Stir in the strained sorrel, cooking it in the oil for 5 minutes. Pour 6 cups of hot water over the sorrel and bring to a boil on high heat. Once water boils, reduce to low-medium heat and cook covered for 10 to 15 minutes, until the sorrel has softened. Add the potatoes, onion, red kidney beans, and spices and continue cooking covered on low-medium heat until the potatoes are fully cooked, approximately 15 minutes. You can add 1 to 2 more cups hot water if needed. Add the garlic, turn off the heat, and allow soup to sit for 5 to 10 minutes before serving.

Suggestion There are other versions of this soup that use wheat or lentils instead of red kidney beans and include dry fruits or fruit lavash. I prefer this version, but feel free to experiment with this recipe!

Note Though dried sorrel may seem like a hard-to-find ingredient, Glendale in Los Angeles, California, has many Armenian shops that carry it—straight from Armenia!

Pairing suggestion Enjoy with a squeeze of fresh lemon and Matnakash (page 138)!

Opo Squash and Chickpea Stew
Դդմիկի ապուր
serves 6 to 8

My father, who grew up on this stew, tells me it was very popular in the Armenian Quarter of Jerusalem, which is why I often refer to it as a Jerusalem-Armenian specialty. Traditionally, it is made with opo squash, which goes by a few other names and resembles a thicker, lighter green zucchini. My grandmother made this soup for all of us, and I'm happy that the recipe passed on to us results in the same delicious stew we were always so fond of. There are times that I have had some difficulty finding opo squash but Siroon's grandmother let me know she substitutes zucchinis (the striped ones used in *tolma*), which require less cooking time and do not need to be peeled. Although I have yet to deviate from my grandmother's recipe, Siroon assures me the zucchini version is just as delicious, so feel free to swap zucchini for the squash, adjusting the cooking time accordingly.

2 large opo squashes, peeled, quartered lengthwise, and thinly chopped
3 garlic cloves, finely minced
1 cup cooked chickpeas
3 tbsp tomato paste, mixed with ¼ cup warm water
3 tbsp oil
1 cup boiled water
2 tbsp lemon juice
½ tsp coarse sea salt (or more, according to taste)
½ tsp to 1 tsp dried mint
½ tsp red pepper flakes (optional)

Add opo squash and garlic to a large pot on medium-high heat. Avoid stirring; instead, shake the pot to combine. Reduce heat and cover with a lid. After a few minutes, once the opo squash has released some water, add the tomato paste—water mixture and oil, and shake the pot to combine. Cover the pot again, increasing the temperature to medium-high heat. Once the opo squash flesh becomes transparent (roughly 8 to 10 minutes), add the chickpeas and salt. Pour in the boiled water, and once it begins to boil, lower the heat to low-medium, add the lemon juice, and cover the pot, allowing it to simmer so all flavors combine. Once the opo squash is cooked, turn off the heat, add the mint and red pepper flakes (if using), and allow to sit for 5 to 10 minutes before serving.

Pairing suggestion *Enjoy with Rice **Yeghints** (with Orzo) (page 198)!*

Vegetable Stew (*Aylazan*)
Այլազան
serves 4 to 6

Aylazan is slow-cooked vegetable stew traditionally made in the summer to use up fresh vegetables and herbs. Often referred to as the "fridge clearer," it is a great excuse to invite friends over for a delicious and flavorful meal, which is also very simple to make. While some of the vegetables definitely make this stew, you can also add in ones you already have in the fridge to stay true to the meaning of the dish.

2 eggplants
2 zucchinis
3 medium potatoes
3 tomatoes
2 bell or Cubanelle peppers (or spicy peppers, if desired)
1 large onion
1 cup green beans
3 garlic cloves, minced
Mixed herbs of choice: parsley, dill, cilantro, finely chopped
4 tbsp tomato paste (or a combination of tomato paste and red pepper paste)
2 to 4 tbsp of oil
Salt, black pepper, and red pepper, to taste

Slice the eggplant into half-inch circles, salting them, and setting them aside for 10 to 15 minutes before rinsing to remove some of the bitterness. Prep the other veggies during this time. Slice the zucchini into thick circles, and cut the potatoes, peppers, onion, and tomatoes into large cubes. Cut the stems of the green beans and chop them into large pieces. Mix tomato paste with 1 cup of warm water. Set aside. Add oil to a large pot on medium-high heat and arrange the vegetables in the pot in the following order: eggplant, potatoes, peppers, zucchini, onion, green beans, garlic, and tomatoes. Pour in the tomato paste—water mixture and allow the stew to come to a boil. Avoid stirring; instead, shake the pot a few times to make sure liquid is dispersed. Reduce heat to low and cook covered for 45 minutes, until all vegetables have cooked. Turn off heat, add the herbs and spices, giving the stew a stir, and cover, allowing all the flavors to blend. Let sit for 10 to 15 minutes before serving.

Tip If a larger batch is desired, simply continue arranging the vegetables in layers in the same order as above!

Pairing suggestion Enjoy with Bulgur Yeghints (page 201)!

Okra Stew
Կուտատուկի ճաշ

serves 4 to 6

Okra is a vegetable (or, arguably, a fruit), that is understandably the stuff of nightmares for most children. My siblings and I viewed okra, which is chewy yet somewhat slimy, as punishment food and refused to believe the adults in our family when they told us they actually enjoyed it. My grandmother would make okra stew at least twice a week, and its popularity could be attributed to how well the pods themselves freeze, something I, back then, wished wasn't true. Fast forward many years later, and while I won't claim it is my favorite meal, I actually do enjoy a nice bowl of hot okra stew, and look forward to eating it, especially when my mother prepares it. My siblings, on the other hand, still refuse to eat it, so I cannot say adulthood is the remedy to the hatred of okra.

7 cups frozen or fresh okra pods
2 garlic cloves, minced
1 medium onion, finely chopped
1 large ripe tomato, finely chopped
1 tbsp tomato paste, diluted with ⅓ cup hot water
1 tsp red pepper paste (optional)
4 tbsp oil
1 to 2 tbsp lemon juice
2 cups hot water
½ tsp coarse sea salt (or more, according to taste)

Sauté onions in oil on low heat until onions are translucent. Add garlic and mix. Add the tomato and the tomato paste—water mixture. Cook on low-medium heat, and once everything is warm, add the okra (if using frozen okra, rinse in cold water right before adding). Cover the pot and cook for a few minutes before adding red pepper paste (if using) and the hot water. Shake the pot to combine. (Avoid stirring as the okra pods may break.) Increase heat and bring stew to a boil, then reduce to medium, cover the pot, and allow stew to cook, gently stirring or shaking the pot occasionally. After 10 to 15 minutes, once the okra has changed color and softened, add ½ teaspoon coarse sea salt. Continue cooking covered for an additional 10 to 15 minutes, until okra has completely softened. Once okra is cooked, add the lemon juice, gently stirring or shaking, and continue to cook covered for an additional 5 minutes before serving.

Suggestion Add cooked chickpeas to the stew when adding the coarse sea salt.

Pairing suggestion Enjoy with Rice **Yeghints** (with Orzo) (page 198)!

Krchik
Քրչիկ
serves 4 to 6

Krchik is a delicious pickled cabbage–based soup very popular in Armenia, especially throughout the northern regions. It should come as no surprise that a soup like this would be common, since you would be hard-pressed to find a home in Armenia that does not have enough homemade pickled vegetables (including cabbage) to last all through the winter. Store-bought alternatives can be used instead, although the soup tastes best when made with homemade pickled cabbage. Spelt is a popular choice in terms of the grain used, but the first time I ever tried and later made *krchik*, was with bulgur, which I personally prefer—due to not only the reduced cooking time, but also the overall taste. If you prefer spelt, just make sure to prepare it in advance and increase the cooking time of this dish.

3 to 4 cups pickled cabbage, store-bought or from Assorted Pickles (page 218), chopped
1 large onion, chopped
2 medium potatoes, cubed
½ cup white coarse bulgur
3 tbsp tomato paste
3 tbsp oil
5 to 6 cups boiled water
Salt, black pepper, and red pepper, to taste
Parsley, chopped, for serving (optional)

Heat the oil in the pot and sauté the onions. Once the onions are cooked, add the tomato paste and mix well. Add the pickled cabbage and allow it to heat up for a few minutes. Add the potatoes and enough boiled water to completely cover the vegetables, about 5 cups. Cook on low-medium heat, covered, until the potatoes soften completely, around 15 to 20 minutes. Add the bulgur, along with the spices, and another cup of boiled water if necessary, and cook for 5 to 10 minutes, covered. Turn off the heat and allow the soup to sit for 5 to 10 minutes. Serve with chopped parsley (if using).

Pairing suggestion Enjoy with Strained Yogurt (page 215)!

Lopakhashu
Լոբախաշու

serves 4 to 5

The first time I heard about *Lopakhashu*, it sounded like what (vegan) dreams were made of: a red bean stew that combines spices, herbs, and walnuts, making it hearty, filling, and protein-rich. A specialty of the town of Vayk, in Vayots Dzor, Armenia, the dish lived up to (and surpassed) its hype, the combination of flavors resulting in one of the tastiest stews I have ever had. It took me a few tries to get it just right, as I realized after a few attempts that small amounts of the finished stew are meant to be blended (or mashed), giving *Lopakhashu* its signature consistency, colour, and taste. Siroon named her son Vyke, a tribute to the beautiful town this delicious stew happens to hail from, making this stew all the more special.

2 cups dry red kidney beans, soaked overnight or for 6 to 8 hours
2 to 3 garlic cloves, minced
1 onion, finely chopped
½ cup ground walnuts
1 to 2 tbsp oil (optional)
½ bunch cilantro, chopped, for garnish
4 cups + 1 cup hot water, if blending
Salt, black pepper, and red pepper, to taste

Drain the soaked beans and rinse them well. Add them to a pot and pour in 4 cups of hot water. Bring the water to a boil on high, then reduce to low-medium. Add the garlic and onion and cover the pot, stirring occasionally. Cook until the beans have completely softened, about 45 minutes to 1 hour. Once the beans are fully cooked, remove the lid and add the spices and oil (if using). Cover and cook on medium heat for another 10 to 15 minutes. You can blend some of the soup now and pour it back in the pot, until the desired consistency is reached. If needed, add 1 more cup of hot water to allow for easier blending and thinner consistency. Turn off stove and remove pot from heat. Add the walnuts, stir, and cover pot. Let sit for 10 minutes. Serve with cilantro sprinkled on top.

Pairing suggestion Enjoy with Assorted Pickles (page 218) and Losh (page 140)!

Chickpea Soup with Prunes
Սալորաչիրով սիսեռապուր
serves 4 to 6

Prunes in a chickpea and potato soup may seem like a strange combination, but soups sweetened or made sour with the use of dried fruit or fruit lavash are quite popular throughout Armenia. Traditionally, dried fruits or fruit lavash were added to soups (or simply boiled with water) during the winter, prepared for those who were ill. Later, the fruit may have been added solely for flavor or as a convenient way to use up some leftover dried fruits. Whatever the reason, the resulting taste, understandably an acquired one, is delicious, unique, and often elevates an otherwise simple dish. If you really cannot get behind the addition of dried fruits in an otherwise savory soup, you can omit that part and still be left with a delicious, though slightly less interesting, meal.

1 cup dry chickpeas
1 large onion, finely chopped
1 tbsp flour
3 tbsp oil
3 potatoes, chopped
⅔ cup prunes
3 + 3 cups water
Coarse sea salt and black pepper, to taste
Parsley, chopped, for serving (optional)

Soak the chickpeas for 6 to 8 hours, or overnight. Before beginning, slice the prunes in half and soak them in warm water while you prepare the other ingredients. Drain and rinse the chickpeas and add them to a pot with 3 cups water and bring to a boil. Lower heat to medium-high, and cover. Cook until they are soft, approximately 25 minutes.

Add potatoes to the pot along with 3 cups hot water, bring the heat to medium and cook covered for an additional 10 minutes. While the soup is cooking, in a separate pan on medium-high heat, sauté the onion in the oil until translucent. Add flour and mix, and then add about 3 tbsp of the liquid from the soup and mix well. Add the onion-flour mix to the soup and stir well, then drain and add your prunes. Stir in the coarse sea salt and black pepper. Turn off the stove, remove the pot from the heat, and allow soup to sit covered for 5 minutes. Before serving, add fresh parsley (if using).

Pairing suggestion Enjoy with Eggplant Salad (page 96) or Mountain Sorrel Salad (page 98)!

Nevig
Նիւիկ
serves 4 to 6

Nevig is a delicious and healthy stew traditionally prepared on Armenian Christmas Eve and Christmas Day, usually to mark the end of a fast, although it can be made and enjoyed anytime. Like many dishes, there are slightly different variations of this recipe depending on where the families making it are from. Even my grandparents made different versions: my mom's side using less chickpeas and more chard, and my dad's side going heavier on the chickpeas and always serving it with crispy bread. Regardless of the specifics involved in preparing *Nevig*, it is a delicious stew that is fit for a holiday table.

....

1 bunch green Swiss chard, soaked and washed well to remove any sand
1 medium onion, finely chopped
2 garlic cloves, finely minced
½ cup lemon juice
1 cup cooked chickpeas
3 tbsp tomato paste mixed with ¼ cup warm water (or 2 large tomatoes, finely chopped)
3 tbsp oil
1 cup hot water
Salt, black pepper, and red pepper, to taste

Slice the Swiss chard in half lengthwise, to ensure the large stems are halved, so they are easier to cook. Trim the end of the stems, chop Swiss chard, and set aside.

Sauté the onion on medium heat in a pot with the oil. Once the onions are translucent, add the garlic and stir. Add the tomato paste—water mix (or tomatoes, if substituting). Add the chopped chard, stir, and lower the heat. Pour in the hot water and cook on low, covered, until the chard significantly wilts and the stems are almost cooked. Add the chickpeas, lemon juice, and spices, and continue to cook covered for about 10 minutes. Turn off heat and stir the stew, allowing it to sit covered for 10 to 15 minutes before serving.

....

***Pairing suggestion** Enjoy with Soy Milk or Coconut Milk Yogurt (page 212) or Garlic Yogurt (page 20) and toasted Losh (page 140)!*

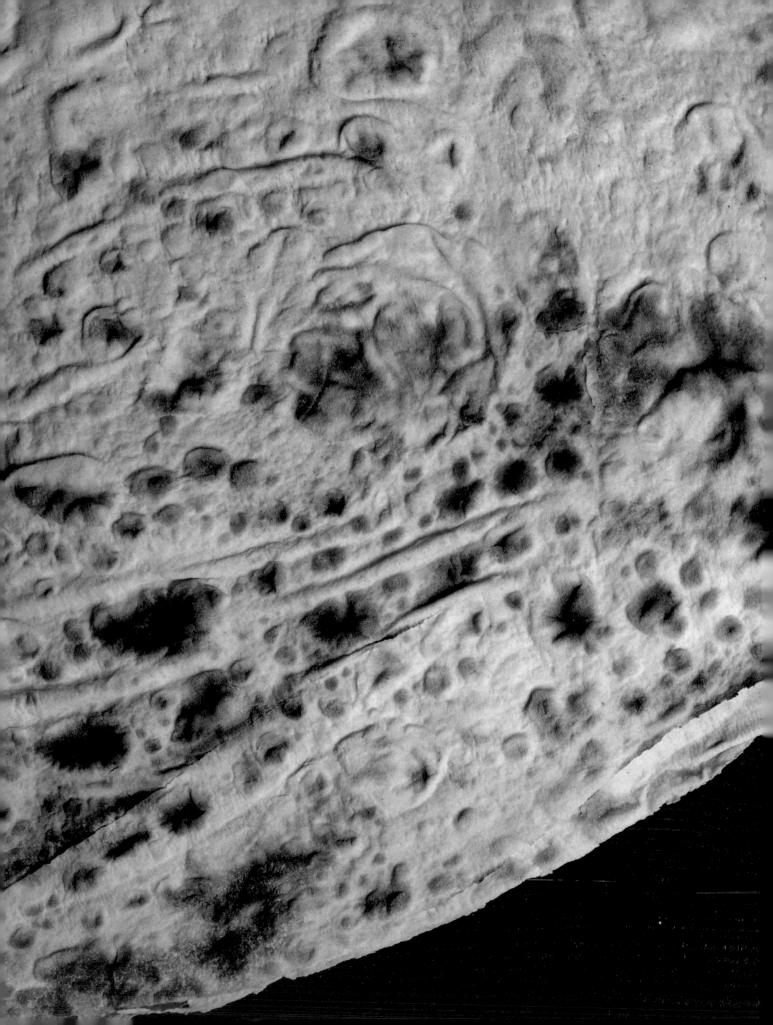

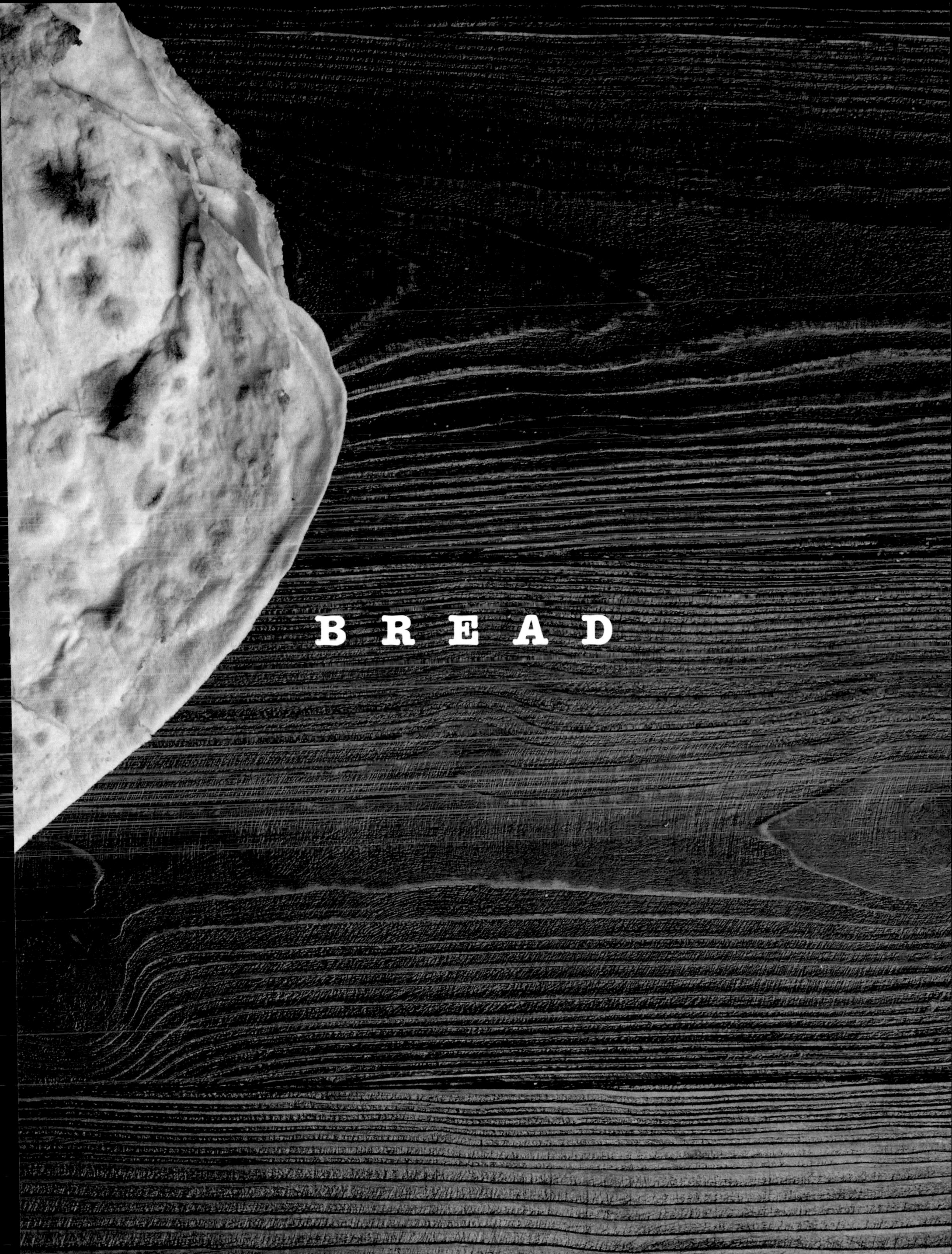

BREAD

Ո՛ւր հաց, հո՛ն կաց:
Wherever there's bread, stay there.

The general revered status of bread in Armenian life can be expressed by the fact that it is often given as a gift to new homeowners, newlyweds are adorned with it, and Armenian priests bring three things with them to bless a new home: water, salt, and bread—as in, all of the essentials. However, nothing can compare to bread's elevated status in Armenia. Tables full of every type of food imaginable, as well as drinks, are not considered complete until multiple baskets of assorted bread ready to be passed around are added. No matter what is being consumed, a piece of *lavash*, a slice of *matnakash*, or freshly baked *losh* will only complement the food, making it even more satiating. In Armenia, the word for bread, հաց, is also used as a generic term for a meal, so if someone says they will eat bread, it is synonymous with food itself, whether that food is breakfast, lunch, dinner, or a snack. This love—or obsession—is also portrayed through the multitude of bakeries throughout the country, as well as in diasporan Armenian communities around the world, that freshly prepare all of the staples along with some stuffed or seasoned bread specialties, creating the most wonderful aromas that effectively lure in helpless passersby. Everytime you bake these breads, it's as if you are creating a little Armenia in your own kitchen.

CONTENTS

Lavash
Լավաշ
makes 4 to 6 breads

Few things proclaim "Armenian cuisine" as much as lavash does—the flatbread to end all flatbreads. In fact, in 2014, UNESCO added "Lavash, the Preparation, Meaning and Appearance of Traditional Bread as an Expression of Culture in Armenia" to its Representative List of the Intangible Cultural Heritage of Humanity. Neighboring countries appealed the designation (the words "in Armenia" were eventually dropped), considering lavash a shared bread among the region. Traditionally baked in an underground clay oven (a *tonir*), lavash is enjoyed as a wrap, a side, a placemat for *khorovadz* (barbecued meat), under a delicious *yeghints*, dried and cracked over soups and stews, and even as a way to grab chunks of food when a utensil just won't do. I've seen it even used as a napkin, though that might be considered blasphemy.

Witnessing lavash being freshly baked is definitely a sight worth seeing. Women effortlessly (or at least seemingly effortlessly) stretch out the dough on a pillow-like rectangular cushion and smack it onto the inner wall of the clay oven, where it will bubble and cook for a minute until perfection. The bread is then removed with a hook and stacked one on top of the other, ready to be served immediately or sold. Besides being versatile and delicious, lavash is associated with many traditions. Most notably, during a wedding, the groom's mother will place lavash on the newlyweds' shoulders, to symbolize prosperity, good fortune, and protection from the evil eye.

*****

Note *Some recipes do not contain any yeast, but a baker from one of my favorite bakeries in Armenia told me a little is necessary.*

2⅓ cups flour
1 cup warm water
1½ tsp instant yeast
1 tsp salt

Combine all ingredients and knead into a soft dough. Place in a bowl, cover, and keep in a warm place for 30 minutes. Separate the dough, rolling it into the size of a golf ball for pan frying or the size of a small apple for baking in the oven. Roll out the dough as thinly as possible in a rectangular shape—a few small tears are okay with lavash dough.

Stovetop method Heat pan on medium-high heat and cook each lavash about 2 to 3 minutes on each side, until bubbles formed turn golden brown. Place on flat plate and keep covered with a damp towel to keep the bread soft until finished. Enjoy fresh or keep secured in a bag once cooled to keep soft.

Oven method Preheat oven to 350ºF (180ºC) and line the back of a large baking tray with parchment paper. Place stretched dough on top and bake for 3 to 5 minutes, carefully turning it over and baking the other side until the lavash bubbles, an additional 3 to 5 minutes.

Lavash Crackers
Լավաշ խրթխրթիկ

Stovetop method Brush the lavash with some oil and sprinkle on black or white sesame seeds (optional). Once cooked, allow to cool without covering, to dry out the lavash. Break into crackers.

Oven method Once the lavash is on the baking sheet, coat the top layer with oil and sprinkle on black or white sesame seeds (optional). Follow directions above to bake. After removing from oven, break sheet into crackers.

Enjoy on their own, in dips, or crushed over Green *Khash* (page 79)!

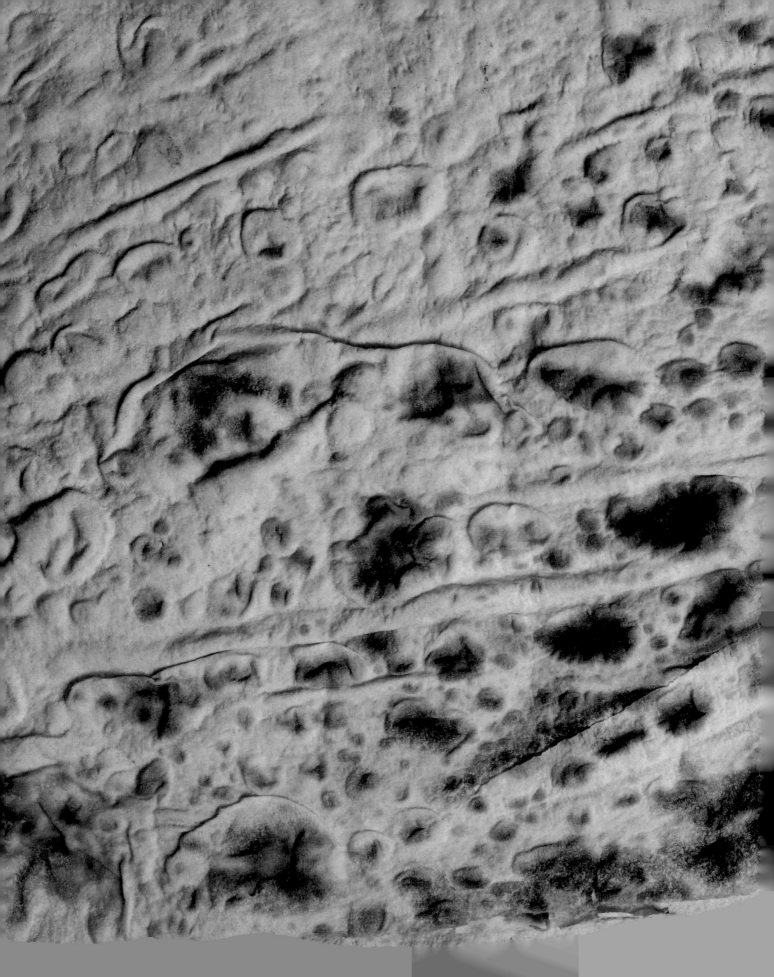

Matnakash
Մատնաքաշ
makes 2 breads

I didn't know anything about *matnakash* until I lived in Armenia, where it is second only to lavash in terms of popularity. It is almost always included as one of the options in bread baskets that are passed around at meals, offering a more filling option. *Matnakash* is recognizable by its signature print, the name meaning "pulled with fingers" (մատ-նա-քաշ) or designed by hand, before the dough is baked. Like most breads in Armenia, *matnakash* is torn apart by hand to enjoy and share, never cut with a knife.

4 cups flour
1 tbsp salt
1½ tsp instant yeast
1½ cups warm water
Oil, for coating

Stir the flour, salt, and yeast together in a bowl. Add the warm water and knead until smooth and soft. Place dough in a bowl, cover it, and keep it somewhere warm for one hour (in an oven with the light on is ideal). Knead the dough one more time to release the air, and cover it again for 30 to 45 minutes. Divide dough in two equal portions, and line two baking trays (or one tray at a time) with parchment paper. Drizzle a generous amount of oil on the parchment paper, and place one of the dough portions on top, shaping and stretching it into its signature oval shape. Make sure both sides of the dough are coated in the oil by flipping it over at least once. Using your hands, create a border about 2 inches into the bread, following the oval shape. Make it as deep as possible to make sure the imprint remains visible once baked. Within the border, using your hands, create two even lines running down (not going outside the border). Allow the bread to sit for 10 minutes.

Preheat the oven to 400ºF (200ºC). Before placing the bread inside, go over the imprint once more to ensure it is deep enough. Bake bread until it is light golden brown, approximately 20 minutes. Enjoy fresh or let cool and store in a bag to keep fresh for a few days.

Suggestion Matnakash *freezes very well, so you can enjoy one fresh and keep the second in the freezer!*

Losh
Լոշ
makes 2 breads

Losh, also referred to as "village bread," is round, fluffy, and easily spotted by its signature doughnut shape. I once made the mistake of casually asking a friend in Armenia if *losh* was essentially the same thing as *matnakash*, just shaped differently. As she reprimanded me, with the word ամոթ (shame) thrown in a few times for good measure, I was reminded of the serious business of bread and directed to the nearest bakery. What I happily discovered is that *losh* is definitely in a league of its own and is traditionally made with sourdough starter created in the New Year, giving it an element of esteem in the Armenian bread community. I've simplified the recipe, and while it still requires a bit more patience than the other breads in this cookbook, *losh* has become my favorite one to bake freshly at home.

3½ cups flour
½ + ¾ cup warm water
1½ tsp salt
1 tbsp + 1 tbsp
**   vegetable oil (plus**
**   more for coating bowl**
**   and dough)**
1 tbsp traditional yeast
1 tsp sugar

Stir sugar and ½ cup warm water in a tall thin glass. Add yeast and stir quickly until incorporated. Set aside somewhere warm until it rises, approximately 5 minutes. Add the flour and salt to a bowl and mix well. Add one tablespoon of oil, ¾ cup water, and the yeast mixture, and stir well. Begin kneading using your hands until a smooth, soft, and stretchy dough is formed. Oil the bowl and place the dough inside, making sure the top of the dough is oiled as well. Keep it covered somewhere warm for 5 to 6 hours, until it has tripled in size.

Separate the dough into two equal portions, and place parchment paper on a baking tray. Drizzle about a tablespoon of oil on the parchment paper, spreading it out with your hands. Knead the two portions of dough again, and place them on the parchment paper, making sure both sides are coated in oil. Shape each piece into a flat circle on the parchment, and using your fingers, create a hole in the middle and stretch it out gently, resembling a doughnut. Repeat with the other piece. Place the tray in the oven on a bottom rack, uncovered, with the light on, to rise a second time, for 30 minutes. Once the dough has expanded, turn on the oven to 425ºF (220ºC), and bake the *losh* breads for 25 to 30 minutes. If a deeper golden brown is desired, switch to broil for 1 to 2 minutes at the end of the 30 minutes. When both loaves have baked, allow to cool, and store in a bag to keep fresh for a few days.

Suggestion Like matnakash, losh *also freezes very well, so you can freeze one (or both) whole or cut them into sections and remove or defrost only what you need.*

Mushroom Flatbread
Մնկալոշ
makes 6 breads

Mushroom flatbread is traditionally made with meat (and called մսալոշ, or meat bread), and is of course more widely known as *lahmajoun* (which also means "meat bread"). It's something I, as is the case with most Armenians, enjoyed immensely growing up and was able to witness its significance by watching my grandmother make it. She would prepare all the ingredients for this family favorite, lay them out on a coffee table, and make upwards of 150 in a couple of hours. Without fail, she would (understandably) proclaim the most recent batch would be the last, and without fail, she would make it again the following week, keeping our stomachs—and freezers—full. There are so many different variations of this recipe, including different ways to serve it, all dependent on the origin of those preparing it. I now even see vegan versions advertised in the Armenian bakeries, restaurants, and shops we used to buy the meat versions from, the plant-based alternatives also differing in terms of ingredients, so not *that* much has changed. This recipe recommends baking your mushroom flatbreads in an oven, but I know many Armenians who, after enlisting the help of all their family members, created outdoor wood-fired ovens in their backyards for the sole purpose of replicating the exact taste of the flatbreads they used to enjoy back home.

Suggestion *As with my grandmother's flatbreads, I always like to keep a bag of these in the freezer for a convenient meal that needs only to be warmed up.*

Pairing suggestion *If not serving with Soy Milk or Coconut Milk Yogurt (page 212), enjoy this flatbread with a cold glass of Tahn (page 46)!*

For the dough
2½ to 3 cups flour
1 tsp instant yeast
1 tsp salt
1 cup warm water
1 tbsp oil

For the spread
20 white button mushrooms
1 tomato, finely chopped
1 green or red pepper, or a spicy long one, finely chopped
¼ bunch parsley, finely chopped
2 garlic cloves, minced
1 medium onion, finely chopped
1 tbsp tomato paste
1 tbsp red pepper paste
Salt, black pepper, and red pepper, to taste

Make the dough Mix 2½ cups of flour, salt, and yeast together. Add the oil and gradually pour in the water, while stirring. Begin to knead the dough and gradually add ½ cup more flour if needed. Place dough on a surface and knead until smooth, soft and elastic, for 5 to 10 minutes. Oil the bowl you had the ingredients in, place the dough inside, making sure the top is also lightly coated with oil, cover with a towel, and keep somewhere warm for 30 to 45 minutes, until it doubles in size.

Make the spread Wash and dry the mushrooms, and halve them. Either finely chop all the mushrooms or quarter and place half the mushrooms at a time in a food processor. Using the pulse setting, pulse them to approximately the size of rice—a few pulses of about five seconds each will do. Place pulsed mushrooms in a pan and repeat for the second half.

On high heat, cook the mushrooms until all the water is released and begins to evaporate. It may seem like a lot of water, but as long as the heat is high, it will all evaporate, 10 to 15 minutes later. Once the water has evaporated, turn off the stove and remove the pan from the heat, allowing the mushrooms to cool. In a bowl, add all the ingredients for the spread, and once your mushrooms have cooled, add them as well, and mix well. Taste and adjust seasonings accordingly.

Assemble the flatbread When the dough has risen, divide it into six even balls and preheat the oven to 400ºF (200ºC). Flour a working surface and roll out each one as thin as you can, in a circle shape. Place 1 or 2 at a time on the baking tray and add one-sixth of the spread on top in a thin layer. Bake for 12 to 15 minutes, depending on preference (longer for a crunchy dough; shorter for a soft dough). Keep cooked flatbreads covered and once cooled, seal them in a bag to remain soft. Serve with fresh mint, soy milk or coconut milk yogurt, and lemon wedges.

Jingalov Hats
Ժինկիալով հաց
makes 8 breads

Jingalov hats, or forest bread, remains one of the best examples of a recipe-less dish I've ever come across in Armenian cuisine. A specialty of Artsakh (Nagorno-Karabakh), it is prepared in both the spring and fall, when wild herbs are aplenty. Depending on who you talk to, you will be told this delicious and flavorful flatbread contains anywhere from 10 to 40 herbs and greens. I was lucky enough to learn how to prepare *jingalov hats* from Saro and Hasmik, the host family I stayed with in Shushi, Artsakh. At what was supposed to be a quick stop at a restaurant on the way to their home, I noticed women carrying huge bounties of freshly picked herbs entering the back, and the purported claim of 40 herbs suddenly didn't seem so absurd anymore. I love to recall how despite the fact that I ordered tea and my friend ordered coffee, we were brought two orders of *jingalov hats* and two glasses of wine instead, the owner telling us we would enjoy that more.

Hasmik had learned to make *jingalov hats* from her mother, and while she did say the bread could easily contain more than 20 herbs depending on the season, most people used the more modest amount of 15 to 20. She explained that the bread, created during difficult times, was proof that "the people of Karabakh do not remain hungry." This is why it is often translated as "forest bread," as it was made with whatever could be found, in order to survive. While I did recognize some of the greens and herbs Hasmik collected, such as nettle and dill, she repeatedly reminded me that this was a recipe-less dish, created with the herbs available at the time. I discovered that this recipe-less dish did indeed have a few rules: at least in her kitchen, thyme never makes the cut and over salting the herbs is a crime. It is also meant to be cooked until the dough is crispy, ideally on a saj pan, but lightly enough so that the herbs remain somewhat fresh and crunchy. It is almost always recommended to be served with a glass of red wine, although *tahn* can be an acceptable substitute.

While I have yet to prepare *jingalov hats* with anywhere near the ideal range of herbs traditionally used, the options I have chosen result in a deliciously flavorful bread that is very reminiscent of the one I enjoyed fresh in Shushi. And when I want the real deal, I am always happy to return.

For the dough
3⅓ cups flour
1 tsp salt
1⅓ cups warm water

For the filling
2 bunches dill
2-3 bunches green onions
1 bunch parsley
1 bunch cilantro
3 cups spinach, packed
Salt and black pepper, to taste
1 to 2 tbsp oil

Wash all of the herbs in advance to ensure they dry by the time you need them. You can wrap them in a towel or paper towels.

Prepare the dough Combine flour and salt, and gradually add the water, mixing it in until it is completely incorporated. Knead the dough until it is soft and smooth. Roll it into a ball, cover it, and set it aside.

Make the filling Roughly chop all the greens and place them in a large bowl. Add salt and pepper, drizzle in the oil, and mix well.

Assemble Divide the dough into 8 balls, covering those not being used. Flour the surface, and using a rolling pin, flatten out the dough as thin as possible, aiming to keep an oval or rectangle shape. Put in a generous amount of the filling, spreading it out on the dough. Press the two opposite sides of the width together into the middle first, before continuing to secure the rest of the dough. Once done, using your palms or the rolling pin, gently flatten out the dough as much as possible. Warm up a pan on medium heat and place the *jingalov hats*, cooking it on each side for 3 to 5 minutes, until the dough is cooked and has lightly browned in some areas.

Tip Feel free to experiment and add or remove herbs and greens to your liking (just no thyme!).

Pairing suggestion Enjoy with Tahn (page 46) or Van Ardi's Classic Blend.

Olive and Walnut Bread
Ձիթապտուղի եւ ընկոյզի հաց
makes 2 to 4 breads

Since this recipe hails from Musa Ler it should come as no surprise that olives and walnuts, as with Olive and Walnut Salad (page 88), are the main ingredients. Musa Ler's mountainous terrain makes it very habitable for olive trees, and as a result, both olives and hand-pressed olive oil were always abundantly available and used in cooking. This unique and delicious bread uses the best of local ingredients and is in constant rotation in my cooking.

For the dough
3 cups flour
1 tsp instant yeast
1 tsp sugar
1 tsp sea salt
4½ tsp olive oil
1 cup warm water

For the spread
1 cup pitted olives, sliced
2 to 3 tsp olive oil
1 small onion, finely chopped
1 tbsp red pepper paste
2 tbsp tomato paste
½ cup crushed walnuts
½ tsp cumin
½ tsp black pepper
½ tsp red pepper
1 tsp dried mint

Make the dough Combine all ingredients for the dough in a bowl and knead until you have a smooth and non-sticky dough. Place dough into a bowl and cover with a towel, keeping in a warm place to rise for 1 hour.

Prepare the spread In the meantime, sauté the onion with oil in a pan until translucent on medium heat. Stir in the red pepper paste and tomato paste. Turn off the heat and add the spices, herbs, walnuts, and olives and combine well.

Make the bread Preheat the oven to 350ºF (180ºC). Lightly knead the dough and divide into two or four balls (depending on preferred bread size). Roll out each ball on a flour-dusted surface until dough is approximately one-inch thick. Evenly spread the filling on each piece of dough. Bake for 15 to 20 minutes.

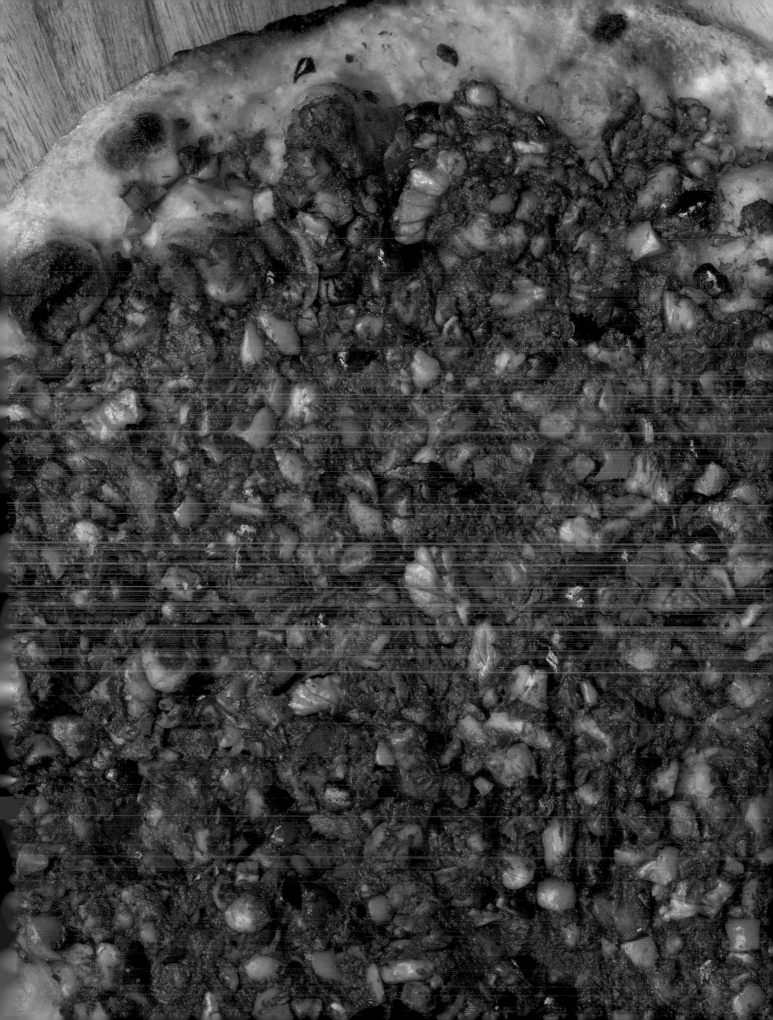

M A I N S

Համբերէ՝ որ համ բերէ:
Be patient, so that it brings flavor.

The guest-of-honor entrée is usually meat or meat-based in Armenian cuisine, surrounded by vegetarian and vegan sides. However, there is a plethora of filling, hearty, and delicious plant-based options that can take the throne at any table—or the center of any plate. Some stand on their own as mains, others were upgraded to fill that role during Lent, and the rest, when combined with a few sides, easily shine as complete meals.

CONTENTS

TOLMAS

Tolma *is a dish that can go by a multitude of different names. Some of the more modern and literal attempts of renaming it include* լիցք *(filling),* տերևափաթ *(wrapped in leaves), and* փաթկած *(wrapped). The case for using the word* tolma *is made by historian Vahe Atanesyan, who says the word derives from the ancient Urartian Kingdom. Grapevines were called "utuli," and wild grape leaves "toli," so Armenians used the word "tolma" to describe stuffed wild grape leaves. Following the same basic concept, they went on to stuff vegetables, and "tolma" became more of an umbrella term, types being differentiated by a preceding descriptor. There are countless varieties of* tolma *available throughout Armenia and the diaspora, and the same type can be served completely differently, based on the specific region's traditions and specialties. Even both sets of my grandparents prepared* tolma *using different methods and ingredients, and I was lucky enough to grow up with the best of many worlds. Tolma can be made with peppers, tomatoes, zucchinis, eggplants, grape leaves, cabbage leaves, Swiss chard, beet greens, and even hemp, stuffed with bulgur (traditional) or rice (contemporary), and can be served hot or cold, as a main or a side. What they all have in common, however, is that since they are special-occasion foods, the important act of preparing* tolma *is always a great way to bring families together, working in unison for the delicious and much-anticipated end result that is* tolma.

Vegetable Tolma
Բանջարեղէնով տոլմա
serves 12 to 14

**12 medium bell peppers
    or 16 Cubanelle
    peppers**
4 medium ripe tomatoes
**1½ cups short-grain
    white rice**
**6 cups chopped onions
    (roughly 8 onions)**
2 tbsp + 1 cup oil
2 tsp dried mint
½ tsp cinnamon
**3 tbsp currants
    (optional)**
**3 tbsp lightly toasted
    pine nuts (optional)**
**Coarse sea salt and
    black pepper, to taste**
¼ bunch parsley
5 tbsp lemon juice
1 cup warm water

Slice the top inch (the "lid") off each pepper and trim the stems. Set the lids aside. Using a knife, remove the seeds and pulp from the peppers and discard them. Do the same with the tomatoes, but use a butter knife or spoon to remove as much of the inside pulp as possible without tearing the skin. Finely chop the tomato pulp and set it aside to use later. Place the peppers and their lids in a large bowl, sprinkle some coarse sea salt and drizzle with about 2 tablespoons of oil, shaking the bowl to distribute the oil.

Finely chop the onions or use a food processor and pulse them in portions. Add them to a large pot on medium heat, cooking for 7 to 10 minutes until completely translucent. Add the rice and cook together for a few minutes, then add the cup of oil and stir. Lower the heat and add the mint, cinnamon, currants, pine nuts, salt, and pepper, and combine well. Add the tomato pulp, cook for a few minutes, then add the parsley and turn the heat off, stirring well. Pour in the lemon juice and taste the mixture, adjusting salt or seasonings as desired.

Preheat the oven to 400ºF (200ºC), and once the rice mixture has cooled somewhat, stuff the peppers and tomatoes using a spoon and cover them with their appropriate lids. Place them in a deep oven dish. Any leftover oil from the pepper bowl can be drizzled over the tomatoes. Pour one cup of warm water into the oven dish, cover the dish with a lid, and bake for 1½ hours, until a knife can easily pierce the skin of the peppers. Allow peppers and tomatoes to cool and gently transfer to a container using your hands and a large serving spoon. Drizzle on some of the remaining liquid over the peppers and tomatoes. Serve warm or cold.

Tip You can use the filling for Grape Leaf Tolma in place of the one here and add zucchini and eggplant to your vegetables for an equally delicious alternative. Serve this option warm.

Suggestion Drizzle Tahini Sauce (page 20) over these!

Pairing suggestion Enjoy with Chickpea Salad (page 94)!

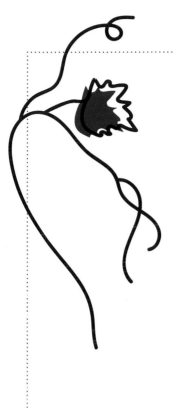

To preserve fresh grape leaves,
simply remove the stems, and rinse the leaves thoroughly. Submerge the leaves in a pot of boiling water, cooking them for about a minute until they soften and change color. Remove from heat and rinse them with cold water to stop the cooking process. Begin stacking the leaves in piles (up to 20 in each pile), with the veiny side facing up. Sprinkle the leaves with pickling salt halfway through and on top of each pile. You can place the different bunches flat in freezer bags and freeze them, defrosting them when needed or roll up each bunch and place them in a sterilized jar or jars. Distribute some lemon wedges throughout the jar or jars. Make the brine by mixing 4 heaping tablespoons of pickling salt and ¼ teaspoon of citric acid in two cups of boiling water and pouring it into the jars with the grape leaves. Do this as many times as needed. Seal the jars and allow them to reach room temperature before placing them in the fridge. The grape leaves are ready after a few days, or they can be stored in the fridge, unopened, for up to six months. Once opened, use up the grape leaves within the week.

Grape Leaf *Tolma* (hot)
Խաղողի տերեւով տոլմա
serves 10 to 12

75 preserved grape leaves (page 157), plus 12 for lining the pot (top and bottom), rinsed

2 cups chopped onions

2 cups short-grain white rice

½ cup oil

¼ bunch fresh parsley, chopped or 1 tsp dried parsley

Juice of two lemons

2 tbsp tomato paste

2 tbsp red pepper paste

Coarse sea salt and black pepper, to taste

3 cups warm water

Cook onions in a large pot on low-medium heat until they are translucent, 7 to 10 minutes. Add salt and cook for a few more minutes. Add rice and stir well, cooking together for a few minutes. Pour in oil, stir, then add black pepper, tomato paste, and pepper paste, and combine. Turn off heat and stir in juice of two lemons and parsley. Remove the pot from heat and allow it to cool.

From the grape leaves, select 12 smaller or damaged ones and set aside. Use half of these to line the bottom of an oven-safe dish. Organize your workstation: bring the cooled off pot of rice, grape leaves, and a baking pot or dish. Place a grape leaf in your palm or on a flat plate, veiny side facing up, and gently remove the stem piece that sticks out. Depending on the size of the leaves, place ½ to 1 tablespoon of the rice mixture on the side closest to where the stem was and roll tightly. Pack the rolled *tolma* tightly in the pot, working in circles, layer by layer, only beginning a new layer once there is no room left.

Preheat oven to 350ºF (180ºC). Spread the second half of the smaller or damaged grape leaves over the rolled ones and place a large heavy plate on top. Pour in the warm water and cover the pot or dish. Cook for 1½ hours, and using oven mitts, remove the plate but leave the top layer of grape leaves in and cover again. After 10 minutes, carefully remove the top layer of leaves and enjoy the *tolma* warm.

Suggestion Drizzle on Garlic Yogurt (page 20)!

Pairing suggestion Enjoy with Yogurt and Cucumber Salad (page 102)!

1

2

3

4

5

Summer *Tolma* (cold)
Ամառային տոլմա
serves 10 to 12

....

75 preserved grape leaves (page 157), plus 12 for lining the pot (top and bottom), rinsed

4 cups chopped onions

1 cup short-grain white rice

¾ to 1 cup oil

½ tsp dried mint

¼ bunch fresh dill, chopped, or 1 tsp dried dill

Juice of one lemon

Coarse sea salt and black pepper, to taste

2 cups warm water

Cook onions in a large pot on low-medium heat until they are translucent, 7 to 10 minutes. Add salt and cook for a few more minutes. Add the rice and stir well, cooking together for a few minutes. Pour in oil, stir well, and add black pepper and dried mint. Turn off heat and stir in juice of one lemon and dill. Remove the pot from heat and allow it to cool.

From the grape leaves, select 12 smaller or damaged ones and set aside. Use half of these to line the bottom of an oven-safe dish. Organize your workstation: bring the cooled off pot of rice, grape leaves, and baking pot or dish. Place a grape leaf in your palm or on a flat plate, veiny side facing up, and gently remove the stem piece that sticks out. Depending on the size of the leaves, place ½ to 1 tbsp of the rice mixture on the side closest to where the stem was and roll tightly. Pack the rolled *tolma* tightly in the pot, working in circles, layer by layer, only beginning a new layer once there is no room left.

Preheat oven to 350ºF (180ºC). Pour the leftover oil from the rice mixture over the rolled grape leaves. Spread the remaining smaller or damaged grape leaves over the rolled ones and place a large heavy plate on top. Pour in the warm water and cover the pot. Cook for 1½ hours, and using oven mitts, remove the plate but leave the grape leaves in and secure the lid on again. Allow the stuffed grape leaves to cool completely, then remove the top layer of leaves.

When ready to serve, remove the rolled grape leaves gently from the pot, arrange them on a tray, pour over the liquid remaining from the pot, and serve with lemon wedges.

....

Suggestion Summer Tolma *can also be served as an appetizer or side in a menu.*

Pairing suggestion Enjoy with Olive and Walnut Salad *(page 88)!*

Lenten *Tolma*
Պահքի տոլմա
serves 10 to 12

....

1 head of sour
    preserved cabbage
    (page 164)
1 cup cooked chickpeas
1 cup cooked red kidney
    beans
1 cup cooked green
    lentils
1 cup fine white bulgur
2 large onions, finely
    chopped
2 + 2 tbsp tomato paste
¼ bunch parsley,
    chopped
¼ bunch dill, chopped
2 tsp dried purple basil
    (optional)
½ tsp savory (optional)
Salt, black pepper, and
    red pepper, to taste
12 prunes (optional)
7 tbsp oil
4 cups hot water

Rinse the cabbage leaves to remove some of the excess salt (optional). Set a few of the smaller or damaged ones aside to line the pot they will cook in. Sauté the onion in the oil until translucent and remove from heat. Combine the chickpeas, red kidney beans, lentils, and bulgur in a large bowl and mix well. Add the herbs (fresh and dried, if using), 2 tablespoons of the tomato paste, salt, black pepper, red pepper, the sautéed onions, and the oil from the pan, and combine well. Taste and adjust spices as desired.

Line a large pot with the cabbage leaves set aside earlier. Place a rinsed cabbage leaf flat on a plate or cutting board, add a generous amount of the bean-and-bulgur mixture in the middle and begin tightly rolling it, folding in the sides as you go. Start arranging the first layer of cabbage rolls in the pot by packing in the rolls as tightly as possible. Before beginning the next layer, insert a few prunes (if using), between the cabbage rolls. Repeat until finished. In a cup, combine the remaining 2 tbsp tomato paste with 4 cups of hot water and a pinch of coarse sea salt and stir. Place a heavy plate on top of the full pot of cabbage rolls and pour in the tomato paste–water mixture down the sides so it doesn't splash up. On low-medium heat, bring the pot to simmer then cook covered for 45 minutes to 1 hour, until the cabbage is soft enough to easily pierce with a knife.

Allow to cool and serve garnished with the remaining prunes (if using).

....

Tip *Lenten* **Tolma** *is traditionally served cool in Armenia, but it is also delicious warm.*

Pairing suggestion *Enjoy with Summer Salad (page 87)!*

To make sour preserved cabbage,
remove the first two outer layers of a large
green cabbage. Using a knife, carefully remove
the core as deep as you can. Fill one-third of
a large pot with water and bring it to a boil,
adding salt and a couple of lemon wedges. Once
water boils, place the cabbage in the pot, core
side down. Cover pot with the lid (even if pot
doesn't initially close completely), and lower
the heat to medium. Allow water to simmer
for 5 minutes, then flip the cabbage so the
core is facing up. Using a utensil, gently begin
loosening and separating the leaves. Leaves
that can be removed completely can be taken
out of the pot. Flip the cabbage over again
and repeat until the cabbage is mostly peeled.
The remaining small center can be left and
preserved whole if desired. In a jar large enough
to accommodate a full cabbage, press the boiled
leaves down to pack them in. Add in the juice
of one lemon. In a separate bowl, combine 1
tablespoon of pickling salt to every cup of room-
temperature water needed to fill the jar, making
sure to dissolve the salt. Once jar is filled,
press the cabbage down again, making sure it
is completely immersed in the salt water. Allow
it to sit at room temperature for seven days,
then transfer to the fridge. Use immediately or
keep unopened in fridge for two months. Once
opened, use the sour preserved cabbage within a
few days.

Tolmakhashu
Snιմախաշու

serves 4 to 6

In a country that is as *tolma*-obsessed as Armenia, of course a few shortcut versions were developed. One option, ծույլ տոլմա, or lazy *tolma*, uses the core and pulp of vegetables often used in *tolma* (tomatoes, eggplants, zucchinis) to make a simple version in a pot with rice and spices. The catch with this option, however, is that you have to already have made *tolma* to be able to use the core and pulp of the vegetables. *Tolmakhashu* fills this gap. It is simply a deconstructed grape leaf *tolma* made *yeghints*-style that is just as delicious and a lot less time consuming—and labor intensive—than the original.

3 cups fresh grape leaves, chopped (or use preserved grape leaves, making sure to rinse before using)
1 cup cooked green or brown lentils
¾ cup long-grain white rice
1 large onion, quartered and thinly sliced
3 to 5 tbsp oil
Salt, black pepper, and red pepper, to taste
3 cups hot water
Squeeze of fresh lemon juice (optional)
Sprinkle of dried mint (optional)

Warm oil in a pot and sauté onions on medium heat until translucent. Add the grape leaves and cook together for 2 to 3 minutes. Pour in 2 cups of hot water, bringing to a boil on high heat, then reduce to low-medium heat and cook for 15 to 20 minutes, covered. (Preserved grape leaves may take an additional 5 minutes to cook.) Once the grape leaves are cooked, add the rice and spices, then the remaining cup of hot water. Stir well and cook covered for 10 minutes. Stir in the lentils, cooking covered for an additional 1 to 2 minutes. Remove from heat, wrap lid in a towel or paper towel, cover pot, and allow dish to sit for 5 to 10 minutes before serving. Squeeze some fresh lemon juice on top of individual bowls followed by dried mint and enjoy.

Tip You can also add 1 to 2 tbsp of Red Pepper Paste (page 18), along with the other spices!

Pairing suggestion Drizzle on some Soy Milk or Coconut Milk Yogurt (page 212) or Garlic Yogurt (page 20) and Marash pepper!

Chortahnjash
Չորթանճաշ
serves 3 to 5

Chortahnjash, literally "dry *tahn* meal," is a delicious and unique centerpiece-worthy dish. Traditionally, Armenians preserved yogurt from the summer in a number of ways, including drying strained, seasoned, and salted balls of it in the sun, or combining it with a grain, crumbling it into a powder once dehydrated. Both were stored for the winter and used as thickeners and/or flavor enhancers in a variety of dishes, including *chortahnjash*. You can follow the traditional process for making this dish or simplify it with the method below.

1 cup green or brown lentils
1 medium onion, halved and sliced in thin moons
1 sheet of lavash, halved
1 cup of Soy Milk or Coconut Milk Yogurt (page 212) or ½ cup Strained Yogurt (page 215), stirred well till smooth
1½ tsp dried savory
1 tbsp oil
3 cups water
Salt, black pepper, and red pepper, to taste

Cook the lentils in the water for approximately 20 minutes, until completely tender.

Sautée the onion in oil. Once translucent, add salt, black pepper, red pepper, and 1 tsp of savory. Remove ¼ of this onion mixture and set it aside. Add the rest to the lentils and combine.

If using yogurt, add ½ tsp of savory and salt (to taste, but it should taste salty like *tahn*) and stir well. If using strained yogurt, stir in enough water to reach a thinner consistency, then add ½ tsp of savory and salt.

Preheat the oven to 375ºF (190ºC). Place one half of the lavash in a clay (or oven-safe) pot, and top with the second half. Place the lentil-onion mix in the pot, and drizzle the yogurt or strained yogurt around it. Top the lentil-onion mix with the sautéed onions that were set aside.

Bake for 5 to 7 minutes in the oven, until the food is warm and the lavash is lightly toasted.

Suggestion *If you do not have savory, you can substitute thyme!*

Pairing suggestion *Enjoy with Olive and Walnut Salad (page 88)!*

Ghapama
Ղափամա
serves 6 to 8

Considering there is an entire song dedicated to the wonder that is *ghapama*, a festive stuffed pumpkin, I'm a bit embarrassed to admit that prior to living in Armenia, I had never eaten it. The song, Հէյ Ջան Ղափամա ("Hey Jan Ghapama"), popularized by Harout Pamboukjian, essentially gives out the recipe for the dish, and states that over 100 ravenous people from "near and far" (including in-laws and distant relatives) came to enjoy the "tasty and aromatic" pumpkin. Understandably, this is another dish you will find present at special occasions, including weddings, as it can serve an abundance of guests. Take one bite of this stuffed pumpkin, and you will understand why every Armenian can't help but sing along the moment the famous song comes on.

1 medium pumpkin
3 tbsp coconut oil
   or vegan butter,
   divided
2 cups long-grain white
   rice, cooked
⅓ cup dried apricots,
   chopped
⅓ cup dried plums,
   chopped, or
   cranberries
⅓ cup raisins or
   currants
⅓ cup walnuts, crushed
¼ to ⅓ cup Simple
   Syrup (page 19)
4½ tsp cinnamon
1½ tsp ginger powder
   (optional)
1 tsp clove powder
   (optional)
½ cup fresh
   pomegranate arils
   (optional)
5 tbsp boiling water
Salt, to taste

Preheat oven to 450ºF (230ºC).

Cut "lid" off pumpkin and remove pulp, setting the seeds aside. Using your hands, coat pumpkin in 1 to 1½ tablespoons of coconut oil or vegan butter. Add a few pinches of salt.

Mix remaining coconut oil (or vegan butter) into the warm rice and stir so it melts. Add the cinnamon, ginger powder (if using), and clove powder (if using) and stir. Add the dried fruits and walnuts and stir. Finally, drizzle in the simple syrup and stir. Stuff pumpkin with the mixture and add the hot water. Cover pumpkin with its "lid," trimming the stem if necessary, and place it on a tray in the oven. Bake for approximately 1 hour, piercing with a knife before removing, to check if it's ready. (It will be very soft when ready.)

Cut the pumpkin in thick wedges, topping each wedge with fresh pomegranate arils (if using).

Note Both butter and honey are used in this otherwise vegan dish, which have been substituted with coconut oil and simple syrup!

Red Lentil Patties
Ոսպով կոլոլակ

serves 8 to 10

I grew up eating and enjoying this dish, which was always served with summer salad. The combination of lentils and bulgur makes this dish surprisingly filling, despite its small size. My grandmother was ahead of her time and would often shape the mixture into burger patties, cooking them with a little oil on the stove for a crispier veggie burger-like alternative. However you plan to serve it, red lentil patties, like red lentil soup, is proof that there is beauty—and flavor—in simplicity!

2 cups red lentils
1½ cups fine white
   bulgur
1 large onion, chopped
⅓ cup olive oil
1 bunch green onions,
   finely chopped
½ bunch parsley, finely
   chopped
1 tbsp cumin
1 tbsp paprika
2 to 3 tbsp red pepper
   paste
1 tbsp salt
5 cups water
1 tbsp red hot pepper,
   to garnish (optional)

Heat the water in a pot, keeping a kettle with boiled water ready in case more is needed. Add salt and stir. Meanwhile, rinse the lentils very well in a strainer then add them to the pot and bring to a boil. Remove the foam that arises and reduce heat to medium, keeping the pot uncovered. Cook for 20 to 30 minutes, stirring occasionally.

While the lentils are cooking, sauté the onion with the olive oil, until translucent. Once the lentils are cooked and "creamy," turn off heat, and let them cool. Rinse the bulgur, thoroughly drain the excess water, and let it sit to soften.

Set aside some of the green onions and parsley for garnish. Once lentils have cooled, add the sautéed onions, green onions, and parsley to the lentils and mix well. Add the cumin, paprika, and red pepper paste, and mix well. Gradually add the bulgur and let the mixture sit for a bit so the bulgur softens completely.

Shape the mixture into ovals or patties, or simply put into a container. Garnish with green onions, parsley, and red hot pepper (if using), and enjoy!

Tip *While these patties are delicious the day they're prepared, they taste even better the following day, once* all the flavors have had a chance to really combine and round out.

Pairing suggestion *Nothing goes better with red lentil patties than Summer Salad (page 87)!*

Vegetable Skewers
Բանջարեղէնի խորոված
serves 2

The moment the weather begins warming up, the smoke from the *khorovadz* fires begins to take over all of Armenia. Swirled metal skewers hold meat, potatoes, vegetables, and sometimes a combination of all three, and are grilled to perfection before being placed on a makeshift plate of lavash, topped with onions and fresh herbs. The lavash holding everything together is just as valuable as the barbecue itself, eaten alongside the meal and often used to pick up pieces of the barbecued food. *Khorovadz* can be served as the highlight of a formal event or as part of a casual summer gathering. We focus on the vegetables in this recipe, creating colorful skewers full of delicious flavor.

---

1 eggplant
1 zucchini
1 medium onion, peeled
1 medium firm tomato
1 bell pepper (or spicy pepper)
3 to 4 tbsp oil
Salt, black pepper, and red pepper, to taste
Fresh herbs, chopped, for garnish

Remove the ends of the eggplant and zucchini and peel sections of skin so the vegetables are striped. Chop vegetables into one-inch-thick slices and add to a bowl. Halve the onion then quarter it, keeping pieces intact as much as possible, and add to the bowl. Chop the tomato and pepper into large chunks and add to the same bowl. Drizzle on the oil, salt, black pepper, and red pepper, and using your hands gently massage all vegetables so they are all coated. Place them on the skewers in individual pieces.

Barbecue or grill the vegetables in the oven for approximately 30 minutes, making sure to rotate them on each side. Once the vegetables are cooked, place them on a plate of lavash and top with chopped fresh herbs.

Suggestion Sprinkle Armenian Herb Mix (page 14) on top.

Pairing suggestion Enjoy with Bulgur Salad (page 101) and Bean Salad (page 95)!

Mantabour
Մանթապուր
serves 4 to 6

Mantabour is a soup made with mante (մանթը), small dumplings filled with meat that have Mongolian roots, and are included in different ways, in a variety of cuisines. Marash Armenians have a unique way of preparing mante, in a soup that infuses a plethora of different flavors and spices for a final result that makes all of the work well worth it. My paternal grandmother, who was from Marash, was an expert at making this dish, and my maternal great-grandmother was known specifically for her ability to make small dumplings (which I'm told are preferred), from dough rolled out thinner than one could ever think possible. The dish is time-consuming and somewhat tedious, and as a result, many regard *mantabour* as a food reserved for special occasions. Witnessing my grandmothers constantly make it at a whim and hearing stories of how my great-grandmothers would happily begin rolling out the dough any time their children or grandchildren expressed a craving for the soup re-categorized *mantabour* for me as a comfort food that we should unapologetically treat ourselves to, as often as desired.

There is an almost identical version of *mante*, called ուլլանչիկ (little ears), in which you shape the dough into a circle using an Armenian coffee cup, place the filling in the middle, and secure it half-moon style, or resembling an ear. You can use this method for a somewhat simpler dumpling!

....

For the dumplings

Filling
25 medium white button mushrooms
1 medium onion, peeled
½ bunch parsley, finely chopped
Salt and black pepper, to taste
Oil or vegan butter (melted), for brushing

Make the filling Wash and dry the mushrooms, then quarter them along with the onion. In a food processor, add the onion and divide the mushrooms into two to three batches, adding the first one on top of the onion. Pulse until finely chopped, occasionally scraping the sides with a spatula. Transfer processed mixture to a pan and continue processing until all the mushrooms are done. If you don't have a food processor, you can finely chop the onion and mushrooms. On medium-high heat, cook the mushroom-and-onion mixture until all the liquid has evaporated, approximately 15 minutes. Reduce heat to low-medium, add salt and black pepper to taste, and continue cooking for a few more minutes. Turn off heat, add the parsley, and stir well. Remove from heat. As it cools, prepare the dough.

1

2

3

4

Dough
2 cups flour
½ tsp salt
¾ cup water

For the broth

2 cups water
2 tbsp tomato paste
1 cup cooked chickpeas
**Garlic Yogurt (page 20),
    for serving**
**Dried mint or Mint-
    Infused Oil (page 19),
    for garnish**
**Red pepper flakes or
    Red Pepper-Infused
    Oil (page 18), for
    garnish**
**Salt and black pepper,
    to taste**

Make the dough Combine the flour and salt, and gradually add the water until completely incorporated. Knead the dough for 5 minutes, shape it into a ball, and cover for about 30 minutes to rest. Flour your work surface, and using a rolling pin, roll out the dough as thin as possible, aiming for a rectangular shape. Using a knife or pizza cutter, cut small squares in the dough. Preheat the oven to 350ºF (180ºC).

Assemble and cook the mante Place small amounts of the mushroom mixture in the middle of each square. Don't be too stingy with the mixture, but don't be too generous, as you'll regret it when it's time to seal the dumplings. Once all the squares are filled, grab both sets of corners of the dough and pinch them together to seal them. If you are having trouble sealing the dumplings, lightly wet your fingers before pressing. Gently press down on the mushroom mixture to keep it in place. As you seal the dumplings, transfer them one by one to a baking tray. Once all the dumplings have been placed on the tray, gently brush them with the oil or melted vegan butter. Bake for 15 to 20 minutes until the bottoms are golden brown.

Make the broth On high heat, bring the 2 cups of water to a boil. Dilute the tomato paste with some of this hot water in a separate bowl, and add it into the pot, reducing the heat to medium. Add the salt, black pepper, chickpeas, and cook for approximately 5 minutes. Gently add the dumplings and cook until they soften, 5 to 10 minutes. Serve warm, with garlic yogurt generously drizzled on top, followed by a few pinches of dried mint or mint-infused oil and red pepper flakes or red pepper-infused oil.

Tip You can bake the dumplings in advance, allow them to cool, and store them in a bag in the fridge or freezer to use in this recipe later!

Sud Mante
Սուտ մանթը
serves 6 to 8

When meat was scarce, or when a "fast-food" version of *mante* was required, there was սուտ (fake) or արագ (fast) *mante*. Though very reminiscent of dumplings, *sud mante* can also stand on its own as an elevated pasta dish.

.....

Mante dough (page 177)
1 onion, finely chopped
2 tbsp oil
Salt, black pepper, and red pepper, to taste
2 tbsp tomato paste (optional)
Garlic Yogurt (page 20)
Dried mint or Mint-Infused Oil (page 19)

Roll out the *mante* dough as thinly as possible using a rolling pin. Using a knife or a pizza cutter, cut it into small squares or rectangles. Sauté the onion in the oil until translucent then add salt, black pepper, red pepper, and tomato paste (if using). Bring a large pot of salted water to a boil, add the pasta and once the pieces begin to float, cook for an additional 4 to 5 minutes. Using a strainer, take out the cooked pasta, removing all excess water, and place on a serving dish. Place the sautéed onions in the middle, drizzle on a generous amount of garlic yogurt, and top with dried mint or mint-infused oil.

Lavash Pasta with Mushrooms
Լաւաշի դդմած սունկով
serves 4 to 6

Lavash pasta, commonly referred to in Armenia as *arishta*, is made from the dough of lavash, but without the yeast. The creation of this pasta is definitely a sight worth seeing. After the dough is cut into cartoonishly long strips, they are hung to dry (often outside), and then baked to a beautiful golden-brown color and stored for use. When it's mushroom season in Armenia, the dried lavash pasta is boiled and cooked with wild mushrooms and herbs, delicious in its simplicity.

....

For the pasta
2⅓ cups flour
1 cup warm water
1 tsp salt

For the dish
1 cup pasta
2 cups mushrooms, sliced
2 tbsp oil
2 green onions, chopped
Salt and black pepper, to taste
¼ bunch parsley, finely chopped, to garnish

Make the pasta Combine flour and salt. Gradually add the water, kneading into a smooth and firm dough. Cover and let rest for 15 to 20 minutes. Flour your work surface and roll out the dough thinly. Using a knife or a pizza cutter, cut the dough into long strips, each about 2½ feet long and ¼ inch wide. Hang them to dry for 8 hours or overnight (less, if hung out in the sun). Make sure to hang each strand equally, adjusting hanging ends so they're both even. Once they have dried, preheat the oven to 350ºF (180ºC) and break the pasta strands in half. Place half on a baking tray and bake for 10 minutes, until they turn golden. Repeat for the second half. Allow the strands to cool and store them in a jar or bag until ready to use.

Make the dish Bring a pot of salted water to a boil and cook the pasta until softened, approximately 12 minutes. In the meantime, sautée the mushrooms with the oil on medium heat until cooked. Add salt and black pepper and continue cooking. When the pasta is ready, use a strainer to remove it from the water and add it to the pan of mushrooms, cooking them together for an additional 3 to 5 minutes. Turn off the heat and add the green onion, giving it a stir. Garnish with fresh parsley.

....

Pairing suggestion Enjoy with Mountain Sorrel Salad (page 98) and a side of Soy Milk or Coconut Milk Yogurt (page 212)!

Lima Beans
Լիմակաև լուբիա
serves 5 to 7

Lima beans are a great example of a vegan side dish that can easily be paired and upgraded to a main. This dish is traditionally served cold with garlic yogurt as a complementary component of a meal, but it can also be served warm with a *yeghints* or rice as a complete meal. My family tends to have bags of frozen lima beans in the freezer, as fresh is not always easy to find, and you don't want to be left lima-less when a craving for these delicious beans hit.

4 cups frozen or fresh green lima beans
2 cups hot water
1 medium onion, finely chopped
1 large tomato
¼ bunch dill, finely chopped + a few sprigs, for garnish (optional)
4 tbsp oil
1½ tsp red pepper paste (optional)
Salt, to taste

Sauté onions in the oil until translucent. Grate tomato on top, add red pepper paste (if using), and cook for 2 minutes on medium heat. If using frozen beans, rinse them with cold water. Add the fresh or frozen beans to the pot. Once the pot has warmed up, add the hot water and allow to come to a boil, then reduce to medium heat, cover the pot, and cook for 10 to 15 minutes. Add salt, continuing to cook covered for a few minutes. Add dill, turn off the heat and allow it to sit for 5 minutes. Garnish with fresh dill.

Pairing suggestion Serve with Rice Yeghints (with Orzo) (page 198) and Eggplant Salad (page 96)!

White Kidney Beans
Ճերմակ լուբիա
serves 6 to 8

White kidney beans are almost always part of the sides or appetizers for special occasions throughout the Armenian diaspora. In many Armenian restaurants, when ordering a sampler or combo starter for a main meal, these beans are automatically an option on the guest list, always set to impress. But once they are paired with *yeghints* and served warm, this dish takes on a completely new personality and shines as a delicious, hearty, and complete main.

2 cups dry white kidney beans, soaked overnight and rinsed
2 medium carrots, chopped
4 tbsp tomato paste
3 large garlic cloves, minced
Coarse sea salt, to taste
¼ bunch parley, finely chopped
¼ cup oil (optional)
5 to 6 cups water

Pour 5 cups of water into a large pot. Add beans, carrots, tomato paste, and garlic, and bring to a boil, making sure to give the pot a good stir. Reduce heat to medium and cook covered, stirring occasionally and adding extra boiled water as needed. About 1 to 1½ half hours later, once the beans have cooked, add salt, oil (if using), and parsley, and stir well. Allow dish to cook, covered, on low heat for another 10 minutes. Then turn off the heat and allow the beans to sit for another 10 minutes before serving.

*Pairing suggestion Serve with either Bulgur **Yeghints** (page 201) or Rice **Yeghints** (with Orzo) (page 198) and/or Beet Salad (page 104).*

Fresh Romano (Cranberry) Beans
Թարմ Ռոմանօ լուբիա
serves 5 to 6

Every summer, without fail, my parents would come home with bushels upon bushels of fresh romano bean pods from farmers markets. Even though the arduous task of peeling each pod still lay ahead, they would still wonder if they made a mistake not picking up a few more bushels. We would enjoy some of it, but the majority would be bagged and frozen for use throughout the year—and for good reason. The fresh beans, in their beautiful red-and-white color, transform into a delicious and almost buttery main, stew, or side dish. Romano beans are easily at the top of the legume hierarchy and are a classic favorite for so many Armenians—especially throughout the Armenian diaspora.

4 cups fresh romano beans
1 small onion, finely chopped
4 to 5 cups hot water
2 large ripe tomatoes, chopped or 2 tbsp tomato paste
2 tbsp oil
Salt, to taste

Place romano beans and onion in a large pot. Cook for 5 to 10 minutes on medium heat, then add the chopped tomatoes or the tomato paste. Add 4 cups of hot water, increase the heat to high and bring to a boil. Once it boils, lower the heat to medium and cook covered, stirring occasionally and adding extra water only if needed. After 20 to 30 minutes, once the beans have cooked, add salt and oil, stir, and close lid, cooking for an additional 5 to 10 minutes. Turn off the heat, allow the beans to sit for 5 minutes, covered, and then remove from heat.

Pairing suggestion Serve with Bulgur Yeghints (page 201) or Rice Yeghints (with Orzo) (page 198), fresh green onions, and a sprinkle of Marash or Urfa pepper!

Flat Green Beans
Կանաչ լուբիա
serves 4 to 6

Flat green beans were in constant rotation for my family and despite their being a tasty and healthy meal, I only learned to appreciate them as I got older. This was another legume my parents routinely bought fresh in the pod, cutting and freezing it to be used throughout the year as a simple but good "everyday dish."

6 cups fresh or frozen flat green beans, ends trimmed, cut into large chunks

1 medium onion, finely chopped

2 large very ripe tomatoes, chopped

3 tbsp oil

2 cups hot water

Salt, pepper, and red pepper, to taste

Sauté onion in a large pot until translucent. Add tomatoes and cook until they are warmed, then add the spices and flat green beans. On high heat, allow the tomatoes to come to a boil, then add 2 cups of hot water and bring to a boil. Reduce heat to medium, cover the pot, and allow it to cook for 20 to 30 minutes, until green beans are completely cooked.

Pairing suggestion Enjoy with Rice **Yeghints** (with Orzo) (page 198) and/or Potato Salad (page 91)!

Ger ou Sous
Կեր ու Սուս
serves 4 to 5

Ger ou sous literally means "eat and be quiet," the meal name to end all meal names. I first heard about the dish from my host mother in Armenia, who told me it was a dish of potato, meat, and vegetable leftovers. When I inquired about the name, she said that when it was served by a wife to her husband, the husband, unable to recognize what he was about to eat, asked his wife what it was. She replied, "Eat and be quiet." He did, and it was good enough to become a staple. I've since heard other explanations behind the name, the most popular being that the husband complained about the meal being too spicy, to which his wife gave the same response. Regardless of the origin story, the name alone inspired me to vegan-ize this meal, substituting mushrooms in place of the meat. I tend to keep it spicy, and if anyone complains, I know exactly what to tell them.

....

1 to 1½ cup assorted mushrooms, sliced in thin strips, or YamChops Szechuan "Beef"
4 medium potatoes, cut into wedges (or 3 cups of *Tatik* Fries, page 211)
1 onion, halved and sliced in thin moons
3 long green hot peppers or jalapeños, finely chopped
1½ cup green peas
2 garlic cloves, minced
3 tbsp oil
Salt, black pepper, and red pepper, to taste
⅓ cup chopped parsley
Sliced tomatoes, for serving

Fry or bake the potatoes. If frying, follow the recipe for *Tatik* Fries. If baking, drizzle the slices in oil and bake in the oven for 20 minutes at 375ºF (190ºC) until cooked.

In the meantime, sauté the onions until translucent. Add the mushrooms and cook with the onions for 5 minutes, adding the spices. Add the hot peppers, green peas, and garlic and cook for an additional 10 to 15 minutes. Add the potatoes, mixing carefully, to keep them intact.

To plate the dish, arrange the sliced tomatoes around a serving plate and add the *Ger ou Sous* in the center, topping with fresh parsley.

....

Tip If you don't want the dish to be spicy, remove the seeds from the peppers or use sweet peppers instead!

Kchuch
Կճուճ
serves 3 to 4

One-pot meals are very trendy now, but they have a long history in Armenia. *Kchuch* means "clay pot," and in the context of a recipe, it is a medley of vegetables, usually accompanied by meat or fish, marinated in a wine, and served and eaten from the same vessel it was cooked in. The pot can be covered with a lid, or covered with a simple dough, which is then eaten with the contents of the pot. The clay pots themselves can be large and shared among many people, or small upright designs meant for one person. If you don't have a clay pot, you can still enjoy a hearty *kchuch* using a ceramic or oven-safe dish!

1 cup cooked green peas
1 zucchini
1 eggplant
1 bell or Cubanelle pepper
1 small potato
1 tomato
1 medium onion
2 garlic cloves
¼ bunch dill (or another herb)
2 tbsp oil
2 tbsp tomato paste
2 tbsp dry red vegan wine
Salt and black pepper, to taste

Place green peas in a bowl. Halve and slice all the vegetables and add them to the bowl. Mince the garlic and finely chop the herb of choice and add those as well. In a separate small bowl, combine the oil, tomato paste, red wine, and spices. Pour this over the vegetables and mix well to marinate. Preheat the oven to 375ºF (190ºC). Oil a clay or ceramic pot and add the vegetables.

If using the bread cover instead of a lid, combine the flour and margarine, gradually adding the water. Knead the dough well. Flour your work surface and using a rolling pin, flatten the dough as thin as needed to completely cover the clay or ceramic pot. Before placing it on the pot, cut a tennis ball—sized circle in the center of the dough with a knife and remove it. This is to ensure the heat circulates and the excess liquid evaporates in the oven. Carefully place the dough on the pot and seal the edges with your fingers.

Continued on the next page

For bread cover (optional)
1 cup flour
2 tbsp vegan margarine
3 tbsp water

Using a fork, poke a few holes throughout the dough. Cook on 375ºF (190ºC) for 1 hour to 1 hour and 15 minutes, until all the vegetables are cooked and there is very little liquid left. Serve in the same vessel it was cooked in and enjoy with pieces of bread.

Tip For a gluten-free alternative, simply omit the bread cover.

Suggestion You can also cook Kchuch uncovered without a lid (bread or otherwise). Just reduce the cooking time to 45 minutes to 1 hour.

Pairing suggestion Pair with Mushroom and Spelt Yeghints (page 202) and/or Chickpea Salad (page 94)!

Harissa
Հարիսա
serves 4 to 5

Harissa is a thick savory porridge, with a place far back in Armenian history, and a special significance in the present day due to its role in the 1915 Musa Ler resistance. It is said that Saint Gregory the Illuminator, the Patron Saint of the Armenian Apostolic Church, was serving a charitable meal of lamb to the poor. As there was not enough meat for the large crowd, wheat was added to stretch the meal, while keeping it satiating. With the inclusion of wheat, Saint Gregory advised his helpers to *harel sa*, or "whisk this," thus creating the name *harissa*. Since then, *harissa* is made with either lamb or chicken, and due to its long cooking process, which is part of the dish's tradition, it is reserved for special occasions, made in large amounts in cauldrons over fires. However, plant-based "everyday" alternatives do exist in Armenian history— as a result perhaps of a scarcity of meat, of Lenten or other fasting periods, or for the use and preparation of seasonal vegetables, greens, herbs, or nuts in a substantial way.

Today, *harissa* holds a very special place in Armenian cooking and culture as it is made to commemorate the resistance that took place on Musa Ler during the Armenian Genocide. For 53 days, the Armenians who refused the deportation order by the Ottoman Turkish government defended themselves against the Ottoman Turks on this mountain, with very few resources. *Harissa* was one of the few ways they were able to sustain themselves until they were rescued by French warships. Every year in September, as part of a *Harissa* Festival, there is a commemoration of the resistance at the memorial dedicated to it in the village of Musaler, in Armavir, Armenia, which was renamed after the mountain in 1972.

Some of the meat-free *harissas* throughout history used potatoes, walnuts, cabbage, Swiss chard, or fresh herbs instead of meat, but in the spirit of keeping it hearty and substantial, I've used white kidney beans. Feel free to experiment with any of these other alternatives.

1 cup peeled wheat
1½ cups dry white
   kidney beans
4½ tsp coarse sea salt
Vegan butter or oil, for
   serving
Cumin and red pepper,
   for garnish

The night (or 6 to 8 hours) before you make the *harissa*, rinse the peeled wheat, add it to a pot with just enough water to cover it, bring it to a boil, then turn off the heat, keeping the pot covered. Soak the beans in a separate pot, also overnight. After draining and rinsing the beans, cook them covered on medium heat with 4 to 5 cups of water, stirring occasionally. Once the beans are cooked, drain all the liquid from the beans into a measuring cup and add water to make 3½ cups of liquid. Add this liquid to the pot with the wheat. Add beans and bring pot to a boil, then lower heat, cover the pot, and cook for at least 2 to 3 hours, adding the salt about halfway through. Make sure to check on the pot and gradually add extra hot water if needed. Once most of the water has absorbed and the grain is fully cooked and softened, start "whisking the wheat," stirring vigorously with a large wooden spoon until wheat kernels dissolve and the mixture resembles a thick porridge. Pour into bowls, make a small hole in the center of the bowl, add a generous amount of vegan butter or oil, sprinkle on some cumin and red pepper, and enjoy!

Pairing suggestion Enjoy with Assorted Pickles (page 218) and/or fresh herbs.

Did you know? The cooking time for meat-based harissa *can range from 5 to 6 hours as both the meat and wheat have to be cooked to the point of dissolution, to then be "whisked" into a porridge-like consistency. This bean-based alternative takes less time to cook.*

Armenian Bowl
Խառն Ճաշ
serves 1

In Siroon's quest to elevate and modernize Armenian cuisine, she suggested that we include an Armenian take on the "bowls," beautifully decorated and with multiple components, so often found in restaurants nowadays. Quinoa, a nutritious and gluten-free grain, is usually the base, and as it does grow in Armenia (harvested by Meline's Garden), I am happy to include it in our recipe. The remainder of the dish is a mixing-and-matching of leftovers to create a filling, flavorful, and colorful bowl of Armenian goodness.

....

½ cup of Meline's Garden white quinoa, or Rice or Bulgur *Yeghints*

1 cup of water (or vegetable broth)

1 skewer of Vegetable Skewers or ½ cup of Vegetable Stew

⅓ cup of Fresh Romano Beans, Lima Beans, or White Kidney Beans

½ cup of either Beet Salad, Summer Salad, or Mountain Sorrel Salad

2 tbsp Tahini Sauce or Garlic Yogurt diluted with water

Armenian Herb Mix or *Tatkhan*

Fresh parsley or cilantro and green onions, chopped, for topping

Cook the quinoa with the water or vegetable broth for approximately 20 minutes. Once cooked, remove quinoa from heat, cover lid with a towel or paper towel, place it back on the pot, and allow quinoa to sit for 5 to 10 minutes. Fluff before use. Place the quinoa or *yeghints* of choice in the bowl first. Add the vegetables, beans, and salad. Drizzle with tahini sauce or garlic yogurt, sprinkle on the herb mix or *tatkhan*, and top with fresh parsley or cilantro and green onions.

ACCOMPANIMENTS

Խոսքով փիլաւ չեփիր:
Rice is not cooked with words.

Once you lay your eyes on a traditional Armenian table, you will understand that sides and snacks are not mere afterthoughts but rather integral components that help create a well-rounded meal. When planning a menu—for family, a get-together, or the holidays—the sides and snacks are what complete the table and give the illusion (however real it may seem at the time) that the food really is endless. Some options may be heartier, others may be lighter fare, but they all play an important role and are sought after due to the love of combining foods. They can even determine what the centerpiece will be, as sometimes the desired sides may not perfectly match the planned main, making a rebrand necessary. Pairing options are suggested throughout this cookbook, but you can always be creative and mix and match to your heart's—and menu's—content.

CONTENTS

YEGHINTS

Yeghints, or pilaf, is a dish that is made when water is poured over a grain (usually rice, barley, or wheat) and cooked until all the water has been absorbed. While these dishes are predominately served as sides today to complement another meal (see Soups and Stews), they used to be prepared as stand-alone filling, nutritious, and simple all-in-one weeknight dinners. The many different variations of yeghints result from the type of grain used, the ingredients included, and even its intention (to be savory or sweet). Although they are so common that most Armenian households can boast making them hundreds (if not thousands) of times, when you witness the commotion that occurs if the yeghints burns or is late to the table, you understand how important and integral to Armenian dining such dishes really are. As they are recommended often in this cookbook as a pairing suggestion, I have included four different variations to keep things interesting, all of which can upgrade any soup or stew (and even some mains) to whole, hearty, and delicious meals.

Rice *Yeghints* (with Orzo)
Բրինձով եղինձ
serves 4 to 5

1 cup long-grain white rice, rinsed
2 cups + 6 tbsp hot water or vegetable broth
2 tbsp orzo
1 tbsp oil
Salt, to taste

On medium-high heat, heat the oil and fry the orzo until golden, making sure not to burn it. Add the water, allow it to come to a boil, then add the rice and stir. Add salt and continue boiling the rice for a few minutes, then reducing heat to low, covering the pot, and allowing it to simmer until the rice cooks and water is almost fully absorbed, approximately 20 minutes. Remove from heat, wrap the lid in a dish towel or paper towel, place it back on the pot, and keep the pot covered for another 10 minutes, making sure to fluff with a fork before serving.

Suggestion *Feel free to substitute orzo with vermicelli.*

Substitution *For a nutritional upgrade, replace the rice with Meline's Garden quinoa and adjust cooking time accordingly!*

Bulgur *Yeghints*
Ձավարով Եղինձ
serves 4 to 5

1 cup coarse white
    bulgur
2 cups hot water
1 cup chopped tomato
    (from 1 large tomato)
1 to 2 small peppers,
    spicy or mild, finely
    chopped
1 small onion, finely
    chopped
¼ cup oil
Coarse sea salt, to taste

Sauté onion in the oil on medium heat until translucent. Add peppers and cook for another minute. Add the tomato and cook until the tomato is completely cooked and softened. Add the bulgur and stir, allowing it to soak up the liquid from the tomato. Add 2 cups hot water and at least ½ teaspoon salt. Lower the heat, cover, and allow to cook until all water is absorbed, about 10 to 15 minutes. Once water is absorbed, remove pot from heat, wrap a dish towel or paper towel over the lid, then cover pot with the lid, allowing excess moisture to be absorbed, approximately 5 minutes. Fluff with a fork before serving.

Tip Dissolve 1/2 to 1 tsp Abukht Paste (page 73) in hot water and add to the recipe after the tomato cooks for a flavor boost!

Suggestion Siroon's grandmother adds 1 cup of cooked chickpeas to her *yeghints*, right after the tomato softens. A great way to make this dish more filling and protein-rich!

Substitution For a gluten-free alternative, substitute Meline's Garden quinoa (grown in Armenia) for the bulgur and adjust cooking time accordingly!

Mushroom and Spelt *Yeghints*
Հաճարով եւ սունկով եղինձ
serves 4 to 5

....

**2 cups mushrooms,
   thinly sliced**
1 cup spelt, rinsed
**1 onion, halved and
   sliced in thin moons**
4 tbsp oil
1½ to 2 cups hot water
**Salt and black pepper,
   to taste**

In a pot, add the spelt and enough water to cover it, and bring to a boil. Turn off the heat, cover the pot, and let sit for 6 to 8 hours or overnight. Then drain the spelt and set aside. Warm oil in a pot before adding the onion. Sauté on low-medium heat until translucent. Add the mushrooms, cooking for 3 for 5 minutes, then the salt and black pepper, cooking for another minute or so. Add the spelt, mixing it in well and cook for 2 minutes. Pour in 1½ cups of hot water, lower the heat, cover the pot and allow to cook for 30 to 45 minutes, until water is absorbed and spelt is done. If water is absorbed but spelt is still not ready, add the extra ½ cup of hot water. (Spelt will always be somewhat chewy in texture, but you can add the water if you prefer a softer grain.) Turn off heat, wrap a tea towel or paper towel around the lid, place it back on the pot, and allow the *yeghints* to sit for 10 minutes before serving.

....

Substitution *For a gluten-free alternative, substitute in Meline's Garden quinoa (grown in Armenia) for the spelt and adjust cooking time accordingly!*

Mshosh
Մշոշ
serves 3 to 5

Part of the traditional Lenten cuisine from the Van region, *Mshosh* is named after one of the main ingredients found within the dish: wild apricots. Although apricot is *dziran* in Armenian, *mshosh* described a specific variety of wild apricot, which is used in this recipe. There are different variations of this dish, some of which include pumpkin, green beans, or beets, but this version is the most popular. *Mshosh* is most often served cool as a side, but it can also be served warm as a main. In the versions I've eaten in Armenia, the apricots tend to be left whole, but I prefer them chopped, to spread the goodness more evenly from the first to last bite.

1 cup dry green lentils
1 medium onion, finely
    chopped
3 to 4 tbsp oil
½ cup dried apricots,
    chopped
½ cup prunes, chopped
⅔ cup walnuts, crushed
¼ bunch parsley,
    chopped
3 cups water
Salt and black pepper,
    to taste

Soak apricots and prunes in hot water. Rinse and drain the lentils, add to a pot with the water, and bring to a boil, lowering heat to medium. Cook until softened, approximately 20 minutes. While the lentils are cooking, sauté the onion in the oil until translucent, then add the drained dried fruits and cook on medium heat for 5 minutes. Turn off the heat, add the walnuts and stir, then add the entire mixture to the lentils. Add the salt and black pepper, and before serving, top with chopped parsley.

Topik
Թոփիկ
makes 8 to 10 balls

A specialty dish from the Armenians of Istanbul, *Topik* is a Lenten food traditionally prepared for Easter, Christmas, New Year's Eve, and other special occasions. Comprising a hearty shell of potatoes and chickpeas stuffed with a rich and creamy filling, *Topik* is meant to be offered as a gourmet side or appetizer, each ball serving four people. My mother tells me that traditionally, women used to include the cloth needed in the preparation of Topik as part of their dowry, as a way to show their future husband and in-laws they were capable of making this revered dish. This is my grandmother's recipe passed down to me, and I am happy to share this unique and delicious dish.

For the filling
10 medium onions
¾ cup pine nuts
¾ cup currants
¼ tsp all spice
Pinch of black pepper
½ tsp cinnamon
Salt, to taste
½ cup tahini
2 tbsp oil

For the shell
4 cups cooked chickpeas, peeled and completely cooled
1 large white potato, (roughly 300 grams), boiled, peeled and completely cooled
Pinch of cumin
Pinch of salt

Make the filling Cut each onion in half and slice in thin moons. Cook onions on low heat with the lid on. They will release liquid. Once they have softened, add the oil and continue cooking on low heat with lid on. Once the onions are completely translucent, turn off the heat, add the remaining ingredients, and mix well. Allow the mixture to cool completely.

Make shell Add the potato, peeled chickpeas, cumin, and salt into a food processor. Process until completely smooth (it will resemble dough). Divide dough into eight portions.

Assemble the *topiks* Place one of the portioned doughs on a slightly damp reusable dish cloth or wipe and flatten it out using the cloth. (The dough should be thinner than a pancake.) Place 2 tablespoons of the filling in the middle of each portion, and using the cloth, fold in the dough. Smooth over outside to round it out and continue for the rest of the portions. Place the balls in the fridge, covered, overnight or for a few hours. When ready to serve, decorate by cutting crosses into each one, drizzling in olive oil and lemon juice, and sprinkling on some cumin.

Tip: Peeling chickpeas may seem like a tedious chore, but it's a necessary step to keep the shell as smooth as possible. To peel chickpeas, take a bunch of cooked chickpeas in your hand and rub them together, loosening the skins.

Potato *Seghmig*
Գետնախնծորի սեղմիկ
makes 6 to 8 balls

Potato *Seghmig* is a popular dish that goes by different names in different regions. Even though the name *prtouj* is most commonly used, in Armenia *prtouj* usually refers to a rolled lavash wrap, made in a hurry. *Seghmig* comes from the word *seghmel* (to squeeze). As this dish is eventually squeezed into a round or oval shape, the name Potato *Seghmig* makes the most sense to me, although *klorchik* (small circles) is a close second. Potato *Seghmig* offers a different way of serving potato, a staple of modern-day Armenian cuisine, and is an easy side dish for laborious days, enjoyed with fresh or preserved grape leaves.

3 Yukon Gold potatoes (roughly 1½ lbs)
½ cup fine white bulgur
1 small onion, finely chopped
2 tbsp oil
¼ bunch fresh parsley, finely chopped
1 tbsp tomato paste
1 tbsp red pepper paste
2 tbsp warm water
Salt, black pepper, red pepper, and cumin, to taste

Boil the potatoes and peel them while they are still warm. Mash them with a potato masher or fork and set aside, covered. Cover the bulgur with water, and thoroughly drain. Set aside. Sauté the onion in the oil until translucent. While onion is cooking, combine the tomato paste, pepper paste, and the warm water in a bowl, stirring well. Add this mixture to the onions and cook for 1 to 2 minutes. Then turn off the stove and remove pan from heat, allowing contents to cool.

In the bowl with the mashed potatoes, add the onion–paste mixture, parsley, and spices, and stir. Add the bulgur and mix very well. Let sit for 10 to 15 minutes, covered, or overnight in the fridge. Form into balls of preferred size using your hands.

Pairing suggestion Enjoy with fresh or preserved grape leaves (page 157)!

Potato Pastry
Գետնախնձորով խմորեղէն
makes 12 pastries

In Armenian cuisine, phyllo-based pastries are a very common side and appetizer, which can be rolled or shaped into squares or triangles and stuffed with a variety of different ingredients—cheese being the most popular. My siblings and I occasionally enjoyed the following vegan-by-default potato rolled version of this growing up, which included different herbs and spices every time, keeping it interesting and delicious.

4 to 6 Yukon Gold potatoes, boiled and peeled
1 medium onion or a small bunch of chives
2 tbsp chopped fresh parsley
Salt, black pepper, and red pepper, to taste
½ tsp oil, plus more to brush and coat phyllo dough
6 phyllo dough sheets
4 tsp black or white sesame seeds, for topping

Roughly chop the potatoes and place them in a bowl, adding the ½ teaspoon of oil. Using the back of a fork or a potato masher, mash the potatoes with the oil. Quarter the onion, and thinly slice quarters into half moons. Salt them directly on the cutting board and using your hands, massage them to reduce the acidity and release some of the liquid. If using chives, omit these steps. Add the onion (or chives), parsley, black pepper, red pepper, and more salt to the bowl with the potatoes and knead.

Cut each phyllo sheet in half lengthwise, making sure to keep the sheets you are not using covered with a damp towel. Brush oil on the side facing up and add about a golf-sized ball of the potato mixture on top of the phyllo and spread it out lengthwise. Tightly roll it in, and fold in the sides as you go along. Brush oil all over the rolled phyllo pastry and top it with black and/or white sesame seeds. Using a fork, poke holes throughout the stuffed phyllo, to ensure it does not open up during baking. Preheat the oven to 350ºF (180ºC), and once all the phyllo pastries are rolled, bake them for approximately 20 minutes, until they take on a goldish hue. Flip them halfway through.

Tatik Fries
Տատիկի տապակած գետնախնձոր
serves 5 to 6

Fried potatoes may be a universal favorite, but when made *tatik* (grandmother) style, they are in a league of their own. While living in Armenia, a friend and I were craving fries and in describing to each other what exactly we wanted, we both said "grandmother-style," almost in unison. These potatoes are made in a pan with a generous amount of oil, then salted generously. They are indulgent and heavy, in true grandmother fashion, and worth every bite.

5 Yukon Gold potatoes, peeled
1 cup vegetable oil
Salt, to taste

Slice the potatoes into wedges. Pour the oil in a pan and heat on medium-high heat. Have a flat plate lined with paper towel ready. Add half the potatoes in the pan, making sure not to crowd them. Cook for approximately 10 minutes, then stir. Cook for a few more minutes until potatoes are golden brown on all sides, using a slotted spoon to remove them directly to the lined plate. Salt them while still hot. Cook the remainder of the potatoes following steps above. Allow wedges to cool, and enjoy.

Suggestion You can also keep the skin on the potatoes. Just make sure to wash the potatoes thoroughly!

Yogurt and Strained Yogurt
Մածուն եւ քամած մածուն

In most Armenian households, yogurt—store-bought or homemade—is always a staple in the fridge. Though also mixed with jams or honey for a sweet treat, yogurt is predominantly a side to savory foods, its creamy texture and tangy taste pairing perfectly with so many dishes in Armenian cuisine, especially *mantabour*, *tolma*, and *yeghints*. The importance of yogurt can be seen in its inclusion in many recipes, as well as in its preservation process of being dried during the summer so it can be enjoyed throughout the winter. It can stand on its own, be strained, turned into a garlic dip, or thinned out into a beverage. I have yet to find a store-bought plant-based alternative that, even when labeled as unsweetened, comes close to the tanginess of the yogurt I grew up with. Since my family makes yogurt regularly, the idea of veganizing it didn't seem daunting to me. After much trial and error, I settled on soy milk, its higher protein content making it ideal for yogurt-making, and, after the initial batch, follows the same basic principle and method as a traditional yogurt recipe. I have also included a creamy coconut milk option, its higher fat content requiring a different method.

Soy Milk Yogurt

For first batch
1 litre unsweetened, unflavored, additive-free soy milk (homemade or store-bought)
4 vegan probiotic capsules (not pills) (free of prebiotics and enzymes)

For all following batches
1 litre unsweetened, unflavored, additive-free soy milk (homemade or store-bought)
3 to 4 tbsp of Soy Milk Yogurt from last batch

First batch
Pour the soy milk into a pot and bring to a boil on medium heat. Remove from heat and allow the milk to cool slightly to approximately 110ºF (43ºC), approximately 40 minutes. The temperature is reached if you can leave your little finger in the milk comfortably for 10 seconds. Pour ⅓ to ½ cup of the warm soy milk into a small bowl. Open the probiotic capsules and sprinkle them on the small bowl of soy milk. Using a wooden spoon, stir well to dissolve the probiotics. Pour the contents of the bowl back to the pot and stir again. Pour the soy milk into flat airtight glass containers (not jars) and secure the lids. Either place these in an oven with the light on for 6 to 8 hours or overnight, or wrap them carefully in 1 to 2 blankets to culture. Just make sure to move the containers gently as too much movement can interfere with the process. After the 6 to 8 hours, transfer the containers to the fridge and allow to sit untouched for 1 to 2 hours. Store in fridge for one week.

For subsequent batches
Take 3 to 4 tablespoons of the yogurt from the previous batch from the fridge, place it in a small bowl, and let it reach room temperature, 2 hours. Stir so it becomes smooth. After following the directions above for boiling the soy milk and allowing it to cool to 110ºF (43ºC), pour in ⅓ to ½ cup of the warm milk into the bowl with the yogurt, and using a wooden spoon, stir together well. Pour the contents of the bowl back to the pot and stir again. Follow the rest of the steps for the first batch.

Coconut Milk Yogurt

For first batch
1 can (400 ml) full-fat coconut milk (just coconuts and water, or with guar gum, a thickening agent)
2 vegan probiotic capsules (not pills) (prebiotic and enzyme free)

For all following batches
1 can (400 ml) full-fat coconut milk (just coconuts and water, or with guar gum, a thickening agent)
3 to 4 tbsp of Coconut Milk yogurt from last batch

First batch
Pour the coconut milk into a bowl and stir with a whisk or spoon until it is completely smooth. Open the probiotic capsules and sprinkle them on the milk. Using a wooden spoon or utensil, stir the contents of the capsules in the milk, incorporating them completely. I prefer my initial batch to be tangier and use 3 capsules, but you can use 2 capsules. Pour the mixture into a clean jar and cover with a cheesecloth or reusable dish cloth or wipe, securing cover with an elastic band. Keep in a warm place or in an oven with the light on for 24 hours. Then remove the cheesecloth and elastic band and cover jar with the jar lid. Place yogurt in the fridge for 2 hours to set. Store in fridge for up to one week.

For subsequent batches
Simply take a few tablespoons of coconut milk yogurt out of the fridge and allow it to reach room temperature, 2 hours. Stir to make sure it is smooth. Then add a new can of coconut milk, and stir well with a wooden spoon. Pour mixture into a clean jar. Follow the rest of the steps for coconut milk yogurt.

Suggestion If the Coconut Milk Yogurt separates, you can simply stir it to combine, or scoop off the thick yogurt at the top and discard the liquid.

Strained Yogurt
Քամած մածուն

**Soy Milk Yogurt or
Coconut Milk Yogurt**

Line a sieve with paper towel or an absorbent cloth like a cheesecloth or reusable dish cloth or wipe. Place over a bowl such that the strained liquid is separated from the yogurt and not reabsorbed. Spoon the yogurt into the strainer and distribute it. Place in the fridge overnight and gently scoop the strained yogurt from the strainer into an airtight container and store in fridge for one week.

Plate of Herbs
Կանաչի

Whether for breakfast, lunch, or dinner, a side of fresh herbs is always welcome on the table as an edible decoration. Seasonal ingredients are used to provide a great addition of flavor—and texture—to any menu. Whether the herbs are stuffed in an on-the-go lavash wrap or eaten with a hearty meal, in Armenian cuisine, there's no such thing as too much green.

One bunch each of the following
Parsley
Cilantro
Dill
Mint
Tarragon
Purple basil (or green)
Radish
Green onion
A few spicy peppers

Soak the fresh herbs (parsley, cilantro, dill, mint, tarragon, and basil) in a large bowl for a few minutes to allow any debris and sand to fall to the bottom. Remove and rinse the herbs, placing them in a strainer or wrapping them in a tea towel or paper towels to dry. Wash the radish, green onion, and peppers, and either leave whole or cut into smaller pieces. Arrange the full bunches or smaller amounts of each on a serving tray, storing the leftovers (wrapped in a tea towel or paper towel) in a bag in the fridge to keep fresh for a few days.

Assorted Pickles
Խառն թթու

Pickles featuring produce like cauliflower, cabbage, celery, beets, turnips, green tomatoes, and more are just as common in Armenia as they are in the Armenian diaspora. A plate packed with these crunchy and tangy vegetables and fruits will always be present on a dinner table or munched on throughout the day. In Armenia, you can visit farmers markets and buy massive quantities of assorted pickles or mix and match a variety from jars of one type of produce to customize your own batch.

My mom told me that her grandparents had a massive clay pot filled with a seemingly never-ending supply of pickles—with red beet added for the signature color we all know and love. My mom makes batches of assorted pickles every year, in addition to batches of only jalapeños or cucumbers, always adding in a handful of dry chickpeas to the large assorted batches. Dry chickpeas to aid the pickling process was apparently common knowledge, and adding dry chickpeas is very popular in Musa Ler pickling traditions as well.

Enjoy assorted pickles on their own or in addition to a savory meal, and personalize the batch by mixing and matching vegetables to your heart's content.

Ingredients (for a 4L glass jar or jars)
1 handful of dry
   chickpeas
A few large garlic
   cloves, peeled and
   roughly crushed
3 to 4 celery stalks,
   sliced
½ head cauliflower,
   florets separated
3 carrots, sliced
3 to 4 cucumbers, sliced
1 jalapeño, whole for
   less spicy pickles,
   sliced for spicy
   pickles
½ a head of cabbage,
   torn into smaller
   pieces by hand
2 medium green
   tomatoes, quartered
1 small beet, peeled
   and quartered
   (optional)
Herbs such as dill
   (optional)

For the brine*
3 cups boiled water
   that has cooled to
   room temperature
1 cup white vinegar
2 tbsp pickling salt
½ tsp citric acid
¾ tsp sugar

*This is the standard brine
ratio. Make as many batches
as needed to fill your jars.

Add the chickpeas to the jar or jars first. Throw in the garlic cloves. Mix the remaining ingredients together in a bowl. Transfer them to the jar or jars. The ingredients will fill a single four-liter jar or smaller jars that, together, add up to four liters.

Make the brine Pour the water in the same bowl used above. In a separate bowl or cup, stir the salt with the vinegar until it completely dissolves. Add this to the water and stir. Add the citric acid and sugar, and stir. Taste the brine to make sure the vinegar-salt ratio is ideal. Pour the brine into the jar(s). Use a spoon to push down all the vegetables to pack them in. If more brine is needed, make another batch. You can use leftover cabbage leaves to keep all of the vegetables submerged in the brine. Seal the jar(s). Flip each jar over for one minute, to make sure the liquid coats all the contents of the jar, then turn right-side up again. Let pickles sit at room temperature (around 73.4ºF/23ºC) for one week, then transfer to the fridge. Store in fridge for up to six months.

Grilled Corn
Խորոված Եգիպտացորեն
serves 4

The most memorable view of Dilijan, a town about 1.5 hours north of Yerevan, Armenia, is the mountainous scenery the area is known for. When I visited in the fall, in addition to the changing leaves and the beauty of the trees, another sight caught my eye: every few blocks or so, there were huge cauldrons of boiling water on the side of the road, with corn being boiled and served to small crowds of people walking by or at pit stops. No matter how close to each other every corn-station was, they each still had a small crowd enjoying corn on the cob, sprinkled generously with salt and red pepper. The corn can be boiled to keep this snack as simple as possible or thrown on the grill as here for a roasted alternative.

4 ears of corn, peeled (husks removed)
Oil, for coating the corn
Salt, black pepper, and red pepper, for sprinkling

Turn the barbecue on medium heat, and allow it to warm up. Coat the corn in oil and place it on the grill, ideally covered (but can also cook uncovered). Flip the corn every couple of minutes and cook until the kernels begin to pop and reach a dark golden brown color. Remove and place on a plate and sprinkle generously with salt, black pepper, and red pepper.

DESSERTS

Ուշ լինի, նուշ լինի:
Let it be late, let it be sweet.

Once dinner is complete and the scent of freshly made coffee or tea fills the air, it's time to end the night on a sweet note. The diversity of dessert in Armenian cuisine means there truly is something for everyone, and if folk wisdom holds true, some of it may even bring about good fortune. Whether it's a cake, pudding, sweet bread, or fruit-based treat, round out your meal (and day) the right way, and համով վերջացուր (end it with flavor).

CONTENTS

Anoushabour
Անուշապուր
serves 8 to 10

Anoushabour, which means "sweet soup," is always eaten in the new year to start the year with something sweet. It also makes an appearance at other special occasions or at large gatherings as it is a favorite, but on New Year's Day it's a must. Since you use only half a cup of grains but end up with such a large amount of dessert, Anoushabour is associated with prosperity and good fortune. It requires attention and patience, but a year filled with good luck is well worth it.

....

½ cup pearl barley
¼ to ⅓ cup dried
   apricots, chopped
¼ cup golden raisins
¾ to 1 cup sugar
2 tbsp rose water
10 to 10 ½ cups water
   (plus more if needed)
Cinnamon,
   slivered almonds,
   pomegranate arils
   for topping

The night before, rinse the barley well and add it to a pot with 7 cups of water. Bring to a boil, remove all foam, turn off the heat, leave the lid on, and let it soak all night.

The morning of, boil water in a kettle and keep it handy in case you need to add more water along the way. Soak apricots and raisins in hot water. Bring the barley to a boil again. Once it boils, remove any foam and reduce the heat to low-medium. Cook for approximately 50 minutes, making sure to stir occasionally. After 20 minutes of cooking, using a potato masher, mash as much of the barley as possible, and add 1 more cup of boiled water. A few minutes before the 50-minute mark, drain the dried fruits and add them to the pot, along with 1 more cup of boiled water. Boil for another 30 minutes, stirring occasionally. Add 1 to 1½ more cups of boiled water if needed. (More water is needed if the barley begins to stick to the bottom of the pan or the porridge becomes too thick.) Add the sugar and cook for another 10 minutes, stirring more often but gently. Turn off the heat and add the rose water. Remove from heat, cover the pot, and allow to sit for 5 minutes. Transfer to a large container (or pour in individual bowls) and let cool completely. Once cooled, serve immediately or place in the fridge to enjoy later. When ready to serve, sprinkle on cinnamon and almonds, or pomegranate arils and almonds.

Rolled *Tertanoush*
Թերթանուշի փաթաթուկ
makes 4 rolls

Tertanoush, more commonly known as baklava, is a layered sweet pastry using phyllo, walnuts, and simple syrup. The rolled option is one of the easiest ones to prepare, and although *tertanoush* traditionally contains both butter and honey, it can be made without animal by-products, making it a great dessert for Lent. I've even heard that the word baklava originates from "bahk" (Lent) and "lavash," which means a butter- and honey-free version may just be the norm!

Simple Syrup (page 19)
4 sheets of phyllo dough
2 cups walnuts
1 tsp cinnamon
1 tsp sugar
1 cup coconut oil, unrefined or refined, depending on preference
Handful of blanched almonds or pistachios, ground, for garnish (optional)
Pinch of salt

If phyllo is in freezer, remove the four sheets and cover them, allowing them to get to room temperature. If making the syrup, do it now, so it cools in time for when you need it.

In a food processor, process the walnuts. Mix processed walnuts with sugar and cinnamon.

Preheat oven to 300ºF (150ºC). In a pot on the stove, double boil or melt the coconut oil so it is easily spreadable. Brush coconut oil all across the phyllo sheets generously, making sure to keep the sheets you are not using covered with a damp towel. Pour approximately ⅓ cup of the ground walnuts onto half of the phyllo sheet along the long edge, spreading it out as best as you can. Place a thin wooden pole on the side with the ground walnuts and begin tightly rolling up the pastry, starting with the side with the ground walnuts. Once you reach the halfway point, brush on more coconut oil on the rolled half. At three-quarters of the way, brush more coconut oil (the more generous with the oil now, the better the end result will be). Finish rolling, and brush coconut oil all over the phyllo, making sure to get the side where the opening is. With your hands, push the phyllo inwards, towards the center, so that it's wrinkled and tight. Slide it off the stick onto a baking tray. Cook for about 30 minutes, until the *tertanoush* is golden brown. Flip midway through. Take the tray out of the oven and immediately pour the cooled syrup over the rolled phyllo dough. When done correctly, you should hear a prominent sizzling sound, which means the pastries will absorb the syrup. Top them with ground blanched almond or pistachio, and a sprinkle of salt.

Let the *tertanoush* cool completely, then cut diagonally. Keep the pastries in a container in the fridge or freeze them—they will taste even better after they sit in the fridge for a few hours or overnight.

Easter Bread
Զատիկի հաց
makes 5 to 7 breads

Most Armenians look forward to this specialty on Easter Sunday, which is easily recognized by its signature shape (a thick braid), topped with black and/or white sesame seeds. One of the important ingredients of this sweet bread, other than the many eggs, is ground mahaleb, which is the kernel extracted from the seed of a species of cherry. This small but powerful ingredient is responsible for the aromatic flavor Easter Bread is known for and will leave any kitchen lingering with its scent. Easter Bread is serious business: Many steps are necessary to ensure the dough rises to its full potential, and the making of it tends to be a family affair. I recall a time I impulsively opened the oven door to see what my mom and aunt were baking (it *should* have been obvious), and after realizing it was Easter Bread, I saw my aunt's face turn white as I had single-handedly stunted the expansion of the bread they worked so long on. Needless to say, I hopped out of the kitchen faster than the Easter bunny, and now use the oven light to satisfy my curiosity.

....

7½ to 8 cups flour
2½ cups sugar
15 tbsp aquafaba
1 tsp mahaleb powder
1 tsp mastic gum, powdered
1 cup plant milk
2 packets traditional yeast (16 grams) + 2 tsp sugar and ½ cup water
1 cup vegetable oil
White and black sesame seeds, for topping

Preparation Prepare the ingredients at least 8 hours before making Easter Bread, or overnight. Make sure all ingredients are at room temperature. Turn on the oven at 350ºF (180ºC), and after five minutes, turn it off, leaving the light on. This will ensure a warm environment for the Easter Bread to rise in.

Make the binding agent In a large bowl, combine the sugar and aquafaba and whisk until well combined. Add the mahaleb, mastic gum, and plant milk, and combine well until mastic gum is dissolved.

Prepare the yeast Mix 2 teaspoons of sugar with ½ cup of water at 110ºF (43ºC) to 115ºF (46ºC) (water should be warm to the touch) in a tall glass until dissolved. Add the yeast packets, stir well, and cover the top of the glass, allowing yeast to rise on a warm surface.

Make the dough Add the oil and the risen yeast to the bowl with the other ingredients. Gradually add the 7½ cups of flour and using your hands, combine well. Continue working with the dough, lightly kneading it for 5 to 10 minutes, until it is completely smooth. It will remain a soft dough, somewhat sticky, but you should be able to lift it off the bottom of the bowl. If not, add the remaining ½ cup of flour and combine well. Shape it into a ball, and if desired, lightly leave an imprint on the dough as is traditionally done (my mother always imprints a cross). Turn on the oven light. Cover the bowl with plastic wrap to avoid the risen dough sticking to a tea towel or blanket. Then wrap the bowl in a towel or blanket and place it in the oven, allowing it to sit for at least 8 hours or overnight. The dough should double or triple in size.

Make the bread If braiding, separate dough into three tennis ball–sized portions, rolling each in your palm and/ or on a surface until they lengthen to about the length of a pencil. Secure the three ends on one side together and begin braiding the strands until you reach the end. Secure the end by pressing it underneath the dough, and place the braid on a parchment-lined baking tray. Do this for the remaining portions of dough, or mix and match different designs. Allow the dough to sit for another 30 minutes for a second rise on a warm countertop.

Preheat the oven to 350ºF (180ºC). Layer on a generous amount of oil on each bread with a pastry brush, making sure to thoroughly coat the braided creases as well. Top with both white and black sesame seeds. Bake for 50 minutes to one hour, until the bottom of the bread is a dark golden brown. Once the breads have cooled completely, use a pastry brush to lightly coat them with oil for a shine.

Semolina Halva
Սպիտակածավարի հալվա
serves 8 to 10

Semolina Halva is an incredibly flavorful and unique dessert that is a common staple in many Armenian households—as both an after-dinner sweet and a breakfast. In Jerusalem, Semolina Halva is traditionally served on St. Sarkis Day, and my father recalls a neighbor who prepared it the night before and left it by the window overnight. In the morning, there were four hoofprints on it, which the neighbor claimed was a sign that St. Sarkis, on his horse, was present, giving this neighbor a bit of a celebrity status in their community.

The reason to serve Semolina Halva is also bittersweet. Traditionally prepared for a funeral service by a relative or close friend of the deceased's family, the halva aims to bring peace to the soul of the deceased as it signifies that they are laid to rest with sweetness in their heart. The halva is meant to serve as a small comfort also for those grieving and can be prepared *yeghints*-style as in the recipe below or as a pressed-down cake. While, understandably, an aura of sadness surrounds Semolina Halva, it is so delicious and universally anticipated that it has the honor of being present, even during a sad time.

---

2 cups semolina
**1 cup vegan butter
 or margarine,
 or coconut or
 vegetable oil**
1¼ cup sugar
**2 cups unsweetened,
 unflavored plant
 milk (higher in fat is
 ideal)**
½ cup pine nuts
Cinnamon, for serving

In a large saucepan, combine vegan butter or oil, sugar, and plant milk on low heat. In a large pot, add the semolina and pine nuts and begin toasting on low-medium heat for approximately 15 minutes until the pine nuts are golden. Once the semolina and pine nuts are almost done, bring the butter-milk-sugar mixture to a boil on medium heat. Once it boils, turn off heat to both the pan and the pot, and gradually add the semolina mixture to the saucepan with the vegan butter, plant milk, and sugar, being careful so that it doesn't boil over or splash. Briefly stir the combined ingredients and cover the pan until completely cooled. Once cooled, you can fluff halva with a fork in the pot or, as my mom does it, be more traditional and remove portions at a time to a flat plate, fluffing the portions with a fork individually, then transferring to individual bowls.

Sharots
Շարոց
makes 6 threads

Walk through the famous Gum Market in Yerevan and you will find vendors surrounded by draped *sharots*, threaded walnuts dipped in a molasses-based mixture, in every color—and in any flavor—you can imagine. Grape is the most common variety, but for those who enjoy things a bit on the tart side, pomegranate is a great alternative. In Armenia, this sweet treat is sometimes referred to as "sweet sausage" because of its appearance after being dipped in molasses, which initially caused me to turn down offers to try this completely vegan dessert, as I took the nickname literally. *Sharots* most likely comes from the Armenian word *sharel* (to line up), and in this case, it refers to the many walnuts impressively lined up on a single thread.

For the mixture
1 cup flour
1 cup sugar
2 tsp cinnamon
1 tsp ground clove
1¾ cup pomegranate molasses or grape molasses
2 cups lukewarm water

String the walnuts Prepare the walnuts first. Knot one end of a string, thread the needle, and carefully thread the 25 walnut halves, by inserting the needle through the walnut halves, convex side first (so the walnuts can hold more of the molasses mixture). The string can be oiled to ease the process a little more, but as long as the needle is thin, it should go in the walnuts smoothly. Set the threaded walnuts aside.

Prepare the area Prepare the area where the *sharots* will be hung. I like to use a towel rack, but you can hang them anywhere. While the *sharots* will not drip excessively, it's a good idea to place some newspaper or parchment paper under the area where they will be hung to catch any dripping.

To make the sharots
6 strong pieces of
  string, long enough
  to fit 25 walnut
  halves each, with
  extra room to tie a
  knot for hanging
1 thin needle
150 walnut halves

Make the mixture Sift the dry ingredients in a large pot. Add the molasses and mix together with a wooden spoon. Place the pot on the stove on medium heat, and continue mixing. Add the water one cup at a time, stirring well. The mixture will begin to thicken. Continue stirring. Once mixture has thickened to the point where it sticks to the back of the wooden spoon rather than drips down, it is ready. Allow it to cool for 5 to 10 minutes.

Assemble the *sharots* Carefully dip the stringed walnut in the mixture, tightly gripping the top and ensuring walnuts are completely saturated. You can use the spoon to coat the walnuts even more thoroughly. Hang the threads of dipped walnuts, one by one, until they are all done. Allow them to dry for 3 to 5 days, until they are no longer sticky to the touch. Wrap them in parchment paper and store in the fridge. To serve, pull out the thread and slice the *sharots* diagonally.

....

Suggestion If you want to use pomegranate molasses but want it slightly less tart, add more sugar to your mixture!

St. Sarkis Halva
Սուրբ Սարգիս հալվա
makes 15 to 20

St. Sarkis Day, a holiday unique to the Armenian Apostolic Church, celebrates Saint Sarkis, the patron saint of love and youth. The holiday is often compared to Valentine's Day and is celebrated every year 63 days before Easter. There are traditions associated with this day in both Armenia and the Armenian diaspora.

In Armenia, I learned about the tradition associated with *aghablit* (salty wafers). These small cookies packed with salt are hard not to notice in Armenia, as leading up to St. Sarkis Day, you cannot walk a few blocks without seeing *booths* of elderly women selling them in bunches. Single people are meant to eat *aghablit* in the evening before St. Sarkis Day, and despite feeling thirsty, they are not to drink (or eat) anything after consuming it. They are then to see their future spouse in their dream, offering them water. I've heard many accounts from people in Armenia affirming this is true and that it happened to them—even though they hadn't yet met the person in their dream. If you don't see this dream, I am told it's because you simply don't remember or you're not meant to get married this year—or in the very near future. My favorite account is from a friend, who dreamt that many women offered him water, but remembering his family's pressure to settle down, he refused their offers and instead went to a lake to quench his thirst.

In the Armenian diaspora, St. Sarkis Halva is a more common tradition, enjoyed on the morning of St. Sarkis Day. Though the halva is traditionally made by whipping the reduced liquid from boiled dried soapwort roots, using marshmallow is a short-cut option used by many, including myself.

I like to combine both Eastern and Western traditions for this holiday and remind myself, as I eat the almost inedible *aghablit*, that even if I don't have a wonderful dream (or can't remember it), I can at least treat myself to St. Sarkis Halva in the morning.

¾ **to 1 cup sugar**
⅓ **cup water**
1 tbsp lemon juice
2 tsp rose water
5 cups (250 g)
 vegan (gelatin-free)
 marshmallows
1 cup walnuts halves
2 to 3 cups sesame
 seeds (won't use
 them all but need
 a good amount to
 properly coat halva)

Place white sesame seeds in the fridge to cool. In the meantime, combine water and sugar in a pot and bring to a boil. Once the sugar water boils, reduce heat to low-medium and add the lemon juice. A few minutes later, add the rose water. Once mixture becomes golden in color, add the marshmallows. Stir until completely smooth and then turn off heat. Pour chilled sesame seeds in a tray. While mixture is still hot, pour scoops of it—making the scoops as round and flat as possible—on top of the sesame seeds. Pour as many scoops as you can fit on the tray. Place walnut halves in the middle of each scoop. Let the halva cool for about 45 seconds to 1 minute, as it will be much easier to roll and handle the scoops. Then fold one side over, followed by the other.

Aghablit
Աղաբլիթ

To make *aghablit*, simply combine 1¼ cups flour with a few tablespoons of salt and stir well. Add enough water to create a dough and roll it out. Cut into shapes of choice (or use cookie cutters) and bake at 350ºF (180ºC) until golden brown, 20 to 30 minutes.

Dried Fruit
Պտուղի չիր

Dried fruits, like jams, were a surefire way of extending a summer fruit's life span well into the winter. Now they are more often treated as delicious and convenient snacks, and beautiful additions to any dessert or snack table. They are also often added to soups or boiled with water to be served as remedies for those becoming ill. A quick stroll through any farmers market in Armenia will bring about pause to appreciate all the types and colors of assorted dried fruits for sale, often decorated into shapes like trees. Making them does require a bit of patience, whether you dry them outside or in an oven. But if you live somewhere with scorching hot summers, use the heat to your advantage!

2 ripe peaches
3 ripe apricots
3 ripe plums
1 cup lemon juice
3 cups water

Halve the fruit and remove the pits from the peaches, apricots, and plums. For a shorter drying time, peel and slice the peaches. Add the fruit in a bowl with the lemon juice and water, gently mixing well with your hands. The lemon will prevent the fruit from browning. Alternatively, sprinkle citric acid directly on the fruit. Allow the fruit to marinade for a few minutes.

To dry in an oven Preheat the oven to 170ºF (76.7ºC). Line a baking tray or trays with parchment paper. Thoroughly drain the fruits and line the pieces on the trays so they do not touch each other. Bake them in the oven with the door slightly open for 4 to 6 hours, flipping them every hour. When ready, the fruit should be wrinkled and chewy, but not stiff.

To dry in the sun Line a pan or baking tray with parchment paper to catch the liquid that would otherwise stick to the pan or tray, and place a drying rack on top for the fruits. Place the drained fruit on the drying rack, making sure not to overcrowd them. Cover fruit with a piece of cheesecloth, securing it under the tray. Leave out in the sun for 3 to 4 days, making sure to flip the fruits occasionally and to bring them inside overnight. The fruits are ready when they're wrinkled and chewy, but not stiff.

After baking or drying the fruits, allow them to sit at room temperature overnight before storing them in an airtight container in the fridge.

Suggestion Use any fruit you like. Larger fruit should be sliced, whereas smaller fruit can be simply halved.

Fruit Lavash
Պտուղի լավաշ
for 1 baking tray

In addition to making jams and drying fruits, the goodness of seasonal fruits can be extended by making Fruit Lavash. Although a sweet snack, Fruit Lavash can also be added to certain soups and stews in Armenian cuisine to provide a different element of taste. I grew up enjoying a thick apricot lavash— almost too tedious to eat due to its stickiness. In Armenia, plum tends to reign supreme, although there is a variety of other fruit to choose from. Thanks to the addition of a very ripe peach, this recipe is both sweet and sour and contains no added sugar.

15 small ripe purple plums
1 very ripe peach

Halve the plums and the peach, removing all the pits. Place the fruits in a pot for approximately 15 minutes, allowing some of their own juices to seep out. Cook them on medium heat, stirring while more liquid is released. Lower the heat and continue to cook until fruits have completely softened and begun to liquify, 15 to 20 minutes. Remove from heat and allow to cool. Pour the liquid into a blender or food processor, or use a hand blender immersed in the pot. Blend until liquid is very smooth. Line a baking tray with parchment paper and pour the blended fruits onto it and using the back of a spoon, spread the liquid out thinly, completely covering the tray. Cover the tray with cheesecloth and leave out in the sun for 1 to 2 days until fruit completely dries, bringing the tray in at night. Roll the lavash and store, whole or cut into strips, in an airtight container in the fridge for up to one week.

The fruit can be dried also in a dehydrator (follow the machine settings) or in an oven (bake on the lowest heat, with the door slightly open until dried).

Suggestion Feel free to experiment with other fruit, or try a combination of fruit. Fruit that releases liquid is ideal, but you can always add some water to get things going!

Fruit Lavash Rolls
Փափթուած պտուղի լաւաշ
makes 1 roll

In addition to the different-colored *sharots* and fruit lavash found at most farmers markets in Armenia, there is also a rolled and stuffed fruit lavash. A more filling dessert or snack, Fruit Lavash Rolls are filled with simple syrup, ground walnuts, and cinnamon.

1 sheet of Fruit Lavash
½ cup of Simple Syrup
　(page 19)
½ cup ground walnuts
　(or other nut)
1 tsp cinnamon
　(optional)
Pinch of salt (optional)

Combine cinnamon, salt, and walnuts, and stir well. Add the simple syrup gradually, until a paste is formed. Spread this mixture on one edge of the lavash and roll like a burrito. Cut the rolled lavash into 4 or 5 sections with a sharp knife.

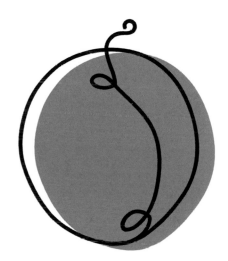

Darehats
Տարեհաց
serves 6 to 8

Like *Anoushabour*, *Darehats*, meaning "New Year's Bread," is made primarily for New Year's Day. In the case of *Darehats*, however, things are not left to chance and instead good fortune is taken via a coin or fruit seed. Besides kneading the dough with good wishes and thoughts, the baker, before sealing the *Darehats*, adds a coin or seed on top of the filling, seals it, and leaves the rest to chance. Once baked, the cake is sliced into as many pieces as there are guests, and whoever ends up with the slice that contains the coin or seed will have great fortune in the year ahead. An unexpected but pleasant surprise for me was discovering that *Darehats* is usually made Lenten, without animal by-products, so nothing had to be substituted in this recipe.

Darehats is a hearty treat, "breadier" compared to other doughs. I was told it is meant to be served with tea that melts the bread in your mouth as you sip the tea. Regardless, *Darehats* is a delicious cake with a flavorful filling, and whether or not you get the coin or seed, you will still feel like a winner when enjoying this dessert!

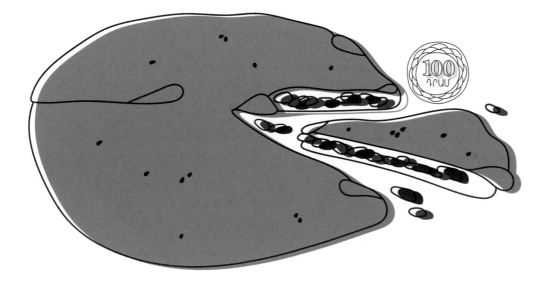

3½ cups flour
2 tsp baking soda
¾ cup sugar
1 cup neutral oil
(vegetable or
canola oil)
¾ cup warm water
1 cup chopped dried
fruits (such as
raisins, figs, and
apricots)
1 cup crushed nuts
(such as walnuts and
almonds)
1 tbsp cinnamon
2 to 3 tbsp Simple
Syrup (page 19)
Handful of white and/or
black sesame seeds
or hemp seeds
Coin or fruit seed

Mix the flour, baking soda, and sugar in a large bowl. Add the oil and water and combine well, kneading the dough. If you want to decorate the bread, set aside a small amount of the dough. Split the dough into two equal parts.

In another bowl, combine the dried fruits, nuts, and cinnamon, and stir. Add the simple syrup to this bowl to bind them together.

In an oiled cake pan 12 inches in diameter and 4 inches in height, flatten out one half of the dough. Spread the nut-fruit mixture across it. Place the clean coin or seed somewhere on the nut-fruit mixture. Flatten the second half of the dough on top, making sure to seal all around. If you saved some dough, make a shape of your choosing to decorate the top of the bread. Brush some water on top of the dough and sprinkle on sesame or hemp seeds. Bake at 350°F (180°C) for 35 to 40 minutes, and then broil on low for an additional 1 to 2 minutes until the top is golden brown. Slice into as many pieces as you like or based on the number of guests.

Tip Make sure to let anyone eating this know there may be a coin or seed in their slice to avoid anyone potentially choking or cracking a tooth on the small item.

Pairing suggestion Enjoy with Mint Tea (page 36)!

Gata
Կաթա
makes 2 cakes

I didn't grow up eating gata, but in Armenia, it is always a go-to dessert, a standard accompaniment to a cup of coffee or tea during a work break, or even a breakfast. It is an ubiquitous dessert for every event or occasion and can be prepared with or without a filling and even layered. You can buy it in a few different forms from any bakery or shop in Armenia, although a trip to Garni Temple and Geghard Monastery is a great way to enjoy freshly baked gata that attracts tourists as well. Although I can't say I understand the mass appeal of this sweet bread, I do appreciate the beautiful design work usually on top of it, my personal favorite being depictions of bezoar goats. Traditionally, families would add an embroidery pattern or symbol associated with them, so the neighborhood or even entire village would know which family baked the gata. Whether you design your gata or not, I hope you enjoy gata as much as 99.9% of Armenians do!

For the dough
4 cups flour
1 cup Soy Milk or Coconut Milk Yogurt (page 212)
1 tsp instant yeast
1 tsp baking powder
⅔ cup vegetable oil
¾ cup sugar
3 tbsp aquafaba

To make the dough Allow the vegan yogurt to reach room temperature, and whisk or stir it until completely smooth. Add the instant yeast, baking powder, vegetable oil, sugar, and aquafaba, and whisk well. Add the flour one cup at a time, combining it well. Knead until completely smooth, and set the dough aside, covered.

To make the filling Melt the coconut oil or vegan butter in a small pot or saucepan on low-medium heat. Add the vanilla. Gradually stir in the icing sugar, then the cinnamon. Once combined, gradually add the ¾ cup of flour and salt, and stir well. Remove from heat and allow to cool.

For the filling
½ cup coconut oil (or vegan butter)
¾ cup icing sugar (confectioners' sugar)
1 tsp cinnamon
1 tsp vanilla extract
¾ cup flour
Pinch of salt

Assemble and bake the gata Preheat the oven to 375ºF (190ºC). Lightly knead the dough again, then split it into two equal portions. If you want to decorate the gata, set aside a small amount of the dough. Work the dough in your hands, keeping it in somewhat of a ball shape. Using your fingers, make a well in the middle of the dough, pressing it in as far as possible without breaking through to the other side. Stuff this well with ½ of the filling mixture, folding the dough back up around it. Place the stuffed dough on a clean surface, flattening it out with your palms or using a rolling pin gently to create a flat circle shape. Place the gata on a parchment-lined baking tray. Repeat steps for the second portion of dough. If desired, create a design— as simple or as elaborate as you like— on top of the cakes. If you didn't set aside dough, you can always use a butter knife to gently imprint a design. Using a fork, pierce the cakes a few times all around. Bake for 30 to 40 minutes, then broil on low-medium heat for an additional 1 to 2 minutes until the tops are golden brown. Allow to cool completely before slicing.

....

Tip I've reduced the amount of sugar in both the dough and the filling, but feel free to reduce it even more or alternatively, add to it for that very sweet authentic gata taste.

Hadig
Հատիկ
serves 6 to 8

Hadig is prepared as part of *Agra Hadig*, a celebration of a baby's first tooth making its long-awaited appearance. *Hadig* means "grain" (which resembles a tooth) and, therefore, is the main ingredient in this sweet treat. At a baby's *Agra Hadig*, objects symbolizing professions (calculator = accountant, notepad = doctor, pen = author, etc.) are laid out on the floor and the object the baby picks up first is said to be his or her future calling. Some of the grain used in the *hadig* is then gently poured on top of the child's head, sealing their future with good luck. The *hadig* itself is then enjoyed by the guests, who will dissect the symbolism of the child's chosen object a little more. You can make *hadig* outside of *Agra Hadig*, as a sweet *yeghints*-style dessert!

½ **cup pearl barley**
3 **tbsp golden raisins**
2 **tbsp slivered almonds**
¼ **tsp cinnamon**
½ **cup pomegranate arils**
1 **tbsp vegan icing sugar (confectioners' sugar)**

The night before, place the pearl barley in a pot, add enough water to cover it, and bring it to a boil. Remove foam, turn off heat, cover the pot, and allow it to soak all night. The next day, add 1 cup of hot water to the pot, bring barley to a boil again, and then cook on medium heat for 15 to 20 minutes, or until cooked. (Unlike *Anoushabour*, the pearl barley in this recipe is meant to retain some of its chewiness.) Remove the pot from heat, cover, and allow to sit for 5 to 10 minutes.

Place the cooked pearl barley in a strainer, rinse with cold water, and drain thoroughly. Remove a handful of the pearl barley and set it aside if using it for the *Agra Hadig* (to pour on the child's head). Add the remainder to a bowl and mix in the raisins, almonds, cinnamon, and ½ the pomegranate arils, and combine. Pour the *hadig* on a serving dish, and sprinkle the icing sugar on top, using a sifter or fine mesh strainer to remove lumps. Traditionally, the remaining pomegranate arils are used to make a cross on the hadig, or otherwise decorate it.

Horseshoe Cookies
Պայտի կրկնեփ
makes 25 to 30 cookies

Horseshoe cookies are a delicious and light treat traditionally made around Christmas. Like many recipes in this section, they symbolize good luck—unsurprising due to their signature shape. This is a vegan version of my great-grandmother's recipe, and I'm happy to report that even three generations later, it's still a favorite.

3 cups flour
½ cup + 2 tbsp sugar
⅓ cup + 2 tbsp vegetable shortening, melted and cooled
⅓ cup + 2 tbsp vegan margarine, melted and cooled
9 tbsp aquafaba
½ cup crushed walnuts
½ cup currants
1 tsp baking powder
1 to 2 tbsp vegan icing sugar (confectioners' sugar) (optional)

Whisk the aquafaba and sugar together. Add 1 cup of the flour and the baking powder but do not mix. Then add the walnuts and currants, and lightly massage them in the flour to coat them. (Doing so will help avoid the walnuts and currants sticking to each other.) Add another cup of flour and using your hands, mix the dough well. Pour in the margarine and vegetable shortening along with the final cup of flour and combine well.

Preheat the oven to 350ºF. Remove walnut-sized pieces of the dough and roll them in your palms to about 3 inches in length. Place them on a countertop and shape them into the shape of a horseshoe, making sure to press them into form, with the middle remaining thicker and the ends slightly thinner and turned inward. Place the cookies on a parchment-lined baking tray and bake for 25 minutes, until the edges of the cookies are golden brown. Allow to cool completely. If desired, dust with icing sugar before serving.

Suggestion *Enjoy with Fruit Jam (page 58)!*

Savory Cookie Twists
Արի կեսկուզ
makes 30 to 35 cookies

These savory Armenian cookies usually make their long-awaited appearance at Easter and are go-to snacks. They are also priest-approved acceptable exceptions to fasting on Easter Day for children and the elderly, who often carry a few in their pockets just in case. They go wonderfully with a hot cup of tea or coffee as a snack or post-dinner savory treat.

2 cups + 2 tbsp flour
1 tsp salt
1 tsp baking powder
2 tbsp aquafaba
3 tbsp water
2 tbsp oil
½ cup vegan margarine, melted and cooled
White and black sesame seeds, for topping (optional)

Combine the flour, salt, and baking powder in a bowl and stir well. Pour in the aquafaba, water, oil, and margarine, and mix everything well, before placing the dough on a clean surface. Knead very well, for 5 minutes. Form dough into a ball, place it back in the bowl, cover, and allow to rest for 30 minutes. Separate the dough into into pieces slightly smaller than a walnut. Take one piece and lightly work the dough in your hands, before rolling it between your palms, to about the length of a pencil. Place it on a surface and form a "U" shape. Hold the open ends together, while using your other hand to flip the looped end two to three times, to twist it. Secure the loose ends by pressing them together and place cookie on a parchment-lined baking tray. Do this with each piece, or shape some into finger-sized sticks instead. Preheat the oven to 350ºF (180ºC). Using a pastry brush, brush a thin layer of vegan margarine or oil on each of the cookies, topping them with white and black sesame seeds. Bake for 20 to 25 minutes, until the bottoms are golden. Switch to broil on a low setting and allow the cookies to cook for an additional 1 to 3 minutes, until desired golden hue is achieved. Remove from oven and allow to cool completely before serving.

Vegan Armenian Table

Whether you are hosting a group of friends or planning for the holidays, these menus are set to impress and will leave you with delicious leftovers for days!

1

Okra Stew
Bulgur Salad, with lettuce for scooping
Bean Salad
Potato Pastry
Drink Armenian Coffee
Dessert St. Sarkis Halva

2

Ghapama
Yogurt and Cucumber Salad or Strained Yogurt
Lima Beans
Eggplant Salad
Drink Mulberry-Infused Vodka
Dessert Rolled *Tertanoush* or Semolina Halva

3

Red Lentil Patties
Summer Salad
Mountain Sorrel Salad
Beet Salad
Assorted Pickles
Drink Mint Tea
Dessert Semolina Halva or Gata

4

Yogurt Soup (topped with Mint- and Red Pepper–Infused Oils)
Fresh Romano (Cranberry) Beans
Olive and Walnut Salad
Plate of Herbs
Drink Armenian Coffee
Dessert Rolled *Tertanoush*

HOLIDAY 1

Vegetable *Tolma* and/or Grape Leaf *Tolma*
Garlic Yogurt
Topik
Green Lentil Salad
Drink Mulberry-Infused Vodka
Dessert *Sharots*

HOLIDAY 2

Nevig
Rice *Yeghints* (with Orzo)
Potato Salad
Garlic Yogurt
Summer Salad
Drink Thyme Tea
Dessert *Anoushabour* or Milk Pudding (*Gatnabour*)

HOLIDAY MENU

Nevig

Rice *Yeghints* **(with Orzo)**

Potato Salad

Garlic Yogurt

Summer Salad

Drink
Thyme Tea

Dessert
Anoushabour or Milk
Pudding (*Gatnabour*)

ACKNOWLEDGMENTS

From Lena

Siroon, for partnering with me on this project and creating such beautiful photos for the cookbook, always making the food look incredible. And for always generously giving me photography advice (even on my terrible Instagram photos).

Adrineh and Maria, thank you for being amazing at what you do and for joining us on this project!

Sossy Mishoyan Dabbaghian, thank you for generously sharing your Armenian language expertise with me for this cookbook!

Mom and Bub, for always believing in me, supporting me, and for all the advice, help, and words of wisdom. You truly are the best parents anyone could ever ask for (confirmed!). Mom, thank you for always sharing your cooking expertise, not getting annoyed when I ask too many questions, and for always patiently telling me the history (and secrets) of every dish. And for always making the most delicious food out of love, giving all your children impossible standards to live up to. This cookbook would not have been possible without your support, patience, and incredible troubleshooting skills. Bub, thank you for teaching me what a strong work ethic looks like through your selfless example, and for for being a never-ending source of sound advice and encouragement.

Varouj, Laura, and Christina, thank you for always being supportive, and being ready to listen to updates (and rants) on the cookbook. And thank you for being the unofficial (but willing) taste testers.

My grandparents, thank you for showing me early on what perseverance looks like. Your warmth, generosity, love, and stories will never be forgotten. I miss you everyday, and this cookbook is for you.

My aunts, uncles, and cousins, thank you for supporting this project from the start and for being the most amazing family anyone could ask for.

Gohar, how can anyone be so lucky as to have a friend like you? I am grateful for you every day, and so happy to have your support, advice, and voice recordings, all of which helped get me through the more challenging parts of this work. You are Armenia's best product. 10/10.

Arpine, thank you for convincing your mom to let me come over and learn how to make Lenten *Tolma* years ago, and not saying anything when I took the credit for how good they were.

Shaghig, thank you for being my #1 cheerleader, for always getting excited about my recipes (sorry about that experimental salad dressing), and for the best OG nights that always took my mind off my deadlines.

Silva Dekirmendjian and Arpi Bozuk, thank you to each of you for generously contributing a recipe to this cookbook.

Ani and Sarkis, thank you for generously sharing your knowledge on coffee, folklore, and Armenian history with me.

To everyone who bought this cookbook, I know pre-ordering something not yet in existence requires some belief and trust, and thank you for believing in and trusting Siroon and I. We are so grateful to every single one of our Indiegogo backers, whether we know you or not, and to everyone who bought the cookbook through our website. Thank you!

From Siroon

Lena, thank you for allowing me to ride alongside you on this journey. I am so proud to complete this project with you. It has been so rewarding to create something so clean, green, and Armenian!

Also, thank you, **Birthright Armenia**, for connecting diasporan Armenians, helping us establish lifelong bonds and friendships that result in the creation of amazing Armenian projects together.

Vartan, you always believed in me and this book and helped bring it to life. You shined a light (literally) when I was lost and guided me back to my path. I love you!

Vyke, you are the greatest joy of my life. Because of you, I am softer and more conscious. Everything I do, I do for you. Thank you for providing me with endless love and kisses. I adore you!

Mom and Dad, this book couldn't have been possible without your hour-long drives to come and help me with my long days and Vyke. You both have always supported my creative ambitions and have been my #1 fan. Thank you for your trust and for always having my back.

To my brothers and their beautiful ladies, I appreciate your endless support and unconditional love and friendship. I am so proud to be in your tribe. Thank you for always coming to my rescue! I love you, all!

Nairie and Meg, you both somehow constantly support my life, creative ambitions, and my mess, and have been there with me through all the beautiful and the ugly. I cannot imagine doing anything in life without your amazing friendship and support. Thank you for lending me your ears, houses, guidance, and strength, and pushing me to make this book a reality. I adore you, my sisters!

It takes a village... **Nene, Ani Morkour, Siroun Horkour, Houril, Arinc, Arpig Nanoog, Tamar, Dzaghig Tantig, and Lena C,** thank you for either cooking a meal for me, sharing your expertise, or helping care for Vyke while I needed to work. I am forever grateful for your generosity and support

Maria, thank you for being my neighbor in Beirut 25 years ago and for putting up with me throughout the design process of this project. I am so proud of this beautiful cookbook we get to all stare at.

My family and friends (you know who you are), thank you for your support and encouragement in bringing this cookbook alive. Especially Nanor, Mary and Sara for being hands-on supporters of the photo production journey. From shopping for props in Armenia to shopping for ingredients in Los Angeles and helping me with styling and cleaning, I will never forget your genuine support. I love you all and I am so proud to share my life with you.

T H A N K Y O U

To our sponsors,
thank you for helping us make this cookbook a
reality and for your generous support.

To our campaign supporters,
thank you for supporting the project early on and for
your generous contributions to our project:

Mary Anadolian, Taleen Asadourian, Houril & Arine
Dekermenjian, Kalia Giuliano, Lara Green, Sahag
Saro Ishac, Alice Istanbul, Gregory Istanbul, Vicken
& Anna Izekelian, Shaghig Kazanjian, Lisa & Varouj
Krikorian, Jake & Rita Masdanian, Greg & Dalida
Nalbandian, Kevork & Hermine Parseghian, Nareg
Parseghian, Laura Tashjian, Vahan & Hermine
Tashjian, Anita Terjanian, Flora B. Vartanian, Nayiri
Yenikomshuyan, Tina Yessayan

CENTAUR

A portion of the proceeds from this book benefits Centaur
Animal-Assisted Therapy & Rescue Center in Ushi,
Armenia. Visit its website to learn more: **www.centaur.im**

INDEX

Authors

Bella Akhmadulina
Vasily Aksyonov
Yuz Aleshkovsky
Arkady Arkanov
Leonid Batkin
Andrei Bitov
Fridrikh Gorenshtein
Fazil Iskander
Yuri Karabchiyevsky
Pyotr Kozhevnikov
Yuri Kublanovsky
Semyon Lipkin

Inna Lisnyanskaya
Yevgeny Popov
Vasily Rakitin
Yevgeny Rein
Mark Rozovsky
Genrikh Sapgir
Viktor Trostnikov
Boris Vakhtin
Andrei Voznesensky
Vladimir Vysotsky
Viktor Yerofeyev

Translators

Christina Dodds-Ega
Martin Horwitz
Boris Jakim
Vladimir Lunis
Carl R. Proffer

Ellendea Proffer
Barry Rubin
George Saunders
H. William Tjalsma

Metropol

LITERARY ALMANAC

Edited by

Vasily Aksyonov

Viktor Yerofeyev

Fazil Iskander

Andrei Bitov

Yevgeny Popov

Foreword by

Kevin Klose

W · W · NORTON & COMPANY

NEW YORK · LONDON

The anthology *Metropol* represents all of its authors equally. All of the authors represent the anthology equally.

FIRST EDITION

The text of this book is composed in photocomposition Electra by Spartan Typographers. Printing and binding are by the Murray Printing Company. Book design by Marjorie J. Flock.

Library of Congress Cataloging in Publication Data
Metropol', 1979 g. English.
  Metropol: literary almanac.
  Translation of: Metropol', 1979 g.
  Published simultaneously in Canada by George J.
McLeod Limited, Toronto.
  1. Russian literature—20th century. I. Aksenov,
Vasily Pavlovich, 1932–   II. Title: Metropol',
1979 g.
PG3227.5.M4713 1982   891.7'08'0044   81–9540
                               AACR2

ISBN 0-393-01438-X

W. W. Norton & Company, Inc. 500 Fifth Avenue, New York, N.Y. 10110
W. W. Norton & Company Ltd. 25 New Street Square, London EC4A 3NT

1 2 3 4 5 6 7 8 9 0

CONTENTS

A Baker's Dozen of Stories, by Yevgeny Popov   85

Translated by George Saunders

Poems and Songs, by Vladimir Vysotsky   154

Translated by H. William Tjalsma

A CREATION IN THREE CHAPTERS 471

FOREWORD

With a broad smile and a cheerful, conspiratorial nod, Lev Kopelev, white-bearded godfather of Moscow's disaffected literary elite, ushered me into his apartment on Red Army Street one bleak January afternoon in 1979 for my introduction to what soon would become a major intellectual and political *cause célèbre* in the Soviet Union and the West.

Without a glance, we passed by the ceiling-high, glass-fronted bookcases lining his narrow study, his careful collections of Russian and German masterworks half hidden behind scores of photographs of friends and family propped against the glass doors. Other Russians clustered in the small room in an intent little group. Heads close together, they murmured almost reverentially over what lay on Lev's desk in the weak winter light sifting through the room's one window. I craned over their stocky frames and got my first glimpse of *Metropol*. The almanac, as Russians traditionally call such broad-gauge collections of prose, poetry, and criticism, was folio-sized, more than four times the dimensions of this page, deliberately large to proclaim its intended public nature. Symbolism with a dash of street theater.

"No smudges, please," Kopelev commanded, his dark eyes alive with derisive adventure. He knew this to be an unneeded reminder; no one there dared such carelessness. This was one of only eight copies, painstakingly produced after two years of thought and effort. As an extraordinarily bold new challenge to Soviet censorship, it demanded respect.

"I haven't read it all," Lev said later as we sat in his kitchen, away from the stream of visitors come to leaf through the collection. "But I can tell you, it is good . . . very, very good." His generous assessment

flowed forth even though he and some of his closest friends had not
been asked to contribute on grounds that their known political dissent
might needlessly reduce *Metropol*'s chance at passing censorship
unchanged. It could be argued, and in Moscow it was, that such
self-censorship by *Metropol*'s organizers was hardly the way to mount
an assault on state censorship. Satirist Vladimir Voinovich, whose
work is not in the collection, tartly observed later that "once you
already establish such conditions, then you don't have a free literature
or a free challenge."
Echoing many others, Kopelev saw it differently. "This is an important event, and maybe something positive will come of it. Perhaps the
time is right to challenge the censor."
Aside from laws barring dissemination of state secrets, censorship
does not officially exist in the Soviet Union. In practice, everything to
be published, broadcast, or filmed is censored, both to protect the
peculiar reality of one-party ideology and to humble the artist by
forcing submission to the state's power. A writer cannot be published
without review of his work by Glavlit, the Main Literary Administration, which carries out detailed censorship according to instructions
from the Communist Party Central Committee. The struggle between
writer and censor is a private affair, with editors of publishing enter-
prises acting as intermediaries. It is invariably painful. "Like tearing
the feathers from a live chicken—and you're the chicken," one children's author described it. Intentional humiliation plays a large role,
too, as another novelist made clear to me. His editor, under pressure
from unseen Glavlit men eager to show their arbitrary power, sought
to convince the author that the virile hero of his new novel should be
made a woman instead. "This would be more fitting," the editor
dissembled vaguely. The disgusted writer withdrew his book, saving it
"for the drawer," that vast repository of some of the best of Soviet
writing.
Under the principal influence of novelist and screenwriter Vasily
Aksyonov, *Metropol*'s contributors aimed for an open crossing of the
line that divides the shadowy world of writing for the desk and
samizdat-tamizdat from the other surreptitious but officially
sanctioned world of state censorship. They wanted to avoid a political
fight, but still achieve a public confrontation with the authorities—
naïve hopes that foundered at the first moment. The authorities
reached out from their lair at the Moscow Writers Union in a classi-
cally absurd act of intimidation that so characterizes Russian life.
The writers had scheduled a reception early in January at a
downtown restaurant to unveil *Metropol* for a few Western corre-

spondents and Russian friends and supporters. But when I arrived at the appointed hour, an elderly watchman in the inevitable dirty smock grumbled through the locked front door that the place was closed for an unexpected "sanitarnyi dehn," a day of kitchen cleaning normally reserved for the end of the month. He couldn't say what had become of the planned reception or why there were no "sanitary workers" busy in the deserted premises.

A public *Metropol* reception never did take place, but from the state's point of view, the damage was already done, for the organizers had boldly smuggled two copies of *Metropol* to the West, simultaneously submitting it to Soviet authorities for unchanged publication inside the country.

By this dual action, the writers sought to force the state to observe freedom of expression which the 1977 Brezhnev Constitution, successor to the debased 1936 Stalin Constitution, affirms as the law of the land in the USSR, but which in fact exists only in the pluralistic West. The organizers hoped that quick reprints in France and the United States would strengthen their hand by shaming the authorities.

However, for the authorities to accept the almanac under such conditions would have violated one of the party's principal reasons for being: denial of free expression. From their point of view, the only question to be settled was one which would preoccupy apparatchiks of any one-party system: how to punish those who dared such a challenge.

But *Metropol* arrived at a delicate moment for Soviet cultural watchdogs. Little more than a year earlier, Moscow had marked its continuing emergence as a first-rate world capital by holding the city's first international book fair. Despite suppression of various embarrassing books offered for exhibit by some Western publishers, such as *Animal Farm* and *1984*, hundreds of capitalist companies had displayed their wares and dozens had signed reprint or translation contracts. Preparations for an even bigger fair in September 1979 were well advanced, and possibly even more hard-currency-rich Western firms would attend. But these hopes were threatened by the continuing storm abroad over the 1978 political trials of dissidents Yuri Orlov, Alexander Ginzburg, and Anatoli Scharansky. Indeed, a number of American publishers had staunchly defended the human-rights activists, and a debate was under way among some of them over whether to boycott the new fair in protest.

That such a debate could even take place underscored how much public-relations progress the Brezhnev regime had made since its early days in power, when it triggered bitter Western denunciations in 1966 for imprisoning writers Andrei Sinyavsky and Yuli Daniel because they sent suppressed works abroad to be published. Foreign revulsion over the harsh treatment made clear to Moscow that the Khrushchev era had altered Western perceptions of Soviet totalitarianism. If the Brezhnev Kremlin were to achieve its long-range goal of improved relations and trade with the capitalist countries, it must find other ways to suppress politically unacceptable writers without resorting to Stalinist tactics. With the egregious later exception of the persecution and expulsion of Alexander Solzhenitsyn, whose power in tapping unredressed Stalin-era agonies made him especially dangerous to the party's claim of rightful moral leadership of the country, the state generally moderated its instincts toward repression.

Full-blown détente in the 1970s forced a further loosening. Some Soviet authors were allowed to smuggle their works abroad without facing the Draconian penalties meted out earlier to Sinyavsky and Daniel, and cultural officials could even find some hard-currency profit—or, at least, solace—in arranging through the ironically named All-Union Agency for Writers' Rights (VAAP) for increasing numbers of translations of contemporary Soviet writers. While the climate for writers improved, it was not without its cynical dimensions. Aksyonov sardonically related to me how VAAP at one time formally agreed to allow French publication of several of his works which the Soviets themselves had rejected as unsuitable for their own readers. Now, he was about to be pilloried for attempting a similar arrangement.

Metropol's major public antagonist was Feliks Kuznetsov, a well-known critic who had recently capped a long climb to power with his selection as first secretary of the Moscow Writers Union, the most important of the many party-controlled writers organizations nationwide. This was not without its own ironies, of course, for Kuznetsov was credited by many Moscow intelligentsia for helping defend the literary avant garde two decades earlier and coining the stirring term "the Fourth Generation" to describe the wave of promising and sometimes fiery young new writers—Aksyonov among them—who emerged during the years of artistic ferment when the "harebrained" Khrushchev ran things.

Addressing the Twenty-third Moscow City Party conference a few days after foreign radio broadcasts (since jammed because of the Polish crisis) beamed news of *Metropol's* arrival to the nation, Kuznetsov passionately denounced unnamed opponents of détente for "subversive activity." Some weeks later, he told the official Novosti press agency that *Metropol* was "nothing but an attempt to palm off literary waste that has nothing to do with true literature." He said the authors had leveled an ultimatum that "the almanac should be printed in its original form with no additions or deletions permitted. I don't think there is a publisher in the world who would accept these terms." Further, he said in accusatory tones, the organizers claimed that "*Metropol* represents all authors in equal measure and all the authors represent the almanac in equal measure."

It was a telling comment about what made the authorities so angry. The extraordinary truth of the effort was that there was little equal among the contributors beyond their shared interest in breaking the censorship that fettered them all. Of the twenty-three, fourteen were members in good standing of the party-run unions of writers, artists, or filmmakers, recipients of many of the privileges available to "official" intellectuals, such as cash bonuses, better health and recreation facilities, personal autos, state prizes, treasured trips abroad. As émigré Soviet constitutional law expert Konstantin M. Simis wrote in "Problems of Communism" that summer, "The publication . . . is a rebellion among those fully integrated into the official establishment of Soviet arts against the unwritten laws, against total censorship." Voznesensky was a Lenin Literature Prize winner; Aksyonov, after a number of scrapes over the years with officialdom, was prospering as a screenwriter; Akhmadulina was publicly revered as the best modern Soviet poetess; Iskander hailed as an innovative and important story-teller; Semyon Lipkin and his poet wife Inna Lisnyanskaya were honored for their years of effort at bringing the rhythms of Central Asian life and epic tales to Russian audiences.

Throughout the spring, party officials and their writers-union min-ions conducted a series of furious private interviews with the con-tributors to turn them against each other. Iskander, for example, was told he was "only twenty per cent guilty" compared with Aksyonov, implying that if he repudiated the group, his punishment would be less severe. Aksyonov took the brunt of the public assault, denounced by name in the official press and ridiculed for attempting to create an "anti-Soviet scandal" that would catch the eyes of "hostile Western forces" so that if he ever emigrated—itself a distinctly unpatriotic act—he would be assured of a cordial reception. When these tactics failed, other things happened. A major comedy film that had pre-viewed to enthusiastic official audiences and was set for national release suddenly was shelved—Aksyonov had written the script. Akhmadulina found that some long-planned poetry-reading tours were delayed. Several of Iskander's stories were being held up for unknown reasons. Permission for Voznesensky to make an American visit seemed mysteriously uncertain. The ways of Soviet power are many.

In the end, as it always does, the struggle centered on the most vulnerable members of the self-styled "kollektif"— Viktor Yerofeyev and Yevgeny Popov, a young critic and a young writer. Privately seeing themselves as members of "the Czech Generation," whose youthful illusions about their society had been shattered by the 1968 Soviet invasion of Czechoslovakia, they nevertheless were seeking entry into the writers union, with its assurance of material and professional benefits. Questions about their qualifications had been raised in the union secretariat, and their membership cards were held up. Aksyonov, Akhmadulina, Iskander, the Lipkins, and Andrei Bitov in letters made public pledged to resign from the union if the two young men were denied membership, a sure widening of the scandal.

In midsummer, William Styron, Edward Albee, Arthur Miller, Kurt Vonnegut, and John Updike, an excerpt of whose novel, *The Coup*, is contained in *Metropol* in a Russian translation by Aksyonov,* joined the fray, denouncing the almanac's suppression and the suspension of Yerofeyev and Popov. Kuznetsov retorted that the issue of membership was "a purely internal affair of our intellectual alliance, and we ask you to leave it with us to determine the degree of maturity and creative potentialities of each writer." By the fall, Yerofeyev and Popov sought to break the standoff, writing a letter to the union in which they refused to denounce *Metropol* as had been demanded, but saying they were "deeply averse" to the kind of "propaganda fuss of no literary relevance" which had arisen. For a time, it looked as if they would be admitted, in itself an important victory in view of their participation in the condemned work. But on December 20, their memberships were postponed indefinitely. Aksyonov and the Lipkins kept their pledges and resigned in protest, casting themselves into official limbo. No one else joined them.

That is the story of *Metropol* in the Soviet Union, where it will never be published. But there is an epilogue.

Most of the more famous *Metropol* contributors have gradually resumed their stalled careers. Voznesensky is being hailed as the librettist for what is said to be a daring, Western-style rock opera. Iskander's short stories can be found again in literary magazines and newspapers. New poetry by Bella Akhmadulina is being published.

Aksyonov did indeed emigrate to the West and now lives in Washington, where he is thinking of settling permanently. Lev Kopelev, the literary godfather, and Vladimir Voinovich, the satirist

* Although, for obvious reasons, not retranslated in this English-language edition.

who didn't like the idea of *Metropol* in the first place, also left Russia and live in West Germany.

Several of the original folio copies of *Metropol* still circulate covertly, joined by compact paperback facsimile copies produced by Ardis Press of Ann Arbor, Michigan, whose owners, Carl and Ellendea Proffer, have been denounced by the Soviets for bringing the almanac into print. So *Metropol* lives on in Russia. At the worst, it is considered a slanderous curiosity; at the best, a brave effort whose time may never come.

Of all the people involved in *Metropol*, perhaps none has suffered the consequences more heavily than Semyon Israelovich Lipkin, the translator of Central Asian epics, and his wife, Inna Lisnyanskaya. Decorated alike for their valor and their wounds suffered during the Great Patriotic War against the Fascists, they live in infirm health, cut off from the medical benefits of the writers union welfare fund, spurned by people who for decades they had counted as friends. Their works are being removed from libraries, and their names expunged from the public record. But amid the wreckage of their shattered careers, they retain their pride.

Last spring, more than a year after he had left the union, Semyon Israelovich kept his monthly appointment at a nearby barber shop "to get my baldness cut," as he put it. In keeping with national custom, this veteran of World War II wore his battle ribbons on the left breast of his suit: three rows of four decorations each, among them, the Defense of Stalingrad (now called Volgagrad), the defense of Leningrad, the Victory over Germany, four "marks of honor" for bravery defending the Motherland.

As he waited for a chair, an apparatchik from the writers union named Mednikov unexpectedly emerged from the barber's chamber, freshly shaved and clipped and smelling of eau de cologne. Mednikov's gaze fastened on Lipkin's ribbons.

"Look how you served your country," Mednikov said in sudden, red-faced anger, "and now look at what you've done by resigning! Scandalous!"

"I'm still serving my country."

"How?"

"I'm continuing my fight against fascism."

KEVIN KLOSE

South Pomfret, Vermont

ABOUT METROPOL

By the editors of Metropol. *Translated by George Saunders.*

It might occur to some that in the background to the anthology *Metropol* there was some sort of "toothache." Not so. The child is healthy, and all its authors are in a positive frame of mind.

Since literature is our business, we take the view that there is nothing more pleasant and healthful than to write and to show others what one has written. Thus, we assume that the birth of our new anthology will be a holiday for everyone.

But why does it have this particular form? A logical question for someone not entirely familiar with certain peculiarities of our cultural life. It would not be overly daring to assert that our culture suffers from something like a chronic ailment which might be defined either as "hostility toward differentness" or simply "fear of literature." The sickening inertia that exists in our literary journals and publishing houses has resulted in an exaggerated feeling of responsibility on everyone's part for each "item" in our literature, which consequently is not only unable to be what it should be but is not even what it used to be. This universal sense of "responsibility" produces a state of silent, stagnant fearfulness, a desire to trim every piece down to size. Works that do not fit established molds are condemned sometimes to many years of homeless wandering. Only the blind can fail to see that such writings are becoming more and more numerous each year, that they already constitute, as it were, a forbidden, untapped vein in our native world of letters. (Our anthology consists for the most part of manuscripts already well-known to editorial boards.)

The dream of the homeless is a roof overhead. That is why *Metropol* is a convenient shelter, a hunter's cabin in the capital, situated above the best "metro" in the world.* The contributors to *Metropol* are literary professionals who are entirely independent (of one another). The one thing that binds them together under this roof is the awareness that the author bears the sole responsibility for a work. The right to have that responsibility seems to us sacred. It is not impossible that the strengthening of that sense of responsibility will benefit our culture as a whole.

Metropol gives a vivid, though not exhaustive, indication of what the homeless stratum of literature in our country is like.

All who wish to read it are invited to do so with a clear conscience.

One request: in turning the pages, please refrain from rough movements.

*There seems to be a three-way play of words and imagery here. The anthology's name suggests, first, the old Metropole Hotel in Moscow, a favorite haunt of writers and artists. Second, the metropolis itself, the capital city, Moscow. Third, the Moscow subway system, which, borrowing from the French, is called the metro(politan). All are places where a "homeless" work or unrecognized author could find shelter [tr.].

PUBLISHER'S NOTE ON TRANSLATIONS
In order to preserve the exact meaning of the writers' words, some of the poetry in the anthology has been translated literally rather than rendered into verse.

.

Epigraphs[*]

YURI KUBLANOVSKY
Return

Rooks have settled on the thorny treetops.
Kremlin brick turns blue in the night.
Screech owl crossroads.

Silence-shattering creak and whistle.
The stucco leaf of the freshly washed metro station.
Rocky cliff of crumbling marble.

A passenger has dozed off, as if to say:
You'll soon be ladling up grief by the spoonful,
Clenching your fists in fear.

Hidden will! Alien fate!
The boxes of the hollow cars rumble.
Hark, the boxes are rumbling.

That's enough joking, brother.
I lift my face. Like a maniac, race
From Radial Line to the Ring.

I'm OK—I'm in luck again today:
Half an hour and you can bet I'll be home.

ANDREI VOZNESENSKY
Derzhavin

To soar above a kingdom dim and mute,
Imagine just how lonely it can get!
Two-headed eagle, how I envy you—
Alone and yet you're always tête-à-tête!

*Translated by H. William Tjalsma.

SEMYON LIPKIN
The Way to the Temple

In the middle of a dry path
To the haven of the gods,
A cow fell to thinking
In the shadow of her horns.

She looked glumly
At the cupola in the distance
And heavily she lowered
Her body into the sand.

The distant smoke of censers,
And the sheen of rusty redness,
And the languor of inkwell eyes,
Were suddenly necessary to me.

Across the sea and ocean,
I shall return to my own city,
When I become a god
With the head of a cow.

There, where there's an iron gnashing,
And heat of day and glint of fire,
I know I won't be slashed,
I know I won't be burnt.

Someday I'll enlist
In the cowshed, ambassador of the heavens,
More likely, thesaurus
Of mysterious words.

I'll whisper on the sly
That we are one family,
That I am confidante to the wolf
And confessor to the snake.

YURI KARABCHIEVSKY

Misanthropy—is just entropy.
General chaos, logarithm of unhappiness,
that measure of loneliness with which
we measure last steps.
Is the weight of the century really at fault in this?
Do even *we* really lose our form under that yoke;

bog down and drain away?
Enviers, jealous lovers, the ambitious,
let us get together, as usual,
fly in, all, pack it in the last time,
clap our hands together, speak a vow,
and turn into the best of friends,
while our hothouse smiles
so heat up the atmosphere
that the central heating may as well be switched off.
Let us play at goodness,
I to you, you to me. Nice business.
While this ball is still in the air,
everything's OK. But if it drops—
it's curtains. Oh, Lord, really,
is no one guilty before anyone?

YEVGENY REIN

Three-headed hydra of a family—
That's my nurturing black earth.
It would be nice to find a place
Of one's own and stay there.

Perchless inhabitant of two capitals,
Dweller in pitiful apartments,
Breaker of my own promises,
I have long been my own commander.

But surplus weight became
A burden to the immortal body,
And I gave myself over to anger and corruption
Like a pilot who hadn't attained the heavens.

Oh, how tough to be a husband and a son,
Orphaned father to a little daughter,
But it's more terrible to remain an errand boy
Ready for anything.

That's enough, enough, quite—
I won't conceal—I must inform you:
Yes, I've lived in a frenzy, basely,
And I'll live worse yet.

You'll not violate inaccessible boundaries,
It's another matter with what's at hand—
For the shelterless, the remaining
Thrice-regal feminine peace.

I'll knock timidly of a morning,
You'll not yet have lit the fire.
Mama, Galya, and my daughter Anna,
Let me in, forgive me!

INNA LISNYANSKAYA

I beg alms from the poor
And give to the rich myself.
And a second wind
Comes to my hoarse gullet.

Grant me your patience
To stand on the church parvis
And grope with a staff
For the steps of the receding earth!

Grant me the defenseless gift
To see from afar the generous
Amidst the insatiable mob—
Let the hand never cease giving!

Grant me your unconcern
Not to think, not to know in advance,
And, placing the cup under the tap of eternity,
To taste the slow honey!

Grant me this, you who are blessed in spirit,
Insensible to slaps in the face,
And gracious toward sin, and I
Shall give to the insatiable.

VLADIMIR VYSOTSKY
To Go to the Bottom

I've had it up to here, to my chin.
Even started getting sick of singing.
Oh, to go to the bottom like a submarine,
So nobody could get a bearing on me!

A friend served me vodka in a glass,
My friend told me that it'll pass,
Introduced me to Verka over a drink—
Verka will help and vodka will do the rest.

But neither Verka nor vodka helped.
I'm hung over and who needs Verka anyway?
Oh, to go to the bottom like a submarine
And not send out an SOS!

I've had it up to here, up to my gullet.
Ah! I'm fed up with singing and playing.
Oh, to go the bottom like a submarine
So nobody can get a bearing on me!

GENRIKH SAPGIR
The Polyphonion

A bottle with a stamped bronze scaling wax,
A case museum chair that's from the dump,
The studio of Sashenka Petrov,
The very dust itself is of *those* days.

And I, the sonorous box, A polyphonion,
An angel etched upon its yellow lid;
Put in a disk a half a meter wide—
And sounds! from Bethlehem! from the Pharaoh's palace!

There truly were galoshes and roadside inns!
I ruffle up myself all over . . .
When will I break the final seal open—

A horn resounds, a goat is in the pasture
In Moscow's Arbat Lane, against the snow
Across from the Italian embassy.

The Many Dogs and the Dog[*]
by Bella Akhmadulina

To Vasilii Aksenov

. . . It was getting dark on the Dioscurian seaboard—that's what the weak-minded and mute Shelaputov, blind from the powerful, cold sun that had floated like an iceberg into the southern gardens, straightaway saw, thought of, and said. He had come out of the lengthy dusk of the alien room that he had rented for an indefinite time into the fleeting, eternal dazzle and thus stood on the threshhold between one thing and the other, taking refuge in his own darkness, and possessed the moment, prolonged the instant at his discretion: he did not look or blink confusedly, but looked unblinkingly into the near barrier of his closed eyelids, extending afar his unclenched palms. For the first time, the common, intrepid assets of closed eyes and extended hands were granted him. Had he actually been healed in Dioscurian bliss? He attentively wounded the dull pads (or whatever they are called) of all his fingers, they, in childhood, having never espied the black and white Goedicke, in huge icy white light, staining its invisible cutting edges with palpable droplets of blood, with a penetrating grope discerning each of the motley seven strings: the thick violet one had muttered in a bass under his thumb without occasioning pain. Every Hunter Wishes to Know Where the Pheasant Perches. Not at all—not every one. Shelaputov loosed the spectrum from his agitated five fingers, opened his eyes, and saw what he had foreseen. It was fiercely light and cold. The measureless sun, not having room enough in the endless sky and limitless sea, did not, to the great gain of glitter, disdain any reflective surface, even Shelaputov's pale skin, which did not tary in bristling up with wretched martial gooseflesh, man's only defense against worldwide calamities.

It was getting dark on the Dioscurian seaboard, day fading not to snuffling dusk—to severe gloom, the death of flowers and fruit, to orphanhood of the forlorn, to winter. In all the coastal gardens, the

* Translated by H. William Tjalsma.

black heads of the gardeners turned together, faces directed to the mountains: there, that night, snow had fallen.

The lonely room in the back part of the house, borrowed by Shelaputov from prodigal fate, had its own independent entrance—a mountainous, rusty stone staircase, from the top of which he now surveyed the changed surroundings. With brazen overstatement, the lodger could claim as his own a separate piece of the garden, bespattered with saccharine bits of persimmon, a wicket gate leading to the sea, and then, well, the sea, too, whose scattered incorporeal azure of yesterday had hardened toward morning into unbending muscular material. Shelaputov had to go down: in the foothills of the staircase, having caught the beloved scent, the powerful dainty wave of air sent out by the man, Ingurka started fidgeting, yapping, bleating.

But who is Shelaputov? Who is Ingurka?

Shelaputov—it's not known who he was. And was he indeed Shelaputov? Where is he now and did he ever exist in fact?

Ingurka was and perhaps is still a cunning and servile dog, when young pronounced a German shepherd and acquired a year before for a (whiskey) bottle of mad plum swill. The pup was dubbed Ingur and chained out to be nurtured in the fierceness salutary for the treasures of the home and the fruits of the garden. Ingur grew modestly, wagged hungry haunches in a feminine manner, obsequiously floundered on front paws and gradually established herself in her present name and sex and aspect: an offhand cross between a comely goat and a homely wolf. The chain lay on the ground questioningly, clawing at the prisoner's absence. As that autumn declined, the dark potent time first came to Ingurka, a ticklish itching under the tail that also elevated the soul for unknown transport and design. In connection with this, beyond the garden fence, unguarded by a watch dog and wound round with barbed wire, there crowded a mob of variously colored males of various countenances: poor wretches, not all of whom had achieved the rank of yard-dog for lack of a yard, but all with the distorted features of a glorious canine species—seedy phantoms of ancestors who had once settled Dioscurias. One looked less battered by life than the others: a bright orange, resonant youngster, the impeccable Sharik, a round ball of fur like a spitz but the color of sunset copper.

In spite of the complex personal circumstances, Ingurka, as was her wont, fell into an instantaneous swoon of love—something sometimes perfunctory and false—for the man. Shelaputov undoubtedly was loved sincerely, with one hitch to trouble the tender feeling: there was not enough room for him in the resourceful imagination schooled by the chain, hunger, shouts, and blows. He leaned over the outstretched, languishing stomach, grinning at the inevitable connection between scratching the dog's armpit and the jerking of the hind leg. This modest example of conformity to convention and all Ingurka's other transformations were easily understood by Shelaputov, who had himself undergone like changes, having fallen into the reverse of that which had been expected of him and desired of him by people, the reverse of that which he had been a short while before. But with his damaged mind that now discerned nothing more than title-page meanings, he could not follow the flickering dotted line between the image of Ingurka that had taken root in his consciousness and the profile of Goethe above the waters of the Rhine. He might have gotten even more muddled, had he been able to recall the story which had once intrigued him about the great German's grandniece, who learned to haul refuse in the environs of northern forests and swamps, far from Weimar but under the intent eye of a purebred German shepherd. What a laugh it was when the little old lady, in out-of-place and difficult-to-achieve ringlets, got the hang of adding to the appellation "Pferdchen, Pferdchen" an indispensable giddy-up, incomprehensible to her but markedly enlivening the horse. No longer cognizant of this gobbledegook, Shelaputov moved to round the house, stepping over the slush of fruit smashed against the earth. Ingurka feared leaving her offstage quarters for the public space of the proscenium once again and stayed behind to sniff the grass, without a glance at her admirers hanging on the spiny fence.

Shelaputov would have been afraid, too, had he been in his right mind.

Having appeared fearlessly from around the corner, Shelaputov appraised the charm of the picture revealed. The fair proprietress of the *pension*, Madame Odetta, aglow in the morning sun, was tragically viewing her roses mortally wounded by the unforeseen frost. Small tender music began to jingle and shed a few tears in Shelaputov's sleeping memory, now abiding with him at one remove, accompanying him like an extraneous cloud, a transparent freedom-loving sphere that slipped away from the touch. This was a sorrowing after something kindredly close, his soul's primordial fatherland, from which it had been abducted by evil nomads. The woman illuminated by the sun, the scarlet jam in crystal against the white tablecloth; the roses and the frost, all betrothed one to the other by a divine joke and now, here, converging in a fateful wedded union. . . . Where had this been, when and with whom? And did Shelaputov, too, have some sort of homeland—dearer than that of speech that wounds the mouth, dearer than the importance of one's own life? But why so far away, so long ago?

Some time back, Shelaputov had appeared at Madame Odetta's with a letter of recommendation which explained that the bearer of said letter, previously in possession of name, mind, memory, hearing, and gift of marvelous speech, having temporarily lost all of that, was in need of rest and tranquility. There was no need to worry about money since everything formerly quite essential and now not even known to Shelaputov was embodied in it without loss.

He had actually suffered these losses, including the unlisted sense of smell. That day and hour of his highest joy and greatest ease, he had been walking through a spacious, crowded hall, taken for the uninhabited Valley of Death by him, if one is to go not in the direction of the beneficent ocean, but has in view smashing forehead and body against the invincible Grand Canyon. Right in front of him, on the horizon, a high point heaved upward—there, at an ordinary long table, twelve times together sat one and the same man whose face had no features at all, even uncomely ones: just an open empty face without any lineaments or details. With the harmonious dozen-member chorus of his loudly prophesying maw, he was saying something that was heard clearly and with revulsion by Shelaputov, transfixed on the cautioning gunsight of twelve index fingers. He went ever higher and higher, and a little pale conductor standing on a clear star beyond the clouds, head down toward the earth and Shelaputov, encouraged him with an indicatory baton, dictated and entreated, sent him the tiding that it was necessary to endure this drawn-out instant and then to give in to the music. Shelaputov ascended to a wooden likeness of a Parisian street pissoir, glimpsed the light of the firmament and, at the same time, a pitcher and an unemptied glass of water in which there teemed and multiplied stalwart, rapacious organisms. The diminutive conductor was still extending his hand to him, when Shelaputov—rather, that man who was then Shelaputov—fell down flat and lost all that which the tiny, all-powerful conductor's stand had been in control of in his head. His undelivered speech, though it produced a poor impression, was forgiven him as understandable and virtuous agitation. No one, including the orator himself, ever found out, or ever would find out, what it was he so wanted, what he was so obliged to say.

And so now, not perceiving and unable to imagine the smell of the dying roses, he looked on Madame Odetta and took joy at her being created of something bluishly ruddy, brittle and puffy together (of porcelain, was it?—he had forgotten the name), at her being fitted out with fair hair and misty eyes that were inclined to moisture dedicated to pity or art, without diverting the sober pupil from a strict, unerring ledger. After all, she was a widow, although she leaned diffidently on Pyrkin's solid arm, without, however, fully accepting this seeking arm and the alien, low-born name. Her husband, a modest zealot of French letters, try as he might to conceal his perverse predilection, had been compelled to give way under the all-seeing, disapproving squint—into the shadows, the sticks, the depths of misadventures. When he stopped, the sea was at his back—between his chest and his back, putrescent inflammation of the lungs—and in front of him, magnolias in bloom, and Pyrkin, in the flower of his power come in person to inspect their documents, to admire Madame Odetta's fear, the weeping mist of her dim eyes and keen, hard pupils. There had been nowhere to go and he had backed, growing chill and burning for the greater glory of France, into the sea that fell away into the universe—of which not one single compatriot of the Orléans virgin knew (Shelaputov's incognito was a native of other parts). He died in poverty, in a hut in a wasteland, all of which was transformed by the mind and labor of his widow into prosperity, a house and garden. "This is all his," Madame Odetta would say, with a weak and brief little gesture linking the portrait of the essayist and his posthumous holdings, her eyes moistening and her pupils focusing on the safety of the feijoa bush—an attraction for any passing sweet-tooth. At that, Pyrkin would send a castigating heel into the gnarls of a nearby tree-trunk or the sinless groin of an oleander bush or into Ingurka, forgetful of the usual prudence for the sake of an unclear dream and of unease. But, as a woman, how to get on without Pyrkin? It is always difficult and actually impossible, given an unsuccessful past, tenacious beauty, and a general system of housekeeping that does not take into account the flourishing of a private *pension* with *table d'hôte*. And then, too, in the impeccable Pyrkin, who honestly and even with a certain richness of zeal carried out his duty—up to and including retirement and pension—there were touching flaws and weaknesses. For instance, bold and indifferent to the inevitable nonexistence of any of the others who overflowed the earth and air, he feared dying in his sleep, and if he weakened and dozed off he would cry out so that even Shelaputov, who was not responsible for his own actions, would hear and grin. Moreover, he would play childishly with the disobedience of things. If a folding chair got tired out or turned wanton and fell part into a double half-split, Pyrkin, his face changing for the worse, would shout: "Get up!"—the chair would get up and Pyrkin would sit down to read the morning mail. In age and general uselessness removed from incomplete activities, Pyrkin would sometimes forget himself and with a cry of "Silence!" tear an indisputable newspaper, struck dumb with astonishment, into shreds, which, coming to their senses, would reunite forthwith. But usually things did not wrangle and fight and Pyrkin would have done with his reading, in a quite inadmissibly frivolous manner—but graciously: "I approve. Carry on." Then Pyrkin would get up, while the forgiven chair could freely sit down on its shaky legs. And he had a secret for the sake of which, becoming dark of visage and sullen, he would ride out once every ten days to the neighboring town, where he had regal living space— Madame Odetta would cast down her moist azure, but her pupil would drily see and know.

A disobedient, deaf and dumb thing, Shelaputov hadn't the vaguest notion that a whole novel would whistle between him and Pyrkin, a reciprocal attraction of hatred like unto love alone in its ineffability and fullness of passion. The entire labor of heavy mutual animosity fell on Pyrkin's shoulders, just as in sawing wood, when one sawyer goes off to drink a beer, leaving his diligent partner to suffer with the back and forth wobble of the saw. This offhanded shirking of the common task offended Pyrkin and inspired shyness in him, something at which he was inexperienced. In Shelaputov's presence, the bewitched Pyrkin did not kick Ingurka, did not fling stones at her ripening wedding and did not grab for his gun when a little flock of children set wing for the coveted feijoa.

This iambic, frosty-pink morning, Pyrkin, behind Madame Odetta's back, catching sight of Shelaputov, rededicated to him the terrible faces that he usually pulled in the direction of the portrait of the enlightened sufferer and true proprietor of the house.

But Shelaputov was already headed for the main exit-entrance: beyond its smart-looking lances there gleamed golden the girl Ketevan. Thin, long, stretched only lengthwise and not having another dimension except oblongness, she extended herself by getting up on her toes, by an uplifting of hands, lengthening space that was cramped for the racing of youthful blood, by an endless gesture streaming into the ether. Thus she flowed into the heavens, brimming over and dancing, curious about and fearful of the attraction between the bewitched dogs and the aloofly nervous Ingurka. The girl was quieter than the silent Shelaputov: he would sometimes talk and say:

"Well, then, child? Who are you anyhow, where do you come from? Is it easy to consist of ripples and a surge, of gossamer specks flying thither into the kindred eternity of the sky and the sea and the snow on the mountain tops?"

He stroked the woven rainbows above her Egyptian hair. She answered him with flashing eyes and her shy laughing mouth, with nightingale pulsing of wrists, temples, and ankles and then shifted, shining in the distance, not a bit darker than the rest of the air, its glimmering shudder.

From behind came the multiple thumping of fruit against the grass: Pyrkin whacking a fig tree—he hated alien beings and had spent the better part of his life on the expulsion of swarthy tribes from their native parts and the herding of them into his.

Shelaputov set off down the crosswind between the sea and the distant mountains, glancing at the autumnal plenitude of the dominion. Peace to you, good people, enough of wandering, enough of scurvy that blackens the mouth. Empty-handed and orphaned, Shelaputov, giving himself over to the hunger and carelessness of his thoughts, was glad at the contentment that lived in the rich, two-story houses. Hello, Varlam, dancing in a wooden hollow up to your knees in the blood of grapes killed for the nonce, soon to be resurrected as wine. Hello, Polina, with the wet ingot of sheep cheese in quick hands. The neighbors still remember how Varlam came back from a long absence with the foreign-born, narrow-eyed Polina, who had saved him from death in distant lands, how he was rejected by his kin and at his own wedding frantically celebrated alone. Polina herself started to speak her husband's tongue about this and that, about the household as about love, learned to make the best cheese in the region and turned out to be fertile as the earth, frankly responding to labor with surfeit of harvest. The humbled kinfolk came for holidays or to ask for the loan of the money lacking for the purchase of an automobile—Polina did not refuse them, gazing with a vindictively burning slant-eyed look beyond the money and these pitiful folk. The children went to school in various towns and only the firstborn Gigo was always with his mother. Hello to you, too, Gigo, idly eating bread and drinking wine. Polina begrudges you nothing for your beauty that rolls waves of strength under your tanned citrus skin. And that you cannot read—that's all to the good: all books bring sadness. Yes, and how many times did the white-skinned northern girls break off their reading and leave the beach to follow you to a pitch-black corner of the garden?

At the post office, because of someone's mistake, from which he could in no way disentangle himself, the resisting Shelaputov was given the correspondence for a certain Foolhardyova and was forced to sign for it. He wrote: "Shelaputov. And if you insist—Fool and Hardy." Tortured by alarm and with bad forebodings weighing down the beat of his heart—this suddenly seemed ill-favored and certain to lead to perdition—he could not get the better of the thought of a subterranean passage, forded a tiny, dusty square, and went into the establishment "Apavillon."

Standing in line, Shelaputov rested as if sleeping, spreading his arms, and flowing on the strong water that knows the way and the goal. Numbered among the members of several unions and societies and an honored member of a foggy, international league, he was in point of fact just a member of the line; that was his place amongst people, a short holiday of equality between semesters of loneliness. The darker and more peevish was the slow current bubbling over the rapids, the more distinctly he sensed something similar to love, to a desire for sacrifice—of course, a trivial and useless one.

He acquired a glass of wine, took a seat in a corner and, suffering, started to read. First, a telegram: "YOU ARE YOUR GENTLY GIVEN NOTICE OF CONTRACT RE REGISTRATION RE PERSONAL MATTER POEM TO NATURE SUM TOTAL OF WITHERING BRINGS ON OCTOBER." Uninvolved, Shelaputov survived this deliberate nonsense, obviously aimed at a different target; he was caressed and consoled by its stupid misfire. If only things had gone just as well after that! But the beginning of the opened letter: "Dear daughter. I ask you—more than that—I demand . . ."— though this could not possibly have anything to do with him, he was terribly frightened and upset by it. The back of his head swelled with pain like a overripe persimmon ready to fall from the branch, and he squeezed it with his palms, trying to save himself from oblivion and collapse. So he sat there, rocking his head, trying to convince it that this was nothing but a continuation of the silly and harmless confusion that was pursuing him, that he had nothing to do with things and that all would pass. He wanted to finish the wine but was mindful of the possible recollection of the tender anesthetization darkening and kissing his brain in exchange for the streaming of his soul, the flying off of that which formerly had been the only thing that Shelaputov had valued. A package remained, preceded by a note calling on him to recover and to return to the vast abandoned brotherhood . . . was it those with whom he had just before stood in line who were writing to him—they were the last thing he could remember and beyond whom he was not seeking kinfolk?—for there was "reason to hope for their joint appearance at the stadium!" "Why at the stadium? What's this? Who are they confusing me with?" thought Shelaputov sluggishly, glimpsing the stone enclosure ringing the arena, the white face of the crowd and a bull's lowered head spewing several streams of blood, the beast more killed than necessary for death. To the communication there was attached a white and black sweater that plagued Shelaputov with irksome questions about the past and the future to which he might have been able more easily to give answers were he possessed of the commonly accessible talent of distinguishing smells. Sniffing it fastidiously and discerning nothing, he tossed the sweater on his back, tying the sleeves under his throat, at which a short man dropped out of the line, choking and crying: "Untie it! I can't stand it! I'm choking!" And emptied the glass forgotten by Shelaputov.

Shelaputov hastened to untie the sleeves and hurried away.

The thing warming his back continued dropping its hints and insinuations, and Shelaputov's shortsighted memory peered intently into distant prehistory, where there glimmered indistinctly voices and faces that came into focus on his bad nights, when he would dream a living, burning fear for someone and wake up in tears. Everything issued in a weaksighted pair of binoculars with which Shelaputov tested the past, where there flitted in and out of view a girl singer or acrobat, torturous for him, gathering mounds of flowers in the fields of her indefinite occupation. Was his sweater actually hers? Was it not from her that Shelaputov fled with loathing, shedding his skin and flitting into the crevice of a new fate? Horrified at this suspicion, he checked his outlines. Fortunately, everything was in order: fleshless, sexless silhouette of a traveler against the background of the firmament, the light step of a hunter who does not want to know where the pheasant perches.

Returning, Shelaputov met the loitering Gigo, who was ridding himself without boredom of a superfluity of strength and time. Elkishly stalwart and well built, he was gnawing on prickly blackberry stems, when he suddenly caught sight of a sweetness sweeter than berries: the white-black sweater that was languidly enveloping Shelaputov.

"Gimme, gimme!" Gigo started begging. "You used to say: 'Gigo, don't beat the dogs, I'll give you something.' Gigo doesn't, he won't anymore. Gimme it, gimme it! Gigo will put it on and show it to Ketevan."

"Take it, take it, good Gigo," said Shelaputov. "Wear it in health. Don't beat the dogs, don't touch Ketevan."

"Ooo! Ketevan! Ooo!" Gigo trumpeted, caressing his new acquisition.

Shelaputov made a little detour in order to drop by a writer's courtyard, where an acquaintance of his, an old Turk, was weaving a summer eating nook out of twigs, an exact replica of a peasant cookery from folklore, with an open hearth in the middle and a hook above it for smoking cheese and meat. Before going in, Shelaputov, bristling up the invisible furry fluff that covered his backbone, peered about a long while at the absence of the master of the house. Having heard about the mysterious Shelaputov, the author's curiosity had been aroused and he had invited him not long before to a supper party, and the terrified not-to-be guest was not lying in the least when he passed on through Madame Odetta that his illness, unfortunately, had taken a turn for the worse.

"Greetings, Askhat," said Shelaputov. "May I come in and sit a spell?"

Affably, the old man waved a hand warped by northern rheumatism but still possessed of agility and beauty of movement. He didn't recall a thing—Shelaputov knew it all: an hour for getting things together, the sobbing of women and children thickening the air, the prayers of the old men, the stolen silver utensils, bloated livestock, death of kith and kin, a long life, perfection of experience, but where did that peace in his face come from, that light? It was in fact people whose calamities also nourished Shelaputov's gathering ailment who were comforting for him, soothing and curative. Askhat wove, Shelaputov watched.

Going up to his wicket gate, he came upon the fascinating, inaccessible Ingurka drawn close up to the fence: she squinted her eyes at him in an alien fashion and fluttered her tail tentatively, a new expression having no relationship to people. The dogs lay exhausted on the ground, breathing heavily with their long tongues, and only the reddish, throaty youngster raged and sang.

And then Shelaputov caught sight of The Dog. This was a big old mutt the color of lions and wastelands, with docked ears and tail; he was covered with marks and scars not concealed by his short fur and had a scrap of chain on his strong neck.

"Behold a lion and not a dog," whispered Shelaputov and, with now grieving heart blazing up, strode straight over to his lion, to his Dog, extending his hand, and immediately the forehead's bulge and the palm's cavity coalesced.

The dog watched severely and calmly with its yellow eyes, knitting its dark brow for thought. Shelaputov carefully stroked the jagged teeth of its lopped-off ears—a dull knife greeted you in this world, but it's nothing, my brother, it's nothing. He tried to disconnect the chain and the collar, but it was steel forever welded to steel—but then you never know.

Shelaputov opened the gate, scolding the orange squaller, who darted under his feet: "Hold it there, go on, git!" Ingurka, freed, dashed along the sea surrounded by her tired persecutors. Behind came the big, old dog slowly.

Thus the day bloomed and faded.

Shelaputov's dwelling, located apart from the amenities of the house, was not heated but did have electricity and lights and glass in its latticed window. Fastidious apartment-dwellers disdained this room, but Shelaputov loved it. He was on the verge of following the example of the frozen roses, when suddenly, in a cap and shawl, Madame Odetta appeared coquettishly and presented him with bottles of hot water for warming up the bed. He attributed this gesture to the softness of heart of her dead husband, who was versed in the cold of vile nights: his shy shadow had earlier shown marked regard for Shelaputov.

The red sun passed with disturbing swiftness behind the promon tory, and Shelaputov followed its disappearance with a sadness exceed ing the everyday circumstances of sunset, as if rehearsing the last moment of existence. Quite near by, the sea labored and sounded. Each night Shelaputov pondered the meaning of this measured, many-throated sound. What did the patient genius of the element know, with what did it address itself to his limitations, beating in a monotone into the stones of dry land one and the same ineffable thought?

Shelaputov ignited a candle and started to look at a white sheet of paper on which nothing resided or came through save for a long-legged, fuzzy little spider, scurrying with a lively dactylic gait along an imaginary line. Night insects that had survived the cold dipped their blind wings into the flame with a crackle. "Why all of this?" Shelaputov thought with sorrow. "And what does this insatiable whiteness want, why does it so easily accept sacrifice in the torment of dying, meaty, and dusky moths? And who is free to make the sacrifice? Really, are contrived letters of the alphabet approximately indicating suffering more substantial and valuable than the flight of a spider and all the petty lives that burn up in alien, unnecessary fire?" Shelaputov, as ever irked by the sight of white paper, blew out the candle with relief and instantly discerned in the rambunctious rustle of night a spiritedly metallic creeping sound. Shelaputov opened the door and said into the darkness: "Come!" Stepping carefully, muffling the sound of the chain with the thousand-year experience of an escaped convict, his Dog came up the stairs.

In the dark, Shelaputov scratched open a can of stew—from the stores with which he had attempted to satisfy all the hunger that Ingurka had accumulated till then. And at that moment, Red rolled in through the partly open door, whining at first at the offense, then as if sobbing and forgiving. "Just shut up, at least," said Shelaputov, giving him part of the meat and grain mash.

Finally, they settled down: The Dog next to the bed, Shelaputov—into the bottles, which were hard to blend with the body and into which he was followed by Red, who started to get arranged capriciously, hotly snapping with his teeth at his furry stomach. "Don't shove, you unbearable creature," Shelaputov reproached him weakly. "What the devil brings you here?" He got terribly agitated from the rummaging around, from his unwarranted hospitality, from the frightening halt of the carefree hammock in which he had dozed and rocked of late. He dropped his hand and immediately met The Dog's big head turned toward him.

It is strange that all of this was, in fact. Not Foolhardyova, not Shelaputov—or whatever they were called after the whim of man—certainly not Shelaputov, who in that autumn of prescribed exultation, in the night of his extreme sorrow, lay in bed squeezed by bottles, Red, and the teeming inside him that was sufficient for several lives and deaths, not this of course but—a room, a storm of the garden and the boiling sea, The Dog and a man who wished to forget it all and who had just now placed his hand on The Dog's head and cried with a love excessive and beyond his strength at that time of his life and perhaps at this time, too.

It was or it wasn't, but in any case from the main part of the house, through the permeable stone wall dots followed by an exclamation point could be heard: Madame Odetta prattled ritually from the bedroom into the dining room on bare feet and turned the portrait face to the wall paper. Red stirred half-awake and barked piercingly at the top of his voice. Chilled, Shelaputov caught and tried to clamp shut his softly defensive jaws. After a pause of bewilderment, in the walled distance there was a knocking and a rumble: the portrait was turned to face unsightly reality, while Pyrkin kicked the foot of the bed. Now no longer hurrying it, throwing back his mug properly, Red gave over to a long and inspired warble. Shelaputov no longer fought him. "Do something so he shuts up at last," he said helplessly to The Dog who understood as well as he that he was speaking nonsense. Red yelped a few more times to get rid of the agitation that distracted him from sleep, yawned melodiously, and all was silent.

Outside the window, slowly, unwillingly, it was getting light. From the night's accumulation of warmth, Shelaputov looked through the lattice at the grey, chilly light as into a dungeon where a pale, painstaking prisoner was obliged to come to. The dog got up and, tinkling the chain with restraint, went down into the garden. Red slept, sometimes whimpering and often rearranging his paws. It was already apparent what a terrible, dandy he was, what a molly-coddle—by his own endowments, by the whim of blood that had strayed into fate's place, where there's no one to coddle dogs. Had he managed to astonish Ingurka with the beauty of his plumage reinforced by the sunrise? Shelaputov did not know, because he woke up late. The garden had already thawed and was all aglow, while Shelaputov was, as ever, too timid to put in an appearance in the Madame's half. This living sensation again brought him into correlation with forgotten actuality, with its usual and once-beloved coziness.

In spite of his misgivings, Madame Odetta, although she looked at him quite attentively, was easy and sweet and offered him coffee. Shelaputov, who had pointedly shunned table joining or any other kind, this time agreed ingratiatingly. Pyrkin made a show of a headlong dash to the kitchen, pretentiously grimacing and repeating: "Coffee pot, coffee pot, hey! Get over here!"—but then fell silent and scowled: today was his day to go to the city.

Madame Odetta, arranging a gracious prop for her chin out of elbow and fist, watched with favor as Shelaputov, unused to the miniature object of the cup, drank coffee clumsily. Her lips rounded, stuck out, harmonized into a pucker for need of consonant and vowel sounds, the sum total of which comprised a phrase whose wild sense suddenly reached Shelaputov's knowing.

"Remember in *Proust that* is called: to do the cattleya?"

He not only understood and remembered but really caught a glimpse of Paris at night, a *fiacre*, the falling light and the dark of the street lamps, the struggle, the muttering, Swan's first embrace of his Odette, his pitiful victory over her complacence—so prostrate and unattainable—directed by a small stuffy mind whither there was no entrée for the suffering Swan. The orchid pinned to her dress was actually damaged then, the orchid with whose name they started to call the nameless inescapable thing between them.

Shelaputov became accustomed to contrived circumstances beautifully and in that sense was slyly practical. As a little child suffering from war and constant winter, he had fallen into the habit of strolling in the oval landscape depicted on the back of an old blue sugar bowl. Over a curved little bridge of faded red brick, caressing its tender moss with his palm, he would pass above a solitary pool and step into the undergrowth of water lilies on the other shore and reckon, for once and all, the charm of yellowish green flowers in the young verdure of the meadow as one of the great joys of childhood and beyond. He also returned there later, emboldened by age, prolonging the strolls. From a bird-cherry ravine along a steep path, he would climb to the precipice of the park, which was crowned by a rotting gazebo, would see in the gap of an allée a big, shapelessly proportioned house, where someone kept starting to play the piano, stopping and laughing. A chaste umbrella sauntered above clipped shrubbery. Self-forgetful, a gentleman sat on a bench, uniting his smart beard and fingers braided round the knob of a cane, gazing immobile through an invisible lens with bright, slightly intoxicated eyes. Shelaputov knew these carefree people well—extravagant, in love with the wrong person, wearied by noble plans and unclear presentiments. He would steal away in order not to awaken them and to conceal from them that there is none of that, that the adored lacy infant chasing a hoop had long since rotted to dust.

Years later, not long before his shameful public swoon, secreted in the ruins of someone's dacha, he had adapted to life in the alien land of a wall tapestry. This was a quite sorrowless place: with the stronghold of a little house entwined with eternal ivy, with a mill on a sweet stream, with fat animals cared for by a shepherdess who resembled a Madame Odetta, though certainly one not versed in Proust. That would have been the place for him, but he fell to grieving, squabbling with the shepherdess, who had annoyed him with her lisping, tender suffixes, and fled.

And so now he easily exchanged blossoming Dioscurias for Parisian gray smoke in which there dwelt a pale yellow, light blue, and lilac pheasant.

Two simultaneous torments hailed Shelaputov and returned him to the geography at hand. The first was the small revenge of an offended wasp that was laboring over the red swelling of his wrist. The second pain, being bigger than his body, clumsily thickened and writhed outside; he was it and stumbled onto it, perhaps because he went blindly straight ahead past the path to the gate and the gate, leaving bits of cloth and skin on the protective barbs.

Senselessly ogling the stumps of antennae that correlate the living creature to the influences and appeals of all that there is around, he again squeezed into the stifling darkness sufficient only for a small part of a man, for a skeleton dressed slapdash in odds and ends. What roses? Ah, yes. The reader is waiting after all . . . The grave on the hill and the small white monastery with the corner dungeon for a monk's punishment: stone fitted tight around the standing sinner, his eyes, ears, nostrils and lips—glory to him, if he stood there of his free will, saw, heard, and breathed the light.

Secreted by deep scorching heat that in good times looks back on the duration of the previous nonexistence and is always laid aside in order to succeed in peering into the subsequent beyondness and expire, Shelaputov discerned and absorbed that which stood in front of him.

This was his singular native property: his life and death. Its grey hair swam in the calm, impelled by the rotation under it; through huge eyes a hell of boiling desperate thought could be seen. They dashed for each other in order to save and be saved, and of course about this there was a word which smoked and foamed on its lips and which Shelaputov saw reasonably and correctly but could in no way understand.

How little torment remained: only to divine and carry out its conjuring cry and press to, press into, once more to acquire the blissful primordial coziness that is guarded by its grumbling, sharp-clawed love. But what was it saying? Could it be proposing a game of billiards? Or all is much worse than I know, and we're talking about golf, bridge, backgammon? Or has it found me a good match? But me, I can't do all that, what are we to do, how am I to atone for your unendurable torment? After all, I am only the outer appearance of the wound that bleeds your poor blood. Oh, Mama, could I really be dying!

They grabbed and scattered inviolable air between them, while of him there was more and more. What mining engineer made a mistake so that they should miss each other in the transparent mass? There it goes further and further away, having extended to him its hand, in breastplate and mantle, in a crown of thorns and shoulder straps.

Again noticing his hand wounded by the wasp, Shelaputov came to: the wrist hurt and itched, the palm embraced the back of The Dog's head.

Leaning on The Dog's head, Shelaputov caught sight of the great multiplicity of sea with its silvery scum and of the garden deceived by the blinding semblance of scorching heat and again desirous of flowering and decking itself out. On the shore, Ingurka, weakening and snarling dully, eluded her inevitable fate. Now without pride and putting on of airs, she shook off first this, then that embrace. Red was dispersing the lot of them with his thin, authoritative bark. Another little pack played not far off: the girl Ketevan was laughing and running away from Gigo.

The Dog's nape rose under Shelaputov's hand, and Shelaputov's shoulderblades tensed. He turned around and glimpsed Pyrkin, who was getting ready to go to the city. He did not at all know this no-sort-of man and was struck by the strength of his gaze, the trajectory of which was distinctly outlined against the light, pierced Shelaputov's crown, exploded where the scrap of chain was, and managed to cause contusions all about. He was sending his gaze along voluptuously and was not able to break off this activity, but Shelaputov also looked at Pyrkin potently.

Bound for the bus station, Pyrkin grabbed the stones of the mountains together with houses and kitchen gardens and flung them at the foreign evil spirits of the dogs and children, at the whole fork-tongued Proustian bunch of pigs aiming to escape hard labor and devour the feijoa.

"Here's what, brother," said Shelaputov. "Go on, do not yield to Red the farewell smile of our sad sunset. And I'll go to town and ask those who understand: what is a man to do, when he wants to depart with his Dog."

The beast set out, downcast. Shelaputov did not bother to watch how he stood there with his head down, while Red, jumping up and falling back chewed the air around his lion's paws superficially, with Ingurka, in his support, wrinkling her nose, her upper lip quivering, hostile thin points bared, to the approval of all the secondary participants.

He didn't bother to watch how Gigo caught the laughing Ketevan. Indeed, can light be caught, a gold column of undefined dust?—but there it was caught and, for a joke, held above the surf, and the surf, for a joke, feigned taking it. But she fell back and back, again flowed out through his fingers, glittered freely in the distance—the equal of a ray, indistinguishable from the rest of the sun.

An ancient bus with a tarpaulin top shook over the potholes until the contents—various appearances, nationalities, subspecies, and breeds—were thoroughly blended by the end of the trip, equally spotted, wrinkled and unified—except for Pyrkin and Shelaputov. Look what a city, what an Athenian-white and colonnaded one, with a crown of structure on the peak of the mountain; oh, not the Parthenon—after all, I don't make any pretenses—but a restaurant where they are out of shashlik—but what a city beloved by Shelaputov. Here it comes, a rich outlander, possessor of pompous excesses of palms, rhododendrons, and eucalypti, gypsum close by and basalt afar off. An azure, acrid, hairy city lusting after a sovereign and inaccessible sister: oh, how it would like to crumple her fleur d'orange, oh Nice, oh!

Shelaputov headed for the Cook office, walking along as always with his hands wound as tight as they would go behind his back, grabbing his right hand firmly in his left. Bewitched Pyrkin went along behind him for a time, trustingly inclining his head to the side for thinking over that peculiarity of his walk, and he even said something encouraging to him, but Shelaputov again forgot to notice him.

Cook not being present, the associates to whom Shelaputov drifted this time without satisfaction through the ins and outs of the line explained to him fastidiously what it was necessary for someone to do if he wanted to depart with his Dog. There wasn't enough room for all that in the time alotted to Shelaputov; there really wasn't enough for the muzzle, repair of the broken chain, and a separate cage for the traveler. Tired and faded, Shelaputov set out along the embankment, burdened by the unmitigated magnitude of the sky, the mountains and scurrying life. The sea was absent whitishly and right beyond the parapet began nothing. The natural born twin of the human crowd that loiters, trades, obtains women or some other prey, he was again entirely alone and leant only on the weaving together of his hands behind his back.

Having taken a seat in a seaside coffee house, Shelaputov took to watching how the Greek Aleko, elegant, wiry, blackishly grey, handled a brazier with burning hot sand. No prattling motion—just the short flight of a strong elbow, the sparkle askant of a capacious eye that foresaw the black brew's every new need, that grinned at the café fortunetellers: not for him answers from an overturned cup, he was sharper than the all-knowing grounds.

Shelaputov remembered nothing, knew everything: that momentary—move it, Chink!—hour for getting things together, graves—there, Aleko—here,

Sensing Shelaputov, Aleko blazed at him lovingly with his eye: wait a bit, I am coming, don't grieve, and prosper forever and ever. There is a look between man and man for which it is worth living in this ineffable world with its shining sea and fragile, gigantic magnolia holding up its porcelain cup of light. Getting the better of the usual batch of copper in the grounds, Aleko came up, with a light touch of his palm greeting Shelaputov's shoulder. About The Dog he said:

"Go to this address and make a deal with the conductor. He'll be here tomorrow evening, the day after tomorrow you and your Dog will go off with him."

Then he extinguished his eyes and asked:

"Have you seen Ketevan?"

"Go there, Aleko," answered Shelaputov, gazing at him distinctly. "Don't delay, go today."

Aleko looked at the expanse of day, at Greece in the distance, briefly played the end of some music on the table with his fingers, and said with a brash grin:

"I'm an old, poor Greek from a coffee house. And she—you know yourself what she is. I'll be going back to my place. Farewell, brother."

But how beautiful you are, Aleko, in you there is everything. You have seen everything under the sun, except the higher whiteness—the beloved homeland of your ancient and valorous blood. The Nike of Samothrace is with you! Let us close our lids and commence to think that sea resembles sea, as one drop of water another. And what gleams white on the mountain top so harmoniously? Not a temple in honor of the beginning and the end of shashlik but a thought without miscalculation, beauty without fault: The Parthenon.

Shelaputov embraced a wrecked column, attending to the rough marble with his forehead. Below, the Acropolis was pulled up tight; farther down and farther out the port of Piraeus bustled with dignity, quite far off, beyond the sea's mirage, twelve men indistinguishable one from the other, entered the coffee house. What sort were they? Probably negotiators successful in trading of musk, ginger, and slaves, celebrating the usual deal. But where had Shelaputov seen them before? The lovesick serving girl was moving the tables, lugging bottles and victuals. Victoria is theirs, no doubt, but do they actually have too few drachmas to win over the hand that greases the features of their faces, that raises their stomachs' sick fat that is dangerous to their happy life? Br-r, however, how they look.

"Get a move on, Greek!" But he's coming with a cup and a copper vessel, irreproachably stately, like Lysippus's fabrications, gaily glancing at them with all-knowing eyes.

"Here, Greek, drink up!"

He takes the glass with a polite bow, fixedly examines the liquid, where something teems and multiplies, laughs with bold fresh teeth and says lighheartedly:

"Your wine is dirty."

He says nothing more, but they, raving, hear:

"Your wine is dirty, thievish curs. A curse on him who drinks it voluntarily; sorrow to him who bends his neck to it. This one's a Greek, that one's somebody else, but you are nobody from nowhere; you've got many holdings but no homeland, because all that is yours is foreign, taken away from others."

Thus he is silent, places the glass on the table and goes back to his place: along the great Panathenaic Way, through the Propylaia, the Erechtheion toward the Parthenon. Farewell.

There was some sort of directive or invitation for Shelaputov, which he forgot but which he responded to. Stepping briskly and officiously along, sincerely and fleetingly stroking the living wool of palms on the way, he went along darkening streets toward the winking lighthouse of an unknown goal. Here is the youthful house with the crumbling plaster, the necessary floor, door, the disinterested bell with wires not linked to electricity. He knocked, waited, and went in.

The gloom of the room was crammed with a smell that made it hard to breathe and to move on forward—otherwise how would Shelaputov have sniffed out the thickness of the fragrant stink?

Everywhere, in pots and boxes, quivered and coiled balletically unearthly, perversely beautiful flowers.

Face to their bell-mouths, back to Shelaputov, stood Pyrkin, trembling, fussing in rapture over his imminent good fortune.

There his hand fell and a howl of triumph and pain resounded.

Having rested and cooled to the tiresome, enticing flora, Pyrkin turned away from the puzzlingly peering, unquenchable plants, caught sight of Shelaputov and shouted at him with dignity:

"I'm on pension! I raise orchids!"

"Hmm-hmm." Shelaputov shrugged his shoulders silently. "That's nice."

They headed for the bus and then home: in front, Shelaputov, closing his hands together at his back, behind, Pyrkin, looking after the back of his head.

Shelaputov climbed up to his place, left the door open, and waited.

There—a cautious ringing in the garden and up the stairs. Shelaputov embraced The Dog's head, pressed his face against it and backed off;—Eat.

That night, Red showed up for a short while: had a bite, hastily licked Shelaputov, squeakily bellowed at The Dog, lay unconscious on his side for a moment, then dashed off.

A grand tender star addressed itself to Shelaputov persistently, but with what? All life long, man tries to divine the meaning of that persistent link, and only in the moment following the last moment does the blinding answer dawn on him, that perfect knowledge which is given to no one to share with another.

Shelaputov woke up, because the dog got up, militarily flexing his fur and his muscles, gurgling in the depths of his throat.

"Stay!" said Shelaputov, and gave the door a shove.

Something poured off the stairs, crackled in the bushes, and abated. Without fear or interest, Shelaputov looked into the darkness. The dog came out anyway and stood next to him: a shot and another and another blazed at random across the heavens' star. An echo and another and another pushed off from the mountains, banged heads with the cry of the had-shot of-a-failure:

"All Frenchmen are kikes! They do the cattleyal Hide fugitives! Steal feijoa!"

"Can't you sleep?" said Shelaputov, "Oh, yeah, you are afraid of dying in your sleep. Be careful, I know a good lullabye."

In the morning, Shelaputov, stiff with cold, tarried in bed, but then, he had nothing to do the while. Out the open door, he caught sight of modest, lacy dandyishness—the earth's primordial delight, which he attempted to elude: on the iron handrails wound round with grapevines, on the dead little bodies of the persimmons wounded-by-frost, northern whiteness glistened icily. Scorching her tiny fingers on it, Madame Odetta, in a most charming padded jacket, climbed the stairs. She had to stop on the threshold in confusion:

"Oh! I beg your pardon: you aren't dressed yet and you aren't even up."

The gallant, well-bred Shelaputov was in fact dressed in all his clothes and got up forthwith.

Madame Odetta viewed him pensively with her sky blue moistness beautifully arranged around vigilant black pupils that knew the thought that was difficult for her to express, something like:

"The reason that prompts me to clarify things between us lies in my past." (The blueness increased and infused the cheeks.) "You see, Pyrkin, devoid of polish and excess education, has a subtlety of his own. His strange trips to the city . . ." (The moisture dried up, but the pupils tried tenaciously to read Shelaputov.) "They are essentially a journey in my direction, an overcoming of hostile symbols that hinder his power over me. He's terribly jealous of my dead husband—and with reason." (Sky blue streams.) "But I want to speak about something else." (The whisper and triumph of black over blue.) "Be careful. He never sleeps so as not to die—he sees everything. Pyrkin is a danger to you."

"But who is he—Pyrkin?" asked Shelaputov, getting absolutely muddled, suddenly terribly agitated, beginning to speak confusedly and as if not sober: "Pyrkin—that is not here, that is something quite other. I swear to you that you simply don't know! There, next to the station, is a hill edged with pines and a lovely church with rather fancy cupolas, one completely gold, and there's a field below and houses on the other shore. So there, if you go toward the top of the cemetery and, not from below but to one side, from the side of the road, you'll be certain to see a forgotten grave above which there isn't anything, only a pole sticking out of the ground with an inscription on it: 'PYRKIN!' Imagine? What ineradicable character, what vitality! To go to the station for vodka, to push your cap down over crazy eyes, to sit in that very cemetery, on a holiday, amid the colored eggshells, to feel in your relieved body a joyous foredoom to a fight, to yell a song until a tear of invincible sorrow wheezes in your throat, ultimately to perish foolishly, and to send this happy vertical cry outside: 'PYRKIN!' "

"You're lying!" called out an invisible, unearthly Pyrkin of the same name. "That's another someone or other, a thief, a drunkard, a loafer with three convictions! Who slept all the time, red-eyed most likely—up and died, the fool!"

No one stood in the door-opening anymore, screening the thawed, unbearably shining garden, while Shelaputov kept looking at the sacred hill so beloved by, so unavoidable for, him.

Having awaited the hour when the sun, which had done all possible for the warming up of these gardens, had begun to look to the impartial care of other gardens and peoples, Shelaputov came out through the wicket gate to the shore and got stuck in the wet pebbles. The sea was already training the slow-witted earth with boxing on the ears and a fist in the teeth, but as befitted her, nobody understood a thing, as before.

Out of nobody's boxtree, tearing free out of somebody's enclosure, Gigo emerged lazily in a striped sweater, once more without occupation and intention. Far away, behind, covering her face with the whole of her long hand refracted in a beautiful wrist dipped in coming, soapy infinity, came the girl Ketevan, not looking golden.

The sun, before departing into the clouds irrevocably, beat the tambourine of orange fur, and Red crossed his forepaws on a wolfishly goatlike, darkly light neck. A structure was erected out of him and Ingurka and froze. The massed assemblage played out its role, sitting around, looking on. Far from the frozen circle dance stood the big old dog, watching.

"Forget it!" said Shelaputov to him. "Let's go."

Ahead was the point of the cliff on the sloping shore; someone else had turned back to look, when forbidden—Shelaputov ran his palm over the thin spine— lion fur took off from the caress, and a wave of wrinkles passed over the scars and marks.

He said: "Wait for me here, and tomorrow we'll leave"—and without looking back, went off to find the conductor.

The place was not too distant, but Shelaputov went far into the depths of quickly-thickening night, staring now into the dead end of a thicket, now at the precipice in the road above a cold trout stream. The sky did not give away in anything its assumed presence, and Shelaputov, discrete from the universe, languished inside the stony, airless dark as in an extinguished, exitless elevator.

There was a glimpse of deliverance, and the sky was bared at once, with its stars and impeccable moon, whose ripening Shelaputov had lost from view behind long clouds, and he was now struck by the sight of it and by its significance. Right in front of him, on an illuminated hillock, stood an arm of the law armed to the teeth and sobbing violently. Waiting out the first pity and respect for the man's grief, Shelaputov, ashamed, turned to him nevertheless for instructions— he, not suppressing his lunar tears, explained with a movement of his hand: where.

Women in black from head to toe met Shelaputov on the porch and took him into a house. He did manage to admire a mournful nobility of their dress that was independent of variegated present time, noting only later how with a light, silky crackle his heart burst, and this was not painful but mint-sweet. An old man, the head of the house, and other men stood around a table, besprinkling bread with wine. And they gave Shelaputov wine and bread. The old man said:

"You drink, too, to Aleko." He poured a little wine on some bread and drank the rest up.

How cool in the chest, what sharp wine, how beautifully blended with its taste was its familiar, blatantly ozonous aftertaste. Was it actually retsina? No, it was a local black brew, while retsina looks golden in the light and sets the teeth on edge and delights the mouth with its gold. But all the same—hail, Aleko. We always die earlier than they; their knife keeps pace with our back, but their death will be more terrible because great is their fear before it. How pitiful people are, in essence. And do they not value their poor life so voraciously because it will undoubtedly not have a continuation and no one will weep over them from grief and not for profit?

Shelaputov drank another glass, though he anxiously knew that it was time for him to go: he fancied he saw the star shake thrice and go out.

"So come tomorrow if you can," said the old man at parting. "I will expect you and your Dog."

Not losing time in the least, in one jump of his hurrying mind, Shelaputov got to the reared-back stone. The Dog was not there. Shelpautov did not know where his Dog was, where his lion was, where he lay on his side, stretched out to the limit, spreading far his head and his frozen-stiff paws. Three bullet wounds and one other that is quite superfluous and indifferent to the body turn black in the bright moonlight. Along the throat and along the velvety, loose excess of the neck necessary to a large dog only for the hand of a man to pat with adoration had passed a knife not bent on causing death.

"So—four," Shelaputov accurately counted. "That's how many little efforts I owe the hyenas who long since are puzzled: am I not their enemy, if the carrion belonging to them raises orchids to this day?"

In sheet-lightning on the other side of the eyes, in instantaneous post-tunnel light that he had hunted for all life long, he remembered everything that he had forgotten under cover of his ailment. It remained only to change the pictures in the magic lantern. The hamlet was called Svistukha, the river Iakhroma; not far off the dead water of the canal lay in its concrete sepulchre. Behind the wall with the tapestry, the unsociable mistress of the cottage gone to wrack and ruin was ailing. Once she called him to her with a knocking and for the first time he entered her room, which gaily surveyed the crimson and gold, October summing up the fading and falling, October sunny and spidery that year. The old and beautiful lady looked at him ardently, stoutly pinching together the lace over her collarbones. He immediately perceived in her a majestic shadow of something bigger than she—a shadow that left to her visage only a narrow detrimental bracket of yellowish light. He was not ready for this; it was just as simple and wild as bowing diligently over a primer and reading there the word: death.

"Sweetheart," she said. "I saw the ones who built this canal. It wasn't permitted to go there, but we got lost after a picnic and inadvertently came upon the forbidden place. They turned us around sharply, but we were feeling gay from wine and from life and went on joking and laughing. And then I met the gaze of a man who was no longer of this world; he had already paved the bottom of the canal with himself but stood there looking at me squeamishly and haughtily. So many years have passed; the claws inside me have clamped shut and are consuming my life. And he goes on standing there and looking. Poor child, you had not yet been born then, but I was obliged to tell this to someone. After all, he had to look at somebody."

All this seemed unjust to the former Shelaputov; after all, he had already fled to saving, miracle-working groves and now he had to make for somewhere out of the serene woods-above-the-grave and sit it out in the tapestry.

A time later, Shelapulov—or that one whose sweater was his—he or she—floated on the canal in an amusing little boat with music and paper lanterns. The twelve traveling companions of the glamorous tour leader in skin-tight velvet and chiming little silver chains responded with garbled platitudes to her most bold quips. Stringing together permissible biting comments, she sipped wine brewed from fat amoebae. And suddenly saw how pale faces gazed at her out of the mermaid moistness beyond the window, squeamishly and haughtily. But why not at those whom they had seen in their last hour— but at her who had happily missed them. The rest of the company looked with gratification at the cozy, trained water, at the cold, lunar night successfully coinciding with the warmth and light inside the swift-winged, roving vessel.

Then there followed the half-flight across the valley of the hall, the innate half-deed, the female feat of falling down senseless and the strained fortitude of getting along without them.

He placed his hand on a void, inadvertently seeking The Dog's large head with its hollow 'twixt pensive knobs above the brows

Nothing could be as cold as that.

Loosed from the bowstring into a near target, Shelaputov soared along the shattering sea and would have stumbled into an obstacle were it not for the sweater the color of a milepost.

Gigo sobbed, rocking his head along wet stones.

"Mother beat me! Mother beat Gigo and she called him a son of misfortune, an idiot. Mother cried: If Ketevan has no father, let my father kill me. Father interceded and wept. He said: Now Aleko will marry her. But she ran out of the house. Mother ordered me to live where homeless dogs live, and together with all the others she said she'll throw stones at me—and no bread."

Responding to Shelaputov's festive lightness, his little resort, his tiny St. Tropez shone before him, igniting all the fires, seeking out darkness with torches.

Toward him ran the fluttering Madame Odetta. Ran up to him, dragged his hands up to her lips, grasping at him and crying:

"Help! He fell asleep! He's dying in his sleep!"

Shaking free of her, Shelaputov went into the house and up to the bedroom (without hurrying). In bed, under the turned-around portrait that looked through the wall into Shelaputov's closet, Pyrkin lay asleep, wheezing and crying out. His face was quickly getting bigger and darkening from the influx of unattractive blood; his hands grasped for something that did not sustain weight, something that was flying off the precipice with him, into the gulf.

His gun rested next to him, once more ready for service.

"Help him!" sobbed Madame Odetta. "For the sake of him who is not above us—wake him up! You can do it! I don't believe that you are so terribly hard." She fell to her knees that protruded white and unpleasant from the open slit of her robe, and spilled over the floor like Saxon haricot, like discordant crocks of thick porcelain.

The diminutive one in a frock coat, hanging upside down from a star, raised his crystal baton, and Shelaputov took up his lullabye. This was an innocent song, in whose soporific powers Shelaputov firmly believed. Pyrkin was noticeably eased by the drowsy recitative: his roving hands found their sought-for peace, the tormented chest gulped the last of the air and stopped—with this its worldly obligations ceased, a sigh being no longer its concern—but that of someone else, higher.

In decent correspondences to the sad circumstances, Shelaputov raised his eyes to the sky and saw that the tiny habitué of the star had tossed aside his authoritative baton and was embracing a ray of light, pressing his weeping body to it.

Shelaputov threw himself on the silent Pyrkin: shook him by the shoulders, blew into his mouth, and ran his palm over his left forearm, where something had awakened with readiness and was starting to pop cheerfully. Slavishly he echoed the lead of the unknown prompter and repeated again and again:

"Not lullabye but beat and kill! I mixed up everything, and you believed me! No retreat! The horn calls us into battle! Death to him who falls asleep on watch!"

A newborn Pyrkin opened unarmed eyes that had not yet taken on color and gaze and, quickly maturing, asked severely:

"What's happening?"

"Nothing much," Shelaputov reported. "The division into murderers and the murdered is foreordained and irremediable."

With an experienced movement of several items: dropping the forehead low, managing to catch it in flight, once more propping up the one hundred and sixty-fifth centimeter from the dirty floor with the crown of his head, with stage machinery above, reproachful star at the zenith, randomly with his back without a hitch passing through the curtain—he bowed, passed by the wall, and ended up in his room that was alien and kindred-as-the-grave. And there, close-fitting velvet tucked into circus boots with spurs was already sauntering, and chains' silver burst, and eyes led hereditarily into hell, but a hell of another, reverse content.

"Greetings, cavalryman-maiden Foolhardyova!" said Shelaputov (Shelamotov? Shuraleenko?). "Have we not overstayed our welcome in Dioscurian bliss? Is it not time to return under the stadium's dome and frighten the simple-hearted public with a song about how the song is sung? No one knows that this is the truth, that the tightrope over the darkness is nearly worn through, as are the vocal cords covered with hoarse nodules. And only for this—bravo and all the preliminary, stupid flowers. Your exit. Time to go."

And so she did.

A tenacious someone who remained searched in the sky where a nonexistent star shone affectedly, and he set out on a moonlit path that was nothing but a reflection of reflected light, the visible aspect of a path into the invisibility beyond the horizon, but, indeed, the rash traveler himself is nonsense, weightlessness, an illusory failure who has outlived his Dog and everything else without which it is possible to get by, but—why?

Two Diaries*
by Pyotr Kozhevnikov

I

GALYA: *April 3*

Sometimes I wonder why I'm keeping a diary. Probably because I miss the man I love. He's far away right now, stationed near Komsomolsk-na-Amure. Why do they send the guys so far away? If he were stationed in the suburbs, we could see each other. But the way it is now, he can't get leave, and I can't go see him. Not to see the man I love for two years. It's terrible! But he won't stop loving me. In every letter Vsevolod writes about how he's going to hug and kiss me when he comes back. We write each other every day. True, sometimes I think I'll finish trade school, they'll send me off to work, and that's how it'll be my whole life, right up to retirement. And what kind of life is there after retirement? Women get old after thirty, and I'm almost sixteen. I've lived half of those years already. And what kind of a life does a woman have anyway? You get married—and that's it. The man does nothing at home. You both put in the same working day, but then the woman has to spend the same amount of time doing housework as well. You have to go to the store, cook the food, serve it, wash the dishes, wash the clothes, have the children, feed them, raise them. . . . You could go crazy! I wonder if Vsevolod will help me. Of course I wouldn't want the man I loved to be washing dishes or socks. But you could divide up the jobs somehow. When there's physical work, for example, like washing the floor, the man could do it, and dusting would be the woman's job . . .

MISHA: *April 3*

Today the thought of suicide came into my mind. This is the consequence of all my misfortunes and failures. But how can I kill myself? If I lived in the states I'd just buy a revolver—and you're all set. But how can you get one here? Take it from a policeman? Become a hunter? Easier to turn on the gas, but if the neighbors smell it it's all

*Translated by Ellendea Proffer.

over. Get some sleeping pills? I really don't know what kind or how many. And how could I get some anyway? I'm afraid to run in front of a trolley, and if I did they'd fix me up and you spend your life as a freak. No, the hell with it! Maybe I could electrocute myself? No, that's unreliable, and I want it to be certain. The main thing's not to suffer, to have no pain. I don't know why I'm writing all this in a diary. For myself? For others? Well, let them read it. But only if I know it and they think I don't. I can even dedicate it to You—read on!

I think that every person has his own thread in life. I lost mine, or never found it. I'm tortured by unanswerable questions. Here's a man. He's born, grows, studies, works, starts a family, and then—dies. Man always dies! I can't bear my mood! Sometimes I wonder how Life appeared anyway, how the Universe came to be. Then it seems like I've gotten off the track. And why is it that a person who was once strong and brave can be insulted by any crummy person as soon as he's old? Why do people get decrepit?

I want to cry.

Go away somewhere.

II

GALYA: *May 16*

There was a Komsomol* meeting today at school. The third-year girls were on monitor duty as early as fourth class, with orders not to let anyone get out. So they made me and Marinka go back. Marinka read her notebook during the meeting. I dozed a little, and then took a look at it too, and began to read. She'd copied down an English story about how a married couple had invited a photographer to come take pictures of their children, while another couple had invited a "state husband" to visit. They have such a job. Families who don't have children make use of this person. So, the photographer goes to the family where they want to have children, and the "state husband" ends up where they wanted the children photographed. The husbands are all away at work, and really funny things begin to happen. After the meeting Marinka and I went to my house. She told me about how she'd kissed this guy. He left suck marks on her lips, and now they're sore. Marinka is a real up-to-the-minute girl. She smokes nothing but Belomor cigarettes and drinks nothing but vodka. She goes out with guys a lot, but even though she seems like she's been around, she's actually a virgin. I don't know how she's managed to preserve her innocence when she drinks with guys so much. And how she swears! Every other word is "mother-this," "mother-that." But you'd never know she was so tough by just looking at her. Really big blue eyes are the main feature in her face. I always imagined that Malvina in the fairy tale had eyes like that. Marinka's face is a little coarse, but her skin is perfect. She isn't tall, but her figure is well-proportioned, so she doesn't seem any shorter than any of the other girls. She acts free and

*Students' political organization [tr.].

easy of course, but she's really shy. And when she talks, she has such a quiet, assured voice, like things couldn't possibly be any other way. My Mama doesn't like her, and I've told Marinka to always give me a call from a phone booth before she comes over. It's just better if Mama's not home when she comes.

MISHA: *May 16*

I never try to rush home after school. But even so, I go down into the subway and in ten minutes I'm at the Vasilievsky stop. Today I got only one two-kopeck piece as change, which is already an accomplishment. There are supposed to be thirty people in our work group, but sometimes there are only twenty-five. Some get sick, some cut. I wanted to get out of the last two hours—it was Special Technology—but the foreman was on duty at the exit and nothing worked out. Spec. Tech. is really a lousy subject. The teacher reads, and we write: "The process of cutting wood is called sawing. The components of the shavings are: sawdust. . . ." And so on for two hours. But the teacher really likes to call people up to the board and make fun of them while they're trying to answer. If you don't snap at him, he gives you a C instead of a D, even if you don't know a damn thing. He considers himself the most intelligent person in the world. Everyone probably thinks that. When I go into the subway a stream of people pass me, and each one is thinking that he's the most intelligent person.

The courses in esthetics are just all junk. The first hour the teacher talks about something and reads definitions, but she's not the one who thought them up. We spend the second hour writing down all the stuff she's said. At home we learn it by heart. I think that each person should have his own views on art or love. But how can we when she does that? The school year's almost over, but we've been to a museum only once—to the House of Technical-Scientific Propaganda.

After school they rounded us up to hear a lecture. A middle-aged man told us how we could actually be committing crimes when we think we're just playing tricks. One guy stole a car—he just wanted to go for a ride, but they sent him to juvenile prison. Another, also from ITS [Industrial Trade School] cut a pistol out of metal and painted it black. And then he went to the Golodai district and threatened a thirty-five year old woman with it. She was carrying her groceries, and he wanted to rape her. He didn't pull off the rape, but they sent him to juvenile prison anyway. They're both fools of course. But sometimes, when I'm drinking, I want to steal a car. And I often wonder what I'd do if I had a gun. Today is Wednesday and there's no night school. I could read that book. I tried to read it twice this year, but just couldn't. There's just no time. I come home from school at three, and then I can't do anything—I just lie around or sleep. And the book has to be returned. The librarian says that there's a waiting list for Sherlock Holmes: Conan Doyle wrote it.

III
GALYA: *May 20*

Yesterday Marinka was late for school and then she acted sick the rest of the day. She didn't go to night school, but asked if she could come over this evening. Mama is working at night today, so I said I'd be home. When Marinka arrived, she told me that she'd become a woman. The same guy who kissed her lips like that said that if she really loved him, she would give herself to him. They were with some people. Everyone was already drunk, and Marinka and Sasha went out to the field. She gave herself to him in the deserted house there. It didn't work out right away, and the next day they went to the house again. Now Marinka doesn't know what to do. What if she gets pregnant? She isn't even sixteen yet, and this guy has to go into the army in the fall. He'll be eighteen in July. He works as an electrician. I'm sorry for Marinka. Mama always scared me with the idea that it hurts to become a woman. I asked Marinka and she said that she felt hardly any pain. But I think it's probably different for everyone.

MISHA: *May 20*

Today I went out with Mama to take a look at the dacha. She wants to have some fresh air on her vacation. I ran into Pashka there. He's turned into a real man. I'm taller than he is, though. Pashka is in the third year of the Energy-Machines Training College. He went in after eighth grade. We were happy to see each other, and arranged to meet in town. We talked about our childhood. We haven't rented a dacha from Veronika Egorovna for eight years now. When my mother and father lived together, they used to rent a cabin in Shuvalov every summer. The first year there, I became friends with the landlady's son. He was two years older than me, but didn't let it bother him. Mornings we would run down and swim in the lake, after dinner we'd fight with raspberry twigs in the garden, and at night they couldn't get us into bed. But there was one incident which broke up our friendship. Pashka was ten then, and it was the last year my parents lived together. The landlady's niece, from her first husband, came to visit. She was nineteen. She seemed like a grown-up woman to us. All of Veronika Egorovna's rooms were in use, so she had to put her in the same room with Pashka. Some buddies would come pick up Rita every day and then she would be gone with them until night. Pashka said that a lot of times when he would fall asleep she still wasn't home. Once after supper, when I'd been out waiting for Pashka in the garden, I went into the landlady's house. When I opened the door of his room, Rita was sitting on the bed. She had on a pink corset and she was fastening a stocking to a garter belt on her full leg. The other stocking was hanging over a colored dress on a chair. Pashka was sitting beside her. I was used to seeing Rita in a dress or bathing suit, and here I was seeing her in her underwear for the first time. I liked her a lot. I wanted to touch the pink brassiere where her breasts protruded. But Rita screamed: why had I come in without knocking? I asked why Pashka was allowed to sit with her, but I wasn't? She said that Pashka was related. I remember I was so angry at Pashka that I wouldn't play with him for the rest of the summer. Now I understand why he was sitting behind her back. Pashka was helping Rita get dressed.

IV

GALYA: *May 27*

A terrible thing's happened. Someone has died—some guy. I don't even know how to write about it. A group of kids got together in a building on a nearby street. Drug addicts. The girl this guy loved got mad at him for something. He asked her forgiveness. She said that she'd forgive him if he jumped out the window. The guy went out on the ledge and jumped. From the ninth floor. He was crushed to death. They say it was awful to look at. The police were called. From the window the group saw the mess on the pavement and they all ran away. The girl, too. Then the other kids got together and waited until there was no one else home at her house, and broke into her apartment. They beat her head against a radiator and stomped on her. They stole a lot of gold things, too. The girl was from a rich family. After that, the police caught the kids and tried them for narcotics and assault. They were all sent to prison. The girl wasn't tried. She's in serious condition in the hospital, and she'll be an invalid for life. They smashed up everything inside her. Now everybody's talking about this incident. Of course everyone has a different view. Some say that if they hadn't all been taking drugs none of it would have happened. The guy was a fool to jump, but after all he wanted to prove that he was ready to do anything, that he loved her so much he was ready to die at one word from her. She was trash, although what they did to her was terrible, of course. A girl who's been beaten is an awful sight. Where we go skating in the winter, there are girls who fight over guys a lot. They take their skates and beat each other on the head and face with them. Marinka and I saw fights like that several times. We were already with guys so we didn't get into that kind of situation. But I've seen girls who were beaten up and it's awful.

MISHA: *May 27*

Yesterday after school Lyokha and I went to the Peter-Paul Fortress. It was too cold for swimming. We sunbathed on top of the bastion, and threw pebbles at the people down below. The people sunbathing by the wall went crazy, but they couldn't figure out who was bothering them. They probably thought it was each other. Lyokha said he was thinking of dropping out of school. He's not much like the rest of the guys. His stepfather's a sculptor and his mother's a singer. He's an intelligent guy, knows a lot, and tells interesting stories. It's true he's pretty tame and quiet, but the guys don't bother him. Probably because we're friends. Lyokha is thin, but he looks a bit like a girl. His muscles don't show at all, his ass is big, and his breasts stick out as well. The changes of adolescence. He lowers his eyes a lot and he's touchy. He's got a face that looks like he just prayed, and you can see something like terror in his blue eyes, terror about something really awful which none of us can see. Lyokha is too honest. When Potapov asked Lyokha if he had slept with a woman, he answered: "I've got to admit it, I haven't." I hardly ever curse around Lyokha. But still I think that people, at least to themselves, call a lot of things by words they don't print in books. For example, sometimes I think in nothing but curse words. They're always running through my head. But for some reason I don't write them in my diary.

At about seven we went to the Kirov movie house. They show old movies there and often there's stuff worth seeing. We wanted to see a horror movie. But this time there was nothing any good. We walked over to the Smolensk cemetery. I love that cemetery. I spent my whole childhood there. When I go there, it's like I'm rereading a book. Everything's so familiar, that it's as if you're in the book yourself. Of course it's not as nice in the cemetery as it used to be. A lot of the monuments are being destroyed. Workers are taking away stones and railings. You've kicked the bucket but they rob you anyway. Be better if they just burned you up. But then some jerk would cop your ashes and spread them over his garden, or on his balcony flower box. We walked through the cemetery to the training field. The field shares a fence with the cemetery, and when we were little we loved to sit on the fence and watch the dogs. But their masters always sicced them on us. We threw stones at the dogs, but we should've thrown them at their masters. Then I dragged Lyokha off to the gulf. He didn't want to go, but I tempted him with the idea of getting some reed nutmeg. But it turned out that there wasn't any nutmeg. They've built up the area there, and spoiled it. Some guys and I used to go swimming and sunbathing by the bay, and then we'd run into the tall grass which hid us up to our heads. Ducks would fly out of the grass and seagulls would scream over the shore. When the grass was dry we'd burn it. Now there are buildings everywhere and swarms of people. We went as far as the excavator. We wanted to go out in a boat, but there was a long line and Lyokha had to go do some errands. We got on a No. 7 and said good-bye at the subway. Lyokha went on to the Vosstanie stop, and I walked to the embankment. What could I do with the time?

V

GALYA: *May 28*

Today I realized that I love him. He lives in the building across the street. He's on the top floor too. I see him through the window or from the balcony quite often. He's half a year older than me. He breaks up fast with all the girls he goes out with. But now he's got one who's three years older than he is. Marinka introduced me to him today. She and Sasha and I were at his place. We bought three bottles of port. After we'd drunk it and listened to the music, we took a walk. Along the way Sasha ran into two of his friends and their girls. We all went together to the railway section of the field. A lot of terrible things go on there. One time Marinka and I were out taking a walk and we went into the abandoned house. It was a small, one-floor place. No one knows what it used to be. There were empty bottles and cigarette butts on the floor. An old, dirty couch. (Marinka became a woman on it when Sasha took her there.)

Our first time there was both scary and interesting. After that we kept an eye on it each time we were in the field. We saw a soldier take a drunk girl into the house. They came out almost an hour later. The girl was crying. Her tears had dissolved her mascara and black streaks ran down her cheeks.

We all walked in the field while it was sunny. Then we went home. There are a lot of tests in school right now, and we've got to study. Final exams are coming up soon, too. But I got home just now, and I can't do anything. I just sit and look out the window, but I don't see Tolya. I really want to be with him again. I got a letter from Vsevolod yesterday. I thought I'd answer it today, but what should I write? I want to talk with Mama. Maybe she'll give me an idea of what to do.

MISHA: *May 28*

I went to see Romin after class. He's the leader of our band. He finishes school this year. He's suffered through three years here and now he knows that his vocation is music and not carpentry, which he can't stand. Romin plays the guitar fantastically, but his singing is weak—he doesn't really have a voice. He's basically a great guy. Even though he's kind of puny, he's very independent and always stands out in a crowd. He really likes to make fun of people. But when he laughs his eyes are serious. At first glance they seem melting, but there's a touch of mustard added. I took a pornographic magazine to Romin. He wanted to copy a photo from it, but I don't like looking at that picture very much. The magazine's in color, from Sweden. I took it away from a classmate two years ago, when he was showing it around class.

I liked Romin's place. There's just a cabinet and a cot in the room, and a stereo tape recorder in the window. Half of the cabinet is taken up with tapes. Romin's really lucky in his neighbors. When I asked if they complained about his loud music, he said that sometimes they yell and tell him to make it louder. In summer they dance in front of his window.

Romin had temporary use of some American stereo earphones. He let me listen to the music with them, and it sounded stronger and more iealistic. I really love to listen to music. Our music is the art of the future. It belongs to us because we are going into the future. We'll take the places of our fathers, and they the places of our grandfathers . . . When you listen to music, a completely different world opens up to you. Sometimes it's not very beautiful or just, but it's always sincere. It's alien and close at the same time. When we hear it, we experience other people's lives. Alien, but close. They are complex lives which seem unattainable, but you fall into them and live some moments along with the people themselves. And when the music becomes more sublime than anything else on earth, then my as yet unspent love flows into this flood, issuing from the shores of human consciousness. And the music floods the very depths of my soul, to which no one ever penetrates. About which no one has any idea. About which no one thinks. I don't understand all of the words of the songs, but they never deceive me. I feel them, have faith, and follow the music where it leads me. Whether I stay alive or die depends on it. It is eternal! I am mortal! But I'm not afraid of death in the depths of my music. Perhaps I'll get to the very bottom of this magnificence when I die and I'll see all the beauty to its very end. I'll be transported by this beauty. Sometimes when you listen the internal rhythm grabs you, and if you dance your aroused body absorbs all of the music. I prefer to listen to it without moving. I become completely still when I listen. All that is real is in our music. The way it is It's diverse. In one piece I see buildings hanging over me, just about to crush me, and the crunch won't even be audible. People are laughing at me. The glass in the windows shines like naked teeth. I see armed drug addicts who in their destructive oblivion rush and kill like animals. I see a sadistic sex maniac torturing a girl, and a body exhausted with longing for what it's never known. I see a suicide drowning in blood, and violence itself, laughing in its inhumanity, bodies scorched by napalm. I see the mushroom hanging over the planet, born of insane human genius, hanging over the frightened, terrorized faces of earthmen in their last moment of horror. But in other pieces I'm struck by the freshness of flowers given to a girl for the first time, and an involuntarily overheard declaration of love—a hysterical one, but identical to the rest of our generation's. I'm impressed by the sincerity of someone else's confession revealed to me by music.

VI

GALYA: *May 29*

I got a letter from Vsevolod today. He asks why I'm silent. He writes that he's really missing me. He can't wait to see me. He's sorry I'm so young, otherwise we'd get married.

I met him in the country, at my grandmother's, where I used to go almost every year for vacation. He would come from Petrozavodsk to see his uncle, whose house was next to ours. Now he's coming back from the army. Even though I don't love him any more, I wonder how he's turned out. He's already twenty-two. I talked about him with Mama. She said not to write him that I've stopped loving him, no matter what. Vsevolod would kill himself if he got a letter like that. I wanted to write him my usual letter, but the whole time I kept imagining him reading what I'd written, so I kept crossing it out. I rewrote it four times. Sent it off.

I was at Tolya's last night. Mama was already asleep when I went out, and I'd arranged with him that he'd open his door for me at two o'clock. Tolya lives with his parents in an apartment like ours. His father drinks a lot. His mother works in the same factory as the father. She's also a house painter. Tolya took me into his room. We sat up until five o'clock. All he did was put his head on my lap. He didn't even try to kiss me once. Rather strange! I've begun to see that he's a very limited person. Tolya only went through eighth grade. He works at the post office. He delivers the mail on a motor scooter. He doesn't go to night school. He drinks a lot. Talking with him is not interesting. We're usually quiet.

MISHA: *May 29*

Today we had practical. That's how they do it: half a week of theory, half a week of practice. They made us a workshop in the factory area—it's an experimental group.

They caught Molchanov at the entrance when we were leaving the factory. He'd stuffed guitar strings in his pants pockets and in the inside pocket of his jacket. All the guys are taking stuff, and it's almost falling out under the nose of the dame who checks the passes. Basically, the whole group steals. Usually strings—you can't buy them anywhere, and here they're loaded with them. They also grab electric guitar pick-ups, cases, and even guitar bodies (they hide them behind the second gates). Basically, everybody's copping stuff. When they took Molchanov to the head of the guards, he almost cried. Molchanov is fat, with a face like a hamster. Freckles all over. He's a quiet guy, pretty tame, steals quietly too, but he's the one who got caught. Now they'll punish him somehow, and he'll get it from almost everybody in our group, for nothing. They nicknamed him "Salty Balls."

VII

GALYA: *May 30*

I've come to realize that I don't love Tolya. He's handsome, but I don't like him. Everyone goes out of their minds over his eyes, but they seem hard and flat to me. All the girls love him, but he's in love with only me. Tolya told me that today. He wanted to kiss me. I didn't let him. I can't kiss someone I don't love.

Marinka came over. She's pregnant. She doesn't know what to do. They say when it's the first time, abortion is often not permitted. She told Sashka about it. He's agreed to marry her. But the main thing is that her whole life will be limited by the baby. She won't even be able to think about getting an education.

My opinion is that she should do anything she can to avoid having the baby.

MISHA: *May 30*

Today Lashin and I stayed after school to wash the floor of the assembly hall. We were late for slide rule class, and they always make the latecomers do something. We washed it fast, and then went to the night school. On the way Vaska said he had a ruble. We went over to the day school opposite ours, and shook fifty kopecks out of the kids there. We got ourselves a bottle of port, went to the Botanical Garden, and crawled through the fence. We settled ourselves in the summer house our whole group goes to. The entire house is covered with the names of boys and girls, the word love, and assorted curse words. There are even drawings with explanatory captions. I don't understand why the kids do this. When Vaska got out his knife, I told him not to write anything.

It's peculiar. Take Vaska. There he is with his clear blue eyes, so clear they're transparent. So rosy-cheeked it seems like he constantly has a fever. In the group they call him "Masha." But here he is, wanting to write or draw something filthy. And the worst thing about it all is that these things were already there in his mind. Somehow it's absurd. And who, looking at his transparent eyes would believe that Vaska steals from the factory, that Vaska shoots pigeons with a homemade gun, and that he swears like a drunk who's lost his mind.

And he's the Komsomol organizer for the group.

VIII

GALYA: *June 17*

Marinka and Sashka were just here. They wanted to drag me off to someone's wedding. But I didn't go. What is this, anyway? A brother and sister?! I know in France they say it's fashionable for cousins to marry, but just imagine—brother and sister?! Now I understand why everything about them was always so peculiar. No matter when you dropped by, it was like they'd just gotten out of bed. Oleg would be dressed hurriedly, his shirt not tucked in, his pants often unbuttoned, and he'd be sweating. His eyes would be shifty, and there was always something unpleasant about him, almost scary. He'd look at you like you were standing naked in front of him—it embarrassed me. Why I went to see them I don't know. And Svetka never had anything on but a robe, her face always dissatisfied. You'd sit down on the couch and see that the spread was wrinkled, and there would be either a bra lying on it or Oleg's underpants. I wonder their parents didn't kill them!? Now they're playing at having a wedding! And if Svetka hadn't gotten pregnant, what would have happened? They would've kept on living on the q.t. Now they'll be pushing a baby carriage soon. What a horrible nightmare.

MISHA: *June 17*

The first final exam is Monday. Genka came over last night, a newspaper-wrapped bottle in his hand. He asked if I wanted to get drunk. Of course! We went over to his aunt's. He told me about her. We took the No. 6 bus, near the embankment, Bursky Lane. A communal apartment. One neighbor's been a guest in the boobyhatch for six months, and the other, a young guy, goes abroad, so his wife rents his room out. A crummy apartment. First floor. The floor is made of plank boards with incredible cracks in them. The pipes are rusted and drip. No bath. Filth.

Genka's aunt is a heavy drinker. She used to have a great room in a different area. She lived with a guy who wanted her to move to another room. But as soon as they moved he dropped her. So she lives here. Her people won't have anything to do with her, Genka's the only one who goes to see her. And not for nothing, I think.

When we rang the bell, no one answered for a long time. Then a voice like a man's asked who it was. Genka answered. There was a buzz and then the door opened. In front of us was a woman you could label neither middle-aged nor elderly. Her appearance was undefined but at the same time—completely defined. The first thing you could tell was that she was a drunk. Aunt Zina looked like a man, with her red mug. Her once-blue eyes were washed out. Her hair was greasy, dyed a platinum color. An upper front tooth was missing. Her face was like a tomato that's unripe, but rotting anyway. Some aunt! Genka hadn't described her appearance to me, but just said she was forty and so on.

Aunt Zina didn't give us a friendly welcome. Probably because of me. "He comes, he brings someone . . . they come . . . they bring people . . ." she muttered almost to herself. She was dressed in a lettuce-green and beige dress of some synthetic material. Genka said it was her pride and joy, and she worried that someone might take it and sell it. Aunt Zina wore white mules on her feet, and her legs were covered with blue veins and scratches. Genka unwrapped the newspaper and gave her the bottle. She took it quickly, and bent her head over the bottle, like a predatory bird. Genka said we wished her a happy birthday and that his dad had sent the booze. It was a full half-liter bottle.

To the left of the entrance door there was a window that was almost level with the ground; opposite was the door of the crazy neighbor. A lock was hanging from it, and on the other side of the neighboring door there was a doorless passageway into the hall. Between the entrance door and the bathroom stood another table and a stove. The entrance hall was also the kitchen. A chipped sink was on the wall facing the windows. Aunt Zina's room was to the left down the hall, and the room of the sailor neighbor was at the end.

We entered her room. A man and a woman were sitting there. Judging by appearances, they were also drunks. The man was middle-aged, unshaven, and had a purple nose, and everything else about him fit with it. He had a mug like a frozen potato with dirt still stuck to it. Fingers like stumps—it was probably impossible to use them to button a fly—which is why his was open all the way. He was wearing an old shirt and pants that belonged to a police uniform. His shoes were the kind poor children wear to school. The woman had hair that was cut too short for her age and dyed black, but it was less shiny than Aunt Zina's. A fair amount of her teeth were missing, but her face was painted up so much that it was like a wax apple. She was apparently once a beauty, but now she looked like a girl who'd suddenly gotten old. She was wearing a cornflower blue dress with white polka dots on it, too short for her age, which didn't conceal her aging body. Genka said her name was Valentina Stepanovna. She works at a refrigeration plant where she checks the passes, and one can always find meat at her house. Valentina Stepanovna is the aunt's friend, and Uncle Sasha—a former policeman—now works with Aunt Zina at a plant where cakes and pies are made. Uncle Sasha works as a loader, and Aunt Zina is a janitress. She gets butter, sugar, and nuts at the plant— she sells what she can on the side, and drinks on the money she makes. When she doesn't want to do something for Genka he threatens her with prison for thieving, and then she does what he wants.

Genka introduced me to all of them and we sat down at the table. I looked around. The room was smaller than ours at home. Low ceilings. A half-made bed with the enamel chipped in places stood by the wall behind which the crazy neighbor lives. On the blanket—the kind they give out in hospitals in summer—was a mound of dirty pillows. A buffet, which was like an old dog who'd gotten mangy and rubbed his fur to the skin, stood against the opposite wall. There were two windows in the room. They didn't give any light because another building stood about two meters beyond them. A bedside table, painted a pistachio color, stood between the windows. A "Volkhov" television was on it. Genka said his aunt was renting it, but the television had broken and she was afraid to take it back. A dining table set for a holiday stood in the middle of the room. Potatoes in an aluminum pan sat on a piece of oil cloth. There were pickles and mushrooms in dishes that had come from a state restaurant. An aluminum bowl held aspic. On top of all this there was a cake which the aunt had ordered from the plant especially for her birthday. Genka said that when employees order for one of theirs, the pastry chefs put in everything the way you're supposed to, not like usual. Nuts and chocolate chips, used at the plant to make chocolate powder for sprinkling on the goods, filled a wide crystal vase. They use the nuts to make halvah. Aunt Zina went out and came back with a frying pan full of meat. Six chairs of different designs were placed around the table, most likely all gotten from the same place—the dump. We sat down on them.

A yellowing photograph, the size of a notebook page, hung over the bed. There were several other small ones beside it. I had seen these at Genka's—they were the family's forebears and relatives. A photograph of Lenin, which had been taken out of a magazine, was pinned up on the wall over the television.

There were six bottles on the table. Two of vodka, four of port, '72. Aunt Zina put out the pure alcohol and said that they wouldn't have started without us. Uncle Sasha put away the cards and poured out the vodka. We drank to the health of the instigator. Uncle Sasha poured again. He offered a toast to the idea that "everything should be good!" We drank. We ran out of vodka. I said that since we'd drunk to Aunt Zina with the vodka, now we should do it with the port. There was a roar in my head and I wanted some kind of action.

The port didn't mix well with the vodka for Uncle Sasha. He threw up half of it on the table, half on the floor. Aunt Zina called him a "parasite" and cleaned it up. Valentina Stepanovna said that men were "all hooligans and bastards." When Genka and I were taking Uncle Sasha to the bed, he tried to take Aunt Valentina by the hand. She called him a "brazen smart-aleck," and said that no one knew how to have fun anymore, never mind how to drink. She called us "kiddies," and described the parties of her youth. We drank to her youth. Aunt Zina said it would be a good idea to invite the neighbors who were renting the sailor's room.

They were young kids. He was about twenty, and she looked to be our age. They said they were married. He was tall, strong. His eyes seemed to get lackluster a lot, and he kind of pouted. The girl was really a dish. Bright like a wet decal. Fluffy hair, with a yellow glint in it. A snub nose. The kind of lips you want to kiss right away. And she's like she's ready to. . . . Full legs, small breasts. Still, a girl in every way. At first they kept refusing to come over, said they were sorry they hadn't known about the birthday, but then they came by.

The guy's name was Vladlen. He behaved quietly, used the formal "you" with everyone. He talked a little with me, invited me to come by and see his work sometime. He's an artist. The girl was silent, but she kept giving Vladlen long looks. She looked at him with such attention and at such length, it was as if she was looking at an icon. There was sadness in her eyes the whole time, like the monkeys in the zoo. They just stayed with us a little while. They had a drink and then left, saying they had to go out on business. On their way out again, they knocked and Vladlen gave Aunt Zina a piece of paper. She thanked him and went over to the buffet, placing the present against a plastic vase. It was a drawing of Lenin's profile, in red and white paint on pink paper.

About this time the lights went out, and Genka and I went to see what had happened. Aunt Zina came out after us, but when she saw sparks flying from the corner we were poking in, she roared like a crazy pig, and hid in the toilet. Aunt Valentina came out to calm her. When the light was fixed and we all went back into the room, I heard somebody having a lively conversation. Someone was proving something to someone, then got incensed and began to curse. I asked what this was. Genka said it was Uncle Sasha. He's usually quiet, but sometimes when he's drunk he starts to curse to himself out loud, and there's no way to stop him.

During all this Uncle Sasha had left the bed and gone to sit at the table. He wanted to explain something, but no one could understand a thing. Genka and I didn't understand it then, but it was their usual kind of conversation. Then it became more understandable. He said that he'd come to see Aunt Zina as a human being, not as a street-walker, but if she was going to sell him out. . . . And at that point, to make them understand what he'd do if they sold him out, he piled on the swearwords.

Then he began to sweet-talk her, calling Aunt Zina a "smart little kitty."

Aunt Zina said that Uncle Sasha had better be taken home because his wife was a "bitch." He turned out to be Valentina Stepanovna's neighbor, and she asked me to help her get him home. I agreed. It was one o'clock. Genka said he'd stay at his aunt's. Well, that's what I thought it was all about anyway. Obviously she feeds him, gives him liquor, so it's all the same to him. We had a drink for the road. Genka gave me a wink at the door. Oh, how I'd like to give it to him right now.

Uncle Sasha was totally drunk. His face was sweating, and starting to look like a frozen potato in damp ground. On the way home he sang a song about a Varangian who wouldn't give up. We got to the No. 1 bus. Their building was close by. Uncle Sasha made it up the stairs with difficulty. We had to push and pull him. We got into the apartment and his wife opened the door of their room and he fell onto his wife. The entrance door closed. I leaned on it and began to sink down. Everything was whirling and upside down. I wanted to sleep, but when I closed my eyes my head collapsed. I shook it and fell against the door. Aunt Valya began to lift me up. I could hear Uncle Sasha cursing his wife. It all began to seem funny to me. I started to hold Aunt Valya's hand. She began to laugh too. I gave her several loud smacking kisses on the neck. She led me along the hall. It was dark. We knocked into the walls. Something fell down. I swore.

We went into a room. I don't even remember the decor. Everything was whirling in front of my eyes. Enormous circles were floating around me. I reached under her skirt. We kept on laughing. She pushed me to the couch. She started to take her clothes off, looking at herself in the mirror. I was probably reflected in it, too. Both of us were in it. It seemed to me that I was riding on a wild and crazy carousel. It was rocking me. I might fall. . . . I fell face down on the couch. Aunt Valya called to me. She stood naked in front of me, and she looked like a horse which has worked a long time: her back sagged, her belly was distended, and the veins in her legs were swollen. Her breasts were large but sagging. Blue green veins showed through her skin. The nipples were dark like raisins. How many men had kneaded those breasts? And I thought about other things like that, so I began to feel bad as I looked at her from head to toe, from toe to head. Actually she was about twenty-five years older than me. An entire lifetime! Horrible! Even when I was lying there with her I kept calling her by her full name, and thinking "aunt" to myself. Despite her heavy body, she had thin legs and looked like a mincing bedbug when she walked around the room. She asked why I wasn't undressing. I began to and she sat on a chair, watching and smoking a cigarette. Her belly arranged itself in several tiers.

I didn't take off my underpants. She said it wouldn't work out if I didn't. So I took them off. We lay down. I didn't want a thing from her any more, but it seemed shameful to just lie there and do nothing when she was waiting for it. She'd think I wasn't a man. I was disgusted by the idea of kissing her, even on the neck. I kneaded her breasts, and then I put my hand lower down. She laughed hoarsely. She said it tickled that way. I lay beside her. She told me to lie a different way. But I couldn't touch her body again! Despair gripped me. I began to cry.

"What are you, a little boy?" she asked.

I pushed her off and got up from the couch. I could feel the tears running down my face. I began to laugh. I started to call her names through my teary laughter. I called her an "old whore," "a dirty bitch," "scum." In the murky dawn she looked at me in surprise, still on her couch which had no legs. She started to cry.

It took me a long time to find my underpants. I wanted to get dressed as fast as possible, but I was unsteady, as if I'd been at sea. I couldn't even tie my shoes or button my cuffs. My hands were shaking. I left the room, half buttoned. I could hear Aunt Valya's quiet crying and sobs in the pitch dark. The floorboards creaked underfoot. I unlatched the hook and went out to the stairs. I got down them and out onto the street. I began running. But I didn't know where I was going. In my ears, Aunt Valentina's sobs sounded through the roof.

I ran all the way to the embankment. I sat down under the sphinx statue and smoked a little. I felt that in another second I was going to be sick. I really hate it when I throw up. It seems like all my intestines are turning inside out. But I couldn't keep it back, and it came out right there on the steps. My head felt better. I put my hands into the Neva and washed up. When I raised my head I saw people up on the bridge. I looked around. People were strolling along the embankment. This is the time of the white nights! And everyone could see me. How awful! Disgusting . . . I went home fast.

IX

GALYA: *July 2*

The day before yesterday we had our last exam. I got an A in Technology. What a brain! Only one B. True, there are three others with the same average, but I'm the best of all of them. Because of my good grades and so on, Mama promised to give me a tape recorder for my sixteenth birthday. That will be just wonderful. Now we have practical every day. When we went to the factory today with the girls, the bus was filled with boys. They're also from the technical school, and have practical opposite us, in the furniture factory. We almost always go on the same bus. I know a lot of the boys by sight. The girls have even fallen in love with some of them. We always discuss them, and we laugh at them a lot. Whenever I see guys, I evaluate them mentally. I imagine several of them alone with me, and wonder how they'd act, what they'd do. It's really interesting. I can't imagine myself with some of them at all. Others are okay, but there's this one . . . I've seen him before; the first time he didn't attract me, but then he seemed funny. We always laughed at him, but this time he was whispering to his friend who's very shy and quiet, only now the friend was smiling off and on— apparently the one I like was telling him something nasty or funny about us. Guys always laugh at nasty things. My guy is both like and not like the others from the outside. He has the same long hair, the same flapping pants, but sometimes it seems like he's pretending when he yells out swear words, hugs the other guys, or gives us nasty looks and just acts like all of the rest of the guys.

MISHA: *July 2*

I studied all night for the exam in Mechanics. I got an A. I got a B in Heavy Materials. School has already ended. I've thrown all the textbooks up into the attic until September.

Practical has started. Now we ride each morning, like we're going to work. It's summer, but we're working hard anyway. We saw and plane. Why the devil did I pick this school, anyway?! It's meant exclusively for cretins. The factory masters are dense beyond belief. The theory teachers tell you stuff that is so simple it's funny. Somewhere I read that one guy wrote a whole talmud on how to sweep snow from a roof. That's what it's like in our shop. They explain what a shaving is, what sawdust is. The only outlet I have is playing with the fellows in the evening. But our band is made up of people from the entire school, and some of the members have different schedules. We

have to get together on Sundays. But that's all right, art demands
it. . . .

One girl attracts me. Of course she's no Sophia Loren, but she's
basically an okay type. She's at the Polytech too. We ride to practical
together. There are thirty of them just as there are of us. But she's the
only girl who attracts me. Today, as we were riding along, I was talking
to Lyokha about this and that. I looked over and she was watching me.
Obviously she's interested too. Some schizzy with a harelip was
standing next to her. I whispered to Lyokha, look, some charmer. He
laughed, of course, and my girl thought that I was sneering at her. She
pouted and turned away. We got to work and separated. They go to the
right, we to the left. It's really too bad . . . I've got to make contact
with her somehow.

X

GALYA: *July 4*

Today the guys were high and they started bothering us on the bus.
One of them, a repulsive redhead, leaned on the back of the seat. I was
sitting with three girls in the back and he asked where we came from.
He knows where. What a fool! When we got off the bus, he stopped
opposite the door, and the guys all followed us. Marina Sokolova told
them they were supposed to go to the other side of the street, but they
walked right up to our entrance. And my guy came up to me right
there. He was even more handsome being a little bit tight. Usually he
mixes seriousness and laughter, but he'd gotten sort of drained from
what he'd drunk. He looked common, but I liked it. His condition was
familiar to me. When you're high, but not drunk, you want to grab the
whole world and make everyone happy. He looked me straight in the
eyes.

"Are you free after work?"

Lord, I would have gone right with him, wherever he'd take me,
would have kissed his hands and given him everything in the world.
But there we were. Right beside us were his drunk friends and the girls,
and they all heard everything . . .

"Free for what?"

"To—"

"Go away!"

He laughed and left. The rest left too. But I wanted to cry.

MISHA: *July 4*

Today my buddies and I really got bombed. We'd received our food
allowance for the summer, and we celebrated this event in our usual
fashion. We rode to the factory in fine shape. Our student group has
the second shift. When we got on the bus, the girlies were already
there. Genka went up to them first. We call him "Crocodile."

He's a pretty unpleasant type. Red hair, pimply-faced, smells of something sweet. Even as he approaches you, he's unpleasant. His breath smells like crushed lake mussels, rotting in the sun. Strangely enough, his eyes are light blue, but that just strengthens the repulsive impression. And exactly what he's after is obvious from his face.

The Crocodile pestered the girls sitting in the back. I look, and at the edge near the exit, I see mine. Well, Genka, I think, all right. But he didn't say anything in particular. And when we all got out I went up to her, wanting to make her acquaintance politely, but I began to speak nonsense. Not at all what I'd wanted to I didn't succeed, because the conversation never came off. But it's better that way. Too bad, of course.

XI

GALYA: *July* 5

I wonder what love is. They say it's like you get so attached, that a person could die from the longing or kill himself. I can't imagine anything like that! Of course I could fall in love passionately, but suffer for a fellow—never! There are so many of them you could always fall for another one.

MISHA: *July* 5

Today Potapov and I were on duty in the shop. He swept the floor and told me how he'd made a girl into a woman yesterday. Even though I don't know any of the details of that sort of thing, he was obviously lying from start to finish. He's a filthy beast! He had to make up the tears which the girl supposedly cried, and if there really were any, that's worse. I wanted to smash him in the face, but I thought, how would the other guys have reacted? Each one of them would think he was a hero if he told a story like that.

Then I thought about how they had all gone out to the suburbs with Lashin, taking a rifle which Vaska borrowed from his uncle. They went over to the field and shot birds. Small ones, like sparrows. I asked them why they did it. If there isn't so much as a feather left when they're done, what's the point? Potapov said it was interesting just for itself. Although when you shoot crows, they keep on fluttering sometimes. But, I said to him, he doesn't eat the crows either, does he!? It's just senseless killing!

Yurka said that he doesn't always kill for no reason. Once he was completely justified. It was to punish a neighbor who wouldn't let him play soccer near her windows. Yurka caught her cat and buried it in earth, leaving only its head above ground. Then he made a bonfire around it and lit it. And he himself sat there, watching and listening.

I called him a bastard. He just guffawed and said he would have had a serious conversation with me, but he had to go see a girl that evening, and I might spoil his face during the fight. Women don't like that.

I thought Yurka was insane, but he's not alone. The devil knows! He has a crazy face: his eyes are round and he rolls them constantly. It seems like he's always about to spit. Yurka's two top teeth in front have been knocked out. He looks like an offended wolf, but he sneezes like a cat.

XII

GALYA: *July 8*

There was a special party yesterday at the Film House. I went with several of the girls from the group. There were heaps of people there. A band was playing. I was so happy when I saw my guy on the stage. He was playing the guitar and singing. His cheeks were burning. It was obvious that he'd drunk a bit. Now all the guys drink, and the girls aren't much better. Five of us girls drank two whole bottles of Khirsa wine, had a cigarette, and then went to the dance. Several guys asked me to dance. I danced with them, but I didn't let them paw me or crawl all over me. My guy played the whole evening. The dance ended at midnight. Everyone began to leave. I was supposed to go too, but I stood up and gawked at the stage like an idiot. Then I figured he might notice this, so I began to look at the people going by, as if I were looking for someone, or waiting for someone. But I still looked at him off and on. All the girls had left with guys except for Lena Zabelina. She has a hairlip and her lower lids are kind of drawn down, and the result is a terrible, funny grimace which makes you look at her a second time. And her body's like it's dead, thin but soft, and Lena always smells awful. When you visit her at home her room always smells of her particular sweat—really unpleasant. Guys don't go out with her, and they call Lena "spoiled meat." I always feel sorry for her; she doesn't even expect that anyone will take her out.

When everyone had left, I started to go too, but suddenly I heard a "Hello!" Even before I turned around I recognized the voice—his voice! And when I turned he was standing in front of me.

"Hello!" I answered.

"Forgive me for that time by the factory. My pals and me had put away a little."

"You're feeling pretty good right now."

"That's okay. When you're playing you have to drink."

"Michael! We'll come for the gear tomorrow. So *ciao*. Don't wear out the girl." A hairy guy in a leather jacket who was still fooling around with the others on stage called out to him.

"Bye, Vadim," Misha answered and turned to me. "Can I see you home?"

"It's pretty far."

"Where?"

"Dachnoe."

"I've been farther. Let's go."

We went down to the cloakroom. Almost everyone had gone. A few guys and girls were smoking while they waited for friends. Zabelina was sitting smoking in an armchair by the entrance. Standing beside her, a cigarette in his teeth, was the redhead who'd bothered us on the bus. His freckly, pimply face might not have disgusted you in itself, but there was so much rottenness in his face that I felt even sorrier for Zabelina. There are people who have what they want engraved on their foreheads. Of course, who cares—everyone wants something. But when it isn't the person who's wanted, not Zabelina with her harelip, but just what she's got that's just like what everyone has, and she's happy even to get that kind of attention . . . I wanted to go up and hit the redhead, but I thought: I don't have a harelip or any defects. My face is maybe not beautiful, but it's nice, my skin is good, and my body's wellshaped. I don't know what Misha sees in me yet, but I'm ready to respond with my whole being even to the kind of attention Zabelina's responding to right now. But I am sorry for her, and she's probably envying me because I'm leaving with a tall, popular guy.

"What are you dreaming about!" I heard Misha's voice. He'd gotten our things and was handing me my raincoat. We put on our coats and went out to the subway.

When we got to my house, Misha looked at his watch.

"Ay-yay-yay! One-fifteen!"

"How are you going to get home? Where do you have to go?"

"Vasilievsky."

"You can get a taxi here."

"How can I get a taxi? I don't even have enough for vodka."

We got quiet. Misha suggested we sit down at the playground.

"Who do you live with?" he asked.

"With Mama."

"You have a separate apartment?"

"Of course, two rooms."

"For two people?"

"No, my father's registered at our place, but he rents or lives with someone else."

We sat near my building for a long time, probably half an hour. We talked about different things. Then Misha asked if Mama wouldn't be getting worried about me not being home yet. What could I say? The truth—that Mama is working at night? Or that she doesn't worry about me? I told him the truth, and said that we could go to my place and stay there until the subways opened again.

I thought that he'd start to come on to me right away, like all guys, embrace or kiss me, but he didn't even take my hand. I thought, he's decided he doesn't like me. Either he just talked a lot with me, or was completely silent.

After getting to our place and helping me off with my coat, he became very quiet and very nice. Now he was like a little boy and not at all the rowdy I'd seen him be earlier. . . . The wind had ruffled his hair into curls and his cheeks were puffy near his lips, like a baby's. I had an urge to caress him. But he sat there and talked, without his usual slang. His talk was simple and interesting, about how he loves his music and his performances. He said his music is real art, and so what if it's produced with the help of electricity! He said that he lives without his father too, in a communal apartment with his mother. His father had registered him at his place so he could get a three-room apartment, but he has another wife and child. Then he talked about his friends. How the one I saw on the stage is a wonderful musician, speaks English well, and knows how to get anything. And there's one guy who really knows how to draw. While he talked I cooked pelmeni.* We ate. Drank coffee. He smoked and so did I. Then we stopped smoking, talked a little more, then fell silent. I wondered: "What's next?" I decided that he probably wanted to go to sleep. I said I'd sleep in Mama's room, and he could have my bed. He was surprised—did I really want to go to sleep? Wasn't tomorrow Sunday? But I made the bed anyway, and then we talked some more, but I wanted him to kiss me, and more, and even. . . . Of course, I didn't want it to go that far. The thing I'd dreamed of not so long ago now frightened me, just the thought of it.

He gave me a pornographic magazine to look at. How can anyone take pictures of such filth? And who does it? After I'd looked at it I raised my head, and he looked at me very steadily, with despair somehow. He leaned over and kissed me right on the lips, pulled me to him and on to his lap, kissing me the whole time. It was so good with him! But when he started to move his hands up, I got embarrassed. I have small breasts and I'm ashamed of them. I began to take his hands away, but he kept on, and then he took my hand and put it on himself. Lord, how frightened I was! I never thought it could be so large. I've heard a lot, and read some, too, but at that point I got scared, and I asked him to let me go.

When I was seven Mama rented a dacha for the first and last time: a little shack in Beloostrov. There were loads of vacationers in the landlord's house. A husband and wife with two sons were staying there. They were younger than me. The oldest was six and the youngest was four and a half. We played different games. We blew soap bubbles and caught insects with nets. Somehow we came up with the game of doctor and patient. The patient would lie in the hammock, and the doctor would examine him and tell him how to get better. We spent a lot of time examining the things which interested us the most. And then, if I were playing the doctor, I'd say that they should make wee-wee (I really liked it when they did that—sometimes

---

*Like small ravioli [tr.].

I even pecked), and then they had to rock me in the hammock, standing by the pine trees with their pants down, all this in order to get better. The boys said it wasn't fair: I should have to take off my pants too and pull up my skirt. I laughed and pulled my skirt up without taking off my pants. We soon quarrelled. The boys pulled on their pants and went away with tears in their eyes. But I kept on rocking.

When I grew up I found out how things were done. But until this moment I hadn't understood anything in practice.

Misha said he wouldn't do anything more, but when I tried to leave he embraced me very tenderly and began to kiss me. He led me to the couch, lay down and began to undress me. We fought in silence and from time to time I'd whisper: "Don't." And he'd say: "Wait . . . what's the matter . . . I'm not doing anything . . ." He undressed me and kissed one of my breasts. I began to get really upset. I lost control completely and started to cry. He let go of me then, and I took my things and left without even saying goodnight. I was burning all over. I got in bed. I tossed and turned. I wanted to cry. But there were no tears. It was as if my heat had dried them up. I wanted to go to Misha. So I went. But he'd fallen asleep and I didn't want to wake him, so I left quietly.

I calmed down after seeing him sleeping. I went to bed and was starting to doze, when I suddenly sensed that he was in the room. Misha stood by the bed in his undershorts. I was trembling all over, and I asked him what he wanted to do with me. He said he wouldn't do anything, but that I should calm down. He sat on the bed and bent over me, pressing his whole body against me. He was trembling, too. He kissed me on the forehead, just like my father used to do before bed when I was a child. He went to the door. I called out to him. He came back toward me. I put my arms out to him. We began to kiss again, and then I threw everything off me and said I was ready for anything. But he began to kiss me less and then stopped completely. He got up and left, coming back with cigarettes. We smoked. I looked at the time. Mama would be home soon. I said it was time for him to go. He dressed quickly, but he looked very embarrassed, as if he'd done something wrong. We kissed at the door. Misha left. I cleaned up everything, and Mama didn't notice a thing.

MISHA: *July 8*
Last night we played at a dance. We did mostly Western things. The dance turned out really great. There weren't many fights, and everyone had a good time. When they were all leaving, I caught sight of my girl near the exit. I guess I'd seen her earlier among the dancers without recognizing her. She'd done her hair: a little fringe on her forehead, all the other hair swept back into something like a lacy pretzel, and curls were hanging down like garlands at her temples and all over her head. Her lips and nails were cherry red. Her eyelashes

were long like a butterfly's antennae, and black as if her eyes were in mourning. Apparently she'd plucked her eyebrows. (Before, they had seemed thicker to me.) Under them was blue shadow. Her face was covered with tan powder. Just like a painted doll.

I've got nothing against a woman using make-up, basically. And even if a guy dyes his hair successfully, that's okay too—I've done that sort of thing myself. But it seems to me that it spoils things when every possible inch is made up. Well, all right, pale lips. Paint them! Your nose is shiny—cover that too! But it's something else again when you cover yourself with make-up from ear to ear and think you're a knockout.

She seemed to be waiting for someone, she didn't leave, but kept on looking through the crowds that were leaving. She wore a gray skirt, short like a little girl's. Long legs in smoky stockings. Platform shoes. A regular stateside chick!

After I got off the stage I went over to her anyway. We said hello. Got acquainted. I wanted to see her home. She was a little high, and chicks allow a lot when they're in that shape. It's true that up to now there haven't been any girls I would've slept with, but I've done a lot of kissing, and I know how to do it. Of course I want to sleep with a girl, but it's just not that simple. I haven't managed to get skin to skin with one. When they start to come on I don't like it. And it's basically sort of awful to get involved with an experienced woman when you've only kissed and nothing more. It seems to me that it'd be simpler for me to do it with a woman I don't know at all: she would just attract me the first time I met her. But is it really possible? When you're well acquainted with a girl, how do you manage to get to it? How would we see each other at that moment, recognize each other?

I didn't know what kind of a girl Galya was, but she did attact me, so I accompanied her home. She lives in Dachnoe.

We walked from the subway stop and got to her building around two. We sat for a while in front of the building. Talked about life. She was worried about how I'd get to Vasilievsky, but I wasn't thinking about that at all. I wanted to kiss her, but I couldn't make up my mind to do it. We sat, talking, and if suddenly—there you go! She'd see that it wasn't serious—but . . . when I asked if her mama would be worried, she said that her mama works at night and invited me to come in.

Her mother and she have a separate two-room apartment. The father's registered there, but like my father, he lives in another place. The building is terrific! Two elevators, a garbage chute. The ceilings are pretty good for a new building. The entrance hall is big, with wall cabinets. Of course the furnishings aren't exactly palatial. Galya's room has a balcony. She showed me the apartment as she boiled water for food. I asked her if it wasn't scary to live on the fourteenth floor. She answered that it was closer to God. I praised her wit.

After we'd had a snack, we talked about different things. Ourselves, our friends. We smoked. Other guys don't like it if a girl smokes, but I don't think it matters. As long as it's the proper way, with inhaling. The conversation flagged and I wondered: "What's next?"

She said I could lie down if I wanted to sleep. She'd wake me before her mother got home. And then I'd leave. I didn't want to sleep, I wanted to be with her a little more. It was really great! Earlier today we'd been strangers. She'd looked like a painted, empty doll. I don't know what I had seemed like. But now here we were, sitting in her house, talking like people who were really close. Probably she and I are alike in some way, since we got together so fast.

I thought about that while she washed the dishes. Then we went into her room. We smoked. I wanted to show her the pornographic magazine Vadim gave back to me today. I asked Galya what her attitude toward pornography was. She said it was awful filth. But she looked at the magazine and said the same thing again. I was conscious that I liked it when Galya was looking at the magazine. When she lifted her head, which had been bent over the magazine, I kissed her. I sat her on my knees, still kissing her. I wanted to know her entire body. She took my hands off her knees and breasts. And I had the inexpressible sense of the vastly different things constructed by nature to be joined into a single whole so that we can see and know each other. What in the world could be more important than that!? She pushed me away and wanted to leave. She asked me to let her go. I let her go, but at the door I wanted to embrace her again. And I took her in my arms and collapsed onto the couch. I undressed her to the waist and kissed her right breast. She was beginning to toss and turn in my arms. She began to cry. I let her go. Then I undressed and went to bed. But what sort of sleep could I have? I heard her come back, but for some reason I pretended to be asleep. She stayed a moment and then left.

I couldn't sleep so I went in to her. When I approached the bed I began to tremble. Galya asked me what I wanted to do with her. A strange question. I said I wanted nothing, and I pressed against her. Then I just kissed her on the forehead and left. She called out to me. She put out her arms. We began to kiss. Galya took off her nightshirt and said that she was ready for everything. In her voice I could hear the triumph of the sacrifice she was about to make. Then I saw that this was the moment. I had a pure girl in my arms, whom I could use. But then I was frightened by the mystery of this business, and the emptiness which had slipped into it. I stopped kissing her. I went and got cigarettes. While we were smoking, Galya said it was time for me to be off. I went to dress. I was ashamed of my past shyness. I'd played the fool again. But she'd think that I'd nobly refused to take advantage of her consent. So all right. The farewell kiss came out short and shy. As if it were the first time.

When I got home Mama was drinking coffee. She's used to the fact that I don't sleep there. She didn't say anything. She can't think about me right now. She's pregnant by the guy she's planning to marry, and she's forty already. Viktor is seven years younger. I wonder where they're going to live, with a baby? Viktor's just got an eleven-meter room, and mother and I together have fourteen meters.

XIII

GALYA: *July 12*

Marinka and Sasha and I got drunk. I didn't invite them over for my birthday because of Mama, but yesterday we killed three bottles of port and got bombed like bedbugs. Marinka shouldn't have been drinking of course, but what can you say to her? You can't take the glass from her, and Sasha is silent. He's strange generally. He has very beautiful eyes, like a cat's, the color of a chestnut shell. They're caressing and soft when he's in a good mood. He himself gives the impression of something very soft, so that sometimes you just want to take him and squeeze him. It's unbelievable that someone like that would take a girl's virginity. He told Marinka that before her he'd had three mistresses—all of them virgins. The youngest was thirteen. He's always dreaming—either about school, or about a career in manufacturing, but I think he's too weak-willed to get anywhere in life, and he's not smart either.

We did our drinking at my house—Mama was working. Sasha told jokes the whole time. Marinka listened and kept telling me that I should have invited Tolya: he told her that he still likes me.

I was quiet for almost the entire evening, and remembered Misha—how he had been on stage, how he kissed me and then went away and didn't call once. And he'll probably never call. What am I to him? He's just a guy.

MISHA: *July 12*

I was half an hour late for the factory today. The master cursed at me. They'd begun making stools. Everyone was planing except Seryoga, who'd hidden himself behind the back carpenter bench, and he slept until dinner. After dinner we go home.

I walked to the tram with Seryoga. He described his various exploits, as usual. Yesterday he got sloshed with the guys. They went out looking for trouble. They pestered some students from the Marine Institute. There were eight of them, too. They all began to fight. Seryoga and his friends grabbed some sticks and threw them at the sailors. The latter did the same. Then the marine students began to fight using their belts. They cut open one guy's head. "Green" was covered with blood, Seryoga said. The police came running and the volunteer police, too. Someone'd called them. They caught "The Count" and "Green." The rest ran off.

Seryoga left by back passageways. He ran into a drunk in one yard, lying near a garage. Seryoga unbuttoned his pants and pissed on his face. He hit the eyes. An eyelid opened, he says, and you could see the white through the stream.

I told Seryoga he'd gotten out of control. I asked him why he did things like that. He answered that there was no damn reason to be lying around in the road.

I'm basically afraid of Seryoga. I wonder how he'd treat me if I weren't his friend? I'm bigger than he is, but I don't have his decisive ruthlessness in me, or the desire to do the things he does. Maybe I might think about things like that, but I'd never do them.

Just after we'd started school last September, they sent us out to a kolkhoz.* They gave us a place in what used to be a bakery. Every year the students or the guys from the school who are helping the collective farm bring in the harvest live there. But what help do they get from us? Everyone goldbricked. We cut faces in the turnips, we threw potatoes. But when the masters said we wouldn't get money for our food from the kolkhoz official, we brought in what they wanted. The masters would drink in the evening, while we'd walk two kilometers to what had been a school. They'd put up a group of jewelers there. There were only six guys in their group, the rest were girls. There were two groups of us, but a lot of the tenderfeet didn't go, so there were hardly any fights over the girls. We set up a dance and then made trouble with the local kids if the girls said they were bothering them.

We stayed at the kolkhoz about a month. Then we began going back. I left with the first batch. Later Lyokha told me that Seryoga tortured the cats which the guys had brought to the bakery from somewhere. They'd given them names: one got Seryoga Svintsov's nickname—"Devil," and the second got the nickname of his best friend Potapov—"Pilot." Seryoga poured iodine on them and threw them into the fire. Then when the cats looked dead, he used them to play soccer with with Yurka. That night, when everyone was asleep, Lyokha went out to the yard to the bathroom. He heard a squeak. He followed the sound. He saw two mounds of fur and flesh lying by each other, just barely able to lift their blind faces and whine. Lyokha started to cry right there, and he still won't speak to Seryoga.

Once I was at Seryoga's house. There was an aquarium in the window. Seryoga knocked with his finger on the glass and the fish swam off. He threw them grub worms. The reflector which hung over the aquarium illuminated the worms dancing in the water. Seryoga said the fish know him. He throws cats in a fire, and talks to fish, I thought.

I was really amazed when Seryoga told me how he stood up for his mother when his drunk old man raised his hand to her. Seryoga probably just wanted to use his fists. He loves to hit. He's used to

---

*Kolkhoz—collective farm [tr.].

hitting. And now he can't do a thing with his ability and his habit. He used to box, was in the first rank, and there were high hopes for him. That kind of man can become a great boxer. Seryoga gave up boxing when his coach changed to a different association. Now he drinks and smokes a lot, and carries on with girls.

Seryoga finished his story by telling how he went over to a girl's house and what he did there. He never tells these things to show off like the other guys do. His best features are primitive.

When I started at the school Seryoga didn't impress me as being a sadist. I can never judge a person just by his appearance.

Seryoga's eyes are brown, but cold, even dead, though they glitter when he's mad. His hair is always short. Light hair. He looks like a horse, with a nice face. Sometimes he seems innocent and languid, but when you look closer you see that Seryoga is like a pair of new shoes which have already been plunged into the mud of the road, the dung of the cattle, and both these things are already eating away the youth of these shiny shoes.

Sometimes when Seryoga is dozing in class, he looks like an old woman. He's a strong guy. But he's burning himself up, just like a bobbin unwinding.

XIV

GALYA: *July 15*

Misha finally called. I was really waiting for his call. I got mad. I wanted to spite him, so I said Vsevolod had proposed. But Misha just wished me a happy family life and hung up. What can I do now? When I go to the factory he's never on the tram. I have to get up my nerve to ask Misha's friend, the one he always hangs around with, how Misha is.

Vsevolod arrived yesterday and proposed to me right away. But I barely recognized him. I'm completely unused to him. He's become very unpleasant. Or was he always? His face is pink, his hands are red. He's balding and his hair is short, but in the back it's longer and curls. His eyes are like pea soup. He's athletic but not very tall, no taller than me. He's serious and businesslike all the time, knows everything. He's planning to take the exams for the Leningrad Institute of Aviation Equipment Instruction. He failed them twice before the army. Now, after the service, he says he'll have priority.

Whenever I start to talk to him about anything complicated, he changes the subject. Obviously he's afraid of being shown up. When I turned on the tape recorder he acted like he was listening, suffering inside, but at the same time he was tapping his foot—is this possible?

He's a man who knows what he needs. So, he's chosen me. That's it, no matter what, I'll be his wife. Maybe he has some human feeling for me? As it is, he's like a machine. He's always dressed in a claret-colored suit with a vest, and of course a tie. A pocket watch, pointed shoes. Even in sunny weather he's got a raincoat on, and a silk scarf.

Vsevolod told me some pretty awful things. In the area where he was doing duty, some eleven and twelve-year-old girls would come over from the settlement, and in the evening their mothers would come running after them, beat them, and drag them home. But the next day the girls came again. And grown women would come to spend the night. The soldiers would give a woman like that a glass of water and a piece of bread. Anyone who wanted to would use her. I can't even conceive of such awful things.

Vsevolod is staying with relatives. We see each other every day. How could I have ever loved him? He taught me to kiss. How could I have done it with him? Now I only let Vsevolod touch me to spite Misha. Sometimes I even want to give myself to him to spite Misha.

Yesterday we drank to our meeting and he looked at me with such sweet eyes that I got embarrassed.

Vsevolod talked with Mama today. She's always liked him. She always told me that she dreamed of a son-in-law like him. Mama said we'd have to wait for the wedding until I finished school, and that's two years away. I'll be eighteen then. In the meantime Vsevolod will enter the institute and get himself set up in Leningrad.

MISHA: *July 15*

I've stopped going to practical. The hell with all of them. I'm sick of those stools! So that my mother doesn't find out, I go out in the morning as if to the factory, but I go to the Peter Paul Fortress instead, crawl up on mine and Lyokha's bastion, and sleep. They say morning sunbaths are good. Then I go to the zoo, I crawl through the fence, and go look at the animals.

I called Galya. She said some guy wants to marry her. I wished her happiness. I won't call again.

XV

GALYA: *July 19*

I told Vsevolod to stop coming to see me or calling. I can't see him.

Practical is over. I curse myself for not talking to Misha's friend. I can't even find out Misha's address—I don't know his last name! It's enough to make me cry! And I cry a lot. I'm ready to forgive him everything. If only he'd come or call. Where is he? What's happened to him? Maybe he's dead?

Marinka was over. She said all my suffering for Misha is nonsense. But she's discovered she doesn't love Sasha—and she lives with him. But she doesn't get anything from him. She doesn't feel like a woman, and it's always painful. But she does it for Sasha; he's very attached to her. They're going to have a baby, and their parents have given them permission to live together. Now they have to go to the Marriage

Administration to get Marinka permission to marry. She said I shouldn't have refused Vsevolod, never mind throwing over Tolya. He's drinking now, because of me.

I told Marinka about how I love Misha. For a long time she refused to agree that it was necessary to wait the way I do, humiliated, but still waiting. Then she said, well, who knows. As she was leaving she said that even though I'm a fool, she envies me.

But I've decided that if I can't belong to Misha then I'll belong to no one. And if I become his I'll kill myself after.

MISHA: *July 19*

I ran into Vladlen yesterday. He recognized me. We said hello. Vladlen was with two of his friends and three girls. They were high. He said if I wanted to get drunk and listen to a foreign tape recorder, I could go with them. I went. Everyone was well dressed except Vladlen. He was wearing old sandycolored corduroys, a pink shirt tied into a knot, and dirty white sneakers. I was badly dressed, and was ashamed of how I looked. We stopped by a corner store. They bought three bottles of vodka and five of port. A guy with a Gogol hairstyle put the bottles into a large leather briefcase. The guy's name was Volodya. His hair was so black there was blue in it. His eyes were hazel like a cow's, and intelligent. Thick red lips. Bad teeth, but he kept smiling a wide smile all the time anyway. Volodya was taller than Vladlen, but puny, only his shoulders were broad. His pants were fashionable, egg-yolk yellow, the kind only foreigners wear. Dark glasses covered half his face. He was wearing a white, sleeveless soccer shirt. A black lion had been drawn on it (Vladlen had drawn it for him). You could see the outline of his sunken rib cage under the soccer shirt. His thin arms hung down like eyelashes. His wrists were all bone, but his hands were broad, with long fingers. An old watch hung around his wrist on a thick leather strap. He seemed drained and worn, but, like a man in the last stages of prostration, he was relaxed and gay.

We caught a bus. We got off at Jubilee station. We went into a gateway at the beginning of Bolshoi Avenue. At the back of the yard was the front door of the "nest," as the guy who was serious the whole time called it. We went up to the sixth floor. A girl in a luxurious robe opened the door. A really good figure. Her hair was the color of ripe wheat, done in a *Gavroche* hairstyle. The roots of the hair were quite dark; it was obviously dyed. She had a Russian face, wholesome. Eyes like forget-me-nots: gay, seemingly casual about what's going on, but actually taking everything in. She said that she'd figured no one was coming. Vladlen introduced us. Larisa looked at me casually.

It was a three-room apartment. The rooms were huge, as was the furniture. In one room bookshelves took up two walls all the way up to the ceiling. There were an old dresser and an armchair in the same style. A piano stood in a corner and a bronze chandelier hung over a round table in the middle. Two fashionable couches were in the second room, along with a cabinet with three doors, a pier-glass, and a very pretty lamp which had a large shade. Larisa lived in the third room. She had a Japanese stereo tape recorder in it and had covered the walls with photographs.

Volodya dragged one girl off to the kitchen. He said she was obliged to fix the eats, it was her professional duty. Sima struggled and refused, but Volodya finally talked her into it. The serious guy, whose name was Kostya, put on a tape. Even Kostya's haircut was serious, and he looked like a cowboy from an American hit. His body looked dry, like dried fish. He was narrow and his shoulders were in line with his hips. He wore really stylish lavender jeans. And a lemon-colored shirt, cut close to the body. And a red calico scarf with big black dots on it. On his right hand he wore a silver ring. A stone, transparent as glass, was embedded in the ring, and under it was drawn the face of a woman with ants crawling over it. (This is also Vladlen's work.)

Kostya's girl, Viktoria, said her head was aching from the music. The fool! Volodya yelled from the kitchen that she should stuff cotton in her ears, and not interfere with the experience of contemporary rhythms. She's really a repulsive girl! A face like a poster run by the rain: it's all faded, except for the lips which are covered with crimson lipstick like a vampire who's drunk blood. She had on white pants that were so wide that each side could have served as a sleeping bag for Viktoria—or a shroud. A rose was embroidered on the left leg. She was wearing a striped vest on top, and over it a jeans jacket. Sort of a combination of the pirate and the cowboy, with platform sandals on her feet.

I asked Vladlen where his wife was. He said I should be more interested in where the hostess was. I went to find Larisa. She was smoking, leaning on the piano and looking through a cloud of smoke at its polish. I asked why she'd left the room. Larisa said she couldn't stand Tamara, the girl Vladlen had come with. And anyway, if you're married, go out with your wife!

Volodya summoned everyone to the table. Sima had made a salad and pelmeni. We ate. Vladlen made toasts which were incomprehensible to me, and we drank. Now he acted common: he kept pawing Tamara, and began to slobber over her. She wasn't bad. A tan face. Hair to her chest, black and curly. Narrow eyes, wide check bones, bee-stung lips. She flared her nostrils. She was like someone who'd been abducted from a wild tribe and forced into suede pants and a lace blouse, and on her feet they'd put sneakers, to which her savage soles were quite unaccustomed. She exuded freshness. She should have done a sabre dance.

Volodya and Sima started to dance. Sima had been silent at the table. She wore a dress the color of spring grass, with black stripes. She looked like a caterpillar in it because the whole time it seemed like she wanted to curl up into herself, and she acted like she was afraid her clothes were about to fall off and everyone would look at her. She was dark and haggard. She had a short haircut which just emphasized the fact that she was older than the others. She wore less make-up than the rest of them. She kept taking Volodya's hand away from her bottom, and looking at him unhappily, but Volodya said she was making a real mistake—after all, he was considered the very best masseur of deep creases.

Vladlen quarrelled with Kostya over something. He said very interesting things to him, the kind you don't hear just everywhere, but Kostya answered with things which I'd heard a lot, was used to, and which bored me. I wanted to tell that to Kostya, but he covered my mouth with his palm, calling me "little boy," and advising me to drink a "seltzer." I didn't take offense, because he was much older, like all of the guys were, and because I'd ended up in their company by accident, having their food and drink for free—what could I say? I lit a cigarette and took a look at Kostya: he had a noble profile, but I'm sure that he's not averse to gaining something for himself, and he said stupid things.

Volodya and Sima stopped dancing and went out of the room. Viktoria went out after them. She came back and told us they were in bed and already "doing it." Vladlen said she was impatient today. He called her a little "chickie," and asked her to dance. I asked Tamara to dance with me.

We'd already gone through half the bottles. The girls did the port, we did the vodka. I was happy I'd ended up in such company. I wanted to kiss Tamara, but someone pinched me from behind. It was Vladlen. He said he wouldn't want to clash with a "kid" like me. I wanted to answer, but Volodya came in suddenly, yelling that he wouldn't get closer than a ten-foot pole to Sima from now on, and that someone should get him a "wheelbarrow." The front door slammed. It was Sima leaving. Volodya started to call for a taxi.

Tamara told me she doesn't like Volodya because of the way he lives. He doesn't work: he plays cards for money at night and lives on that. He's an intelligent guy, but he spends the whole day in the Saigon. No matter when you drop by that cafeteria, he's there. And he's always trying to get people involved in all sorts of conversations.

Volodya heard Tamara and said he was now settled down at the Ulster, and he advised her not to "defecate" his life story so casually. At that point the telephone rang and they reported to Volodya that the "wheelbarrow" was on its way. He left, making a two-handed gesture of a farewell, regards to all.

Larisa and Vladlen went out of the room. We all joined hands and danced a circle around the room. After whirling around we all fell down. I fell on Tamara and quickly kissed her on the lips. During the fall Kostya and Viktoria rolled under the table, but it was obvious they had no plans of coming out soon.

Vladlen came back in, called Tamara "Mama," and said it was time to beat it. They left. Larisa told Kostya and Viktoria that they could use the bedroom. They left holding hands. Larisa became more modest when we were left alone. I asked her to dance. We danced calmly. I kissed her neck. She pressed herself to me. Besides the sensation of being drunk, I could feel that some kind of force was now kneading me into a ball, and that it would throw me at her feet, after which I would straighten up into a different person. I got on my knees and kissed her hands. She smelled very good. I lifted her in my arms and carried her to the couch. Her emerald slippers, embroidered in gold, and with red fur pompoms, fell off onto the floor.

After we lay down I undressed her. She kept repeating my name. I grew quiet and waited for her to say something, but Larisa only bent her head to my shoulder. I kissed her and realized that the new feeling was already gripping me. And when she wanted to interfere I commandingly hissed: "Lie down . . ." And she obeyed.

XVI
GALYA: *July 20*
Mama offered to send me to Grandma's until the end of the summer, but I wouldn't agree to it. Of course there's no hope, but I'm waiting anyway. I hardly leave the house. I listen to music for days on end. Mama kept her promise, she gave me the tape recorder as a present. Sasha brought over cassettes of the most popular pop music.

I love music. Not the monotonous wild kind, but the more human kind, not as nasty as the guys like. I often start to shiver when I listen to it. As if the music is telling me something, answering my thoughts. I can't convey it in words, but my heart understands, and sometimes it seems like the music is saying Misha has a girl who's prettier and smarter than me, that he's kissing her now, and that he doesn't love me. But if Misha and I see each other, I know that some kind of enormous events await us, and I can sense how important and big they are. But mostly it seems like someone in the music is longing too, sitting and waiting for their beloved, and maybe they'll never meet him. Then I feel the wall between me and Misha with my whole body, and the more tender my feeling, the less hope there is that he'll break through this wall, and I see myself with disturbed eyes.

MISHA: *July 20*
So I'm a man. But it's strange, like I've done it before, and that it was even a habit of some kind. When you get used to something it doesn't touch you any more. After it happened Larisa became divided for me, like a film: the people on the screen and the sound from the speakers.

XVII
GALYA: *July 28*
Sometimes I think I hate Misha. I'm mad at him, and I know I'll never think about him again. But then I remember and I want to be

near him for a moment, just so that I can look at him carefully. And sometimes I even want to catch Misha and lock him up so he can't go away. Then I could be with him my whole life.

MISHA: *July 28*

I can't go with Larisa anymore. She understands I don't love her at all, I just need her as a woman. But she says she fell in love with me from the first time. Before she used to love Vladlen, but although he's a talented artist, he's a bad man, and he wants to have lots of women, like handfuls of berries. She's proud and didn't want to share him with anyone. I arrived at the moment when all of this had fallen apart, and she'd called him from the room that time to tell him she didn't love him, didn't want to see him. She said that even though I'm a barbarian, she loves me.

But I keep on thinking about Galya the whole time, even imagining that she's the one I'm with when I sleep with Larisa. I really want to see Galya. How strangely a man is made. Take me: a woman in her prime (she's twenty-two), as much money as anyone would want, and always an empty apartment. Her parents are in Hungary right now at some congress. Her father is a big scholar, and her mother doesn't work at all, but has just spent her life taking care of herself. They don't deny Larisa anything. She's finished the third year of a theater institute, and she's going to act in the theater. But I'm hot for a girl who has neither house nor home (though she does have living space), who hasn't read Shakespeare or Goethe. I can't do anything about it, and I don't even know why I love her. I keep imagining her eyes—big, chocolate-colored and offended, like a child's. Are we really never going to see each other again?! But how can I go see her? I've deceived her!? And she's probably with that guy now, what's his name, Vsevolod?! Misery!!!

XVIII

GALYA: *August 26*

He slept on the couch in his clothes. My couch is by the window. Misha lay with his head facing the window and the sun was on his face. I came over and sat beside him. His burning face was sweating from the sun, but it was calm. There were several pimples by his nose. It's strange, but it didn't seem repulsive at all, like with other guys. I wondered what he was dreaming of. Probably about the zoo he wanted to take me to.

Misha was with me tonight. He called me last night and asked if he could come over. Yes, of course! Mama is on vacation right now, and she's gone to the resort rest home for two weeks. But even if she were home I'd let Misha in.

He was high, but not too much so. And we sat there together and he was like a little boy, and then he got serious, but serious like a child.

He took my hand, kissed it, and began saying that he couldn't live without me, that he knew how dear I was to him, that he had no one but me. And I said I couldn't go on without him and I began to sob like a fool. He kissed me. I wanted to become his, but he said better later, and we slept the rest of the night together, just like that.

Misha wants to marry me! I said I didn't want to cramp his freedom in any way. And I don't demand anything from him. And if he falls in love with someone else I won't say anything.

MISHA: *August 26*

Yesterday I couldn't stand it so I called Galya. She said that I could come over. I went, hemmed and hawed, and then said I didn't have anyone in the world except her. She cried and said she'd been waiting for me all this time. I almost started sobbing myself.

I really want to marry her. It's too bad we're only sixteen.

Poems 1959-1978[*]
by Yevgeny Rein

Vologda

In a strange provincial city,
When you're sitting and smoking above the river,
Just listen and have a look around.
Your sorrow will be repaid with interest.

Horns and voices can be heard in the distance,
The barking of dogs, dance tunes.
Do not die.
            The heavens are accessible
Without that.
            And your head's in order.

1. The Monastery

I implore holy providence:
Leave me my distressing days,
But give me iron patience.
But harden my heart.
Let me come, without change, to
The mysterious gates of new life
As the Volga's white-haired billow,
Whole, to the shore!
                —N. Yazykov

Beyond Sokolniki Station, where there's a meat store
And the Old Believers' cemetery, there was a monastery.
A ruin and a sea of mud, wreckage, disintegration:
In the twenties they set to turning it into a dwelling.
There's no other communal house like it today.

[*]Translated by H. William Tjalsma.

Why I did it, I'll not explain I, worn-out, scandal-ridden,
Bum and lout, exchanged Leningrad for a monastery cell.
There was a corridor a mile long, where forty people
Wandered day and night. There were invalids, night
Watchmen living there—a half-liter bottle away
From the knife. And all the same, when they could,
Our lives flowed on there in sympathy and camaraderie.
People were invited to visit, they shared a ruble,
There was gossip, plotting, as in any society.
But there was compassion, too; no one held a grudge.
On my right, there was a crafty invalid, Adamov.
He'd knock on my door with his crutch, early,
Come in, fidget with his stump under the desk,
Where I kept a jar of kefir and some wine.
He'd ask for the bottle to use for a sample,
And I'd give it to him with some change once in a while,
And Adamov would leave. While next door, busy
With sorting out sturgeon, nibbled cutlets,
Curd tarts and snacks, not yet twenty,
The waitress Zoya, mother of ebony twins.
Next to her, lived Georgii Odintsov, a defrocked priest
Who worked in the Priboi Publishing House
As a cloak room attendant and was a walking
Reference book on literature. He had seen Sholokhov
And knew Pasternak; he had been given a drink
From Nobel money and had handed Yuri Olesha
His galoshes. But I knew that, in secret,
He performed baptisms and funeral services.
But it's not a matter of the characters, here.
Whoever has seen life knows what things cost,
How much for a bottle of vodka and a clean john,
And that a Roman liar said people are wolves.
They aren't wolves. Though what they are is beyond me!
I could present evidence—the best theologian
Would break his neck over it.
And all the same, thanks for everything, for bread
And shelter, for him who assigns us our rations
And fate, to him who teaches shamelessness and shame,
Who instructs us in patience and steels our soul,
Who teaches plain singing and the singing of the muses,
To him who sends us a house or disaster
And sends on further the white-haired billow.

2. The End of the Monastery or the Last Morning

They wrecked the monastery beyond Sokolniki Station,
Near the Old Believers' cemetery a vacant lot was opened up.
It was the sixteenth of May, the capital, and hot.
But Klavdiya Petrovna had lived here for forty years.
Valentinov next door built the Dnieper Hydro-Station,
And was shipped back and settled here,
Brought his wife and granny, who soon died.
His wife Valentina can't imagine how she survived.
She drove her tram from the thirties on.
And now a bulldozer finishes off what's left.
Mattresses smolder; a chiffonier thunders.
Pilots and sailors fly all over the place
Out of old family albums and curled frames.
Antonov stands there; Chenykh's lying down.
He drank last night and started again in the morning.
Sergei Ivanych Chernykh lost a daughter here.
Pudgy little Sasha, who worked as a messenger girl
For the paper and used to get up with the chickens
And grease her lids with soot.
There's a housewarming today on Boitsy Street,
Refreshments and gaiety. The sum. The very end.
The cemetery crosses stand there and the Church of Protection.
A raspberry-colored bedbug crawls out of
Serezha the crane operator's sleeve.
                          I too wail.

Oh, all-powerful God, I implore—
Teach me to weep with the masses and the muses,
Include me in legend, the kind that gives you the shivers.
Burn me to ashes and turn me into grey sand.
Dress me for the holidays in your bright heavenly jerkin.
Send me, for god's sake, an apartment and refuge.
And pour out the white-haired billow on the threshold.

The Spring

What say you, muttering wind,
Stream, leaf-fall?
Wine keeps you from midnight,
Tobacco from the wetness.
Pitch blackness keeps you
From the kerosene lamp.

Without rubber overshoes
You'll not get along.

I always feared
Ill winds and insanity,
You and the full moon,
And moisture around my temples.
Oh, merciless autumn,
You're no doubt close by.
The plank step creaks
From the wet sand.

And somebody small comes in
In top hat and cloak,
And looks around like a poor gourmand
At the vodka and stuff.
That's a furious genius loci
Whose rheumatism's in his shoulder.
What truth springs, Lord,
From the spring!

* * *

Of a cold summer day
Near Sretensky Gate,
There's no seeking out
Your bounties with firelight,
Moscow,
Putting aside the "Evening" paper,
I see that the day is done!
Still alive the while,
It casts a shadow.
Greener than grass,
Redder than stout wine.
In the virgin soil of the heavens
Moscow's night shadow,
Multicolored as a harlequin,
Switches on a semaphore,
Narcotics of sorrow
And samovar of thirst.
The disorder of great cities
Is great in that nobody bothers
To sort the good fruit
From the bad.
The day's affairs are done,
The paper read,

And all that you gave
You have taken back again.
Do not forget me!
Sometime later
Send me, too,
A melted spot of fire.

The Thirtieth of September

At a dacha outside Moscow a yellow leaf falls,
The last warm month, the thirtieth day.
A child races about the yard, playing soccer,
A sagging chaise lounge stands out in the sun.

At the dacha there's desolation and spilled cognac,
Slept-in beds and hairpins on the floor.
And I sit in the chaise lounge, sighing: "How is it
that it came out so, that I fell into such bondage?"

Oh, how we celebrated here and drank
In June and July in the rain and the fog!
What people would come by here!
I'll write a novel about it sometime.

The guests would arrive late, after eleven.
Dusk was right around midnight—it was midsummer.
The toastmaster was marvelous and not a bit drunk.
While the guests, alas, were quite the opposite.

They laughed, kissed, tormented themselves as best they could.
Somebody was commemorated while the apple pie was consumed.
Somebody else was forgiven words, sins, debts,
Others were shown the door.

A brunette with glossy lipstick from ear to ear,
A girl student in white jeans who made tea,
A pale boy, lover of colored pencils—
I once told them all: "Farewell, farewell, farewell!"

The suburban train hurried away, a taxi hustled up.
Some left, others found fault with trivial things.
And only our well-known toastmaster
Did not notice the dessert and poured a glass.

Wine, wine, wine flowed over on the tablecloth.
The dishes were a jumble and the starch turned red.
"Tell me, toastmaster, who's at fault here?"
But the toastmaster was leaving, as if he were tired.

And so, the last chance, autumn heat.
After all, we spent the summer here waiting for it to be over.
And I've been sitting under this maple since eight A.M.
As if all of my honor and my arrogance hung in the branches.

Fifteen Years Ago

In a cornflower blue suit,
In a vest, under an umbrella,
With Serezha Vasiukov
(I'll talk about him later),
On an Estonian street
Around bars and cafes,
With a typhoid hairdo
On his drunken head
He walked at the beginning of summer,
Fifteen years ago,
Glancing into the pale
Shimmering sunset.
A bit behind came his girl,
(I'll speak of her now!).
Over the small horizon
The amber moon
Clambered through chimneys
Like the bubble in a level.
In garrison khaki,
Dark-haired and pale,
Know-it-all and ignoramus,
Mistress of words and deeds,
Still the intended
And first love,
Striding along briskly
On spike heels,
You passed by here once,
Cursing Serezha Vasiukov roundly
For his banal taste in movies.
In a cornflower blue suit
Fifteen years ago,
We walked, the three of us,
Through Viru Square.
I walk now alone.
But I see the apartment.
The same wine labels.
At the Cannes festival

Serezha Vasiukov
Is on a pedestal,
Covered with prizes and laurels.
Amid the concrete block comfort
Of the Moscow outskirts
Her burner glows,
Her stockings hang there.
In the nursery, children play,
Whose blood is foreign-born.
While dawn over Tallin,
Like first love,
In the middle of a sleepless night
Fifteen years ago.
But life is shorter still.
And stitched together
haphazardly.

* * *

Flights canceled. Winter. The airport is packed.
The way we live isn't worth a plugged nickel.

Where are we all flying to? Why are we getting tickets?
When only a light in the window is really necessary.

I went out into the winter forest, walked a mile,
and then a damned TU flew overhead.

It hovered above like a watchdog of the evil skies.
I waved a glove at it—it disappeared.

I went back along a frozen ski-trail,
quite frozen myself. And I felt like going

back to the warm house with my light in the window.
There's no justifying yourself with wing and wheel, no.

Inscription for a Torn Portrait

Gazing at the cranes, the passenger boats,
Sailboats, barges, motor launches,
I remember you, you, you.
I recall how easy it was without the prodigal woman,
The lying, hypocritical, tender whore
Who transformed Vasilievsky Island
Into the shore of meeting and the port of parting,
Sigh of relief and air of frenzy.

The years have not adorned you with shadow.
Like scarlet rouge on rosy skin
I remember you in tears of impatience.
Oh, do not change. I'm that sort myself.
From this multistory height
I see not only the gulf and the factories—
Prolonged chronos opens out for me
And presents the past years.
I see the whimsical furnishings of rooms—
Photoportraits, bouquets, flacons.
All that we did was in vain,
We won't be paid by the days nor the distances.
Gazing from here, I'm not sorry for
The gilt of a winter day that darkens early—
Only conversations survived,
As in Eckermann's* bosom.
How you resemble, with your clock-dial face,
Nimble muse of history Clio,
That girl with the fanciful ribbon
Who lived so frenzied and askew
In crumpled time, in an unclean house,
In the confusion of frustration and quivering.
Midnight key, ring with an amethyst,
Only one pair of shoes and still preferring
Even wine that's always ready,
Even Eros with goose-flesh to legal love,
Eternally falling, not into fury, not into heresy.
Gazing from here into the last darkness—
The light of the night lamp tears out of the gloom
The highest stage of frenzied tenderness,
In letters, as in life, pencil-marks with verve.

* * *

A flock of crows over the boulevard.
The skis smell of turpentine,
And the skier himself is obstinate.
He makes his way on stiff legs
Near the Nikitsky Gate,
At midnight sharp.

It's the middle of winter,
Life itself is at the middle—
Neither beginning nor ending.

*Eckermann—Goethe's secretary.

In the warm-blooded core
There's not a trace of sorrow—
Like the mob in the store around the corner
Without a salesman.

Someone will wiggle under the snow,
Kiss, hug,
Tickle with wet fur,
Rummage through holes—
Maybe this one will understand!
It's a half hour before dark,
So now let's say "thou."

While all around lies the huge
Stretched-out block
Like a crumbly bed in a garden.
On a night like this I too
See all with my own eyes:
what I wanted and what I did not become.

The Fountain

I debark at the wharf, go up the stairs.
Go down Odessa's Pushkin and Deribassov Streets
And into a little courtyard where
Next to a stack of firewood there's a fountain with a broken vase.

It drips rusty tears drowsily,
And formerly was famous for its fresh spray—
And I shall recollect cheap life
And southern Sunday luxury.

A white shirt and wholesome youth,
You in the courtyard under the towels.
And I'll not do anything
Under the striped half-shadows.

How marvelous in August, just a trifle needed—
A little wine in a bottle, a bit of meat on a fork,
But you, silly fool, stand there clowning around
In your Odessa back alley.

When we go out in town of an evening,
Where loners mope about,
And naked swimmers pass by,
And steamers move beyond the sea,

Silly Europe flashes before your eyes,
Before mine—stupid mattress sacking.

Oh, fierce youth, populous Odessa,
On the beaches—what large pebbles!

Twelve years passed—not much, hmm?
I'd be in town from time to time,
Lived on Chicherin Street, Gogol Street,
Was here with wives and fiancées.

But your alley was forgotten entirely.
And now I've ducked in by chance—
And without laughter, without hallo,
The little fountain drips its rusty tears.

At the Crescent Shore

At the Crescent Shore, there's a green oak,
Meaty, thick, and salty soup,
And a cloudy bottle.
For the fourth day, crazy rain—
The tour guide, the tourist, the artist
Drink with me—all's rubbish!

I brought some bread from Rostov.
There's one good thing about
A bachelor's lot—
Unexpected reversals
In connection with grief, the weather.
It's dark at noon.

Without observatory passes
Dark advances like Batorii,
Who moved on Pskov
Through these sacred spots.
Under the moist blue illumination,
Am I ready? Not ready?

Shadows huddle around the fire, the little circles,
The broken steps thump.
Who's there? It's nobody!
When I left the house,
What was it—sleep or languor,
What sort of happiness?

I don't know. The twists and turns of life,
Or maybe the girl from the tourist center,
Who drops in unexpectedly,
Or the noise of the rain against the roof,
The sheepskin that covers me,
And the voices of old women.

They prattle over the milk.
Is my age over? It's not begun,
I've just been born.
I chewed through the umbilical cord myself,
Today I've lived through half,
Tomorrow afternoon I'll pass on.

Krestovsky Prospect

It'd be easy for me to recall Krestovsky Prospect,
Where the Baltic waters ring in a singsong,
In November, in a flood, when the islands
Are inundated by the gulf and the Neva on a binge?
It'd be easy for me to recall the window above the water curtained by
    windy darkness?
It'd be easy for me to remember you, my beauty?
How you'd gaze half-awake, smoothing your hair over your
    temples,
Arranging a reddish lock. I'd like to know—
What all of this was called?
Arrant 1960? Or your striped French scarf?
Or the Georgian Tsinandali that we guzzled then?
Or Armstrong's horn we loved so much?
Or Tatiana or Anna, weird Oktiabrina,
Strange Violetta or dear old Mariia?
Or the poor prospects of the five-year steel plan?
Or the first intelligence report and the last war?
It'd be easy to remember. But then I can't!
There where the island thrusts up on the big bank,
Beyond the empty stadium, storing up sobs,
I stand like a mastodon, forgetful of itself.

The Four

To A. Kushner

The four chimneys of the heating plant
And the bridge over my Fontanka—
That's my homeland, that's an impartial
Picture that is dearer than the others.

How happy I am that we both didn't die,
Just got coated with grey varnish,
How familiar the dusks,
The little bell over Haymarket Square.

With the mossy face of a hairworm
The snowy evening soared.
Four familiar gardens
From the house to the schoolyard railing.

Now it's a matter of indifference,
Senseless to sob on your breast.
But I always listened, hoping
To hear your maternal love?

Wasn't the pitiful singing heard,
The singing that is useless to others?
Isn't the guardian angel visible
On your four chimneys?

Here I was, a hero and a schoolboy—
What could be dearer on earth than that?
Let the foursome become the ruler
Of life and death for me.

The Balcony

Home, home! —Not so simple
From the Author to Tolstoy's day.
But it's too late to stay over,
And the relationship doesn't have
The sort of basis for spending the night.
In the morning it would be reproaches or a spat,
And simple tears without hysteria
Would be a sheer miracle.
But it's a sugar-coated pill,
Today is the fifth of July,
2:30 by the clock—
Which is about dawn.
Stay? No, what for?
There are even taxis
In this forgotten part of town.
Right through Narvsky Gate,
Then a smooth turn onto Gaz Prospect.
What is this city? It's a disease,
An addiction and infection.
Across the Fontanka and Kalinkin Bridge,
Fastened to the river by chains,
As if by way of a garden wicket gate
And onto Garden Street. Bumping through
Maklin, Haymarket, Demidov, and Chernyshev.
—Now, soon! It'd be good!

Engineers Castle is darker than blood,
Awaiting conspirators as before,
And here the daily sunrise comes in all its hope.
The Neva stretches like an admiral's cutter
From Ladoga to the Baltic fleet.
And I already grasp a bank note
Since it's close to the debarking area.
The wharf. My house is on Kamennostrovsky.
The balcony is huge.
I dwelt here as infant, boy, adolescent.
And it is built.
For me too. Although it's possible
It was built much earlier.
Not for nothing is my luxurious balcony
held up by two naked female giants.

The Sea of Japan

The beer that we drank in the Sea of Japan,
Weak beer, oh, weak recollections,
Various things that happened—
Fights and pretenses, did we really understand them.
The Sea of Japan crawls in, hissing with whitened foam;
Electric light will whiten both foam and elbows.
A single military islet pushes into the sea,
Where submarines are put into the water.
Radio music plays over the decks.
People dance and cry and love.
Vodka is laced with other weaker stuff,
And mixed and drunk. We must drink to parting!
Oh, don't forget one single intentional hurt, there are
Deaths of all kinds and Lugovskoi's* marvelous death.
People sail as they lived, look—everything is clear,
The age runs out, the fresh sea is gloomy.
It's stifling in the cabins from the velvet and the ebonite,
Gay in the heart from the sound of the ship.

1959

599/600

To V. Aksyonov

At kilometer No. 600 there's a well by the rail line.
The water in it is deathly deep and too cold.

---

*Lugovoskoi—a poet, who, according to legend, died in 1958 of a heart attack while climbing after a
flower in the mountains.

But there's no other water around and I crank the windlass,
And lick away a drop of sweat before it slides under my collar.

And I get out my pack of Dzhebels, sit down on a wet bench,
Pull out not my fortune but a nibbled cigarette.
My eyes run over the line. At first in the direction of Warsaw,
Where the distant trains are covered with sable clouds,
Where there's the city of Kuznitsa on the border, and not a step
    beyond, though
There's an allied country there, our friend mighty Poland.
But it's sweet for me to hasten in the other direction
Toward my native Leningrad, and urge the sluggard road crew
On the way. Oh, steam engines with engineers,
Yesterday's fun, like imaginist books—you're the technology of the
    past century.
And I don't understand satellites, transistors, or radiation,
While I do understand profligates who change clothes
Three times a day, take leisurely meals, and follow women around
    slowly,
Posing in front of a photographer out of this exposed-to-light
    eternity.

On earth what is less constant than life?
Having fallen behind this fast age, I'll not make up the distance,
Like a local behind an express.
I finished my cigarette and the pain of it passed to my tired mitral
    valve.
God grant me to drink the waters of oblivion from this terrible well.

31 December

When I discern the scarlet vault
Of the frozen sunset,
It seems to me that somehow
My whole life will pass under it.

Oh, this illuminated dusk,
And long path on the embankment.
I am, as it were, someone's faithful companion,
Always ready to turn and follow
Behind a dear and valiant leader,
Through the snowy gloom
That turns red just like a white flag
Under the bloodthirsty sunset.

I bet everything on the turn,
Foresaw it and there,

Where there's a stack of wood,
I stand staring into the firmament;
Until the carmine and cranberry of December wanes,
Until the cupola of the blind man's aerial guide
Is extinguished.

Until the city that's dark blue
Exposes to the yellow snow and wide world
Its pretentious evening newspapers.
And under the light of a shop window,
Incorrigible stay-at-home,
Shivering in a threadbare coat,
I give myself advice:

"Calm down, fate has already decreed
The taking back of all promises,
The understanding that there's nothing better
Than the city, snow and sunset."

Quarantine

In that year of 1960, an unclean train carried me
Through hill and dale, across the Volga and the Urals.
It smelled of sweat, shag, and a yarn was spun.
I was still young, that is, I hadn't yet started to live.
But then I got off in Tashkent, looked around on the platform,
And a Central Asian appeared, tapping
On my suitcases, picked them up as if on command,
And remarked to his rival: "Joking apart—there's a brother!"
I spent some time in Samarkand.
There where Gur-Emir glimmers
With its sky-blue tiles like cold glass.
I found myself in quarantine. It happens, it happens!
I report to you: "The time passed all right."
In the prerevolutionary hotel rooms, the corridor
Twisting and turning three and four ways at once,
Where never once were we given dinner à la carte,
Where the tomatoes were stacked in heaps, I lived and contrived
To spend two rubles—no more—on food, since I needed
The money for Fergana and Bukhara,
And it happened—and probably that was the first slip—
I picked out dried fruit at the bazaar in October.
I washed it off with tea, then indulged myself,
Though it's not very interesting, tea taken sugarless.
And then I rapped on the door of two girls in the end room—

Demonism and paradise. The demon was just Nina, the
      angel—Angelina.
They had tea brewing on a hotplate—and plenty of wine;
Two weeks of quarantine and it was heartfelt picture—
Angelina or Nina looking me straight in the face.
Oh, the brunette and the blonde, the lab technician and the
      botanist,
The one from Leningrad, the other from Kostroma.
A cigarette, sweater, Petrograd moll,
While the other—whatever ya need—as she said herself.
Oh, how I loved them both and squeezed and kissed
Those strong, salt-stained hands, blew
the last of my money on port wine and drank the nights away
to the radiola; we danced a bit. Nina or Angelina?
Angelina or Nina? Dark white concern, pale black love!
The one tilted her head, the other was higher than flight—
Nina or Angelina? Angelina! The blood cools.
I love you, I love you, I never saw you again.
Two weeks flew past and the suitcases were packed again.
But my sorrow is immortal. I loved you, I really did.
What if the empty net of space has gotten threadbare at the edges.
Never again, oh Lord! Not in a single hotel of the world,
Not in the capital's Astoria or Monaco's casino
Shall I see you again. It'll never be again!
Something will happen, I'm awaiting a sign. But for now, it's all the
      same to me.

Melancholia

We'll screen ourselves from the city
With curtains and glass,
It's uncomfortable and expensive
to say goodbye to heat.

To go over to the windowsill,
Lean on it, light a cigarette—
The warmth dissolves in the blood
Little by little.

Everything tighter and more painful,
Further, bigger, sicker,
Deeper and more disgraceful,
Better, narrower, smarter.

The miracles of melancholia
Surround you,

The bristles of the brush
Pretty you up.

Do you want it in oils and tempera,
Do you want it etched deep—
But the further on, the more sacrificial
Is your connection with the model
In the etching by Dürer,
Where there's a magical square.
God save me! Otherwise
These cyphers and symbols
Will get too wise.
We'll live in simplicity,
Though it is more beyond one's strength
At times, than those

That are tighter and more painful,
Better and narrower and smarter,
Deeper and more disgraceful,
Further, bigger, sicker.

* * *

Twice in ten years. On the same day.
The sixth of May, it was Sunday.
Honeyed Moscow lilac,
Dense violet vision,
Dangled around corners. I was
Heading for The Telegraph for some reason,
Squeezed by the crowds, then—
Suddenly, nose to nose. She with her
Hooked-Roman nose in the air, since she was with
Something like a cross between a pig and a polecat,
And so was especially haughty,
Though we certainly had things
To remember. At the same time
To shed a tear over, onto the warm sidewalks
Of alien Moscow, empty, like all capitals
On Sunday. And the wind blew
Through Tverskaya Square and couldn't calm down.
It carried along empty Marlboro packs,
Lilacs, somebody's letters.
Oh, life, you appear in final copy
As song torn from the soul!
You arise by chance, in the dark,
As you fumble for the switch.

And there the windows go flaring up—
We headed for Pushkin Square.
She was the friend of two friends
In other parts and times once.
It's time to sell her underwear to a museum,
And I assure you they'd pay plenty.
All of that was in the best of systems,
Where Hippocrene surges on the black grain.
Why, I ask you, why?
And what for? And what's more absurd than anything,
Both were left holding the bag.
Then she smelled of champagne,
Could hardly stand on her feet,
Here in Tverskaya Square with her foreign freak.
He was out of work,
An art historian or repair man of some kind.
—How come, old friend, you got burnt out?
My pupil, my brilliant boy.
How come another brought your girl (no joke)
To this paltry altar?
But here the sidewalk ended,
And they didn't want to start down another.
I saw how they got into a taxi,
And how the Volga raced off down the boulevard.
I'm finishing. With neither ardor nor sorrow
Nor cursing. But still, whatever it was,
It was worth something? Something? If only tears,
Half-words, a hole in a glove?
I turned my lascivious eyes to Babylon, where life is still in embryo,
Where toward evening southern tops used to slip out of their jackets
          toward evening into coats,
Where the crowd gurgled near the Theater Society,
Turning blue in jeans of all description.
The sixth of May, a day renowned of old.
Fifteen years ago it meant a lot.
My wife's name day. But the calendar,
As proper, has altered that.

Nikodim

It was in the fifties.
Stalin had croaked. A Pioneer camp.
Everybody was wearing crêpe de chine and covert.
"In a Distant Land" was the big hit.

Then, in our narrow pioneer world,
There appeared, riding a bicycle,

A kid from a nearby dacha.
He was a year older, really somebody,
a master of badminton and lotto.
He was good at everything.
Even the governess Née
was more attentive and tenderer

To him than to the other children.
Née Irène Lvovna, a Frenchwoman,
No doubt by blood. She was loving
To him; that is to be explained
By the fact that Nika or Nikodim
Is good-looking and unbeatable on the playing field.

He's into everything. Right wing in soccer.
A magician on the racing bike.
He's got it over everybody
In defense of our sports' banner.
At sixteen, the champ of the region,
An old-timer around the stadium.

And the girls from all four ranks—
From nine years to sexually ripe,
Ninety-six carat diamonds,
Uglies and those a little bit backward,
They all answer "Nika" glowingly
When playing "tell-the-truth."

The passage of time, as ordered on high,
Is unavoidable and implacable.
Already, I see you as a graduate,
Wise Nikodim, pride of our scientific establishment.
Machines and girls and sports parades
Always served him well.

On the distant peninsula of Chukotka,
Testing a new device,
He thrives. Asthma and consumption
Don't bother him. They say
That he doesn't even smoke. He's rejected
The bottle, only indulging in the ladies.

He comes to Peter and Moscow,
Basking in glory amidst well-known maestros.
I saw a picture of him—on a bridge somewhere,
Standing in a fresh breeze

With an actress from Lenfilm,
Skinny, in a leather jacket.
The vector changed

its swift course to cruel deceleration.
And Nikodim cracked up some contraption.
What are rumors? A reflection of ideals!
It wasn't his fault, and they say
That he tried to pull out of it
'Till it was time to go for the parachutes.

But thank God, he escaped jail and death.
Landed in the tundra in a cedar wood.
Just try it yourself. Could you manage,
When the bolts are cracking off
And it's forty-two seconds till death
And the chance of survival is zilch.

So, he wasn't at fault and he was.
He was kicked out, a doctor and not a doctor.
He comes to Leningrad,
Where he proposes an atomic reactor
Combined with a turbine,
and sticks his foot in his mouth forthwith.

As with the turbine reactor,
So too x-rays, taxis, fast-food dispensers;
Saving the Dvuglavaya Katarina*
Is beyond him. And they say
That he lives with an uncle and works
As a weight clerk in a warehouse.

His wife leaves him. But that's rubbish.
Another one arrives the same day.
And his ex-father-in-law Sergei Ilych
Even takes a drink with him,
And they head for the stadium
To a soccer game.

Now, it's no longer fashionable poets
And music-hall actresses . . .
He goes fishing next to a parapet
on the Little Neva. Has a beard.
Drinks beer and port at the railway station.
And here's what I was told recently:

He's happy. He's so at peace.

*A (Polish) Roman Catholic Church in Vilnius [author's note].

He took a look at life and saw
That the rat race and the social whirl,
Like the stadium, like science—all vanity,
Full of fateful emptiness.
He stopped trying to rise above the mob.

So there he goes across the Chernyshev Bridge*
That's chained to the river Fontanka.
A terrible seam across his face
Turns blue from the cold. Cold shadows
Cover airy Leningrad in May.
He's got a fishing pole in his hand. He's happy.

He's happy that the day ahead will be filled
With fishing and Pepper Vodka.
He stands there absolutely alone
In front of a noisy tram stop.
Only the outlines of the clouds
Tell of how he, too,

Like those shapes in the sky,
Was once full of brilliance and glory.
They're like a combination of continents,
And animals like wild boars, leopards, lions,
And other heraldic figures,
Unlike anything in nature.

So far as the lion in the local zoo goes—
It turned up its toes from colitis.

* In Leningrad [author's note].

A Baker's Dozen of Stories*
by Yevgeny Popov

1. "Voryuga"†

One time Galibutayev showed up at home with a half-liter of vodka in the inside pocket of his padded jacket.

What with the price of vodka and other hard liquor nowadays, just the thought of it is enough to bring a bitter smile to a drinker's lips—something Galibutayev passed on to his wife Masha.

Who answered, "Don't start blowing off. Take a seat; it's time for chow."

"Hush your mouth, Voryuga," Galibutayev barked sternly and planked the vodka down on the table. But he was smiling.

And started washing up, after taking off his jacket and boots and unwinding his footcloths.

Barefoot, washed, and in his undershirt he sat down at the table, where the cabbage soup steamed and the vodka gleamed in the drinking glasses like so many bright and shining eyes.

"Yeah . . . vodka," said Galibutayev, and drank up.

So did Masha.

"What was that you said? 'Voryuga?' How many times do I have to tell you not to talk like that. I'm a working woman." She started in.

"I know. Galibutayev knows everything. But what that 'Voryuga' is for, is to luminate you. Understand?"

"I don't know . . ." said the woman.

"Well you better know. I want to see a luminated object. An unluminated object is not what I want to see, and I don't see it. I want to see you luminated, which is why I call you Voryuga. Got it?"

---

*Translated by George Saunders.

†Literally, "thief woman." The underworld of the Russian thieves (*vory*) is a separate subculture with its own rough customs and colorful slang. To call someone "Voryuga," then, is insulting, since it classes the person in the disapproved criminal world. On the other hand, it adds a certain glamor and luster. An American equivalent might be "gun moll" or "tough broad" [tr.].

"Laminated? What is this?" Masha asked uncertainly.

"Not that. *Lu*minated. Lume. Get it?"

She was insulted.

"I get it. You keep up that kind of talk, and I'll get you right out of this house. Out you'll go . . . That's all we need, a luminated man on our hands."

And the leftover half a glass went down in one gulp.

Galibutayev fell to thinking. And he had something to think about. The problem was, he didn't have his own place. And Masha was his wife, of course, but with no papers, no certificate from the marriage registration office. So she could ask him to leave any time.

"Now don't get all worked up over nothing." Galibutayev was conciliatory.

"I'll kick you out for sure," Masha promised. "As soon as the kids come, out you go. You wait."

"Mmm, the kids." Galibutayev poured out what was left in the bottle and kept eating.

That was the problem. The kids. Masha had four of them. But the two daughters, thank God, had married demobilized soldiers and gone off with them somewhere.

Then there was Sonny Mishka—a real nemesis. He worked at the same factory as Galibutayev and constantly had an eye out for him. One minute he'd be asking Galibutayev some filthy question, the next he'd be shoving him, the next he'd be trying to get Galibutayev to read something from the paper out loud, knowing full well that there was no way Galibutayev could read the paper because of his severe near-sightedness and problems with literacy. Always after him. Galibutayev kept out of his nemesis' way. But he would also let Sonny Mishka have it, when he got the chance. Tit for tat.

And Seryozha, the youngest. That one might seem harmless, maybe, because he was still young enough to be in the Pioneers, but he was also a potential threat to Galibutayev, his love, and his apartment. Because Seryozha would soon grow up and start feeling ashamed of his mother's behavior, which the whole street knew about.

After eating, the couple's spirits rose considerably, and they turned on Masha's TV.

"The American bourgeois professor in this case reveals a total lack of familiarity with the fundamentals of Marxism-Leninism," the lecturer was saying. Etcetera.

Then there was a concert. And a movie, *Stakes Higher Than Life*, about the indomitable Captain Kloss.*

After which the day's programming ended and the lighted screen went out.

The day had gone out too. The day had ended. The evening had

*Captain Kloss—a Soviet Television hero, a superspy—like James Bond [tr.].

ended too. Night had come, and after that Galibutayev and Masha would have to go earn their living again.

"Like to smash the loafing fuck-offs," said Galibutayev stretching.

"Huh," Masha didn't hear. She was getting ready for bed.

"The fuck-offs, I said. What's the matter? You deaf?" he roared. And went out on the porch.

On the porch, too, night had fallen. A full moon shone. The barns were white in the darkness. Almost all the lights in the barracks were out. It was night. Galibutayev went back inside and got in bed. But in bed he was master and king.

"Masha, tonight let's do it like I was forcing you," he said. Masha was interested.

"What do you mean?"

"Like this. You pretend to resist, but for real, with everything you've got. And I'll try to get you as you fly."

"Okay," she said gladly. "Let's go."

"And I threw myself on her like a wild animal," Galibutayev related the story. "Ripped off all her clothes, and she twisted and turned, and scratched, and squealed. Any other rapist would have given up long before. But Galibutayev's not like that. Ripped everything off her and was just getting ready, when suddenly she rams me so hard that I fall off the bed, hurting."

"And then what?"

"Then this. I broke the big toe on my right foot. Fell on my toe."

And Galibutayev let out a string of curses.

"So? Then?"

"Well, listen . . ."

In the morning Galibutayev had come limping to work and, taking the chief of the work gang aside, told him the whole story. The gang boss said nothing, and they set to work unloading boxes of cucumbers.

The gang boss, working with Galibutayev, got up on top of the load and ever so gently, with extreme care, let the corner of a box down on Galibutayev's foot. On the left one, at that.

"Oh-oh-oh," Galibutayev began to shout and whimper. "Oh, my poor foot! Oh my beautiful little foot. Oh. Oh."

After which an accident report was filled out. Galibutayev went to the hospital, where they did an X-ray of his big toe. The X-ray fully confirmed the presence of the trauma indicated, and Galibutayev was given authorization for leave with one hundred percent compensation.

And Galibutayev went home, where Masha laughed her head off when he told her the whole story.

"You mean, they're even going to pay you *money* for all that? What do you know!"

"And for a whole month I sat home," Galibutayev went on, his eyes gleaming. "Didn't do a thing. And me and Masha did such numbers together, such numbers no one could dream of."

"And then?"

"What do you mean, then? Then she kicked me out, anyway. Mishka, the scum, came back from his business trip, and Seryozha from Pioneer camp. She kicked me out, weeping. 'I can't bear doing this,' she says, 'but I can't bear that, either. After all, I've got children to take care of. Thief woman! Broke my toe! You know what she weighs? Ninety-six kilo. And she's ten years older than me."

"That doesn't matter!"

"No, not ten," Galibutayev started counting. "I'm thirty-two. And she's forty-three. So that's eleven years older.

"She gave me everything back," he continued the tale of his unhappy love. "Everything that was mine she gave back, plus her first husband's leather jacket. He used to be a technician at the airport. Everything. My padded jacket, my overalls, my overcoat from the GDR, my felt boots, and my cap. The only thing I left at her place was my tar."

"What tar?"

"Tar. I had a little jar of tar for patching my boots. I left it there. Got to ask Mishka to bring it, or stop by for it myself."

"So where are you living now?"

"Now I'm not living. I'm spending the night. I spend the nights in the factory garage. But they're promising to give me a room. Right on the factory grounds. Winter'll be here soon. I'm not afraid of winter in general, because she gave me everything back, including my felt boots and cap. But we did such numbers together that no one else could dream of."

Galibutayev broke into a happy laugh.

When he finished, he resumed his story.

"I'll tell you one thing. Since childhood I've had this disability with nearsightedness. They used to call me 'squint eyes' because of it. I only finished second grade. Because I couldn't study. What I needed was real careful teaching. You know, special instruction, after hours, consideration for my moods. But how could you get that in an orphanage?"

"Was it bad in the orphanage?"

"Why bad? It's like family to me still. They even took me to the top eye doctor, Filatov. Trouble is he said they had brought me too late. He even tried to rip the medal off the director's coat."

"What medal?"

"How should I know? He had a medal on his coat. And Filatov wanted to rip it off. 'This child,' he said, 'you've ruined him.' But why come down on them? They were concerned about me. They're the ones who brought me to Filatov. The only things was, they didn't know they should have taken me to Filatov right way.

"That's why I can only see a luminated object. An unluminated object I can't see. And unluminated objects include everything that's written down and everything that's out there around me.

"A luminated object, though, that was my Voryuga." Galibutayev didn't want to talk with me any more. He figured any more questions I might ask would only be to poke fun at him.

2. About Cat Catson

They were sitting, one hot August night, in the stifling kitchen next to the bathroom, facing each other across the table with its colored oilcloth.

"The ways of the Lord are hellishly far beyond human understanding," said Garigozov. "Hellishly! People today have been so shaken up they've lost their clear outlines, like from vibration. That's the thing, that's the thing, you understand? That's what's depressing. It's frightening! Did I ever think, for example, that she could do something like this?" complained Garigozov, who had been educated at the local Polytechnic Institute, to his friend Kankrin, educated there also.

Kankrin, though, maintained a concentrated silence. Then he sniffled a bit and came out with an answer:

"Absolutely, I agree with you, brother. Why, just look at this, right here, in this particular case, in the given instance: outside it's August, but they go and turn on the radiators. Is it hot? It is. Is it stifling? It is. And why do they do it? They just do, that's all. So what if they suffocate you. But in the winter, wait and see. In the winter, brother, in the winter the wind will be howling and the snowdrifts will come and then you'll wait your ass off for them to turn the heat up full blast. And what's the reason for it? You just try to figure it out—whether it's simple, swinish mismanagement, or . . . or, in general . . . in general, Christ knows what!"

"You've stated the question correctly," Garigozov approved. "Correctly, although too concretely. What you've got to understand, and I don't think you'll argue too strenuously on this point—you've got to understand, after all, that we *ourselves* are to blame for a lot of this. Understand? Because a lot of things are literally simple to correct. All you have to do is not get shaken, not vibrate, but somehow take yourself in hand, d'you understand? To feel yourself to be the master, understand? —master of your destiny, your family, your work, your country, after all! Understand?"

"Well, then, shall I—what d'you say?—shall I pour it all out?" said Kankrin.

"Uh-huh," said Garigozov.

The remaining clear vodka began to gurgle and lap into the green wine glasses. After drinking it down, the two friends gasped, sniffed at some individual crusts of black bread,* and fixed their glistening, lively eyes on one another.

But—they stayed silent. In this silence, arising not out of scarcity but abundance, a certain small quantity of double man-time went by. Until some new sounds intermingled with the faucet-dripping silence of the kitchen, a cautious scratch-scratching of some kind, a rustle-rustling, and even a certain rumbling.

"You?" Garigozov came to. "You hungry?"

"No, not hungry," Kankrin answered tensely, trying to hear something and tilting his head floorward, in the direction of the dresser with the remarkably carved fretwork.

"I also say," Garigozov began rambling, apropos of nothing. "I also say it's about the soul, about the soul that it's time to think—for this shaken and shaking individual of our age, who has completely lost his outlines."

"Yeah," said Kankrin.

"And our age has lost its outlines, too, completely," Garigozov moaned. But a new person arriving on the scene would have realized right away that his share of the vodka had simply gone straight to his head and he was suddenly very drunk, as sometimes happens in the still of the night in intimate conversation with strong drink.

"There you have it," Garigozov summed up.

But Kankrin was no longer listening. He suddenly lurched to his feet, and with one bound whirled over and began dragging out from under the carved dresser a poor cat of enormous size that kept holding fast and putting up stiff resistance. The guilty beast's fur was all puffed out in a frightful state, and its pupils were enormous, burning with an unpleasant glint.

"He rolled a tomato!" Kankrin excitedly denounced the beast. "D'you realize? He rolled a tomato under the dresser. Va-aska cat," he began intoning. "Va-aska cat! Vaska must get thrashed!"

"Yeah . . . uh . . . we can thrash him," Garigozov confirmed, cracking his fingers fastidiously. "Here it is. Nighttime. Quiet. Conversations. And he starts in."

Garigozov waved his puffy little hand vexatiously.

"Oh, you, Vaska-Vaska! Vaska cat!" Kankrin was overjoyed for no apparent reason. "Vaska cat! Vaska must get thrashed!" he kept chanting.

And hearing this bitter resolution of his solitary fate, the martyred Vasily now heroically closed his yellow eyes and without a murmur prepared for the torture. I will not make any bold assertions, but evidently they would indeed have punished him—maybe only a little,

---

* A Russian custom is to sniff bread after swallowing vodka [tr.].

but the two friends, who'd had a bit too much, would surely have given him a licking if it hadn't been for what happened next.

What happened was that on the threshold of the kitchen there appeared the austere figure of a tall, slender, curly-headed boy in black satin shorts and full Young Pioneer uniform, consisting of a white shirt and red tie. The boy was silent for some time and gazed steadily at the crimson faces of the merry-making brothers of the bottle. Then he coughed.

Kankrin saw him and spoke.

"Pashka? Well, hullo. What's up, brother? How come you're not asleep? When I was your age I was always in bed by this time. And you've even got your tie on! Well, look at you, what an important personage in the middle of the night." Kankrin was effusively good-natured.

"My son here was taken into the Pioneers three days ago; so now he won't part with the relics of that occasion," explained the proud Garigozov, and jokingly gave the command: "OK, be prepared. Day is done. Off to bed, you little shit!"

Suddenly, to Kankrin's horror, the boy cried out in a voice that rang with strain:

"Stop shouting, Papa! And I'm not gonna say that the way you and Uncle Kankrin are behaving might wake up Mama who's really tired from work. But I *will* say you mustn't get any idea you can beat poor Vaska. I love Vasenka and I will fight against this. You are grown people, and actively building communism, and you must know it isn't allowed. One can't lose one's moral bearings. One can't beat a cat, or hit a rabbit, or throw stones at a bird!"

And with great dignity he extracted the cat from Kankrin's hands.

"Ah, you. . . ah, you. . . . What's that old song you're singing?" Garigozov turned pale. "How does that old song go? It isn't allowed? But it's alright to torment a man?"

And at this point Garigozov leaped to his feet and loosed a hail of obscenities upon the child, to which the Pioneer with great dignity made no reply, but merely continued to stare proudly, courageously, and honestly at them, holding the cat next to his heart and his Pioneer tie.

What a group of statues froze this way! And who knows how things would have ended, but suddenly the floorboards creaked and into the kitchen burst a sleepy, rather stout, cheerful woman in her middle years, wearing nothing but her nightshirt. She squinted from the bright light and surveyed those present myopically:

"What's all this noise you're making in the middle of the night, comrades?" she said in a lilting voice. "Pashka! You march off to bed this instant, naughty rascal. I don't even want to see your shadow! And you, Yegor, it isn't right of you to cause a disturbance," she turned to Kankrin. "So you drank the whole bottle—I won't say anything against that. But it's wrong of you to cause such a commotion, upsetting Andryusha* and getting yourself upset too. Are you really going to be happy, dear *friend*, if he ends up in the asylum again?"

"They were going to beat the cat," the boy reported.

"The ca-a-at? Well, what artists!" The woman began laughing. "No kidding, you'll really make it into the nuthouse together this time. But come on, Andrei. Andryushka. Don't you remember what you promised Pavlik and me? Don't you remember? Not to *drink!*"

"Hey, what the hell are you carrying on for?" said Garigozov angrily. "What nuthouse are you talking about? You better drop that nuthouse stuff. I know why you're bringing up my nuthouse! But the only thing Doctor Gusakov said was go easy on the drinking, not stop it competely. We had two bottles, and we finished them. And we're going to beat the damn cat anyhow, because he rolled a tomato under the dresser. And I'm gonna give Pavlik a whipping too, because he can't start talking to his own father that way. And you're gonna get a punch in the smush too, because when I was lying in the hospital, you were running around with that waiter from 'The North.' Tell me, isn't that so?"

"Of course it's not so," the woman dissented sincerely. "Seryozha and I are just friends. Besides, he's a married man. Pavlik loves you. And the cat? Well, why beat up on a little cat?" the woman was astonished. "There's absolutely no reason to beat him up. We'd do better to put a pretty red ribbon around his neck and dance a happy dance with him in the middle!"

Garigozov and Kankrin froze in place, their mouths hanging open.

"O Mama!" The boy became ecstatic. "Look at you! You and your Uncle Seryozha must have had a few, too—"

"Hush," said Yevdokia Apraksiyevna sternly and at the same time jokingly, because meanwhile she had deftly outfitted Vasily in the above-mentioned costume. The cat hissed but was bought off with a dish of milk which it began to lap up adroitly.

And taking hands in the middle of the night in the quiet kitchen, they began to circle around the beast as it drank its fill.

Mama began:

> We'll sing,
> We'll sing,
> About Cat Catson,
> About Cat Catson . . .
>
> Ya, about Cat Catson.
> Ya, about Cat Peterson . . .

came the answering refrain from Garigozov, Kankrin, and the representative of the rising generation.

---

*Endearing form of Garigozov's first name, Andrei [tr.].

And they quietly danced in the night in the quiet kitchen around the animal filling his belly, these quiet people of a vast country. They felt empty; they felt muggy; they felt OK; it was fun. Kankrin did a fancy step. Garigozov stomped his feet.

"Awright now, tell the truth, shitface! Did you sleep with the waiter or not?"

"Quiet," said the boy. "Quiet, or the neighbors downstairs will start thumping with their mop handle!"

"Yeah, and then we'll let 'em have it," said Garigozov.

It was still night, and the street lights had gone out. Garigozov, stumbling, was escorting Kankrin through the dark entryway of the building, seeing him off.

"Brother, what emptiness!" he whispered hoarsely. "What damned emptiness, brother! What did we ever get an education for?"

But Kankrin refused to agree with him and, in answering speeches, gave a multitude of well-argued examples.

3. That's Why No Money's Coming In

"Yeah? What's that? Drunk, you say? Excuse me. But did you give me something to drink? No. So there. And what'd I do to you? Lost my balance and stepped on your foot. But not on purpose, you know. Now forgive me, forgive me for it. Just dozed off a bit. Waiting for the train. The electric to Kubckovo. Forgive me, please. I was just sleeping, and I woke up. I was just . . . I'm not drunk, you know. Forgive me, OK? I didn't mean anything by it."

An ordinary Russian scene, dear to the heart. An old guy in a rumpled hat and rumpled trousers, coming to in the waiting room of a suburban train station. His neighbor, a man with the look of an intellectual, maintains a fastidious silence in response to the gushings of this recently intoxicated individual. Peasant women, peasant men, peasant girls with their long-haired boy friends and transistor radios, shelling seeds, popping them in their mouths, and shouting in a shrill, unnatural frenzy the words of a popular song:

"Hey, you really messed me up! . . ."

And the waiting room itself—with its famous Ministry of Railways benches, hard and uncomfortable, its ancient smell of carbolic acid, its enormous fig tree and, even larger, a scene from the life of the leaders of the world proletariat—was apparently designed, in the subtle scheme of the station authorities, to have an aesthetically uplifting effect on the turbulent passengers, to allay their passions and soothe their minds.

"Yeah, but it was the meatpie, the *belyashik*, that was to blame," said rumpled-hat, although his tidy neighbor, nose buried in *Pravda*, had turned away and by his whole appearance made clear that because of his importance in life, if nothing else, and even because of a certain goodness of heart, he was refraining from shoving this dissolute individual out the wide doors of the station, after grabbing him firmly by the scruff of the neck, or even snapping that skinny neck in his fat hands.

"Oh, that *belyashik*, that *belyashik*," the man who had just woken up repeated in a monotone. "If it hadn't been for that *belyashik*, maybe everything would have been different. What do you think?"

"Although . . ." the questioner began to reflect. ". . . who the hell knows? Who the hell knows?"

"Hey, Grandad-Saucepan, what you gettin' all worked up about? Got a smoke?" a tall, young fellow with a guitar accosted him.

"Yep, and why not," said the "grandfather" judiciously.

"Comrades!" the civilized gentleman was about to tear himself away from his paper, but he saw the steep brow of the fancier of light music, who had settled down on his haunches with his mighty paw outstretched for a "Far North" cigarette, a paw tattooed with reminders of that same distant part of the world, and with that the gentleman simply breathed a light sigh and sniffed disdainfully, trying not to inhale any of the tobacco smoke from those cheap and filthy cigarettes, which was poisonous to himself personally of course, as well as to other working people.

"So tell me, what was you gabbin' about," the dauntless young smoker absent-mindedly addressed his older comrade.

"So, this is what. I was telling about the *belyashik* that did me in. Because they had given me one last chance."

"Oh yeah? What *belyashik* and what last chance?" the impatient young man cried out. "You gonna tell me about it? Or you gonna beat around the bush? Huh?"

"Hey, the minute I start telling you, you start butting in!" the old guy flared up. "If you wanna hear, listen. If you don't, get lost."

"I'm listening," said the young man.

And the older guy's rough story poured out in a smooth stream.

It all began in the sixties, those hard years of our era. I had an important job with good pay in supply work. I was forging ahead and got a little dizzy with success. Began drinking too much, cognac and hard liquor, because those days they were a little cheaper than now, and I always had money, more than I needed.

Well, my mates and my boss kept warning me, sooner or later things would turn out bad in this respect, but in my impunity, I wouldn't listen to them, because I was having success in my work all the time and that softens a person's head a lot.

But time showed that they were right. Because I began having all kinds of setbacks on the job, not to mention personal ones, because my wife soon left me, after a lot of little incidents. And disasters kept popping up on the job, one after the other, like devils. It was on a bench just like this, to be exact, in Savelovsky Station in Moscowtown, where I was passing the night in an inebriated condition, not having a hotel room, when some stinking bastards I didn't know stole a roll of government-issue silver wire that I'd been sent to Syzran-town to get. Our shop was at a standstill as a result of the lack of this wire, and they, the bastards, stole it from me. You know yourself what that gets you . . .

"Gotcha," said the youth.

Well, it was plain as day I was going to pay for it all, although in this case the rules had been broken. They had no business sending me for the wire. It's the kind of wire that's supposed to go by special messenger, because it's silver. But I didn't make a big fuss because they had other goods on me.

And so, having blown it completely, I was standing, not so long ago, in front of Gerasimchuk's steel-frame glasses. And he says to me, "OK, Ivan Andreich, here's your last chance to keep working at our factory. And if you don't take it, we'll part company with you for good, because we've gotten sick and tired of your escapades, despite your good work, and we've been flooded with letters of one kind or another about you, asking that you be penalized, which we've been lax about. So this is your last chance!

"Our contract's about to expire with the hothouse farm, and if they don't extend the contract, that devil of a German, Metzel, will make us forfeit. And we'll have to pay five thousand. And that damn German will hold us to the letter, because he's not a Russian and he can't understand any way of doing business but his own. On top of that he has a real hot temper. He has his hotbeds, and all the creeps in the world go to see him to beg for onions, cucumbers, tomatoes, radishes, carrying orders from higher places, which they get with pull. And since these orders are from higher up the German has to grit his teeth and fill them, so as not to be thrown out of his job. So he fills them, and has to sell his German hothouse wealth dirt cheap, which is why he has such a nasty temper, and you can see exactly why he'd take that five thousand out of our hides for sure."

"So what am I supposed to do?" I ask, trembling because I can guess well enough.

"What you have to do," says Gerasimchuk with this brazen grin, "is see to it that he *prolongs* the contract half a year. Then we won't have to pay the five thousand."

"And what does that mean—*prolong?*" I ask with fainting heart, guessing the answer again.

"That means he puts off the deadline, sweetheart," Gerasimchuk keeps smirking. "And then we don't have to pay the five thousand."

"So what is he, a fool?" I burst out. "Why would he extend the contract when he knows he can get the five thousand out of us?"

"That's what we're sending you for," the devil coos. "It's your last chance to keep working at this factory. Do it and you'll get a raise, and a bonus, and all past problems will be buried and forgotten. If you don't—well, you know very well." He spreads his hands, in this murderous way.

"So what you're saying is it's just like a fairy tale, right?" I ask, quiet as a mouse.

"Yeah, like a fairy tale," Gerasimchuk confirmed. And I left his office ever so quietly, deciding right then and there I wasn't going.

Because there was absolutely no point in going. I knew this German inside out, just like he knew me. I had made this aforementioned contract for delivery of goods with him myself. And the German hadn't wanted to sign it one bit. I had sworn up and down that everything would be done on time, with top accuracy and promptness.

And so I had nothing to expect from a friendly visit to Fritzie but that he'd have me thrown out on my neck. Which is why I went to the bulletin board outside the Employment Bureau to look for a new job.

There I see "Position Wanted" posted up all over the place, and I think to myself, "What the hell, I'll go. Maybe something'll turn up while I'm there. Maybe by now the German's gone out of his mind completely and will sign anything, giggling as he does it. What have I got to lose?"

With thoughts like that I arrive at the farm, which is a model farm if you've got the pull. And proudly holding my balding head up high, I come trailing in among the rows of hotbeds, lit from within, full of cucumbers, onions, and tomatoes for the boys upstairs. After which I come into the office and, without stopping for a minute, ask the secretary—who's real rude from constantly dealing with visitors—I ask her before she has a chance to catch her breath:

"Is Vladimir Adolfovich in?"

"He's in," she answers snidely.

"I'll go in then—"

"Just a minute," she yells, but I had already taken a step, opened the leather door, and found a small conference in session. And the man in charge, orating away, was some guy, but it sure as hell wasn't my dear, brave *guter Kamerad*, Metzel; it was some other character acting as boss.

"Sorry," I say, "for interrupting."

I take a step back.

And there the secretary, Ninka, lands on me with stuff like where do I think I'm sticking my nose, that Metzel is *in*, but *in* his own *house*, because he retired on pension a month ago and is sitting at home, now, offended because they pensioned him off.

"And if you're here for onions or cucumbers, we don't have any. We'll have some in March or April, but those are crops for which we've just put in the seedlings," Ninka tells me.

"Dear Ninochka," I answer her. "What are they to me, your cucumbers? When I'm here on totally different business, strictly related to production, and not to eating up and selling off everything."

"Well, that's a horse of a different color," Nina says in a reassuring way and tells me, "Wait a while, he has some comrades from Norilsk in with him. They'll be through soon, and he'll see you."

"Sure, I'll wait, I'll surely wait." And I think to myself, "Jesus Christ! Can it be that I'm saved?"

Well, I only waited an hour and a half. They all came out of there, like out of a steambath. And I ups to the orator.

"Huh? No!" he barks. "Me? We're on our way to lunch. No onions, no cucumbers, no tomatoes."

"Yeah, but I—"

"No onions! No cucumbers! You should stop these shameful practices, you know! What do you have? A letter? Where from?"

He takes my papers in hand and looks at them for a long time, without understanding a thing.

Then sly little Nina, to show how smart she is, says to him with a titter, "No, Multyk Dzhangaziyevich, he's here about a different matter altogether. About extending a contract for delivery."

"Ah-h-h," the new boss softens. "Why didn't you say so in the first place?"

He takes out his ballpoint and my heart damn near stops beating.

"Where do I sign? And how come you comrades are letting us down so much on the deadlines?" He holds my document and his pen together.

"Well, we have . . . there's new construction under way. Only half a year is all the extension it needs," I jabber away.

And as I watch—oh, Lord above!—this remarkable and efficient individual, this beautiful Mulliuk Varpakhesovich, who's standing there now like a Caucasian cliff, on guard over the state's cucumbers and onions, signs everything for me in a dash and says to Ninka, "Slap a stamp on it. We're off to lunch."

After which he leaves with his Norilskers, who've been standing there, impatiently pawing the dust like so many horses.

And—oh my God!—I'm saved. Painted Ninka, still tittering, stamps the papers for me. I give her the box of "Tales of Pushkin" brand chocolates I have all ready and, just like in a fairy tale, I fly out the door of that nerve-wracking establishment on the wings of Joy and Victory.

"Saved," I think. "Saved! The raise is mine, the bonus is mine, and the deeds of the past are dead and buried."

But just then the phone rings in the office. I hide behind the door.

"Yessir. No," says Ninka. "He's gone already. Just a minute. I'll take a look."

She comes running out. I'm hidden behind the door.

"Comrade! Comrade!" she shouts down the stairwell.

Ha-ha! No comrade down there for you!

She goes back, all down in the mouth, and says into the phone, "No, it looks like he's gone."

Even from behind the door where I am, I can hear loud cursing, with an accent, over the phone.

"Aha," I think. "He caught on. But it's a little too late, brother. Your signature's already on the line. And the stamp's there too."

I fly away on the wings I mentioned. The sun is shining brightly. Hello you beautiful country! The sky is blue. It'll soon be spring. You can feel the warmth. And me—what a fine fellow I am! I've looked out for all my own interests, including the interests of my home factory.

Only I get this tremendous urge to eat, because by now it's already two o'clock. I go here and there and everywhere but there's no place for me to get anything to eat. Because some places are completely closed from two to three, and some places have lines full of guys like me. And I don't have any taste for hanging around, wasting time.

And just then that damned *belyashik* that caused my ruin appears on the scene.

The thing was, I had a terrific craving for a bite to eat. And so I bought some stuff off these two pests standing at a bus stop with an aluminum warming pan with steam pouring out of it.

And these pests are shouting: "Hot meatpies. Get'em while they're hot. Thirty-eight kopeks a pair."

"Fresh?" I ask.

"Made today . . . get 'em while they're hot."

"Fish, are they?"

"What do you mean fish? They're real. Meat. Thirty-eight a pair," they answer me proudly, these two lying fat-asses wearing unsavory white smocks over their quilted jackets.

And in that instant I was lost. Because only after I had bought and eaten those two highly-touted *belyasha* did I understand what the problem was. And what it was, was that they'd been lying around somewhere in their shop window and gotten all dried out, and then they had heated them up and peddled them on the street to fools like me. Right away of course I started feeling bad. But I didn't lose my head, because for every lock there's a pick. Right then and there—I pull a flask out of my briefcase (I always carry a flask with me), pour some salt down its mouth, wipe it off, and to stop the burning in my gut I drink it all, right out of the mouth of the flask. And this all happened in some snack bar—I don't remember the name exactly.

And then. Well honest to God—I don't know what the hell I'm supposed to be judged for. My old man always used to do that, you know. He had two sure cures. Vodka and pepper for a cold, and vodka and salt for stomach trouble. And he would have lived to a ripe old age if the goddam Germans hadn't killed him at the front.

So what do they judge me for so much? And why do they say I was in a state of alcoholic inebriation. And they're bastards you know, the ones that apparently called up my job and said that I was in a state of inebriation. Those bastards lied the whole time about me being in a state of alcoholic inebriation. Because when I was at their place I wasn't in any such state. And when I called them up later in an inebriated condition, they couldn't see over the telephone wires whether I was in a state of alcoholic inebriation or not in a state of alcoholic inebriation. And what they said, about me supposedly talking funny, they're definitely lying about that, telling vicious lies to suit their own needs.

I wasn't talking funny at all. They were just insulted that I was smarter than them and had fooled them. So they decided to let me have it. Ukkh, and I fell right into it.

And here's how I did it. Sure enough, you know, as soon as I had drunk down the vodka the burning in my belly stopped. But if I'm gonna tell it to you straight, the truth is that all of a sudden I had to go real bad.

It was already getting dark. This toilet, which was the real thing, I went into right away; it was next to the train station, and I took an instant dislike to it. Because it was awful dark in there. And some guys came in, and you could hear all sorts of crude jokes, which I'm not about to repeat. Then I took a seat, real carefully too, and started thinking hard.

What I started thinking was how strange life is, how strange all its ups and downs are. Like, what had I been that very morning? A candidate for the scrapheap. And what was I now? A wise member of the team who had brilliantly carried out an industrial duty of great responsibility in spite of all difficulties.

Only—because of the vodka, maybe, or some premonition—I suddenly began feeling really scared. Maybe because the water was gushing and roaring underneath me. And I felt scared first of all by the way the damn water was roaring and on top of that I saw this apparition—I start thinking some hand from under the water is gonna suddenly reach up and grab me from underneath.

I took care of my painful business real fast and got out!

Then it hits me like someone had clubbed me over the head. You fucking fool, what'd you wipe yourself with? You let that dreadful roaring water gush off with the *contract!*

Oh man, did I let out a moan, and covered with teensy little beads of sweat, I ran to call up that hellhole of a hothouse farm. And there they tell me I must be drunk, that I had fraudulently tricked the comrade director into a signing a paper, which he had signed without being fully brought up to date on the matter. And again that I was not in a sober condition and that a tumbril was on its way to my home establishment with the signatures of two witnesses.

"They from Norilsk, these thieving witnesses of yours, by any chance?" I growled into the phone and hung up after telling them off, not knowing any other weapon to use against the misery of life coming down on me like a leaden weight.

And then? What next? Then what did I have to lose? That damn *belyasha* poisoning was still gnawing at me, so I had some more vodka with salt. To make a long story short, I keeled over on the street, but thank God I wasn't taken to a drunk tank but to an emergency ward. And there this doctor, Tsarev, honest to God, I'm not lying, he could barely stay on his feet himself, a great big, fat guy, bearded like a wild animal, and he grunts:

"How your family can put up with you, I can't imagine. It's types like you who are destroying the family as an institution."

"Ah, you hog! You can go straight to hell, if your fat ass doesn't beat you there!"

I couldn't take this guy any more, vomiting the way I was. So then a tumbril got sent for me from there too. And now I'm of two minds, my very own self—whether to go after them or to go on to other things. So there you have it, lad.

Having finished, he opened his eyes, which had been closed from strong emotion since the beginning of the story, and discovered that the waiting room was almost empty. The women with their bags, the girls with their suitcases, the peasant men and women, and the citizen with his newspaper—all were gone. Only the tattooed youth was still there, sleeping peacefully, resting his curly head on his massive fist.

"Hey, Kent," the storyteller shook him.

"Waddya want, waddya want," the lad mumbled in his sleep.

"Get up! Get up!"

A stern cleaning woman stood over them.

"What are you yelling about, troublemakers?" she shouted, leaning proudly on her high mop handle.

"We—we weren't doing anything," the old guy quieted down. "We're waiting for the electric. To Kubekovo."

"To Kubekovo!" she smiled sarcastically. "Your electric to Kubekovo left long ago. Clear out. I have to mop."

"But can't we," he became even more timid. "Can't we wait for the next one, little mother?"

"The next one, little *cousin*," she said spitefully, "won't be here till tomorrow, your next electric to Kubekovo."

"That's OK, we'll wait till morning," the old guy suggested.

"But this here, didn't you see this?"

The dame was giving him the finger. The guitarist woke up.

"Hey, what's all the noise?" he barked. "What's with you woman, you trying to mess us over? One more minute and I'll let you have it."

"And me—I'll call a cop," she began to squeal as she retreated, this woman well on in years.

"Hey, don't do that," the old guy yipped like he'd been stung.

"You're exactly right, what you say, dad," the young man loftily agreed. "We don't have any use for a policeman at all. Let's get out of here, old man."

"Where to?"

"Somewhere. We'll find somewhere."

"Yeah, but where? Where?"

"Well, come one, we'll go sing . . . that's why no money's comin' in."

"Well, let's go," said the old guy.

And off they went somewhere.

4. The Gold Plate

Acch, fellow citizens! Listen for a while to an unceremonious person who is totally disillusioned with time, because I'm not going to lie! Because *there's no fooling around with time*, and I'm telling you straight. You see I had this terrific Victory wristwatch, of native manufacture, with "shockproof" printed on it. It ran just fine till one day when I accidentally dropped it on the sidewalk and it stopped dead, requiring six rubles, ten kopeks for the repair of a "hair spring," as the watch repairman told me, in his white coveralls and with a bright purple pimple on his forehead, exactly like the beauty spot on a Hindu woman's brow in a movie.

OK. I still didn't know that *you can't fool around with time*, and I handed over six rubles, ten kopeks, along with the watch, to the care of this pimply Hindu, and he told me to come back in six days. There you go.

But I don't despair. I have hope in what's left. And what's left is a grandfather clock of an ancient type, with a cuckoo that pops out. But in an instant that too starts to groan and hiss. And this prerevolutionary cuckoo sticks its head out, says "cuck—" in a sickly voice, and that's all it says, and it doesn't go back inside, and its weights just hang there ugly and limp.

What of it, you say? But knowing from the experience of my own wallet a trifle can run as high as the aforementioned six rubles, ten kopeks, I wasn't about to revisit that efficient representative of the watch and clock industry. Instead I kept modestly hoping that *some-thing* would turn up. Because, first of all, it's characteristic of a normal person, who isn't sick, to always keep hoping for *something*. And second, I still had an ordinary, three-ruble workhorse of an alarm clock which always woke me up, plain working man that I am, to get me to the office, where I had always showed up late, and where I was about to start showing up later than ever. Because it must be said that after these few incidents I was getting totally disillusioned with time.

Still, that doesn't have any special relevance. And you should stop thinking I've gotten disillusioned with time in any *specific* sense. I—well, I didn't express myself exactly right, probably, because I said you can't fool around with time, but what I was disillusioned with was timepieces, seeing no good in them at all and justifiably seeing nothing in them but harm, verging on criminal injury. And I'll explain why.

The reason is because of the *strange* thing—excuse me, comrades, but a really *strange* thing happened with my last line of defense, my workhorse-alarm clock. And what happened was right out of either the movie *Romance of Two Lovers* or some musical romance by the composer Glinka, as sung on Channel One by some velvet-voiced singer with a piano in the background.

My girl friend Svetlana, Light of my Life,* all ruddy from the bracing Siberian air, comes in. All red in the face from the icy air, and sly as a fox, with her naughty brown eyes gleaming deep and unfathomable as our Motherland itself. This rotten scum, all red in the face, announces to me:

"I've come to tell you, because it's the only honest thing, that I'm getting married."

"And you've already applied for your license?" I express my interest, sitting there all the while on a little stool with nothing on but my underwear and socks.

"I have," she answers me bravely.

"So tell me this, dear Svetochka," I continued to show curiosity. "Does your shithead know where you are at this very moment? Or should I call him so that he'll fly here on the wings of his love to gather up his spoiled goods once and for all, full of amazement and suffering and numbness, just like the Lensky fellow in *Onegin*, who in the end caught a bullet, one he didn't deserve maybe, but still an honest-to-God bullet in his dear little love-enflamed brain?"

At these bitter but justified words of mine, Svetlana, Light of My Life, burst into real tears and began to be wracked by deep, authentic sobs.

But before that she threw the alarm clock at me. A jet-propelled throw, but still she missed.

I was pretty upset too and suggested to Sveta, after putting my arm around her neck, that she calm down. Sveta sobbed for a while. We showered each other with numerous kisses and soon got real close and tender, like never before. We cooed and cuddled each other, but when I announced at last that we should have a serious talk, Sveta

---

*The author uses the Russian word *svet*, meaning light, to make a series of puns with forms of the name *Svet*lana, such as *Svet*ka, *Svet*lyachok, etc. [tr.].

started laughing insultingly, roughly pushed away my probing hand, got up, and quickly began to get dressed.

I was about to start saying: "Of course you can't say that I never told you this before . . ."

But, without directing one nasty word at me, she silently kissed me goodbye and walked out, slamming the door on me, it would seem, forever. I figured this out right away as soon as I heard that her application was already in at the marriage registration office.

I understood. And I also realized that I had been left alone, sorry creature that I was, all alone in the world without Sveta, and with a total absence of time.

Oh, how dreary! There you are, your Sveta has left you, your last bulwark in a cruel world, wearing her fuzzy wool scarf. Svetlana, Light of My Life, maybe I love you badly but I love you all the same and I don't want anyone else, because they're all alike. Here, my Sveta has gone, my symbol of light, and I don't even have a TV, because it's a symbol of philistinism, and they've turned off the radio in my place because I didn't pay the bill, and I can't read the paper, because some heartless maniacs keep stealing it out of my mail box. Oh, how dreary! How lousy!

And it gets to be dark. Myself, I live on the fifth floor of a large apartment building, and I work with moderate and steady success at my main profession—in a laboratory for the scientific organization of labor, which supposedly determines certain norms and rates, but in fact, if I had my way, I'd close it down completely and for good, as an extremely dangerous breeding ground for parasitism and negligence. Judge for yourself. As an engineer I get 120 rubles plus a 20 percent differential for working in Siberia, and every day I suffer miserably because I have—precisely speaking—absolutely nothing to do at work. No more than any of the other sixty-nine members of the staff, who scurry around the corridors with preoccupied looks or sit dumbly at their polished desks. We don't till the soil. We don't sow any grain. We just attempt to organize scientifically what we can't do ourselves. And I'm simply amazed that the government puts up with the existence of such a gang of spongers, who collect their salaries for nothing—one of them being me, because I haven't the courage not to. Oh how dreary! How lousy! And where the hell did that idiot toss my clock?

Deeply vexed by such thoughts, I crawl under the bed and realize with horror, as I crawl out, that never before have I encountered such a strange kind of time, that my alarm clock is ruined now, along with all my other instruments and my life itself.

Because I pick up the clock and see—acch, fellow citizens, I'm not lying!—I see that all three hands of the clock are *bent in a wave pattern!*

In a wave pattern! Imagine. Like the ripples in a Russian pond, where an athlete is resting next to the bathhouse, waiting for his Olya, who's wearing white—a gal with a braid, with a kind of waxen complexion. Or like the scraggly piece of string of a child at play, who makes a snake out of it among the municipal sandboxes and brightly colored mushroom stools for children. Or like . . . but what's the point of comparisons? I always knew Svetka had a poetic nature, but this! To chuck an alarm clock in such a romantic way? Without even breaking the glass, to make all three hands, as though wracked with passion, bend in a *wave pattern!?* I gained a great deal more respect for Sveta and, longing for her with immense feeling, I began to cry, because I realized once and for all that this was a total fiasco.

After which I went to bed. Someone who's suffered a total fiasco needs to sleep and not to dream, and as much as possible, not to wake up. Because when he wakes up he's got to participate in something, be doing something wholeheartedly. But someone who's suffered a total fiasco can't and shouldn't participate in anything. I'm telling you straight, based on this bitter experience which I'm recounting.

Right. So I went to sleep. But I woke up again right away, because the wavily-bent alarm clock went off just then, with piercing tones, golden and sad, although there was no call for it to do that. I, for example—excuse me for the clumsy joke—but for example, I never asked it to do that.

And then it began. And later it all ended up badly, very badly, because—Christ!—that goddamned ex-alarm clock kept *ringing and ringing all by itself!*

Whether the mechanism had subtly shifted into the realm of perpetual motion or whether it was some other antiscientific thing, I don't know, but I swear, and I'm not lying—may I be frozen to the spot—I swear, all I had to do was tremble slightly and it would start, ringing and ringing and ringing.

Well, what's to be done, in your opinion, in such a nightmare situation, when a person's feeling a lot of grief and needs to sleep? Smash the clock with a hammer? Take a sleeping pill? I couldn't use a hammer; enough noise was already coming from my place. As for the sedative, what would I want to use narcotics for? They always give me a headache and my eyelids stick together, and in the morning I flounder around like a broiled carp in heavy sour cream.

That's how the wee hours of the night found me. Tossing and groaning, while the springs of the bed groaned and squeaked, and the crystal in the cupboard kept up a steady conversation with the glass.

Acch, Svetka, Svetka the creep, I always knew, dear Svetka Svetlanochka, that someday this would happen. Svetochka would up and tire of me, and go off with some faker or other. And no one is capable of understanding why I wouldn't try to keep her, wouldn't kiss her and pronounce her my lawful wife in the local marriage registration office. What was holding me back? Was it time or what? Time? Or what?

Tossing from side to side and groaning, I rolled over with a groan, and tossed around some more. I tossed around till I was all tossed out, with the dawn beginning to show through the frozen wintry windows and the audible shutters of houses beginning to bang, out on the street. People were on their way to build, to construct, and here, poor, weak thing that I was, I hadn't even slept yet.

Well, then I really began to go wild and came close to passing out.

Time! That hateful agglomeration of jerky little gear wheels that jostle and catch on each other and supplement and negate each other, shuddering and shaking. And the ringing, the ringing, the goddamned ringing.

I looked and looked at this savage thing, listened and listened, then picked it up and threw what was left of time out the window.

But you can't fool around with time.

Because immediately after the process of throwing the alarm clock out the window there came from below the woeful cry of a wounded individual.

"Ay-ay-ay, I've been killed," a man cried.

I stuck my head out the window and saw such a sight that right then I flew down the stairs pell-mell. "Ay-ay-ay. I've been killed."

There on all fours in the white snow was a total stranger, dyeing the snow red with blood from his head, which he was holding onto, shouting: "Ay-ay-ay, I've been killed."

"Ay-ay-ay, I've been killed," he continued to shout. Although if he'd really been killed, he'd be lying on the snow dead, whereas what had happened was a simple thing, a fairly substantial alarm clock had landed on him pretty hard.

"Well now, who's done you wrong, poor soul?" I shouted at him as I drew near.

"Don't get gloomy! Don't get gloomy! Just don't get glum!" shouted the wounded man, getting up off all fours and holding his wounded head. "I swear you won't have to sit in jail because of me."

"There's no reason for me to sit anywhere, most noble and unfortunate soul," I shouted when I came quite close to this craftily smiling fellow with his ruffled exterior and outlandish behavior.

"You know very well, my friend, that when the question is considered properly you will sit in jail, like a good fellow," the man stuck to his guns.

I got depressed.

"Yeah, but no need to despair," the good man consoled me. "No problem. Better if you give me what money I'll need and I'll go to the doctor and, with you paying the bill, he'll put a gold plate in my head."

"But maybe it'd be better to put in a plate of some lightweight material, like aluminum?" I cautiously inquired.

"No, a gold one's what I need," the poor sufferer insisted.

"Yeah, but why a gold one?" I still didn't understand.

"So it'll cost more," the cheerful vagabond brazenly explained.

And he added, looking at me searchingly.

"What do you say? Shall we go to the police and put it on the record?"

I opened my mouth, intending to give him a razor-sharp tongue lashing, but suddenly I felt sorry for this beggar, as though he was my comrade in some lonely misfortune.

"Stay here," I ordered, and I flew upstairs and was back in an instant with five rubles paper money.

"Now that's something!" the injured party went into raptures.

A moment after which, he went out of his mind, that is, started acting like an idiot again.

The blood is streaming down and he's singing:

> *You feel light at heart*
> *From a pension so fine . . .*

This seeming idiot took my money and went off singing and bowing, assuring me not to worry. That he'd have a gold plate in his head for sure, so there was nothing to worry about.

But was I worrying? I had only done what I had out of feelings of humanism. You think it was because the clock fell out the window? No. That was an occurrence that could unquestionably be called an accident. An accident and that's all! Do you think such things happen so rarely? Acch, you alarm clock! It's as though you had fallen on my head and not this fool's. As though you'd landed on me and knocked all the sufferings out of my fool head, all my worries and torments.

Because actually everything worked out fine real soon. I got to know another girl. Her name is Katya and I've promised her some day we'll go to the marriage office. At work I've been made group leader, and of course you can laugh at me but I've actually fallen in love with my work and even get a certain kick out of it. My wrist watch now is fixed and gleams upon my arm. The cuckoo is cuckooing again, and I've got a new three-ruble alarm clock. Everything, nearly everything, is straightened out.

And I really love that fool of a man for that. I love that hard-core long-time resident, who's lived in our city from way back, Misha the fool. I'm always glad to see him when I run into him in the least expected places.

Here he is dealing in second-hand goods—used radio tubes and photo portraits of various stars. His clothing: worn velvet trousers, a knapsack, and a bowler hat.

Here he is in a bookstore. Conversing importantly with the salesgirls on some salacious topic. Unshaven. Spit spraying from his gap-toothed mouth.

And here he has climbed up on a high pedestal alongside the

executive committee building. He's climbed up and he's shouting something. What's he shouting? Let's get closer and listen:

> Golden plate! Golden plate!
> Life's tragedy I turn to farce.
> Golden plate! Golden plate!
> From New York to Resheta!
> From Kozulka—to Mars!

And I look at him, resting my hand on the hand of my dear and charming Katya. I look at him and think. I think. I think. What do I think? Have no fear. I don't think a damn thing.

5. "A Night Watchman—He Went Out of His Mind"

On that special day for him, the watchman Kudryavtsev showed up toward evening as usual for his nightly stint guarding the *sharashka*[*] across from the five-story, multiple-apartment residential building where the scientist Valka Kuzmicheva lived and where she was visited by her lover, Abramov, a former engineer and office worker.

Valka had put some chicken soup on to cook, but when Abramov, with his own key, opened the door, she turned her back on him.

"Oho, how angry we are today. And still pouting even," said Abramov.

Valka said nothing.

"What a weird dream I had this morning," said Abramov, "There was this woman, all in tears, dressed in old clothes, and you couldn't see her face. What does a dream like that mean, do you know?"

"The application for work. Did you put it in?" Valka asked, staring at the wall.

"Look, Valek, don't you see?" Abramov began to whine. "Work? Work's just alienation! An office? I can't work in an office. I go out of my mind in one. The percentage ratio between fantasy and reality in an office doesn't agree with me—"

"But loafing around agrees with you, reading your idiot books," Valka cried out, turning at last to face her beloved, a man of complex psychological make-up.

"Besides, I keep falling asleep and hurting my head from hitting it on the desk, in an office," Abramov explained in a smooth voice. "I'll wait and see, Valek, look into things more—"

"Time for you to be a doorman! Sweep the streets. What'd you get a college education for? Why waste the people's money?" Valka was on the offensive. But just then the soup boiled over and Valka rushed to save it, leaving Abramov in peace for the moment.

Let us leave them too, and go back to the watchman. He showed up

[*] Special, top-security research establishment [tr.].

for duty with the usual watchman's supply—a piece of smoked lard, a hunk of heavily salted bread, and the magazine *Ogonyok*. However, as has been stated, this was a special day for Kudryavtsev, which is why he also brought along a full 0.25 liters of home-distilled sugarbeet vodka.

"Okay," some impatient reader will exclaim. "What was so special about this watchman's nightly round?" And I hasten to explain. The only reason this became a special day for night watchman Kudryavtsev, Dmitry Alekseevich, was that it was the day Kudryavtsev went out of his mind. But prior to that, he had decided to take possession of the sharaskha manager's sofa. (Don't worry. I'm not about to clutter up the mind of the reader—neither the impatient reader nor any other kind—with this manager's last name.)

The boss in question owned a very beautiful sofa. It was all leather, down to the last little crease; and, along with a small mirror, it furnished the boss's office, on the wall of which a portrait of the leader hung, in the corner of which a scarlet banner gathered dust, and the entire middle of which was occupied by a polished desk forming a large, fat capital letter *T*.

The watchman, exulting, drank down his vodka, devoured his lard, and finished off his bread. But before lying down on the sofa in the office, the keys to which he had lifted, he began to reminisce.

He recalled his whole long working life. How he had always dreamed of sleeping on a sofa like this. And how he had first seen a leather sofa back in '34, when he was just a boy. And how his heart had pounded! And how he had striven since then, and raised himself up and fallen down, and risen and fallen again, enriching his life with much experience. But he had never despaired because he knew in the future *it* would be—it, the sofa. Dear little sofa.

The memories dragged on, and the watchman felt weary. He yawned and headed over to close the blinds, so that the yellow moon would not be blasting him in the eys when at last he met up with his sofa.

"Shish! Wouldn't give me the keys!" the watchman muttered sternly as he made his way toward the window. "You'll start sleeping on the sofa, they said. Now they'll see what they get. I'll sleep on it all right, and every shift from here on out, goddam them," he muttered sternly, making his way through the darkened furniture to the window.

And when he got there, he was lost in an instant, for as he looked mournfully out the window he saw the multi-apartment residential building in which, on account of the late hour, only Valka's light shone through the blinds. And through the blinds—or more exactly, over the top of some thick curtains—Kudryavtsev the watchman saw a sight that made him grab for the window jamb, barely managing to keep himself up on legs that had turned to butter.

Valka Kuzmicheva and Abramov had eaten their soup, drunk a bottle of wine, and now had embarked on a serious conversation about Abramov marrying Valka officially through the registration office. A serious conversation they had had every week, twice a week, for the past five years.

The conversation always ended up this way. And since—through lengthy training, practice, and repetition—they had each acquired such superhuman skill, artistry, and inventiveness at what they did, the night watchman could only stare at their union, and stare and stare and stare. Then he let out a howl and began to tear the cheap but sturdy clothing off his back.

The next morning, Abramov, a worn-looking man of thirty-two, was leaving the house at dawn, ever so cautiously, so as not to compromise the lady of his heart in the eyes of her neighbors. So that this learned woman, holder of a candidate of sciences degree, would not be asked some boorish question, prefaced by a hollow remark like, "Excuse us, Valechka, it may be none of our business, but. . . ."

So then. Abramov was leaving on tiptoe. And as he came tiptoeing out, the dashing and solicitous young Abramov became a witness to two unique events simultaneously—the disintegration of a personality and the first stage in the care of the mentally ill.

On the peak of the slate roof, with his unshaven face turned to the rising sun, a man sat naked and blue, swinging a scarlet banner before him. He was singing a song, the words of which could not be distinguished except for the word *sofa*. Actually, all the other words could be distinguished, but they are all unprintable.

"_____ _____, sofa," sang the watchman.

"Who in the world is tha-at!" asked Abramov avidly of a bored but pleasant-looking young man, wearing sideburns, a white medical coat, and jeans. The young man took a drag on his cigarette and languidly observed the watchman.

"It's a night watchman—he went out of his mind. And we're a psychiatric team," explained the young man, flipping his cigarette away and pointing to some other young men clambering up the fire escape with something white in their hands.

"And what's that white thing? Isn't that a straitjacket?" Abramov began to get excited.

"Those are special restraining garments. Our medical science stopped using straitjackets long ago," the young man looked condescendingly at Abramov.

"And how come you're not up there?" said Abramov.

"I've been going to night school," said the young man. "Completed all the requirements at the food-industry institute. Tomorrow I'm taking charge of a restaurant. Got sick of this. Deadly! But they pay you, man, I'll tell you straight, they pay fucking good!"

"Take off that white coat, fella. It's an orderly's life for me!" said Abramov.

6. An Old Idealist Fairytale

Under the direct rays of the sun beating down on the Ukrainian Soviet Socialist Republic, three roommates at a health resort were basking on the pebbly beach—Doctor Valery Mikhailovich Tsarev, Colonel Schein, and a certain Ryabov, not an altogether ordinary person.

The conversation dragged along listlessly. The doctor's remarks dealt mainly with the miraculous properties of a cure with the idiotic name *mumiyo*. The doctor himself had headed a research group the previous year, hunting for this medicinal substance in the evergreen forests near the Sayan range. And had found it. And now was telling about it. The colonel puffed and wheezed in reply. But Ryabov remained silent, stretched out on a chaise-lounge, wearing gold-rimmed spectacles. He was timid, withdrawn, a mournful type. He didn't hit it off with people very easily.

Gradually, as tends to happen, the conversation turned from the particular to the general. Tsarev started talking about all the miraculous things which, in spite of science, still exist in our life.

"Because science is the enemy of everything miraculous," he averred, stroking his black, wiry beard, "where there is science, there is no room for the miraculous. And vice versa."

"Absolutely true," Schein agreed. But Ryabov again held his tongue.

"Dogs, for example," the doctor rambled blandly on. "They don't need any medicine. They seek out certain grasses by themselves. And so, as it turns out, all of our scientific research institutes are nothing in comparison with an ordinary Rover's sense of smell."

"Well now," puffed the colonel, "What you say there, heh-heh, there's a definite denial in that of your own science of Hippocrates."

As you can see, the conversation was taking an interesting turn.

"Nuh," suddenly said Ryabov.

The friends looked at him.

"What does your 'Nuh' mean, lad?" asked the colonel, tensing.

"You don't agree with me?" the doctor was curious.

This made Ryabov terribly embarrassed. He took off his glasses, wiped them, put them back on, and said in a trembling small voice: "What are you saying? I'm *with* you. But also," he hastened to clear things up with the colonel, "I'm not against *you*. I—that is, you and I, doctor—don't deny science as a whole. We simply stress the multifarious nature of existence, isn't that right? You know, only 0.000001 percent of human potential has been tapped. Man, for example, can do anything. He can even, by an effort of will alone, it goes without saying—he can hang in mid-air."

"Wha-at?" the officer was astonished.

"Fly," Tsarev explained with a thin smile. "Our friend is trying to say that a man can fly, all by himself, without anything else, if his mind wishes to. But this," he paused for effect, "this is an old Idealist fairytale."

"Hear-hear," the colonel backed him up.

"Not fly," Ryabov took the liberty of specifying precisely. "Simply —hang in mid-air."

The doctor smiled. These words, however, gave the colonel a terrific urge for some beer. The colonel swallowed, but the doctor addressed Ryabov almost politely:

"And is it given to any ordinary person to do this, or is it only for select individuals?"

"Dunno," Ryabov averted his eyes.

"And you couldn't demonstrate such a miraculous occurrence for us, could you?"

"I could," Ryabov said quietly.

"But of course you don't want to," the doctor chuckled.

"Don't want to, but I can. In fact, I can in spite of not wanting to," Ryabov sounded all mixed up.

The doctor politely clapped his hands.

And at that Ryabov partly folded up the chaise, turning it into a chair. He sat on the chair. He tensed himself, and immediately rose slowly into the heavens.

Imagine what a silence followed then.

The colonel breathed with his mouth open.

The doctor asked, hiccupping:

"Well? What can you see up there?"

Ryabov's mournful voice came down from above.

"The cosmos! An abyss of stars has opened. Tremendous! A cloud's eternal heavenly pages! All of philosophy! Besides, it seems there's a women's beach next door, covered with naked female bodies."

"Completely naked? Really?" the colonel caught his breath.

"Naturally naked," Ryabov shouted down, mournful as ever.

"And can you see all their . . . er . . . charms?" the doctor grew animated.

"Well . . ."

"So come on now, Ryabov. You take us up with you," the colonel began bustling about. And he turned to the doctor:

"Valery Mikhalych, tell him to take us!"

"Ryabov!" the doctor shouted. "You hear?"

"Can't be done," replied Ryabov, dejectedly but emphatically.

"Well, Ryabov, we didn't know you were such a selfish pig," the colonel said bitterly.

"You said it," the doctor drily supported the colonel's position.

"It's the truth; can't be done," said Ryabov plaintively. Nevertheless he came down fast and hard.

The doctor and the colonel leaped over and grabbed on. But the chair couldn't take the extra weight and soon fell back onto the spot where it had stood before. It fell, causing a definite hush to come over the people on the beach who had been the unwitting and amazed observers of what we have described.

All of the roommates except Ryabov went rolling down the pebbled beach, doing a certain amount of harm to their bodies. The doctor made a grim joke, as he wiped away a trickle of blood:

"There you have it! A fact, as they say, hits you right in the face."

A black and blue lump was emerging under the colonel's eye.

But Ryabov said nothing. He sat quietly on the chair. One glance at him made it clear that he was not an altogether ordinary person. Such people are dangerous for society, and as soon as they make their appearance anywhere in a public place, they should be made to show their documents! Such people are dangerous to society. It wouldn't be a bad idea to isolate such people from society entirely, somewhere as far away as possible.

7. A Manuscript Consisting of One Poem

Once upon a time on Zasukhin Street they decided to tear down or move all the old wooden houses, so they could build a laboratory for the Polytechnical Institute in their place.

For this purpose three workers came and dug a seven-meter trench, long and narrow, and when they were finished someone from the engineering and technical staff (ETS) showed up, and after sliding down into the trench, climbed back out with samples of the sand and clay, which constituted a cross-section of the Quaternary deposits in this locality.

The local residents, who by then had formed a crowd around the trench, began to tug timidly at the ETSer's sleeve, eager to learn the results of the investigation; some even invited him home, promising to regale him with vodka and cold cuts.

But he turned out to be a cynical, arrogant, and bilious type. He gave the finger to the assembled public, and drove off in a GAZ-51 car, pursued by unpleasant looks, having seated the workmen in the car and himself taking the wheel.

And not right away, not the very next day, but two days or a week later another official appeared on Zasukhin Street, not an engineer this time but a social worker.

He listed all the residents in his little notebook and said that the tearing down and removal of homes was actually going to happen and that, where their wooden miseries had once stood, soon there would be the gleaming glass of a new Polytechnical laboratory; and that they themselves would be given well-furnished living quarters, at the equivalent of nine square meters per person, in the new, experimental, northeast district—with bathrooms and toilets, the like of which they'd never seen.

Hearing this news, many burst into tears because they felt sorry for their old nests, and many began shouting because they couldn't wait to have their own bathroom, toilet, and hot running water, and the sooner the better. And not to have to go to the street pump for water, which up until then sometimes had frozen in the winter, so that they had to pour gasoline over it and set it on fire.

Some began to weep, some to laugh, but they were all listed on the pad of this man who had come from wherever it is they decide what to tear down and what to build, every last case.

So what then? Well, being on the list, they actually were soon given well-furnished apartments in a new microdistrict.* Of course there was a lot of dissatisfaction and some disputes. Some people weren't given apartments on their desired floor. Some felt uncomfortable with the amount of living space assigned them (expressed in square meters)—it seemed small after their own roomy places. Others were angered by the whole thing—it was much too far, they said, to drag yourself from the microdistrict to the places they usually went to for work, for shopping, for the drugstore, and for the movies.

But all the relocated persons, without exception, were happy about the hot running water and, especially, the gas. They turned the gas on this way and that, large burner and small, and would surely have blown the building sky high if the inspector from CITGAS, the municipal gas works, hadn't made the rounds every day and showed them how to handle the gas properly, so as not to mess it up.

So, on the whole, in spite of everything, they were all eventually satisfied.

And the conversation—or more precisely, not the conversation but the story—now turns to how the residents dealt with the wooden immovable assets which had belonged to them for so many years, property which by no means ceased to belong to them upon their being transferred, as renting tenants, to goverment-owned apartments.

The residents disposed of their properties in extremely varied ways.

Some simply chucked everything. Spat once and that was it. Hell with it, damn house, so to say.

---

*In Soviet town planning, a microdistrict is a neighborhood complex built to include both residential units and essential services [tr.].

Others sold their houses cheaply.

Still others, luckiest of all, sold their houses as homes, for real money.

They were purchased by social organizations—for example, collective farms—so that, by carting the timbers and lumber out to the village, they could set up a store there.

The houses also were purchased by individual citizens, so that they could haul the lumber out to the suburbs and reassemble it to make cheap summer houses.

On the whole, they all disposed of their houses somehow or other and received money for them, some more, some less—it varied from one to the other.

The only one to miss out was Vaska Kharabarov. This was very odd considering Vasily had spent five years in jail for some shady dealings, knew everything there was to know, and feared nothing.

His trouble was, he kept hemming and hawing, looking for a better deal. When they offered to buy his house for firewood, he wouldn't agree to that, and of course, from one point of view he was right.

But why, one wonders, did he refuse when the Eighth of March producer's cooperative wanted to take his house as an infirmary? That was incomprehensible.

He fiddled and fooled around so long that suddenly no more offers were coming in and the houses were going to be torn down within a matter of days.

Not in vain, however, had Vasily been in trouble with the law and been absent so long from his native haunts. He found a way out of this trying situation, and a brilliant one at that.

There were two young specialists living with some people in a temporary barracks. They had come from Moscow, but they hadn't been given the kind of quarters they were supposed to get as young specialists. And they weren't getting the 150 ruble salary with the 20 percent increment that they'd been dreaming about all through those long years as students eating margarine.

They were only getting 108 rubles, including their travel allowance *and* the 20 percent bonus. On top of that this city didn't please them because of its industrial grime, old-fashioned way of life and, apparently, the savage Siberian boorishness of its inhabitants.

They longed for Moscow. For some reason they yearned to be back at the institute, warming themselves in the sun, sitting in some little university garden on the Manezhnaya, since renamed the Fifty Years of October Square. They yearned for the Kazbek shashlik house by the Nikita Gates, yearned for the Metropol movie house, even yearned for the Lenin Library, which they had entered only on extremely rare occasions.

It was to them that Vasily made an offer to sell his fine home.

And when they courteously refused, stating they didn't have the kind of money you needed to buy a house, he filled them in on his scheme.

He told them that it really didn't matter so much whether the house was standing or not, that they should draw up a deed of purchase, and if they had a deed of ownership, the executive committee would be obliged to assign them an apartment too.

At first they laughed. But they they got to thinking—what if they didn't succeed in making their escape from this assigned location as soon as they thought?

So they paid Vasily Kharabarov almost all the money they had in their pockets and moved into his house expecting someone to arrive and give them an order to relocate into the northeast district, which consisted exclusively of glass and concrete structures.

It was evening and in their hands they had the notarized deed for which they had paid Kharabarov, but they didn't know that Kharabarov had tricked them, as well as another comrade to whom he had also sold the house, and had tricked the state too, getting an apartment from it for the twice-sold home.

It was evening when the two young specialists arrived at their new quarters. They brought hardly anything with them except some vodka, and they made themselves at home, nipping at the bottle, and waiting for morning to announce to some official that they were homeowners and that the government was obliged to give them an apartment in the new microdistrict, where there was brick, there was glass, and there was concrete.

They were cheerful and full of ideas. They talked about this and that. They cursed many things and praised many things, getting pie-eyed, with only onions to snack on.

And late at night they went out to get some air and to get away from the stifling heat that had built up in the peasant house after they had stoked Vaska's old stove red hot.

They saw that there were myriads of stars in the sky, and on the earth an absence of light. And there were houses—some half-demolished by bulldozers, others still fully intact, but dark, empty, black; and some weren't even houses, but only foundations, with the houses gone, holes full of the rubbish of many years, with fresh gray snow filling them fuller.

"I feel a little scared," said one young specialist. "I'm afraid they might not give us an apartment."

"That's not excluded," the second young specialist put in his two cents worth as he continued to gaze at the stars. "But you and I, do we give a damn?"

"I only feel bad about the money," the first one concluded, and the drunken young specialists went back inside their low-cost acquisition.

And they drank on. And on. Already they could see themselves in the gleaming new experimental microdistrict, already they had settled in as permanent residents of this town, putting their roots down here, each raising a family, becoming respected old-timers, making a fuss over their grandchildren. They would speak at Young Pioneer assemblies, in years to come, in their capacity as honorary Pioneers, as people who could still remember our stormy and disaster-ridden times.

And one of them then said to the other:

"Did you know I have a manuscript consisting of one poem dedicated to you?"

"No," replied the other.

And they stood up and put their hands on each other's shoulders and began to look into each other's eyes.

Just then there came a terrible crash. The house shook and the plaster began to break and fall on the young specialists' heads. They quickly removed themselves from the danger zone—out to where an SMU-2 bulldozer was knocking houses down even before dawn, doing its part to enlarge and consolidate the area for new construction.

At this the look of serious and deep emotion passed from their faces. For the manuscript consisting of one poem, which one of them, drunk as a dog, had dedicated to the other that very night, had perished forever in the debris of their new home.

8. Dark Forest

Many messy situations in this life can be explained, it seems, quite simply—by differences in temperament. One person, let's say, is so cheerful and jolly that no matter what happens to him, it doesn't bother him a bit; he just shrugs it off and goes on living. But another will take any bit of nonsense as solemnly as a judge, put on a long face and be so hypersensitive that you can't do a thing with him.

That's how it was in this case too. Tsarkov-Kolomensky went and blurted out to Vasilyev's woman that on Saturday he and Vasilyev had taken a trip into the forest "to feast our eyes on the autumnal grandeur." But the woman, whom Vasilyev stubbornly refused to marry, knew right away that if they had taken a trip into the forest, they couldn't have gone in any direction but the state farm "Successful" where Vasilyev's old heart-throb Tanya was teaching at a school for idiots (who called her Tanya the Inquisition). Supposedly she was living in a godforsaken backwoods area, but in fact she was a whore the likes of which the world had never seen. And she was working in this "hole" because it wasn't far from the city and because she earned a 15 percent bonus for the alleged "hardship conditions," although what those were it was impossible to tell.

So Vasilyev's woman went to his place and made a scene. Vasilyev broke out in red blotches all over and began yelling at her that she was depriving him of his freedom of thought, and after she had sobbed her fill and powdered her face he sent her out the door. But he remained and began to pace around the room, senselessly seating himself over and over in the armchair, touching his forehead, chewing his mustache, and rumpling his hair.

Again someone knocked at the door. He opened it and there, kneeling like a clown, was his friend-betrayer, V. Tsarkov-Kolomensky, who said:

"Come on now, forgive me, brother. I don't know how a thing like this ever happened. Well, so I made it with her. But who was to know? Come on now, you forgive me, brother. What do you say we have a drink in expiation of my guilt?"

Vasilyev looked down at him. He looked and looked and then he slammed the door, without saying a single offensive word to the other man, his friend.

And therefore Tsarkov-Kolomensky didn't feel offended. Still it was rather awkward to stay on his knees. The jolly fellow stood up, brushed off his trousers, spat down the stairwell, and began heading down in the same direction his spit had taken.

However, as he was leaving the entryway he was nearly knocked over by an agitated young man in a mohair scarf.

"Easy on the running there, young man," lectured Tsarkov-Kolomensky. But the young man looked at him blankly, didn't answer, and went flying up the stairs.

Soon he was knocking at the door of Vasilyev's apartment.

"What do you want?" Vasilyev inquired drily, because he vaguely recognized this young man. His name was something like Sanechka.

"Me? What do I want?" the young man suddenly started to smile. "First of all, hello," he said.

"Hello," said Vasilyev sullenly.

"And second, won't you give me a sip of water? I'm very thirsty."

"I don't begrudge you the water," said the man of the house, "but look for it some place else," and he tried to close the door.

"Hey, wait a minute, wait a minute . . ." The young man rolled his eyes wildly, sniffing like mad, and even rose on his tiptoes for some reason, craning his neck in a disgusting way. Vasilyev was thoroughly fed up and began shoving him out the door. But the young man proved difficult, hard to handle. Breathing heavily, they tussled but subsided again, ending up in their original positions in the narrow hallway.

"Maybe now you'll let me through!" the young man exclaimed. "I want to see everything with my own eyes."

"But . . . you're here for that?" The man of the house suddenly understood, and sneered. "Well come in, brother, go ahead, be my guest."

The young man plunged into the room.

"But she's not here!" the youth cried out, wringing his hands. "Where is she?"

The man of the house smirked.

"So it turns out she's cheated on us both!" cried the youth. "And you? You accept that?"

"Get out," said the man of the house. "You get the hell out, sucker, rube, greenhorn, ignormaus, cretin, jerk. Get out of here."

"You . . . take it easy. You know I'm a boxer," Senechka (or whatever) shouted with his last bit of strength. Then he broke down in hysterical sobs and, backing up sideways, dragged himself out of the place. He tumbled out of the apartment like a key from a pocket.

The man of the house locked the door. The smirk was still on his face. He went over to the mirror and drew himself up. His handsome head, slightly touched with gray, looked back at him, with a face that was no longer young. He grimaced, stuck out his tongue at himself, sat down at the desk, and began to write:

Many messy situations in this life can be explained, it seems, quite simply by differences in temperament. One person, let's say, is so cheerful and jolly that no matter what happens to him, even something, let's say, that would make others go crazy or hang themselves with a rope, it doesn't bother him a bit. He just shrugs it off and goes on living. But another will take any bit of nonsense as solemnly as a judge, put on a long face, and be so hypersensitive that you can't do a thing with him.

Just then someone knocked on the door again. Vasilyev sighed and went to open it.

In the doorway stood Vasilyev's woman, Tsarkov-Kolomensky, and the recent young visitor.

"I'm just dreaming it's the three of you, right?" said Vasilyev.

"Hey, aren't you awful? You're terrible," the young man said gloatingly, and addressed Vasilyev's woman: "Witty old man, isn't he?"

The guests tumbled into the room in a bunch and spread out to the various chairs. A bottle of wine appeared on the table.

But near the state farm "Successful" at a school for disturbed children a boy named Vanya Kulachkin could not understand at all what this strange Auntie in make-up wanted of him. What little squares? What little birds? Why? Where? Who was she, this Auntie? Where was Mama? Why was Mama white and shaking her head? Why was the spider eating and eating the fly, but never eating it all?

"Vanya, you know, I asked you a question," said Tanya the Inquisition angrily.

Vanya stood up and slammed down the desktop. "I'm not going to do this anymore," he said.

His eyes were dark, dark blue.

Auntie didn't answer him. She only cracked her slender fingers and went to the window to stare for a long time into the dark forest, which came right up to the school.

The pines and silver firs had been refreshed by a rain. The stern trees had grown still, not moving at all. The road looped through the village like a rope. A bird, heavily flapping its wings, disappeared into the depths of the forest . . .

"Shishkin and Levitan* should be here. Let them sit down opposite one another and paint and paint and paint, the scum!" thought Auntie.

And the picture of those nineteenth-century greats sitting there like that cheered her up a little.

9. Song of First Love

I was at the time frightfully young, had started at the Literary Institute, was working as a loader for the railroad, had rented a room on the outskirts of town, and was writing my *Song of First Love*.

Once when I had eaten my cold soup to carry me through the night and had sat down to work, it sounded like they were about to start in again on the other side of the thin wall. But I stubbornly kept writing, line after line, trying not to be distracted.

For Stepan this was the first time. Never before had he experienced anything like it.

The bed squeaked.

At first Stepan was amazed—where had this unknown, unfamiliar feeling come from? Maybe he was getting sick or was overtired from the heavy physical labor, this young and easily embarrassed fellow from Siberia.

"Stop, stop," the woman murmured, "Wait a little, darling . . ."

And then there came one lovely summer day, when it seemed that all of nature was sunk in a drowsy slumber . . .

The iron legs of the bed went thunk, thunk . . .

It happened to be a rainy summer that year, with incessant fogs starting at dawn and lasting late into the day, and the woods were ghostly—without a twig stirring . . .

"This is simply swinishness," I said quite loudly.

And then as they came out onto a clearing, having carefully parted the damp fern leaves with their hands, a slanting ray of sunshine . . .

A howl or moan from deep in her belly seemed to signal the end, but as usual I was mistaken. They were fighting. Were they strangling each other? I didn't know, but a pleading, hissing whisper, a cry, and the sound of bodies striking against the thin wall were replaced by a blood-curdling song—or was it a hymn? I don't know how to

*Russian nature painters [tr.].

categorize that stupefying stream of vileness with its broken notes, moaning, sobbing, and tears.

She: Oh, finish up; hurry, finish, finish, finish!

He (in a bass voice, breathing heavily): Finish up, sure; but how about starting again?

She and He: We finish, finish in the afternoon,

> In the evening we start again soon,
> Finish in the evening, start again at night,
> Finish in the morning, finish in the afternoon,
> finish in the evening, finish at night.

He (bass voice, heavy breathing): And that's for sure!

Immediately after that, I heard a woman's ratlike squeal. Everything inside me turned over. I flung down my pen and began to bang on the wall. At first the only answer I got was silence and emptiness, but then they began banging on the wall themselves—apparently with all four fists, because my copperplate statuette of Gorky flew off the shelf and hit me hard on the back of my head. I let out a howl and, not knowing what I was doing, leapt out the door and into the snow.

The snow in the gathering dusk was devilishly beautiful, freshly fallen, a pale violet. I nervously started to ring the doorbell at their entranceway, intending to say that after all one couldn't carry on so loudly, that there's a limit to everything, there are certain bounds. . . . But the doorbell didn't seem to be working, so I began kicking the door with my foot.

Then the door flew open, and coming at me I saw a thick-set bearded man with raised fist. Without saying a word he immediately smashed me in the face, drawing blood. But I hadn't been working at the railroad, heaving sacks of grain, for nothing. I hit him back with a sharp uppercut, but didn't knock him off his feet, although he swayed a bit. We grappled, breaking down the fencing. It was late at night, a pointy moon was rising in sharp relief, and the jagged teeth of the pine forest were almost indistinguishable against the sky, although the forest was located right next to our hamlet. With inhuman effort I dodged, grabbed him by the throat with the left hand, and with my right landed another powerful blow. My blood was surging higher and higher. I wanted to hit him again, but just then that vile woman appeared on the porch, barefoot, with a coat flapping open over her bare body. She flew over the snow barefoot and with a screech fastened onto my hair. Her hot, sweaty skin touched my face . . .

It was all over for me right then and there. I was wracked by convulsions. On all fours I crawled off to the side. The bearded man was spitting black blood into the snow. "Hooligan! We'll see you in court," the woman shouted.

I dragged myself home, gathered up what little I had to my name, and left the apartment that very morning, although I had paid the landlady for the whole summer. I finished *Song of First Love* elsewhere, and soon it was published, at first in a magazine and later in a separate edition. With that my literary biography properly begins. Of course I never met those people again and why I even told you this nasty little story I don't know.

I don't know, young man. I don't know . . . Possibly to warn you, because your sincerity strikes a sympathetic chord in me, your belief in "genuine art." Warn you against what? That too I don't know. I just don't know. Figure it out for yourself, young man. Nowadays you're all extremists and you think we of the older generation were all totally blind. No, you can see that wasn't so. But we made our choices, and as for how you are going to live—well now, that's your business, that's up to you to decide. . . .

10 The Reservoir

At first even Buhlik seemed to us a decent sort. He paid good money for a two-story house, with cultivated lot, to the grass widow of Vasil-Vasilka. Vasil, an embezzler of the people's wealth, was sent up for selling things on the side—roofing tin, ceramic floor tile, and steam radiators—which he also offered us in his "good neighborly" way, and we heard him out, heard what he had to say, but we didn't get involved, preferring to walk the straight and narrow. Because we're old time residents of Siberia. Besides, do you think in my own town I couldn't get hold of some damn ceramic crap? What a joke that would be. Besides, that would partly go against the policy of raising living standards and the principles of harnessing the outlying regions of our vast Motherland. Now we're not any of your kulaks, you know; it's just that these days everybody lives well this way, and they're a whole lot better off than your former kulak fools, who tried to get ahead when the time wasn't ripe, tried to leap over the backs of others and not bring anyone along with them. For which they were very severely but justly punished.

But Lord, Lord. God in heaven above. What for, really? How much effort they put in. Used to deliver bottled gas on Saturdays. That was Kosorezov, a wise and clever man. Went to a lot of trouble, thank you very much—could put a machine or a man on a job when he had to. . . . Bushes and bushes of raspberries, beds and beds of strawberries. It was an elegant and heady sight to see, easy on the eyes and comforting to the soul . . . a beautiful, elegant, heady sight to see . . .

But best of all was our reservoir. Lord in heaven, what a reservoir! Constantly fed by crystalline, subterranean waters. Truly, it sweetened our lives on our stifling summer days. In its tender waters our mischievous lads would splash, a merry flock. And our girls, our maidens, like Youth itself, would lie stretched out, like kittens, on the crunchy quartz sand. Studying for their exams or just surrendering themselves to the usual girlish dreams—the life of proud labor before them, a family, marriage, raising children, proper relations between the sexes.

And round about them us—the parents. The women knitting something out of mohair or talking about who was vacationing where in the south or who had bought what new acquisition for the household. Under the willow trees Colonel Zhestakanov and Professor Burevich would do battle in a game of checkers. Mitva-the-Bark-Beetle would argue with the physicist Lysukhin about whether the numbers for different grades of Czech beer corresponded to their actual alcoholic content. Some people worked on crossword puzzles, others on production problems they had encountered on their jobs. And me? I would look at all this and, honest to God, my heart would rejoice, but it would also roll over. The years of hunger during the war, when I was left in the reserves, would come back to me, and I'd remember the time when me and my spouse were number 261, standing in line for corn flour in the black morning blizzard next to the movie theater Rote Front. My leg had gone numb from cold; I couldn't feel my foot in its thick felt boot; couldn't feel it at all. Afterward they rubbed it with goose grease. When I remember that, honest to God, I'd like to personally strangle all these loudmouths and troublemakers with my own two hands. They badmouth everything but they guzzle their fill of shashlik and Pepsi Cola. I wish all those stinking bastards had been in my place, standing in line in 1947. I'd like to see what kind of tune they'd sing then, the sniveling rats.

As for those two young men, who had the look of artists about them—I won't start trying to hide or justify our blunders—at first we actually took a liking to them.

It was theater director Bublik who brought them here, to our town, along with his good-looking wife, the singer. The only good thing about Bublik, the scum, was that during his time as director he often cheered us up by having various celebrities visit Pustaya Chush* (that's the name of our workingman's town). One time you'd see the singer M, parading around, dangling a handkerchief and bellowing "Live in fame and glory"; another time the magician T would amuse everyone by making Zhestakanov's pocket watch disappear and turn up in Mitya-the-Bark-Beetle's boot. Then another time our celebrated portraitist Spozhnikov would be sitting up on the heights, painting a portrait of our reservoir against the background of its natural surroundings. Strange that those intelligent people didn't detect the rotten inner core of this Bublik before we did. Very strange.

Now, at first glance those two were the simplest, most ordinary long-haired kids. But it's not by chance, you know, that we have the

*Literally "Empty Nonsense" [tr.].

old folk saying: some simplicity is worse than thievery. Although it's also true that modesty is a virtue. Well, one of them was kind of tall, a blue-eyed athlete type. The other was more of a weakling, on the dark side, and a little brighter than the first one. Our gals, our young maidens, crowded around in droves when they saw how skillful these fellows were at table tennis. And these boys, no way would they say any low words to the girls or make any vulgar or suggestive gestures. Oh no. They were all modest and above board, you see, those bastards whacking away at their little white ball. Until it happened.

But once it happened, everyone started yelling that we had made it up. What was there for us to "make up"? We didn't have the slightest inkling of anything until all of a sudden the most honest-to-God, out-and-out swinish scandal erupted, the consequences of which are ineradicable, sad, and shameful. Even the dachas are being boarded up tight, the second-hand dealers are scurrying about, rustling through the autumn leaves, the fruit trees are being dug up and carted off for transplanting, and there's no joy in anybody's face, just depression and weariness, disillusionment and fear.

Although with only half a brain we could have guessed right away. They even went around holding hands, not to mention the fact that they obviously, *obviously*, avoided our gals.

And the gals, the little pranksters, were glad to have a laugh. They put the smaller one's hair into little braids, like the Uzbek women do. They smeared some bright lipstick on his mouth. Then they went and looped a spare, empty brassiere over his fairly hefty chest, which was more then standard size. And laugh! My how they laughed.

And all of us, at the time—we laughed too—in our ignorance, and had a good time, while also being aware of a certain vulgarity in this relatively pointed joke. We laughed and had a good time—until it happened.

Lord in heaven! I'll remember it for the rest of my life. You see, the disposition of forces was like this. The pond. Those two on a raft near the shore. The gals right there with them. All of us sitting under the trees. Bublik the director and his wife the singer nowhere to be seen.

The girls had no sooner fastened this harmless female ornament over the younger one's chest than the older one jumped up, turning pale, with his blue eyes getting all dark, and he gives poor Nastya a trained boxer's jab right in the solar plexus from which the poor child, without a murmur, not even an "Ow," falls over on the sand.

We all stood there with our mouths hanging open. But he didn't waste a second. He cut loose the raft and in the wink of an eye the pair of them were out in the middle of the reservoir, where they started cursing in the foulest and dirtiest way. The tall one was all in a fury. The short one would only mutter in reply, but using filthy language. Also he stuck his tongue out at the tall one. At which the first one, twitching and jerking in the strangest way, shouted: "Ah, you whore!"

And smacked the shorter one in the face. Then that one goes crashing
to his knees and starts kissing his comrade's bare and dirty feet, half
covered by the waves washing over them.

And Lord, Lord. God in heaven above! The tall one kicked him
with all his might and with a piercing scream, the first one landed in
the water. But this threw the raft off balance, and one end shot up,
throwing the second one in the water too. The two of them, without a
gurgle, began to disappear beneath the waves. Then they surfaced for a
moment, apparently not knowing how to swim—after which, again
without a gurgle, they sank to the bottom for good.

A terrible silence fell.

We all stood there, thunderstuck. Our gals hovered around like so
many frightened little animals as Nastya came to. The nurses woke
up. Infants began to cry. Dogs began to howl.

Colonel Zhestakanov was the first to gather his wits together. With a
shout, "I'll save those fairies—so they can answer to a people's comradely court," this superb swimmer, who had won more than a few
swimming championships in his youth, plunged into the water and
disappeared for a long time. Coming back up, he floated on his back
for a while, after which, without wasting words, he dove again.

But neither Colonel Zhestakanov's second, nor his subsequent
soundings of the reservoir bottom produced any favorable results. The
Colonel muttered, "How can it be?" But they had disappeared.

We figured out that we had better hurry over to Bublik's, since he
was to blame, so to speak, for this "triumph." But he had disappeared,
too, along with his good-looking wife the singer. The wind from the
pine forest was blowing freely through their empty dacha, ruffling the
tulle curtains. A coffee cup rolled on its side on the rug, having
dumped its contents on an issue of some glossy magazine that was
obviously not one of our Soviet magainzes. Bright orange flowers
languished like abandoned waifs in their pretty ceramic vases. Bublik
and his good-looking wife the singer had vanished.

And when, a few days later, we sent a delegation of our people to the
musical comedy theater, the administration there, staring at the floor,
informed us that Bublik had already made a clean escape and had
taken off for parts unknown. And it was only afterwards that we
understood the embarrassed look on these honest people's faces, when
it finally came out exactly what unknown parts director Bublik had
taken off for. Turned out it was the United States of America, and the
two of them had brazenly emigrated right under everybody's nose—
him and his good-looking wife the singer. Well, what the hell, it's not
all that surprising that they went to the USA. Seems it'll be easier for
them there to engage in degeneracy, which in our country is barred by
good, hard roadblocks. So it's not surprising.

What's surprising is something else. What's surprising is that when
the militia arrived at the lake and the scuba divers got there too, they

didn't find anyone either. We begged the scuba divers to keep at it, and they really tried to cover every square centimeter of the bottom, but it was all in vain. The two "artists" were gone.

You know, later on we discussed another idea—maybe we should go to the necessary expense and drain the pond, find out what was going on, and get to the bottom of everything, so that there wouldn't be this leftover smell of the devil's work or papistry, so that there wouldn't be this weariness and depression, disillusionment and fear—what the hell, we had enough money. But we missed our chance, and now we're really paying for our foolish gullibility, negligence, and dizzy-headedness.

Because literally on the very next day, after everything seemed to have quieted down, the town was suddenly treated to the terrible screams of someone being killed. It turned out to be Comrade Zhestakanov, who loved night swimming. The poor soul could barely get his breath, his eyes were popping out of his head, and all he could do was point at the watery traces of moonlight, repeating: "It's them! It's them. There. There."

After being revived with a glass of vodka, he got hold of himself. But he still insisted he had swum out to the raft at twelve midnight, the raft out in the middle of the reservoir, and on this raft there suddenly appeared two skeletons sadly embracing and singing a song ever so softly, "No need for sorrow, all of life lies ahead." How do you like that?

And even though Zhestakanov was soon being treated by the psychiatrist Tsarkov-Kolomensky, it didn't help anyone. The skeletons were also seen and heard by Professor Burevich, Comrade K., Mitya-the-Bark-Beetle, (and Mitya's mother-in-law), the metalworker Yeprev and his buddy Shenopin, Angelina Stepanovna, Edward Ivanovich, Yuri Aleksandrovich, Emma Nikolaevna, me, and even the physicist Lysukhin, who as a man of science was so shaken by this spectacle that he began to drink dangerously.

People tried to scare them off by shouting "Scat" and firing a double-barreled shotgun, but none of it helped. The skeletons weren't always visible, it's true. But the damn raft moved around literally on its own, and you could hear yelling, singing, lamentations, hoarse curses, smacking kisses, and prayers at night *all the time!*

I'm not one of your Zhestakanovs, I grant you. I never was at the front. And I'm not your physicist Lysukhin. Never had higher education. I'm just a normal average person, and not an especially big vodka drinker either. *But I personally swear to you myself that I heard this with my own ears:* "My darling, my darling," and then a wheezing sound, but such a sound it made my hair stand on end.

And after we tried everything over and over again, guns and stones and chlorophosphate, the end came—the end for us, the end for our town, the end for the reservoir. The dachas are being boarded up tight, and the second-hand dealers are scurrying about everywhere, rustling through the autumn leaves, the fruit trees are being dug up and carted off for transplanting, and there's no joy in anybody's face, just depression and weariness, disillusionment and fear.

So what would you have us do? We're none of us mystics or priests. But also we're not fools enough to live in a place like this where some degenerate corpses with their lustful skeletons gleaming in the moonlight try to lure people or get close to them and scare them and drive people straight into the psychiatric hospitals, leaving the women without any courage and the men without good sense and the children without their happy childhood or a clear vision of their perspectives in life and of working for the good of our vast Motherland. O Lord, O Lord. God in heaven above.

11. Vera* or Additional Information About Life

I wouldn't say that my visit to the friend I had known throughout childhood, adolescence, and young manhood left any unpleasant traces on my soul. I was even invited to come again. I was treated to cucumbers, tomatoes, squid, stewed duck, fish *kunzha*, and wine from the Caucasus. Besides, I enriched myself to a considerable extent with additional information about life.

Because when the parquet floor had creaked its last creak and the whispery murmurings had finally stopped, and the bedsprings clunked hollowly, then . . .

"Vera! Vera! Are you asleep?" Sasha cautiously stuck his head out of the kitchen.

No answer.

"That means she's asleep." He was satisfied. And he remarked vaguely: "In her condition sleeping is very desirable."

"Why desirable?" I asked.

"Just a minute," Sasha pricked up his ears. "Step out there in the corridor. Now, when I talk, can you hear me?"

"I hear you."

"Now I'm going to close the door tight. How about now—"

"Can't hear you."

"Then everything's shipshape," Sasha decided. But still he fiddled around some more—put his ear against the wall panel depicting little cornflowers, turned off the overhead light, turned on the table lamp, filled up the cut glass goblets once again, and . . .

"You understand, old man. You understand," he began his story in a sibilant whisper.

Aleksandr E. Morozov (our "Sasha") was a bespectacled young man

---

*Vera, short for Veronica, in Russian also means "faith."

of thirty-five and a bachelor when he was sent by his production unit to work for two weeks on a collective farm. His job was to help the toilers of the Red Lighthouse farm in the village of Sikhnevo with their burdensome rural labor as grain-growers in the non–black earth soil region so that there would be more grain, meat, poultry, and vegetables, and people could live the good life. His group traveled out of the city singing cheerfully. The entire well-harmonized chorus was put up in the school (not in session owing to the summer holidays) on bunks. Again they sang and drank a toast to their arrival. Shishaev and Koshkin got into a fight in the hallway, and the following morning everyone set to work in unison. During the first phase Sasha got bored. Sleepily carrying a small pitchfork, he walked along behind some sort of orange-colored machine which was attached to a tractor. This machine cut and devoured the grass all by itself, without a snag. The tractor driver was a tall, taciturn fellow, with high cheekbones, about twenty years younger than Sasha. So Morozov was bored. And here came another machine and ate up the rest of the grass. So Morozov asked to be sent home. But the leader of the group, department chief Fiyurin, said that if someone had come here to help the collective farm, let them help, adding, "What kind of philistine gossip-mongering is it to say there's no work? There's no work for fools. But if you have some brains, you can go lie in the sun or hunt whortleberries in the woods. Or look for odd-shaped roots or handcarved folk art. You're getting your pay, your travel allowance has been made out, the better for you to help on the collective farm. So what more do you want? You're an idiot, Sasha, if you want to be sent away from here. Where to? To the dusty city, to the carcinogenic asphalt, to sitting at your desk in an office from 8:30 in the morning till 5:45 when the bell rings? Phooey."

"You've got a point there," said Sasha and calmed right down. "The weather is beautiful. The birds are fooling around in the forest. The air is so fresh you could seal it in jars and send it to Japan, so that the people there could open the jars and gulp it down—the newspapers say that's what they're doing there already."

Morozov grew to like walking barefoot. And not out of affectation, by the way, but for the simple reason that his feet were pinched something awful by the new fake leather boots his mama had bought him. She bought them because she thought it might be too rainy but also because she didn't know what the real working atmosphere is like now in our contemporary agriculture, where there is much less filth and muck than there used to be back then, when the great minds and prophets were just beginning to imagine and dream about this. . . .

However, there was one shortcoming, to tell the truth: that is, the way people were fed was rather poorly handled at the collective farm—why try to hide the fact? And so, out of urgent necessity Morozov had to seat himself in the dusty wormwood bushes alongside the road, leaving his boots standing on the edge of the road. The mosquitoes were biting. It was getting dark. A wagon carrying two drunken peasants trundled by. Some fool was running along behind the wagon. The fool was also barefoot, but not out of necessity, as in Morozov's case, but simply out of doltishness, the guy being an idiot. He was pounding the thick dust with his grimy heels. And as he ran past our Morozov squatting in lonely solitude among the bushes, this fool, without reducing his speed, snatched up Morozov's boots and raced on in pursuit of the wagon.

Morozov didn't sit there like a lone eagle for long. Half buttoned up, he shot like a bullet out of the bushes and chased after the wagon too, grabbing at the boots. But the fool wouldn't let go of them. Morozov knocked him in the chest with the boots and the fool fell in the dust, still not parting with them. At that moment the wagon backed up. The peasants watched the scene with pleasure, winking at one another.

"You shouldn't beat him, comrade," said the first peasant, holding his ear reflectively.

"He's just a fool. He doesn't understand, no matter what, comrade," said the second peasant, scratching himself.

"Stealing someone else's boots—he understands that well enough," said Morozov, finally getting the boots away from the fool.

"Hey there, hey there, what are you talking about? You shouldn't even think such a thing, comrade," the peasants smacked their lips reproachfully. "He's an honest lad. He would have given 'em back to you later on; that's the kind of fool he is. Absolutely, he would have. He's honest. He'd come over with 'em and give 'em back."

"What're you trying to tell me? You take me for a fool too, comrades?" Morozov was about to start in. But the peasants weren't listening anymore. They had crossly urged their horse on and were already galloping off, these peasants, catching up again with the fool, who was pounding along on his bare heels, holding to a course along the road toward the distant church without cross, most of which was hidden behind a far off hill. Our Morozov shrugged his shoulders and wandered back to the place where he'd been sitting, but soon . . .

. . . Soon he got up again. This time he carefully buttoned up his beautiful trousers, a new pair of jeans made in one of our fraternal socialist countries. But the sun, the sun was already setting, turning the emerald iridescence of the rolling fields to gold, and also turning to gold the rust-red domes of the distant crossless church, and Morozov began to feel sad. The young man looked sadly at the lushness of nature that evening—with all the flowers pollinated, the pine cones ripening, and the potatoes radiant with white blossoms. Only he, A. E. Morozov, thirty-five years of age, somehow still felt awkward and ashamed and, anyway, he had no time to be doing something especially nice for somebody else—for attracting someone and warming their heart and making them happy. The sun was now hidden completely behind the hill, the golden domes turned back to rust, and from these sad thoughts Morozov quietly but forcefully belched.

And instantaneously, as in the mountains of Ala-Tau or the Pamirs, where, as everyone knows, one small pebble can set off a colossal avalanche and the awful power of the elements can come crashing down on a defenseless city, so too the belching of this young man produced an explosion, but of a biological kind, which came crashing down on his entire organism, weakened and slack from these elegiac thoughts. Morozov's eyes grew damp with tears, we know not why. His nose began to sting. He belched again and then something calamitous happened, and he realized he'd made a terrible mistake in thinking he was "through"; he had the sudden, horrifying feeling that all was not well for him in his new pants.

Groaning and cursing through his tightly clenched teeth, turning pale, and keeping his legs closed, Morozov went hopping like a gopher in the direction of the local pond, where the local lord's daughter had once drowned herself.

Now, this pond was all overgrown with alders and sedge, like a description from Turgenev, when that author had gone off to France for many long years to listen to the songs of Pauline Viardot and to write novels about his dearly beloved native land, about every last bush, every inch of soil, every blade of grass, etched into the surrounding limitless, fathomless patriotic expanse. (So we were taught in public school No. 10 in the Siberian city of K— and the Polytechnical Institute of the same city, where Sasha and I studied all the different sciences together for many long years . . .).

"Sasha, Sasha! Is that you, Sasha?" Sasha heard a woman's sweet voice calling. Never slackening, he turned his head. Fairly far away he caught sight of some red and black clothing and light-colored hair, encircling a face that was difficult for the weak-eyed Morozov to distinguish. Sasha sped away, then hunched down again in the heavy grass. The woman was amazed. She came closer and gazed about in astonishment, turning her head this way and that. Now Sasha could see her better. It was Veronica, the secretary from the typing pool, of whom it was said she was "a joker and a hot ticket." She was always running around the workplace with her big clodhoppers, whispering with her women friends in the hallway, and, in the same locale, asking the men for a smoke in a loud voice. In the bus it was Veronica who rallied everyone, and everyone sang loudly:

> My address ain't a street or a number,
> My address is the USSR.

Sasha's breathing stopped.

"Where'd you go Sasha? I saw you," the woman hailed him once again uncertainly, sighed sorrowfully, and headed for the pond, parting the high grasses and pulling her red jersey off over her head.

Now in fact, about sixty years earlier the unwed daughter of Lord Sikhnevo had drowned herself in that pond. He had been the lord of the local area at that time and since then the collective farmers had always refused to swim in the contaminated waters, crossing themselves and muttering, "This is an unclean place, this is where the lord's lady drowned." This amused the already highly amused city people, who invariably kept coming here in the summer to help in the collective farm work. And these city people would make up highly successful anecdotes out of this material, to tell their friends, as illustrations of the idiocy of rural life . . . snacking and drinking as they'd tell them . . .

Morozov crept along. The pond was deserted. Even the reliable helpers of the collective farm didn't come here after dusk because it was absolutely dark on the pond at night, the frogs croaked in their creepy way, the mosquitoes committed their depredations, and the silt-covered bottom of the pond slithered and sucked under your feet, the bottom which served as the resting place for Sikhnevo's daughter.

Morozov was surprised. What the devil had brought Veronica to this lonely place? Why couldn't she pick some better place for her evening promenade? But speak of the devil, an unclad body appeared nearby at that moment. Morozov stood rooted to the spot. By the light of the already-risen moon he could see from behind how Veronica's plump, white, surprisingly large breasts first sank in the dark water with a sucking sound, then seemed to reappear on the surface in the moonlit dazzle as she swam on her back, out into the depths of the darkness, with springy sweeps of her powerful arms.

Sasha realized that the swimmer could not hear what was happening on the shore because of the noise she herself was making. Therefore he crept down through the bushes, no longer trying to hide. After choosing a suitable inlet, he pulled off his boots. Then grimacing and turning away in disgust, he removed his soiled jeans, turned his underpants inside out, and began to wash and scrub them ever so quietly in his little inlet. Slowly he calmed down, and found himself in a very good mood for no apparent reason. Also, without knowing why, he felt a rather sweet and pleasant sensation. His imagination suggested a certain *something* to him. Morozov grunted and scrubbed furiously at the soiled fabric.

"There you are. Now I've got you. What are you doing, you rascal?" Sasha heard a familiar voice behind him. The engineer trembled in surprise and dropped his dark blue drawers in the water. They didn't float off, because there was no current; instead they slowly folded over in the warm water and sank to the bottom. Sasha swung around.

"There you are. I wasn't mistaken, Aleksandr Eduardovich. But where'd you disappear to? Why didn't you answer, you nasty thing?" Veronica kept repeating these questions, coming closer and closer to

Morozov. Sasha doubled over, made a face, and waved his arms. "You—you shouldn't," he stammered.

The young woman stopped, uncomprehending. Then she laughed slyly seeing that he had on only his spectacles, gleaming in the moonlight like windowglass high up on a windmill.

"Oh dear, I'm naked. I'm completely naked," she suddenly began to sob and sat down on her haunches.

"That isn't the problem," Sasha growled.

"But what if I *am* naked?" the typist straightened up determinedly. "Look at me, look, Aleksandr Eduardovich. Look, Sasha. Am I so badly built? Anyway, in the West they have entire colonies of intelligent people who go around naked and no one's ashamed of it. Why do you have to think nasty thoughts? . . ."

And she kept coming closer.

"Hey, what are you doing?" Sasha was again thrown into confusion. And he jumped away, covering himself with his hands.

"Aha, so you're washing something." She was simply overcome with laughter. "But let me help you. I can do it better."

She was about to bend over Sasha's stinking clothes. But he grabbed her by the hand, pulled her to him, and they both fell laughing and gasping into the warm, shallow water. And there came to pass between them, right there in the warm water, in the muddy shallow water, all that which apparently was inevitably bound to pass between them . . .

Then again they parted. Pushing off with a powerful shove, Veronica once more swam to the middle of the pond. She splashed and sang and threw up a spray. And Sasha quickly rinsed all his things out, wrung them dry, waved his trousers in the breeze, and put them on, right over his bare body.

"I'm going," he said.

"Wait, I'll go with you. Be there in a jiffy," she answered. She swiftly came ashore, and off they went. Morozov's drawers spent the night there on the muddy bottom.

"You're shivering. You're all wet, you crazy thing. Why'd you mess your pants? Come here, I'll warm you up," she said.

They lay next to one another, having dug a hole in the warm hay, and gazed at the stars.

"You're a funny guy. I noticed you a long time ago. You're sad all the time. Everyone's singing and you don't say a word. The guys play volleyball, and you go off for a walk in the woods . . ."

Sasha said nothing.

"Why don't you say anything?" She touched him gently.

"I hate everyone," said Sasha.

"How can you hate everyone?" she reproached him. "You must be joking," she reflected.

They were both silent.

"Say, do you believe in God?" Veronica suddenly asked.

"What do you mean, God?" said Sasha, rising on his elbows with astonishment. It seemed she was looking at him quite seriously.

"I believe," she said simply. "I believe that God brought us together today. I saw you chasing after the wagon and for some reason I felt a miraculous happiness in my soul and like a little girl I ran and ran and ran. Don't think I'm some sort of shameless hussy," she flared up. "I only. I . . . I suddenly wanted you terribly," she looked down. "I love you and I simply couldn't do anything else. All around people are so indifferent and cruel. I couldn't be like this with them. I didn't want to at first, but at the last moment, you know, at the last moment I understood that I love you. You think that's strange, don't you? I've seen you so many times. You bought pirozhki at the cafeteria, and some liverwurst. I've seen you, and I never guessed that I loved you. We were with the whole laboratory when we saw the movie *The Big Race*, do you remember? With Yves Montand. And I didn't realize that I loved you. Or working on volunteer Saturdays. Remember, I was filling your wheelbarrow with the shovel and neither of us knew or ever could have guessed what would happen between us. But now I see that I love you and I believe in God, because God gave me my love and gave me you. And do you love me?"

Sasha said nothing.

"You close-mouthed bastard!" she cried. "Take your time. You don't have to admit it right away. And most of all, don't believe in the nasty things they say about me. It's true I had a husband, a really creepy drunkard. He and his friends used to talk about God all the time. They'd drink and eat and I'd wash the dishes. They'd found the perfect sucker . . . but I'm no fool anymore, and you don't have to be in a hurry. Don't break this . . . magic. We've only met and we have a great deal of this . . . magic ahead of us. I trusted you and I believe you won't deceive me. Don't deceive me, darling. I couldn't bear it. I'd lay hands on myself. I'd put an end to myself and no one would ever know what happened. So swear to me in the eyes of God under these stars that you love me."

"Vera, what the devil do I have to swear for?" Sasha said with embarrassment groping for her with his hand.

"Oh no. You swear first. Otherwise it's all over, it's all over. No more." She thrust his hand away.

"OK, I swear," said Sasha.

"No, you say 'I swear to God'," she insisted.

"God?"

"God."

"God," Sasha mumbled and finally got angry. "Hey, how would you like to? . . ."

"What?" the young woman didn't understand.

"Shove it," Sasha clarified.

She looked at her beloved wildly, then spat pungently right in his mug. After thinking it over Sasha decided to spit back. And he did. Veronica jumped up, let out a roar, and began to shake with rage . . .

"So you spat yourselves out?" I laughed.

"Quiet, quiet! Why so loud?" Sasha hissed.

He went on tiptoe out into the hallway but came back satisfied.

"It seems she's still asleep. Said her prayers and went to sleep."

"What is this? Does she really believe in God?" I was genuinely surprised. "Come on, tell me about it. I want to enrich myself with additional information about life."

"It seems she does," Sasha looked down.

"Hey, wait a minute, my friend; then maybe *you believe in God, too?*"

Sasha went over to the black window.

"I won't lie," he said to the window. "I won't lie. I believe. But not in her foolish sense of the word. I'm not about to lie about that. It's entirely possible that I do not love her, but, but . . ."

Sasha whirled around.

"But a child. You understand. Of course I didn't want to get married. But you know I had a sudden clear and piercing realization that a child of Vera, a child of faith, is something altogether different than faith itself, or Vera herself. You understand, even if it wasn't from Vera, wasn't from faith, but in general, you understand? With a child I wouldn't be alone in this world, because with a child I would *continue!* I, and I hope this won't sound like blasphemy to you, but I look forward to having a child with great delight. I, my friend, suspect that that is the greatest high there is. Of course that's something you can't understand. But you should understand that it's pure bliss. I, Morozov, A.E., am thirty-six years old, and suddenly it turns out I have another dimension. And I am a child again, and the whole world is a child and nothing will ever die. Do you understand? If I have a son, a fat little thing with a big head, fat cheeks, and a mouth reaching back to his ears, I'd cut anyone's throat for him—anything, as long as my kid was OK. Do you understand? Do you understand what I'm saying? You ought to, you really ought to understand. I don't believe for an instant that you don't understand me. You should understand me. You yourself must have something that's sacred, don't you? Or do you?"

But unfortunately I wasn't able to tell Sasha what was sacred to me. Because through the glass doors of the kitchen in the semigloom of tobacco smoke there appeared a round, bulging figure.

"Give me a chance to sleep sometime, pig," the figure began to scream. "The minute I fall asleep they start in again with their yakkityyakkityyakyak . . ."

"I'll give you something to sleep about, I'll give you 'pig'," Sasha got tense and nasty.

The woman opened her mouth and was about to holler and howl and shake but I reacted instantly and got up from the table quick as a wink.

"Quiet, quiet, comrades." And again, "It really is late and time for me to head home. Sasha, you're not right. But you too, Vera, you're going after him for no good reason. I'm the one to blame," I played up to her. "Don't get angry at him, Verushka. It's just we haven't seen each other for so long. Promise you won't be mad at me, OK?"

Sasha breathed loud and heavy through his nose and Veronica began to smile through her tears and gestured with her hand to indicate she wouldn't be angry at me. So I can't say that the visit to the friend and comrade of my childhood, adolescence, and young manhood left any unpleasant traces on my soul. On the contrary, I enriched myself to a considerable extent with additional information about life, and Vera even invited me to come again, "Only not so late."

So what then? In her way she's right. In general she is quite a normal woman, and I am sincerely happy for Sasha. Maybe because he was so lucky. It's not everyone who manages to enter their charmed circle so easily and painlessly. And sooner or later everyone has to, everyone, hear me? Everyone. Remember that. Everyone . . .

12. The Hills

A quiet, unassuming man was on his way one evening to get a bite to eat at the corner of Zasukhin and Semenyuta at the Shashlik House, which, to tell the truth, didn't deserve such a fancy name but should have been bluntly and honestly called The Dive. Because the people who always hung out there were bums, vendors from the bazaar, dudes, drunken workmen, and other lowbrow individuals of the type that we won't be able to take with us into the coming bright future, which is already "just beyond the hills."

Also, the selection and quality of food in this miserable establishment left a great deal to be desired. Naturally there wasn't even a hint of any shashlik here. The only thing they served was some murky sauerkraut soup and a standard type of flatfish, criminally fried in some nameless brand of machine oil. From this last substance an odor of unbearable foulness spread over not only the eating-house corner itself, but all the adjacent area, which consisted of wooden and concrete-block houses in the suburb of a great city. It was odd that the local sanitation and epidemic service hadn't closed down this vile source of infection and boarded it up solid with crisscross boards. It was surprising and attested to definite dereliction of duty on the part of the aforementioned public service.

But this quiet, unassuming man, Omikin by name, was by no means one of your thrill-seekers or speculators or alcoholics, but simply a quiet, unassuming Russian man whose wife had left him because he was too timid. A man who was too lazy at eight o'clock in the evening to go hunting for some place better suited to a cultivated taste in food. Moreover—why hide it?—his income did not permit him to sit down at a fine table in a fancy restaurant to consume something more moderate to the taste and higher in caloric content. His income. Possibly this too was a material factor in his beautiful wife's decision to leave him.

It happened this way. He and his wife were riding in the front section of an overcrowded bus from the downtown area when suddenly a young hooligan of average age began misbehaving. Apparently he had drunk too much vodka or smoked too much marijuana. Long-haired and unshaven, he seemed at first to be sleeping, pressed against the door. But he awoke and found Omikin's beautiful wife next to him. So he said loudly, "Ah, my girl. Poetry. Stars. Do you know what they are?"

This kind of statement was an unpleasant surprise for the quiet, unassuming Omikin and he addressed his wife in a restrained way, reminding her that tomorrow was the nineteenth, the day on which the family linen was due to be picked up at the laundry: sheets, pillowcases, underwear. The young ruffian began to laugh with deliberate malice, and Omikin's wife, filled with inexplicable rage, began, as it were, to dissociate herself from her husband and dissociated herself completely at the bus stop, where—as they got off—she made the following declaration:

"I don't want to live with a man who cannot defend me as a woman from the first rampaging hooligan who comes along."

Omikin, the husband, timidly said that the hooligan was not entirely on the rampage and perhaps wasn't even a hooligan at all but some sort of young, unrecognized poet or inventor, at which his wife fell into prolonged and scornful laughter. "Coward! Sissy!" she flung at him, after laughing her fill. And soon she left Omikin altogether. Never to return, as Omikin should have understood. Because her new husband, a former widower, was a clean-cut, manly, outgoing type. He served in some military unit, had a summer house, and a three-room apartment, and was always going off on long business trips. Who would leave such a remarkable husband to go back to an Omikin? Granted, she'd loved him once; nevertheless, he was the kind of husband—dawdler that he was—who still lived in a dilapidated wooden house that the authorities kept talking about tearing down but never got around to, a husband who had no money and never would have because it wasn't fated to be. He didn't have the right kind of energy. Who would go back to such a husband? Only a total idiot, obviously, and Omikin's wife was anything but that.

She had married Omikin back then, for a special reason. In a world of universal, unrestrained hooliganism and brashness she had been impressed by his peculiar gentleness. To all the insults and misunderstandings that still occur in our not entirely perfect life he responded with a defenseless smile and a total mildness of manner. And only when people bore down on him especially hard would he mumble, "You know it isn't nice to do that. It's wrong to do that. You should be ashamed of that."

And he didn't climb all over her—she who at the time was a virgin, with the maiden name Milyaeva. He didn't come after her rudely or demandingly, but courted her at length in the old-fashioned way. He took her to the planetarium to show her the various planets, and it was only a good long time after that that he said to her, looking at the dormitory doorstep, "You know, Lyusya, it seems to me that I love you. Wouldn't you agree to become my wife?"

That's how he said it, "*I love you. Wouldn't you agree to become my wife?*" What a weirdo. At first Lyusya wanted to laugh out loud and make a cutting remark, but then she looked at his troubled face, all clouded over, and somehow she no longer wanted to laugh. She suddenly thought that of course she had other more brilliant and dashing cavaliers, but all of them were sort of—too clever for their own good. This one at least wouldn't devour vodka by the quart or go dropping his trousers at someone else's house. Besides, she was sick of knocking around in dormitories. On top of that, job assignments for graduates were about to be made at the institute of light industry, where she was a student.

"I don't insist, of course, on a hasty reply," he continued stiltedly, sensing her lack of response. "But we do know one another a little, Lyusenka. So I think you would be in a position to understand the seriousness of my intentions."

Well, she soon agreed. Secretly she placed great hopes in her own decisiveness. "It's a good thing he's like that." She was even happy at the thought. "I'll be his manager. He's so polite. I'll manage him and we'll show *them*."

But they didn't show *them* anything. After all, how can you manage jelly? It just dribbles through your fingers. Omikin worked steadily as before at his economics laboratory, earning 110 rubles a month, and as before his old house remained standing, and Lyusya Milyaeva-Omikina, a specialist with a diploma, began to get bored stiff in her spare time. Omikin would sit in his soft slippers in front of the television set, reading some boring thick book, and she, after washing the supper dishes in water heated on the electric stove, would stare lazily at the same TV set, and now and then Omikin would address her as follows:

"What now, snookums? Want to go beddy-bye?"

"Yeah, I wanna," she would answer coarsely for some reason.

"Oh, why didn't you say so?" Omikin would get scared. "Well then, you make the bed, and I'll go in the kitchen and read just a little more."

That's how it went. And after suffering with this for a certain length of time and having had her fill of "beddy-bye" and "snookums," Lyusya rebelled in the manner described above, leaving Omikin for good.

And what about Omikin? This event of course shook him up quite badly. He even cried helplessly, like a little child, when she informed him of her decision and convinced him that she meant it.

"But it's not right to do that, Lyusenka. What did I ever do to hurt you?" he sobbed.

"Ah, drop it. I know damn well," she said, exasperated, as she packed her various bottles, jars, tubes, blouses, and shirts in her large, gray, artificial-leather suitcase.

"Have I been such a bad husband to you?" he asked, perplexed.

"Drop it. Why go over it a hundred times when it's already been decided." She knitted her thin, fashionably plucked brows and hurried on with her work.

"Probably I'm to blame. Probably I didn't pay enough attention to you," he kept repeating.

Well, what's to be said to such a person? That no one, none of her friends lived like that? Ask him, Did he ever once buy her Arabian perfume or a gold ring or take her to Sochi or Yalta? No money? Well, he didn't have to steal. Just earn more if he didn't know how to steal. Instead of reading pointless books and sitting there in an armchair with, she had to admit, the stupidest possible expression on his face.

"What are you thinking about?" she asked once.

"Huh?" he woke up.

"I asked you what you're dreaming about with such a blissful expression on your face."

"Me? Oh yes. You guessed. I was dreaming," he said with a smile. "You know, I was dreaming about you and me and the bright new day that's just beyond the hills. You know, maybe it's an overused expression—'just beyond the hills'—but you know I can picture those hills so clearly. They're covered with a kind of magical, pure, clean, open forest—these emerald hills, beyond which there is a bright and quiet future waiting, where there's no noise or cursing or shoving. Where there's no envy and no filth. Where the houses are covered with red brick tile and the roads are filled with yellow sand. Where there are warm lights on the porches. And you and I walk hand in hand, eternally young, eternally happy, eternally tender. We touch the quiet flowers, hear beautiful music and the sound of Siberian pine cones popping, and go swimming in a dark, dark blue lake."

"Yeah, and what are you doing to bring this bright future of ours closer?" she asked, trembling with rage.

"Why 'of ours'?" he asked in surprise. "It's for everyone. It's an objective process. And I simply take my place, work honestly, and try to be honest in day-to-day life."

"And do you get much for your honesty?" she couldn't control herself any more.

"But don't you think we have enough?" he smiled. "We're well fed. We have clothes to wear and shoes on our feet."

And he acted as though he didn't notice her anger at all. And maybe in fact he didn't.

But she had dumped him. At first Omikin missed her terribly. He even drank a hundred grams of vodka on one occasion, but he didn't like it. He grieved in a lost kind of way, abandoning his reading for a while, and for a while his television set stayed off. He sat home alone in silence in the evenings and went back over everything. How had he offended her? How had he failed to please her?

"Not enough. I didn't pay enough attention to her," frowning, he said to himself. "Couldn't see beyond my books to where a living person stood."

But somehow he gradually calmed down. He never felt any jealousy toward the unknown military man, who remained a mythical figure to him. Even in his thoughts he couldn't imagine Lyusya undressing, taking everything off, and lying down next to another man. That would be monstrous and preposterous. It was something he couldn't conceive of. And gradually the idea somehow formed in his mind that everything that had happened was simply temporary. How could it, in fact, be otherwise? For then who would he walk with beyond the hills, through the groves of happiness? With whom would he greet the dawn and watch the sunet? Gradually the pain and sorrow receded, and life returned to its normal course again.

He sat at his desk at work, gentle and dependable as ever. Once a month he took a trip to the grave of his parents, who were buried outside the city in the distant cemetery of Badalyk. And he read a lot. Read and read his peculiar books, which in all fairness couldn't be said to have ruined him by themselves, reducing him to the status of the quietest thing in the world. It couldn't be. Other people read books too, and you see how sharp they are. Always on the go, never daunted by any obstacle.

And so he ate at the so-called "Shashlik House," and he was mistaken of course to do that. There are grounds here for reproaching him. He should have either fought against this improper Shashlik House by filing complaints, or have overcome his laziness and visited a more suitable place. It's not all that expensive, you know, if you don't try to get too fancy. Another thing: if you don't know how to cook for yourself, at least you could order something to take out, say, once every three days. You know how convenient it is—you get the pan out of the fridge, warm it up on the stove, and you're always fed.

But he kept going to the Shashlik House. He kept going and going until he got into this eerie situation.

That evening the Shashlik House was filled as usual with devil-may care alkies. Omikin looked at the menu on the wall, ordered the usual, handed the cashier a bill, carefully counted his change, and soon was looking for an empty place to sit. But where could he find one? Under the potted palm they were drinking their own private vodka. At one place a guy with his bare mug sticking out was sleeping at the table. At another they were gambling by flipping matchboxes. There was no place for Omikin.

He was forced to put his tray of food down on the empty corner of a table occupied by two young men of hippie appearance who had had quite a bit to drink and were discussing something confidentially. At their feet were fat, black "diplomat's" briefcases, which lately had become the surest sign of secret traders in goods that are in high demand. "This place isn't taken, is it, young men?" Omikin asked just in case.

They didn't even hear his question. They were discussing terms in a mystifying way about returning to some place. Therefore, Omikin unloaded his food, took his tray over to the used-tray stand, and at the same time picked up a bottle of Borzhom mineral water at the bar. This was quite easy to do because the bartender had already sold her day's supply of the cheap red stuff, and the only thing on the mirrored shelves now was French cognac, round which the drunkards, leary of the price, were buzzing like bumblebees.

Omikin drank a glass of the tasty water and quickly set about eating his dinner, trying as hard as he could not to listen to the private conversation of these disgraceful representatives of the younger generation, because the conversation they were having was an exceedingly vile one.

One of the young men was a bit sharper than the other and kept grinning more and more; the second one, apparently rather dull-witted, kept frowning during the conversation, needing more and more persuasion by his partner.

"OK now, we're gonna drive over there, sonnyboy," the sprightly one was saying in a crafty way. "And when we drive over, man, are we gonna get *high*."

"Yeah, you try and get high," his partner responded gloomily, "when we didn't sell any 'platters'* today."

*The Russian slang word, *plasty*, means "*foreign* records" [tr.].

"So? We'll sell some tomorrow. For sure! You think I can't get fifty off of Drovyanoi for the Beatles *Sergeant Pepper's Club?* Then you don't know me very well, old buddy."

"Know you? I know you. But there's no cabbage. How're we gonna get it on? I'm a gentleman, a *caballero*, not a penny-pinchin' piker, muvvah."

"Hey, what's with you?" the sprightly one looked surprised. "Don't you know Valka the Cheek? You think Valka won't fix me up, if she's got some cabbage. But what am I hangin' around here for? The Cheek! Do you know how she takes it?" the young man whispered, looking around lasciviously.

"What vileness," thought Omikin in disgust. "No, something has got to be done about our young people. "Platters?" "Cabbage?" Surely beneath this outwardly unhinged talk, some corrupt content is hidden. Something has got to be done. Something has definitely got to be done."

"Oh, how she takes it," the young man cried exultantly. "What a woman! Even though she was born in '42."

"Yeah, and who is she?"

"Christ knows who. Seems like she's got a husband, some old guy, kind of a big wheel. He's all the time off on business."

"She got a girl friend?" the frowning man asked bluntly.

Lord, what vileness, Omikin thought again and drank down the remaining Borzhom at one gulp.

"Sure. She's got a whole bordello going there," the young man said, getting more and more excited. "I took a shot of 'em last time. Wanta see? I tell you, this is one *graphic* shot."

With trembling hands he groped in his "diplomatic pouch," and pulled out a black envelope.

"Wow, they're somethin'!" His partner was entranced. "Those broads are somethin' else!"

A photograph fell from the envelope. It fell to Omikin's left, so that unintentionally he glimpsed it out of the corner of his eye.

And was struck dead. There *she* was, fallen asleep, drunk, completely naked, stretched out on a rumpled bed with her legs disgustingly parted.

"My God," Omikin groaned, reaching for the photograph. But with a skillful movement, quicker than the eye, the young man snatched it from under Omikin's hand and said rudely:

"Get lost, old goat. Who asked you to sit here? Get lost. No one's bothering you; so you just sit there, you creep, and eat. And chew your food real good."

"Cut him in the face," advised the young man with the frown.

"Lyusya. But that's Lyusya, my wife," Omikin groaned.

"Or let me cut him," the one with the frown said again.

But the young man in charge vetoed any rough stuff, because he was feeling good again. "What are you blabbing about, old man? What's that you say? Hey, hey! Well, take a look then if you want; if you want to so bad," he winked at his partner.

With trembling fingers Omikin took the photograph. It was the same disgusting picture as before. The disgusting woman lay there still, but it wasn't Lyusya.

"That's The Cheek herself," the young man said, beaming. "Well dad, it looks like you got overanxious, about your hearth and home being tampered with. You ought to buy us a drink," he addressed Omikin.

The latter, however, suddenly felt weak; he sat back on the steady legs of the chair, filled his lungs, and uncontrollably vomited. Whether the Borzhom had played its part, or the quality of the food at the Shashlik House had finally reached rock bottom, we don't know. But he spouted forth uncontrollably— right on those grimy plates and that bespattered table.

"Hey you, what you doin'?" The young men backed away.

But Omikin retched and shuddered, was thrown and twisted about, and from the strain he even gave vent to an abrupt, unseemly sound.

"Someone throw him out of here, the pig!" a drunken bystander shouted.

"Yeah but . . . he's not a drinker, I don't think," said the woman behind the bar.

"Drinker or no drinker, what's he stinkin' up the place for?" the drunk argued.

"Could be he's sick," the bartender took Omikin's side. "You feeling bad, comrade?"

Omikin lifted his beclouded eyes.

"You don't have to throw me out. I'll go myself," he mumbled. "You don't have to. I'll go."

He rose, then stretched himself to his full height and shouted wildly:

"I'm going, but you stay here. And so-and-so your mother!"

The drunks began to laugh.

"We thought you said he wasn't a drinker."

"Gee, I don't know." The woman behind the bar grew hesitant.

Omikin, however, had already gone weak again. He was swaying, wiping the heavy sweat off his brow with a dirty handkerchief.

"Forgive me. I know it's not right to do that. It's shameful to do that. It's wrong. Forgive me."

"Go on. Get out of here while you're still in one piece, or else I'll call the cops," the bartender said in tender tones.

But Omikin no longer heard her. He bent over, sat down, swayed, and slowly toppled onto his right side.

He was struck dead—this time for good.

13. The Blue Flute

Fate dropped me once at S., a station on the eastern Siberian railway along the line from Abakan to Taishet. My train had already left for Krasnoyarsk and I realized I'd have to while away the boring hours of the night alone until the morning bus.

In my boredom I looked around. A station like any other. Hard wooden benches, a magnificent fig tree, a cooler with boiled water, a dented drinking cup fastened with a thick chain, and a tin trashcan. Plus a painting! I suddenly saw this *painting*. A huge thing, done in oils, taking up almost an entire wall of the waiting room. And it completely overshadowed the other visual propaganda, which consisted of statistics, slogans, appeals, promises, and the wall newspaper *Typhoid Fever*.

And here is what the inspired hand of the artist had depicted on this magical canvas: in the background, near some emerald hills, cheerful multicolored cows were grazing and an airplane was flying blissfully by, through azure skies; and in the foreground, coming right out at the viewer, on a smooth, clear field, in high grass, weaving little wreaths for one another, *he* and *she* were tenderly amusing themselves, about the same age as Daphnis and Chloe, but with clothes on.

Wearing a scarlet shirt, he was dreamily following the sure and steady flight of the airplane with his large eyes, and she, in a bright-red peasant skirt, was playing some unknown, softly trilling song on a blue flute. Underneath was a caption in white, "Arrive, O Fabled Time."

"Wow, who the hell did that fantastic painting?" I exclaimed without realizing what I was saying.

"Why? You like it?" came a question from the bench across from me, where a man of middle years was sitting, dressed all in black, with a black cap on his head and a bandage on his unshaven cheek.

"Yes, I like it," I said sincerely. "But who painted it!"

"Mitya Pyrsikov painted that," said the man, whose name, I found out later, was Viktor Parfentyevich, a mechanic in the local machine shop. "He made a vow, and then he painted this picture and went off to work on the Baikal-Amur Mainline."

"A vow?" I asked.

"A vow," said Viktor Parfentyevich.

"And then went off to work on the BAM?"

"Yup, with his wife," Viktor Parfentyevich confirmed it, grabbing again at his aching jaw.

"Maybe a bit of vodka would help," I said. "I've got a little here."

"OK, let's have it. Maybe it'll quiet this damn thing down," Viktor Parfentyevich quickly agreed.

We drank out of the dented cup, punctiliously sniffed some bread crusts, and he began his tale.

Hey, there you go. The goddam tooth has quieted down all right. It shouldn't ever have had to hurt, but it started up anyway. All because of that goddam dental technician Seryozha Malorubko. He gave me a wrong filling; he's a complete drunkard now, that goddam Malorubko. He wasn't a bad young specialist before. But you know how vodka and women will ruin anyone you can think of, even the most brilliant specialist . . .

Well now, I'll tell you, when the wedding ceremony was held in the Wedding Palace of our town for this famous pair of young working people, no one knew then how things would end up, how our troubled hearts would long for calm. Just the opposite. A lot of people thought that everything would work out smoothly, and you can be sure no one ever suspected that Mitya would wind up having to go to Leningrad, make a vow, and so on.

Because the two of them, Mitya Pyrsikov and Masha Khareglazova, made a really fine young couple in every way and they were just right for this kind of Young Communist marriage. Both of them were not only tall and handsome, with healthy, ruddy complexions, but they had other good points too—they both had high ratings in production and took an active part in social activities at their factory.

Our hometown lad Mitya, even when he was at the municipal technical and trade college, stood out from the rest of the troublemaking crowd from the factory schools, because he was pretty well behaved, and applied himself to his work. His late mother even got a letter about his good conduct from the education assistant at the factory school himself. For example, Mitya never got involved in those club-swinging fights (using fence palings) with those thieving Kachinsk peasants. The peasants had it in for the future working class on account of their nature walks and necking and other fine doings in the Kachinsk woods along the river with the wives, adolescent daughters, and even little girls of those same peasants. All the others fought, but Pyrsikov didn't, because he didn't go walking there or necking or other things. He was busy in the evenings, not with the flesh and the devil, but with painting in color on cardboard at the amateur painting circle or sitting quietly in the library, studying the words of Professor Paton on the subject of welding.

It was in the library that the first youthful encounter took place between Mitya Pyrsikov and Masha Khareglazova, Masha also being a reader, who was working her way through the writer Dumas' novel *Queen Margo* at the time. She had these magnificent full braids and was fifteen years old, sitting there quietly turning the pages till the library closed at nine o'clock. After that she would head for home, which was the building called "Dormitory, Women's Entrance." And there she'd fall asleep ever so quietly in her pure little bed, where there were photographs of actors on the wall, and of doves kissing. She'd fall asleep without being disturbed by the emotions troubling her overly indulgent roommates. And when they would ask her straight out, "How about you? Have you ever?" she would smile at them without any embarrassment, opening her splendid big eyes, and say, "No, I haven't. I don't even think about those stupid things." Still, she felt terribly embarrassed about her name.

Well, Mitya's name wasn't all that common either, it must be said. It was a long time after they first got acquainted before he could bring himself to tell her his name, and when he finally got around to telling her, well, she up and answered him this way: "I knew that long ago. I like your name a lot."

He would walk her to her building and they would stand there for a long time by the women's entrance, glancing at the passers by— Masha Khareglazova, all resplendent in a nighttime veil of snowflakes, and Mitya Pyrsikov, full of attentiveness. They'd stand there for a long time, and then they'd go their ways, each to a separate entrance. You see, things were arranged back then so that people of different sexes weren't put together, God forbid. That's why there was a women's entrance and a men's entrance and at twelve o'clock at night both the one and the other were locked tight. So that if someone was off fooling around, they had to climb in through the window, and all along the sidewalk the windows were broken.

The passersby, comrades and friends, were burning with curiosity to find out what Mitya was whispering to his Masha. And they asked both Mitya and Masha about it and didn't believe a word of their proper and righteous replies. But the fact was, he hadn't been saying anything special to her. Usually he just told her something he'd learned from the works of Professor Paton or some funny incident from the life of the talented director of the amateur art circle, the artist Pyotr Ilyich Saltykov. Masha would listen and laugh.

And it was logical, what happened next. They both graduated from the Institute as outstanding students and were sent to the same big prize-winning factory, famous for its production of the aluminum so vital for the needs of our country and for foreign industry. They were sent to the same factory but to different work brigades.

And there, because of their hard work, they were soon both promoted, becoming leaders of neighboring work brigades, and their brigades would alternate in winning the socialist competition for the highest output.

A great deal of this was useful and important. Everyone benefited from the resulting close productive links and exchange of exemplary industrial experience, and the unfurled red banner passed back and forth, again and again, between these two work brigades until some brilliant mind came up with an extremely clever idea.

This bright brain called Mitya into his office and, after shooting the breeze about this and that for a while, came around to the main point.

"What do you say, lad, isn't it time for you to get married?"

"Well, I haven't thought about it so far." Mitya got embarrassed.

"It's a little early. I haven't done my army service yet."

"Ah, that doesn't matter. You know the saying, 'Don't cry, little girl, the rain'll stop soon,' " the tall comrade laughed. "Well, is there a bride on the horizon?"

"Yeah, there is," Mitya swallowed. "But I don't know how she would feel. She and I never talked about *that*."

"Why don't you go ahead and talk with her about it. And if you want, I can say a word to her for you, a little matchmaking so to speak. What do you say?" The comrade kept smiling and smiling.

After which the wagon rolled straight to the finish line, that is to the Young Communist wedding of these two exemplary team leaders. A wedding with correspondents flown in and generous gifts, both material and symbolic, consisting of solemn vows by the members of both work brigades to raise the productivity of labor still higher and achieve greater success for the good of the five-year plan. On the whole this new type of ceremony came off real well.

And then it was over. All of the speeches had been made, and Uncle Fedos, the old veteran, had cried; and the brass bands had played; and a dance called *lyotka-yonka*, performed by beautiful young working women, had been filmed; after which the young Pyrsikovs moved into a beautiful one-room apartment provided for them by the factory in the New Way of Life apartment building. Their apartment had a main room of twenty-four square meters, a kitchen of eighteen square meters, an electric stove, a dryer, aluminum cabinets for the dishes, built-in closets, and an entrance hall of 7.2 square meters; and that's not counting the deeply recessed bay window with balcony. So you can see for yourself what all this meant for the two young people who had spent their entire conscious lives in and out of dormitories, or renting little niches on Kacha Street or Nikolaevka.

Oh dear friend, dear ironic reader friend. Forgive me for the digression, but I know what's on your mind.

You're sneering, dear reader, and saying, "I know what's coming next, sweetheart. You and this Viktor Parfentyevich of yours are going to treat me to a scathing satire on the theme that all this artificially organized happiness goes flying to the four winds, that the only results of it all are tears, squabbles, and the dividing up of the apartment. Exactly the kind of thing we sometimes have the chance to read in that special part of the Young Communist newspaper which sternly criticizes formalistic attitudes, impersonalism, and insensitive work with living people, right?"

"No, not so," I answer.

"Aha," you guess. "Then it's something even worse. What it is, most likely, is you're going to pull that old, bearded, dull-witted, foul-smelling joke about the boss calling him in at his wife's request and telling him to go ahead and *do it*, right?"

"Ah, if it were only that, dear friend. Then everything would be a lot simpler," I sigh. And sadly I continue, because here comes the most important part . . .

Because in actual fact, what? Because in actual fact they entered their marvelous new apartment happily and began to live there very happily, gradually putting the blare and kettledrums of the wedding behind them and gradually getting used to this new phase of life. And they didn't even think at first, either at work or in their off-hours, about any kind of foolishness except innocent kisses, tremulous touches, and tender stroking.

Nevertheless, one fine day that decisive moment came when all the furniture they'd been given was situated in its proper place and at midnight the television set had been turned off after good weather for the next day had been announced, and Masha had already fixed herself up for the night in the bathroom, undid and redid her heavy braid, undressed, and put on all her tender, rosy things. So that when she came out of the bathroom Mitya suddenly got so hot and grabbed her so hard she retreated in fear.

"What are you doing, Mitya?" she asked.

"Darling," Mitya swallowed the lump in his throat.

"Let's go to sleep," she said.

"Yeah, let's," said Mitya.

And afterward when everything was over in the dark, and all worn out and limp, he was stroking her and touching her silken skin with his hot lips, she suddenly began to toss around restlessly.

"What's wrong?" Mitya whispered.

"I'll be right back."

She got out of bed and, after turning the kitchen light on, said in a guilty voice, "I forgot to iron your shirt."

"The hell with my shirt. Come here," the happy Mitya said, all throaty-voiced.

"But how can you go to work in a wrinkled shirt tomorrow? That's no good."

"Ah, the hell with it. Hell with it," said Mitya who still didn't understand anything.

"Oh no, it just won't do. It's not right for you to wear a wrinkled shirt." She stuck to her guns.

The iron was already hot, and from the dark room he could see that she was pushing it back and forth, her head bent low over the white material, back and forth, back and forth, senselessly.

"What are you doing?" Mitya shouted.

"Me? Nothing," she said.

"Come on, what are you doing?" Mitya got up.

"I'm not doing anything," she answered.

But when he, all naked, embraced her, almost fully dressed, from behind, a cold tear suddenly slid onto his hot hand like a piece of ice.

"What's wrong with you? You're crying?" Mitya was thrown for a loop.

"No, I'm not crying," she answered swallowing her tears.

"So why are you crying?" he asked.

"I'm not crying at all," she answered. But her body was stiff as a board under his hands. He realized with horror that she felt cold, cold, and not all hot, not all sweet, the way he felt. And oh my God, he felt so hot, and it had been so sweet for him with her, and it still was, and he wanted so bad to do it again and again every minute, every second, three hundred times, five hundred times, every moment—with her, with her, with her—no one else in the world could do that for him.

Well, what can you say? That's how their joyful nights rolled by. Should we say she did not love him? Whose tongue would speak such foolishness? She loved him. She loved him something awful. She loved to make soup for him and tasty porridge; she liked to wash his shirts; she simply adored buying him the socks that he threw at the wall one day, making her cry. Yes, she loved.

But he began to waste away. He grew dark and gloomy. He developed a twitch in his cheek. He went drinking once with a super clever guy by the name of Kunimeyev, and this rat Kunimeyev said to him in response to what were only little hints, that's all, just hints: "Hey, why chew over the same old lyrics? We'd do better going over to the women's place on Zasukhin Street."

"Well, let's go," said the slightly tipsy Mitya.

And they went to the women's place on Zasukhin Street, taking 3.08 liters of rosé with them. The lovely girls surrounded them, and everything there was great—good conversation and group singing and then everyone off by themselves, at the height of which for some reason he began looking intently at the playful little Lyubya Kryukova and suddenly said in a dreadful whisper, "You get the hell out of here, you slime."

"What do you mean get the hell out of here when I have a permit to live here?" Fun-loving Lyuba was totally surprised. But when she saw the weird way his face was growing pale, she just went limp and whispered, "What's wrong with you, man? What are you doing?"

And in his hatred he shoved her away, quickly got dressed, and went running off, stumbling and skidding to where his beloved wife Masha was anxiously waiting for him, not sleeping, heating up the tea several times, and listening for his nighttime footsteps.

"Mitya, what are you doing?" she also whispered when, with the same strange smile, he appeared before her—his matted hair sticking to his forehead and the light gone out of his shriveled eyes.

"What am I doing?" he repeated her question. "I'll show you what." And with all his might he hit her with his fist. "Oh-oh" Masha gasped. But he beat her and beat her and beat her. Then he smashed through the window and flew down headfirst from their second-story apartment.

When she came to see him in the hospital she was almost completely healed. The big round bruises under her eyes were carefully powdered over, and where there had been a big ugly scrape, just a little rosy spot was left. And for some reason she was in very good spirits, even happy.

"Here Mitya, look what I brought you," she said and busily began digging out all sorts of cookies and roast chicken and *shanezhki** from her shopping bag.

An orderly hovered not far away. Mitya was sitting quietly on the cement bench next to some bald-headed old man, with a full gray beard up to his eyeballs.

"Gimme something to eat," the old man uttered distinctly, reaching for the string bag.

Masha shuddered.

"Give it. That's Marshall Zhukov," Mitya grinned crookedly.

Masha made herself cheerful again.

"Mitya, get these things out of your head," she said with conviction. "As soon as they fix up your nerves and you're released, you know how *well* we're going to live!"

"Yeah, I know," Mitya grinned again.

In the hospital, among other things, he had gone a little soft. Started making these skeptical sniffing sounds. But Masha kept buzzing on, full of conviction.

"After all, is that what love really means? Just to do *that* at night over and over, countless times? Anyway, you get released from here real soon and I have a little surprise for you."

"What kind of surprise?" he frowned.

"The sooner you get released from here, the sooner you'll know," she smiled.

"And it's no lie," Viktor Parfentyevich suddenly cried out in a high, thin voice. "May I be a scoundrel and a rat if I'm lying. May I never get up again from this yellow bench we're getting callouses on till morning if I'm lying. You know what happened next? Next the *collective* helped them out. No lie."

"Viktor Parfentyevich," I said cautiously, "What are you saying, brother? How could that be? Think about it yourself. In such a ticklish and intimate problem how could the collective help? Aren't you putting me on a little? You ought to be ashamed."

"It's no lie," Viktor Parfentyevich insisted stubbornly. "Someone once wrote that the will of the collective is stronger than the gods, and you know that damn well yourself. If you admit that Love is also a

*Pastries with a layer of curds or sour cream [tr.].

God, well, look and see what came of it. I'm not lying. And don't interrupt anymore, because my story is coming to the end."

What happened was that Mitya was still in the hospital when Masha had to go to the factory committee office about the question of his disability pay form. Well, they quickly got everything she needed together but for some reason she hung around, and Svetlana Aristarkhovna Lizoboi, who just happened to show up there, started talking with her in a kind and tender way, "What's wrong, honey? Things bad?" she asked point-blank.

Masha began to cry.

"There, there. No use crying. Tears never solved anything," Svetlana Aristarkhovna said with deliberate crudeness. She took her into the office where she worked as chief bookkeeper, and at the same time performed the social function of chairperson of the women's council of the factory.

"Now then, what's the problem between you two?" she appealed to Masha.

Masha looked into Svetlana's sympathetic eyes and, without thinking about what she was doing, went and told her literally everything.

Svetlana Aristarkhovna nervously lit a White Canal cigarette.

"Damn, I thought it was something like that," she blurted out. "They've begun whispering all sorts of unkind things to me about you, but I had faith in you. Ah, you young people, young people. Why didn't you come earlier to the collective for help?" Masha looked at the floor.

"Ah, you young people," Svetlana Aristarkhovna repeated. After which she pulled out some sort of official form from her desk and, with her eyes suddenly gleaming bright blue, the penetrating, deep, dark eyes of an old textile worker, said:

"This is a travel authorization. Go together to Leningrad. There you'll find a certain famous professor." She spoke his last name. "And without fail he will help you. Do you understand?"

"Yes, but it's so embarrassing," Masha whispered hiding her face in her hands.

But Svetlana Aristarkhovna took Masha's embarrassed face from behind her hands and tenderly embraced her, and apparently they even cried together a little then, the two of them, Svetlana Aristarkhovna Lizoboi and Masha Pyrsikova—there in the office of the chief bookkeeper, with the working day in full swing—the bookkeeper who simultaneously performed the social function of chairperson of the women's council of the factory. A very important function.

And that's how they came to be in that phantasmal city on the Neva, which began its existence with Peter the Great and now is all bedecked in granite, marble, and bronze. In fact, it proved to be not at all easy to break out of those fog-drenched Leningrad streets and reach the clear light of day—the professor's illustrious presence. But the certificate, with its many stamps and signatures, finally got them there. And at the appointed hour the professor admitted them to his large, high-ceilinged office, where a cream-colored lamp gave off a warm glow. Beyond the thick drapes a narrow strip of some nearby body of water could be seen, and on it a small steamboat was sailing, and a small sailor bending over the rail was bitterly spitting in the water. Masha and Mitya were very impressed with the office and liked it a lot.

But they absolutely did not like the professor. He was a young-looking man with a totally stylish appearance and thinning but long hair. He was wearing bell-bottom jeans, red wool socks, and platform shoes, which did not detract from his impeccably white doctor's coat and round, gold-rimmed glasses.

He was obviously bored, this balding doctor. He smoked, wrinkled up his eyes, and crossed his legs. He continued in this way, bored, grimacing, smoking, and listening to Masha, who stammered the whole time as she kept one eye on Mitya, who for his part had completely turned to stone.

"Get undressed," the professor said to them at last.

"Totally?" Masha's voice trembled.

"Uh-huh," said the professor, indifferently swinging his modish shoe.

So they got undressed, burning with shame. The skinny professor got up briskly, examined them, and ordered them to get dressed again. He himself said nothing, he only buried himself in a pile of papers.

"What's going on?" Masha couldn't restrain herself.

The professor lifted his head and smiled.

"You may go," he said.

"Yeah, but what about us?"

"You?" The professor was surprised. "There's nothing wrong with you, my dear exemplary working people. Most of our citizens could only envy you. You are an ideal couple, absolutely normal, healthy people . . ."

"But—," said Masha.

The professor interrupted her: "Please let me finish. I've written about this in the press more than once, and now I'll repeat it to you, since you obviously don't read the papers. You simply haven't studied one another at all, my young friends. It's an elementary matter of investigating the repulsive thing called sex education."

"But what are we to do?" Masha was dismayed.

"I'll tell you . . ."

And in an everyday tone of voice the professor began to tell them such surprising pieces of filth that Masha couldn't believe her own ears. She got red as a beet, but Mitya kept saying nothing, saying nothing, till finally he barked out at the professor:

"You better shut up. You should be ashamed to talk that way in front of a woman."

"Well now, I just don't know, my kind and gracious comrade," the professor said ironically, spreading his hands. "Which is more important to you and the young woman—shame or health?"

Mitya: Masha, let's get out of here.

Masha: Wait, Mitya. Comrade professor—

Mitya: What kind of professor is he? Professor of sauerkraut soup—

Professor: And yet you'll thank me to the end of your days, and send me telegrams.

"Sure, right away," said Mitya. "We've sent them already."

"Maybe we should argue this out?" the professor screwed up his eyes.

"Sure, yeah, go ahead," said Mitya. And apparently it was there and then that he made a vow to paint this picture back in his home town and go off to work on the Baikal-Amur Mainline.

They left. A fresh wind was blowing off the Neva, down which ice from Lake Lagoda was floating to no one knew where, along with the usual garbage. Staid middle-aged Leningraders were carrying their fashionable shopping bags. The two of them stood on a bridge. The wind tousled Mitya's curly locks and filled Masha's beautiful skirt. The fresh wind blew off the Neva, and Mitya looked into the distance, unseeing, to where Peter the Great, on a horse with a serpent at its feet, was cutting a window open onto Europe, where the cannon of the former Peter and Paul Fortress once had boomed and thundered. He could see the golden dome of Saint Isaac's Cathedral, witness to tremendous upheavals, and the sea gulls soaring proudly overhead.

They stood on the bridge.

Suddenly Mitya embraced Masha roughly. Masha cried, "Oh."

Mitya: Masha, what are we going to do? Maybe we should throw ourselves headfirst off of here. Do you really love me?

Masha said nothing.

Mitya: If you really love me, let's. What good is this kind of life? Let's throw ourselves off.

"Let's," whispered Masha, growing faint with fear and realizing that there was no one to call to for help because night was falling and there wasn't a living soul around, let alone a hospital orderly. And why call for help anyway, when it would be better to die this way—calmly, quickly, beautifully. Suddenly in a frenzy Mitya seized her, because somewhere in the heavens he had glimpsed the foxy snout of the professor. He crushed her to him and kissed her, and suddenly he swung her back, but she grabbed the cast-iron railing of the bridge and held on with a death grip, listening to the sound of his labored breathing.

All at once the light of day began to dim before her eyes, then it flared up again, and a green spark appeared and grew larger, in time with his movements, and the light on the water grew sweet as though someone was walking on the water and light was coming from him, and the light from the one walking on the water grew greater, and then came an atomic explosion of light. Blinding light exploded and devoured everything living all around. It exploded painfully and blessedly. It exploded so blessedly, so-o-o . . .

"Oh-oh-oh," she said.

"What?" he asked hoarsely.

"Oh-oh-oh," she said.

"What?" he asked.

She looked around. She kept looking around and sucking in air with her open mouth.

"What? What?" he kept asking and asking.

"Oh-oh-oh, my darling, I love you," she said at last.

And, my dear friend, on that high note, Viktor Parfentyevich ended his "true story." After which, grabbing at his cheek and demanding some more vodka, he began going on about all sorts of utter nonsense. That he himself was this Mitya. And when I reminded him that Mitya had gone off to work on the BAM, he shouted that he was going to work on the BAM too, and that everyone was going there who had any conscience, unlike me who wouldn't give him more vodka. And only then did I, entranced by his mysterious tale, guess the truth—that in all the commotion he had drunk up what vodka we had left. I grew terribly angry, accused him of cheating, and said that in a decent place people like him would get a punch in the mouth.

He then began to cry, covering his face with his tattooed hand and saying from behind his hand something like this.

"God take it, the bottle. There's plenty of bottles in the world, but this is what I think, sonny. And most likely you're not going to disagree with me. You know what? In life, you don't pick your woman. Just like you don't pick your parents either, for example. Either she's there with you, your woman, or she's not. The same way you either have your parents with you, or you've buried them."

By this time I had reconciled myself to the loss of the vodka, and somehow this trickster had touched me.

"The same way, a woman doesn't choose you. Same conditions apply to her," Viktor Parfentyevich went on, muttering and mumbling.

Again I found myself agreeing with him. He was mumbling something else, but I was no longer listening. I was thinking about something else altogether.

I was thinking, dear friend, about how we look at the world and we don't know it. We don't know what, where, or how. For example, the story presented above, seemingly a rather tasteless one—what is it really, a piece of cynical philistinism? Or on the contrary, something light and sweet and good? Or maybe actually, it's all those things mixed together, both good and bad and vile and holy. And the blue flute? Maybe it's actually all those things together. Maybe it's the complete wholeness of the world. That's what I was thinking, dear friend, on that wearisome night, when fate abandoned me to while away the heavy hours of the night at station S. on the Eastern Siberian Railway on the line from Abakan to Taishet.

Everyone around me was sleeping. Viktor Parfentyevich had fallen asleep, slumped against me, with his pointy shoulder bone digging into me. Yawning and staring, a silent policeman walked by with a round, childish face and a unique set of whiskers. The windows filled up with the dawn. The shepherdess played on her flute.

Poems and Songs*
by Vladimir Vysotsky

Write me a Letter, Lads

My first term was too much for me.
They'll slap on maybe a year or two more.
So write me a letter, lads.
How are things in that free world of yours!

What are you drinking out there?
There's nothing but snow here, nothing to drink.
So, lads, write me all about it.
Nothing happening here. What do you think?

I'd like a look at your ugly mugs!
It's really tough for me without you.
What's with Nadiukha there, who's she with?
Alone? Let her write me a letter, too.

Maybe only the Last Judgement is final!
A letter, for me, would be a lifeline.
Maybe they won't hand it over.
But a letter, lads, that'd be fine . . .

* * *

That evening I didn't drink, didn't sing,
Spent the whole time looking at her,
The way children stare, the way children stare.
But the guy who was with her before,
He told me I'd better leave,
He told me I'd better leave,
That I didn't have a chance.

And the guy who was with her before,
He insulted me, he threatened me,

*Translated by H. William Tjalsma.

And I remember everything, I wasn't drunk!
When I did decide to leave,
She said to me: Don't be in such a hurry!
She said to me: Don't be in such a hurry, ·
The evening is still young.

But the guy who was with her before,
He didn't forget me, I guess,
And once in the fall, once in the fall,
I'm walking along with a friend,
And they're standing there in a row,
And they're standing there in a row,
Eight of them in all.

I've got my knife with me, so I say:
You won't take me so easy.
Beware, you bastards! beware!
Why cash in for nothing? Then,
I was the first to strike,
I made the first move.
It had to be that way.

But the guy who was with her before,
He cooked up the whole mess,
Serious about it, too, serious:
Somebody jumped me from behind.
Valiukha yelled: Watch out!
Valiukha yelled: Watch out!
But it was too late!

You can only die once.
And there's an infirmary in jail.
I spent some time there, some time.
The doc cut me up and down.
He said to me: Hang on, brother.
He said to me: Hang on.
And I hung on—

The parting passed in an instant . . .
She didn't wait for me,
But I forgive her, forgive her.
Of course, I forgave her.
But I'll not excuse the guy
Who was with her before, with her before.
The guy who was with her before,
The guy who was with her before—
I'll show him!

The Red-Haired Broad

What's with you, shaving your eyebrows, slut?
How come you've put on your blue beret, whore?
And where are you off to, bitch?
I saw the other ticket to the club!

You know I dote on you, don't you,
That I'm ready to steal for you night and day!
But of late I've noticed something about you,
You've started to be unfaithful too much.

If it's with Kolka or even Slavka, OK!
I've got nothing against friends.
But if it's with Vitka from Pervaya Periaslavka—
Then I'll break your legs, I'll send you back to God!

Red-haired broad, I'll not keep it from you:
If you go on wearing your blue beret
I won't touch you—I'll bury you in my soul
And have you covered with cement.

And when summer comes—you'll come back again!
But I'll pick me a lady the likes of which
Will turn you green with envy, bitch.
You'll say: Forgive me, but I won't give a damn.

On Great Karetny Lane

Where'd you spend your seventeenth year?
On Great Karetny.
Where did your troubles begin?
On Great Karetny.
And where's your black pistol?
On Great Karetny.
And where aren't you today?
On Great Karetny.

> Do you remember the house, buddy?
> No, you'll never forget it!
> I say he's missed half his life
> Who's never been on Great Karetny.
> And how!

Where'd you spend your seventeenth year?
On Great Karetny.
And where are your seventeen misfortunes?

On Great Karetny.
And where is your black pistol?
On Great Karetny.
And where aren't you today?
On Great Karetny.

> It's been renamed, you know.
> Everything's changed—believe it or not.
> But wherever I've been, wherever you roam,
> You'll pass down Great Karetny yet,
> And how!

Where'd you spend your seventeenth year?
On Great Karetny.
And where'd your misfortunes begin?
On Great Karetny.
And where is your black pistol?
On Great Karetny.
And where aren't you today?
On Great Karetny.

* * *

If I was rich as the king of the sea,
I'd just call out: catch the bait—
Without a thought I'd splash out for her
My underwater and above water world!

> The crystal house on the hill is for her!
> Myself, like a dog, I grew up in chains . . .
> My silvery springs,
> My gold in the ground!

If I'm sick like a dog, alone,
And the house is deserted, empty,
Then help me, Lord!
And don't let me mess up my life . . .

> The crystal house on the hill is for her!
> Myself, like a dog, I grew up in chains . . .
> My silvery springs,
> My gold in the ground!

I'd never compare you to anyone,
Kill me, shoot me, I won't!
Look how I gaze on you
As if you were a Raphael Madonna!

The crystal house on the hill is for her!
Myself, like a dog, I grew up in chains . . .
My silvery springs,
My gold in the ground!

In No-Man's Land

On the border with Turkey or Pakistan,
There's a neutral zone. On the right by the bushes—
Our border guards and our captain.
On the left side—their post,
       And in no-man's land there are
       Of extraordinary beauty.

The captain's lady decided to move in with him,
She arrives and says: Darling! This and that . . .
You've at least got to give your bride a bouquet—
A wedding without flowers is just a drinking party.
       And in no-man's land there are
       Flowers of extraordinary beauty.

While, just as if on orders, their captain's girl decides
To come and live with him—taken by a whim!
And also: Darling! she says—in Turkish—
There'll be a wedding, she says, a wedding and that's that!
       And in no-man's land there are
       Flowers of extraordinary beauty.

Our border guards, brave lads—
Three volunteered to go with the captain.
How were they to know that the Asians had decided
That very same night to go after flowers, too.
       And in no-man's land there are
       Flowers of extraordinary beauty.

Our captain's dead drunk from the smell of flowers,
And their captain, he's flat out drunk, too.
He's sprawled in the flowers, grunting in Turkish,
And, crying in Russian "motherf——," our captain collapses.
       And in no-man's land there are
       Flowers of extraordinary beauty.

The captain's asleep and he's dreaming
That they opened the border like the Kremlin gates . . .
He didn't need a foreign border worth a damn.
He felt like taking a swing around no-man's-land.
And why not? The earth belongs to everyone!
It's actually neutral! . . .

And in no-man's land there are
Flowers of extraordinary beauty.

Parody of a Bad Detective Story

Fearing counterspies,
Shunning social life,
Under the English pseudonym
Of Mr. John Lancaster Peck,
Eternally in leather gloves—
No fingerprints, you know—
In the "Sovietskaya Hotel"
Lived a certain non-Soviet chap.

Usually at night and all alone,
John Lancaster
Clicked whatever it was
That he hid
His infrared lens in.
And then in normal night
There appeared in black and white
"That which we value and love.
That in which the collective takes pride."

The club on Nagornaya Street
Looked like a public toilet.
Our own Central Market
Became a dirty warehouse.
Distorted by the microfilm,
GUM resembled a little hut.
And it would be indelicate to say
What the Moscow Art Theater looked like.

But working without subordinates
Can be sad, can be boring.
The enemy thought about it. Diabolically clever,
He wrote a counterfeit check
And, somewhere in the bowels of a restaurant,
Good Citizen Epifan
Was led astray
By the non-Soviet chap.

Epifan turned out to be hungry,
Sly, smart, voracious.
He knew no bounds
In women and beer
And didn't want to know any.

So it turned out like this:
John's subordinate was a find
For the spy. It could happen to anyone
Who's drunk and wishy-washy.

The first assignment:
At three-fifteen, next to the public baths,
Maybe earlier, maybe later,
A taxi would drive up.
He'd get in, gag the driver,
Play a simple thief, then later,
Blare it over the BBC.

And then: change clothes
And go to an exhibition at the Manège,
Where a man with a suitcase
Would come up and say:
"Would you like some cherries?"
And you answer: "Of course!"
He'll give you a loaf of bread
With explosives.
Bring it back to me.

"And for that, my drunken friend,"
He said to Epifan,
"There'll be money, a house in Chicago
And lots of women and cars . . ."
The enemy didn't realize, the idiot,
That he was ordering around
A Chekist, a major in intelligence
And a fine family man.

Even that master of such tricks,
The very Mr. John Lancaster!
He really slipped up,
The notorious Mr. Peck.
He was neutralized and even
Clipped and thrown into jail.
Then a peaceful Greek arrived
At the Sovietskaya Hotel.

About a Sentimental Boxer

Bang! bang! Once more, bang!
Again, bang! And then
Boris Budkeev (Krasnodar)
Gives me the old one-two.

Then he gets me into a corner,
And I just barely get out,
Then the old one-two and I'm
On the floor feeling bad.

And Budkeev thought, while shattering my jaw:
"It's good to live and life is good!"

At the count of seven, I'm still lying there.
The local fans are moaning.
I get up, lunge, dance back—
Glasses would look good on me.
Not true, as if I'm saving up
For the end.
Since childhood I've been unable to beat somebody's face in!

But Budkeev thought, shattering my ribs:
"It's good to live and life is good!"

In the stands, they whistle and howl:
"Get him! He's yellow!"
Budkeev closes in,
And I press back on the ropes.
But he gets through, he's Siberian—
An insistent and nasty lot.
And I say to him: "You character!
You're probably tired, so rest!"

But he didn't hear me. He was thinking:
"It's good to live and life is good!"

And he keeps on hitting . . . tough devil!
I see there's going to be trouble.
True, boxing is not brawling—it's a sport
Of the brave, and so on . . .
So he hits me one, two, three
And runs out of strength.
The ref raises my hand,
The one I didn't use in the fight.

Budkeev lay there thinking life is good . . .
Good for some, for others a bunch of crap!

About a Wild Boar

In a quiet and harmonious kingdom,
With no wars, cataclysms, or storms
A wild boar appeared, an enormous one,
Either a buffalo or a bull or an aurochs.

The king himself suffered from a bad stomach
And asthma. Just his cough caused others great fright.
Meanwhile, the huge and terrible beast
Was eating folks or dragging them off to the woods.

So the king issued three decrees at once:
The beast must be subdued, at last!
Whoever dares to do it, to do it,
Will win the princess's hand in marriage.

And in this desparate kingdom, the minute
You enter, then crossways,
In reckless boredom, living the life of a hussar,
Was the former-best-but-out-of-favor archer.

On the castle floor there were skins and people
Singing and drinking mead . . . and then
Troubadours trumpeted the call from the castle
To seize the archer and bring him in.

And the king coughed out to him: I won't
Read you a lecture on morals, youth.
If you're victorious over this monster tomorrow,
You'll receive the hand of the princess.

But the archer says: What sort of reward is that?
Roll me out a barrel of port instead!
I've got no use for a princess in any case—
I'll beat the monster for you anyway.

The king: You'll take the princess—period!
If you don't, I'll toss you in jail just like that!
She's the king's daughter after all!
The archer: Even if you kill me, I won't!

And while the king was wrangling with the archer thus
Almost all the women and hens were eaten up,
And the buffalo or aurochs sort of thing
Was hanging around the castle wall.

The king was powerless: the archer
Got his port, captured the monster and beat it . . .
Thus the former-best-but-out-of-favor archer
Insulted the princess and the king.

Concerning Evil Spirits

In the forbidden and sleepy
Terrible forests of Murom
All kinds of evil spirits

Wander at will,
Sowing fear in passersby.
They howl like the living dead,
If you hear a nightingale—it's a nightmare.
'Tis terrible, oh, horror!

In enchanted swamps
Dwell night frights
That'll tickle you to death
Or drag you off
To the bottom of the river.
Be you on foot or on horseback,
They'll grab you. The wood goblins
Ramble through the forest so.
'Tis terrible, oh, horror!

And a peasant or a merchant or a warrior
Comes along in the enchanted forest,
Drunk or for some other reason,
Stupidly crawling into the grove.
And for one reason or another
They disappear
Never to be seen again. Vanish.
'Tis terrible, oh, horror!

They've come from all over the world,
From places that are downright hell,
Where the demons are so evil
They all but eat each other up
In order to get together
And share their evil experiences.
'Tis terrible, oh, horror!

Solovei-Razboinik, chief among them,
Arranged a stormy feast.
Zmei Trekhglavyi was there
And his servant, a vampire.
They drank brew from skulls, ate bagels,
Danced on graves, the blasphemers.
'Tis terrible, oh, horror!

Zmei Gorynych climbed a tree,
Just to rock it back and forth.
Bring on the girls, Razboinik,
Let 'em show their stuff!
Let the wood goblins dance and sing.
Otherwise, you mother, I'll rot them all.
'Tis terrible, oh, horror!

Solovei-Razboinik was something else.
He whooped and whistled: Dope!
Pig! Foreign parasite!
To Zmei Gorynych swinging in a tree:
Get out of here, scram,
And take your vampire with you!
'Tis terrible, oh, horror!

They all started yowling like bears:
"We've suffered!" "All these years!"
"Are we witches or not?"
"Patriots or not?"
"Roll your eyes, bloodsucker, you got yours!"
"He was ogling our ladies, too!"
'Tis terrible, oh, horror!

But now the grey-haired folk
Recall previous affairs:
The evil spirits clambered all over each other
Till they were trampled to death.
The clamor was silenced forever.
A man comes fearlessly into the forest.
Ant 'tisn't terrible the least bit!

Ice Sheet

An ice sheet on Earth, an ice sheet,
All the year long!

> An ice sheet on Earth, an ice sheet!
> As if there's no spring, no summer,
> The planet dressed in something slippery,
> People falling slam onto the ice.

An ice sheet on Earth, an ice sheet,
All the year long!

> Even when flying around the planet,
> Not touching it with their feet—
> If not one then the other will fall—
> Ice sheet on the Earth, ice sheet!—
> Boots trampling across it, trampling.

An ice sheet on Earth, an ice sheet,
all the year long!

> As if there's no spring, no summer!
> People falling slam onto the ice!

Ice sheet on the Earth, ice sheet!
Ice sheet all the year long.

The Crescent Beach Is No More*

The crescent beach is no more,
There's not a trace left of the oaks.
Oak is great for parquet—
So that's that:
Some husky slobs
Came out of their hut
And cut them down
For coffins!

Take it easy, take it easy, the grief
I've got in my heart!
That's only the opening line
Of the fairy tale ahead!

It's great to live in houses
On chicken, on chicken legs,
But a doltish sort
Arrived, putting people in a fright!
A great guy he was,
Got the old witch drunk
And did a brave deed—
He burned the house down.

Take it easy, take it easy, etc.

Thirty-three bogatyrs
Decided they'd been had,
Guarding the Tsar
And the seas.
They all grabbed a plot of land
And started raising chickens, sitting there
Guarding their own,
Not on the job!

Take it easy, take it easy, etc.

Stripping a green oak,
Their chief
Turned it into firewood.
The troop

---

*This song refers to a poem of Pushkin's, *Ruslan and Lyudmilla*, about a cat in an oak tree by the seashore, who tells fairy tales about "old Russia," the "real Russia."

Started getting crude with the folk.
And day after day
Their old sea chief cursed and screamed,
Though he had a place
Near Moscow.

Take it easy, take it easy, etc.

There is a cat here, true,
Walking left—he sings,
To the right—he tells a joke!
Real learned son-of-a-bitch,
Took the golden chain
To a pawn shop,
And then off
To a liquor store.

Take it easy, take it easy, etc.

Once it happened that as a gift
He got some royalties—
And Crescent Beach
Stank to high heaven
Of booze.
But he got apoplexy,
And to escape the wrath of God
He's dictating a memoir
About the Tartars!

Take it easy, take it easy, etc.

And the water nymph—what a tale!
She didn't keep her virtue for long,
And gave birth, best she could.
Thirty-three muzhiks
Don't want to know
Their little son.
Let him be, for now.
The son of the regiment.

Take it easy, take it easy, etc.

Once it happened a certain wizard
And liar, blatherer, and laugher,
As an expert
In the ways of the ladies,
Suggested to her:
Water nymph, I'll understand,
I'll take you and your baby!

So she went off to him
As to a prison.

Take it easy, take it easy, etc.

The bearded Chernomor
Crescent Beach's top thief,
He made off with Liudmila long ago—
Oh, he's cunning!
He takes advantage of the fact
That he can fly.
You're standing there with your mouth open,
And he's gone.

Take it easy, take it easy, etc

And the flying carpet
Was turned over to a museum last year;
The inquisitive folk
Shove through!
Carefully the old codger
Steals women—no matter how much they weep—
Oh, let him be a cripple,
The taster!

Take it easy, take it easy, etc.

Once it happened
That a wood goblin didn't get enough to drink,
So he beat up his wood goblin wife.
He yowled:
Gimme a ruble, otherwise I'll nail you!
Am I the breadwinner or not?
Gimme it or I'll drink up
The chisel!

Take it easy, take it easy, etc.

As for unheard-of animals
And stuff—there's none of that anymore:
The hunters came in droves,
And that was that!
So that it's no secret
That the crescent beach is gone!
Everything that the poet wrote of
Is blather!

Take it easy, take it easy, grief,
Don't wound my soul!

If that's the opening line,
Then the fairy tale is poppycock!

* * *

And people keep murmuring, murmuring,
People want justice:
We were first in line
And those behind us are already eating.

They were told: So that there won't be any cursing,
We ask you to leave, dear friends!
The people eating are foreigners!
And you—excuse me—are who?

But the people keep murmuring, murmuring,
The people want justice:
We were first in line
and the people behind are already eating.

The administrator explained once again:
I ask you to leave, dear friends!
The people already eating are members of a delegation!
And you—excuse me—are who?

But the people keep yelling, yelling,
The people want justice:
We were first in line
And behind us they're already eating!

On the Death of Shukshin

The cold hasn't come, nor the ice.
The earth is warm, the guelder rose is red.
But one more man has lain down in the ground
In Novodevichii Cemetery.

> Probably he didn't know
> What the frivolous common folk say:
> Death takes those first
> Who play at dying.

So then, Makarych, don't be in a hurry.
Undo the pegs, loosen the clamps.
We'll shoot it over! We'll rewrite the script!
Play it again! Stay alive.

But, you took a bullet in the stomach
That would make strong men weep,
Fell to the ground like a faithful dog,
And there a guelder rose grew,
A red, red guelder rose.

He would have been Razin this year!
What's reality? The Onega! The Naroch?
Yes! Stoves-benches, Makarych,
That kid of yours is no longer alive!

You caressed the white trunks of birches
In the hollow, cinematic dawn,
But settled down in earnest,
More decisively than in the movies.

Death takes the very best,
Drags them off one at a time.
What a brother of ours has departed!
It went badly with him!
He does not rage or grieve.

So after a temporary hitch
Fate muttered through its teeth:
"Remove the taboo from the one with the high cheekbones
For having seen in the grave
All the wakes and memorial services!

Take that one with the great soul in his body
And the heavy burden on his humped back,
Take him out of bed on a warmish morning,
So that he does not experience his fate."

And after the obligatory bath,
Clean and smiling and sober,
He up and died in earnest,
More quietly than in the movies.

Letting his coffin into the earth
Amidst the birches of Novodevichii,
We howled, lowering our friend
Into the roar without time or boundary,
Next to a lilac bush growing there,
Autumnal and naked.

Wolf Hunt

I'm at my wit's end, tendons taut.
But like yesterday, again today

They've surrounded me, surrounded me,
Driving me happily for the flags.

From the pines—double-barrel flashes.
Hunters lurk there in shadow.
Wolves somersault in the snow,
Living targets.

> It's a wolf hunt, a wolf hunt!
> The drivers yell at the gray beasts of prey,
> At old-timers and pups alike!
> And the dogs bay until they vomit.
> Blood on the snow and the red spots of flags.

The hunters don't play fair with wolves,
And their hands never quiver!
Fencing off freedom with flags,
They blast away happily.

A wolf shouldn't break with tradition:
As blind pups we sucked our mother's milk,
And with our mother's milk we learned—
"Don't go beyond the flags!"

> It's a wolf hunt, etc.

We're fast of leg and jaw.
Leader, why not give us an answer—
We're being driven by their guns—
Let's break through the boundary!

A wolf should not, cannot do otherwise . . .
So this is the end of my life:
The one I was destined for
Smiled and raised his gun . . .

> It's a wolf hunt, etc.

I disobeyed, passed through the flags,
—The thirst for life is stronger!
Only afterwards did I hear the surprised
Cries of the people behind me.

I'm at my wit's end, tendons taut,
But today is not like yesterday!
They surrounded me, surrounded me,
But this time the hunters
Were left holding the bag!

> It's a wolf hunt, etc.

Bathhouse Blues

Make me a steambath and let out the smoke,
I need a world without smoke.
I'll pass out, I'll go out of my mind,
The steam will loosen my tongue.

Make me a steambath, lady,
I'll roast myself, I will.
On the very top bench,
I'll burn out the doubt in myself.

I'll get obscenely mellow,
A mug of cold water—and everything is in the past.
And the tattoo on my left breast,
From the days of the cult of personality, will glow blue.

Make me a steambath and let out the smoke,
I need a world without smoke.
I'll pass out, I'll go out of my mind,
The steam will loosen my tongue.

So many truths and forests have fallen!
There's been so much grief, so many roads!
And on my left breast—Stalin's profile,
On my right—Marinka *en face.*

Make me a steambath and let out the smoke,
I need a world without smoke.
I'll pass out, I'll go out of my mind,
The steam will loosen my tongue.

I remember how early one morning
I just managed to yell to my brother, Give me a hand!
And two pretty bodyguards
Carried me out of Siberia into Siberia.

And then, in quarry, in swamp,
Choking on tears and the dust of the mines,
We tattooed that profile over our hearts
So that He would hear how they were being torn to pieces.

Don't end my smokeless steambath,
I need a world without smoke.
I'll pass out, I'll go out of my mind,
The steam will loosen my tongue.

Ay, you're shivering! Getting sick listening?
The steam has driven things out of my head.

Out of the cold fog of the past
I plunge into the hot fog.

Thoughts start beating in my skull.
It turns out that I branded myself with Him for nothing!
So I beat myself with a birch branch
On the legacy of these gloomy times.

Make me a steambath and let out the smoke,
I need a world without smoke.
I'll pass out, I'll go out of my mind,
The steam will loosen my tongue.

The Horizon

So that there won't be a trace—sweep everything clean,
Curse me and shame me and roar.
My finish line is the horizon, my ribbon, the edge of the earth.
I must be first at the horizon.

Not everybody approved of the conditions of the bet,
And the stake was unwillingly held.
The conditions were this: to drive down the highway
And only the highway, without turning back.

Winding the miles on the axle,
I speed along parallel to the wires,
But every now and then there's a shadow in front of the car—
A black cat or somebody dressed in black.

I know that they'll poke a stick in my spokes,
I can guess how they're going to deceive me.
I know how they'll cut off my race with a grin,
And across what road they'll string a wire.

But I step on the gas. At these speeds
A grain of sand acquires the force of a bullet.
And I squeeze the wheel until my bones ache,
I must get there before they start tightening the bolts!

Winding the miles on the axle,
I speed along vertically toward the wires.
Faster—they're twisting the nuts—
Or they'll pull a wire right up to my neck.

And the asphalt melts, the tires boil,
My heart aches from the nearness of the denouement.
I tear the stretched line with my bare chest.
I'm alive—take off the black bandages!

Who forced me to make such a harsh bet—
They argue and calculate dirtily.
The rush intoxicates me, but, say what you will,
I break on slippery corners.

> I wind the miles onto the axle
> To spite ribbons, lines, and wires;
> It will only bring the losers to their senses
> When I appear on the horizon!

My finish line, the horizon, is just as far off as before.
I didn't break the ribbon, but I have done with the line.
My jugular didn't cross the ribbon,
And they're shooting at my tires from the bushes.

It wasn't the money that turned me on to racing.
They told me: Don't waste your chance!
What if there's a boundary at the edge of the world?
And is it possible to push aside horizons?

> I wind the miles onto the axle.
> I'll not let them shoot at my tires.
> But the brakes refuse to work—coda!
> And I cross the horizon at full tilt.

* * *

He was a surgeon, neuro, even—
Although he didn't know the difference between miles and
    hectares.
At the congress in Rio de Janeiro
Everybody else was small fry next to him.

> He could turn folks who had just about had it
> Into normal people again, but
> This big star, alas,
> Was a Jew.

In science he was used to fighting,
Everything was done step by step.
He put a new brain into the head
Of a certain pioneer.

> He could turn folks who had just about had it
> Into normal people again, but
> This big star, alas,
> Was a Jew.   .

Dialogue

Oh, Vania, look at the clowns!
They're grinning from ear to ear.
And they're all painted up, Vania!
And they talk like drunks.
 And that one looks like—no really, Van,
 Like my brother—same sort of booziness!
 No, no, just take a look, take a look.
 No kidding, Van!

Listen, Zina, leave your brother alone.
No matter what—he's kin!
You're painted up yourself, smoking like crazy . . .
Look out, I'll show you!
 Instead of blabbing, Zin,
 You go get some booze at the store!
 What? You won't? OK, I'll go.
 Get out of my way, Zin!

Oh, Vania, look at the dwarfs!
They're dressed in jersey, too, not worsted.
In our clothing factory No. 5
There's nobody who could make the like.
 But all your friends, Van,
 They're such riff raff!
 And they start drinking such crap
 So early in the morning!

Even if they don't have fancy outfits
My friends care for their families.
And they drink garbage to save money,
Even if they do start in the morning.
 But you've got such friends yourself, Zin,
 That guy from the tire factory,
 He actually used to drink gasoline.
 Remember Zin!

Oh Vania, just look at the little parrots!
Honest to God, I've got to yell!
And who's that in the tee shirt?
Van, I want one just like it, myself.
 At the end of this quarter, right, Van,
 You'll make me one like it, won't you . . .
 Whadaya mean "shove off"? "Shove off" again?
 That's not nice, Van!

You'd just better shut up.
You can kiss the quarterly bonus goodbye.
Who sent complaints about me to work?
Whadaya mean "no"—I read them.
    What do you need a tee shirt like that for, Zin?
    It would just be a shame,
    Just a waste of cloth.
    Where's the money, Zin?

Oh, Vania, I'll die from the little acrobats!
Look at how that one spins, the imp!
Our Director of Entertainment
Jumped just like that in the shop . . .
    So you come home, Ivan,
    And have something to eat—then onto the sofa.
    Or you yell when you're not drunk.
    What's with you, Van?

Zin, you're asking for trouble.
You're always aiming to hurt someone.
I race around all day,
Then come home and there you sit.
    Well, then, Zin, the liquor store beckons,
    My friends are there, waiting for me.
    I don't drink alone,
    You know . .

Oho, you gymnast!
Ouch, what are you doing, at your age!
In the "Swallow" milk bar at work
There's a waitress who likes to do that stuff.
    And you've got friends, Zin,
    Keep knitting caps for winter.
    I go out of my mind from just looking
    At their ugly mugs!

What, Van? What about Lilka Fedoseeva,
The cashier from CPCR?
At the housewarming you kept making up to her.
She's not so bad, is she?
    But why fight, Van?
    Better let's take a vacation to Erivan.
    Whaddaya mean "shove off"?
    That's not nice, Van!

Steps[*]
by Fridrikh Gorenshtein

I

Grigory Alekseevich took a piece of bread from the porcelain bread dish and held it aloft with his arm tilting slightly backward.

"In terms of the historical law of opposition between the great bread-producing plains and the breadless peoples who had to struggle for their bread, Russia was always a great bread plain," he said, "whereas ancient Rome, Germany, and England always went after their bread . . . And believe me, Yury, it's not national arrogance; it's simply that we people of the bread plains are particularly open to notions like goodness, happiness, and justice, since we have not been deprived."

Grigory Alekseevich tossed the piece of bread back into the dish and drained his glass of cognac.

Yury Dmitrievich finished his cognac, too, and chased it with a swig of sweetened cold water colored with tea. He began to feel queasy from the sweetish concoction, and he felt a familiar churning under the left side of his rib cage, just intense enough to be annoying.

"We often cling to certain ideas," said Yury Dmitrievich, "not because of their substance but because of the literary form we've so aptly found for them . . . in any case, I'm tired . . . the thunderstorm kept me up all night . . . flashes of lightning . . . I had a dream, or maybe just a memory, as I was lying there awake . . . just amazing . . . a childhood fantasy of mine . . . once, when I was a child, I was starting to feel ill . . . my late mother came over to me, felt my forehead, and asked me what was wrong. I said, 'A spear.' 'What spear?' she asked, growing alarmed . . . and I replied, 'The kind they use to kill animals.' Then I lost consciousness, but those words were deeply embedded in my brain . . . the onset of delirium . . . from time to time I remember. . . ."

Yury Dmitrievich lumbered to his feet and went over to the window. It was the end of May. The leaves had already begun to lose their

*Translated by Barry Rubins and Vladimir Lunis.

spring freshness. The morning was as sultry as midday. A tram crawled laboriously up the hill along the cobblestone road. From a cathedral that was nearby but hidden from view by the rooftops came the thunder of bells.

"Grisha, I've stayed at your place for a week and a half already," said Yury Dmitrievich. "I have to find myself an apartment. . . . Your Galia and Shurka aren't returning before the middle of June?"

"Never mind that," said Grigory Alekseevich, "we've got three rooms. You're not a hindrance to me. What really matters is—"

"But you're a hindrance to me," said Yury Dmitrievich. "I like you . . . but I've got to get to work instead of engaging in fruitless arguments . . . what nonsense . . . students are on vacation now . . . I have to make use of the time off . . ."

"Yura," said Grigory Alekseevich, also rising to his feet. He was wearing a handmade Russian shirt embroidered at the neck and silk pajama bottoms. (Grigory Alekseevich had recently sprouted a little blond beard and had taken to wearing handmade Russian shirts he acquired in some remote village up north to which he had gone to collect folk material.) "Yury Dmitrievich, forgive me . . . I don't understand . . . what I mean is, don't you feel that your divorce is absurd . . . humorous, even . . . ah, humor, humor. I'm sorry, but do me a favor, try very hard and find a kernel of reason in my confused babbling. You're forty-six years old, Nina is forty-four . . . and that regrettable incident happened so long ago. . . ."

"No," Yury Dmitrievich shouted, "it wasn't twenty years ago that she was unfaithful to me, it is now . . . , today . . . a month ago. She was unfaithful not when she slept with another man but when I learned about it." He suddenly went limp and sat down at the table at a slight angle. He sighed deeply several times. "I've known her since I was fifteen, don't forget," he said softly. "She was my first date, and then my first girl friend and first woman. . . . I'm forty-six but I haven't known any other women . . . she went off on study trips . . . for months, for years I didn't know any women . . . they'd fall in love with me . . . I had this beautiful assistant. . . . And nights . . . at night a person is not the same as he is during the day . . . everyone knows that . . . daylight makes a nighttime feeling shameful and absurd . . . in the daytime a person can reason coldly, be ironic . . . but night consumes irony. When Nina wasn't home I'd imagine her, I'd picture her down to the smallest detail, and as I lay in bed I'd kiss my own forearms. . . ."

Having finished what he wanted to say, Yury Dmitrievich became silent and averted his eyes, as though he had done something shameful. Grigory Alekseevich didn't say anything either, and just looked out the window.

"I think I'll be going," said Yury Dmitrievich after a few moments of silence. "I have to see the lawyer . . ."

"You look dreadful," said Grigory Alekseevich. "I suggest you see Dr. Bukh. After all, he is a colleague of yours at the institute."

"Why should I see Bukh?" Yury Dmitrievich said, smiling wryly for some reason. "Bukh has a Zhmerinka accent . . . Benedict Solomonovich . . . if I go mad, I'll probably start singing Hebrew psalms." He thought he had made a good joke, but instead of smiling Grigory Alekseevich responded with a look of alarm.

Yury Dmitrievich put on his jacket, went out onto the staircase landing, and stood there for a while in a state of uncertainty. He took several steps downward, then quickly ran back up, opened the door, and started rummaging through the desk drawers that had been set aside for him.

"Grisha," he called.

"I'm in the bathroom," came Grigory Alekseevich's muffled reply.

"I hope you don't think I wanted to insult Bukh," said Yury Dmitrievich. "If I go crazy, I'll think I'm Don Quixote, not a rabbi. . . . But then again," said Yury Dmitrievich, speaking louder and starting to feel hot, "then again, modern Don Quixotes are just as uninteresting as modern bureaucrats. The sole advantage of Don Quixotes is that they're ridiculous and go unrecognized. The medieval term for Don Quixotism is delirium. One's perception of reality becomes distorted. Fear, rapture, affection, and complacency alternate with one another. Ah, dear Grisha . . . the archenemies of modern-day Don Quixotes are tranquilizers, not windmills. If Christ appeared today, he wouldn't be crucified; he'd be given an injection of aminazin and reserpine, judiciously followed by something to stimulate cardiovascular activity. At the current level of neuropathology grand delusions are impossible. . . ."

Yury Dmitrievich pulled on his tasseled skullcap and went out still greatly agitated, but looking focused rather than disconcerted.

He headed uphill. The ascent was so steep that there were steps built into the sidewalk. The higher he went, the louder the church bells sounded; as if acting out a dream connected with the Bible, he walked straight toward the firmament. Yury Dmitrievich looked back at the countless steps he had already climbed. He was totally alone on the blazing-hot asphalt steps. Bordering them on both sides were thickets of thorny acacias. On one side, the shrubs touched up against the grillwork fence of a park scarred with ravines; on the other side, they covered a grassy slope that ran down to the cobblestone roadway. Farther up the hill the bells continued ringing; before each heavy copper boom died away, a set of smaller bells hastily chimed in. Yury Dmitrievich ascended a few more steps, and suddenly an unfamiliar blissful feeling welled up in him, as though his chest had been laid open and with one breath he had become so utterly filled with life that living was now insignificant. He had gone beyond his own being and looked at himself from a distance with wise dispassion, though not without feeling a certain sadness about the human frailities that were now inaccessible. He was not a human being, he was mankind. All of this lasted no more than a moment, however, so it wasn't possible to comprehend anything in detail or retain any of it. He sat down on the steps; they were sticky and had an acrid smell of asphalt. He felt so drained that he could not bring himself to look in his pockets for a handkerchief to wipe the sweat and tears from his face. He was sitting in the shade of a bush, and beyond the hedge of acacias, at the bottom of the slope, the trams were busily grinding their way past. That, evidently, was why the sidewalk stairway was empty: nobody wanted to climb the hill on foot in such heat.

"Nevertheless, I'm getting sick," said Yury Dmitrievich. "I should see Bukh . . . what a bother . . . still and all, it *is* quaint. Unbalanced people usually imagine themselves as great personalities— Napoleon or Mohammed, but I thought I was all of humanity at once. Of all the instincts a human being is born with, the greatest and the saddest is the passionate urge to live . . . and here we find the chief contradiction between a human being and mankind. For mankind, death is a blessing, a guarantee of eternal renewal."

The bell up the hill had stopped. Getting up, Yury Dmitrievich took out his handkerchief and dried off his face. The final flight of steps was guarded by an iron railing. As he walked on up, he counted the steps and tapped the hot iron with his palm.

Coming from the deserted stairway and finding himself in a crowded square, Yury Dmitrievich was momentarily frightened and confused; however, he soon got used to the people and returned to his previous sensations which he had forgotten or, rather, repressed on the empty stairway during the tolling of the bell. To test himself, he went up to an ice-cream stand and bought himself a fruit-flavored ice cream in a waffle cone. He looked probingly at the woman vendor, who wore her white smock directly over her slip, without a dress. Although his look was obvious, it did not embarrass her. Nor did he himself, apparently, make any impression on her.

"Everything's all right, I guess," thought Yury Dmitrievich. "Just an ordinary neurosis . . . emotional trauma plus four nights without sleep . . . I'd better finish my work and go south."

He tried the ice cream, but it tasted sour and, at the same time, sickeningly sweet.

"How can that be?" Yury Dmitrievich puzzled. He didn't stop to wonder about it very long, however, and he threw the ice cream into a smouldering trash can.

The square was ringed by old multistory buildings of gray brick. On Yury Dmitrievich's left, the entire side was taken up by a cathedral set back in a courtyard skirted by a low granite wall. The cathedral was white, with many grilles and porticos on a roof covered with galvanized tin. Its gilded domes were engulfed in a sea of blue. A lot of old women were selling flowers in the courtyard, and it was noisy and crowded. Through the wide-open main doors of the cathedral something glittered and singing could be heard. So close to the dusty, hot trolleybuses and the listless faces of passengers and passersby dulled by the heat, the cathedral seemed to Yury Dmitrievich the only place where he could prolong the unusual state he had been in today; and even if he couldn't re-experience it, at least he might clearly recapture those sensations which had enticed him back there on the steps like voluptuous nocturnal sin whose purity could be destroyed and turned into an obscenity by a single careless move or look.

"Incidentally," thought Yury Dmitrievich, "there are some fine paintings by Vrubel in the cathedral . . . Grigory Alekseevich mentioned it . . . and I've never been inside . . . I should be ashamed, an educated person . . ."

Yury Dmitrievich entered the courtyard and walked up onto the parvis, where some beggars were standing. One beggar wearing a quilted jacket with nothing on underneath came up to Yury Dmitrievich. Crossing himself and whispering something through swollen lips, he held out his palm. He was a young man, about twenty-five, but his skin was yellow and wrinkled like an old man's. He had lean, protruding collarbones, a fat, sagging belly, and hips that were plump and womanish.

"You, my friend, need medical attention," said Yury Dmitrievich. "Your adrenal cortex is impaired and, evidently, your blood pressure is low . . ."

The fellow hiccupped and uttered something inarticulate. He had a black eye and reeked of bad vodka. Yury Dmitrievich slipped him a ruble and quickly moved on. The flickering of the candles, the glitter of the brocade and gilt, and the cool semidarkness, through which singing drifted from somewhere above, under the dome, calmed him down and dulled the unpleasant effect of his encounter with the beggar.

Yury Dmitrievich looked up. The walls were faintly lit, and the biblical frescos were barely discernible in the gloom. In one area he could only see a part of a human hand and beautiful, sensitive fingers; in another, the head of a young man, which exhibited a vague autumnal melancholy, typical of cyclothymia, more than it did the unworldly and the sinless.

"The characteristic feature of the depression associated with cyclothymia is the patient's inability to cry," thought Yury Dmitrievich. "How awful that is. The patient often complains that his heart has turned to stone, but this insensibility causes acute suffering . . . sometimes even suicide. Yes, cyclothymiacs have a high incidence of attempted suicides. . . ."

"Remove your headdress," someone said in a rancid breath at pointblank range.

In front of Yury Dmitrievich stood a bald-headed man with a

pointed nose; he was training an angry stare right between Yury Dmitrievich's eyes.

"The Tartars and Mongols have been here," said the man, "so have the Germans. We've had a committee from Moscow, too, and still, they removed their hats."

"Oh, I'm sorry, I was preoccupied, lost in my thoughts," said Yury Dmitrievich, yanking off his skullcap.

Behind him there was a burst of stifled laughter. Some teenage boys in warm-up suits were standing there with colorful bags over their shoulders. They kept elbowing each other and winking. The man with the angry eyes rushed up to them and tried to push them, but the boys dodged him and giggled.

"Never mind, Sidorych, let them be," said an old woman.

Yury Dmitrievich looked around and saw that there were many idle people in the cathedral who had come merely out of curiosity. People stood crowded together, but there were gaps in the crowd, like ice holes. After making his way around, Yury Dmitrievich saw and realized that in those gaps, contorted on the stone floor, lay the believers. He was particularly struck by an old man and a young woman. The old man's gray head and knobby hands were resting against the floor and his face was flushed like an acrobat's. Yury Dmitrievich nearly stepped on the young woman but started back in alarm. She had on a kerchief and sandals and was holding some flowers. She seemed alone with herself, not aware of anyone, oblivious to the assemblage of legs wavering near her face. Yury Dmitrievich carefully made his way out of the crowd and started to walk up to the second floor along the well-trodden runner of a winding marble staircase. On the stairs he met a nun carrying a box similar to the ones that are brought to the homes of people too sick to get to the polls during an election; only, it was black instead of red. The box bore the words, "Donations for the maintenance of the temple." The nun looked at Yury Dmitrievich questioningly. He took out a five-ruble bill and pushed it through the slot in the box, like a ballot. The nun crossed herself and continued down the stairs. Yury Dmitrievich went on up to the second floor, which had a highly waxed parquet surface. In the corner by the icons a middle-aged woman in a black dress and a pince-nez was resting her hands on a voluted marble barrier and whispering her prayers. Just below her left hand Yury Dmitrievich could read a graffito that had been made with a nail or a small knife: "George + Lucy = Love. 1906." Yury Dmitrievich couldn't help smiling but then quickly walked over to the opposite barrier, from where a view of the crown below and the prostrate believers in the midst of it brought to mind the parterre in a theater.

"Really," thought Yury Dmitrievich, now even a little irritated, "it does bear a strong resemblance to the theater . . . a common spectacle . . ."

To the right of him, in the balcony, was the choir. He saw the music stands with their electric lights, and the scores. A gray-haired, withered man wearing glasses—the choir director—was waving a baton. The choristers were mostly women, still fairly youngish, in knitted blouses. There was one man about thirty-five who had on a nylon shirt and a red tie. His cheeks were cleanshaven and well-fed. Another man was wearing an embroidered shirt. In the interval between prayers they exchanged remarks, emitted yawns. In front of one woman was a small dish of candied fruits, and there was an open bottle of mineral water in front of the choir director.

First, a bass resounded from below, and then the choir in the balcony rang out in response. Down on the stage appearances were made by some shaggy youths and an old man in brocade. After circling the stage they would disappear, and a silk curtain with a cross on it would jerk closed.

"It *is* theater . . ." thought Yury Dmitrievich, feeling annoyed. "And not very talented at that . . . why are these people lying about on the floor . . . that woman . . . I can't understand it."

He went downstairs again. Another nun came up the stairs toward him, carrying a black box lettered "For the support of the choir." When the nun stopped in front of Yury Dmitrievich, he was already very irritated; the nun just glanced at him and quickly walked on by, crossing herself. The singing stopped and the sermon began. The old man in brocade was standing at the edge of the platform with his arms crossed on his chest and was saying something. Yury Dmitrievich began to listen.

"The power of harbored insults is very great and enduring and only in prayer can it be vented completely. But is everyone capable of prayer? Some people even become offended. I prayed, they say, and asked the Lord, but He didn't hear me; my prayer was of no help. Prayer must come from the bottom of the heart, and if a person harbors even a single drop of selfishness or animosity at the moment he is praying, the Lord will not hear him. . . ."

As he went on, the old man started to repeat himself in the monotone of a dull lecturer mouthing vapid truths. Yury Dmitrievich stopped listening to him. He gazed in fascination at the young woman who earlier had been lying on the stone floor. She was about twenty-eight. She was wearing a cotton blouse that revealed the edge of a lace slip at the neckline. Around her neck was a cross and a strand of glass beads, and she was holding a slightly crushed and wilted flower in her hand. Her face seemed plain, at first glance at least, but after studying it more closely, Yury Dmitrievich sensed in it—and in her figure, too—something not yet awakened but attractive and promising. What fascinated him most was the childlike openness, the intensity and trust with which the young woman listened to the tiresome, insipid words of the sermon, sometimes even rising on her tiptoes so as not to miss a single word. It was particularly noticeable in contrast to the people standing idly by, yawning, looking around, whispering, and, in some instances, pushing their way to the exit. After the singing had stopped and the sermon had begun, the crowd had grown conspicuously thinner.

"With your prayers and your good deeds you are fighting for peace throughout the world," the preacher was saying, "and by working well in your own appointed field each of you performs a godly act in behalf of peace on earth, against war, and to the glory of our government."

"Right you are, pop," said a citizen in a polo shirt. "Public-spirited. A useful act. . . ."

The choir began singing again, and once more the worshipers got down on the floor, creating gaps in the crowd. The young woman had gotten down and tucked her knees in close to her stomach, so that one could see the worn soles of her sandals. The choir thundered louder and louder, candles crackled, the brocade curtains rippled, the gold of the icons glittered, and the woman prayed more and more fervently, more and more tempestuously, her face radiant and happy. Yury Dmitrievich stood there looking dull and faded, and what had happened to him on the steps today now evoked only a feeling of mean irony and shame. But suddenly something extremely unexpected occurred, an episode which many people talked about afterwards and which even to this day in those parts continues to be the subject of rumors that take on the most fanciful shades of embellishment.

At the very moment when the singing of the choir started up again, far back in the cathedral, where the icons glimmered in semidarkness, appeared the vague outline of a naked body. The silhouette started to drift slowly across the wall. Its right arm was upraised as though it were blessing everyone. A frightening, painful silence descended on the cathedral; the only sounds were the crackling of candles and someone's heavy breathing mixed with sobs. The tense silence lasted several minutes, until a shaggy-maned young man in vestments, standing next to the old man giving the sermon, started bellowing: "Kondraty! Kondraty, grab him . . . the police, call the police. . . ."

Kondraty, a broad-shouldered young stalwart in a monk's cassock, rushed toward the silhouette, which was now slipping away. An old woman began yelling, something fell with a crunch, noise and commotion erupted.

"Kondraty!" shouted the fellow with the mane. "Move in from the right, he's in the niche."

"Comrade monk," yelled the citizen in the polo shirt, "he's over there . . . there he goes, he jumped out . . ."

Kondraty dashed over and raised a hefty fist, but the woman in the cotton blouse suddenly interjected herself between the naked body and Kondraty and took the blow intended for the nude. She fell but immediately sprang to her feet and grabbed hold of Kondraty's cassock at the neck. Yury Dmitrievich hurriedly forced his way toward her. Her face was bloody, and there was a cut over her eye. The skin around it had begun to swell and turn dark blue. Kondraty vainly tried to tear her fingers loose from his collar as he gasped for breath, then with an enraged grunt swung his elbow menacingly. But Yury Dmitrievich shoved him aside and drew the woman to his chest. Her fingers relaxed and her head in its skewed kerchief sagged backwards. Glass beads slipped off their broken strand and softly clicked against the stone floor. Puffing angrily, Kondraty ran off to the other end of the cathedral, where the naked silhouette was now wavering. Two policemen with embarrassed faces entered the church and looked around uneasily. One of them, after a moment's hesitation, even removed his cap. They disappeared along with Kondraty in the semidarkness of the cathedral but soon reappeared, escorting a naked man. As they led him along, they kept his arms outstretched to either side, in the standard police grip, with one policeman holding his left arm and the other his right. From a distance it looked very much like the Crucifixion.

Yury Dmitrievich could feel the woman against his chest shivering, as though she were feverish. Her face had turned pale and the temple she had pressed against his chin was cold and moist. When the policemen got the prisoner into the light, he turned out to be a fellow about eighteen with a crew cut and a nice tan. He was wearing white, woolen swimming trunks. His face bore a wry, intoxicated smirk. As he was being led away, he passed close by and Yury Dmitrievich experienced a twinge of fear and, at the same time, disgust—the feeling one gets from seeing a crocodile or a swarm of rats. From behind the icons Kondraty appeared, squeamishly carrying in his outstretched hand a warm-up suit he had found.

"It's the atheists, the blasphemers, they instigated it," said Sidorych, the bald man who had admonished Yury Dmitrievich for not removing his skullcap. "They did it, to make fun of the feelings of the worshippers. No, it is rightly said: you shall fight your enemies first with a cross, then with a fist, and then with a club."

Sidorych went around with a list, looking for witnesses. He approached Yury Dmitrievich, too, as someone directly involved in the skirmish, and Yury Dmitrievich perfunctorily stated his name and place of employment. Then he walked towards the exit, holding the woman around her shoulders and pressing his handkerchief to the cut over her eye. The woman submissively walked with him; she was in a half-conscious daze. They crossed the courtyard and Yury Dmitrievich sat her down on the granite parapet of the wall around it, in the shade of some overhanging tree branches. The cut on her brow was not very deep, but her black eye was getting more and more livid, turning a shade of yellowish violet.

"A cold compress of Goulard's extract would help," said Yury

Dmitrievich. "I think there's a pharmacy nearby."

"I'm cold," the woman whispered.

She was shivering so violently that the heels of her sandals were tapping. Yury Dmitrievich moved her out of the shade into the sun, but even though she was now sitting on scorching granite she continued to shiver.

"They've killed him again," said the woman.

"Be quiet," said Yury Dmitrievich, "you need rest. You've got to lie down . . . where do you live?"

"I get a stabbing pain right here," the woman said. She took Yury Dmitrievich's hand and placed it on her breast near her left nipple. Her breast was girlishly supple and Yury Dmitrievich instinctively pulled back his fingers.

"Cardioneurosis," said Yury Dmitrievich. "Don't worry, now, it's only nerves . . . do you have any pain in your arm or in your shoulder blade?"

"My palms hurt," the woman whispered feverishly, "my feet hurt, too . . . right where they pierced him with nails . . ." The woman fell silent, then unexpectedly produced a faint but happy smile. "Love, love," she repeated. "What a pity I'll never see my heart . . . I'd like to smother it with kisses because it's so full of love for Christ. . . ."

The woman's fingers were cold and her pulse rapid.

"I'd better get an ambulance," thought Yury Dmitrievich. As he looked around for a passerby whom he could ask to make the call, he noticed a weird old man hurrying toward them. He had bushy gray eyebrows, long gray hair, and a long gray beard. He was wearing an old felt hat pulled down low over his head. From a distance, Yury Dmitrievich thought he was dressed in a cassock, but it turned out to be simply a shabby old raincoat without a back belt that the old man was wearing in spite of the heat. He had sneakers on his feet, and around his neck, together with a cross, hung a small oval portrait of Leo Tolstoy.

"Zinochka," the old man cried out when he saw the bruises on the woman's face, "I told you not to go, I told you—"

"Papa Isai," said Zina, and as she embraced the old man and kissed him she began to cry. "They crucified him again—"

"They won't crucify him," said Papa Isai, "and even if they do crucify him, he will rise again three times over . . . I was on the bench, I waited for you on the bench. . . . Do you also believe in the Christianity of the Church?" he asked, addressing Yury Dmitrievich.

"I don't know," said Yury Dmitrievich, "I don't understand you . . ."

"There is the Christianity of Christ and the Christianity of the Church . . . have you read Tolstoy's "Destruction and Restoration of Hell"? Christ destroyed Hell, but the Church restored it."

"I've thought about it," said Yury Dmitrievich. "That is, about Christ and religion in general . . . right now, though, we should call an ambulance . . . or better yet, I'll get a taxi . . . we can go to my place . . . it's not far. She needs a dressing and some rest . . . she should lie down for a while. You stay here with her, I'll be right back . . ."

Yury Dmitrievich went out into the middle of the street and hailed a taxi. With Papa Isai's help he put Zina on the back seat.

"Who gave her the working-over?" asked the driver.

"She fell," Yury Dmitrievich said, and then told the driver the address.

II

As they got out of the taxicab at the entrance to the building, a number of passersby and tenants stopped and watched them. They did, in fact, make a rather unusual looking group. Yury Dmitrievich was a tall man with graying blond hair. His face, though now a little haggard, still looked well-groomed. He was wearing heavy tortoise-shell glasses, a cream-colored silk suit, and expensive imported sandals. He was holding on to the hand of a poorly dressed young woman who had a cross around her neck and, what was more, bruises on her face. From the other side the woman was being supported by some half-deranged old man. The situation was complicated by the fact that deep down Yury Dmitrievich felt ashamed of his companions, a feeling that was beyond his control, and that made him even more tense. Consequently, he was even happy to see a barking dog come bounding out of the gateway, and he stepped toward it so energetically that the enormous German shepherd abruptly shied away with its tail between its legs.

Yury Dmitrievich hoped that Grigory Alekseevich would not be at home but he was, and he met them in the front hall, surprised though relatively calm. Apparently, he had seen them from the window and his first reaction had already passed.

"You see, Grigory," said Yury Dmitrievich, "the young lady has had a mishap . . . If you mind, of course, we'll go to the hospital."

"Don't be silly," said Grigory Alekseevich. "The first-aid kit is in the kitchen, you know where."

Yury Dmitrievich led Zina into the kitchen, sat her down on a chair, took off his jacket, rolled up his sleeves, deftly treated her bruises, put on some adhesive bandages, and applied an astringent compress to Zina's black eye.

Zina sat there tired and indifferent. Whereas earlier she had looked pale, now her face was red and profusely covered with beads of sweat. Yury Dmitrievich wiped away the sweat with a piece of gauze. Then he guided her to his room and installed her on the divan, slipping a pillow under her head. Papa Isai was still standing in the front hall with his coat on, and opposite him, just as silent, stood Grigory Alek-seevich.

"I guess I'll be going," said Papa Isai. "I'll sit awhile on the bench downstairs and wait for Zinochka."

"No, no," said Yury Dmitrievich, "we haven't finished our conversation. As a matter of fact, we just started it . . . I want to talk now . . . I want to think . . . take off your coat. . . ."

He helped Papa Isai out of his raincoat. Underneath it he had on a velveteen Tolstoyan tunic.

"Take off your jacket too, it's hot," Yury Dmitrievich fussed, becoming more and more animated.

Papa Isai took off his jacket too, and under it he was wearing a fresh white Russian-style shirt. A portrait of Tolstoy hung from a neat little moiré ribbon.

"I'll put on some tea," said Grigory Aleksecvich.

"So then, what was it you were talking about?" said Yury Dmitrievich when Papa Isai had seated himself at the table. "The Christianity of Christ and the Christianity of the Church."

"It was faith and not the Church that brought the Gospel down from Heaven to earth," said Papa Isai. "Faith made it applicable on earth."

"Now that's interesting," said Yury Dmitrievich, picking up the thread. It was his own thoughts, rather than the words of Papa Isai, that had roused him. "Christianity changed from a religion into a form of government . . . the materialization of an ideal. . . . That's right, Grigory. You look surprised, but you and I have lived nearly all our lives during an era in which contemplation has been replaced with unambiguous slogans . . . I don't mean the false slogans . . . I'm talking about the true ones: Thou shalt not kill . . . Thou shalt not steal . . . All men are brothers. . . . Ideals that, instead of soaring in the air, became firmly planted on the ground, satisfied immediate needs. I can see that there might have been a brutal necessity for it. Nonetheless, there was an enormous danger lurking in it, since it violated the natural way of thinking. . . . What was I trying to say?" Suddenly confused, he put his hands to his temples. "Ah, yes, I was talking about an ideal, an ideal that was enclosed within a slogan and sent down to earth. The meaning and the grandeur of any idea is in its ultimate conception, its ideal, and the truth is always simple. That's right, I agree . . . the meaning and grandeur of any mountain is in its peak, but if you were to chop off the peak of Everest and put it in the middle of a field . . . all you'd have is a sorry little mound . . . and that's precisely why an ideal is called an ideal, because it can never be achieved, like a steak or a woman . . . when it materializes, it vanishes. . . ."

Yury Dmitrievich circled the table. He could feel an unusual surge of strength. His eyes had a feverish gleam and his face was hot. Papa Isai, sipping from a saucer the tea served by Grigory Alekseevich, said:

"The earth is just what it is—the earth, a hodgepodge with its ups and downs, its tripe. . . . Go and save this planet here and not one flowing with honey. That's just a pipe dream . . . this is why Jesus came down to the earth. . . ."

"Now here's where you've got it all wrong," Yury Dmitrievich cried out with a certain delight, like a child. "This is an important point . . . this is a very important point . . . I want to take issue with Jesus . . . and in order to do so I have to accept him, for now at least. What I want to dispute is the key principle, the central idea: love your enemy . . . nonresistance to evil . . . answer evil with good. Agreed . . . but only evil that is still in gestation, still unborn . . . this is the kind of evil that needs good. Remember Dostoevsky's idea that the salvation of the world is of no use if it comes at the price of even one child's destruction? That idea expresses the height of man's humanism . . . an ideal one cannot live without . . . an ideal that in fact vanishes or even becomes its own opposite when it materializes. . . . So then, to summarize, the main thing I disagree with Jesus about is his interpretation of the slogan "nonresistance to evil," not as a philosophical notion but as a guide to action. "Love your enemy" is not a slogan for today, it's an ideal to strive for . . . when there aren't any more enemies . . . when all men become brothers. . . ."

Yury Dmitrievich stopped talking. He was so keyed up that no sooner had he sat down than he jumped up and began unbuttoning the collar of his shirt.

"What you've been saying is interesting, though debatable," said Grigory Alekseevich, "but take it easy, have some tea. You haven't been sleeping at night, I can hear you pacing when I wake up . . . you need some rest. You've attacked slogans here, but a slogan is a thought that has assumed the form of dogma. The thought of any man is finite, it has a birth and a death—dogma, that is—like any living thing. The only thoughts that don't end in dogma are those of barren dreamers. Progress of any kind is a movement from one dogma to another . . . in any case, let's have some tea . . ."

In the meantime, Papa Isai had wilted from the tea and the heat and had dozed off. His head drooped on his chest and the portrait of Tolstoy made gentle taps against the edge of the table. Yury Dmitrievich moved his glass of tea closer and spooned out some jam from the pot, but suddenly sprang to his feet, dropping the jam on the table cloth, and hurried to his room. Zina was not asleep. She was sitting with her legs curled up under her like a child and was looking at the wall. Her face had taken on a pink tinge.

"I have to go home now," said Zina. "I feel uncomfortable about being here . . . you're such a busy man . . . you look like a professor."

"No, I'm not a professor," said Yury Dmitrievich, "I'm a physician, a doctor. It was my duty to help you."

"Do you believe in God?" asked Zina.

And suddenly Yury Dmitrievich realized that right now, standing before this naïve young woman in the chintzy blouse, he had to clear up some very important notions for himself. And the naïveté of this woman would not allow him to get by on his experience, to say just anything, to lie or toss off some apparent truth without doing a bit of soul-searching.

"I want to believe," he said after a few moments of silence, "but there is no God, my sweet . . . there isn't, my dear . . . because for ages man has hungered for him and dreamt of him in a way that he could only hunger for and dream of something that never existed and couldn't possibly exist . . ."

He said this with such passion and such pain that the woman stared into his face and suddenly understood him and believed him.

"There isn't," she said mournfully, craning her neck like a bird, "and cannot be . . . there never will be." Tears flowed from her eyes as she reflected, but they were not tears of protest and this was in no way a lament. There was no longer any reason to protest or any reason to cry.

"I was only joking," said Yury Dmitrievich in alarm. "I believe in God . . . I go to church . . ."

He moved closer to the woman, touched her hair— and at that instant, as though jolted back to her senses, she shoved him away, jumped up, her face distorted with terror, and socked Yury Dmitrievich in the shoulder, rather painfully hitting a muscle. With her other hand she knocked off his glasses. Yury Dmitrievich tried to protect his face with his hands and instinctively crouched down, then grimaced as he brushed against the end table that had a vase on it. The vase fell with a crash, and shards of glass skittered across the floor.

Grigory Alekseevich ran to the room and for a few seconds stood dumbfounded in the doorway. Then he rushed at the woman, grabbed her by the shoulders, and shoved her away.

"What *is* this?" he yelled, astonished and frightened. "What's going on here? What is this? . . ."

"It's my fault," said Yury Dmitrievich, grimacing as he rubbed his injured shoulder and fumbled on the floor for his glasses. "I committed an outrageous act . . ."

The old man, looking drowsy-eyed, edged his way into the room. He stood there yawning pleasurably and made the sign of the cross over his mouth.

"Papa Isai," Zina said, weeping, and embraced him. "Papa Isai, let's get out of here . . . let's hurry . . . quickly . . ."

"Yes, it's time for you to go," Grigory Alekseevich said hasteningly. "Yury, I'd like a word with you . . . come on, come with me to the kitchen . . ."

He took Yury Dmitrievich by the shoulders and led him into the kitchen.

"Yury," he said, "Nina called. . . ."

"Yes, so . . .?" said Yury Dmitrievich.

"She wants to see you . . ."

"Fine," said Yury Dmitrievich, "later on sometime . . . she can see me later . . . right now I'm in a hurry . . . I have to see them off . . ."

"They've already gone," said Grigory Alekseevich. "What do you need those holy fools for? She's not just religious, she's a fanatic. Don't you think all this might have unpleasant repercussions? You are a respected man in the community. You publish articles in medical journals."

"Oh, please . . ." said Yury Dmitrievich, anxiously looking over Grigory Alekseevich's shoulder at the door. "What have medical journals got to do with it. You can see I'm in a hurry, I'm busy . . . I've got visitors . . ."

"Yury, you're ill," said Grigory Alekseevich. "It's my duty as your friend . . . as someone who cares for you . . . and for Nina, too . . . I won't let you go . . . I'm calling Bukh immediately . . ."

"I refuse to be watched over," Yury Dmitrievich shouted so loudly that he felt a pain in his chest. "I'll move to a hotel."

"I won't let you go," said Grigory Alekseevich. "You want to fight me . . . cause a public scandal?"

"Grisha," said Yury Dmitrievich in an unexpectedly calm voice, "please understand that I must . . . please . . . sleep is out of the question . . . I've committed a despicable act against that woman. Maybe I *am* unwell . . . I'll go and see Bukh myself. As soon as I finish up things I'll go south . . . I need a rest. If you like, we can go together . . ."

"All right," said Grigory Alekseevich, "what can I do with you . . . but go wash up, you really look wild—"

"I haven't time," said Yury Dmitrievich, "they'll leave . . . they'll disappear . . ."

He quickly smoothed down his hair and ran out onto the stairway landing, and without waiting for the elevator he started down at a run. When he covered three flights and reached the second floor, he collided with Zina, almost knocking her down.

"I'm sorry," he said, stunned and overjoyed, "I was looking for you. It's a good thing I didn't take the elevator . . . what luck. . . ."

Zina looked at him and suddenly bent forward and pressed her lips to his hand. Then she knelt and kissed his feet, both of his dusty sandals.

"What are you doing," Yury Dmitrievich shouted in embarrassment, "for God's sake, get up . . . for God's sake . . ."

From overhead came a burst of raucous laughter. Hanging over the railing one floor above were two pulpy faces, and Yury Dmitrievich couldn't tell if they were male or female.

"Hey there, you grovelers, I'll give you a buck if you lick off my shoes!"

And the other one chanted: "What's the matter, what's the matter, someone knocked out someone's tooth . . ."

"You scoundrels!" Yury Dmitrievich yelled.

"He's swearing," said one of the faces. "He's frowning. I think he's having stomach trouble."

"Can't you see? He's an armed crackpot," said the second face. "One minute he'll start crowing like a rooster, the next he'll wail like an accordian . . ."

"Most of all beware of vengeance on men's vulnerability," Zina said softly. "I stand guilty before you and before these people, and before everyone . . . I doubted the Lord . . . darkness came over me . . . I caused you pain and I want to atone for it. I will serve you . . . I will wash your feet and drink that water . . ."

"No, no," said Yury Dmitrievich, "I'm the one who is guilty. Please forgive me. Let's go downstairs, I'll take you home."

Papa Isai was waiting for them by the entrance.

"Well now," said Papa Isai, "I can see your faces are calm . . . Your faces are beautiful now. . . ."

"I'm going to take Zina home," said Yury Dmitrievich.

"All right," said Papa Isai. "I'll head for the train station. I want to go out to the forest . . . to lie on the grass for awhile and listen to the birds . . ."

He doffed his hat and bowed to them, walked along past the wall, and then turned the corner.

"Where do you live?" asked Yury Dmitrievich.

"A long way off," said Zina, "on the very outskirts of town . . . It would only put you out. I'd better come to your house. If the floor needs washing, or your clothes. . . ."

"No, no," said Yury Dmitrievich, "I take them to the laundry. As for putting me out, don't worry . . . I enjoy this. . . ."

They got a taxi and drove off. They rode for a long time without saying a word, except when Zina once in awhile gave directions to the driver. Finally, they arrived. They were, in fact, in a suburb. Not far away, on a knoll, one could see the remains of a small village with a little church and a graveyard. The fields that once surrounded it were all dug up with trenches and foundation pits, in the midst of which several five-story standard boxes were already standing. The fields receded beyond a small river, a swampy tributary of the larger river that flowed through town. On the left were the crumbling moss-covered walls of a monastery, with twigs growing right between cracks in the bricks and through loopholes. One of the towers housed a kerosene store and there were drums standing about.

"I live here," said Zina. "I used to live over there, in the village, but they demolished it and moved us to the monastery."

They walked around and came up to some massive gates bound with rusty iron. Not far off, in the weeds, lay the rusty barrel of an ancient cannon. A wicket made out of newly planed boards was set into the gates; tacked to the wicket was a small piece of paper bearing a message in rough hand-printed letters that read: "Please don't slam the gait, nock lightly."

They squeezed through the wicket, held fast by a tight spring, and walked under an arch that resonantly echoed their steps. They came out into a cobblestone yard overgrown with grass. In the middle of the yard was a dilapidated gray church showing traces of a fire that had occurred long ago, probably during the war. The lancet windows of the church were vacant and twigs were growing out of them, also. The only panes were in the basement, which was now a city commerce department warehouse stacked with cases of bottles. There were crates, hanks of wire, and drums out in the yard, too, under enormous oak trees whose girth it would have taken three men to span. The oaks were so old that their bark had peeled off in many places and their trunks had developed bald spots. Under a roof by a wall that still bore a soot-blackened fresco, construction workers had set up their storage area. It provided refuge for some toilet bowls and gas ranges, plus some bags of cement. Some distance away, far inside the yard, stood a two-story, white stuccoed building, evidently constructed at a later time. Standing by the entrance on wooden gun carriages were two ancient cannons with their barrels tilting upward.

"There used to be a museum there," said Zina, "but now it's an enterprise of industries for the handicapped. I do work at home for them, knitting blouses. We're supposed to have a meeting; we're going to be criticized for not fulfilling our quota . . . I have to find out when—tonight or tomorrow. Right now the deaf-mute division is having a meeting—"

Just then there was an outburst of noise and a disheveled man in a ripped tee shirt emerged from the doorway. He was being steered along with his lone arm pinned behind his back by a stocky man in dark glasses, paramilitary jacket, and blue pants.

"Peregudov is making a ruckus," said Zina. "He gets drunk every day and comes here for a fight—either over the rates or because his pay's been docked for skipping work. If it weren't for his handicap, he would have been in jail a long time ago. He also beats his wife. The other man, the one in the glasses, is Akim Borisych, a member of the Board. It was through his efforts that I got a separate room, but I'm afraid of him," she said, suddenly drawing close to Yury Dmitrievich trustfully. Her face now looked like an ordinary girl's: a bit frightened and helpless, blue eyes, delicate cheeks tinged with light fuzz. And to Yury Dmitrievich the feel of her warm body against his own, through the clothing, had become pleasant.

Several more men came spilling out after Peregudov and Akim Borisych—deaf-mutes, judging from their gestures. They were vigorously moving their hands and smiling. Suddenly Peregudov bolted and broke loose. Then he picked up a stick from the ground and charged at Akim Borisych. Akim Borisych made no effort to evade him; on the contrary, he stiffened, then, raising his head and extending his hands forward with the fingers spread out, like a hypnotist, he slowly turned his torso, as though he were sniffing the air with his fingers. With a lightning-quick movement he snatched Peregudov's stick-wielding hand in midair and gripped it tightly. As Peregudov helplessly waggled the stump of his other arm like a fin, Akim Borisych began slapping his face, raising welts on Peregudov's neck and cheeks with his well-developed, sensitive fingers.

Yury Dmitrievich rushed over to them and instantly felt an intense pain from a blow to his cheek. But the blow was even more frightening than it was painful, since it had come from something more like a rigid flipper than a human hand.

"That's not him!" shouted Zina. "That's not Peregudov . . . Peregudov ran away . . ."

Peregudov had indeed broken loose in the confusion and run off toward the gate.

"Why are you butting in, citizen?" Akim Borisych said angrily. "I wanted to hand that rowdy over to the patrolman. We've had enough of him. He's knocked over the inkstand in the accounting office, smashed the typewriter. . . ."

Akim Borisych spat angrily and walked toward the door of the office. The deaf-mutes also walked away.

"What a stupid day," said Yury Dmitrievich. "Fights. You and I get hit, Zina."

"That's all right," said Zina. "Maybe it's for the best. Maybe God is beating the sins out of us."

"Is he blind?" asked Yury Dmitrievich, holding his aching cheek.

"He was born blind," said Zina. "But he's not really handicapped, he's been used to it since he was little. . . . I'll be right back, I'm just going to find out about the meeting," she said, walking off toward the white building.

Yury Dmitrievich stood there for a while in the yard. He looked around for a shady spot to sit down in and then he, too, walked off toward the white building. The front door of it led into a long corridor filled with the smell of boiled potatoes. Evidently, behind one of the doors along the corridor there was a dining hall or cafeteria. Yury Dmitrievich's mouth began to water and he remembered that he hadn't eaten since morning. He started following the smell, but stopped when he realized he might miss Zina. He stood in front of a door left half open, probably to allow some fresh air into a fairly large room, almost an auditorium, where a meeting was in progress. A good number of men and women sat crowded together on benches. In front of them was a table at which several men were sitting—the presidium, most likely—and a lectern. Strung along the wall was a long banner emblazoned with two-foot-high letters that read, "Deaf-mutes in the

U.S.S.R. enjoy the same civil and political rights as those who can hear." An announcement of the meeting, artistically embellished with curlicues, was tacked to the door. Item number one was "Production problems" and item number two, "The personal matter of carpenter Shmigelsky." In all likelihood, it was the second item that was now being considered, the man at the lectern being in fact carpenter Shmigelsky. Repentantly, he put his hands to his heart, pounded his chest with his fist as if he were making a vow, and with his finger he alternately kept touching the tip of his nose and his earlobe. On closer look, Yury Dmitrievich speculated that touching the nose indicated the name of the hook-nosed gray-haired old man sitting on the presidium, whereas touching an earlobe signified the chairman, who was making a vain attempt to establish order. The deaf-mutes on the benches were angrily gesturing all at once and, odd as it might seem, or at least as it seemed to Yury Dmitrievich, the room echoed with the clamor of many voices.

At that moment Zina returned. From her Yury Dmitrievich learned in detail the story of Shmigelsky's misconduct. While Peregudov, who could hear, was an inveterate old rowdy, Shmigelsky, a deaf-mute, had up till now been quiet and well behaved, and his act was a surprise to everyone. Though his behavior could not be justified, still, there had been mitigating circumstances. Carpenter Shmigelsky had failed to report for work for three days because his wife had been sick. Since he hadn't submitted a medical certificate on time, the accounting office docked his wages for being absent without reason. Carpenter Shmigelsky then went to the accounting office to clear up the matter. Although the bookkeeper in the payroll department, Haim Matveich, the hook-nosed old man, was not a deaf-mute, he had learned their language fairly well. He was able to talk to them in signs and the deaf-mutes liked and respected him. This time, however, Shmigelsky got worked up and began gesticulating wildly. For the first time in fifteen years of working with deaf-mutes, Haim Matveich couldn't understand a thing, and that in turn began to irritate him. A confused argument took place, ending with Shmigelsky, in a state of great excitement, gripping his nose with his fingers and twisting it from side to side. Inasmuch as this gesture was construed as anti-Semitic by the local deaf-mutes, and since it was witnessed by the chairman of the local trade union, who happened to be walking by, the matter was duly prosecuted. And that was the background of this stormy meeting, which was now apparently coming to an end. After a few gestures by the chairman, the deaf-mutes raised their hands in a unanimous vote and the repentant Shmigelsky embraced Haim Matveich effusively. Haim Matveich bent his right arm at the elbow, formed a circle with his thumb and forefinger, and waggled his other three fingers. This evoked applause and rejoicing from the deaf-mutes. The meeting was over. To the sound of scraping benches the deaf-mutes got up and started to leave, continuing to exchange impressions. Yury Dmitrievich and Zina also went outside.

"We can go to my place," said Zina. "You must be hungry . . . I'll make you something . . ."

Zina lived in a one-story structure with thick walls. Her room was a small cell with an oval window shielded by an iron grating. The walls were papered and in spots discolored with damp stains. The room was rather clean and comfortable. It had a couch, outmoded but not threadbare, with a new vinyl seatcover. Shelves rising from the back of the couch held all sorts of knickknacks: celluloid ducks, little porcelain elephants, two identical porcelain Uzbek girls in skullcaps and baggy trousers, sitting cross-legged. One of them was painted but the other was not—apparently a reject or a second. On a special stand in the corner, under an icon, lay some skeins of wool and knitting needles, and a sweater with one unfinished sleeve. A reproduction of "Christ's Appearance to the People" hung on a wall. The table was foreign-made, from Finland, with a polished white surface edged in black. In the corner opposite the icons, behind a folding screen, was a kitchenette of sorts, furnished with a small kitchen table, an enamel pail of water covered with a board, and some pots hanging from nails hammered into the walls.

Yury Dmitrievich made himself comfortable on the couch, stretching out his legs, cracking his knuckles, and pleasurably taking in the smell of fried onions coming from behind the screen, where Zina was puttering over a kerosene stove.

There were two knocks at the door and, after a pause, three more. Zina hurried to the door, drying her wet hands on her apron. Yury Dmitrievich was amazed by the change that came over her face. It looked frightened and confused, and her small ears had turned crimson. In the doorway stood Akim Borisych sporting a haircut, smelling sweet, and holding a bouquet of flowers.

"Come in, Akim Borisych, I'm making supper," said Zina fussily.

Akim Borisych thrust the flowers right at her face and patted her cheek. Actually, he was slightly off the mark at first and his fingers grazed the back of her head; but then he quickly found her cheek. Akim Borisych smiled but his smile immediately faded. Apprehensively, in a way that was unnaturally stiff and precise for a human being, he straightened up, as he had done earlier in front of Peregudov, and his dark glasses, like the eyepieces of some cybernetic mechanism, began scanning the room, until they locked onto Yury Dmitrievich. Yury Dmitrievich felt a slight nocturnal chill begin to creep up from the small of his back toward his shoulder blades.

"This is Yury Dmitrievich," Zina said hastily, "an acquaintance of mine . . ."

Akim Borisych's face, as if obeying a new signal from within, instantly lost its mechanical stiffness and broke into a smile.

"I accidentally hit you, please forgive me," he said, and after taking a step exactly in the direction of Yury Dmitrievich, he offered his hand.

Yury Dmitrievich looked at his own palm disconcertedly, then desperately thrust it forward, as though putting it into the gears of a machine. Akim Borisych's handshake was gentle, supple—too gentle and delicate for a human being. The machine simply operated in a different mode and this frightened Yury Dmitrievich even more.

"Are you religious, too?" asked Akim Borisych.

"Actually, I'm a physician, a doctor . . ."

"I see, I see," said Akim Borisych. "It's good that Zina meets people like you . . . because she's got all those religious zealots around her . . . she ought to be torn loose from the shackles of religion."

"Akim Borisych," said Zina, "I fulfill my quota. My belief doesn't interfere with my work."

"I'm not talking about your work," said Akim Borisych. "Religion interferes with your life. You need to meet a good man, have a family. I managed to get her a room, even though our enterprise was only recently organized. The deaf-mutes, blind, and other handicapped were consolidated . . . an appropriate step . . . reduces the size of the managerial staff."

He seated himself at the table and from the wicker basket he was holding he took out a bottle of vodka and a jar of marinated tomatoes. Zina set down a platter of sliced fresh cucumbers and onions dressed with sunflower oil, a plate of boiled new potatoes sprinkled with sizzling cracknels, and some thick slices of light brown smoked pork fat. The first round was drunk to Zina. Yury Dmitrievich followed it down with assorted bites of everything: a piece of pork fat, a couple of cucumber slices, two potatoes. He was soon high, and after his second glass he unceremoniously moved closer to Akim Borisych and asked:

"Were you born blind?"

"Yes," said Akim Borisych, whose movements were no longer precise. "I have often thought of you," he said with a scornful smile, "the sighted . . . you're unfortunate . . . I read your books . . . I hire a reader expressly for that purpose. All your misfortunes stem from your ability to see. Eyes are the instrument of man's enslavement by external space. Take the notion of beauty, for instance. Beauty is out of your reach . . . instead of it belonging to you, you belong to it . . . beauty can only be captured by feel—"

"Why capture it, blind man?" said Yury Dmitrievich, feeling his heart begin to pound, as if his national honor had been insulted. "Maybe beauty is beauty precisely because it *is* unattainable . . . and the moment it comes within your reach it vanishes. Have you ever seen . . . I mean, have you ever imagined the stars . . . not in January, when they're small and harsh, but in August, when the sky is alive with them?" He knew it was cruel to ask a question like that but he asked it anyway because the blind man irritated him so much. In response the blind man merely broke into hearty laughter.

"I know from a textbook on astronomy," he said, "that stars are hot and cold also. Outward appearance is deceiving . . . reality is in the feel . . . sometimes I dream and I dream only of touching . . . I dream something hard or soft, or hot or cold, or wet or dry . . ."

"But what about form?" said Yury Dmitrievich, now experiencing a totally new sensation, or, rather, having a presentiment of something unknown but near at hand. "Surely you must have a sense of line—"

"You're mistaking me for someone who has lost his sight," said Akim Borisych. "Those people are absolutely pitiful . . . worse than people who can see. They miss their slavery. I was raised by a mother who also was blind since birth . . . my father lost his sight . . . he was a pitiful man. When he woke up in the morning he'd curse and cry . . . he'd shout that he hated the darkness, and when he got drunk he would threaten me with eternal darkness . . . a fool. The only thing I cannot visualize, even approximately, is darkness. Form, line, convexity—I can imagine, but it always has to be warm or sharp or wet. I once got very sick and while I was delirious I imagined three lines intersecting each other at their ends, and the lines had no sensation attached to them. They seemed to be squeezing my head from three directions . . . and I thought that I had either died or else had just understood something of great significance . . ."

"That was a triangle, a geometrical figure" said Yury Dmitrievich. "You saw it in your delirium, like a sighted person . . ." And the thought suddenly occurred to him that this was no man across from him but some other intelligent being who had simply become adapted to living among people and had adopted their habits. For a moment or two, Yury Dmitrievich stared intently at Akim Borisych, until the latter reached out and scooped up some salad, though not without clumsily spilling some on the tablecloth; he was slightly agitated.

"The same thing happened to me," Yury Dmitrievich said softly, "this morning on the steps. You know that steep street that juts right into the sky . . . the sidewalk has steps built into it . . . and up above you can hear the church bell peal . . ."

Akim Borisych scooped up more salad, but this time with a firmer hand; he had evidently gotten over his agitation and Yury Dmitrievich's story about the steps in the sidewalk had no effect on him.

"There's a blind man who goes to the church in the village here," said Zina, breaking her silence, "a holy man . . . he exhausted himself, lives on prayer and bread."

"He went blind," Akim Borisych said crossly, "I'm sure he went blind, he wasn't born blind. Someone born blind lives entirely in himself . . . he doesn't need God . . . the sighted invented God in order to justify their own enslavement. Thousands or millions of years from now, man will be born a blind creature."

"Eye sockets may be all that's left," said Yury Dmitrievich, "just like the rudimentary tail in the vertebrae of the coccyx. But it won't be a human, it'll be some other intelligent being . . . completely immersed in its brain, not in the external world . . . and among those beings any child will have a depth of understanding that even Einstein couldn't reach. But they'll see the shape of a triangle with their brains after thousands of years of effort by the best minds, and maybe that will actually be the high point of their civilization . . . because they'll be moving in a direction counter to human civilization . . . from cognition to observation . . . and maybe that is in fact the antiworld and antiman."

When he finished speaking, Yury Dmitrievich was surprised to notice that instead of sitting upright, he was leaning forward with his head pressed against the sharp edge of the table and a smarting crease was imprinted on his forehead. Akim Borisych was no longer listening to him, having drifted away long ago, and was now talking in whispers to Zina.

"I'm going to see off Akim Borisych," said Zina, but not without a certain uneasiness, as though she were reluctant. "Why don't you splash some water on your face, you look all wilted . . ."

Akim Borisych got up, nodded politely, and walked toward the door somewhat unsteadily, even bumping against the doorjamb with his shoulder. Zina threw on a shawl and followed him out.

III

Yury Dmitrievich sat there feeling slightly dizzy—a result, he thought, of his conversation with the blind man. Outside the window there was a noise and commotion, and even something akin to a faint scream. Yury Dmitrievich looked in that direction with alarm but promptly sank back into the oblivion of his thoughts. He reached for a marinated tomato and just sat there sucking in its cool, agreeably tart juice. Zina walked in. Her dress was torn at the breast.

"He has gone berserk," Zina said angrily. "He's blind but there is no fear of God in him. 'Marry me,' he says 'Stop knitting blouses . . . I have a house of my own, a garden. If you don't marry me, I'll report you as a parasitic element. The police have been watching you for a long time, you get young people involved with sects . . .' Am I a sectarian? I go to church." Zina sat down at the table and started crying.

"Never mind," said Yury Dmitrievich, walking around to the other side of the table and sitting down next to Zina. "We'll take care of him . . . don't be afraid . . . I'll phone tomorrow. I'll report him . . . he's concealed his origin . . . he's an antihuman . . . he's a creature from a different civilization . . ."

Yury Dmitrievich carefully stroked Zina's hair; it was soft and chestnutbrown, and pleasantly tickled Yury Dmitrievich's neck and chin.

"My little kitten," he said, "let me rub your ears, let me stroke your tail . . ." He went on talking for a long time and said a lot of silly things, but oddly enough, he enjoyed feeling silly and rhapsodical, like some infatuated high-school student.

"You're old already," said Zina, "and all gray. But I like you. You're kind . . . and your face is handsome." She kissed him on the cheek and slipped out from under his arm, somehow instantly changing from a votary into a mischievous girl.

"I'm going to tell your fortune," said Zina gaily, without a trace of her former fear. "Now we'll find out about your future . . ."

She found an old blanket in the corner and curtained off the window with it. From a chest of drawers she took a small box containing gray ashes that were clean and sifted, and sprinkled an even layer of the ashes into a shallow porcelain dish. She poured some clear water into a glass, set the glass in the middle of the dish on the ashes, and securely positioned three candles around the dish. Then she took a thick solid-gold ring and dropped it into the glass.

"Sit still," she whispered. "Don't look around, just watch the candles."

To please her, Yury Dmitrievich sat quietly, smiling skeptically to himself. The wooziness had passed and his head was clear and empty, as though he had had some sleep. Gradually, however, Yury Dmitrievich was again overcome by drowsiness. The candles crackled and the room smelled of burning. Suddenly there was a tinkle of bells overhead; a powerful stroke resounded, then another, though this time more like a light scraping, as if the tongue of a bell had merely been drawn across copper, and then it all rapidly died.

"Look," Zina whispered.

Yury Dmitrievich leaned forward and saw a little house inside the ring, but he was not particularly surprised now, as though he were seeing something perfectly natural. The house was standing on a hillock; it had two windows, and there was a light in the front one.

"A house on a hill," Zina whispered. "You see . . . and the front window is lit . . ."

"I see," Yury Dmitrievich replied, also speaking in a whisper, "and it's nice . . . and there was a bell ringing . . . weird. . . ."

"That was the old clock on the roof," said Zina. "It's broken but sometimes it begins to strike . . . sometimes the ringing wakes me up at night. . . ." She quickly blew out the candles and in the dark Yury Dmitrievich embraced her.

"I want to see you tomorrow," he said. "I'm married but I'm getting a divorce . . . my wife was unfaithful to me twenty years ago, that's been established now beyond any doubt."

"Come and see me," said Zina, "I'm at home during the day . . . I go to the village church in the morning, I rarely travel all the way to the cathedral. But watch out for Akim Borisych, he asked about you."

"Never mind," said Yury Dmitrievich, and missing her lips, he kissed Zina somewhere on the chin.

It was very late when he came outside. The night was warm and moonlit. He felt strong, more youthful, and his walk had a spring to it. A light breeze from the river, coming in unimpeded through a caved-in section of wall, was refreshing on his face and rustled through the branches of the oak trees. Far back in the courtyard could be seen the thin figure of Shmigelsky, the deaf-mute carpenter. With both hands raised to his head, Shmigelsky stood there enjoying himself among the bags of cement and the toilet bowls, rubbing his nose and twisting it from side to side. His upturned face was bathed in moonlight. His eyes were rolled back and his mouth was half-open. Only short, anguished sighs of gratification periodically escaped from his breast.

For a while Yury Dmitrievich was unclear in his mind, until he remembered something and touched the tip of his nose with his finger.

"Self-abuse," he said. "Masturbation . . . artificial stimulation for sensual gratification . . . anti-Semitism that produces sexual pleasure . . . sexual racism . . . this is something for a pathophysiologist. Pathology gets down to the core."

Yury Dmitrievich was aware that Shmigelsky was deaf; nevertheless, he spoke aloud, holding his moonlit palms outstretched toward him. With his palms still outstretched, he stopped at an intersection. By now he was in a different world. The small garden out front was enclosed by a fence of brick pillars with metal pipes fastened between them. The garden smelled strongly of damp soil and flowers. Yury Dmitrievich lay down on the grass and, resting on his elbows to avoid crushing the flowers, he thrust his head into a flower bed and closed his eyes, delighting not only in the smell but in the feel of the petals and leaves against his skin. Then he walked along deserted streets; only entrances to buildings were lit. From time to time a taxi would pass him. One even stopped and the driver peered out, but he evidently took Yury Dmitrievich for a drunk and drove off. It was already getting light when Yury Dmitrievich reached the center of town and the streets he walked along every day. For a while he stood in front of the library of the republic's academy of sciences with its antique lamps by the entrance. He had often worked here; it was here he had written his dissertation. Now he simply stopped and sighed, though he didn't know what about. The first passersby began to appear on the streets, porters rustled their brooms. A tram crawled past but it was only half past five and Yury Dmitrievich decided to keep on walking a little longer and not wake up Grigory Alekseevich. By the time he turned for home, not only rooftops but upper stories as well were sunlit. He rang the bell and immediately heard footsteps behind the door or, rather, the tramping of feet, as if someone were running. The door burst open and Nina threw her arms around his neck, hugged him, and cried.

"What is this?" Yury Dmitrievich shouted at Grigory Alekseevich, who was approaching from the far end of the hallway. "What's going on here?" He had to throw his head back in order to evade his wife's kisses. "I dislike this woman . . . and anyway now . . . it looks like I'm in love with someone else. God Almighty, when someone dislikes *me* I do my best to steer clear of him. . . ."

"All right," said Nina, sobbing, "I'll leave. But you have to get out of your clothes and go to bed. I was so worried . . . Grigory Alekseevich phoned me. We were up all night . . . we kept calling and went out looking. . . ."

"Grigory," said Yury Dmitrievich, "you're an intelligent man . . . I had such a wonderful day. The night . . . I saw so much that was new . . . I thought about a lot of things . . . I'll tell you about it—"

"Later," said Grigory Alekseevich. "Now you're going to take a bath and go right to bed. Later on we'll talk about it. . . ."

Yury Dmitrievich found the warm jets of water from the shower refreshing.

"I thought a lot today about Christianity," he said, "about religion. Religion is a primary stage of cognition . . . because giving form to man's unknowing is the first step in cognition. But religion hardened too soon into dogma. . . ."

He could hear Nina sobbing and he felt ashamed that he was standing naked and uttering serious words. He was still feeling ashamed when he fell asleep, and maybe that was why he had nightmares. First, some teenagers were peeping through the windows, even though he lived on the seventh floor; then one of them threw an object through the glass but without breaking it. The object resembled a soccer ball bladder, except that it was oblong. This was followed by something totally jumbled. Ghosts moved about with red vertebrae showing through their bodies. A sick friend—who in particular never became clear—disappeared and two fat, jolly cooks turned up in his bed.

"Cooks!" Yury Dmitrievich shouted. "Love one another!" In response the cooks burst into merry laughter.

Their laughing may have been what awakened Yury Dmitrievich. It was already evening. Nina and Grigory Alekseevich were sitting some distance away at the table and by his bed sat Bukh—small, neat, wearing a clean shirt with mother-of-pearl cufflinks and breathing peppermints into Yury Dmitrievich's face.

"Hello, colleague," said Bukh.

"Hello, Benedict Solomonovich," said Yury Dmitrievich, propping himself up on one elbow. "What is it, delirium? Or is it amentia already?"

"Yury Dmitrievich," said Bukh, "I have deep respect for you as an anatomic pathologist and as an intelligent, interesting person to talk to. But now I'm asking you to be reasonable . . . you are exhausted and unless you undergo a course of treatment, you may become seriously ill."

"Well, what of it?" said Yury Dmitrievich. "Suppose I do become ill . . . or suppose I already am . . . after all, I have come to understand things that are beyond your grasp. What do we know about man? Our knowledge of man is on a par with that of past philosophers who thought the earth was flat. For instance, can you imagine my feelings on the pavement steps as I walked skyward and the bell tolled . . . or the ring . . . with my own eyes I saw a ring dropped into a glass of water and a little house on a hill appear inside it, with a light on in the front window. . . ."

A nurse entered the room, apparently having been in Grigory Alekseevich's study. She took out an ampule and attached a needle to a syringe, at the same time discussing something quietly with Bukh. The nurse took Yury Dmitrievich's arm and raised his sleeve. He caught the smell of a cotton pad saturated with alcohol, felt the needle gently enter his body, then lay back submissively on the pillow.

He slept through the night undisturbed. Just before he awoke, he dreamt that Bukh had not left. Bukh was sitting there as before, though not on a chair now but directly on the bed, on top of the blanket, and he was dressed in a jacket and white long johns. This cheered up Yury Dmitrievich and, after waking up, for a long while he lay in bed and smiled. In spite of some weakness and dizziness he felt good. He had breakfast sitting up in bed in his pajamas. Nina served him a cup of thick broth that had a chicken liver floating in it. Since his weakness made it hard for him to hold up the cup, Nina supported it from the bottom with her fingers. At eleven, the nurse came in to give him an injection. Her fingers were soft and delicate and for some reason Yury Dmitrievich asked her, "Are you married?"

"I've got a daughter who's married already," the nurse said. "She's a student . . . she took one of your exams. . . ."

"That's interesting," said Yury Dmitrievich, "she must be a good-looking girl. You know, it's occurred to me that people should fall in love often . . . they can only love one person but they can fall in love often . . . it's so purifying, so revitalizing. You're going to ask, what about morality? In the last analysis, however, bromides render us invaluable service . . . Bekhterev's mixture, and so forth . . . despite the fact that bromides are toxic if handled improperly and can cause asphyxia, burn the lungs—"

"Lie still," said the nurse, "I'll break the needle. . . ."

Bukh arrived.

"Well, you're doing very nicely," said Bukh, examining him. "Very nicely."

Bukh was in a hurry to get to a meeting. In spite of the heat he was wearing a black suit with a white handkerchief peeping from the breast pocket. In a corner Bukh set down his heavy briefcase with its suitcase-type locks. Yury Dmitrievich remembered Bukh sitting on the bed in his white long johns and burst out laughing. Bukh wiped his hands with a handkerchief—not the white, ornamental one but a checkered handkerchief he took out of his side pocket—walked away, and began to say something to Nina quietly.

They had lunch at the table. Yury Dmitrievich refused to eat in bed, getting up and even pulling on a pair of gray slacks over his pajama bottoms. For lunch there was a delicious vegetable soup, stewed shoulder of veal, fresh hothouse tomatoes, and strawberries.

Grigory Alekseevich had been outside town today with a commission and had seen an old, twelfth-century church that had been converted into a warehouse and was falling into ruin. Just as he began to share his impressions and express his indignation, Nina signaled him with a wink and he steered the conversation to something innocuous. When the meal was about finished, the phone rang and Grigory Alekseevich answered it. "Yes," he said, "but he's ill . . . he isn't able to—"

"It's for me!" Yury Dmitrievich cried, dashing to the phone and knocking over the plate of strawberries. "It's Zina . . ."

"It is not Zina," said Grigory Alekseevich.

Yury Dmitrievich snatched the receiver away from him, however, and shouted: "Zina, I've been thinking about you! I dreamt about you. You're a good girl but your body hasn't been awakened . . . and you're wrong . . . you're mistaken . . . a human life should expire physiologically . . . a human being ought to use up every bit of himself as he ascends stepwise toward something supreme, what you call God but what I refuse to give any concrete name to, because it's not the name that matters. A human being must go through sin, temptation, passion, pain—without missing even a single step. It's the easiest thing to be a righteous man or a villain. . . ."

Nina made an effort to get the receiver away from him, but he fended her off and stopped talking only when he heard agitated voices on the other end of the line. The receiver there had evidently been put down on a desk without being hung up. There was a click and a woman's voice said: "Yury Dmitrievich, this is Yekaterina Vasilyevna, the assistant director's secretary. Good afternoon."

"Good afternoon," Yury Dmitrievich said.

"Please forgive us for disturbing you . . . you're unwell—"

"Never mind, it's all right, please go on," said Yury Dmitrievich.

"Nikolai Pavlovich would like you to see him, but I'll inform him that you're unwell—"

"No, I'll be there," said Yury Dmitrievich. "It's just a slight indisposition. I'll be there tomorrow."

He hung up the receiver and sat down, covering his face with his hands.

"Anyway, I had a very strange experience," he said. "Grigory, has it ever occurred to you that someone born blind can reach out at any time and touch Ursa Major or Cassiopeia. What, in fact, is a star to a man born blind? It is an incandescent gaseous substance that one can produce in any lab . . . and wearing a special safety device. But that's getting into technical details. Someone born blind can't live by our laws, since what for us is an ideal, for him is a way of life, and conversely, our way of life is his ideal. He's shrewd. He has adapted himself . . . he's an infiltrator . . . and if a thousand years from now they take over the earth, they'll be less tolerant toward us . . . they'll simply put out our eyes. Grigory, our civilization is too careless . . . man is a seeing creature and he has to fight for his eyes . . ."

An acute pain suddenly struck Yury Dmitrievich deep within his skull and blinded him. Nina got down on her knees and, swallowing her tears, unbuttoned his slacks and pulled them off. Together she and Grigory Alekseevich carried Yury Dmitrievich over to the bed. Grigory Alekseevich phoned Bukh. Bukh arrived in fifteen minutes. Since he had just returned from a meeting, walking in the door right before the phone rang, he hadn't had time to eat, and Nina fixed him several open-faced sandwiches with salmon and cold cuts.

"The attack was brought on by an external irritant," said Bukh, taking Yury Dmitrievich's pulse. "The main thing is rest. The window should be covered with a heavy curtain. Keep the moonlight from shining on his bed at night."

Bukh made a few more suggestions and left. Grigory Alekseevich made up the couch for himself in his study, and Nina lay down in her clothes on a folding cot next to Yury Dmitrievich's bed.

Yury Dmitrievich was awakened by a noise. Somewhere above the ceiling there was a drone like that of an airplane, but the sound did not recede. From time to time it would suddenly break off, then start up again with the same intensity and in the same place, as though the plane, like some large beetle, had gotten caught on the roof and was now suffering and languishing. Yury Dmitrievich sat upright, and Nina immediately got to her feet. Her face looked weary and pinched with sleeplessness.

"What is it?" she asked quietly. "Do you have to step out?"

"There's a plane up there," said Yury Dmitrievich. "It's caught on the roof and is suffering . . . it has to be freed . . . what about the crew, the people. . . "

"It's the wind," said Nina, "it's the wind howling."

Grigory Alekseevich came in from the next room and turned on the light. Standing barefoot in his pajama bottoms and undershirt and with his little blond beard, Grigory Alekseevich brought to mind a vagabond in an opera.

"Grigory," said Yury Dmitrievich, "why deceive me . . . I'm ill, but why this deception . . . I can't stand it when people suffer . . . I can't endure physical pain not because I'm afraid of it, but because it's degrading. Physical pain is the lot of animals. Man was born to conquer a higher, moral pain. . . ."

"Give him his medicine," Grigory Alekseevich said to Nina.

Nina poured some water into a glass and sprinkled a powder into a spoon. Yury Dmitrievich swallowed the medicine obediently and wiped his mouth with his hand. "Send me to the clinic . . . I have no right to make you miserable."

He looked to the window. It was covered over tightly with a curtain, but beyond the curtain was the deep, dead silence that prevails at the peak of night.

"I wish it were morning already," Yury Dmitrievich said dejectedly. "You remember the biblical curse . . . at evening you shall say: would it were morning. And in the morning you shall say: would it were evening."

He became pensive and sat that way for about five minutes, until his expression brightened a little. Instead of dejection, his face merely reflected a thoughtful sadness. Even a trace of a smile appeared — apparently the medication had begun to take effect. Yury Dmitrievich pulled himself up toward the head of the bed, lay down, and closed his eyes. He woke up again before dawn, hearing the sound of the janitor's broom scraping outside. Nina lay asleep with her eyes shielded by one arm that was bent at the elbow. She was wearing her skirt, but she had taken off her blouse, and her full shoulders, banded by the silk straps of her slip, gleamed white in the darkness.

"Even at forty-four she's still attractive," Yury Dmitrievich thought. "And what was she like twenty years ago. Whenever I had to be away, the books that meant the most to me were guides to railroads, airlines . . . I'd study the routes to her. . . ."

He got up quietly so that he would not awaken Nina and walked toe-first over to the window. He drew aside an edge of the curtain. The sun had not come up yet, but it was already light outside and the strong aroma of early summer came drifting in through the open vent window. Yury Dmitrievich's heart beat with anxious delight, perhaps because of the aroma. Or maybe it was because he had gotten up after a stifling, delirious night feeling buoyant, fresh, and—to his mind— perfectly fit. To avoid making noise and waking Nina he gathered up his clothes in his arms and tiptoed out into the hall. As he passed Grigory Alekseevich's study he listened attentively. A light snoring and whistling emanated from inside. Yury Dmitrievich displayed considerable shrewdness and ingenuity in opening the lock. First, he went to the kitchen, got dressed, and shoved his sandals into his pocket. Then he got a bottle of olive oil and liberally poured it into all the crevices of the lock, leaving the lock shiny and glistening. After wrapping the handle with some cotton from the medicine cabinet, he began to pull on it and the catch slid back smoothly, without making a click. He headed down the stairs in his stocking feet, realizing, though, somewhere around the second-floor landing, that he was being overcautious. Whereupon he sat down and put on his shoes. The janitor was hosing down the parched clean-swept sidewalk, raising the hose from time to time and directing the stream toward the leaves on the trees. The thought struck Yury Dmitrievich that it would be good to leave a note for Nina and Grigory. He sat down on a post of the fence enclosing the grounds, tore out a sheet of paper from his pad, and wrote: "Feeling fine. Went for a walk." What he had actually put on that piece of paper, though, were some lines and dots—diagramming the growth of a malarial plasmodium in the body of a mosquito and a human being.

"Say there, my dear sir," Yury Dmitrievich said to the janitor, "would you deliver this to Apartment 47 . . ."

The janitor took the note and stuffed it into the pocket of his apron. Feeling reassured, Yury Dmitrievich headed off down the street.

He decided he would go to the zoo. He hadn't planned to; the thought just came to him all of a sudden, and from then on, Yury Dmitrievich felt that were it not for this idea, it wouldn't even make sense to go out. For half an hour he rode in a broiling-hot trolleybus and then sat for two more hours in the blazing sun, waiting for the zoo to open.

The heat had fouled the water in the zoo's pond. Swans, ducks, and other water birds had been herded into a small fenced-in area, and workmen in high rubber boots busied themselves in the muddy excavation. In a concrete-lined basin where the seals had crawled off into the shade and were languishing in the heat, two broken floor lamps lay about for some reason—apparently part of the inventory of the administration building nearby. The cages housing the predatory animals gave off a powerful odor. A raucous, cackling crowd had gathered around the cages of the anthropoid apes. A monkey was holding up its bloodied paw while an attendant and a vet painted its fingers with iodine. From time to time the attendant stuck a cigarette between the monkey's lips and the monkey took a deep puff and, like a true smoker, exhaled the smoke through its nostrils. In the next cage another monkey sat hunched over with its paws covering its face.

"She's depressed," said the attendant. "Bit her friend and now she's suffering . . . conscience-stricken . . ."

Yury Dmitrievich walked over to a stand, bought some chocolate candies, and tossed them to the depressed monkey. The monkey picked up a candy, carefully unwrapped it, and put it in her mouth. Then she crumpled up the wrapper and with pretty good aim flung it in Yury Dmitrievich's face. The crowd burst into a chorus of laughter.

Yury Dmitrievich walked to the other end of the zoo, where the snake house was. A boa constrictor was being fed. A live rabbit, though trying desperately to resist, was creeping on its own toward the boa.

"The boa has it hypnotized."

"It oughtta shut its eyes and scoot away," said a towheaded fellow.

"It doesn't stand to gain anything," said Yury Dmitrievich. "The rabbit and the boa have a common ideology, and that leads to their bodily merging. The rabbit is even flattered to have an ideology in common with the boa. The rabbit ceases to be a rabbit and turns into a boa . . . except for physiological wastes, of course . . ."

"Early morning and he's already drunk," the attendant said, looking at Yury Dmitrievich. "The day before yesterday some drunk jumped in with the polar bear . . just try and keep an eye on you people. . . ."

Next to an enclosure in which some ponies, zebras, and donkeys were walking around, Yury Dmitrievich gave his spirit a rest. And although a zebra did try to bite him, it was only because Yury Dmitrievich had failed to notice the warning sign and tried to pet it.

Yury Dmitrievich remembered yesterday's phone call, looked at his watch, left the zoo, and took a taxi to the institute. Inside the building, which was unusually empty and quiet, there was a smell of calcimine and paint. Painters were walking around in the hallways and the dirty parquet floors were covered with newspapers. Yury Dmitrievich walked up to the second floor and pushed open a leather-upholstered door. Here it was clean; the waxed parquet gleamed and a breeze from a table fan rippled the lowered silk curtains. An unfamiliar young man in a plain cotton jacket, evidently the supervisor of the work crew, was dictating to Lusya the typist from a contentious piece of paper, constantly emphasizing the word "supposedly."

"The claim made by the general contractor that supposedly the painting of the lower floor . . ." the young supervisor dictated, "the painting supposedly does not conform to established standards. . . ."

When Yury Dmitrievich walked in, Lusya and Yekaterina Vasilyevna looked up at him at the same time and their faces registered identical expressions—of astonishment and fright.

"Good morning," Yury Dmitrievich said.

"Good morning," Yekaterina Vasilyevna replied hesitantly. "Actually, I reported that you weren't feeling well. We were going to forward the summons to your home."

"What summons?" Yury Dmitrievich asked.

"You received a summons from the police."

"Let me have it."

"It's in Nikolai Pavlovich's office."

Behind him Yury Dmitrievich heard Lusya whisper something to the supervisor and the supervisor grunted, then forced a yawn in order to choke back a laugh.

Yury Dmitrievich took a step toward the door at the side, but Yekaterina Vasilyevna, with an agility one would not expect from her heavy body, got up quickly and said: "Just a moment, I'll announce you." She edged through the door and slammed it in Yury Dmitrievich's face. Inside, she may have even been pressing up against it with her rear end.

Soon afterward, she emerged and, anxiously looking Yury Dmitrievich in the face, she said: "You may go in."

An entire wall of the office was lined with lustrous blond shelves on which books with gold-embossed spines stood in close ranks. In a corner was a skeleton. Nikolai Pavlovich, a flourishing, very hairy man, was sitting not directly behind his desk but in a chair next to it—a position he had apparently assumed for democratic reasons. He was wearing a nylon Japanese shirt unbuttoned at the chest and a dense mass of graying hair billowed right up to his throat. During the war, Nikolai Pavlovich had been deputy chief for political affairs in a large military hospital. Later on he worked for the Ministry of Health, and since 1952 he had been assistant director of the medical institute.

"How are you feeling?" Nikolai Pavlovich asked, rising for his visitor and smiling.

"All right," Yury Dmitrievich replied. "So I've gotten a summons? That's interesting."

"Yes," Nikolai Pavlovich said. "By the way, you look pretty well . . . I assumed you . . . Bukh, as usual, has been exaggerating. In cases like this I would rather have Solovtsev than Bukh. In spite of his experience, Bukh is nevertheless overly . . ." Nikolai Pavlovich gave some thought to finding the right word. ". . . Overly specific."

"What do you have against Bukh?" asked Yury Dmitrievich, gazing at Nikolai Pavlovich's hairy chest. The hair curled in ringlets, like lamb's wool. "I was the one who composed the letter about you to the ministry. It was on my initiative."

"I like the straightforward type," Nikolai Pavlovich said brusquely. A Russian, even if he's led by the nose, still retains—albeit in spite of himself—certain noble qualities."

He walked around the desk and sat down, solidly planting his elbows.

"Sit down," he said, beckoning curtly.

Yury Dmitrievich sat down.

"Your collective smear," Nikolai Pavlovich said, lowering his head as if he were getting ready to butt, "your smear is in my hands. It was forwarded to Georgy Ivanovich, but since Georgy Ivanovich is ill—"

"It hasn't reached its proper destination, then," Yury Dmitrievich said gently, as though he were patiently explaining a difficult point to a student. "We'll write again . . . or else I'll just go . . . you, Nikolai Pavlovich, simply must not be assistant director of the medical institute. At the beginning of this century, Nikolai Pavlovich, people died mainly of tuberculosis and intestinal disorders, whereas now they die of heart disease, cancer, and disorders of the nervous system. These are diseases of movement . . . mankind is collapsing from its own tempo . . . cancer is killing millions of defenseless people. Every doctor, when he wakes up in the morning, must first of all have a feeling of shame. . . ."

Nikolai Pavlovich buzzed discreetly. The door creaked but Yekaterina Vasilyevna did not come in; she must have merely peeked inside.

"Go on," said Nikolai Pavlovich, "I'm listening. Incidentally, what a magical recovery. Only yesterday talking gibberish on the phone, and today you speak like a shrewd opportunist taking advantage of a squabble in order to appropriate someone else's job. . . ."

"I have no interest in the job," said Yury Dmitrievich, "but it should be given to an experienced specialist, especially in view of Georgy Ivanovich's advanced age and illnesses. Actually, he is director in name only—"

"Why, of course," Nikolai Pavlovich shouted. "And Bukh, then—"

"Bukh is an experienced specialist," Yury Dmitrievich said.

"Just a moment," said Nikolai Pavlovich, leaning his whole body forward. "And in '52, when Bukh was exposed . . . or should I say, when all sorts of doubts arose . . . you too signed the letter."

"Yes," Yury Dmitrievich said. He was sitting with his head pressed against the high back of the chair and he could feel the blood throbbing in the veins near his ear. "I was at the zoo just now. There was a rabbit merging with a boa constrictor. In '52 I did sign against Bukh, and in '51 Bukh signed against Sokolsky . . . and before Sokolsky hanged himself he left a note. Not a word to his wife or his children. Just slogans. . . . History has known many executioners and victims, but never before have a victim and an executioner been so united, never before has a victim loved his executioner so much. . . ."

"Of course, I don't have Bukh's keen faculties for diagnoses," Nikolai Pavlovich said with a smirk, "but I could always spot a malingerer with just one look. When I was a company medic, the malingerers all reported for duty. They fell into line," Nikolai Pavlovich suddenly shouted, turning red. "We are aware that you are connected with the zealots. We cannot entrust the education of students to a man ideologically hostile to us. You are trying to discredit Soviet medicine with your statements. And now that you've been exposed . . . when the police call you as a witness in a case of an obviously deliberate provocation during church festivities in a cathedral, you try, with Bukh's help, to feign mental illness. You've started divorce proceedings against your wife, a respectable woman, because you're involved with some zealot . . . and we, as militant atheists, refuse to allow this. Every word you have said has been taken down in shorthand by Yekaterina Vasilyevna and will be turned over to the proper authorities. Here, take your summons," he said, flinging the piece of paper in a blatant fit of temper.

Like a paper dove, the summons described an arc and fell to the carpet. Yury Dmitrievich bent down and picked it up, and for some reason read it syllable by syllable. He then looked at Nikolai Pavlovich and knew he would slug him but hadn't decided where to land the blow. Everything looked inviting: the frontal bone, rather prominent and knobby; the pointy mastoid process; and the superior maxilla, with a slight recess that a fist would fit against very neatly and, at the same time, overlap the lips, which oddly had just begun to quiver. Those lips slightly distracted Yury Dmitrievich from his thoughts. They began descending lower and lower and were soon level with the desk.

"Allow me," Yury Dmitrievich said. He was afraid of losing his listener, whom he needed in order to express some very important thought that was slipping away, however. "Allow me . . . just a moment."

Yury Dmitrievich extended his hand and restored Nikolai Pavlovich to his former position.

"Do you know why you are dangerous, Nikolai Pavlovich? Because you continue to be a problem . . . and you obstruct mankind's view of real problems . . . urgent ones. No, that's not quite right . . . I can put it more precisely . . . there's a stairway . . . you know, the street where the steps lead up toward the sky . . . civilization . . . every step is a problem . . . don't you find that mankind is like a madman climbing a stairway higher and higher into the unknown and at the same time dismantling it behind him as he goes. Isn't it about time to start building steps not only upward into space but down to earth as well . . ."

Yury Dmitrievich looked but didn't see Nikolai Pavlovich. He wanted to keep on talking but without his listener he couldn't, so he started to look for Nikolai Pavlovich. He found him behind a bookcase. Nikolai Pavlovich was sitting there very comfortably with his knees drawn up under him. Yury Dmitrievich placed his hands under Nikolai Pavlovich's shoulders and lifted him. Nikolai Pavlovich yielded but it was only a ruse; as soon as he was out in the open, he made a feint to the right, ducked, and bolted for the door, at which blurry faces kept appearing, astir like ants in a routed anthill. Yury Dmitrievich easily caught Nikolai Pavlovich and shouted at the unshorn nape of his neck: "While the sighted are engaged in strife, the blindborn are not asleep . . ."

The anthill by the doorway spit out a face that came running up and grabbed hold of Nikolai Pavlovich from the other side. A lively tussle ensued. Yury Dmitrievich pulled Nikolai Pavlovich in one direction and the face pulled in the other. Nikolai Pavlovich himself remained neutral, totally incapacitated by fear. At first, Yury Dmitrievich out-pulled his opponent, but then the face was joined by several more vague outlines. At this point, Yury Dmitrievich let go and they all instantly disappeared from view. Yury Dmitrievich walked out of the office. There were a lot of people out in the waiting room; something had happened. The painters were craning their necks and Lusya the typist was leaning over. There was someone standing in the doorway, but Yury Dmitrievich moved him aside and started down the stairs. He walked rapidly and once outside, he quickly turned the corner, not with the specific thought of escape, but in response to the taut muscles of his legs and to his accelerated breathing. Nearly out of breath, his mouth contorted, his ribs heaving convulsively, and his back sopping wet, he slumped down onto a bench. It was a quiet shady street in the midst of small one-story houses—one of those outlying streets that sometimes turn up in the center of town, just a few steps from the noisy main thoroughfares, and afflicted with this noise only at their start.

Yury Dmitrievich raised his hand and wiped away the cold sweat from his forehead and temples. His heart was pounding and it hurt. He felt his wrist and, looking at his watch, took his pulse. It was 130 instead of the normal 70. Yury Dmitrievich was sitting in a little park. About fifteen feet away water splashing from a pipe flowed in a little stream and some sparrows were flitting about close by it. The street was deserted and Yury Dmitrievich waited for about ten minutes, until a little boy on a two-wheeler appeared along the sand-strewn path. Yury Dmitrievich took out his handkerchief, motioned to the boy to come over, and abruptly, in a strange, gruff bass, he said: "Wet it . . . bring it back. . . ."

The boy took the handkerchief, parked his bike, and thoroughly wetted the handkerchief so that water streamed from it. Yury Dmitrievich grabbed the handkerchief and splashed himself in the face with it. The boy just stood there watching curiously. "You can go now . . . thanks," Yury Dmitrievich said.

No sooner had the boy ridden off than Yury Dmitrievich thirstily pressed his lips to the handkerchief and began sucking on it. He felt better. His heartbeat had slowed down and a sudden breeze felt pleasantly refreshing. At last, Yury Dmitrievich got up, walked over to the pipe himself, and drank his fill. Then he wetted the handkerchief, went back to the bench, and applied the handkerchief to the back of his neck.

IV

Yury Dmitrievich took the crumpled summons out of his pocket, read it, walked over to a tram stop, and rode for about fifteen minutes down a long hilly street. All that remained of his attack was a slight weakness in the small of his back and a metallic taste in his mouth.

The police precinct was located in a high-rise building that also had a garden out front. Sitting on benches were several devout old women, Kondraty in his cassock, and Sidorych in a sailcloth cap.

Yury Dmitrievich sat down a short distance away and was immediately approached by a broadshouldered, suntanned man in a short-sleeved jacket of unusual cut.

"Excuse me," he said, "I've been looking at the list of witnesses. Do you teach at the medical school?"

"Yes," Yury Dmitrievich said.

"Pleased to meet you," said the man, extending his hand. "Khlystov, master of sports."

"A pleasure, a pleasure," Yury Dmitrievich replied, shaking hands.

"I'm also a professor," said Khlystov, "in the soccer department. Been assigned to the public defense." Khlystov smiled. "However, I'm thinking of switching to the public offense."

"I'm not a sports fan," said Yury Dmitrievich, "I don't understand the terminology."

"That's a shame," said Khlystov. "Well, anyway, what I mean is I'm a public defender. If only those church rats bring the case to trial it won't be Kesha who'll be prosecuted, it'll be the clericals . . . I've had a word with the investigator. Ultimately, the boy was expressing his instinctive protest against age-old obscurantism . . . against the auto-da-fé . . . against the burning of Galileo, see. . . ."

"Galileo wasn't burned," said Yury Dmitrievich.

"What d'ya mean 'wasn't burned'?" Khlystov bridled. "I saw a movie about it with my own eyes."

"Your Kesha is a son of a bitch," said Yury Dmitrievich.

"Let's suppose," said Khlystov, "the boy did commit an improper act. He was taking upon himself the functions of the state . . . I mean the function to fight against religion. We'll punish him for it, we'll suspend him for two games. Maybe he'd had a drop . . . made a bet with the boys . . . he did it on a bet, after all. Those clericals, though . . . I'm sure you read the literature on atheism . . . they're involved in shady things . . . *they* are the criminals. How do they get people? With a spectacle . . . and in that sense our Soviet soccer plays an atheistic role by attracting the masses. So how in our day and age can we allow clericals to prosecute an atheist . . . under the Soviet system. . . ."

"What comes to my mind," said Yury Dmitrievich, "are the people who defend the foundations of a system solely because they happened to be born under that system and live there. If they'd been born into some other system, instead of Soviet soccer they would be playing some other sociopolitical soccer just as rapidly. By the way, speaking of atheism . . . what is it, a belief or an absence of belief?"

"I don't understand what you're talking about," said Khlystov, stunned. "As for your insinuations—"

"I haven't made any," said Yury Dmitrievich. "I'm not even addressing you, Comrade Soccer-player . . . it's myself I'm asking . . . religion is a belief that there is a god . . . atheism is a belief that there is not a god . . . a belief in what isn't . . . it's an odd play on words . . . if religion gives form to human unknowing, atheism demands concrete answers to questions that mankind won't be able to grasp for a long time to come. Religion says man exists at the behest of God . . . atheism says man exists in order to understand why he exists . . . it's a circle. Yes . . . true atheism has nothing in common with those shabby newspaper caricatures of lecherous little priests. . . ."

"Pardon me," said Khlystov, "I'm a professor too . . . it's strange, even . . . you're also a professor, but your head's full of ideological mush."

"That may be so," said Yury Dmitrievich, "but a man has only three possibilities: religion, atheism, or playing soccer. In other words, either steps or a vacant lot . . . you and the lecherous priests run around the lot . . . Zina and Papa Isai are happy because they can see, and standing on a bottom step they can see the heavens . . . and me, an atheist, I crawl up the steps, skinning my hands and knees, so that I can touch the heavens . . . a star . . . and maybe somewhere halfway up I'll meet a congenitally blind atheist crawling down the steps because he's incapable of being happy that he can touch a star—he wants to see it. The opposite of our civilization. . . ."

Two more people appeared in the garden, and the soccer professor hurried over and began quietly speaking to them. Yury Dmitrievich tried to listen in. One of the new arrivals had a crew cut; the other was bald and had a large birthmark on his cheek with blond hairs growing from it.

"I could see there was something wrong," the soccer professor was saying. "I was stressing public duty to him . . . to rescue our boy from the clutches of the clericals. But then he answers me with such a line of anti-Soviet propaganda that, well, you know, any normal person ought to be brought up on charges for saying things like that. . . ."

"You're an ass," Yury Dmitrievich shouted. "The Soviet system currently has no more dangerous, no more mortal enemy than its own domestic ass . . . that's more dangerous than intercontinental missiles."

"You shouldn't provoke him," the bald man with the birthmark said to the soccer professor, "he's stirred up enough as it is. We got a call from the hospital, he gave them the slip. But I told them I won't go . . . let them give me a reprimand. They must have psychologically damaged him there. Let them call out a squad of police. On my miserable salary why should I get my teeth knocked out."

"Let's give it a try, the police are right over there," said the crew cut. He moved closer to Yury Dmitrievich and said, "Good morning, may I see your summons, please."

Yury Dmitrievich held out the summons without saying a word.

"You're to come with us," said the crew cut. "Come on, you'll have a rest." He motioned with his head toward a car with a red cross on it and firmly gripped Yury Dmitrievich by the elbow. The bald man came up and took Yury Dmitrievich by his other elbow. They lifted him up and led him off toward the car.

Yury Dmitrievich felt so weary, so exhausted by his words, that he didn't care in the least where he was being taken. But at that moment his name was called out and he saw Zina emerging from the doorway of the police precinct.

"Zina," he shouted, "I've been thinking about you. Darling, how many faces I've seen before me today . . . how many useless faces . . . I want to be with you but they're taking me away. . . ."

Zina ran after him in tears.

"Where are they taking you?" she asked. "Why are they tormenting us? They won't let us love. They asked me about that naked fellow . . . and about the Lord . . . and about belief. It wasn't Christ, it was a naked blasphemer . . . Papa Isai explained it to me . . ."

"Wait," Yury Dmitrievich said to the hospital attendants, "I have to talk to her . . . you see what a state she's in."

The attendants, however, tightened their grip and increased their pace. Then Yury Dmitrievich bolted and shoved the bald man into a fence, causing him to smash his elbow.

"Help us!" the attendant with the crew cut yelled to Khlystov.

"And have that nut rip my jacket?" the soccer professor said, walking farther away.

Zina, in the meantime, leaped at Crew Cut and sank her teeth into his wrist. Crew Cut groaned and let go of Yury Dmitrievich's arm. Yury Dmitrievich hopped over the fence, catching his glasses in mid-air, warded off some eager-beaver civil patrolman, and ran down a sidestreet. Zina ran with him. Behind them police whistles started blowing. Yury Dmitrievich drew Zina into a narrow passageway between buildings. After stumbling on pieces of broken brick and leaping across faintly malodorous puddles that refused to dry up in the damp shadow of the damp wall, Yury Dmitrievich and Zina reached a rusty fire escape and began climbing up it. Zina went first, with Yury Dmitrievich following slightly behind, looking down at the receding earth to keep from staring up at Zina's shapely legs. The attic was dusty and large; it had an odor of cat excreta and baked clay. Yury Dmitrievich noticed that a strip of flypaper dotted with dead flies had gotten stuck to the heel of his shoe. It must have come from the refuse piled between the buildings. As he was about to remove it, there was a loud noise outside. Yury Dmitrievich and Zina went over to a dormer window and saw a police motorcycle rush by, followed by an ambulance.

"There they go," Yury Dmitrievich said and laughed wickedly.

He removed the strip of flypaper and sat down on the wooden rafters. Zina sat down next to him and buried her face in his chest. It was hot, and they could hear the tin overhead crackling from the heat.

"I'm going to marry you," Yury Dmitrievich said. "We'll go to the Carpathians . . . the health department promised me a job as chief doctor in a hospital. Come to think of it, no, I haven't raised the issue yet . . . but I definitely will and they won't turn me down . . ."

In a corner behind the chimneys a pile of rags lay in view. Yury Dmitrievich picked up Zina, not at all conscious of her weight, carried her over to the rags, and put her down on them. He started unbuttoning his jacket but the buttons were tight, and since they would not go through the buttonholes, he ripped them off and put them in his pocket. He suddenly lost Zina in the semidarkness of the attic and in order to find her he got down on his knees. Zina lunged up at him and threw her arms around his neck. He fell forward and instead of his face ending up against Zina's, it became embedded in the soot-glazed rags, which he now felt against his lips and breathed into heavily. Zina tensed her whole body, uttered a cry, then immediately went limp. He too went limp, lifted his head from the rags, moved it over to Zina's face, and pressed his lips to hers. Then they sat together for a long while in an embrace.

"This will pass," said Yury Dmitrievich, stroking Zina's neck and hair. "Everything is all right . . . tell me about your life . . . tell me about yourself."

"My mother died when I was eight," Zina said. "We lived in another town. There was this very long street, with a bank on the corner. She started to die and my aunt and my grandma let out a cry . . . I was frightened and I said, 'Mama, tell them not to yell, it scares me.' I turned to her, as though she were the boss now and in charge of everything. She heard me and motioned with her hand as if to say, 'Stop your yelling.' Then I couldn't stand it any longer and I ran out . . . I ran all the way to the end of the street, to where the bank was—the cries just barely reached that far. People walked by, paid no attention; why should they care about cries somewhere. I stood there and was the only one who knew the reason for those cries off in the distance. . . ." Zina straightened up, probably engrossed in some new thought that had been unexpectedly awakened, and Yury Dmitrievich could see that her eyes were glistening in the darkness.

"Tell me," she said, "when the nails were being driven through Christ's hands, don't you think there were a lot of people who heard cries but didn't know the meaning of them?"

"There's a special branch of medicine that studies the illnesses of ancient peoples," Yury Dmitrievich said. "Paleopathology . . . a science that links medicine and history . . . radiologists are studying the bones of Neanderthals, Khazars, Polovtsy, Scythians—and are finding cancer, joint diseases, tuberculosis, leprosy. To a neuro-pathologist, the Gospels, as I see it, are the history of the illness of an ancient Jew from Nazareth. If he reads the Gospels carefully, a neuropathologist will find all the symptoms and render a fairly precise diagnosis of hebephrenic schizophrenia. In Greek, schizophrenia means a splitting of the soul. When the soul is split, energy is released, under proper conditions—very high energy . . . all of ancient and medieval European civilization was built on the energy released by the splitting of the soul of one ancient Jew born in a stable . . . built on the nourishing power of that energy, or else on the resistance to it. Let's look at the case history, at the period preceding the illness . . . it's very important to a doctor. In the beginning, he was an intimi-dated, sickly boy who had innocently experienced unchildlike shame and humiliation, since an illegitimate child in ancient Judea was considered a terrible disgrace. . . . Then as a young man girls avoided him because of his poverty and his disgraceful origin. A lean, young southerner bursting with ardor and passion . . . seminal fluid tyrannizes him, colors his impressions of life . . . his bile takes on a deep green cast and, acted upon by psychic trauma, it solidifies in the gallbladder, forming gallstones. . . . Added to his spiritual sufferings and intensifying them, there are now physical sufferings . . . sharp pain in the right hypochondrium radiating to the right scapula, vomiting, chills. . . . At this stage Jesus required a special diet: lemons, apple sauce, stewed fruit, seedless and skinless grapes . . . Borzhomi and Yessentuki mineral waters are good, too . . . but there was no chance of maintaining a diet in the family of the poor carpenter Joseph; antibiotics and Novocain were unavailable. . . . By the age of thirty the illness usually becomes chronic . . . please take note of the age," said Yury Dmitrievich, extending his hand toward a chim-ney. "It was precisely at this age, according to the Gospels, that Jesus began appearing as the emissary of God . . . the tyranny of seminal fluid reaches its peak, corrodes the brain, and is transformed there into something strange and illusory, yet steeped in genuine suffering and pain already become habitual and indispensable, made permanent by conditioned reflexes, and now a source of pleasure. There is not a particle of falsehood or sham here, it's all true, it's all a prod-uct of suffering. A change in the psyche had caused a change in personality. . . ."

Yury Dmitrievich walked back and forth across the attic, stumbling over rusty scrap and broken crockery. An oblique shaft of sunlight filled with dancing specks of dust filtered through the dormer. It had moved slightly to the left and now illuminated the object of his love lying on the pile of dirty rags.

"Just like Mary," Yury Dmitrievich said with a tremor in his voice, "like Mary, who had given herself in a stable to a Jewish shepherd . . . the father of Jesus . . . a carefree man, perhaps, who lived for the moment . . . how must one love, how must one be able to surrender to love in order to disregard pitiless custom, to transgress the callous laws of Jehovah . . . the Gospel account of the virgin birth is a trivial circus wonder, compared with the true fortune of that woman. . . ." Yury Dmitrievich touched his burning forehead. "Mary," he said. "If we have a son . . . what I mean is—I'm getting mixed up . . . let's get back to the son . . . let's leave the father and get back to the son and the holy spirit . . . because I haven't the slightest wish to refute the sanctity of what took place . . . even fallacious movements of human spirit, if based on nobility and strength . . . at first people are taken with them, then oppose them in a struggle . . . European civilization is built on Christianity and on the struggle against it. Christianity as an idea existed even before Jesus. Jesus was one of the believing Christians, but his belief in Christ was so powerful that he merged with him, and at first, when the human mind was stagnating in ignorance, this made the idea of Christ more accessible and tangible. In time, however, Christ thus materialized began to have the opposite effect . . . I'll get that later, though . . . I still have to give some thought to it . . . Yes. . . ." He began to speak erratically, omitting phrases. "In the beginning, a doctrine requires titans; later it needs mediocrities who will carry it to the absurd, to a natural death, that is, since doctrines are mortal and succeed each other like human generations. But let's get back to the history of the illness. And so, the patient retires to the desert . . . that's the early course of the illness . . . he becomes withdrawn, has a change of interests and emotional reaction . . . he loses interest in his previous activities and, conversely, begins to show interest in what formerly held no attraction for him . . . in philosophy, religion . . . Today he might get excited about mathematics, designing, or collecting. He alternates between listlessness and vitality, ponders things, keeps going off somewhere by himself . . . then he gathers a few of the same sort of mentally unstable people and he begins to preach . . . this is already the next, paranoid form of schizophrenia . . . the patient thinks that he has acquired a significance and that everyone is interested in him . . . he starts having delusions, thinks he can influence people . . . a patient today, for example, may think that some radio announcer is talking about him, that the newspapers write about him, that billboards and even signs refer to him. Then comes a new, depressive-paranoid period. The patient thinks that enemies have cropped up and are threatening him with torture, betrayal, slander . . . one of you will betray me and another will deny me before the third cock crow . . . today a paranoiac will often claim he is being affected by electricity, radio waves, magnetism, atomic energy . . . he's jealous of his wife, checks her underwear. . . ." Unsteady on his feet, Yury Dmitrievich stepped within the shaft of sunlit dust particles, gripping the collar of his jacket with both hands.

"You're like a saint," Zina whispered. "You were speaking . . . I didn't understand . . . you're like a saint, though . . . you have an aureole around you. . . ."

"No," said Yury Dmitrievich, laughing, "in ancient Judea there were no neuropathologists but there were executioners. But then again, at the age of thirty-three Jesus was already suffering from the hebephrenic form . . . it was incurable. At that stage patients stop eating; they say their guts have all rotted away, they're already corpses . . . they look to suicide, death—" Yury Dmitrievich broke off suddenly. A large ginger tomcat scratched up on one side was looking at him through the dormer.

"Scat!" Zina yelled.

The cat grunted and disappeared.

"There were a lot of young men like Jesus later on, too, in the Pale," Yury Dmitrievich said, "in squalid little towns. Gaunt, wasted dreamers . . . the grief of their parents . . . a disgrace to the family . . . Jesus could have been one of Sholem Aleichem's heroes if he had been born later. . . . But he was born at a moment of psychic upsurge, when his people, without realizing it, offered themselves in sacrifice, doomed themselves to crucifixion for the sake of giving birth to Christian civilization. There's a paradox here . . . the destruction of the Jewish Temple was a harbinger of the destruction of pagan Rome . . . yes . . . Christ was the great literary image of Hebrew literature, a literature capable of arising only at moments of psychic upheavel . . . I've lost my train of thought, though," Yury Dmitrievich said, touching his hands to his temples helplessly, and for some reason smiling apologetically.

"Come here to me," said Zina, holding out her arms to him.

"It's strange somehow," Yury Dmitrievich said. "This attic, these chimneys, that cat . . . I'm sick, you know . . . I went through a terrible night . . . I thought some airplanes were suffering . . ."

"Come here to me," Zina repeated.

Zina's face was slightly flushed; it was the face of a happy, loving woman.

"Yes," Yury Dmitrievich said, "to you and only you . . . because at this moment you are so far removed from impurity . . . lying here on these rags . . ."

Yury Dmitrievich lay down beside Zina on the rags. Taking her in his arms, he brought his lips close to hers and began to inhale her breath, savoring the aroma and the purity of the air she exhaled. They lay there like that until evening. A ray of sunlight from the dormer had reached in toward the opposite corner of the attic; it faded and there was a patter on the roof.

"It's the rain," Zina said. "You were asleep and I was watching you . . . your face looked different when you slept . . . your face is like an infant's . . ."

Yury Dmitrievich got up and stretched, and bumped his head against a rafter.

"Let's climb down," he said.

The fire escape was slippery from the rain. They started down cautiously, expecting to hear a shout at any moment. Fortunately, everything was quiet. It was evidently rare for someone to come by that dirty alley, especially in the rain. They set out openly along the glistening pavement, allowing the warm rain to revive them and wash the attic dust off their clothing. Record players blared from open windows. A gaggle of teenage girls ran by laughing and splashing through puddles barefoot, holding their stylish shoes in their hands.

"In the classic Hindu concept of medicine the human body has three main constituents: airy matter, phlegm, and bile," said Yury Dmitrievich. "The practical applications of Hindu medicine are now thought to have had good results, even though the theory is based on pure fantasy. How beautiful it is, though . . . and it's true . . . airy matter is love, phlegm is vegetative existence, and bile is carnal pleasure . . . how simple, how intelligent. . . ."

Water streamed down the hilly streets, forming eddies among the cobblestones and gurgling in the gutters. Silent flashes of lightning flickered in the distance. Out at the monastery, where Yury Dmitrievich and Zina had arrived by bus, the rain was only just beginning. The rain cloud was moving in from the center of town, but over the river and the fields beyond, the sky was still starry. With a hard wind at their backs, Yury Dmitrievich and Zina squeezed past the stiff gate and hurried across the monastery courtyard, mindful of the wind growling through the oak leaves. A light was burning in Zina's room.

"It's Papa Isai," Zina said happily. "He's back. How nice . . ."

Papa Isai was sitting at the table eating bread with salt and mustard. He was barefoot and wore his shirt unbuttoned. The portrait of Tolstoy dangling from his neck lay right against his bare chest.

"Papa Isai," Zina said, kissing him, "I'm going to make you something to eat right now . . ."

"I've been visiting churches," Papa Isai said crossly. "For two hundred years throughout the Russian land, under the pretext of making repairs to churches, the old church style was done away with. In place of seven-tiered iconostases, they began installing low screens in the Western manner . . . and the icons derive from the French school, not the Russian . . ."

"You should talk to a friend of mine," Yury Dmitrievich said. "He's a Slavophile, too."

"And the clergy," Papa Isai yelled out, disregarding Yury Dmitrievich's comment, "the clergy goes flat uncontrollably, like a liquid in an open container. If a priest is entrusted with souls, then all the more reason to entrust church funds to him. That's the way they talk. They interpret the spiritual and material needs with which the Orthodox Church confronts us as her spiritual children in their own particular way. . . ."

Zina set before him a dish of kasha that had been heated up on the kerosene stove, dropped a piece of butter in it, and Papa Isai began to devour it, emitting fierce wheezes.

"Let's get back to our debate about Christian dogma," said Yury Dmitrievich, sitting down on the sofa but immediately jumping up again. "It's a problem of ordinary good versus ideal good. Let's consider the personality of Jesus, that is, the history of his illness . . . I contend that after analyzing his actions, one may arrive at the conclusion that he had gallstones. Patients with gallstones are usually irritable and unkind . . . especially when there's an accompanying effect of seminal fluid. On the other hand, however, Jesus' followers attest to his gentleness and kindness . . . there's a contradiction here . . . or, what's more likely, a mix-up . . . if you closely analyze even the Gospels, you can find that many of Jesus' everyday actions aren't really that kind . . . all the same, one factor is enough, the principal factor—that is, the Crucifixion—which has everything. Some seditious theologian, I think, has written about it . . . I don't remember, though . . . doesn't the cruelty of the executioner pale before the cruelty of Jesus himself, the omnipotent god who perpetrated his own crucifixion right before the eyes of his earthly, suffering mother? It's legend, but there are echoes of reality in it . . . the Crucifixion was done for the sake of man's salvation, for the sake of good, but in relation to the actual time when the Crucifixion was carried out Jesus' act was cruel and unkind. And this is where paleopathology cames to our aid . . . this is where medicine assists history and philosophy . . . gallbladder patients are rarely kind, but the feeling of good as something inaccessible yet enticing and beautiful, a striving toward good, is developed in them to an unusual degree . . . even though it may be hidden, at times unconscious . . . they often feel good as an ideal much more intensely than do so-called good people, for whom good is accessible every day and is buried in the daily routine. What I want to say . . ." Yury Dmitrievich fell silent for a few seconds, as though confused. "Ah, here's what I want to say . . . to be sure, there are a lot of stories in the Gospels and you can look at this from different viewpoints. But the main thing, nevertheless, is the Crucifixion . . . it should be the basis for judging the fundamental postulate of Christianity . . . nonresistance to evil . . . I've already talked about that, though . . . the point is simply that physiology corroborates philosophy and makes it more precise . . . nonresistance to evil as an ideal is wonderful . . . as an everyday rule it's absurd . . ."

Papa Isai had eaten up the kasha and was now finishing off some reheated cabbage cutlets drenched in sour milk. Gusts of wind made the windowpanes rattle; a heavy rain was already coming down. A flash of lightning momentarily lit up the darkness outside the window, revealing shiny, wet walls and wet branches disheveled by the wind. Before the glare of lightning died away, Yury Dmitrievich caught sight of a wet face pressed up against the glass.

"The blind man," he whispered, cringing from a sudden chill. "He's peering through the window . . ."

Papa Isai likewise shrank back in fear toward the folding screen and crossed himself; Zina blanched, then rushed to the window and lowered the blind.

"He often does that," Zina whispered, "just stands there and looks, or, I should say, listens . . ."

There was knocking at the door.

"Zina," the blind man called out, "open up, I want to talk to you."

"Akim Borisych," said Zina, "it's too late now, I'm already asleep."

"You're lying," Akim Borisych shouted, "your light is on, you're entertaining your lover." He pounded on the door again.

"Don't open it," Papa Isai yelled, "he's drunk . . . ugh, that devil . . ."

"Open it," Yury Dmitrievich said. The fear had passed and he was calm again. His face bore a look of determination.

Yury Dmitrievich went over to the door and pushed back the hook. The blind man burst into the room. He looked dreadful. Water ran off him in streams. His tunic, trousers, hair, and even his dark glasses were spattered with mud and his shoes were swollen. His left hand was holding a tattered, bedraggled bunch of flowers. His breathing was heavy, punctuated by gasps, and his warm fetid maw emitted an acrid stench of alcohol that blasted Yury Dmitrievich right in the face.

"Doctor," the blind man said, "I recognized you, Doctor . . . and that damn zealot is here too . . ."

Papa Isai sat himself behind the screen and Zina backed off into a far corner. Yury Dmitrievich alone stood motionless; only when he adjusted his glasses was it apparent that his hand was trembling slightly.

"How could you tell the light was on, blind man?" Yury Dmitrievich asked.

"The panes are warm," the blind man answered, disconcerted by Yury Dmitrievich's calm question.

"Akim Borisych," Zina shouted from her corner, "stop coming to visit me . . . I love someone else . . . and you I'm scared of . . . I'm going to go to the police—"

"What police, you zealot," said Akim Borisych. "You're a disgrace to a Soviet organization, a disgrace to our collective—"

"The infiltrator has adapted himself to our words, our slogans," Yury Dmitrievich shouted. "Let's go where there aren't any slogans, where there's just rain, just nature—"

"Don't leave," Zina cried, "he's drunk. He's a terrible person. He'll cripple you, he'll maim you."

"He's not a person," Yury Dmitrievich said, "he's some other intelligent being . . . if they take over the earth, they're not going to respect our ideals . . . the ideals of the sighted . . . they'll simply put out our eyes . . . people have to fight for their eyes . . ."

Yury Dmitrievich hugged Zina and started out the door. Akim Borisych stood there for a few seconds, plainly taken aback; he then tossed the wet flowers at Zina's feet and went out after him. The lash of the rain was so hard that Yury Dmitrievich felt engulfed in water. He was instantly soaked, and his sandals squished. The blind man walked ahead without speaking, never once stumbling, while Yury Dmitrievich kept slipping on the wet clay, ending up in puddles, and bumping into rocks. He even fell once and skinned his knee painfully.

A small fretwork door was set in the wall of the monastery. They entered through it and went on walking among the saplings that were growing between the outer and inner walls. They continued along this passageway that was some ten feet wide. The blind man ducked into an opening. Yury Dmitrievich climbed in after him, groping at the damp walls, but he soon halted.

"It's dark in here," he said. "You crawl down the steps while I crawl up them . . . and here we meet . . . but you were clever to choose this place . . . you want to nullify my advantage and still keep your own . . ."

"Stop seeing Zina," the blind man spoke out of the darkness. "You'll find yourself many others, but I can't live without her . . ."

"Neither can I," said Yury Dmitrievich. "I'm amazed, though . . . You mean you're really capable of longing and suffering for a woman? . . . It's not her you long for, though, it's touching her . . ."

By now the blind man was very near; he had approached soundlessly and Yury Dmitrievich sensed his presence only from the reek of alcohol. Yury Dmitrievich managed to take a step backward as the blind man's fingers nearly knocked off his glasses. Yury Dmitrievich slowly retreated toward the light but the blind man relentlessly groped for his eyes: Yury Dmitrievich's eyes, apparently, were what the blind man found most hateful about him. The passage became wider and already reflected a gleam of light from a streetlamp. In the lamp Yury Dmitrievich caught sight of the blind man's face, which seemed like a visage from a nightmare, as though the mask that had given him at least an outward resemblance to a human being had been removed. Whereupon Yury Dmitrievich understood: the dark glasses had disappeared and now one could see those soft, pink eyesockets, which were especially terrifying, though not because they looked like mutilations. On the contrary, it was because their appearance had achieved such perfection that for an instant Yury Dmitrievich's own eyes felt like mutilations. The feeling was so abhorrent that Yury Dmitrievich cried out and started to run. The blind man ran after him. Yury Dmitrievich could already sense the breathing at his back, but when they ran out of the cellar into the rain the blind man fell behind. There was suddenly a cry and the sound of his footsteps ceased. Yury Dmitrievich looked around. The blind man was gone; he seemed to have simply vanished. Lightning struck the dome of the crumbling church, splashing light on commerce department crates and trees bowed by the wind and rain. Yury Dmitrievich was shaken by the thunder; it reverberated in his chest and temples . . . Hearing some sounds coming from below the ground, he approached them and saw the blind man floundering in a watery pit that had probably been dug by construction workers. The blind man struggled vainly to climb out but kept slipping on the sodden clayey earthwork.

"Give me your hand," Yury Dmitrievich said. He lay down at the edge of the pit and extended his arms downward, trying not to look at those fleshscarred eyesockets. The blind man raised his head and his face became distorted. He leaped up and sank his teeth into Yury Dmitrievich's left hand so ferociously that instead of pain Yury Dmitrievich first felt astonishment on hearing the crunch of his own skin. He yanked away his hand and, holding it up in the air, he seized the blind man by the collar with his other hand and started to pull him up. Tiring from the weight, he kept pulling until the blind man's head appeared at the rim of the pit. At this point, the blind man himself grabbed on to the wet grass and crawled out. He stood up and took a few steps but immediately stumbled. His movements had lost their precision and confidence, and now, instead of resembling someone blind since birth, he looked more like an ordinary man gone blind, still unaccustomed to his blindness and thus especially helpless. Yury Dmitrievich got up from the ground arduously, holding his bloody hand in the air. The blind man looked totally exhausted; he had clearly spent his last ounce of strength tugging himself from the pit. In vain he tried to find the way out, groping about in a circle and bumping into walls.

Yury Dmitrievich walked over to him, took him by the elbow, and led him to the exit. The blind man followed along submissively. His feet tripped on rocks and landed in puddles even though Yury Dmitrievich made an effort to guide him carefully. When they emerged from the gate of the monastery, the rain had abated. The wind, however, was blowing with even greater force and the moon, appearing through rents in the clouds, was racing across the sky madly. Yury Dmitrievich and Akim Borisych soon adjusted to each other and walked along like a blind man and his long-standing guide.

"I feel sick," Akim Borisych said, "I finished off a whole bottle of booze. I was miserable . . . jealous . . . but now I know very well what I should do. She needs someone bright-eyed. I'm going to marry a blind girl. . . . we've got one in our blind society . . . she likes me . . ."

"I just had this odd thought," Yury Dmitrievich said. "There used to be an intelligent being, dangerous, let us say, but mysterious and unlike us, and it fought against us and made us fight. Our brutality and strength proved to be ineffective and undependable against it. We then resorted to a more powerful and cunning weapon that men use to make their conquests . . . we resorted to our nobility and our goodness . . . we tamed that being and turned it into a helpless blind man . . ."

Someone approached and shone a light on them. Two small vicious dogs jumped out and began barking. It was the nightwatchman in a canvas raincoat with a hood.

"Akim Borisych," he said, recognizing the blind man, "you got a phone call from the blind society. There's a board meeting tomorrow at five."

"Konovalov," Akim Borisych said, "ask your wife to take me home, I can't get there by myself right now . . ."

"Are you sick?" Konovalov asked with concern.

"I blinded him," said Yury Dmitrievich, "I committed a crime . . . I'm a human . . . a human who from the very beginning felt like a conqueror. He conquered the planet with brutality and good . . . he killed and tamed. Look at these dogs . . . sorry mutts waiting to be tossed a bone . . . there's a lot being written about dolphins nowadays . . . smart, mysterious creatures . . . as long as man hunted them they were safe as identities . . . but now man is preparing to bring out his terrible, overpowering weapon . . . good . . . and dolphins face the threat of being turned into dumb sea cows . . . in heated pools. We don't know how to work together on an equal basis, we know how to tame . . . civilization would have progressed who knows how far, if from the very beginning man had worked together with animals instead of taming them . . ."

"Uh-huh," said Konovalov, noticing Yury Dmitrievich's bloody hand, "they've been looking for you, mate, for a long time . . ."

He clamped a painful grip on Yury Dmitrievich's elbow and yelled, "Nayda, go and tell 'em the nut they're looking for is here . . ."

Some fragments of conversation followed, and Akim Borisych disappeared. Grigory, Nina, Bukh, and a few others arrived. Yury Dmitrievich was seated in a car and, right there in the car, dry clothing was put on him. He then found himself in his own apartment, to which he had not been for nearly a month. It was stifling inside; the apartment had probably not been aired out the entire month.

"It needs an airing," Yury Dmitrievich said. "It's hot."

"Does this hurt?" he was asked as his ribs were squeezed painfully. "And how about this? . . ."

"My spear hurts," said Yury Dmitrievich, "the one that's used to kill wild animals . . . I'm not sure, maybe killing them is nobler than taming them. . . . Until mankind realizes that, it won't have the normal right to go out into space and encounter other intelligent beings . . ."

Yury Dmitrievich sat down, took hold of a lap robe with one hand, and with the other fended off Nina, who was trying to get him to bed.

"A metaphysician once stated that life is a form of disease of matter . . . matter is actively opposed to life. Well, what of it, I say to him . . . you're frightened by the word 'disease' . . . isn't typhoid fever the life of a typhoid bacillus two microns long, whose universe is a man's intestine? . . . Let's think of what healthiness means . . . the healthiness of an intestine means death for a typhoid bacillus . . . health is death . . . disease and cure are a form of the Darwinian struggle for existence . . . except that one would like to believe that if man is a disease of the universe, he is its prolonged, incurable disease . . . by experiencing pain nature comes to know itself. . . ."

What followed was incoherent raving. A tranquilizer was administered to Yury Dmitrievich. In the afternoon, besides Bukh, Professor Parotsky and an internist came to see him. In addition to a severe mental disturbance, Yury Dmitrievich was found to have double lobar pneumonia.

V

In November Yury Dmitrievich returned from the South. The illness had radically changed his disposition. He had become reserved and taciturn. He was ashamed of what had happened to him and he suspected everyone of mocking him. Bukh, however, tried to reassure Nina that these were normal relapses that would gradually disappear. And in fact Yury Dmitrievich did find diversion in the Crimea and became more cheerful. Formerly, prior to his illness, he had paid no particular attention to food or to his appearance. Now he took a liking to delicious, unusual cuisine and good-looking clothes. On his dressing table were bottles of expensive cologne, skin toners, wrinkle creams, tweezers, brushes, nail files.

At first Yury Dmitrievich and Nina stayed in Alushta; later they moved on to Yevpatoria. In Yevpatoria they made friends with an elderly couple—nice people, but dull and not very intelligent. Every evening Nina ended up strolling with them along the esplanade, since Yury Dmitrievich—scented, eyebrows tinted, dressed in an elegant suit and tastefully chosen tie—would leave to, as he put it, "admire the sea in solitude." Nina knew that he had had an affair with an actress and, after the actress left, with a waitress from a local eatery. Lying on a couch in the hotel, Nina would cry and at the same time berate herself for crying; she called herself an egoist, since she had persuaded herself that living like this would build up Yury Dmitrievich's health.

One day Yury Dmitrievich returned just before daybreak and found Nina lying fully dressed on the couch, not having slept. He sat down beside her, embraced her, and said with a smile:

"Ah, Nina . . . how often we forget . . . rather, we don't know how to appreciate our own body. It's the only thing that belongs to us in this world . . . our spiritual life doesn't belong to us, it belongs to something universal . . . something still not clear enough. All our mental illnesses are the vengeance of our body, which in revenge for being ignored withdraws its support from a person and hands him over entirely to the spirit . . ."

Yury Dmitrievich smelled of wine and meat and spices, and when he deftly started undoing the buttons of Nina's blouse, she experienced a feeling of terror, as though Yury Dmitrievich had vanished and a drunken rapist had broken into her room. Moreover, they had not been intimate for a long while; Nina had grown unaccustomed to him. She sat up and, shielding her chest with her elbows, said, "Later . . . not now . . . for heaven's sake. . . ."

Yury Dmitrievich, however, inflamed by the wine and by her resistance, employing strong, skillful movements, forced back her head and brought her down. Instead of getting up to go to sleep by himself on the sofa, as he usually did, he remained next to her. Nina lay awake feeling like a dishonored maiden at the age of forty-four. When she fell asleep it was already morning and the laughter and footsteps of vacationers on their way to the beach floated in from the street. And when she awoke she saw Yury Dmitrievich bright and cheerful, wearing sneakers and nylon swimming trucks and working out with dumbbells. She felt ashamed of the feelings she had had during the night, and in her heart she felt young and joyful, as if it were the morning after her wedding night. She got up, threw on a robe, kissed Yury Dmitrievich on the nape of his neck, and went out to make breakfast. They had their meals in, since Yury Dmitrievich didn't find the restaurant fare tasty enough. A hotel employee who lived on the first floor and had her own kitchenette let Nina use it for a fee and even shopped for the groceries.

For breakfast Nina made some open-faced sandwiches on toasted bread. On each piece of toasted light bread lay a slice of hardboiled egg. A mound of pressed caviar rose from the center of the egg slice and around the edges of it was a thin strip of butter. Besides the sandwiches there was tongue in white sauce with raisins and lemon juice, an apple omelet, and whipped cream with powdered sugar.

After talking it over with Yury Dmitrievich, Nina invited the couple for breakfast. The husband's name was Osip Leonidych. He had a cane with him which he did not lean on, however, but carried under his arm with the head pointing forward. Sitting down on a chair, he began massaging the bridge of his nose with his fingers.

"It doesn't offend you, does it," he asked Nina, "if I massage the bridge of my nose?" A packet of the latest metropolitan newspapers was protruding from his jacket pocket. The buttons on his white linen trousers were always undone, allowing his long underwear to show, and Nina was afraid that Osip Leonidych or his wife would notice this bit of carelessness, become embarrassed, and then the pleasant atmosphere of the breakfast would be spoiled.

The wife's name was Klavdia Andreevna. She was very fat and old, older than Osip Leonidych. She had a growth of whiskers and a skimpy Tartar beard. She had adopted many of her husband's habits and mannerisms, even speaking the way he did, in a slight singsong. About the hotel manager she said:

"I warned him that the next time I'd make it so hot for him he wouldn't be able to tell his own mother from his own father."

Yury Dmitrievich liked the old people. He ate hungrily, laughed, tried to speak in a singsong too, and argued with Osip Leonidych about politics.

That very evening Yury Dmitrievich and Nina left.

November was exceptionally warm, a real Indian summer. In the daytime, the sun's rays were so warm one could go without a jacket. During the first week, Yury Dmitrievich was busy with the reassignment formalities at his new place of work, to which he had gotten himself transferred so as not to lose his seniority. His new employment was with a fairly reputable biomedical journal. The pay was better and there was a lot of free time left for working on his dissertation. The dissertation had nearly been finished back in the winter of the previous year, spring was when the first signs of mental disturbance had appeared and Yury Dmitrievich no longer slept at night. In the spring, his dissertation seemed like a trivial, untalented hashing-over of an isolated problem.

He found the dissertation in a remote desk drawer. A number of pages were wrinkled and crumpled, and a few torn. Rummaging in the drawer, he found a folder of papers labeled in a neat hand: "The History of Jesus Christ's Illness and an Anatomical Study of Jesus' Body; a Determination of the Exact Position of the Body on the Cross and of the Reason that Jesus, in Dying, Inclined His Head toward His Right Shoulder." Yury Dmitrievich took out the folder and, holding it in his outstretched hand, like a snake, he went to the kitchen with his heart pounding. Suddenly he felt terrified, as though that gray, cardboard folder could take away, could swallow up this quiet day, now golden from the yellow foliage, the apartment, the smell of the delicious food that Nina was preparing in the kitchen. He got a sack from the pantry, dumped the folder into it, put on an old, velvet jacket, and picked up some matches.

"Where are you going?" asked Nina, viewing him with alarm. "You're not feeling well . . . you're pale."

"No, it's nothing," Yury Dmitrievich said. "I'm just going down to the furnace room. I've got a few rags to give to the stoker, some old clothes . . ."

It was damp in the basement and the smell of fuel oil and soot made it hard to breathe. Yury Dmitrievich stopped in a narrow passageway, shook out the folder from the bag, and began tearing it up, breaking his fingernails on the stiff heavy cardboard. Only when a pile of torn paper lay in front of him did Yury Dmitrievich calm down a little. He lit the paper and took pleasure in watching it writhe on the cement floor. He then stamped on the ashes and scattered them, and walked out into the courtyard, to the sound of clicking dominoes, music drifting out of windows, and kids chasing a soccer ball. Yury Dmitrievich looked at all of this and, as though he had just awakened from a nightmare, breathed a deep sigh of joy.

He ate heartily. Nina had made a mushroom pudding with finely chopped white mushrooms baked in a casserole with fried onions, white bread crumbs, and walnut oil. In addition, there was fish soup made with perch and flavored with pressed caviar crushed in a mortar, and stuffed rabbit with garlic sauce.

In the evening Yury Dmitrievich received a visit from his new co-worker Aleskovkin, whom everyone called Kononovich for short. They were supposed to go off to some fraternal supper, and Kononovich had come by since Yury Dmitrievich didn't know the address and this was the very first time he was joining this group. Kononovich was accompanied by an ample young woman, a dyed blonde in a dark dress that was swelled out by her high bosom, with large, red, evidently frostbitten hands. On her massive left wrist she was wearing a tiny gold watch. The dyed blonde's name was Rita. While Nina was changing her clothes in the bedroom and Rita was looking at fashion magazines in the dining room, Kononovich talked about her in a whisper, with knowing winks. Rita had once worked at a construction site where she had gotten her hands frostbitten. At the time, she went by the name of Glafira. Later she went to work as a domestic for a professor, an old bachelor, started an affair with him, and married him.

"A terrifying woman," Kononovich was saying, "a vampire . . . devours men . . . I advise you not to slight her . . ."

The apartment they went to was noisy and crowded. The first person Yury Dmitrievich saw was Nikolai Pavlovich. Yury Dmitrievich was embarrassed but Nikolai Pavalovich calmly walked over to him and shook his hand.

"You look wonderful," Nikolai Pavlovich said. "I'm glad, very glad . . ."

Nikolai Pavlovich was not deputy director of the institute now; he was head of the epidemiology station. He still gave the appearance of someone in charge. Yury Dmitrievich heard him say to someone wearing a pince-nez: "First of all, I adopted measures aimed at tightening financial discipline, since financial control is a criterion. Namely, a criterion as distinct . . ."

Yury Dmitrievich drifted away and, after drinking a toast to the health of some Anton Antonovich Kroshchuk, he began to listen in on other conversations. The talk at Yury Dmitrievich's part of the table centered on the race problem.

"Race exists," said a man with protruding ears, "and a difference exists which we mustn't close our eyes to . . . especially doctors. On the contrary, as soon as we close our eyes to difficulties, to differences that have to be overcome, it's immediately taken advantage of by the cannibals, racists of all stripes—"

"Hogwash," exclaimed his opponent, who was still quite young, ruddy-cheeked, and wearing a cheap, mass-produced suit. "Race means external biological characteristics. Markers of the human body: skin, nose, eyes, and so on. Race marks the boundaries between biology and psychology. Depth biology, which in fact constitutes the essence of man, is connected with the nervous system and the brain, and forms the basis of the human individual in respect to whom race is an external characteristic that merely furthers development as a result of psychological influence. In other words, race is psychology invested with an externally biological form—"

"And genetics?" shouted the man with the protruding ears. "Is heredity an external form, too?"

"Hereditary features transmit for the most part the character not of a race as a whole, but of an individual," the young man replied, "an individual . . . In a colony of coral each single organism is only a part of the whole; man, on the other hand, is biologically independent of fellow creatures. You confuse biology with psychology . . . and don't say they're inseparably linked, mixed up, and so forth. People always use these expressions in order to get away from the concrete, to avoid clarity and indulge in superficial chitchat. There is depth biology, concerned with man's internal organs, and there is external biology, concerned with geography, climate . . ."

"That's foolish," said Kononovich, who was sitting next to Yury Dmitrievich. Kononovich's cheeks had turned pale from the vodka he had consumed and he was spitting out olive pits on the table cloth. "Foolish . . . there *is* a difference . . . and the item on the questionnaire hasn't been eliminated yet, understand . . . the order hasn't been given. Now when *I* meet someone, I always think: What does it say on your I.D., fella? Only a *woman's* nationality doesn't interest me, and that's only when she's performing as a woman . . . when that's finished she's branded with her origin and becomes just another broad . . ."

Kononovich raised his head and listened to the sounds coming from the record player. "Yura," he said, "let me have your wife . . . for a dance. . . ."

"Of course," said Yury Dmitrievich.

Nina was disgusted by Kononovich, who for some reason stank of urine. But she was afraid she would irritate Yury Dmitrievich if she refused. No sooner had they stepped out into the middle of the floor and started moving to the beat of the music than Kononovich led her off into a corner and began feeling around between her shoulder blades through her dress for the hooks of her brassiere. Nina shook off his arm with her shoulder and said, glaring into his blondish, foxlike face:

"One of us stinks of turpentine."

"Oh, really?" Kononovich said. "It can't be me, unless maybe I stepped in something."

Rita sat herself down beside Yury Dmitrievich. As she sat she pulled up the hem of her dress so high one could see the silvery clasps of her garters on her ample fleshy thighs.

"What I want is a man," said Rita. "I don't care about nationality."

Her hands were moist and touching them left white blotches that slowly flooded with redness. Before long Rita and Yury ended up in the front hall among the clothing, and Rita, her eyes wild and hungry, silently began grabbing Yury Dmitrievich.

"Is it true you went psycho?" she asked after several minutes of silent grabbing and breathing. "I've never tried a psycho. . . ."

"I was ill," Yury Dmitrievich said. "Man consists of air, bile, and phlegm . . . I was filled with air . . . it bore me above the earth . . . now I want to live on bile. Bile is produced from blood that has gotten free of lymph components . . . it is overladen with fatty substances . . . if seminal fluid can't escape, the fluid interacts with it and corrodes the brain . . . but I'm going to let the seminal fluid escape and direct the bile into another channel. Write down your phone number for me . . . we'll get together . . ."

A noise came from inside. Something had smashed. Yury Dmitrievich hurried back, straightening his clothes which Rita had roughed up, and fastening buttons. Nina was sitting on the sofa and the biologist in the mass-produced suit was giving her a cold fruit drink. Her hair was disheveled and there were sauce stains down the front of her dress.

"Nina Ivanovna began to feel sick," said Kononovich. "It really is hot and smoky in here."

"Yura," Nina said forlornly, lifting her eyes to Yury Dmitrievich, "what are you doing to me and to yourself?"

"Well, what of it?" Yury Dmitrievich said, his head ringing from vodka and from Rita's strong, masculine hugs. "Our relationship may not be forever, you know . . . that's right . . . I'm sorry I didn't go through with things . . . since you're to blame for my breakdown . . ."

Nikolai Pavlovich was standing nearby and when he detected a familiar note in Yury Dmitrievich's voice, he quickly moved away.

But the quarrel ended benignly. Kononovich called a taxi and Yury Dmitrievich and Nina left.

Everything remained the way it was. Nina ran herself ragged shopping in stores and farmers' markets for food. She ransacked cookbooks and made a mayonnaise of game, mushroom borscht with prunes, *gateau de crêpes*, and other "goodies," to use Yury Dmitrievich's term. Yury Dmitrievich usually went to his office or to the library of the republic's academy of sciences to work on his dissertation. To get away in the evening he used various pretexts such as a conference or an anniversary celebration. Once he even said he was going to the morgue to see an interesting specimen. He would come back home in the middle of the night. Nina pretended to be asleep and saw him walking about in the dark in a state of excitement. In the morning she would notice black and blue pinch marks and scratches on his body. One day Nina overheard Yury Dmitrievich talking to Kononovich on the telephone: "There's something about the woman that's like a female spider who devours her mate . . . . I'm not sure if one should feel sorry for the mate. It's more like Buddhism than Christianity . . . Buddhism is also based on a legend of self-sacrifice, but a sacrifice that may be more noble than the Crucifixion . . . when the Buddha encountered a sick, hungry tigress, he offered himself as food . . . specifically to a tigress, a female. There's a subtlety here . . . the basis here is not good but gratification , not everyday gratification, of course, an ideal gratification . . mutual love here leads to a merger into a single organism. Then again, in the Gospel according to John, Christ offers his flesh to be eaten and his blood to be drunk . . . but this isn't the basis of Christianity; it's one of Christ's miracles. . . ."

Nina heard the crackling of Kononovich's laughter coming from the receiver, and added to the hurt she felt as a woman was her annoyance with Yury Dmitrievich for confiding some of his thoughts to that idiot.

Yury Dmitrievich again began having trouble sleeping; when he woke up he felt as if something were pressing on his stomach and that if he just screamed the feeling would ease. Lying there in the darkness, his feet hot and his forehead cold, he would fearfully anticipate the instant when his scream would erupt and everything which he thought was now going smoothly in his life would thereupon collapse . . .

This didn't occur very often, however, and at that only at night and always at the same time, at two or three A.M. In the daytime, though, Yury Dmitrievich felt very well. His appetite was good, he took care of his appearance, he even gained some weight, and his face took on a healthy color. Nina made a trip to get Bukh's advice.

"Relapses are possible," Bukh said, "but let's hope that these are just residual occurrences. Heightened instinctive behavior—appetite, sexual attraction—is frequently above normal even after a total recovery. One has to be tolerant and understanding . . . this is something that goes beyond the realm of medicine, by the way. More here depends on you than on me. You're his wife, a woman . . . and in this struggle . . . or, I should say, rivalry with the animal . . . yes, it's really terrible . . . I deeply sympathize with you. . . ."

But day after day went by and nothing changed, until the second of December. When he got up in the morning, he immediately sensed that it was not just another day of the month but a date; today something was supposed to happen. It's possible, of course, that he convinced himself of this only later, after the fact. First of all, Yury Dmitrievich noticed that the room was lighted unusually. It had become cleaner, as it were, but the cleanliness was sterile, uneasy, like that of a hospital ward. He glanced out the window and saw white roofs. It was the first snowfall. It had apparently snowed all night and maintenance men were scraping it from the walks and sweeping it into piles. He ate breakfast hurriedly and without the usual satisfaction, though this too might have just seemed that way to him later on. He then put on his winter coat, which smelled of mothballs and had a Persian lamb collar, his ear-flapped hat made of young deer fur, picked up his squeaky briefcase with the chrome suitcase locks, and went off to the library. He decided to walk so that he could enjoy the first bit of freezing weather and relax before work. The library had three reading rooms: one for undergraduates, one for specialists with an advanced degree, and one for scientists. The undergraduate reading room was always crowded and noisy. The seats had no numbers on them and people sat close to one another, several to a table. The scientists' reading room was small and usually half-deserted. Massive potted palms and soft armchairs made it hard to concentrate. Yury Dmitrievich preferred working in the specialists' reading room. The room was enormous, like a stadium. It was over thirty feet high, with a ceiling made of thick, opaque glass set in aluminum frames. Yury Dmitrievich filled out a call slip, got his books, found the seat he had been assigned to, and immersed himself in his work. After about ten minutes, however, he began to feel that something was interfering with his concentration. He laid aside the table from which he had been copying figures, got up, and walked over to a window. It too was very tall, about the size of a store window. Some trolleybuses with snowcovered roofs were crawling along outside. The cold had diminished and the snow was melting. The roadway was covered with a yellowish brown mush.

"The thaw," Yury Dmitrievich reasoned, "I guess that's what's making it hard to concentrate . . . there you have it, the influence of the weather on people's behavior . . . in London the number of suicides goes up in October because of the wind and fog."

He sat down again in his seat and spread out the table. He took a sharp-pointed red pencil and suddenly looked at the reader sitting across from him. Actually, he had looked at him earlier also, but with indifference then; now, however, he looked closely and for some reason concluded that it was this particular reader who was disturbing his concentration. The reader was a man of about forty with reddish hair and red eyelashes, though on the whole quite ordinary-looking. He was wearing a dark jacket, a gray knit vest, and a gray tie. He had slender fingers with neat fingernails that looked polished. On one of the fingers was a wedding ring. Yury Dmitrievich figured that this man liked his reflection in a mirror, in spite of his reddishness, which he was used to and didn't notice. But maybe he even liked the reddishness. At the same time, there was something elusively disquieting about his face, something that distinguished it from other faces in the vicinity. Perhaps it was the slight tremor of an eyelid that became noticeable if you looked closely. Or it may have been the small crescent-shaped scar covered up with powder next to his right eyebrow. In the meantime, the man realized he was being stared at. At first he merely frowned in annoyance while he continued to write something rapidly on a pad, turning the pages of a weighty tome with his left hand. Then he became fidgety, stared angrily at Yury Dmitrievich, and finally, unable to bear it any longer, he slammed the book shut, moved aside his pad, fished out a pack of cigarettes from under a pile of papers, shook one out and pressed it between his lips, rattled a box of matches, and got up and walked away down the aisle, evidently to the smoking room. As soon as the man left, Yury Dmitrievich felt calmer. He turned to the table again and concentrated on his work for a while.

Suddenly, there was a violent crash accentuated by the quiet of the library, the sound of shattering glass and cracking wood, shrieks, and the tramping of feet. Yury Dmitrievich looked up. The first thing he saw was a torn apart lampshade. The chair in which the redheaded man had been sitting was smashed and had an aluminum rod embedded in its back. Sharp pieces of glass, ribbed and a centimeter thick, with wire mesh fused in the middle, were lodged deeply in the seat of the chair. The table was also covered with glass. The books and papers on it had been cut and torn by the shards and by pieces of aluminum. A woman sitting on the left, about fifty years old, was holding her cut hand, but it wasn't a deep wound, only a scratch. Yury Dmitrievich looked up and saw a gaping hole in the ceiling through which he could see beams. An entire frame had broken loose and fallen thirty feet, crashing into the table and into the redheaded man's chair. The readers had leaped from their seats. An attendant came trotting across the room down the carpeted aisle.

"Where's the gentleman?" she asked, out of breath.

"He went out for a smoke," Yury Dmitrievich replied.

"It would have smashed his skull in no time flat," someone said. "You never know when it's going to get you."

The redheaded man came into the room. He looked rested; maybe along with his smoke he had had a cup of coffee at the snack bar. As he walked along the aisle, he wiped cookie crumbs from his mouth with a handkerchief. When he noticed the crowd of readers, he raised his eyebrows in amazement. In addition to contentment his face took on a look of curiosity. He walked faster, craning his neck and trying to peer over people's backs.

"It's you!" the attendant shouted when she saw him. "It's him . . . the man who was in this seat . . . see how lucky you are. . . ."

People made way for the man. He saw the mutilated chair and the table covered with sharp fragments of glass and aluminum. For an instant his body shivered as though from a chill and his face became distorted. But only for an instant. The next instant his face assumed a pensive, even drowsy expression, like that of people who have lapsed into philosophical contemplation. He stood that way for a moment or two in total silence with his head leaning slightly to one side. Then gently and carefully, as though he didn't want to dirty his suit and were selecting the cleanest spot, he sank to the floor. His cheeks had turned pale.

"He's fainted!" the attendant exclaimed. "Some water . . . the nurse . . . go telephone . . ."

Yury Dmitrievich began to gather up his books and papers. He saw them sit the man up. A nurse was giving him a vial to sniff and the man jerked back his head. His unbuttoned shirt was wet from the water.

"It's all very clear," Yury Dmitrievich muttered. "Very clear . . ." He returned the books, put away his papers in his briefcase, put on his coat and hat and walked out, breathing in the raw air. The morning's snowbanks now looked like dirty little mounds. He felt hot in the winter coat and hat.

Nina met Yury Dmitrievich in the front hall and, looking directly at him, she asked in a whisper:

"You know already? There was a phone call! . . Oh, good Lord . . . but there's no need to get excited, I suppose . . . it can all be settled . . . the main thing is your health . . . any court will be on your side. . . "

"What court?" Yury Dmitrievich asked, taking off his coat. "What am I supposed to know? . . You've always got some news . . . you spy on me like a Jesuit."

"Yury," Nina said, wrinkling her brow as if she were about to cry, "Yury, now is not the time for an argument. Some important things have to be settled . . . I'm sure you know . . . I could tell it right away from your expression when you walked in—"

"Oh, come off that telepathy of yours. What expression? What's going on?"

"Grigory's here," Nina said, "he wants to talk to you. But you mustn't forget about yourself . . . about your health . . . and your family. . . ."

"Grigory?" Yury Dmitrievich said, somewhat confused.

Lately Yury Dmitrievich's relations with Grigory, and with his old friends in general, had gone sour. They had stopped seeing each other. Yury Dmitrievich had run into Grigory by chance on the street about two weeks ago. They said hello, exchanged two or three words, and parted. Grigory Alekseevich was sitting in Yury Dmitrievich's study and leafing through last year's calendar for women.

"This *is* a surprise," Yury Dmitrievich said, trying to give his face a look of audacity. "I can't believe my eyes."

"Hello," said Grigory Alekseevich. "Actually, I've come to see you on business . . . I should say, there's a letter for you. . . "

"Grigory," Nina said, "Yury has had a serious illness. I'm asking you, in fact, I insist—"

"Oh, stop it!" Yury Dmitrievich cried, feeling his heart beating more intensely. "What is it, a letter from whom? What is it I know . . . what's going on, anyway?"

"Sit down," Grigory Alekseevich said. "I belong to the Society for the Protection of Ancient Monuments . . . which are barbarically ruined because of ignorance. For example, a monument of Russian architecture . . . twelfth century . . . used as a warehouse by the city commerce department . . . construction workers . . . toilet bowls lying around . . ."

"Oh, you want me to join the society too," Yury Dmitrievich said with a sigh of relief.

"No," said Grigory Alekseevich. "That is, you can certainly join the Society . . . it's the duty of every cultivated person. To safeguard history . . . forebears . . . yes. But, actually, I'm here for another reason. I went with a commission to visit a monastery . . . in fact, it was that same one . . . I met a girl . . . a woman . . . religious . . . she recognized me . . . Zina. She's pregnant. . . ."

Finishing what he had to say, Grigory Alekseevich emitted a deep sigh and caught his breath, as though he had just climbed a hill. Yury Dmitrievich heard Nina begin to cry behind him.

"Yes, of course," Yury Dmitrievich said softly, "But what can I do? . . That is not to say I'm asking you for advice; I'm just thinking out loud."

"You were ill," Nina cried out, "you aren't responsible for your actions . . . I've discussed it with Bukh. During an illness, one's instinctive behavior, one's sexual urges are heightened . . . yes . . . there are known cases of patients frivolously marrying chance acquaintances. And besides," Nina shouted spitefully, "those religious hypocrites are depraved. In those sects they have relations with preachers . . . and monks. She's trying to take advantage . . . it's not your child. . . ."

"She doesn't belong to a sect," Yury Dmitrievich said softly, thinking about something and guarding his thoughts from those around him.

"Here's the letter for you," said Grigory Alekseevich, handing over a soiled envelope.

Inside it was a sheet of paper at the top of which was imprinted: "For the Delegate to the Sixth Congress of the Republic Society for the Dissemination of Political and Scientifc Knowledge."

"I let her have a sheet of paper from my pad," said Grigory Alekseevich.

The paper was covered with a scraggly but conscientious handwriting, like that of a semiliterate:

"My dear husband Yury," wrote Zina, "greetings from your wife Zina. Even though we have not been married in church, I still write to you this way because we are man and wife before God, and I pray for you as my husband away on a long journey. When you come back we'll be married and we'll be husband and wife in the eyes of other people, too. In the very first lines of my letter I wish to tell you, my beloved husband, more wonderful news. We are going to have a son. I have taken a leave from the cooperative and with Papa Isai, who also loves you, I am now going to Pochaev, to the holy monastery, to pray for our son and for our love. I don't know your address, but when I come back I'll write to your friend and he'll forward it to you. Your faithful loving wife, Zina."

"Grigory," Nina said, nervously cracking her knuckles, "what are we going to do?" Her face looked imploring and even obsequious, as though, instead of asking, she were pleading with Grigory Alekseevich for advice and as though his advice could solve everything.

"I don't know," Grigory said. "Try to talk it out with her. Maybe she'll agree to get rid of the baby . . . I'm making no sense, I'm just saying the first thing that comes into my head, but I don't know . . . it's so complicated . . . or maybe alimony, after all. Then again, in the absence of a legal marriage—"

"What difference does that make," she exclaimed joyfully. "You've got a real brain, Grigory. You're a true friend . . . you've found a brilliant way out. Of course, if she doesn't want to have an abortion, we'll pay. We'll give the child love . . . that's right, Yury . . . he's your son and I'll love him as if he were my own. We'll buy him presents, we'll visit. . . ." She pressed up against Grigory Alekseevich's shoulder and burst into sobs.

"Be still now," Yury Dmitrievich said, stroking her hair, her neck. "Don't . . . come on now, please . . ."

His face became gentle and pensive.

After Grigory Alekseevich left, they had dinner. They moved and spoke in a way that seemed like an effort to protect each other from their own imprudent words and movements. Toward evening, however, Yury Dmitrievich's mood took a new turn. He grew sullen and uncommunicative. Settling into an armchair, he gnawed on a pencil and gazed out the dark window against which the wind drove flakes of wet snow.

"Go to bed," he said to Nina, "I've got insomnia . . . I'm going to sit up for a while and do some work."

"It's not good for you," Nina said, "I discussed it with Bukh. He is absolutely opposed to your working at night. Take a pill . . ."

"Stop watching over me," Yury Dmitrievich shouted so loudly that his throat began to tickle. ". . . You and Bukh . . . that's right, leave me alone!"

He jumped up and went off to his study. Locking the door, he put out the light and lay down on the sofa with his hands behind his head. He lay like that until morning, shifting his body from time to time, putting his left hand behind his head instead of the right. In the morning he applied some powder to the puffy circles under his eyes and left for work.

VI

Two weeks passed. Real December cold had set in. As usual, a lot of work had piled up at the end of the year and Yury Dmitrievich wasn't able to get home for lunch now. He ate in a restaurant not far from where he worked. It was a second-rate establishment that had more waiters than customers, though one still had to sit and wait a long time for service. The waiters were mainly young kids who looked like small-town dudes in their dog-collar ties with a glass bead at the throat, their dingy shirts, tight pants, and down-at-the-heel pointed-toe shoes. They congregated in small groups toward the back of the dining room and read *Soviet Sports*. There were also some experienced middle-aged waitresses who, like porters in a railroad station, would go out into the lobby to greet lucrative patrons and escort them to their tables. Lucrative patrons were fought over. Yury Dmitrievich found this unpleasant, so he stopped tipping and in turn was no longer noticed. Now, however, he had to wait a long while for one of the youngsters to serve him.

One day when Yury Dmitrievich was sitting there restlessly, glancing at his watch and playing with the salt shaker, someone called over to him. Sitting at the next table was Kononvich, and he was being fussed over by a fat waitress in a starched lace cap.

"Sit over here, we'll have lunch together," Kononovich said.

Yury Dmitrievich thought about it a moment and moved to the other table.

"So you've been avoiding me lately," Kononovich said. "Someone's been whispering, I guess. There's no shortage of slanderers nowadays . . . and you've forgotten Rita, too. But we're your friends, as a matter of fact. You've been rough on Nina as well . . . she's complained to me . . . the woman doesn't look herself anymore . . . she's running a fever; she's coming down with something, I think—" "Hold on a minute," said Yury Dmitrievich, "not so fast . . . I want to get this straight . . . where did you see Nina?" "I've seen her, "Kononovich said. "Don't worry, there's nothing to be jealous about. That's not the point right now. Let's just say she paid Rita a visit. Don't be surprised: we—your friends—we may have our disagreements, but we all love you and are concerned about your welfare. You're in trouble, you've been reported—" "Reported?" Yury Dmitrievich was quick to ask. "By whom?" "Some blind man," Kononovich said, "a member of a cooperative board. You seduced a girl and left her pregnant. The blind man wrote to a newspaper and the paper sent the letter on to the old man, Rita's husband. The situation, you see, has taken a very bad turn . . . the girl died . . ." "What do you mean 'died'?" Yury Dmitrievich asked rather calmly. "She went to Pochaev . . ." "So what?" said Kononovich. "If someone goes to Pochaev, you think he becomes immortal? . . . After she got there, she died from an abortion. She had it done by some old woman. That's ignorance for you; they don't even know how to sin . . ."

Yury Dmitrievich got up and walked off, weaving his way through the closely spaced tables. Stacks of dishes rose from the tables, threatening to fall over and smash into countless fragments, since the floor was laid in ceramic tile. Numerous people were sitting and standing in the most inconvenient positions, legs outstretched, leaning on bony elbows, or simply blocking the way with their bodies. In the lobby there was a telephone on the wall by the checkroom, but some colonel was using it. Fortunately, there was a phone booth outside the restaurant. Yury Dmitrievich went out but that phone was in use too, so he headed for the booth at the end of the street. He drew looks from passersby, since he wasn't wearing a coat or hat and his jacket was covered with snow. The phone booth at the end of the street was unoccupied. Yury Dmitrievich dialed a number.

"Grigory," he said, "Zina's dead, is that true?"

"Yes," said Grigory Alekseevich. "I didn't know how to tell you . . . I wavered . . . Nina wrote to her . . . five days ago . . . I read the letter. Nina said everything we talked about . . . she offered to help with the child's upbringing . . . I tried to persuade her, too . . . do you hear me, Yury? . . . You shouldn't blame Nina . . . of course it's sad, it's terrible . . . but these religious fanatics, bigots . . . are you there? . . . Where are you calling from? . . ."

"I hear you," Yury Dmitrievich said, and he hung up the receiver.

He returned to the restaurant, put on his coat and hat, and headed home. He was wet under his coat. The melting snow had seeped through his jacket and shirt and the moisture made his body itch. On the landing in front of his door he could no longer stand it. He took off his coat and jacket and began scratching his itchy body between his shoulder blades, under his arms, and even behind his knees. He then opened the door with his key. He could hear the sound of voices and the clatter of dishes coming from the dining room. He walked in and saw Nina and Rita sitting at the table. The table was replete with dishes of preserves. There was also a platter of candies and cookies and oranges were heaped in a mound.

Rita was wearing a fluffy knit blouse that clung tightly to her broad, mannish shoulders and high bust. When Yury Dmitrievich came in, both women turned their heads toward him, intending to say something.

"Quiet!" Yury Dmitrievich shouted. "Since the two of you have reached an understanding . . . or, I should say, have become friends . . . Zina is dead . . . yes . . . I have lost my humanity . . . but you, Nina, how could you have anything to do with this animal . . . this female spider. . . ."

"Well, listen to him!" Rita cried out and jumped up. "Out of the goodness of my heart I agreed, but now I don't give a damn. Some family! . . The wife herself invites in a mistress so her husband can have some fun . . . Listen, you booby, you should know that she asked me to give you a good time . . . so you wouldn't get too upset about that dame . . . the one you got pregnant and who died from an abortion. It's a riot . . . the wife asks me. . . ." Rita burst out laughing and when she stopped, she cried out once more: "Enough of this! . . . They'll put you on trial . . . I'll testify against both of you. We'll see who's a spider. There's a letter with a charge against you, action'll be taken. . . ."

While she was yelling, Yury Dmitrievich stared at her gums. Tiny bubbles of saliva welled up between her strong, white teeth. She was holding on to the back of her chair with a tight grip, and her red frostbitten hands had turned white around the joints, at the bends of her fingers. Rita went out into the front hall, where she could be heard getting dressed. Then she slammed the door.

Yury Dmitrievich went over to Nina and sat down next to her.

"I went out of my mind," said Nina. "I lost my reason . . . I was hoping . . . I was clutching at everything . . . I don't know . . . life isn't possible any more. . . ."

"Easy now," Yury Dmitrievich said. "Let's be quiet for a moment. If there is anyone I feel more guilty toward than I do toward the deceased, it is you. Now I'm going to go there. . . ."

"I'm worried about you," Nina said. "I'll go with you—"

"No," Yury Dmitrievich said, "you're a good girl, you know you can't go there. You're nice, you're so sweet . . . have some tea, rest for a while, read a magazine . . . I'll be back soon." As he got dressed to go, he talked to her like this, as though trying to persuade a little girl.

When he was already out on the street, he saw Nina come running out after him, apparently having regained her senses. Since he had paused behind a newsstand, she failed to notice him and hurried off down the street looking in several directions. Yury Dmitrievich took a taxi and went out to the monastery. It was very quiet and clean outside of town. The monastery walls and courtyard were covered with a thick layer of snow, and even the scorched church that was now a commerce department warehouse looked clean and elegant. The door to Zina's apartment was unlocked. An unshaven man was seated at the table, making an inventory. An icon lay on the sofa among the pans, the kerosene stove, and some small bags of food. The bureau drawers were pulled out, and on top of the bureau lay a small pile of clean linen smelling of mothballs, glass beads, a box containing inexpensive but still brand-new shoes, a skirt, two dresses, several skeins of wool yarn, and an unfinished knit sweater. The heavy ring in which Yury Dmitrievich had once seen a little house on a hill was also lying there.

"What do you want?" the man asked Yury Dmitrievich.

"I'm here to find out about the deceased, about the funeral."

"You a relative?"

"No . . . a friend."

"I see," the man said disappointedly. "Someone's got to sign the list here."

"They've taken her to church," said an elderly woman, apparently a witness.

The woman was sorting the dishes, piling those that were a little better in one stack and tossing the old and chipped ones into a rusty basin that already had a lot of broken pieces in it.

"There'll be a funeral service," the woman added. "Here in the village. You have to go past the construction site."

"Thank you," Yury Dmitrievich said, and he left.

The church was set back in an old park among beautifully snow-covered paths. A bus and a truck were parked next to it. There were some people walking around wearing black armbands. Inside the bus one could see musicians and a rolled-up banner trimmed with black ribbon. A tall, gaunt old woman in a black kerchief was standing at the entrance to the church. Facing her was a short, stocky man wearing a Persian lamb hat with earflaps, a fur-lined jacket, riding breeches, and felt boots trimmed with leather.

"My dear woman, try to understand," the man was saying. "Come to your senses before it's too late. By this action of yours you are undermining the ideology which your son fought for all his life. He was decorated by the government, remember; he was a Party member, after all."

"In this world he may have been a Party member," the old woman said, "but in the next world everyone's the same . . . I won't let you bury him without a church service. I was the one who gave birth to him but all his life he was yours. And I never even saw him from the time he left home at the age of seventeen," she sobbed. "Never any time . . . always in a rush . . . always just for the day . . . just to spend the night. But now I'll see him all I want. Now he's mine, not yours. . . ."

"That's just not proper," said the man, wiping his eyes furtively. "We all remember Pyotr and always will remember him . . . our entire staff . . . as a good public citizen, do you understand . . . as a skilled leader and a caring friend. But this mustn't be, it mustn't, don't you see? . . . We don't infringe upon your ideology, there's freedom of religion in our country. So why do you infringe upon the anti-religious ideology of your late son, who was dear to us all?" The man remained silent for a moment, looking at the woman. Then he sighed and, making a hopeless gesture of frustration, said, "The district committee is going to tan my hide." And he walked off toward the bus.

Yury Dmitrievich walked up the old steps worn smooth by many soles and, removing his hat, entered the vestibule, a rather spacious room lined with steam radiators and benches. Over by one wall stood the lids of two coffins, one opulent, covered with red fabric bordered in black, the other simple and newly planed. On a bench in the antechamber a young woman was diapering a crying baby. Next to her sat a boy of about seventeen, and a girl with dyed red hair combed over her forehead, wearing black ribbed stockings. The boy's hair was parted right down the middle and glistened with pomade. The boy and girl were listening to the singing inside, exchanging winks and smiling.

"He's joining in, praying to God," the boy said, nodding toward the crying baby.

The church was divided into two halves. The left, the side closer to the door, was empty, except for the oil lamps burning in front of the icons and the glitter of gilt. The right side, separated in part by a wall and in part by columns, was where the service was being conducted. There were not many people, mostly old women in kerchiefs. The choir, situated somewhere up front behind the columns, sang softly and off-key. From time to time, those who were praying kneeled down and crossed themselves. Behind them, closer to the doorway, were two coffins readied for departure, resting on special supports. One of the coffins was covered with red calico, and the man lying in it was engulfed in flowers. He was dressed in a black suit with a shirt and tie; his forehead was taped over with something. Alongside, in the newly planed coffin, lay Zina. A white kerchief was tied around her head, and her body was covered up to her neck with a white sheet. On her chest lay some object whose purpose Yury Dmitrievich did not know. It looked like a square piece of leather or heavy cardboard studded with sequins. The man's face and Zina's, both waxenwhite and pointed, looked amazingly alike, as though they were related. A number of people were crowded around the man, including a woman dressed all in black, apparently his wife, whose face was sallow and tear-swollen and who continually shuddered as though she were waking up. Next to Zina were only Papa Isai and the blind man. Papa Isai must not have recognized Yury Dmitrievich, and the blind man did not sense his presence as he had done in the past. The blind man was now hunched over and tapped a cane when he walked. A church attendant came over to him and said something. The blind man followed him for several steps, then stumbled, nearly knocking over an icon lamp. Tears ran down his cheeks from beneath his dark glasses. Papa Isai, though, stood there looking detached and calm, mumbling, shaking his head, and crossing himself. Yury Dmitrievich squeezed in closer.

"And this is the Father's will which hath sent me," Papa Isai muttered, "that of all which he hath given me I should lose nothing, but should raise it up again at the last day . . ."

Standing brass candelabra were placed around the coffins. Each candelabrum held several thin wax candles. Nearby there were also several lecterns covered in black fabric with white edging. On the lectern at the head of the coffin lay a small pile of unused wax candles and a sheet of paper with a prayer printed on it in type.

"The Jews then murmured at him," Papa Isai muttered, "because he said, 'I am the bread which came down from heaven.' And they said, 'Is not this Jesus, the son of Joseph, whose father and mother we know? How is it then that he saith, I came down from heaven?' "

Yury Dmitrievich walked over to the left side, the empty half of the church. On one wall hung a painting, *Christ in the Temple. Christ Heals the Infants* was on the opposite wall. The wall directly across from him was entirely filled with gilt frames; it was covered from top to bottom with images of saints. In the center of the top row, in the largest frame, was a depiction of God with a beard. Seated on his lap was his own bearded image, only smaller. To God's left and right were the patriarchs, four on each side. On the left was the patriarch Jacob, on the right the patriarch Abraham. In the next row down were the prophets: Moses, King David, and so on. Eight prophets in all. Below them were the archangels. The seventeen-year-old came up to Yury Dmitrievich and stood next to him. Looking upward, he asked:

"Whose picture is that? I can't make out what it says."

"The patriarch Isaiah," Yury Dmitrievich replied.

"They're all kinds of people," said the boy, "Jews, Georgians. . . ."

The boy exuded a pure, immaculate stupidity, like a happy puppy.

"Lord have mercy, Lord have mercy, Lord have mercy," drifted over from the other side of the church, and one could still hear the baby wailing in the antechamber.

Yury Dmitrievich left the church. The man in the felt boots was standing by a snow-covered bench and talking to someone wearing a fur cap and eyeglasses:

"I've made the arrangements . . . two hundred rubles . . . a farewell dinner in the factory cafeteria . . . the factory committee will chip in too. . . ."

Yury Dmitrievich walked away down the steep village street. Along one side of it were old log houses; the other side was lined with recently built high-rise apartments. At the end of the street was a wooden booth.

"How about splitting a bottle?" someone in a pea jacket proposed.

"No," Yury Dmitrievich said. He walked up to the booth and bought himself a bottle of vodka. Then he walked away and, after he had rounded the corner of a fence, he drank half of the vodka, straight from the bottle. Afterwards, he walked along without knowing where he was going and with no idea of whom he was with. But toward evening, when the sky had cleared of clouds and the stars hung thickly overhead, he found himself exactly where he wanted to be—at the foot of the asphalt steps leading straight up into the firmament. Yury Dmitrievich had trouble seeing because his glasses had disappeared and his right eye was swollen. The whole side of his face, in fact, was smashed up. His cheekbone and the corners of his mouth felt as if hard foreign objects had been sewn into them.

Yury Dmitrievich started up the icy snow-covered steps toward the sky, and he fell down, painfully banging his elbows, knees, and ribs. Whenever he got tired of walking, he crawled, and the snow near his face would melt a little from his heavy breathing. Midway up the stairs, Yury Dmitrievich stopped to rest. He got the bottle out of his pocket and finished off the vodka, accompanying it with a bite of icy twigs off the shrubbery that bordered the steps. The steps that he had already climbed disappeared in the darkness, leaving behind him a precipice, with the abandoned earth as far away now as the starry sky. Exhausted, Yury Dmitrievich lay still for a while, then continued his climb. He crawled out onto a quiet snow-covered square. The buildings were already dark, a part of the night. Only here and there were windows lit. Lacking the strength to stand upright, Yury Dmitrievich remained on all fours. With his head tilted back he stared up at the huge somber cathedral, whose domes leaned against the stars. The castiron gates of the cathedral were covered with silvery frost, and from up above, coming from the cornices, he could hear the little groans of dozing pigeons.

"I've got to get up from all fours," Yury Dmitrievich murmured. "But to get up from all fours one has to take up a stone with one's paw . . . I'm weak, but it wasn't the strongest, it was our weakest forebear who first took up a stone in his paw to rival the strong . . . it was weakness, not strength, that gave birth to men . . . weakness begets strength, and strength weakness."

Falling forward, Yury Dmitrievich sank his swollen cheek into the snow. The square was quiet and deserted as before. One lone man walked toward him in squeaking boots.

"Man," said Yury Dmitrievich, full of hope and joy, "man, teach me . . . I am your little brother . . . I am down on all fours . . . enlighten me . . . steal the fire . . . light my way . . . lead me, man. . . ."

The man bent down, pulled Yury Dmitrevich's arm behind his back, locking it in a skilled grip, and firmly and painfully pressing his forearm against Yury Dmitrievich's shoulder blade, he led him away.

When Yury Dmitrievich came to, he saw Bukh. Bukh sat there, his breath again smelling of peppermint, and palpated Yury Dmitrievich's body with his small fingers.

"Benedikt Solomonovich," Yury Dmitrievich said, "Benedikt Solomonovich, what a bother . . . your coming here in the middle of the night. It *is* the middle of the night now, I can tell by the silence. . . ."

"Lie still," said Bukh.

"Benedikt Solomonovich," Yury Dmitrievich said, "you took the course on nervous diseases with Professor Narotsky—Ivan Ivanovich. You remember, he always gave the same example . . . patient X goes hunting . . . like arithmetic . . . two pedestrians leave point A and walk toward point B. . . ." Yury Dmitrievich sat up and pulled the blanket over his shoulders. "So patient X goes hunting and he develops a fear that he has accidentally shot and killed a boy picking mushrooms. The fear develops despite his certainty that there wasn't any boy in the woods and that it isn't mushroom-picking season. Nevertheless, he combs the woods within the maximum range of his rifle. But maybe this patient X is right, right because he is troubled. He's concerned whether he lives cautiously enough in a world where it's easier to kill a human being than to kill a sparrow. . . ."

Yury Dmitrievich spoke hurriedly because he knew that the nurse was about to appear with a syringe. She did in fact appear, but a little late, enabling Yury Dmitrievich to finish what he had to say. He held out his arm voluntarily and heard the tiny crunch of the needle piercing his skin. . . .

For ten days he remained in very serious condition. At times he managed to raise himself up by holding on to a wall hanging, and with his voice choking and his eyes agleam he would begin to ramble on about various subjects, jumping from one idea to another, having episodes of so-called "leapfrogging thoughts."

"Do you know what the basis of our consciousness is? . . ." he said once, ". . . our height, our size . . . Einstein was approximately five feet six inches tall . . . Euclid's height was in that area, too. It's not a

question of inches but of order of magnitude . . . inches, not microns
. . . in the microworld, which certainly exists, our second is equal to
an eternity . . . in the macroworld, our eternity is their second. And
perhaps all our history, all our suffering, all our prophets, all our
tyrants, and all our most complicated philosophy exists for the purpose
of keeping man in his second. Man can breathe only within the limits
of his second, which he himself in fact created, as he can within the
limits of the atmosphere. . . . His own second—there is man's
greatest creation, made by him in his own image and likeness, that is,
in his own dimensions. Animals and even plants feel time too, but
aren't capable of creating its concrete image. The notion of time is the
notion of God. But if Albert Einstein demolished the notion of an
eternal second, if the concept of one single instant in the whole
universe is devoid of meaning, then isn't the idea of one God also
devoid of meaning? . . . I say this with pain, not joy, because I need
Him now so much that for one second of belief I may be ready to give
my life . . . I killed the boy who was picking mushrooms. It's absurd
to pray to time because it's impassive . . . even our own man-made
time is indifferent to human life . . . of all the gods created by men,
the closest to time was the Judaic god Jehovah, and now I understand
why it was the ancient Jews in particular who created Christ so
hurriedly, so feverishly. They, like no one else, felt a need for goodness, and having felt it, they recognized good as a force helping them
to assert themselves in the world; like the ancient Greeks, who felt a
need for beauty and, having felt it, recognized beauty as a force. Since
Christ was created in a hurry, he was created with serious mistakes
. . . I don't mean the chronological and tautological confusion
which the Gospels are full of. . . . Read the Gospels . . . the
essence of Christianity can be stated in half a page . . . all the rest of it
is parables and miracles whose purpose is to debate the Pharisees, the
non-believers, those who doubted the truth of Jesus' origin as God's
emissary. . . . But the Pharisees and the scribes aren't Christ's main
adversary. Christ's main adversary is Jesus, the son of Mary and the
stepson of the carpenter Joseph. From the very start of Christianity, a
bitter invisible war is carried on between them—the conflict between
the flesh and the incorporeal . . . every parable, every miracle of the
Gospels is a strange combination of dogmatic code and poem . . .
Jesus is reality, Christ a dream. . . . Jesus demands action, Christ
demands an idea . . . Jesus sacrificed himself by allowing himself to
be crucified. That is, by allowing to be done to him what was done to
thousands of people before him and to thousands after him, and what
for those thousands was not a heroic deed but simply a torturous
execution. Christ's sacrifice was not through bodily suffering or
through crucifixion, but, on the contrary, through resurrection . . .
the highest sacrifice in Christianity is in fact the Resurrection of
Christ, and it is that which contains the essence of Christ as Savior

. . . let's leave that for later, though . . . I'm tired now, let's leave that for later. . . ."

Such outbursts most often occurred during the night and were unexpected, since earlier in the evening the patient was usually peaceful, ate heartily, and fell asleep quickly. In the beginning, Nina tried to calm him down; subsequently, however, she realized that her interference added further to Yury Dmitrievich's trauma. She even learned not to cry in his presence, not to show her despair. She would simply hold his shoulders and head to keep him from injuring himself if he banged into the side of the bed or the wall while gesturing. Occasionally a seizure was followed by a state that showed signs of a coma: modification of the rate and depth of breathing, feeble pulse, and coldness of the extremities. Nina would call the nurse and summon Bukh. Gradually, however, the patient's health began to improve. The seizures stopped and his sleep became more restful. Yury Dmitrievich started to get up and walk around the room. At first he was so weak that after walking from his bed to the armchair, he felt his heart beating as if he had run several miles. All at once he seemed to have aged considerably; he walked with a stoop and spoke little, probably because of weakness. And when Nina addressed him, he would look at her and smile guiltily. Nevertheless, by spring he had recovered somewhat; he had put on some weight and his spirits had become more lively. When the first warm days arrived and Nina peeled off the strips of yellowed paper from the window frames and threw them open, Yury Dmitrievich moved his chair over to a window. For hours at a time he would sit looking out in silence, his elbows propped on the windowsill, resting his chin in his hands like a child.

"Impressions," said Bukh, "new impressions, that's what he needs. A small town would be best. . . ."

In April Nina and Yury Dmitrievich went off to live in a small town in the Southwest. They traded their apartment and now had two small rooms with a kitchenette half taken-up by a huge Russian stove. They were in an old two-story building that was occupied mainly by employees of the local public utilities department. The ceiling of the apartment was sculptured; the work was rather crude: birds and fruit that must have been gilded at one time—the gilt still showed through a coat of whitewash. There was a very beautiful tiled stove in one corner. It only served as a decoration, though; the other stove, which had been installed at a later time and hooked up to the gas lines, was the one that was heated.

Down the hall from them, in a tiny room on the other side of their wall, lived a woman named Liza. She was thirty years old and had a three-year-old daughter named Dashutka. Liza worked as a cleaning woman in a bathhouse.

"I work in a bathhouse and I live in a bathhouse," she would say. "Under the old owner there used to be a bath here. . . ."

Dashutka was reddish and small, like a bedbug. At the age of three she looked a year and a half. Nina immediately became attached to her, and Liza would often leave Dashutka for the entire day, since she worked from morning to night every other day and had had to lug Dashutka to her mother's at the edge of town. She refused to send Dashutka to a nursery school because a few years ago there had been an accident in the local nursery school—some boy swallowed a needle.

For some reason Dashutka took a liking to Yury Dmitrievich and followed him around like a shadow. When Yury Dmitrievich sat down to have some milk, Dashutka would climb up on the table, look right at him and ask: "Are you tirsty?" When he went to the toilet, she would stand right there with her head thrown back and ask very seriously: "Do you have to pee-pee?"

Yury Dmitrievich liked Dashutka, too. He would stroke her head and ask: "Who do you like more—the rooster or the chicken?"

Often, however, Yury Dmitrievich wanted to sit by himself and do some thinking, but Dashutka would disturb him. He would stay out of sight in the bedroom but he still couldn't concentrate as he listened apprehensively for the patter of her feet. Dashutka went looking for him, and then she would look into the room and find him. Yury Dmitrievich didn't know what to do. He tried threatening her with his finger. He made terrible faces, hoping she would get scared. But Dashutka merely laughed gaily, walked in, climbed up on the bed, on a chair, or on Yury Dmitrievich's lap. She would often have a piece of black bread and a pickle in her hand. She loved black bread and pickles.

"Why aren't you going to work?" Dashutka would ask Yury Dmitrievich.

"In September," he would say with annoyance, getting angry at Liza and at Nina, "in September I'm going to start teaching anatomy at the local midwifery and paramedical school . . . understand?"

"What's that?" Dashutka asked.

"That's science," Yury Dmitrievich said, "about people. What they are like inside, under their skin."

"Draw me a picture," Dashutka would say. "Draw me a person."

Dashutka herself liked to draw too. She had paints and brushes, and she would guide them over the paper and say, "This is a carrot, this is a radish, this is the moon. . . ."

Gradually Yury Dmitrievich stopped getting angry and was glad to see Dashutka. He would tickle her slender, little neck. As soon as she left, however, he would close the door tightly. He anxiously listened for her footsteps and shook his finger at her when she looked in. Dashutka also liked to wash the sink and the dishes. First she would put a stool in place and then climb up on it. She would roll up her little sleeves, turn on the faucet, and then take a rag and in great earnest—

obviously imitating her mother—scrub the sink and the lids of the pots Nina gave to her. At moments like these Yury Dmitrievich felt truly loving toward her because she worked away so humorously, keeping busy and not disturbing his thoughts.

One day Yury Dmitrievich found his old rough drafts at the bottom of a trunk. By some miracle they had survived; after going down to the furnace room and destroying the folder containing the history of Jesus's illness, he had made a careful search for all the notes he had made while he was sick and destroyed them. The drafts were studded with hieroglyphs and little lines. He had trouble recognizing his own handwriting. There were excerpts from biology journals, from Engels, Weismann, Dostoevsky, Einstein, the Gospels . . .

"From the viewpoint of a physiologist," he read, "emotions represent a special nervous system that has developed during the millions of years of evolution of the organic world. The function of this system is to compensate immediately for a lack of information necessary to purposeful behavior. Because of emotions a living system continues to perform when the probability of achieving a goal appears very slight. Emotions activate all segments of the brain and sensory organs, extracting additional information from involuntary memory; they provide those particular types of quest whose resolution we associate with intuition and illumination. Living nature has contrived to use both ignorance and knowledge, making them the starter mechanisms for emotional reaction."

"Yes, that's true," thought Yury Dmitrievich. "It's true not only for man but for mankind as well. Emotions are what religion used to be. They are art, which now takes the place of religion that exhausted itself . . . Christianity too soon changed from a designation into a type of knowledge, a form of governance, and Christ into a government official. And the basis for the change was laid by the early Christians who suffered for their faith and lived underground in catacombs, since persecution does not serve to develop nobility in either persecutors or their victims. Moderation, gradualness, and timeliness—those are the three temporal mainstays, and if they are not adhered to, any cause, even the most useful or the most just, can become a terrible scourge of humanity, more terrible than an epidemic of the plague. After all, even light, a source of life, can turn into a deadly poison for plants that have been placed in the dark for a long time. Man is not a servant of God, but neither is he the lord of nature. The two formulas are equally absurd . . ."

Yury Dmitrievich leafed through several pages and read an excerpt from Engels:

"Let us not get carried away with our triumphs over Nature. For each of these triumphs she takes vengeance on us. At first they each have consequences that we expect, but in the second and third instances, quite different, unforeseen consequences that often nullify the meaning of the original ones."

Next, he read an excerpt from the Gospel.

"When the unclean spirit is gone out of a man, he walketh through dry places, seeking rest; and finding none, he saith, I will return unto my house whence I came out. And when he cometh, he findeth it swept and garnished. Then goeth he, and taketh to him seven other spirits more wicked than himself; and they enter in, and dwell there: and the last state of that man is worse than the first."

"What is evil and good," Yury Dmitrievich thought, "the devil and God. Maybe there is neither evil nor good, neither devil nor God, it's all the same. . . . Is light for the leaves evil or good? . . . Evil is good that is ill-timed and ill proportioned . . . man cannot free himself from evil when he is surrounded by dry deserts. . . ."

Yury Dmitrievich leafed through a few more pages, but then someone rang the bell and he heard the voices of Nina and Liza and the patter of Dashutka's footsteps. The door slammed again, no doubt indicating that Liza had gone away and left her little daughter. If Liza had brought Dashutka over an hour later, Yury Dmitrievich would have been delighted, because he was starting to get tired and would have liked to play with Dashutka for a while, relax, take a rest. But now Yury Dmitrievich still had a batch of unsorted-out papers lying in front of him and his thoughts had been set in motion and were working acutely and efficiently. Yury Dmitrievich knew how rarely this happened and that once he was interrupted this stage of his would be lost for a long while and his thoughts perhaps forever. That was why he listened to the cheery voices of Nina and Dashutka with irritation.

"Look at my vibimins," said Dashutka. "Mama says a lemon's got vibimins . . ." Then he heard the splashing of water.

"Thank goodness," Yury Dmitrievich thought, "she's washing the sink. That means she won't come in here."

But he couldn't concentrate any more because he kept listening to see whether Dashutka was coming. The splashing of water ceased, he heard the tread of her little feet by the bedroom door, and in she came. She was wearing Nina's tinkling coral jewelry and had a pickle in one hand and a piece of black bread in the other. Yury Dmitrievich began to shake his finger at her and make nasty faces, but Dashutka laughed and climbed up on his lap.

"I met a wolf," Yury Dmitrievich said with utter despair.

"Where?" Dashutka asked brightly.

"At the vegetable market," said Yury Dmitrievich, trying to read his papers by peering over Dashutka's head.

Dashutka laughed. Then she began to play a peculiar game. She would bite off a little piece of bread and put the remainder on the edge of one of Yury Dmitrievich's sheets of paper. When she finished chewing, she would take another bite and put the rest back again, but farther this time. She continued eating the bread until all that was left at the opposite end of the paper was a tiny scrap, which she snatched up in her little mouth, barely reaching it and dripping a fair amount of pickle juice onto the papers.

"Go and see Aunt Nina," Yury Dmitrievich said. "Go and wash the sink . . . I'm busy . . . Come back later on."

He picked up Dashutka, put her out in the hall, and closed the door. Dashutka went away but soon returned. He could hear her giggling by the door. Blocking his ears with his hands, he tried to read, and suddenly he felt a surge of wild, totally instinctive vexation, the sort that occurs in dreams, when a person loses control of his reason and lives only for the immediate needs of a given instant. For example, he's thirsty but he can't get anything to drink, or he wants to scratch himself but for some reason he can't. Dashutka opened the door part way and Yury Dmitrievich looked malevolently at her crafty, jam-smeared little mug.

"Vibimins," Dashutka said, opening the door wider, "vibimins . . ."

Suddenly, however, she took an awkward step and stumbled, and the door jerked shut, pinching her hand. Dashutka shrieked. Yury Dmitrievich, as though he had just awakened, also shrieked, but it was somehow soundless: his mouth was wide open in a convulsive yawn. He yanked open the door, then fell on his knees in front of Dashutka and caught her up in his arms.

"It was me," he finally shouted, "I slammed the door . . . I broke her hand. . . ."

Nina, in her flour-smeared apron, shuttled between Yury Dmitrievich and Dashutka, trying to calm them down. Fortunately, the door had merely scraped the skin on two of Dashutka's fingers. Nina went and got a bottle of Mercurochrome, painted Dashutka's fingers, and then put a bandage on them.

"It hurts," Dashutka said, sobbing.

"It was me," Yury Dmitrievich repeated, "I ought to be isolated. . . . Nina, I'm dangerous . . . I'm a doctor and I understand this very well. . . ."

"You're mistaken, Yury," Nina said, hugging Dashutka with one hand and stroking Yury Dmitrievich's head with the other. "It wasn't you . . . I saw what happened . . . by accident the child simply gave the door a clumsy shove."

"No, it was me," Yury Dmitrievich reiterated, covered with perspiration. "I desired it from the bottom of my heart . . . like Jesus, who reduced a fig tree to ashes with desire. . . ."

"It wasn't you," Nina repeated, "you're just tired. Why are you constantly thinking . . . writing . . . you need a rest . . . Dashutka, be nice to Yury Dmitrievich—it hurts him too."

Dashutka reached out with her other, uninjured hand and caressed Yury Dmitrievich's cheek. Yury Dmitrievich immediately jumped up and began kissing Dashutka on the neck, both hands, her back, her fanny. Nina caressed the two of them and tears rolled down her cheeks. Nina then washed Dashutka up, and as the wet, soapy skin of Dashutka's hand was being rubbed, it made squeaking noises.

"My hand is crying," Dashutka said and smiled.

In the evening, Yury Dmitrievich and Nina went out for a walk. All the way from the railroad station to the center of town promenades extended along the main street. The benches on the promenades, manufactured by a local cooperative, were long—holding about ten people and not conducive to intimacy. The people who sat on them, therefore, were not lovers, for the most part, but senior citizens. The little town was clean and verdant, the entire center paved with asphalt. It was very warm, and although the sun had long since set, the walls of buildings, which had become scorching during the day, remained as hot as before. One side of the street was mobbed with people, mainly young. The strollers passed by the movie theater, the prosecutor's office, the sports arena, the supermarket, the local church, and the town council, as they headed toward the municipal park. In the park the crowd moved along the central walk in two streams: one heading toward the dance pavilion and the other, in the opposite direction, from the dance pavilion to the movie theater. This was known as "being noticed." And people were accordingly noticed in the course of the evening—at the movie theater and the dance pavilion. All the individuals in this flow were known to one another, were tired of one another, and, at the same time, needed one another, because even though they made life boring, they made it secure and certain. Once he saw some familiar faces out for a peaceful stroll, everyone realized, albeit subconsciously, that his life was not being threatened and that tomorrow, just as today, the street lamps would burn just as peacefully, there would be shows at the theater, and there would be supper at home. Everything would go right, everything would be fine.

Yury Dmitrievich walked over to a wall and started reading the notices.

"Here's an apartment for exchange," he said. "Let's write down the address and go and see the house . . . just for the fun of it, to give our walk a little meaning. Otherwise it'll become boring."

The house was situated somewhere near the river. They came out by the town beach. It was a bit cooler there, but the water was warm and one could hear the snorting and splashing of bathers. It was dark, and only in the distance, by the pedestrian bridge, was there a string of lamps burning, plus one single lamp being swayed by the breeze near the boat dock. This lamp was illuminating a statue of a one-armed athlete holding an oar. Yury Dmitrievich approached the lamp and checked the address.

"It's somewhere around here," he said.

"You're odd," said Nina, smiling. "Why do you care about that house? Let's just breathe the air. It's so nice. Hear that? Ducks quacking in the reeds on the opposite bank . . ."

They walked along the shore. There were lights glimmering in the riverside gardens. The owners were spraying trees that had become infested with insects during the hot weather. Standing on rocks and moored boats, women rinsed out clothes. Cows and goats roamed about tinkling their chains as they nibbled the grass and drank water. While the center of town was paved with asphalt and lit by daylight lamps, the streets down by the river looked very rural: small houses ascended the hillside slope, and some were even thatched and had white painted walls and low wattle fences.

"There it is," Yury Dmitrievich said all of a sudden in a constrained whisper breaking with excitement, and at the same time he gripped her arm. "There's that little house."

"Do you feel all right?" Nina asked anxiously. "Let's go back home . . . you're tired today, let's go to bed early—"

"There's the little house," Yury Dmitrievich said. "I recognized it . . . the two windows . . . and the light in the front one . . ."

The house he was pointing to was situated off to the side, on a hillock. It had a galvanized tin roof and was surrounded by a solid high fence. Coming closer, Nina did in fact make out the address indicated on the piece of paper.

"Let's exchange our apartment," Yury Dmitrievich said, "let's move here."

"You can't be serious," Nina said. "This place has no gas or plumbing."

"What do you need gas for? The house was in the ring . . . at the bottom of the glass standing on the ashes. The little house on the hillock . . . it's just the way the deceased foretold it . . . we'll come and look at it tomorrow."

"All right," Nina said, "but let's go home now, it's getting cool. I'm chilly in this sleeveless dress."

After he had walked away a short distance, Yury Dmitrievich turned and looked back. Now, however, the house had three windows instead of two and all of them were lit. And there was some sort of glass terrace added on in front, so that now the place looked completely different. Then again, it may have actually been a different house, since they had not taken the same path back and had headed more to the left. The first house might now have been hidden by the hillock or by neighboring houses.

"I want to tell you two parables," Yury Dmitrievich said. "They're odd and not to the point. Not exactly parables, I should say, but stories. For some reason, however, I see them as parables, even though I can't grasp their meaning. One parable is amusing and the other is sad. Here's the amusing one. When I was three years old, or at most four, my late mother took me with her to the baths. This was in a place and at a time when, of course, there weren't any individual rooms, just one common facility. It's amazing how clearly I remember all this . . . the bathhouse was made of logs, and soot-blackened. Wooden lids covered the hatches on the floor . . . and there was this woman, along in years, a huge mound of a body drenched in sweat, and she lit into my mother. 'What right do you have,' she yelled, 'taking a boy with you into the women's side'. . . or something to that effect. My mother replied I was only four years old. But the mound yelled, 'no, he's a big boy already.' She went out and brought back the manager . . . they yelled at each other for a long time, and then the mound left, covering herself from me—a four-year-old—with a wash basin. And it was then that I first took an interest in looking at that basin . . . actually, not at the basin. . . . Basically, you understand what I mean , . "

Nina laughed and took Yury Dmitrievich's arm. They were walking along a cinder road. To the right, in the village of Brodok across the river, dogs were barking; to the left, from the center of town, came the sounds of the local House of Culture jazz band that played on Thursdays and Sundays in the municipal park.

"The second parable is sad," Yury Dmitrievich said. "This happened many years later, during an army exercise. It was winter and the snow was very deep. We were observing an air drop, and one man's parachute failed to open in midair. We saw the man fall like a stone and could hear him scream. Then he hit, bounced up for an instant, began shaking the snow off his jump suit, and keeled over once and for all. The autopsy revealed that his lungs and heart had immediately been torn from him as he fell . . . he'd been shaking the snow from his jump suit with his heart torn out. There really is a parable here, you see, but I can't grasp its meaning . . . the final reserves of blood in the vessels, the final split seconds of life in the brain are spent on trying to shake the snow from a jump suit . . ."

With her own shoulder Nina could feel Yury Dmitrievich's shoulder trembling as though from a chill.

"There it goes again," Yury Dmitrievich said. "Nina, I'm incurable and dangerous to the people around me. You're a strange woman . . . you were advised a long time ago by both Bukh and Narotsky . . . and I advise you, too, to put me in a clinic. Then again, for me, of course—no—I, of course, get depressed just from thinking . . . but what can be done . . . perhaps that really is a way out . . . even a road to recovery. Furthermore, as a result of overall stimulation this type of patient becomes susceptible to all sorts of infections. . . ."

They climbed the creaky wooden steps. There was a light burning in the little hallway on their floor, and Liza was peeling potatoes. When she saw Nina and Yury Dmitrievich, she pursed her lips angrily and turned away. Dashutka was sitting right there on the kitchen table singing a lullaby to her doll.

"I'm rocking my doll," she said to Nina, "so she won't get hungry. . . ."

"Now you keep still!" Liza scolded Dashutka. "What did I tell you? You promised me. If you talk I'm going to put you in a dark room. . . ."

Yury Dmitrievich and Nina went into their apartment and turned on the light. On a post near their balcony there was a lamp burning. It was enmeshed in a cobweb and had a cloud of gnats swarming around it. Their movements were so rapid and chaotic that they merged into scintillating, intersecting lines. The cobweb was thickly covered with dead gnats.

"What a stupid thing," Yury Dmitrievich said. "That lamp ought to be smashed, it irritates me. It would be so easy to do, you know . . . just splash some cold water from a children's enema syringe onto the hot bulb. . . ."

"Don't be silly, Yury," Nina said. "Liza has already threatened to complain about us to the housing management."

She came up to Yury Dmitrievich and embraced him.

"We shouldn't have moved," she said. "It was Bukh who told us to . . ."

"It's not Bukh's fault," Yury Dmitrievich said. "A change of environment really helps in certain cases . . . and I did feel better . . . but now I'm worse again . . . somewhat. . . ."

He sat down on a chair and tried to unbutton his shirt collar, but his hand slipped past the collar and clung to his left side, to his ribs. Nina ran out into the hallway and started knocking on Liza's door.

"Liza," she called. "Yury Dmitrievich is ill . . . I want to call an ambulance. You look after him while I go and make the call."

"My child . . . you maimed my child," Liza replied angrily from behind the door. "I'm going to complain about you to the housing management. . . ."

"Never mind, Nina," Yury Dmitrievich called to her from their room, "I feel better already. Come in here, let's sit for a while and talk."

Yury Dmitrievich had in fact recovered somewhat.

"Come here," he said. "Sit down next to me, wife of mine . . . I want to read you the Gospel . . . the entire Gospel . . . it's only one page, or, I should say, the main essence of the Gospel . . . it's the first page of the Gospel according to Matthew . . . it's the only one that belongs entirely to Christ. To a considerable extent everything else belongs to Jesus, the son of Joseph the carpenter. All the rest is heavily mixed with the history of the mental illness of an ancient Jew. And what's more, this page is the best narrative poem I've ever read."

Yury Dmitrievich opened the Gospel and read: "Abraham begat

Isaac; and Isaac begat Jacob; and Jacob begat Judah and his brethren; and Judah begat Pharez and Zerah of Tamar; and Pharez begat Hezron; and Hezron begat Ram; and Ram begat Amminadab; and Amminadab begat Nahshon; and Nahshon begat Salmon; and Salmon begat Boaz of Rachab; and Boaz begat Obed of Ruth; and Obed begat Jesse; and Jesse begat David the king. And David the king begat Solomon of her that had been the wife of Uriah; and Solomon begat Rehoboam; and Rehoboam begat Abijah; and Abijah begat Asa; and Asa begat Jehoshaphat; and Jehoshaphat begat Jehoram; and Jehoram begat Uzziah; and Uzziah begat Jotham; and Jotham begat Ahaz; and Ahaz begat Hezekiah; and Hezekiah begat Manasseh; and Manasseh begat Amon, and Amon begat Josiah; and Josiah begat Jeconiah and his brethren, about the time they were carried away to Babylon. And after they were brought to Babylon, Jeconiah begat Shealtiel; and Shealtiel begat Zerubbabel; and Zerubbabel begat Abiud; and Abiud begat Eliakim; and Eliakim begat Azor; and Azor begat Zadok; and Zadok begat Achim; and Achim begat Eliud; and Eliud begat Eleazar; and Eleazar begat Matthan; and Matthan begat Jacob; and Jacob begat Joseph the husband of Mary, of whom was born Jesus, who is called Christ. . . ."

Putting aside the Gospel, Yury Dmitrievich stood up and walked over to the balcony door, from where he looked at the gnats flitting around the lamp lights. . . .

"This long, monotonous list," Yury Dmitrievich said, "indicates both a fear of the end and a longing to see the end. Man has a complex relation to his death, much more complex than it first seems . . . the relationship between mankind and its death is no less complex. The sun has already lived half of its life—astronomers have established that—and sooner or later it too will die, it will become a 'white dwarf.' Engels put it very well: 'Death as an essential element of life. Living means dying. . . .' Death is a biological necessity . . . the ages of mankind are just as fated and inevitable as the ages of man. The mission of applied medicine is to alleviate disease symptoms even when it is a long way from understanding their meaning . . . God for a long time was mankind's applied medicine . . . I say 'was' because now He is no more. That's a fact, regardless of the joy that some feel about it or the sadness felt by others. Mankind has outlived the idea of God, but the idea of Christ hasn't disappeared. This son who was orphaned after his father's death now takes on a special, fundamental, and, perhaps, sole meaning. If the legend of Adam is a legend about the first sinful, and thus living, man, the legend of Christ is then a legend about the last ideal man . . . and Christ's sacrifice is not at all to be found in his crucifixion but in his being resurrected in order to be last. Christ is the Savior because he embodies all of man's longed-for harmony with the universe, and while serving unattainable ideals he takes upon himself all of the 'weeping and gnashing of teeth,' as the last day is referred to in the Gospel, because harmony signifies the end of the concept of a being called man. But if the death of the ancient Greek gods, pagan gods, did not destroy Apollo, Venus, Hercules— that is, did not destroy the ideal of physical beauty and strength that were engendered by them, then why should the death of modern God destroy the ideal of spiritual beauty represented by the poetic image of Christ the Savior, devoid of flesh, separate from the bilious, mentally ill Jesus—perhaps the greatest and the most living image ever created in literature. We've never had occasion to hear an atheistic lecture on the subject 'Was there a Venus?'; yet 'Was there a Christ?' is given as often as 'Is There Life on Mars?' and just as vaguely. Fearing death, mankind has been striving toward it with all its life since the moment of birth, but only Christ, the son of man, will die, since every person comes into being again in his children. Christ will die childless because he himself was conceived devoid of flesh, not through the body but through the heart . . . and there is one other important point I want to make . . . on a somewhat different subject . . . but then again, no, the subject is the same . . . the contradiction between man and mankind . . . maybe the reason God came into being was to smooth over this contradiction. Dostoevsky's Ivan, you remember, doesn't accept God's world or universal harmony in the end if they come at the price of even one child's suffering. Dostoevsky, of course, was a powerful intellect, but the hundred years since his time have made a lot of things clear . . . made them clear, that is, only to obscure them even more, because the more knowledge man acquires, the less he has the right to dictate to nature his own conception of her. That is, he loses the privileges that were afforded him in that respect by his ignorance, which gave his imagination unlimited possibilities. What Aristotle had the right not to know and to confuse thousands of years ago, and what Dostoevsky had the right to confuse a hundred years ago, has been lost forever by modern man, who has come to know the theory of relativity and is on the threshold of cosmic discoveries. Dostoevsky confuses man with mankind and man's striving with the striving of mankind. The ultimate goal of an individual human being is probably happiness . . . the ultimate goal of mankind is knowledge. No, that's not quite right, I want to put it more precisely. The ultimate goal of each individual is also knowledge; that's why man was created by nature. But man self-assertively, in defiance of his mother, nature, displayed his orneriness and changed his ultimate goal. Happiness was in fact the apple of Eden . . . and it's what man suffers torment for . . . but the world is by no means an absurdity, as Ivan says, nor for that matter is harmony an absurdity, because Dostoevsky proceeds directly from man to the world, even though between man and the world there is mankind. Mankind, however, is unable to change its ultimate goal no matter how hard it tries. Nature was very clear in arranging this, since mankind is devoid of flesh and is only a philosophical notion, like Christ, and man's happiness is absurd without man's body. There is yet to be invented an apple that can seduce mankind as a whole. Or take Tolstoy . . . Tolstoy ends *Resurrection* with the commandments from the Gospel, urging as well that they be put into practice in the belief that they would immediately change the world if everyone applied them as everyday rules."

Yury Dmitrievich hunted around in the bookcase and got out a small volume of Tolstoy. He opened it to one of the bookmarks in it and read:

"Not only would all the violence that filled Nekhludov with such indignation be done away with by itself, but the greatest blessing attainable by mankind would be reached—the Kingdom of God on earth."

Yury Dmitrievich put aside the book. "This is another striking example of subordinating a fact to an idea. The earthly world belongs to mankind, not to man. Man's life is measured in decades; the life of mankind is measured in millions of years. One must not equate two such different organisms, which are contemplated on such different scales of time. Tolstoy wasn't familiar yet with the theory of relativity. He didn't know that man and mankind have seconds of incomparably different magnitudes . . . mankind is an adolescent for whom the truths of the Gospel are not yet attainable . . . they become attainable somewhere toward the end of life, and there are millions of years to go before the natural death of mankind. The Mosaic "eye for an eye" is not that absurd . . . it saves the adolescent from a violent death . . . it is not a call for cruelty, it's the effect of instinct when intellect is still immature. Yes . . . a very sad sight—an adolescent in a coffin . . . the death of boys and girls who have barely begun to awaken to life. Chekhov understood this incongruity between man's time and mankind's. It's evident in his writing, maybe because he lived a little later than Tolstoy. Actually, he died earlier, but his work is linked to later and more mature conceptions of the world. On the last page of *Resurrection*, when he cites the Gospel parable about the husbandmen who were sent by their master to work in his vineyard but instead imagined that they themselves were the masters and enjoyed themselves to the full, killing anyone who reminded them of their master and their obligation to him, Tolstoy is too one-sided and categorical in his condemnation of the husbandmen. One shouldn't assume, however, that I am calling for nationalization of the vineyard . . . the husbandman is man and the master is God, or nature—what name we use isn't important. The master will receive his due when the vineyard ripens, but a human life is so triflingly brief that man cannot wait for the grapes to ripen. And while condemning the arrogance of the husbandman, Tolstoy fails to notice the spiritual tension by means of which the husbandman derives pleasure from unripe grapes, a pleasure requiring human talent that is unavailable to the omnipotent master . . . and the main psychic energy is expended not on imagining oneself the master of the vineyard, but on enjoying the sour berries, the same enjoyment that the master will experience only in the end, in millions of years when the berries are ripe. . . ."

Yury Dmitrievich had a restless night, waking up often and sitting up in bed. He had stomach pains, so Nina prepared hot water bottles, made tea, and peeled lemons. They finally got to sleep toward morning, but not for long: around ten o'clock there was a knock at the door. In walked the neighborhood policeman carrying his shoulder bag, the building manager in a sailcloth jacket, a doctor, and two hospital attendants. The policeman and the doctor called Nina aside and tried to convince her of something. Nina kept shaking her head angrily and saying, "You have no right . . . I'll file a complaint. . . ."

Liza appeared in the doorway holding Dashutka in her arms. "If they are not removed," Liza shouted, "I'll write to the Supreme Soviet . . . I am a cleaning woman, I'm a working person . . . he crippled my child . . . they keep running around all night making noise—"

"Nobody asked you," Nina shouted. "Everything you've said is a lie! Nobody crippled your child . . . you're a despicable creature!"

"Nina," said Yury Dmitrievich, frowning, "why do this? Everything is going the way it should . . . when they came to get Jesus, Peter cut off the servant's ear . . . the servant's name was Malchus . . . it's so absurd . . . I mean, it's not absurd that his name was Malchus . . . I'm getting things confused . . ."

"Why did we ever move to this miserable place?" Nina said, sobbing. "We'll go away . . . I'll get on the phone . . . it's all Bukh's fault. . . ."

"Benedikt Solomonovich made a mistake," said Yury Dmitrievich, "and so did I. This poor woman and her child . . . we really are bothering her . . . look at how you've distracted me . . . I wanted to say something . . . to continue . . . now they're going to take me to the hospital . . . we won't see each other very often . . . and you want me to be like that paratrooper . . . you want my last living movement to be to shake the snow off my jumpsuit. Wife . . . what I wanted to continue about . . . was the contemporary significance of Christ. Something living cannot be a symbol, that's absurd. Remember what it says in the Epistle to the Hebrews: 'Be fearful of the living God'. So that succeeding generations are not disrupted, there must be constant symbols of some sort . . . something living is a combination of many things; a symbol is the repository of one single thing carried to an extreme . . . like Venus, the repository of eternal beauty, and Moses, the repository of eternal wisdom, Christ is the repository of eternal good. When the last day of mankind comes, beauty will disappear along with the flesh, and wisdom will merge with universal wisdom—how, I don't know; maybe through cybernetics . . . but eternal good will remain on earth, since cybernetics isn't in control here. Eternal good will be man's last deed on earth, his last breath, his last thought, which will outlive the flesh . . . what is good, after all, and what is eternal good? There's a contradiction here . . . eternal, ideal good is something that has long been known to people but will only be necessary in the end . . . everyday good is something that is needed today, every hour, every second, but is unknown, and people rush about and suffer in pursuit of it. The ideal, great good is the overall answer, "Thou shalt love thine enemy." Like arithmetic . . . all you have to do is look at the last page . . . but in a problem the answer is divided up over dozens of questions, millions of questions. . . ." Yury Dmitrievich became disconcerted and fell silent.

Seated on a chair, the policeman inconspicuously shifted his shoulder bag from his right hand to his left, just in case the psycho jumped at him. The building manager, looking around apprehensively, moved away toward the door. Liza and Dashutka had disappeared.

"There now," the doctor said to Nina. He was young and had a gold tooth that glittered. "You see . . . his condition is very serious. It calls for special monitoring and care, which can only be provided by trained personnel. With this type of patient attempted murder and suicide are usually carefully planned. . . ."

"Young man," Yury Dmitrievich said, "have you ever heard Professor Narotsky's lectures on nervous diseases? He cites a curious parable about a patient X who goes hunting in the woods and a boy who picks mushrooms . . . I can tell from your eyes, though, you skipped that lecture. . . ."

"Yury," Nina said, holding back her tears, "here are your socks . . . See, I'm putting them into the suitcase separately . . . and here are your handkerchiefs—"

"Come here," Yury Dmitrievich said. "Forget the handkerchiefs . . . come sit next to me, my wife . . ."

"Your wife is greatly to blame," the doctor said to Yury Dmitrievich. "For selfish motives she prevented us from employing clinical methods of treatment."

"It's all right," Yury Dmitrievich said, "her sins, which are many, are forgiven; for she loved much. But to whom little is forgiven, the same loveth little. . . ."

Yury Dmitrievich got dressed and took his suitcase. The two hospital attendants took up positions on both flanks. The policeman walked in front, with the doctor taking up the rear. The neighbors watching from their windows and doorways pointed their fingers and whispered to one another.

It was very hot outside. A breeze that stirred from time to time brought swirls of dry, abrasive dust instead of coolness. Chickens were roaming the street in search of a cool spot. A listless dog barked lazily at the hospital attendants. Before getting into the ambulance Yury Dmitrievich hugged Nina. She cried as she stood there with her cheek against his chest. "I'll get in touch with Bukh," she sobbed. "They'll transfer you to a clinic in the capital . . . I'll move there too. For now, I'll stay at Grigory's . . ."

When the ambulance drove off, Nina returned to the empty apartment to get their things together and pack up. Liza was standing in the doorway with Dashutka. Nina and Liza looked at each other hostilely, but Dashutka smiled and offered Nina a piece of chewed pickle.

For a long while Nina just wandered about the room, half-starting to pack some books or fasten suitcase straps. When she got tired walking around, she would sit down on a chair and take a short rest. Then she would start walking around again, gather some cups and spoons . . . and suddenly she thought: How good it would be to leave all this and go to the station and get on the next train out. On the table she found a quarter sheet of paper. Yury Dmitrievich had covered it with irregular, hurried script, probably just before leaving with the hospital attendants.

" 'Can the blind lead the blind?' " Nina read. " 'Shall they not both fall into the ditch?' The Gospel according to St. Luke." Farther down, the lines ran into one another and the letters were so small that trying to read them made her eyes hurt.

"Soon, however, Nina regained her composure and was on the go again, gathering things together in preparation for her departure. When she felt tired, she sat down to rest on a window ledge. It had gotten darker outside. A low rain cloud crept slowly from the direction of the villages across the river. It was as sticky and hard to breathe as in a steam-bath dressing room. In the middle of the cobblestone street stood Dashutka, barefoot, wearing only an undershirt, and holding a piece of dark bread smeared with cottage cheese. She was eating the bread with her head tilted back, looking up at the cloud. The sight of the lone, defenseless child made Nina leap up and run out to the street. She picked Dashutka up in her arms and carried her home. Liza was standing over a washtub full of laundry. Beside her there was already a pile of washed shirts and sheets that she had taken in. Seeing Nina with Dashutka, Liza shook the soapsuds off her hands and took Dashutka. She sat her down in the corner and gave her a peeled young radish, which Dashutka began gnawing on with gusto, alternating it with bites of bread and cottage cheese. Outside it had turned completely dark. A heavy rain began, becoming harder and harder, and mixed with hail. In five minutes, it was no longer a rain but an avalanche of water rushing down from the murky heavens and inundating the earth like the Great Flood. A turbid clayey stream filled the whole courtyard, flowing around the shed, filling the cesspools, sweeping along tree branches, downed foliage, newspapers, fragments of broken bottles, then merging with other streams and coursing down the cobblestone street.

"My God," Nina gasped, choked with sobs, "why must I know the great eternal good, which I will never need, if I don't know everyday good, which I cannot live without. My husband left me a note as a legacy . . . I want to read it to you, Liza . . . even though it's absurd . . . particularly in light of our relationship." She took out the note and read it:

"Eternal good will merge with everyday good only then, and millions of questions will merge and be reduced to one answer—"Thou shalt love thine enemy"—only when man stops being the prodigal son of his mother nature and returns to her original design. When man recognizes knowledge as his ultimate goal instead of happiness . . . only then will suffering disappear. But man will never agree to this, and nature will never forgive him for his defiance and his rebellion . . . and so it will be until the last day . . . Human happiness and human suffering will disappear only when the human body does . . . and then eternal good will come, which nobody will have a need for. . . ."

Liza looked up at Nina, straightened her tired back, and stood that way for a while, resting. Then, without saying a word, she bent over the washtub again and plunged her hands into the dirty sudsy water.

Poems[*]
by Inna Lisnyanskaya

On St. Vladimir's day, Sunday eve,
I entered the church by chance,
And again through indistinct singing
The secret of the days broke through.

And a young suppliant
Came into the temple for holy water,
Her collarbones sticking out of her cardigan,
Bangs hidden under a kerchief,

Forehead free, but a bit narrow,
Like a path down a side street in winter,
Then her gaze free like a prisoner
Forever reconciled to his prison.

The suppliant falls to her knees,
Kisses the edge of an icon: Have mercy!
And shadows of things to come flicker by
As if things to come have already been . . .

* * *

Of fire and wood,
Of grain and the path,
Let us speak whimsically
And not just any old way.

Bold from shyness—
Let us cense the phantoms,
Attire them
In visible detail.

Oh, dowerless muse,
How can I go on?

*Translated by H. William Tjalsma.

Without a stone on my heart
I cannot live for one hour!

Should I force myself,
Try fate—
Take the bronze horn
In my hand like a lily,

Blow marsh music
From my breast
And stick fingers into
The heavy soil ahead.

* * *

Time and I, we're so alike!
We look like twins.
How can you tell us apart, God?
So, tell me, aren't the escort
And the fugitive
One and the same?

Bright pink palms,
Each capillary aglow—
I'm on the run and time is in pursuit,
For both of us the world is two-sided
There, our ashes, and here—fire!

Time and I. We're so alike!—
Separately, eyes gaze askance.
How do you tell us apart, God?
So, tell me, aren't a look ahead
And a look back
One and the same?!

Neither one nor the other
Is any better, time nor I—
Deprived of hearth and roof,
We race as one word after another
In the maddened silence.

* * *

Above the sanatorium section,
Above the population of the town,
Puffy clouds lay
In the March sky.

And every day before dinner
On a stool next to the porch,
The sick man endlessly wrote to his Judas,
Anti-Semitic delirium.

His Judas was curly-headed,
Snake-like, without a rib,
One hand bloody, the other
Covered with silver spots.

An artist mixed his colors
In a crumpled tin can,
And another sick man kept glancing at him,
Not without caution.

Thus in March in the hospital town,
Exhausted winter went slowly
Out of its mind and huddled
Against the brick buildings . . .

In Gegard

My truth and my untruth
I drag along behind me.
In stone—in the church of Gegard
I light a candle.

Slowly before the icons,
I burn like a candle:
Lord, even with Thee
I speak with the words of others!

Outside—the slime of spring,
Layers of clouds and trees . . .
I weep. But I've had enough of weeping.
The tears—are not mine, either.

Blind Man

In our Caspian city,
Unnoticed by the crowd,
A blind man lived and acted
With no little risk, for himself.

There was paper in front of him,
And a needle in his hand,

And mortal courage
He carried in his chest.

A concentration camp in the East,
A war in the West.
He was reading with his fingers
Near the dark window.

The earthly world and the world above
The old man reconceived.
By stages, in prisons
He kept a secret day-book.

But once at dawn
They took the blind man away
And burned those pages.
But his offspring read them,

Because there was the Word,
And he had learned to write
With a pine needle
In an aerial notebook.

Poems*
by Semyon Lipkin

Fantasy

I also learned to talk nonsense
Like present-day rhymers, and these
Details grow dim in the even light
Of demands, essentials, and desires.
But believe me, I walked the planet
Where angels are the only two-legged
Flesh, where in a thick glade
Fading does conversed
With the two-dimensional contour of a steed,
Where the bright bustle of light colors
Now took away my sight,
Now strengthened internal vision—
But perhaps that was illumination?

I learned to comprehend blissfully
That bird and nest, wave and calm,
And the glint of a butterfly barely perceptible,
And the cuneiform of the plant's shape—
Are not indicators, not signs, not visions:
They are things, they are objects!
The dead by Providence's will
Rose again according to that will,
But in life unearthly, unusual,
In which there is neither passion nor desire,
Life which cannot be considered secondary—
Or must it be seen as higher?

And the angels, superb, like beasts,
Occurring in the lair of books
Or in the revelation of myth and legend,

*Translated by H. William Tjalsma.

Did not move through these or past them,
But talked with every speck of light,
With the living hieroglyph of matter,
Assured: they are creatures
With unrepeatable image and face.

I didn't think that soon I'd part
with all that I saw here—because
I didn't see much. I noted a strangeness
In the angels. It seemed to me as if
They were afraid—just as in Gomorrah,
Where a caper bush spewed its fruit and an almond tree
Was in blossom; riffraff roamed the streets,
A grasshopper grew heavy and forbidden desire in women's gazes
and in men's . . . In languor and alarm
They covered their legs with their wings
And waited voluptuously and ineptly
For the devil. The matter has long since passed,
So whence the present fright?

Neither sinners nor demons around,
The peculiarity of this place is quietude and beauty;
Glow dissolved in glow. Where do the angels get their shyness
And their hopeless despondency?
Or have they understood—the demons are not outside,
That the demons grow inside themselves, languish
In idleness and strain to act—
Then reason dies in war
And altars smoke with lambs' blood.
How to live in the devouring fire?

Their gaze did not rest on me:
To them who were cast into this strange world by the Most High
No doubt I seemed superfluous; meanwhile I was attracted
By the weak-willed omnipotence of the chiaroscuro,
Some sort of magical glass—
Splinters of forgotten observations.

Here was what I had seen before:
No, not a body and not even a deed,
But say, the laughter of an Austrian soldier,
Of a Croat, in captivity not pining
For badges and the brooms of yardmen.
Memory brought me quanta of light,
And I see the friend of my youth again,
Passportless, smart, and evil,
Whose shelter is midnight railway cars

And suburban cold outside the window,
The railway stations of upside-down Moscow
And a camp cut into the Mordovian region,
Where he first knew the speech of grass,
Which is more intricate than poetry or chess,
And how people wither and how they smell
And later dig their own graves.
With me always is my blondish head
And furtive, arrogant grin.
Thus another poet grinned too,
Irate, prodigal, sad sweet-tooth . . .

A sign from my earthly years still shines for me:
"Crimping, Pleating, Embroidery."
But the embroiderer could not stand greens
Nor whites nor Petliura's troops nor cavalry,
Nor drunken soldiers nor infantry.
Innovation displeased this craftsman.
"Thievery! They grab for work!
For things to be OK, we need a tsar!"

You here, too? Are you here, Monsieur Tarrar?
Oh, but the way they killed you, There, in the slaughter.
You thought it was more peaceful waiting for the Germans—
With five or six neighbors—at a dacha:
Not far from the sea and with no shortage
Of food foreseen, the hot sand of the
Steppe, the thyme, wormwood, and poppies,
While the German—he's cultured, not riffraff.

So there'll be a ghetto. In what way is a ghetto worse
Than this? God of vengeance and covenant,
There, as here, summer was ending
And it was quiet, too, but another
Silence enveloped the earth.
All that had been something became
Nothing—grass, sand, smiles, sighs.
It seemed the city had grown deaf and dumb
And time had stopped forever
For several families. But so it seemed.
The day waned unnoticed, like pity.
And what was it everybody at the dacha
Said to himself, to the others in the long nights?
What would the victims have done, if successful?
Couldn't they have turned into executioners?

And they weren't even betrayed: they headed
For the police station, as if drawn there

By an oath or slavish craft—
To idolize the edict, the ukase, the orders.
They set out—at first by Preobrazhenskaya,
Then after, turning, by Kherson slope.
A marvelous city had become alien, unRussian.
It smelled of semirural distance,
Estuaries. . . . They didn't take mama
Along to the dacha—well, there wouldn't have been room.
What's more, she was a different sort,
And without her the ones who were shot lay down
In a pit. Now mama's with them—
Fleshless ones, others, unearthly.

Acacia, is it, from our courtyard,
Grey and big-eyed and kind,
Or has mama suddenly started talking with me:
"Dear son, check: Did I close the door?
Not that, not that. . . . But how's my grave
In Vostriakov Cemetery? Nothing's right, nothing's right . . .
You needn't think that the world is Nothing.
We are all and in all and all is in us.
Did you fall in love, dear son? Well, good luck—
No longer young, but for the first time.
Was the road to her long?
Does she look like me, a little?
That's why you noticed each other!"

And I touched the grey flowers with my hand:
"Love is God. And, actually, is it possible to love
God the last time or the first?
I remember that which I myself had wanted to forget.
I did not come to love—I returned to it."

1974

Khaim*

There, where the retinue of the GSR raced
And of late—the colonel of the gendarmerie,
Where now still we'll find a yellowed prayer book
In the hut of an Old Believer,
Where the Buryat's Buddhist books
Have made their way through the remote villages—
Silvery-bright and ample,
There's a river called Khaim.

*Khaim, or Chaim, is the Hebrew for "life."

Let's not put too much stock in tradition:
Either he was returning home by a path through the taiga
And cut up by ragtag convicts (moreover, they say
He was carrying gold),
Or he kept an inn on the high road
And concealed fugitives
And paid the price for his kindness . . .
There's a river and a Khaim pass.

The eternal spirit abides in the idol,
In the ancient scroll and in the tiny cross.
How do you like it, Khaim, in Siberia
Flowing as a river, serving as a mountain pass?
What glimmers in the silvery splashing?
Could it be the smile in the taiga of him
Who confounded the wisemen of Benares
And preserved his people in the wilderness.

1973

In the Desert

Like sojourners in elevated meekness,
We move in the fourth dimension,
In the desert of years, in the swirling of sand.
Now a mirage glimmers, now a whirlwind swirls up,
Now a well-crane flickers in the distance
Amid the dreamy centuries.

Let us go there where we once were,
So that our forefathers' stories
Will transform our great grandchildren into dreams.
It seems to us that we are wandering in circles,
But we discover new lands
Without thinking we shall reach our goal.

The first traveler is always forgotten.
So what gives joy on the way? The well.
It is here, in the desert, where there is sand and heat.
Suddenly you feel time as freedom,
As if you're drinking
This stagnant water
From a bucket on the verge of eternity.

1974

Gulls' Cry

A family of fattened gulls
Chatters on the seashore.
I cannot come to
From the cries of those beggars.

I recall how we buried the wife
Of an office mate. It was evening when
She was put in the grave.
But we and our grief

Caught the last bus.
And then, like an infection,
Out of wailing, oaths, gossip and cursing
A mixed cry arose.

The flock of cemetery poor,
Drunken oldsters, men and women,
Bent, one-legged, rotten,
Wandered and wondered aloud . . .

Earth, human moorage,
You've revealed to us what
The scainy side of senseless life
Is like, where words replace the word.

The final sum has been revealed,
And we sense what sort of
Eternal engine turns,
While eternal peace is moved by it.

1976

* * *

As I was arranging letters into words
And helping meaning to be born,
Already I darkly divined
How fate would dispose of me.

How I'd not grow as tall as the window vent,
And my body would be squeezed into a harness,
How till death I would retain traces
Of the fearful common folk.

The insane century goaded me,
Raising its fearsome pikes and pitchforks,
And in childhood I already had a presentiment
Of my rebellious weak will.

But my life was mysterious,
And I lived, understanding curiously
That truth does not exist in the world,
Life-giving, unearthly,

And if I became desperate
At the all-victorious collapse,
I found joy in repentance,
And weakness gave me strength.

1976

Days of Leavetaking*
by Andrei Bitov

1. The Last Bear

*On April 8, 1944, Lieutenant Lapshin, Hero of the Soviet
Union, and his rifle platoon took the bridge on the zoo
grounds with a surprise attack from both sides, destroying
30 Hitlerites and capturing 195. This decided the outcome
of the battle for the zoo.*

—Inscription on a Monument at the Kaliningrad Zoo

I live no one knows where. Now and then I return home. My
daughter, reddening, says from a distance: "Papa, remember? Last
time you came you said we would go *somewhere?*" Some of these
words she says loudly, some softly—the whole art and meaning lies in
this. Immediately I am made uncomfortable by this knowledge of
hers, this experience she already has, that once again we won't go.
And the "somewhere" (said in a whisper), I remember, means: *to the
palace.* Palace in general.

And I, with the defunct dignity of a man who has known success
and lost it, abruptly stand and say, "Let's go." This is almost more
humiliating than once again to say, "Later; another time." I say,
"Let's go," hating myself, but she believes it. Then again, she knows
much more than people usually admit about children (for the con-
venience of adults), about "that age," as they say. There's nothing
awful about it to her (that I have agreed to go, with no intention of
actually going); it's only awful to me. She is content with my verbal
agreement, it seems, exactly in the sense in which it was given—
without any "fancy frills."

We go. We go outdoors, and there the day is revealed to us. Such a
sudden and surprising day, with the flavor of another life passing you
by, with the remorse and inaccessibility of yesterday, which has
already been with you and gone. . . . The awning has been removed

*Translated by George Saunders. From the book, *Remembrances of Reality.*

from our narrow courtyard. We smile at the sky, smile into ourselves, as corpses do. Even the cross old women of the courtyard are like well-watered flowers behind the newly washed windows. Forgetting the need for caution, someone unexpectedly exchanges hellos with me, condemning us both to the necessity of greeting each other hereafter.

However, it's time to pass the yard by and get on to business.

Thus I go out, squinting shyly, with a sweaty, obedient little palm in my hand, not sure that it is I going out, nor that those are my footsteps and this is my daughter. Not sure that I haven't been filmed beforehand on that length of film I used to watch back during endless classtimes in school. . . . One must know the world day by day to live to see such unreality! The beautiful weather stretches out around you—that and only that is reality—this lovely day. We'll leave individuality to cloudy days. "Do you think I'd drink if for three kopeks I could order up the sun for half an hour!" Edik K. once said, eternal memory to him . . .

"Such a beautiful day," I say perfidiously. "Let's go to the palace another time." There isn't even despair or hurt as my daughter agrees—just resignation, a knowledge of life: we aren't going after all. She hasn't yet lived to see the day.

We go our way, not to the palace and not to the circus. We come to the zoo.

After the trampled areas in front of and behind the turnstile—soldiers and schoolchildren ten kopeks—the magical veneer of the ticketbooths, the signboards with diagrams and regulations, the ice-cream carts, and the portable laboratory equipment from the Lomonosov era for making seltzer water, it is natural to expect the same kind of fairyland, plywood animals with white bull's-eye targets on them and always with left-facing profiles—easier for the artist to draw, apparently. That is why the first animal is so unexpected.

Let's say, an elephant. But you don't yet believe in it. Moreover, it's hard to believe in one, in general. But there it is. An elephant. Just so. An elephant. You're more inclined to look at the attendant, who's sitting right there either to see that the elephant isn't fed some totally inedible garbage or simply to serve as a comparison. It's enlightening to watch the elephant's keeper. Between his large friend's legs he sees the tower clock whose big hand is inexorably, but too slowly, drawing closer to the little hand.

The elephant has understood everything, so as not to go out of its mind. The elephant is also serving as an attendant. You pass on, not having fully ingested it into your consciousness.

You come to the horn-and-hoof section—colorlessly heaped-up nonlikenesses of cows. . . . Here, too, are the northern reindeer, whose cage you pass by especially quickly—for some reason this very reindeer is nothing new to you. Then a few gnus and some sort of

llama. And a bison, shall we say, which won't come out from the
darkness of its shelter. You quickly leave this lowly cattleshed behind,
almost without having registered in your brain the surprisingly unim-
posing quality of the reindeer and the roe deer and without having
switched your consciousness to the land of savannahs and selvas.

Now there will be a pool with something pathetic, something you
have dreamed, but not at all frightening—a hippopotamus' side.
What will be swimming is a huge, slow-moving loaf. You won't live to
see any life from that.

You will marvel at the tapir, ever so smooth and new—synthetic.
Your little girl will say: "You can tell right away it's African . . ." A
philistine will read the plaque to his pregnant wife: "Has no commercial value. Aha, it's only good for show then . . ." The wife will look
with unseeing eyes, abrupt as eggs—and see her own belly, one more
proof the earth is round. What sort of manners are these? They
invariably take their pregnant wives to the zoo? Haven't you noticed?

The birds are too numerous to sort out. They are some sort of little
black things—all carrion-eaters, from the look of them. At the very top
is a stuffed animal, the color of slate. Because of this you will carefully
inspect the sparrow. An absolutely staggering bird. It is free.

The sparrow, though the least, is surely king of beasts.

The monkeys are closed for repair. The chimpanzee is being
displayed separately. He is sad: before him stands humanity. With his
inhibitions he shocks us once again into seeing that he is human. He
digs at himself, looks around; scratches, looks around. He is surprised
at his hands—nothing has turned up in them. Empty. Lacking.

You become unaccountably sad and dull. The false desire to be
enlivened with the help of your child, to look at everything with
motion-picture eyes, remains sterile. They are simply attentive, children. Their eyes are on the borderline of fear. Fear, not of an animal's
frightfulness—how could the poor thing be frightening? In a cage? But
of life itself. They, the children, are before; you are after. You cannot
eat at the same table with their way of seeing.

Here again we must add: the sun. The city's air is unaccusomted to
it, so long ago grown colorless. Colors come out in Leningrad only
when the light is gray. Like the skin of a blind man. Nothing is lit up.
The amplitude of sun—a thing in itself—is squeezed in between
objects without touching them, without affecting them, without sticking to them. The animals are the same—without color, or the color of
khaki, earth, and spring. A rubbish heap of plywood, fences, and
hides. The light caught everything unaware, nothing managed to take
on color, everything seemed lost, lit up and blinded, with nothing to
use as a screen. A pale blue dome over a rubbish heap.

Thus far you have not come to the carnivores. Only the carnivores
have color. Only they, properly speaking, are animals. That's how
things are, at any rate, in terms of success with the spectators. For here

there is a crowd; there is liveliness and conversation—immediacy. Extraordinary immediacy is evident on the faces of the philistines, the way it is after an accident or someone else's funeral.

Time to shift from *you* to *I*.

Bear was written on the cage. Which is to say it was precisely that—a bear. I met its gaze.

And suddenly it was as though all the animals I had seen were looking at me. It was rather strange. One and the same creature may look at you in different ways. But to imagine that so many different creatures, so distinct from one another, could look at you at different times with one and the same gaze could mean only one thing—either you are crazy, or they all are. A tinny madness at high noon was seated in the eyes of the bear. Not dread and not anger, not fear and not fierceness, not longing—madness. This was a bear that had gone out of its mind, and it was eating and eating pieces of candy just as they were, without unwrapping them, indifferent to the spectators, to itself, and to the candies. Drearily and unfailingly it caught the pieces if they came flying conveniently near its maw. If it wasn't convenient, the bear didn't bother. In that case the sweet would strike against the bear as though against some nonliving thing and fall to the ground. The bear sat in a circle of candy, and there were so many pieces it must have been sitting there a long time without stepping over them.

This steady, even madness in the bear's eyes, without any glimmerings whatsoever, could have seemed simply to be blindness, if it hadn't been opening its maw to the pieces of candy with perfect timing; which is to say, it wasn't blindness. As an image one might suggest some age-old toothache, some pain since the time of birth, pain that was the only known form of existence of the world, pain that would be unendurable if for even one moment in one's entire life it had not existed, but endurable because it had always been; pain of such permanence and intensity that candy after candy is tossed indifferently into the heart of it, like twigs into a bonfire. If not blind, the bear could have been mute. And then its gaze would have been the howl of a dumb creature. But in that case, it would not have been catching the candy in its maw. If it were howling, that would mean it understood the pain. And so it (the madness) was not muteness, either.

But all these suggestions have only approximate value, as attempts to somehow define and delimit by a ring of similes (too wide and incomplete as yet) a concept of madness that is new to me; that is, for this particular madness all of these analogies are annoyingly imprecise. In the middle of the ragged, overly extended ring of similes is its gaze, burning dully and evenly as before and having no relation to my attempts at definition.

And so at first the bear, then all the animals that we had passed so carelessly, were suddenly looking at me with the same unseeing mad stare. (Actually a certain goat once looked at me with the lively slyness of a schizophrenic who has understood everything about the world and continues to understand it as he looks at you; that is, his type of insanity alone had been familiar to me.) One's thoughts might follow a handy, ready-made channel: they have gone mad because of the lack of freedom, life in a zoo, a prison—but no. If it were that, there'd be something more here. And that something *more* would be more frightening, more important, and more novel to the human observer.

With what suddenness and sorrow I realized that this bear before me no longer existed; what's more, *could not exist*. If modern man had not ascribed everything to himself, had not appropriated everything to such an extent that even a statement made about some object in the external world is said to describe for us, not the object at all, but the one speaking about the object, then the celebrated joke about the Jew who, upon seeing Behemoth the hippopotamus, said "It cannot be!" would ultimately have been, not about the Jew, but about Behemoth.

It's absolutely true, Behemoth cannot be.

It's not that I was feeling sorry for the animal in its cage. I was about to give the zoo my blessings for still having this bear, which no longer existed. Otherwise how would I have learned about it? This was a bear miraculously preserved, the last bear, just as all the other animals were the last ones. It seems that the bear itself did not believe it still existed. Again I describe a circle of approximations to the center of its madness and come no closer. But I am convinced that in its gaze there was precisely the madness of the final survivor. It may have been that the bear had given up on living any longer; not that this particular bear (individually) had given up—but that *in him* bear in general had given up; that in him there no longer remained the vital energy *to be bear*. And really, if among the animal instincts that have not yet diverged, compared to humans, from the logic of the Creator and Creation, if among these the precise awareness of oncoming death, when animals go hide, crawl away, etc., has not been lost, then why can't they sense death in a more global sense—of the species, of the genus, or of life itself? The animals in Noah's ark had a better chance of surviving amid the terrors of the elements than this one in the absolute safety of the zoo, the kind of safety the condemned have between sentencing and execution. Here there were no pure and impure left. They were all the last of their kind, pale blue in the dimness of leavetaking.

I wanted to run back to the elephant, to look at all of the animals with these newly opened eyes, to look into their dear, last eyes, feeling guilt and brotherhood, the brotherhood of all living things on earth in the face of death. Any why after all shouldn't I embrace that very same gnu as my sister and say, "I am found. Your brother who was lost in the wave of progress, with no news of his fate, is found again. It is I. I am still alive and have not forgotten you."

If someone were to say I have forgotten about my daughter in telling this, it isn't so. I lifted her up at every cage at which she couldn't see well enough. She experienced everything deeply, which is to say in silence, and she didn't prevent me from experiencing this mute business that I have just tried to convey. But—and this is the heart of the matter—she experienced something *different*, and what it was I really am unable to say. At any rate, these animals, because of the imprint of their finality so suddenly revealed to me, became for me—amid the plywood, the hawkers' trays, the fences, and the cages—something nearly as conventional as those things, a group of bumpy metal compatriots from the shooting gallery. But if these animals were also implausible for her (my daughter), it was precisely because of their reality and life. And when, not far from the merry-go-round, I saw a poor, rundown little pony, whom you couldn't tell apart from a papier-mâché horse on the merry-go-round, I said to my daughter dubiously, as though to apologize for the pony, for the fact that it was as unreal as it was, "Do you want to get on the pony?" she suddenly nodded with such ardor and conviction, growing so red with emotion, that I understood that the living world still existed in all seriousness.

Isn't it strange that we make more and more books with fairytales and pictures about wild rabbits and wolves and foxes, and we still make fish and reindeer and teddy bears out of rubber and plastic and stuffing and realize less and less what it is we are doing. And our children already live in a world where there are thousands of times more toy animals than there are animal animals. Animals are no longer objects of first-hand knowledge and acquaintance with which to spend your life. They are objects of mythology. And the day is not far off when the fabulous quality of animals in fables—the hare, the wolf, the bear—will extend beyond allegory and take on the dimension of make-believe, like dragons and griffins. And it's really so. Objectively speaking, if the wild hare no longer exists, it will be no easier to produce it than a griffin. And it's rather frightening to think that all our toys and fairytales might be nothing but relics of a bygone day, when kind old nursemaids thought that such games and amusements planted in a child's soul the first seeds of the Christian injunction to love thy neighbor.

2. Nowhere Street*

Among the evolved characters which frequently occur in the self-replicating systems we call living organisms is the termination of the individual. This "natural death" of the living units which carry for a time the unbroken line of descent from the first primordial origin of life is of little

---

*Literally, Gluxhaya Ulitsa—Godforsaken, Remote, Out-Of-the-Way, or Dead-end Street [tr.].

consequence to the vast majority of living things, for the
places of those that die are soon occupied by other individuals.

—Bernard Strehler, *Time, Cells, and Aging*

THE PEASANT

I am on my way to the store and the post office; just that. . . .
Not to forget to buy butter, soap powder. . . . Not to forget to call
the editor in town, and if he's not there. . . .

Forget to buy chocolate for my daughter; forget to drop my mother-
in-law's letter in the mailbox (I keep touching the letter in my pocket,
so as not to forget it, but later take my hand out of my pocket) . . .

Not to forget, on the way to get the butter, to think over the article,
an extremely topical one, on the state of contemporary criticism, so
that when I get back I can sit right down to it and send it off tomorrow
to Moscow, where for some reason (they have nothing better to do
with their lives) they're anxiously awaiting it. (I won't have sent it this
time either, a month later, for which I will curse myself terribly
instead of praising and reinforcing within myself that fidelity and
attachment to life which has not yet died out completely . . .)

And so I go, remembering some and forgetting some of the tasks
urgently pressing upon me. I don't forget and I do forget about the
butter, the nails, the milk, the soap powder, the kerosene, a telephone
call, two visits, three farewells. . . .

I definitely do forget, however, that all around me life is going on,
with its weather, passersby, and clouds; that I myself am hurrying
along in this flood, which is lit up by the sun for the sake of my eyes;
that I will find it "some day a painful torment to have spent without
purpose" this very second—because whether I forget or don't forget
this or that little curlicue of duty (imposed by whom?), I am nevertheless preoccupied with *not forgetting* instead of with the present moment, which in the meantime has passed irreversibly. And that you
can never recreate—not ever.

My brain is a saturated solution. The poisons and salts of memory
have eaten sponge holes in it, and into them the quivering moisture of
life disappears with apparent ease, the outer surface staying dry and
porous. But I am still alive. At least the little toe of my foot still moves,
unafflicted by necrosis, and the callus on it still pains me. And since I
am still alive, I cannot pass life by entirely. Ah, no. It will touch me.
Maybe it won't press close or embrace me; but in its pensive liveliness,
in which the plague of formulated thought has not yet shown a trace,
life will brush against me, like a young girl, not noticing me, heading
for a rendezvous not with me but with some lucky fellow, handsome
and well built, brushes you with the edge of her cloud of health and
well-scrubbed youthfulness as she passes you by on the bus. And
though I am no longer a direct relative of life and though I show up

sometimes, nameless, at her name-day feast, still an extra place is found for me with some peripheral tidbits to snack upon.

And so I do not always pass life by, with my hands full of an awkward package wrapped in embarrassingly torn and shredding newspaper, a package of duties to which I've been assigned, which look like the lids of empty mayonnaise jars that haven't been thrown out, duties reminiscent of unwashed socks and unpublished manuscripts. And although I don't throw out this package with two passport photos, several buttons, some test tubes, some pre-reform kopeks, and many little hanks of twine, and a nail as well . . . and on top there's also a phone number, I've forgotten whose . . . still the newspaper shreds and tears, and I am one week short of thirty-three, and can't go home, and can't in any way forget it. Not to lose home or the package . . .

Something is spilling out of the package more and more. Then, when one more little bit has spilled, I suddenly feel—beyond the terror of loss—the relaxation of freedom. I see the corner of a mouth, the edge of some water, a scrap of sky. And before you all at once is a flowering field, and no one has noticed that you have gone there (not there); no one has called you;, no one will. . . . There, at that moment, into that free space in the package, into the space left by nothing more than a little nail, rusty and crooked, or a dried-out cork—into that place come woods, a cliff, birds . . .

You can't pass life by after all; you can't unintentionally raise your eyes to life and not forget at least some little thing immediately! Blessed be everything I have not done, everything I've overlooked, dropped, lost, let go of, forgiven, or been forgiven. Blessed be my laziness. Cursed be the greed that never threw anything away, never chucked anything out, but always kept waiting for that merciful moment when something would be lost.

Thus I come tumbling into this narrative, all red in the face, sweating, with a package in my hands, pressed against my chest, a wire from a champagne cork poking me in the neck (for some reason it was this that made the surface hole); little bits of candy wrapper sticking to my trouser legs, and extraneous confetti—lucky street car and lottery tickets—always a sure winner—gift certificates worth 2.87 rubles each, rounded off to the nearest full number; and here's a ticket to the American production *Porgy and Bess*, which they put on for a new New Year's celebration fifteen years ago; and a coatroom ticket in my watch pocket pointing exactly, without hands, at either the day or the year or the hour when it all happened. . . . In my hands I hold several tickets for exams in botany, constitutional law, and explosives; the elevator doesn't work, my feet are killing me, my heart is pounding against the package; I still have enough sense to take from my back pocket a rusty ring of keys for locks that have long ago disappeared and use it to open the window in the bus speeding down off the bridge. . . . And that's the shape I'm in when I meet my beloved; and as luck would have it, there's no place to put my package down so that I can throw my arms around her; and it's no good putting it down, even if there were some place, for then I could hardly keep it together, and it would come unwrapped immediately, before my lover's eyes, which wouldn't be a pretty sight at all. Besides, how can you throw yourself on someone's neck if first, fastidiously, you set aside a package? How gauche. I throw myself on my knees—the package is before me, the fresh wound from the champagne is bleeding on my neck, and I bow my head to the ground in deep obeisance to a rubbish can. . . . But what I wanted to say was that if through some misunderstanding life drops in at my little cell, that means that I have lost the recollection of one more small scrap of life gone by, for in a saturated solution the addition of a salt, even with constant stirring, results in the precipitation of the exact same quantity of salt and its immediate crystallization.

That is the kind of unreal being who is roaming like a phantom amidst the real bushes and grasses, where real birds chirp and real insects crawl, on his way to buy butter and soap powder at the village store. But this being, actually, doesn't even do that, not only because the paper clips and straight pins of errands allow him no opportunity to look around and find himself in a reality that is surprising to him but that constantly goes on without him, but also because neither the butter nor the, what is it?—soap—neither are realities for him. On the contrary, they are something alien and offensive, rejected by his soul, not recognizable as reality. Within this gap in reality, this very gap whose edges on the right and on the left appear as little fibers and woolly hairs—in this dead zone, the shadow of my being roams, crosses a little stream, goes up a slight rise, and finds himself in a brightly lit corridor between low fences and birch trees, at the end of which, among pines, an azure hollow shows. . . . Soap and butter slip out of his head, and I suddenly feel a sharp pang of happiness: the sky comes tumbling down upon me, of rarest blue and luminosity— how long it's been since there was such a day—the leaves began to rustle, a child shouted, a swallow chirped at my feet, and a ladybug landed on my finger.

The ladybug flew off into the sky, and from the sky three apples fell: for me, for you, and for the narrator. That is, no sooner had I come in step with life than I was, in the same instant, visited by a revelation (and forgot it). But to make up for it, in its wake some agency of unreality sent me a new, seductive idea, which I was fated to suffer from, along with other unrealizable ideas, to this very day. . . . Instead of a fresh, green, curly revelation, as alive as a new twig, not even a thought but a direct contact and convergence with the world— instead of that, at the end of the bright corridor, hardly a hundred meters long, there was a ready-made idea for a new book. The green twig was shaved off, and the thought, rounded like a club, came down upon my head.

It was a totally new kind of *Autobiography*, the only honest and sincere kind, as it were, the only genuine autobiography—not at all about what is regarded by society as the achievements and events of a lifetime; not a report on the fulfillment of some social duty, the life's work assigned to each person; not reminiscences of childhood, school, university, marriage, and the historical events one has witnessed; not about the fact that you lived among others, not about others at all—but truly about yourself. After all, there must be something that distinguishes an *Autobiography* from a biography, and a biography from memoirs. After all, your life differs from others', not simply as a variant, although it may be a sole variant, but by your uniqueness, the fact that it was you and only you that lived on this earth. That is the only thing that can have general significance.

It was in these oblique terms, lacking immediacy, that I later told myself about the pure, precise, and correct thing that passed into me in an instant, at the moment of contact. . . . An azure hollow opened up between two infinite pine trees—a lake was there. I was swept up and out of that narrow and constrained corridor of consciousness and found myself spread out upon the shore. Limp and prostrate, I recalled those dull and tarnished words, pulled out at random, one by one. They no longer meant anything; they had dried out and turned gray like pebbles from the sea. . . . And how could you take hold of that ever-so-slender, breaking thread of the poetic high and not belittle the subject, which—it must be said—gets along quite well without you, anyway?

I sat on the shore of my lake. It was precisely *my* lake—no better than others I have seen or not seen—because it is the mental image that appears before me at the word *lake*; lake in general. With boats, black ones, half-submerged, or brightly painted ones, bobbing lightly before me like floats on fishing lines. With a steep sand embankment to the right, over the top of which, connecting it to the woods as though by stitching, the cars of a train flashed by between the pines; and on the left, the flat carpet of a marsh. And jutting out into the lake, a spruce-covered promontory, which usually looked like a bear at a watering hole. With hills in the distance, on the opposite shore, where at the very top, against the sky, there stood a grove of trees, indistinguishable from the wood and merging with it, but resembling by itself a ruined castle. In the foreground, an island with a sparse growth of gnarled pines floated before me, and the marshy carpet came right up to it. And on the marsh, like decadent little lanterns, there glimmered some special kind of marsh flowers, which as one looked farther into the distance merged into a single, solid field of white. The sun was falling into the marsh, turning more and more crimson, and the water, rather gray at your feet, just a little way out glinted and flashed with mother of pearl, then turned violet and gold and scarlet and dark blue, then quite far out along the opposite shore (where the "castle" was) suddenly turned black. There was no place for one's gaze to rest—such was the weightlessness of looking. One's gaze established such a direct and unstrained connection that there was no such thing as where you were, where the lake was, much less where home was, or in general, where *everything* was that was not *here*.

Where on this lake could I look and not be myself but be this lake, if only so long as the sunset would allow? But despair at the idea that was slipping away (as though they had shown it, then tried to take it away, but I had fastened onto it and now am pulling it in; however, I had taken a poor, sorry hold on some miserable little store of things, and there is no strength in my fingers)—despair forced me, slightly ashamed and covering my face with my hand, although there was no one on the shore, to jot down a note on a cigarette pack (as a reminder), as though merely to avoid doing violence to it, to avoid letting go of it at that second, now, but at the same time with the idea of later, suddenly, encountering it, to resurrect everything when I was more ready—some day. . . . And now the cigarette pack is before me and I copy out the following:

AUTOBIOGRAPHY (Apology for Reality)

(This title was spaced out generously, in large letters and then the lines took shape, smaller and smaller and closer together, as they went down, as though under the "mighty pressure" of those above; finally, unable to withstand it, they were squeezed out and up, as though from a tube, until they encircled the title like the vapor of an idea whose dimensions had been fixed in advance by the size of the cigarette pack. However, room was found for the date: "May 1976.")

No dates. Only that which was. Then it will come out very concisely. Only the real moments of existence. Even memories of childhood should be approached in such a way as to sift out any that are *restored* with someone else's help (as though they were your own). And even *your own*, which were understood only later, should be presented not when they happened but when they were comprehended. Thus many things from childhood will be moved to now. Unreality is to be presented only at the moments of your awareness of it, that is, at real moments—in the same step-by-step sequence by which you became aware of that unreality (biography within biography). That is, write down at last what actually was *real* in this life, write without reminiscing, drawing pictures. *Test out* a method, and thereby *measure* the deviation of the true picture from the accepted standards, i.e., all those *imposed* concepts of reality that exist in society.

Surely you know now what I then had in mind?
A perpetual-motion idea.
Least of all did I recall that autobiography in thinking over these

"Days of Leavetaking," linked together, if by nothing else, by sunshine, which I am writing now—and there, you see, I've suddenly discovered that a writer's first attempt is indeed a stab in the dark. . . .

Must you strive so hard in pursuit of an idea that it catches up with you?

The following is apparently what I thought on that shore:

"I never thought about death (not afraid?), but isn't that a kind of suffering every second from the desire and the inability to merge with reality, which exists only at the present moment—my active (inborn?) desire for nonexistence? I might be happy (no way of knowing) even in my unreality, a hammock suspended between past and future, if I could recognize this unreality as *mine*. In the final analysis I was always this way, was never consciously present in my own sense of what is 'programmatically and desiredly real.' So what does the surrounding world matter to me? However, if love and happiness were, in my experience, only those moments when I did not exist, childhood didn't exist; 'I don't remember' didn't exist; the act didn't exist; death didn't exist—that means, above all, that it was the desire to disappear that possessed me throughout my 'conscious' life."

THIRTY-THREE YEARS

But where is "The Peasant"? Where in the world is he?

All this time he has been walking toward me along the shore of the lake.

He has been walking toward me for a very long time, and today he woke up, had a hangover, but later had something more to drink, because today is a holiday, Victory Day, and he had fought and fought, and reached Berlin. (Berlin was a deviation, of course, from the line of march, but a strictly and carefully thought-out deviation that would bring him precisely to this day, to the moment when I would be sitting by the lake and thinking about . . .)

And here we can place an exact date after all. It's passing and now the aforementioned week has passed and I have completed . . . here knocking on my door was . . . my thirty-third year. The nails in my new heels were aching and on this day, memorable to Christ, I was busy with an approximate resurrection from curly and flowering Dilizhan* to my lake, to meet my peasant apostle, to my now gelled and solidified home territory. I carry myself, resisting, a deliberate deadweight, over to the other shore and drive the new heels of my shoes into the firm, dry sand. Clearly I see myself from the side—distraught and cowardly, standing on the shore, in a land of unfrightened themes, and I smile bitterly. But too late. It's as though someone were warming a mixture in a smoke-blackened, waste-heat

---

*A resort in Armenia [tr.].

boiler corresponding, in this case, to an early-morning form of the head, over a smoking kerosene wick—some yesterday's mixture of stale beer, coffee grounds, burned-down cigarette butts, and loves-me-loves-me-not petals. The rising current brings to the surface—now a cigarette butt, now some spittle—and swirls them down to the bottom again in a cycle . . . the bubbling and boiling of creation. Come here, dear peasant . . . I will now put you out . . . and down in writing.

He draws nearer to me from the right. He emerges from either a boiler room or a pumping station next to the railway track, narrows his eyes at the light, and sways assuredly in his honest, positive inebriation, and sees me. . . . Consequently, I am writing my autobiography three years ago. But how am I to grasp the ever-so-slender breaking thread of the poetic high, which is already under pressure from reflection and formulas, a thread coarsened by the drunkenness of spasmodic existence?

Still and all, it is he. He built a tile stove for me last fall. Just as diligent, slightly awry, and honest as himself. No matter. It works. . . . He took a liking to me then for no apparent reason. Was it that I, out of the lack of desire (today) to write, too eagerly mixed the cement and handed him the bricks, as I was not at all required to do? Or was it the conversation that started up between us—about how it was alright to drink but you had to know how much, and how he never overdid it, so that nothing had would happen to him, although of course things happen; but everything in its own time and season. Or about how it was no good that we were feeding the Arabs. Or about how, back in 1945, we shouldn't have stopped at Berlin but should've gone all the way to America and now we wouldn't have all these conflicts the way we do now. Or about the Jews—a cautious, tentative conversation. . . .

For whatever reason, one day that thickheaded slyness—all that peasant's narrowing of the eyes from being tricked so many times—one day it disappeared, and from the five-ruble note that I gave him for vodka as a tip, he gave me back two rubles. He'd take enough for a quarter-liter and no more. From then on he needed me when he wanted a conversation, when he would come out of his yard and take a stand in the middle of our Nowhere Street and stay there that way, swaying assuredly as though on the deck of a ship, always keeping his balance, never a misstep. And he would look at the street over which night was falling, where even in the twilight many little trails braided together. He stood there that way, patiently waiting, with an age-old longing for communication in his eyes . . . and there were no passersby.

You tell me now, Andrei . . . from your father's name you'd be Yegorevich, right? So you come on now, Andrei Grigorevich, tell me this . . .

I smile, weary of my own insincerity. I lean my head to the side as though to be warm and friendly and hear him out. I answer painstakingly, choosing my words and then—

"Hey, you got an education. Graduated from college. I didn't have the chance. . . ."

He listens, he chews, and suddenly his eyes are filled with injury. He grunts, lifts each leg separately off the ground as he sways and walks off without looking around. "You insulted me, Andrei Grigorevich. Why'd you say no? I've still got a quarter-liter." And he turns to go and drink it, and sure enough, he grunts again and gestures a couple of more times in irritation.

Here he comes toward me and again tears me off at the perforated line, like a page from a calendar. I was just going for soap, engrossed in my busy list of nonexistence, when suddenly the revelation descended, I merged with the world and with real time for a moment, then was torn away from life immediately, back into nonexistence, but seemingly into an inspired, poetic nonexistence, and again I ask you . . . who the devil is this peasant walking toward me?

"Today's the Ninth of May, Victory Day," is what he says, "And I got all the way to Berlin, three times wounded and shell-shocked. Twenty years gone by. Why not drink? You can't do without drinking." Nobody would say anything against him for that or anything like it, absolutely not. . . . He was coming toward me, consequently, from the Reichstag and had been for twenty-odd years and had guessed exactly that I would be sitting here by the lake and thinking at this very second that. . . .

I will forget about him completely as he comes up to me. The neighbors will put on a record, the sounds of rotation winding the landscape around into a gray, dusky mass . . .

"What're you," he'll say to me amiably, "just standin' there for?"

"Thinking," I'll say roughly. And from that moment not a single thought will come into my head, and that remarkable feeling inside me will be dissolved in hot waves of shame. I'll apologize immediately, lying: "You understand . . . I was walking . . . sunset . . . thinking . . . the lake . . . pity . . . the earth . . . sky . . . birds . . . where to?"

Thus I played up to the honesty of his inebriation, without looking at his eyes, expressive of the joy of wine, at the mother-of-pearl sunset of reason in the smoothness of eyes for which night is falling. Effusiveness and vigilance, slyness and guilt, devotion and churlishness, complacency and the wish to oblige, respectfulness and strong doubt about my, his, yours, their words . . . I gathered within myself the thoughts of the people so that I could forever doubt and underrate them.

"No, nothing exists any more!" I exclaim. I could barely keep from weeping out of insincerity, wallowing in pathos and apotheosis.

"How that bear looked me in the eyes! . . . . They should have mercy, at least a semblance. . . ."

The peasant fixed me with a piercing look and bore down hard . . .

It seemed like this: A drunk was rolling a wagon wheel down the road so it wouldn't be lost; such a useful thing, almost completely intact, which would hardly ever be there when it was needed, undoubtedly useful, a reminder of the horse, which cannot be. The wheel had the shape of an irregular circle and rolled the drunk lopsidedly along behind itself, tugging him forward with a jerk, then shooting away from him. Starting to fall over, it careened from side to side, equally far in opposite directions; it to the left, me to the right. It would stop to bump, trickily, and abruptly leap ahead. Oh hell—it's fallen over again. Just then the feeling that had come over me began to grow again. Who knows what the devil it is when such a perfect thought comes along, so useful and worthwhile that it's of benefit right away? Something to drink, and the wheel, and suddenly it had come back!

"Alright, I'll show you," he thought, overtaking the wheel and slowing it down with difficulty, so that this time for no good reason it shuddered and came at him. "So you wanta . ." he said, spreading his legs carefully, sitting down and taking a firm hold of it as it reached him. "Heave ho," but it proved to be suspiciously lightweight, like a child's hoop, or maybe stronger, like a spring; maybe it wasn't he that threw it back over himself with such skill but *it* that threw *him*.

"You're full of it." (Crawling up to it expressively from the other side.) "No way am I going to sober up or leave you, not on your life"—having in mind this time his wife, against whom the honor of his intentions would bump as the wheel, with a sigh, rolled at last into their yard, knocking into the porch. But *she* doesn't appreciate it, letting him choke on all the heartfelt tenderness welling up in his breast . . . He, she, and it—the graphic image of the rolling wheel. He-she-it—a naive tribe that has survived civilization. The ritual dance of the wheel of endeavor, of life and death, of words with man. And while the procession moved off down the road with an obscene dance, ashamed of nothing, circling and changing places, driving before itself its own mirror image . . .

The peasant, gazing at me with the furrows of his brow, bent deep down inside himself, to the bottom of his being, picked up a single, weighty word that had been saved for future use, a word whose time had come, brought it to the surface, and with a reproachful look at the dried-out wheel in the ditch, said:

"That's just it. If man does in all the animals, he still won't be able to get along without them. He was made from nature along with the animals—so there would be both man and animals. . . . So if there aren't any animals any more, he will have to make them out of himself. To even things up again."

"Yes, yes!" my confirmation was ecstatic. The world was still beautiful, it still *was*, if it had saved for me, the ingrate who had turned against it, a present once again. Who was it that had broken off my thoughts? What in hell kind of thoughts were they in fact? They were the stuff the air itself, the water, and the forest were made of. They had chosen us at random . . .

We stood on the shore, with our heads together like calves, a two-headed seed of radiation and professional union, and his intoxication flowed over into my head, my thought flowed over into his; we swayed on the shore, attached by a dried-out stump of a cord, through which weak juices from the earth suddenly began to run.

"Thank you, Lord," I offered up. "Each of us two is not yet alone on the earth."

"So you believe in God too?" the peasant said, simultaneously doubting and flattering me.

"How can you not believe in Him when there is this?" I said, sweeping my hand over the munificence of the world still remaining to us, as though to caress the object of our mutual thoughts, our child who had given us birth.

"I don't believe in Him hardly," he said, "I believe in nature. If He was above it, how could He allow it to perish? No real lord and master would let himself do that."

He was right and there was no denying it. I say:

"Faith doesn't mean agreeing with God. Faith means not doubting Him, never in any case."

"Then the Last Judgment has already begun. Is that it, do you think?"

"Why of course," I snatched it right up, overjoyed at the logic. "We've lived to see it."

"But I feel sorry for my son," he said. "How do you figure? If I love him and I feel sorry for him, what then? That doesn't make sense either, I tell you. . . . You, maybe. And me. We deserve it. But the kid, what's he guilty of? There again. It's unfair."

"What you said about the animals is right," I said, extricating myself. "The same for children. We kill the child in them, and raise ourselves within them."

"Uh-huh," he said. "But while he's still real little, what about then?"

"As long as he's like that there is no end," I told him confidently.

"Then that's right," he confirmed.

"It's like you said," I spoke with increasing proximity, pleased by his agreement. "When there are no animals, human beings will have to create animals out of themselves, to keep everything equal. That means there will be only half as many people. And then when children grow up, hardly any people will be left. So gradually we'll be reduced to nothing."

"Then that's right," the peasant nodded my head in agreement. "If

at first there's half as many, later on there'll be a quarter . . ."
Thus we stood, embracing upon the last shore, still able to do arithmetic and pleased with this ability of ours.

"Man is always a minority," he said profoundly, bringing the very last word up from the depths. "Of us there's two. Let's go up to my place, to the boiler room."

The boiler room was a homunculus.

THAT IS THE QUESTION

We sat in the boiler room, which was, properly speaking, a pumping station. It was on the shore of the lake under a railway embankment and trains passed overhead. It was cozy here. The place was so out of the way and isolated that you had to remind yourself where you were—under a railway embankment, between a lake and a thick, green reservoir, shaped like a bomb crater, out of which it was hard to imagine they took water. When a train would pass over and slightly increase the steady humming and trembling of the boiler room equipment, you could imagine that the sea was beyond the walls and that you were at the seashore, which was probably the reason it was so warm here too. I would forget where I was and when I remembered, I would pass through some stage of prerecollection as though it was night and I was in the midst of a great expanse of water on a barge or something like that, something isolated and powerless, like a small wave or a balloon.

All around us stood the kind of machines which, unlike ocean liners, jets, or lasers and masers, you could really call *machines*, the way kids do. (Boy, look at all those *machines!*) Thick pipes stood shaggy in the corners; big valves, like ship's wheels, curled ornately; on the floor, as green as frogs, two pumps were chugging; and in the middle, very large and blending bulkily into the darkness of the corners, sat some sort of great-grandmother of the modern missile with two inoperative pressure gauges as though she were wearing glasses tied on with cord. She was quietly snoring, with the slack mouth of a fire box hanging open.

The peasant took good care of her. She was thoroughly lubricated in her safe and secure old age, and gleamed with a rare variety of copper plating. It was good for her here; it was good here in general—warm, clean, and dimly lit by a thrifty light blulb. And Lord, what smells! Old rags, coal, oil, whitewash, stale heat, the darkness of the morning shift, and the dark blue of metallic shavings. In an empty bucket was a broom made of twigs; on the shelf over the wash basin, a drinking cup; on the shaggy elbow of a pipe a half-liter . . . Everything had its place, its own special roost.

I complimented him on everything here and patiently he heard me out.

"What else? . . . the proletariat . . ." he spoke incomprehensibly, and we drank. "You're an educated man; you write books. Can you tell me somethng? How come they publish bad books and they won't publish good ones?"

"It can't be!" I thought delightedly. "To suddenly find a kindred spirit. And just like that, ingrate."

"For the same old reason," I said.

"For instance, *The Cavalier of the Gold Star*. Who wrote that?"

"Babayevsky—"*

"Right," he said. "You know it. Now why don't they publish that?"

"But they did publish it!" I was astonished. "They even gave it the Stalin prize, first class!" I smiled grimly and was about to add that maybe the only good thing was that even if they don't publish quality works, at least they don't republish that . . .

"Oh yeah? They published it?" He was dubious. "I read a hand-written copy."

"Handwritten?"

"Copied by hand. Now that's a true book. It writes about the owner, the master. About the land. You explain to me now why a book about the land and about the master can't be printed?"

I didn't know what to answer. An apocryphal *Gold Star!* It was bound to be . . . worth a Solzhenitsyn . . .

"It writes about the kulak. Now you explain me another thing, why they treated the kulak so unfair? His whole crime, you know, was that he worked and worked, never straightened up, never saw the sky . . . there's a real proletariat for you . . . when he finished his shift, when he'd nothing to do, he'd read a novel. Got to be a real brain, big as that," he indicated the breadth of his shoulders. "And away he went!"

This said everything. We drank another half-liter.

"Well, how's the tile stove?" he said. "Keeps you warm?"

You see, it was he who had built it for me . . .

"Yes, yes it keeps me warm," I nodded, "only the bricks keep falling out."

"It doesn't smoke?"

"No, it doesn't."

"Doesn't matter then. If any more fall out, you call me."

"No, don't worry about it," I say. "It keeps me warm."

"And the bugs don't bother you?"

"Bugs?" I didn't understand.

"I remember some bugs were bothering you—"

"No, no, they're not bothering me . . . what kind of bugs?"

*Semyon P. Babayevsky (born 1909), Soviet novelist. To progressively minded people in the USSR, Babayevsky typifies the false, rosy-colored optimism that flourished in the form of "socialist realism" in the late 'forties and early 'fifties, when Babayevsky was thrice awarded the Stalin Prize for his novel *Cavalier* *of the Gold Star* and its two sequels. Babayevsky's trilogy describes miracles of reconstruction and economic progress on a postwar collective farm under the leadership of a local youth devoted to the party line on rural electrification [tr.].

"Woodbeetles. Eat wood. They bother me a lot."

"Those little, dark, hard beetles?"

"Yeah, you seen some?" He got alarmed.

"At my parents' house, I saw some. They had eaten the legs of their chairs . . ."

"Yeah, but you never saw this kind," he became inspired. "You saw furniture beetles. You didn't see a real woodbeetle. I'll show you . . ." he jumped up and disappeared through a small emergency door.

He soon reappeared.

"I still have a few of them left," he said (carefully sliding open a box that was ever so tiny in his big machinist's hands). "Two or three specimens." That's what he said, *specimens.* "Two," he said disappointedly. And in some absolutely incomprehensible way he carefully avoided crushing the "specimens" between the pliers of his thumb and index finger (the same way they use to surprise us in the documentary movies—*Science and Technology*—with the spectacle of a jointed, H.G. Wells–type mechanical hand that skillfully poured some sort of liquid, the symbol of Radiation, out of a fragile flask into various test tubes), and he triumphantly held it out to me.

Truly I had never imagined such a thing. It was a rather disgusting, soft, rust-colored creature, halfway between a fly and a cockroach. What struck me most was its softness. In order to gnaw wood a beetle would have to be imagined as black as anthracite, something like a tiny drilling machine designed by nature itself.

"Soft," I said.

"So-oft," the peasant sang the sounds in a poisonous way. "You *said* it. Slimy!"

His eyes glistened with inspiration, his face grew hot. His speech poured out smoothly and drunkenly, like a Pharisee easily drowning out the awkward speech of an Apostle. It was rhythmic prose about how the beetle at first has wings, flys away, lands, lays eggs, loses its wings; later it all seemed the other way around to me: at first it lays its eggs, then flys away. The males have a special chitinous little key with a complex ridge; the female has a keyhole. Locked up tight like a money box; can't get in there with the wrong key, not on your life . . . The main thing is, when they lay their eggs or fly away, one or the other, they devour people's houses with great speed. The major culprit is the female, while the male is harmless, or maybe it's the other way around . . . but above all they are devouring his (the peasant's) house . . .

The peasant closed his eyes and his speech took on a new intonation, shifted to another key, an epic mode, and the saga was about how he, the peasant, had gone forth all alone against the countless multitudes of beetles, had thrown down the gauntlet and rushed into battle; how he had hacked off their heads with insectide, dust, chlorophosphate, kerosene, but they just kept growing. How he had pasted over the little nest holes with wax, stopped them up with resin, smeared them over with tar; how he had changed the beams of his cottage and had begun to tire in the uneven struggle. The beetles fed upon the poison dust, multiplied especially rapidly in the insecticide, and developed terrible destructive strength and hardness from the kerosene. He had written letters to the newspapers *Village Star*, *Red Living*, *Medical Truth*, *Yesterday*, and many others, subscribed to several specialized journals, tried out forty different kinds of advice, but never gave up. He had tried burning them out with hot iron (literally a heated nail) and had burned down his porch. . . . Apocalyptic clouds gathered over his narrative, which took on renewed force, the fury of the Apocrypha. The locust jangled the steel of its wings, bearing something secret within itself, within its live, wet, greasy body.

If the misfortune he told of had not been so natural and grand I would have marveled at the figure he made, grown suddenly large and monumentally impassioned, expressing the Passion and Death of the warrior in a way Vuchetich* would have envied. Just then the flashing, precious essence of his eyes grew narrow and smeary again.

"But now I've understood," he whispered voluptuously. "The only way you can fight them is one by one."

A slight shiver ran through my body.

"You don't believe it?"

He gently and insistently took me by the hand. I ducked down to pass under the shaggy pipe, which seemed alive and insectlike to me, the belly of a bumble bee, and thus diminishing, with housefly steps, we went through the emergency door. It was a small hole eaten through a hard substance, as in the case of the woodbeetle, only done by people for people.

I found myself in a small laboratory, where in cramped quarters, as in the Middle Ages, in confines determined solely by the narrow aims of the work, an enormous pulsating forehead labored in torment, performing wondrous feats. In the total purity of philosophical commitment, it was engrossed in a task beyond its powers: the materialization of the Idea. Here, making the weight of the world equal to itself by an effort of thought alone, without even the cunning Archimedian trick of the lever, it would reach the verge of accomplishing its task, and each time be defeated by a sudden fainting spell, a treacherous coma, right at the very gates, upon the threshold, as the hand touches the goal. . . . Where nevertheless it regained consciousness after an eternity of swooning and, without noticing the madness that had set

---

*Yevgeny V. Vuchetich (born 1908), a leader of the "socialist realism" school of Soviet sculpture, famous for the heroic poses of his figures, as in the monument to the Soviet soldier-liberator in Berlin and the statue at the United Nations in New York representing the beating of swords into plowshares [tr.].

in, buckled down to the happy, disjointed, and light-minded elegance
of discovering and inventing, as an end in itself, objects that had once
served the Idea. . . . Thus it had acquired, through the refined
sophistication of lenses, finely molded bronze spigots, and the curved
subtlety of chemical retorts, the skill of selling the instrumentalities of
the Idea itself—that is, unable to bear the straining of the spirit any
longer, it had made a turn in midstream toward technical progress,
and further on, with another easy leap, with the ticking and donging of
clockwork from Solomna, of hydroscopes and crystal watches, micro-
and macro-cephalic, it had moved time forward a little to perform the
exploits of industrial production . . . where the enterprising spirit of
home-grown genius à la Kulibin and Polzunov,* embodying in itself
the inquiring mind of the people, had twisted time into a spring that
gave impetus to the productive forces up to and including the Kremlin
chimes.

And where a naïve Yid is now inventing integral calculus in the
euphoria of genius for the professional amusement of the creators of
the infinitely small, there stood my big lug of a peasant, who had
recently invented a clockwork mechanism activated by the trains that
pass over the pump house. I suddenly found myself here, across the
ages, and—never mind clockwork!—the peasant was holding in his
hands a syringe and, after taking aim like a surgeon with a thin little
spurt, he stuck the needle into the next hole of the deathwatch beetle.
Several blocks of wood sawed from the beam he had replaced last year
were carefully piled in the corner for experimentation.

"Right now I'm injecting chloroform, but soon I'm going to have
invented my own new formula." And he winked at me slyly instead of
saying, "And then . . ."

I looked at the transparent row of test tubes, at the bulky row of thick
jars full of poisons on the long shelf, at the clipping from the *Evening
News* hanging under glass ("our reader, I—ov, a resident of I—vo
Junction, asks us . . . ," it begins; and red crayon underlines the
"I—ov"), at the bronze shapeliness of the sprayers, at the flashing top
of the hypodermic needle, held vertically, frozen in midair, an incandescent dot representing the focal point (mediastinum) of the moment, capturing the entire compass of its surroundings. . . . The
pause stretched out, silence hung, a long, thin sound extended from
ear to ear.

I looked at the injected block of wood—myriads of little holes,
precisely focused, distinct, representing black constellations of day,
whirling spirals of galaxies, worlds and pathetic antiworlds, where the
density and substance of the remaining wood was simply a constella-
tion of cosmic emptiness, where the wood was somehow suspended in

---

*Ivan P. *Kulibin* (1735–1818) and Ivan I. *Polzunov* (1728–1766), early Russian inventors and
mechanical geniuses [tr.].

a mass of holes . . . worlds, holes, world holes.

"The same for every hole?" timidly I breathed the question.

"Sure," his voice suddenly sounded quite normal and natural.

Time went by overhead, the test tubes tinkled delicately in their well-ordered row, silence was broken, the dizziness left me, and like the country bumpkin in the story who asks the touring lecturer how they get that sweet, gooey stuff inside of chocolate candies, I discovered normalcy in what was thick-headed and habitual, I lost the fearful world and found surroundings free of fear—and I asked:

"But listen here. How did you get the beams out? When the house was sitting on them?" At first he looked at me dumbfounded, then visibly returning by foot from bottomless reaches of consciousness, he saw me at last, from far away.

"Ah you," he said with affectionate superiority. "I raised the house! A cultivated mind . . . educated people," he said in mock dismay. "Course not all of it at once. First one corner, then another. What an oddball." His laugh was genuinely cheerful. "We better go have a drink. I've still got a quarter-liter left . . ."

"But we drank it."

"You don't understand anything. I always have a quarter-liter left."

I went out in the nightly night. It was big and dark like a bear. The moon was shining, a senseless, wall-eyed thing. The world had closed its bright, clear eye. The wall-eye was directly over the chimney of the house of the woman who owns the cow, from whom we get our milk, and who for fifteen years now has rented a cottage in the summer to an old woman who translates from Old French, and she knows about me, but I know nothing of her (although she moves entire epochs in the proper direction toward our present day, I do not think she will translate this to be read yesterday). The house was still darker than the sky in its stubborn determination to be a household with the aim of living on at the expense of its own corpses, feeding itself and its own land, forming the likeness of a cycle on an area of ten hundred (square meters), where the cow's peaceful fluid was filtering through the pores of the earth to the unsleeping potato tubers. Beneath the ground the skim milk has congealed, while the cream is being digested in the people sleeping above. But in the still greater darkness of the field the cow *was*, and its sleeping and breathing made the world more real now than the deathless configuration of physical bodies and quantities. She breathed about me. I was swathed in a warm puddle of air, lingering between two haystacks. And I would have liked it if on that night there were more cow than bear. There would have been inequality, but not loss of equilibrium.

It can't be said I was remembering the same bear mentioned above. But everything was one and the same. The peasant and the beetle and the moon. "Don't forget to tell them at home the difference between the peasant and a boor." I was brightly carrying this sentence along with the earthenware jug of milk I had taken off the porch. The jug was full. My feet did not know the micro-relief of the previously existing puddles. The soles of my shoes lost their sensitivity. Milk ran over my fingers and up my sleeve, signifying to me, as a consolation, that there still were cows now. Nevertheless a few more would be even bet-ter . . . .

And if you must know, I was drunk.

Don't forget to tell about the kulak-bloodsucker. A passion for verse overtook me.

> The peasant eaten out of house and home by beetles
> Will not be outlived for all eternity.
> And here a cow is breathing still (still willing?)
> Although there is nobody listening.
> Bend your ear to the topic of the day
> And you'll go deaf and curse your life away.
> Thanks to all that's in the world, some day
> You will understand these words I say.
> O Lord above, I'm thankful for
> Equivalence to the calendar . . .
> The calendar, the calendar . . .
> I calendar to Thee, O Lord.

There was an old woman back when I was a child—Aunt Paula, Pelageya Pavlovna, a kulak woman, a woman good as a cutlet. They've buried her, already buried her; I didn't notice that she died; don't remember when. . . . She used to tell, as I now recall, about how she led the horse out to do the plowing, and young Pelageya wouldn't let go of the reins. She couldn't let go. She feared for the horse. She feared for her husband; stronger than pain, stronger than blood, was the earth. The earth already was her blood. "All they grow is rocks," she said, and how could there be any doubt about it? And that story, so literary that it seems to have come out of the black disc of the loudspeaker under which she was cutting onions, it turns out was the truth breathed out by the cow in the night tonight.

The milk ran down my fingers in the night of the mad bear; not to forget to tell . . . who? What? Not to forget . . .

What?

This is what, it turns out, shouldn't be forgotten. This is what, it turns out, I was thinking on the shore when the peasant came up to me and broke my thread.

Remember or forget, that is the question.

Exactly that. You see, I am not living, because I'm remembering yesterday, not living today and getting ready to live in my memory tomorrow as well. That means you have to forget in order to be alive and real now. But the world perished because they forgot. Doesn't that mean we *must* remember? Remember so that not every last thing will perish, the way the owner of the cow, the repulsive old thing, remembers her cow, the way old Pelageya dragged her horse along—that's the way to remember.

But in remembering I don't live, I perish in everything, with everything. In forgetting, the last one who remembers leaves the world. In forgetting, I perish completely for everything. Not to remember, so as to live without noticing death? Or to remember, so as to fear death and not *live* in general? To leave the world, forgetting about it, in order to live for oneself, or to remain in it, so as not to be in it ever, not to be in it *now*?

And that's how I rolled the drunken wheel home off the road. In my pocket a fruit drop was melting, a treat for pay day.

To forget or to remember? To be aware or let it be? Hamlet—rambles . . .

FATE

In Memory of N. Rubtsov

Every spring when I moved to the summer cottage I brought myself up to date on the events of our street over the winter.

It's a strange street. It has no beginning and no end. It suddenly spreads out from a path in the marsh, stretches along, all solid and respectable, past houses, orchards, and neighbors—then suddenly breaks off, tapering precipitously down into nothing. There emptiness yawns, a blue hole between trees. . . . And someone who doesn't live here but finds himself here for the first time can't figure out right away what in the world this is—where did the street go? What exists is a steep bank, a drop, a little stream, and a meadow—flood lands. But to see this, you have to walk right up to it, keeping your eye, to the very last step, on the expanding emptiness of the end of the street—only then do you understand. . . . Maybe that's why they call it Nowhere Street, because it's without end or beginning. And there in that greening current of air which I dreamed of in light sleep after irreparable sorrow, I see a word written, erased, and written again—*fate*. That is, at the word *fate* this little spot swims up, like a fish, before my mind's eye. . . . And I don't even notice.

A little house stands there which apparently cannot *be* in this life any longer. People live there who didn't even have time to become bad. They took over half the street, creating a kind of straits, or narrows, and a dead end of their own, because they didn't have a building lot per se, but had to have some room outside the house to live on. And the house. What a house! Someone's abandoned bathhouse, in which some newly arrived stranger took up residence no one noticed when, and though he outlived everyone, he remained unknown and an outsider nevertheless. And though there were people living all around, who had come later than he, later than I, just yesterday even—so stubbornly do they build, sink in, put down thick and blunt roots like carrots and fingers that of course it turns out to be *they* who live there—a man with some woman; another woman with some man—but not *he*. He's crowded off to the edge of the street as though shoved aside. His whole uneven plot of land inched up to the street like a patchwork quilt, one edge dipping into the little stream. The bathhouse somehow or other expanded, as needed, with tiny rooms and sheds, because time passed, the family grew, and no one's going to go away after having grabbed half the street and a little piece of ground on a falling bank. They surrounded their household plot, their little piece of meadow, with a wavy little fence made of stakes that you could see through—and their life showed through for everyone to see, shadowy and unrecognizable. A hammock hangs, a tub has been thrown out; the only garden is a tiny one, like a grave, just to keep up appearances, to be "registered" in this world as part of the population; and all there was in this little garden were two carrots, three dill plants, and one sunflower. It had the rights of a flower bed: it was watered the way a kitten gets milk or a puppy, leftovers. Nothing from it could be eaten. Above all there was no reason for it. It didn't produce anything.

Nothing can be heard there. They don't argue or fight or yell or explain things loudly. Someone is swinging in a hammock, forgets a book; someone goes out barefoot onto the meadow, looks at the tub . . that's all. Never in your life will you find out who it was. And everything else all around, full-blooded and straining, full of self-affirming existence, was forced to exclude this little spot from its consciousness, from the range of its concerns, as an invisible part of the spectrum, as an inaudible part of the scale—as nonexistent. This accidentally revealed piece of simultaneity from another life, proceeding (it's hard to believe in such luck) within the frozen and awkward fortresses of confirmed and well-implanted forms, like a little blade of grass in a barren, rocky crevice—it's so awful—will suddenly start up at a sharp sound, then catch itself, remembering it has revealed itself—and once again close up, go under wraps. But no, Lord be praised, thus far they're still with us, within us, incorporeal, looking through us, and we through them. This is the only place on earth where something happens.

It was he who had been run over by a train one night while drunk—which I found out about this spring or that one, and so I spend the summer as though he no longer *was*. But nothing had changed. Something was even reinforced in the little house on the edge. I meet him alive in the autumn without a leg and am amazed that I hadn't noticed earlier that he was legless. But those are two different stories, and it isn't known which was first, or whether he was legless first and then run over by the train. Well, it was just yesterday that I met him, hale, hearty, and alive. Or is it, on the other hand, that time is going backwards on their little plot of land, toward us or away from us?

Among us it doesn't move. Their time passes through us, and soon a grandfather appears at last, to live with the grandson. Over at their house, now and then a new person is added, as though someone had made up his mind and run over to their side, deserted. Yoo-hoo, I'm here. And he looks happily over the fence, which is speeding away from us, speeding away for good. Everyone there loves—what business is it of anyone's?—milk spilled in passing . . .

But they are solid, not for our sake, but for themselves; and what is it that lives in their solidity, the way they live in us? Isn't there a cloud there, on which they come to us and contract with us in our sleep to meet someday, only don't tell anyone, and you aren't able to say in time what you wanted, bursting from the muteness of love, to say "Till tomorrow"—then a finger goes to the lips, "No, no. It's our secret, just you and me. . . ." So that in the morning, after splashing your face with water, you notice the morning and wonder, "What in the world was that? What *was* that?" Then you remember you're not supposed to remember—and you smile: it's your secret, between you and them. Isn't it *there* that all of that lives? Keeping itself off to the edge without any convulsive clutching, indifferent to the instability, poor adhesion, and thin rope? And there, in their solidity, in which they are form manifested and become fixed, these loving and lively people are "not us"; so that there, for them (in their onerous corporeality, which for us is incorporeal), to this day still lives the only girl, who hung herself, shot herself, whom I killed, whom he killed, under whose assumed name someone continues to live on the surface of the deep, sent outdoors to awkwardly imitate her former gestures and words, the killer bearing her name, wearing her dress, with hopeless cynicism made up to look like the murdered girl. Oh, isn't it obvious it's not her over there? So it seems I was foolish to put on make-up, so that everything would be obvious to everyone, that this is how we live, that this is the way it is over here . . .

So you see, it's all so awful if you're among them, in love, over there, beyond the provisional, see-through fence, and from over there, from your own genuineness to look out upon your own street, your own house, at yourself, at the awful vampire that has put on the clothing of the child whose blood it sucked and whose nametag it has pinned to its own pocket, so as not to forget. We are all there, God bless us, which is why in that little house it's so crowded that it's frightening to leave there; and you can't leave; and he alone, to show up everyone, yes, he, the grandfather, who once found this little spot, is still alive, has come out from under the train after cutting off two of its locomotive wheels. . . . He asked me today for enough for a "little one" (a liter) and yesterday he paid me back; he's a good man, though why should he insult me so, even though I'm dressed up to look like the boy I killed—I would gladly have forgotten about the ruble he owed, but he doesn't want to have anything to do with me; he takes a ruble off the next liter and pays me back. It's sad. What could I do for them that would be just as nice? Nothing, never. Burn them out maybe? . . .

There's a fire at their house, there's a murder; there's a prison at their house; there are children one after another; there's no cow. And a garden—they have one, which we don't. They have everything, even the lack of what everyone else has; you have nothing. "Can I come in?" They don't hear you. The gate is always hanging open—you can never go in there through it. Conscience won't allow it. That is what won't let you ask them if you can come in—that too, it seems, is conscience . . .

Another new spring is here—a little boy, a son, so fine-looking, who last spring got married, such a beautiful young woman (it was she who was added at that time, beyond the garden in the little lake of their emptiness creeping down to the stream) . . . a boy, a son, Now, yesterday, he was cut down by a bullet, by a knife in the temple; he had gotten involved with a gang, then disentangled himself, then got married, tied the knot. It may have been that; it may have been something else . . . They found him day after tomorrow, dear child, cut in little pieces, beside the Finland Station.

That's how it is; that's how. They are all *not with me*—never, not for any reason, by nature—not with me. Suicide in reserve. Fate in retirement. Soul on pension. Conscience on the stake. Body in repair. Mind in the cupboard. I hunt for the door out to the fields.

It's a family trait. The accomplices—they devoured the child in silence; an old woman found him later in the garden; now she is singing him a lullaby. The happy couple is going down to the stream; the husband is carrying a basket, full of underwear removed from people they have killed, people who had been suitable in size and quality for murder. See how the stakes in the fence are reflected upside down in their pupils—and the meadow has grown empty following them with the look of the thrown-out tub. When everyone rushed into their bathhouse out of fear, they forgot the tub.

In that house is fate. It happens to those who couldn't become us even if they wanted, and who have thus remained where they were, settling down on the edge of our argillaferruginous forms, our forms compounded of iron ore and clay, taking their place in this life just as deliberately as a mother to someone, someone's grandmother, or simply a distant aunt . . .

This then is the concept of *the people*—not folk songs, not birch trees—the people, that is, Divine Fate, which still happens to some people on earth. Among them are all those who were, who are not, and who were not. Everything that I loved, everything that I still love because of its leftover, residual quality, everything that I had, and everything that remains to me—very little. But that is now *everything* that I love. Fate is the people; the people are fate; I am off to the side, removed. Until all envy leaves, until I place the generous remaining crumb of myself upon the greedy open palm, until then, I will never get over there, where everything is out in plain view as though upon an open palm, where the gate is always wide open.

3. The Doctor's Funeral

In Memory of E. Ralbe

A sunny day reminds us of a funeral. Not every such day, of course, but the kind we really call sunny—the first, sudden day of sun that comes at last. It is also translucent. Maybe it's not the sun but the translucence. At a funeral, first of all, there is the weather.

My aunt by marriage was dying, the wife of my uncle by blood. She was "such a *lively* person" (the words of my mother) it was hard to believe she was dying. She really was lively, and it really was hard to believe, but in fact she had long been preparing for this, though unbeknownst to herself.

First she tried the foot. Suddenly there was something wrong with her foot; it swelled up and wouldn't fit in her shoes. But Auntie didn't give in. She tied a prewar slipper to the "elephant" (her word) and, thus shod, came out to us in the kitchen to wash the dishes. Later Aleksandr Nikolaevich, her chauffeur, arrived, and she drove off to her Institute (disability examinations), then to a meeting of the executive board of the Society (Therapeutic), then to an alumnae activities group (she was a Bestuzhevite*), then to a consultation on some titled gangster, then she went by to visit her Jewish relatives, who because of a tacit forty-year-old conspiracy never visited us; after that she came home for an instant, fed her husband, and laboriously tried to decide whether to go to the banquet on the occasion of Nektor Beritashvili's defense of his dissertation. (Beritashvili was a lecturer at the Tbilisi branch of the Institute.) She was very tired (that was *more* than was true) and she didn't want to go (that was *not quite* true). Unbeknownst to herself, she wanted to go (in repeating this "unbeknownst to," I'm beginning to understand that such an emotional capacity can be maintained in old age only by people who are very . . . lively? pure? kind? *good?*—I mutter this unintelligible, no longer existing word— unbeknownst to myself). And she went, because she took all human gatherings for good coin and loved them. She had a passionate attachment to the signs of acknowledgment, to all the brocade of honor and respect. And as though to forestall any possible irony, she

*Bestuzhevite—a graduate of the "Bestuzhev courses," a form of higher education for women founded by democratic and populist circles in St. Petersburg in 1878 (named after the first director, the historian K.N.

Bestuzhev-Ryumin). This was essentially the first university in Russia for women, who before the 1870s were barred from higher education [tr.].

taught our bigoted family the Yiddish word *kovod,* meaning respect that doesn't come from the heart, but respect for form, for status, respect for appearance as such. (Russians don't have this concept, nor such a word, and at this point the anti-Semite, unbeknownst to himself, may smile warmly and say, "The Jews are different." Well, it's true we don't have this insincere word in our language, but it's well established in practice. Another thing—why is everyone so convinced of the sincerity of boorishness?)

"You know, Dima," Auntie said to her husband, "He's the son of Vakhtant. You remember Vakhtant?" And sighing grievously, she went. Her desires were still stronger than her weariness. Nowadays we don't understand this kind of thing. People were different then.

At last she returned; she hadn't stayed long, just for the ceremonial part, which she found very moving in all respects. She instilled all tinsel and falseness with her own generous faith and meaning. (It's interesting that they sincerely considered themselves materialists, these people whom we will never be like; one must possess exceptional . . . goodness? . . . the same unintelligible word—to act out this paradox.) She came back quickly because, besides her foot, she suffered from diabetes and couldn't indulge in anything at the banquet; nevertheless she came back a little tipsy. The ceremonial speeches had had an effect on her like champagne—she seemed younger, was all flushed, and animatedly told her husband how fine it had all been, how warm. Gradually it came out that the one who had spoken best was she herself. And if you looked at her face at that moment, it would be hard to believe that she was almost eighty, that she had a foot, but the foot was a has-been—that it had a slipper tied to it, enough to make you avert your eyes. And after chatting, after giving her husband some tea, while he went to bed, she filled a tub with hot water and sat there a long time soaking her foot, which had suddenly swelled up "like a big lump" (to use her expression). She sat there for a long time like a lump and stared at her already dead foot.

She was a great doctor.

They don't make doctors like that any more. I easily catch myself falling into this standardized formula, which has seemed foolish to me ever since childhood. They would say (with a "sober" smile) that everything had been better before; it was always the same, nothing was ever better now . . . I often catch myself doing this and easily let it go. From the vantage point of present-day experience the formula, "They don't make them like they used to" seems to me both fair and accurate. It's true; they don't . . .

Not that Auntie was able to cure everybody. Least of all did she have any illusions about medicine. It was not so much that she thought everyone could be helped as that she thought everyone *must* be helped. She might know very well, not in words and not through science, but by her very . . . the same unintelligible word . . . that there was *nothing* to be done; but in that case, if there was even some small way to help, you can be sure that she would do everything. She was unable *not* to do everything she could, even if that everything was something very small, and that necessity she felt to do *absolutely everything possible*—that imperative—was the essence of "doctors in the old days," the kind "they don't make like they used to," the kind Auntie was the last of.

And it was provocatively simple. For example, you have a cold, and she asks you," Are you sleeping well?" You're surprised; what does sleeping have to do with it? She says, "Whoever doesn't sleep well catches a chill, and if you catch a chill, you come down with a cold." She gives you a soporific against a cold. (Allergies, after all, were an invention of the capitalist world.) And you suddenly feel so happy and so comforted by this forgotten way of talking, phrases like "catch a chill," that everything seems right, everything is as it should be, everything lies before you. You become aware of the unparalleled morning with its gray sky and white snow; the felicity of the temperature; someone has passed beneath the window on a horse; smoke curls from a chimney. You say, "My nerves are playing tricks on me, Auntie; there's something wrong because of my nerves." She looks at you icily and passes judgment, "Get a hold of yourself; nothing is caused by nerves." But one time, you don't even ask, yet she presses into your hand an authorization for relief. She saw you yesterday evening, smoking in the kitchen—you need a break.

And if some observant intellectual were to describe Auntie to herself this way, she wouldn't understand it. "What are you talking about?" she'd shrug. She doesn't know the mechanisms of experience. How she goes in to see a patient! No mastery over yourself would allow you to make such a transformation. She simply changes and that's that. There's nothing but lightness and ease. Not eighty years, not a handsome, young husband, not thousands of snotty, black-and-blue, sweaty, pathetic patients breathing in her face—no experience of the past, neither professional nor personal, not a shadow or a patch of herself, with her life, her own urge-filled life. How she lets the patient complain! How reassuringly she asks. "It hurts a lot?" Exactly that, "A lot." She doesn't say "Don't worry" or "It'll go away." None of that. Only two people in the world know how much it hurts at that moment, the patient and the doctor. They are the elect in the matter of pain. After she leaves, the patient is almost proud to be one of the initiates. Never in my life have I seen a greater capacity for *sympathy*. They don't test for sympathy at medical school. Auntie expressed sympathy instantaneously and in that instant renounced forever her own age and pain. All she had to do was turn around and see your face—if you were really ill—and with the speed of light her sympathy would flood down on you. By this, I do not mean at all the presence of a sympathizing person; rather, a total awareness of how you feel, of what it's like for you. This amazing ability, devoid of any element outside itself, this *sym-pathy*, fellow-feeling in the truest sense, became for me the Essence of Doctor. The word for physician. This, and not any false or put-on doctors, none of your Moscow Art Theatre "kindly old souls" or "dear friends." (Although she faithfully believed in the Moscow Art Theatre, and when they showed it on television she would settle down in her armchair with a ready-made expression of satisfaction, as much as to say, "Isn't it true, Dima, none of your modern things can compare with this?" Not that the actor Kachalov was so special. Tarasova was her ideal of beauty. At the word "Anna" she would adjust her elegant coiffure with trembling hand.)[*]

It is with her splendid coiffure that I begin to see her. To the end of her days she wore the hairdo that at one time had been the most becoming to her. Someone's compliment had caught her ear as a girl—something perhaps like "My, what lovely hair"—and that was enough to convince her to keep the style for half a century, for a lifetime. Every morning that gray wave, almost the color of sulfanilamide, would be fluffed up, and the tortoise-shell comb would strike –her hands trembled terribly—in three ways: from front to back, from the top down, and finally right in the middle, always in exactly the same place. Very deft and skilled were her uncertain hands, and now I also see the artillery fire of their shakiness: the narrow teeth of the comb fall short, then overshoot, then hit directly on target. That is, I see before me her hands erratically bustling, but always striking at a target, always doing something. . . It's not my typewriter clattering now; it's Auntie washing dishes; it's her typical way of hitting the cups against the faucet. If she broke a cup—which was known to happen, and she had very expensive cups—of course she felt very badly about it, but with the same ineffable maidenliness surviving from the time of her first hairdo, she would immediately announce the calamity to all observers in the kitchen, presenting it as her eternal endearing failing. Something like, "Oh, there I go again." And even her posture would change as she threw the pieces in the trash; even the bend of her waist (what waist could there be any more?) and the tilt of her head were again like a girl's. The most taboo form of behavior for an observer at such a moment was pity. To notice age in her was absolutely forbidden.

Even now I want to reach out and kiss Auntie (which I never did, although I loved her more than many I have kissed) . . . now while the cups are clattering against the faucet.

She would throw out fifty or a hundred rubles worth in the trash with the gesture of a very rich person, forestalling our false chorus of sympathy. Next came the most difficult thing of all for her. But she

---

[*]Vasily I. *Kachalov* (1875–1948) was a leading actor of the Moscow Art Theatre, which he joined in 1900. Alla K. *Tarasova* (1898–1973) began her career with the Moscow Art Theater in 1916 and was especially famous for her "Anna Karenina" [tr.].

was a decisive person; she didn't put things off, didn't procrastinate. For an instant, in front of the door, she would lose heart, with a variety of cups in her hands—and she would become even more trim-looking; even her rounded back would straighten. It was hard not to believe in this optical illusion. Then she would push the door open, and go sailing through with almost the same summery chirping as in a painting by Serov from the same 1910s when she was young. It is morning: through the washed leaves satiated sunlight has spattered color over the worn parquet floor; a bouquet of dawn-plucked lilacs has frozen in its drops. Almost a peignoir and an étude by Scriabin—as though the print on the wall was not a print but a mirror. "Dima, what a shame. I broke my favorite china cup."

Ah, there's no denying it: we remember all our lives the way we were loved.

Dima was my dearly beloved uncle by blood. In these remembrances he remains beyond the door, in the shadow, one leg over the other, next to a bouquet, himself a variety of bouquet—his surgeon's musical fingers drum on the tablecloth, he waits for his tea, he smiles attentively and gently, like a good person who has nothing to say.

And so at first I see her coiffure (or more precisely, her comb), then her hands. Now she's fixing some jam; the old fashioned, scoured-out copper tub, back before the catastrophe, gleams like the sun; its bottom is covered by a scarlet layer of select strawberries, the most expensive at the market, and on top coarse and fine fragments from a large, old-fashioned sugar cake glisten. All of this is precious. The crown, the scepter, and the globe—all of it together. (In the family we loved to say that Auntie was as magnificent as Catherine the Great.) And over this entire empire ruled her hand with its golden spoon. She would catch her hands trembling and pretend these were the very movements she wanted to make. (Just as in painting—the use of accident as an artistic method.)

I see her comb, her coiffure, her hands . . . and suddenly I see all of my aunt distinctly, as though I had been rubbing and rubbing the back of a decal, then finally, holding my breath, torturing my own hand with smoothness and slowness, I pull the back away and—it worked! The strip didn't break anywhere. The bright, strong colors of her Chinese jacket (quilted, silk), her rounded back with the jacket's bouquet between her shoulders, and the foot with the bandaged slipper—they all show through clearly. The flowers on her back are elegant and curly, a Chinese type of chrysanthemum. She loves to be given these for her jubilee celebration, which never passes. (Every day a basket is brought from the thankful, and Auntie's room is always like an actress's after a benefit; and every day, to make room, another faded basketful is put out on the stair). The flowers on her back are the same as on her coffin.

In our extended, live-together family there were a number of established formulas, legitimized ways of expressing our admiration for Auntie. The only thing I don't know is what served as the coefficient for organizing her *personal data*, the information from official questionnaires—age, sex, marital status, nationality. Of course our family was too intelligent to descend to the personnel-office level. No one ever spoke of such things, but the hundred-percent silence always spoke for itself. The silence said that people did not speak about these things, but *knew*. She was fifteen years older than uncle. They had no children. And she was Jewish. For me, the child, the adolescent, the young man, she never had age or sex or nationality. At the same time all other relatives had these things. Somehow this contradiction was never noticed.

We all played the game of accepting without question all the conventions she required. Our indulgence was encouraged too generously, and our awkward scenes had an ever grateful audience. Who knows who was better at acting noble, but everyone overacted. I think nevertheless that she saw through it; not we. Weren't her exaggerated conventions a lofty reaction to our unconventionality? Wasn't that why the only person she was afraid of and catered to (beyond all measure) was Pavlovna, our cook? Pavlovna had the option of not playing our game. She *knew* that Auntie was Jewish and that she was an old woman and who her husband was . . . and that there were no children . . . and that death was near. Pavlovna knew how to reveal her not very clever but ruthlessly accurate knowledge, with exaggerated servility, and without giving it verbal expression; in return for her silence she would take, with vain and fussy gratitude, as much as she wanted and whatever came to hand, including those same cups.

We really did love Auntie, but this love was declared quite openly. Auntie was a Real Human Being! This has a bitter sound to it. How often we put words in capital letters in order to conceal the very requirement for "personal data," the automatism of our own membership in the human race, the automatism of races. Excessive admiration of someone else's merits always smacks of something. Either fawning or apartheid. She was a real human being—big, expansive, passionate, *very lively*, generous, and very *distinguished* (Distinguished Scientist—that title too had been awarded her.) In general I think now that for all the forty years of her marriage she *worked* at being Auntie to us, with all of her remarkable abilities and came to be *like one of the family*. (That's also why she and Pavlovna were able to reach a mutual understanding; the latter was also a real human being.) I think that for my family she was still a Jew, if for no other reason than that I did not know it and that no one ever once said it (the word *Jew*).

We had every reason to extol her and idolize her. She did so much for everyone. None of us did anything like it, even for ourselves. She saved me from death, and my brother, and three times my uncle (her husband). And how many times she simply helped us (when our lives were not in danger) can't be counted. The list grew longer and with the years was canonized as the items rolled backward out of sight. It was the custom, however, to refer to this indirectly, not to *remember* it; thus, what I just said was right—she was *like one of the family.*

Another thing I found out much later, after her death, was what she was *like a wife.* It turns out that throughout the forty years of their marriage she and uncle were not registered. This old news suddenly became an up-to-date legend, stylish and chic, a model of two truly civilized persons' independence of empty form. All the others had registered their marriages.

Time gives way beneath the feet like a muddy bottom. The structural components of the story stick out, all rusty. This is not life; it turns out to be the subject of a story. And in the retelling it is no longer alive. Many years after the fact, information germinates and sprouts up in our family in the form of a funeral monument.

Out of it I am now building a pedestal.

She was a great doctor, but there's one puzzling question I cannot escape: "What actually did she know about her illness?" Sometimes it seems she could not have failed to know; other times it seems she knew nothing.

She tried her foot and then she tried a heart attack. She almost lost her foot as a result of the heart attack. Somehow or other she dragged herself back from this attack. And from the realization that this time she'd had a narrow esacpe. (In the given instance, as a doctor, she certainly could have told herself that.) She grew so cheerful and young—her foot even began to fit into her slipper again—that none of us could express our happiness enough. Again there came meetings, executive boards, the defense of dissertations, consultations (the title-bearing gangsters again). (To cure a murderer is without question a sacred principle for a physician. But you can't try to cure them with greater effort and attention than you give to their potential victims, can you? But you can. The ironies of the law are the proof of its existence, as in England.) And now I see her again in the kitchen, ruling over her gleaming sun-tub.

But the tub had risen not for long.

Auntie was dying. That was not yet true for anyone—except herself. She so lost her strength that, weary and forgetting, every day she would take an unwitting step closer to death. Then she'd wake with a start and once again stop dying. Her foot turned completely black and she firmly insisted on amputation, although it was clear to everyone but her that by now an operation was beyond her strength. Her foot, a heart attack, her foot, a stroke. . . . And then she fastened onto life with new strength; of all of us, only she had so much.

The bed. She demanded a *different* bed. For some reason she especially looked to me for physical assistance. She summoned me for instructions. I understood her mumbling poorly, but agreed to everything, saw nothing very complex in the assignment. "Repeat it," she suddenly said very clearly. And oh, with what vexation she turned away from my unparalyzed prattle.

We brought in the bed. It was a special bed from a hospital. It was fouled up in that awkward way that only happens with people remote from technology. Of course none of the fixtures for adjusting the position of the body could be made to work. Countless times this bed covered with institutional paint, lost not only its form but its contour and became literally ungainly. We carried this monster into Auntie's shelter of mirrors, crystal, carpets, and polish, and I couldn't recognize the room. It was as though all the objects had fled from the bed, taken refuge in the corners, shrank back with a premonition of social change. In reality it was just that a place had been hastily cleared for the bed. I remember that youthful sense of muscles and strength, exaggerated and inappropriate to the task of the laborer—showing your muscles; your veins sticking out for an old, paralyzed, dying person to see. An especially uncomfortable feeling haunted me because of this. I clutched at the corners, tripped, knocked my knuckles, and it was as though the bed was making me into its likeness.

Auntie was sitting in the middle of the room, directing the operation. That's how I remember it. But she couldn't have been sitting in the middle; she couldn't sit up; and the middle had just been cleared for the bed. Her gaze burned with the light of red hot coals. Her eyes had never been so deep. She desperately wanted to move from her resting place of forty years; she was already in that other bed, the bed we were just bringing in the door; that is why I remember her in the middle. We were not supposed to injure the "unit," we who didn't understand anything about it. We were simply supposed to open it and partly reclose it to produce higher, lower, and higher positions in its deadly, immobile, flat surfaces. But nothing would work for us. It was impossible to be such fools. It was obvious she would have to do it herself . . . I still have the recollection that she finally got up herself; fixed everything as it was supposed to be—"See, it's not so hard. You just have to go about it with some intelligence"—and having arranged things, lay back down in her paralysis, leaving it to us to move the pillows, quilt, and mattresses, work more suitable to our level of development. Although here too we committed grievous errors.

My God, in thirty years she hasn't changed a bit. During the winter of the blockade of Leningrad, when she and I were sawing wood together for the stove, she, fifty years old, lost her temper at me, a five-year-old, in exactly the same way as now. She was offended to the point of tears by an argument about who was supposed to pull in which direction. Our saw bent and groaned while we tried to save each other's fingers. "Olga!" she finally called my mother. "Take away your hooligan. He's deliberately tormenting me. He won't saw in the right direction and he's doing it on purpose." I, too, was terribly offended by her. Not for yelling at me, but for suspecting me of "doing it on purpose," when I hadn't the slightest ulterior motive and would never do anything bad on purpose. I wasn't such a bad child then, it seems to me now. Sobbing, we left the saw sticking out of the half-sawed log. Ten minutes later, all cheerful, she came to make peace with me, bringing "the last bit" of some trifling thing, some crust or crumb. So it seems that only I have changed. She could never get used to the only change in her life, one that was still in the offing. Of course she did not believe in the other world. (Oh, no! But I still don't understand it. Their generation was sure there was no God; yet they upheld the Christian commandments far better than I.)

We moved her into the other bed; for a long time she adjusted herself with obvious satisfaction, never looking back at the abandoned marital couch. I had the impression, I realize now, of a great sigh of relief when we lifted her away from it—away from everything that, despite her medical experience, she continued to not understand; it seems she understood it then irreversibly. She would never return to that bed. We didn't understand; we, like idiots, understood none of the things she knew so well, knew better than anyone: what a sick person is, how they feel, what they really need. Now she herself needed that kind of understanding, but none of us could repay what we owed her. When she had gotten herself settled she said to us, with the most profound, original meaning: "Thank you."* As though we had actually done something for her, as though we understood. "Was it very heavy?" she asked me sympathetically. "Of course not. What're you saying, Auntie? It was light." I should not have answered her that way.

This bed also did not suit her after all. She was objectively uncomfortable. And then we brought in the last bed, grandmother's, on which all of us, all our family, died. And on this bed, straightening the pillow for the last time, stroking the smooth fold of the sheet over the quilt with her trembling hand and closing her eyes, Auntie sighed with relief: "At last I feel comfortable." The bed was in the center of the room like a coffin and her face was at rest.

On that very day that other woman's life suddenly ended, that subject of a story.

But Auntie survived her. "At last I feel comfortable."

The bed was in the middle of a strangely emptied room, where the objects had abandoned the owner in the nick of time, a moment before the owner abandoned them. They had cheap expressions on their faces. These precious-since-childhood surfaces and boundaries turned out simply to be old objects. They shun the iron object in the center; they are lovely objects; they are from Karelia. And Auntie feels comfortable. She can't take them with her.

*In Russian, literally, "God save" [tr.].

But she took them.

In the middle of a burial mound stands a bed with nickel-plated pine cones, worn down to the brass beneath. Half-sitting and comfortable on the bed, with her eyelids closed and her jaws bandaged, is Auntie in her favorite Chinese jacket, with her sunlike tub full of strawberry jam on her knees. In one hand she has a stethoscope, in the other an American thermometer reminiscent of the timing mechanism on a bomb. An apparatus for measuring blood pressure is at her feet. Not forgotten are those cups which are still intact, the dissertation submitted for consideration, the yellow Venus de Milo which she brought with her to our house (according to the stories). Uncle, and behind him the chauffeur, stand modestly to the side, already half-covered by the dirt flying down from above. Noiselessly an automobile rolls up, with a gleaming reindeer on the hood. (As a regular thing she would have the reindeer remounted from one model to the next, ignoring the fact that it was out of style.) That means the reindeer is here too. . . . And our whole apartment is already here, under crumbling time, spilling down, snatching at my entire past with the broken pieces of blockade ice. Everything to which I am in some way obligated is being buried in this mound; time comes pouring, crumbling down into it, with live humanity and Darwinian humaneness, with principles and decency, with everything that her bearers had not taken away, with everything that has made of me the pathetic creature they call a human being because of the generally similar traits; that is, comes spilling down with me. But I myself have time to throw down the last spade and turn around shaggily to face the darkly gleaming warmth of an honest animalism . . .

For since the time when they ceased to exist—at first my grandmother, who was even finer, even purer than my aunt, then my aunt, who, carrying on the torch, replaced my grandmother (and now that place is empty for——. . . I will not forgive them for it)—for since the time when those last people ceased to exist, the world has not grown better but I have grown worse.

Dear Lord, after death there will be no memory of Thee. I have already looked upon Thy countenance. If a person is sitting in a deep well, why would it not seem to him that he is looking out of the world and not into the world? But if one were to get out of the well . . . and find that in all four directions it's ever so even, ever so empty; there's nothing; except the well hole, out of which you crawled? I hope, Lord, that the terrain where you are is at least slightly broken.

Why is a pupil—granted, not very competent, but hard-working—placed at the bottom of that bottomless prison and forgotten? Is it so that throughout my life I could observe that single star—granted that it is farther away than is visible to an eye not furnished with a well hole? I have already mastered it.

Oh God! Uncle! Auntie! Mama! I cry . . .

In one's own city sometimes there are little places where one has never been. Especially in the vicinity of tourist attractions, famous sites that overwhelm their surroundings. Smolny (with the flag and the statue of Lenin), and to the left the bell tower of the Smolny monastery. You always know they are there; that travelers are being brought right up to them and will pay no more attention to them than to a postcard. Then there will come an occasion when you will have to hunt for an address (it turns out there are houses there too, and streets, and people live there), and to the left of the bell tower, to the left of the regional committee building of the Komsomol, to the left of the monks' honeycomb cells, there is a crooked street (a rarity in Leningrad), hundred-year old trees, and your aunt's Institute (the former House of Invalids, which is why it's so beautiful; there aren't many medical institutions so well designed and built—they're usually just some old building). Suddenly everything is so fine that even the out-of-the-way fence looks like a thing of beauty. It's as though everything here has remained intact within the shadow of the tourist attraction. A fence instead of the iron grating, which has been removed, and a checkpoint instead of a sentry box. To make up for it, the gates are still in one piece, and an elderly, invalid janitor stands in place by the gates of the House of Invalids (one of their own, undoubtedly). The ornate, baroque gatepieces are obligingly open, and finally I read on the board the exact name of Auntie's institution (Ministry of Health, Regional Executive Committee . . . a great many words had replaced three—House of Invalids). I have to step aside and let a black Volga pass. From its depths an epaulet flashes. The invalid leaps on his stump of a leg and salutes. There is a hefty rustling sound as the general, sitting back, is swept down the brick pathway, wearing his black Volga like a fat fur coat. I drag along in his wake onto the "territory" of the hospital.

"Going to the funeral?" the invalid asks, not to be strict but to show he is one of the initiates.

"Yes."

The pathway bricks are red, in keeping with the maple leaves that are being swept to the side with great care and thoroughness by an idiot. He looks like a homemade stuffed doll, a cheap toy soldier; another one, a little brighter, priding himself on the tool that has been entrusted to him, is going after cigarette butts and scraps with his paper spearer. A cripple with a brick-red snout, standing confidently on a wooden leg with a black sucker on the tip, is breaking up bricks for the pathway with a heavy instrument that looks like his wooden leg turned upside down. Gray, laundered old women hover here and there about the park like those same autumn spider webs. Ophelias who have survived with bouquets of luxurious leaves . . . There is work therapy in the air, it is a beautiful, sunny day. The air has grown empty, and the sunlight has spread out evenly, unimpeded, as though it were the air itself. There is no shade. Shade has been illuminated from within by the radiance of the leaves all aflame; and there is premature smoke (don't let children play with matches) gathered over the heads of the concentrated group of retarded persons. The ancient smell of rotting leaves, the rejuvenating smell of burning leaves. Autumn cleaning. Everything is thrown around, but a hasty order is discernible through the chaos. Space is tidied up. The air has been aired out. The path is newly red. This morning the retarded aren't yet fully awake; the early rising wounded veterans (wounds so early?) and the autumnal old women have entered into a great agreement with the autumn. "You going there?" said an extreme oligophrenic with respect. Where was I going? I stood at the end of the walkway peering into the hospital yard, I had to step back off the edge into a pile of leaves, which pleasantly gave beneath my feet. The oligophrenic intelligently withdrew to the other side. Two Volgas passed between us, two at once. Aha, they're going there. Where I'm going. Auntie's there.

At the mortuary there had been a problem. We couldn't recognize her. Her hairdo wasn't full enough. None of us could raise a hand to fluff it to its usual fullness. With her was Nektor Berilashvili, who turned out to be very near and dear to her. He brought a hairdresser, virtually in irons. "No one wants money anymore," he was incensed. "How much?" we were curious. "Agh," he waved his hand. "A hundred." The words had the crisp sound of a new bill. Auntie didn't stint herself.

Now Auntie looked okay. Her face was properly important, lovely, and at peace, though just a bit wary. She was obviously listening to what was being said and wasn't entirely happy with it. Her merits were being enumerated languidly. Corpses of epithets piled up—not one living word. "Her bright countenance . . . never . . . always in our hearts . . ." The first general, who had been the first speaker (a good general, a full one, four stars, lifeless in his preoccupation), drove off. Through the doors of the conference hall, opened to the autumn day, we could hear the disrespectfully hasty roar of his departing Volga. "Rest in peace," he had said again, lowering his gaze before the coffin, and already the car doors were slamming. "To Smolny!"—to get to a meeting on time. He had had time mainly to dwell on her wartime services: "Never will we forget them." They'd forgotten already. The war, the blockade, the living, and the dead—all forgotten. There was no time anymore to remember Auntie. I knew she had been written off long before her death. Changed historical circumstances allowed them to show up at the memorial ceremony. And that was fine. New times had come, in which old men had to hurry. And if the general would still have time puffing, out of breath, to reach his next star, it would be on only one condition—that he not step off the carpeted racetrack for one moment. After the general there was a reluctance to speak, as though in driving off, he had left behind an ear encircled by graying hair and reflecting the golden gleam of shoulder braid. And the next speaker droned on the exact same way, and the ones after him. They just couldn't warm up. The kin of the deceased, divided by the coffin like streams of water by the bow of a ship, looked like the poor relatives of the speakers. On the left, we crowded together; on the right, the Jewish relatives. I hadn't known there were so many of them. Not one familiar face. It seemed to me I had seen one of them fleetingly in the entrance hall. He had caught my glance and nodded. Gray, attentively distraught eyes, as though nearsighted. Why was it I had never? . . . any of them? I still didn't understand, but I felt awkward, uncomfortable—ashamed in general. But I assumed it was the speakers that displeased me, not we ourselves, not I myself. "Services recognized as they deserved . . . with a medal." Auntie was a human being. Impossible to reward her "as deserved." Death is death. Nevertheless, I was beginning to understand something. The ritual, cultish rouge was coming off the cheeks. Stalin was dying a second time, fifteen years later. Because for that whole era there was nothing for me to remember any more but my aunt, a crystal pure representative, it turns out, after all, of Stalin's times.

Auntie was more and more strongly displeased by the funereal droning of the speakers. At first, her attitude was, it's not bad: why, there are academicians, professors, generals among the guests . . . But after a while she finally died of boredom. At a certain moment, I had the distinct impression she was about to get up and give a speech herself. She would have found the right words! She knew how to talk from the heart. The urge to cheer people up was always strong in her, and she always contrived a way to speak praise from the heart to people who were not even worth one degree of her warmth. It is not an exaggeration, not just imagery, to say that Auntie was the liveliest one at her own funeral. But here too, just as when she died, she couldn't come to her own assistance, and no one else came either, though everyone had crowded then around her bed and so too now, around her coffin. And now, too, there was nothing for her to do but turn away in vexation. Auntie lay back in the coffin, and we carried her out along with the bed, totally dissatisfied with the ceremony. Out into the autumn sun of the hospital yard. And of course I once again held up my end . . . side by side with the attentively gray-eyed man, who again nodded to me. "What are you saying, Auntie? It's light . . ."

The yard had become unrecognizable. It was thick with people. Nearest to the doors, the nurses and aides were sobbing with unusual respect for the merits of the deceased as expressed in the importance of those who had come to the funeral. Glowering orderlies, not yet recovered from their hangovers, mixed in with cripples, formed the next row, with their collective dark blue shoulders pressing back the crowd of the retarded, who in turn pressed back the old women, standing timidly behind an invisible line. Their faces were lit with a steady glow of shy delight. The light spilled over onto us. We grew more dignified. The relatives at a funeral are also important officials. Tassels on the coffin, the gold braid of the cover, a pillow with a medal on it, sobbing chief nurses . . . a general! . . . (there was another, not in such a hurry) . . . automobiles with drivers opening the doors . . . the autumn gold of a brass band, the short-winded sunshine of a bass horn—and cymbals! They stood there in shy delight, not breaking discipline in the slightest way, in patches, but clean, leaning on their rakes and shovels—this anti-insurgent group. The general took his seat in the car and gleamed there, within, as though the bass horn was being driven away. They all followed him with a single look, unblinking. The coffin sailed past, its bow cutting the human wave into two humanities—the lesser ones flowing off to the right in larger numbers than the normal, successful, and deserving ones to the left. Behind the coffin the water did not meet again, separated by a jetty of border-guard orderlies. "We come from them!" Such is the pride I read on the generalized, uniformed face of an idiot. They gazed with rapture upon what they would have become, if they had ventured out into the world as we had. It was from them that we had come, so that now, at the end of the laborious path, we could flash with noble gray on our heads and tinkle with medals. They come from us, and we from them. They had not ventured out, fearing the orderlies—whom we had bribed, then subjugated. Difficult and glorious had been our path into the ranks of doctors, professors, academicians, generals! Many of us had possessed unusual talent and energy, and all this energy and talent had gone to progress, so that a medal might tinkle and a door slam obligingly upon a prestigious coffin on wheels . . .

But if they are half human, we are too . . . they didn't take hold, we lost our hold. What we lost was precisely the half they still have in its entirety. To break into pairs, as in kindergarten, to take hands, to pretend to be one. Only in that way would it not be terrifying to come before Him. Never, never to have forgotten what we were; never to have agreed to all this. Here we stand in a gray, distinguished line, with large and small heads, like so many flowers, micro- and macro-cephalic, with the border-guard orderlies, and the coffin of the last living person in the world between us! Here we go, shedding our last drop of blood to become what you deservedly take delight in. Dead, we are burying a living person; and with our brilliance we blind the living. For they are alive, the retarded ones! That was what ran like autumn cold between my shoulder blades, between my youthfully straining muscles. Alive and without sin. For what sin do they have on their souls other than what's in their fists or pockets? Besides, their pockets had prudently been sewn shut. And here we are, with coffins of worthiness and experience on our shoulders. And if one were to glance first into the soul of an idiot, see the close, pale blue bottom in his eyes, and then suddenly look into the soul of that same general, or of any of us—then Lord God, it would be better not to look at what we're worth. We are worth a lot, worth as much as we've paid. And we have paid everything. And I am far, oh how far, from looking into the worn, treacherous blind alleys of our life's ways, the inevitable peristalses of each career. I deliberately assume that our entire procession is made up of crystal-pure, industrious, talented people who have devoted themselves to the cause (even if in capital letters). And I propose to look into our souls, totally free of all suspicion—and I pull back in fright. They don't come running over to us either, frozen stockstill not only out of rapture, surely, but also out of terror, out of fear! Not only the halfwits but we too have difficulty separating horror from ecstasy, ecstasy from fear, and we can't separate them, because we don't understand them. More power to the retarded. From the very first, wise as he was, he took fright; even then in the cradle—or even earlier, in the belly—he wouldn't come over to us. He stays there in the cradle with his toy rakes and shovels and does not cry for his doctor. The doctor is alive; you are the dead ones. None of us could really look Death in the eye, and not because it's frightening but because we have already. Souls not born to Paradise; souls that died in Hades; Auntie flows between us like the Styx.

We walked in an unliving line down the bloody path through the park. It had already been cleaned up thoroughly. (When had they had time?) Not allowed through by the orderlies, the retarded stayed back at the end of the path, spreading out to form a gray wall; then they blended into the fence and were gone. My last glimpse was of a thoroughly emptied world—beyond the still and painted park rose a burial mound, to which patients one by one were going to see their doctor.

Which of us two is alive? I? Or my idea of myself?

She was a great doctor, but even now with all these pages I have not freed myself of that same old banal uncertainty. What did she know, as a doctor, about her own illness and death? That is, as far as knowing goes, to judge by these written pages, she knew, she must have known. But how did she handle this knowledge of hers? Thus I haven't answered my question. I continue, as before, preoccupied with what methods professionals use to deal with their knowledge in cases where their methods can be applied to themselves? How does a writer write to his beloved? How does a gynecologist sleep with his wife? How does a prosecutor take bribes? What kind of a lock does a thief use? What kind of treat does a cook make for himself? How does a builder live in his own house? How does a gigolo treat himself when he's alone? How does God view the crown of his Creation? When I think about these things I naturally conclude that great specialists are people too. Because the narrow and secret pathways by which their consciousness moves in such acute cases, circumventing their own craftsmanship, intelligence, and experience, is such a victory of the human over man—always and in every case!—that one can only thrust one's face once more toward Him, who for our redemption, consists of blueness, clouds, and stars, and ask: Lord, how much faith can one have in Thee if that too is foreseen by Thy Providence?

Three Songs*
by Yuz Aleshkovsky

Lesbian Song

Let them frisk us all they can during watch.
When the warder goes into the barrack,
we'll cry our fill to a concertina
and set our wedding table.

My little mate is a good-looking lady,
he pours me a glass of thick tea,
and instead of red caviar spreads lipstick
on a hunk of grey bread.

He doesn't wear lipstick himself,
and he walks with a masculine gait,
he seems like a man to me,
only his whiskers don't grow.

The girls stamp "The Gypsy Girl" tap-tap,
the old gals cry out "Kiss the Bride,"
and one lesbian weeps in the arms
of the unmarried girls.

Oh, let's have a smoke of Siberian weed,
the girls will have another drink,
to the bitter kiss, the lesbian kiss,
to our first married night.

It's sweet in the zone here and unbothered,
I don't send my husband outside any mail,
and he shall never, never know
that I love Maruska Belova.

*Translated by H. William Tjalsma.

Cigarette Butt

We were walking back to the zone
from the white hell of Kolyma.
I spotted a cigarette butt smeared with red lipstick
and broke ranks to pick it up.

"Stop or I'll shoot," yelled the escort.
His damned mutt tore my pea jacket.
"Take it easy, chief, old boy,
I'm already back in line."

I haven't seen a lady for years.
Finally now I'm in luck. Probably
oh, cigarette butt, fierce wind
carried you from a TU-104 to me.

And all the way back to the zone
Kopalin, who strangled his wife,
and one active fag couldn't
tear their eyes from my cigarette butt.

With whom are you fooling around now, bitch,
sucking on a single cigarette with whom?
You get drunk, you don't buy a ticket at Vnukovo
just to fly over me here.

I threw drinking parties in your honor,
gave everybody French cognac to drink.
I got drunk myself from the way you smoked a Troika,
the one with the golden rim at the end.

I lost that cigarette butt at cards,
though it was dearer to me than a thousand.
Even here I haven't any luck
from grieving for my queen of hearts.

I've lost all my clothes playing cards
and my sugar ration two years in advance.
So here I sit on my bunk hugging my knees
with nothing to wear to roll call.

That cigarette butt was my downfall,
cursing no one, blaming nobody.
The big guys here among the cons
were impressed with my style.

I went to the guard shack barefooted,
like Christ, calm, quiet.

For ten days I painted my hand-rolled cigs
with my bloody lips.

"Scoundrel, you blew a million
on fancy women on the outside,"
"That's right," I say, to the citizen warder.
"Only, no point, citizen warder,
Wiping my lips with your cuff!"

Personal Meeting

I was serving my time in Siberia,
was considered a hard working guy,
and broke my back to get
a personal meeting with my wife.

I wrote: "Show up, wife, I miss you,
living here three miles from the camp station."
I waited, then stopped waiting, worried myself to death,
kept climbing up on the roof to watch.

My heart started aching when I saw the poor thing
bent to the ground from her rucksack.
But the zeks looked at her, hungry, from the roof,
they looked at my plain-looking woman.

I stood there in front of the guard shack,
as the warder frisked my wife,
but my letters had told her clearly
how to hide homebrew under her skirt.

So they locked us in the room,
the silly fool neither alive nor dead,
while I'm like at my trial, red-faced
and mixing up my words.

She perched on a bench
and I lay down on an old mattress.
Yesterday, the embezzler Lavochkin slept here with his wife;
day before that, the pickpocket Monia Kats.

The gray wallpaper was pretty faded,
there was a peephole in the iron door.
In the corner the portrait of Comrade Kalinin
was silent, like the icon in our shack.

We grabbed a bite, I drank the homebrew
and smoked a hand-rolled cigarette. . . . Ah, life,

make the bed wife, the government bed,
then lie down beside me like you used to do.

The duty warders toss jokes through the peephole,
the zeks roar sorrowfully outside the window:
"Stepan, give us your spouse for a minute,
we'll stretch her out for the lot of us."

Oh, people, people, people, you're not serious,
you need your heads examined.
This is my wife here and it's not
kolkhoz bulls servicing your cows.

I'm mad at them all and sorry for 'em too,
you don't share your wife with everyone . . .
. . . at dawn it was like the escort
beating an iron rail in my heart.

Pour me something, wife, it's goodbye.
Get into the greenish railroad car yourself.
Don't grieve, they'll give us a chance next winter,
don't forget- -no, not me, you dope- -
don't forget how to hide the home brew.

Poems and a Design*
by Andrei Voznesensky

Shchipov Lane

For Andrei Tarkovsky

Thieves' yards beyond the Moskva River,
you didn't know, our Bethlehems,
that the women beat their rugs
with a woven Olympian emblem.

Not only for the cap do I thank you,
for Moscow's courtyard leaven,
that, having cut "I love you" on a poplar,
slashed my skin with a safety razor.

I thank you for the fairy-tale lexicon—
not Oxford's, not Massachusetts's—
when a gang leader, in lunar terror,
came to a dance with a blackjack.

We made a cosmic mess of things, Andrei,
but we'll come and help at a whistle . . .
Long ago they put asphalt on the yard
and on our first meeting place beyond
the rubbish heap.

After the Rain

Grove, you are as a pagan woman,
cleansed and led into Christianity.
How bright is the echo after the rain.
How responsive your heart after tears!

*Translated by H. William Tjalsma.

Hexameter

Don't stoop to words against
inadmissible abuse.
The philistines dash in unexpectedly?
Don't offend asses.

Esenin

Light bulbs hang
by eternal cords from the ceiling.
Only the poet
hangs there by his white spinal cord.

After

—Here's the little apartment of the poet. His pen on his
        Empire-style desk . . .
—But what's a "pen"?
—It's been guided by the hand of Derzhavin, Matthew, and Luke
        . . .
—But what's a "hand"?
—That's a kind of lever
that transforms an idea into a creation, chiseling it for the centuries:
"Man—that is the meaning of the universe"
"Man shall be glorious forever and ever."
—How did you put it? —"Man"?

Two Stories[*]
by Fazil Iskander

A Sexy Little Giant

I think that the best, most idyllic period of my friendship with Marat was the early period when he worked as a photographer on the quay boulevard opposite the theater. He had a small stand for displaying samples of his work there, but he would either sit on the seawall over the shore or walk back and forth nearby. From this vantage point he would cast an eagle eye, or something which was supposed to be an eagle eye, over all the approaching women, as well as the women who stopped by the stand to look at his samples.

He often cast the eagle eye on women who were walking away as well; and I was always amazed at their insensitivity, because his gaze was so eloquent that it struck me as impossible not to feel it and turn around.

He liked me then because I was a good audience for his stories of romantic adventure. There was no end or limit to these adventures, and my patience as a listener was inexhaustible.

A lot of people took an ironic attitude toward his stories, but I showed only attention and amazement; and this was enough to make him share his many secrets of the heart with me.

Still, we must be precise: he shared the secrets of his heart with everyone; but not everyone catered to his effusions. And I think I did more than others.

Marat was of short stature, solidly built, with thick grown-together brows which he controlled the way a horse controls its tail. That is, he could bring them together menacingly, or arch them both in surprise, or one sarcastically. This apparently made quite an impression on women, when combined with the other features of his face, among which we should note (of course, we have to do so rather delicately) a fairly large hook nose. Besides everything else, the general expression of romantic energy which was typical of his face made his stories seem more realistic, to me at least.

[*]Translated by Carl R. Proffer.

Sometimes, most often coming back from fishing, I would walk past his domain; and if he was not busy with clients, I would stop, we would sit down on a bench or on the seawall, and he would tell me his latest story.

When telling a story, he never took his eyes off the women who were walking on the boulevard, and he simultaneously surveyed those who were passing on the quay street as well. Sometimes to see the latter better he would have to tilt his head or slightly lean to one side to find an opening in the growth of oleanders through which he looked at the street.

If he was busy with a customer when I came, he would tilt his head a bit interrogatively in my direction, which meant: do you have time to wait until I get rid of these people?

Sometimes, seeing me, but busy with clients, he would wave his hand ironically, as if to say: there are many new impressions, but now is not the time or place to talk about them.

The stories themselves were accompanied by a graphic acting out of certain details of amatory propinquity. This demonstration of the various positions of love often embarrassed me, all the more so that he forced me to assume the role of mannikin-partner. Usually I tried to avoid these efforts of his, attempting to guide his story into the realm of pure verbal art, in which area he attained no little eloquence.

The great variety of rendezvous settings in his stories was amazing by itself: parks, beaches at night, groves of trees at the edge of town, ship cabins, photolaboratories, rooms in a Turkish bath, out at sea, in the back seat of a car, deep in the earth in a labyrinth of cavern stalagmites, and finally, high above the earth in the control booth of the port's cable car, where he had several vertiginous meetings with the cable-car operator.

The stories about successful rendezvous always ended with the same sacramental sentence:

"Well, what can I tell you? . . . She was satisfied, really satisfied . . ."

Sometimes, emphasizing that he had managed to avoid the threat of forced marriage, he would end his story this way:

"Well, what can I tell you. . . . I kept my passport clean . . ."

Sometimes he would stun me with an unexpected question. For example, once he asked me:

"Have you ever drunk pomegranate juice from the breast of your beloved?"

"What?" I said in disbelief.

"Pomegranate juice from the breast of your beloved," he repeated; and to make this more vivid, somewhat bending back, he thrust his own breast out as if trying to remind me of the generally-accepted pose for drinking pomegranate juice from one's beloved.

"No, of course not," I replied, my voice indicating that not only was

I unacquainted with this method of quenching thirst, but that I doubted its possibility on technical grounds. Understanding this without any words, without words he showed me how it is done.

"Very simple," he said, and continuing to thrust his chest out he brought his palms together beside it, as if closing up the sides of a dam. "He who has not drunk pomegranate juice from the breast of his beloved," he observed instructively, "does not know what true ecstasy is. It's even better than sipping cognac from your beloved's navel . . ."

"Oh, come on," I said to him, "there can't be much room for cognac there."

"The point is not in the quantity . . . you drunkard," he interrupted me, "the point is in the ecstasy . . ."

Sometimes he brought his photographs to the offices of *The Red Subtropics*, where I worked. They were shots of picturesque parts of our region, popular singers, or scenes from plays on road tours.

Occasionally, as I was looking at his picturesque photographs of our landscapes, he would point to some spot in the picture and say:

"Right here is where she and I were sitting at first. . . . And then we went down here, into the grove. . . . Well, what can I tell you. . . . She was so satisfied, really satisfied . . ."

As a rule his photographs were accompanied by fairly extensive captions which, as a rule, had to be recopied cleanly. But I did this for the sake of his stories and our friendship, because as soon as I started to grumble he would launch into one of his interminable stories, and I became an involuntary listener.

The captions to the pictures which he gave me were both clumsy and stunning in their monstrous messiness. Sometimes they were started in pencil, or with a loose piece of lead, and then finished in ink. Sometimes vice-versa. The handwriting looked as if he had done the captions in a car racing along at 100 kilometers an hour.

The photographs, I have to say, were always of the highest quality; and if many of them did not make it into the paper, it was only because when photographing women on stage he often managed to get them from an angle that made it appear that he had snapped them after jumping down into the orchestra pit.

Apropos of the photographs: one time after a trip to Moscow, besides stories about his conquests of credulous Muscovite girls, Marat brought back an original photo. In the subway he happened onto, and photographed, the following scene: on one side of the car all the passengers are sitting reading books or magazines, but on the other side all the passengers are either dozing or sleeping.

It really was an unusual photograph, and it was so sharp that one could almost feel the subway's underground wind. At any rate, one could see that a girl reading a book (naturally she was in the foreground) was patting down her windblown hair with a nice gesture, without looking.

Everyone in the editorial office liked the picture and they wanted to use it, but suddenly one of the fellows at the meeting said the photograph might be misunderstood. People could interpret it as saying in our country half the people sleep while the other half are awake and studying. In spite of the absurdity of this interpretation of the comic scene, our editor Avtandil Avtandilovich decided to hold the photograph back.

"Yes," he said, looking at it, "it says that half of our population is illiterate, and the other half is literate, which does not correspond to reality . . . but it is an interesting moment he has caught . . ."

Marat asked about his picture several times, and each time he was promised that it would be used eventually, but that time never came. However, Avtandil Avtandilovich hung the amusing photograph in his office.

Finally, one day at a meeting one of our colleagues proposed cutting the photo into two pieces and printing them side by side with the legend: "In *our* subway, in a subway *abroad*." Avtandil Avtandilovich liked the idea a lot, and he was already starting to nod his head in agreement when the same skeptic who had spoken before said something—and, incidentally, unlike us he had been to Paris. He said that the construction of the subway cars in Paris was quite different from ours, and we could be caught in our own trick. And though someone tried to save the situation by saying that there are subways in other capitalistic countries besides France, Avtandil Avtandilovich agreed with the skeptic's remark, and publication of the photo was again postponed indefinitely.

From this incident alone one might guess that Fate was holding an implacable arm over Marat; but at that time no one had looked that far ahead, and Marat himself was not very worried about what happened to the photograph.

One evening when Marat and I were strolling along the quay—he was very nattily dressed, incidentally—he nodded toward one of the old women who was selling sunflower seeds in the distance, not far from the port.

"Take a good look at her," he said.

When we got even with her, I looked at the old woman but didn't notice anything special about her. True, her face struck me as rather good-looking.

"Well, what do you think?" Marat asked.

"An old woman like any old woman," I said.

"Fifteen years ago," he said, "she was in her prime. One taxi driver stabbed another one over her. And me, when I was still a green youth, I had an affair with her. Yes, she worked as a waitress in the airport restaurant. After every rendezvous with her I would find a ten-ruble note in my pocket. And then one day I come to the restaurant and she says to me:

" 'Today is our last rendezvous.'

" 'Why?' I ask.

" 'I'm getting married—to a guy without a permit to live here, a rover,' she says.

" 'But what about me?' I ask.

" 'Well, you're still young,' she says, 'you'll have a lot more like me . . . I'll bring you some beefsteak, the *shashlyk* isn't fresh today.'

" 'O.K., do that,' I say, but inside I'm really burning.

"I ate the beefsteak and left. We had a favorite place in the old park. I went to the park, found some stinging nettles, carefully tore some out by the root, wrapped them in newspaper so as not to get pricked, and put them under some low box trees right beside where our rendezvous would take place.

"She comes running up, all out of breath. We nuzzled and kissed and so on, and we said our goodbye—but then I got out the nettles and started raking her naked rear with them."

" 'Take that for your rover! Take that for him!' "

"But you didn't intend to marry her," I interrupted him.

"No, of course not . . . but I was young and hot-headed . . ."

I wanted to ask him if he found a ten-ruble note in his pocket that evening, and if he did, what he did with it. But I didn't. What was there to ask? That's the way Marat is, and you have to either accept him that way or reject him.

We got to the end of the quay and headed back. When we walked by the old crone, I took a sidelong look at Marat and then at her.

As he went by, Marat assumed a dignified air, as if sternly warning her against any attempt to renew the acquaintance. The crone didn't even look at us.

I felt strange looking at her and remembering Marat's story. Taxi drivers had a knife fight over her; she had come running out of breath to a rendezvous with her young lover; she had been raked with nettles—and there she was now, such a peaceful old woman, selling seeds. God only knows where her rover was now. Yes, I experienced a strange feeling then, as if I had looked into the cruel and bottomless well of life and seen my own face grown old. Marat walked alongside me as if nothing had happened.

"You are immortal, Marat," I told him.

"You don't have to give me lessons," Marat replied, and looking around imperiously, he added, "We'd better go have some coffee."

Precisely the same way, he pointed out a plump matron to me at the bazaar one day. She was standing at a counter in the distance, her breast touching a whole tableful of greenery: parsley, fennel, green onion.

"I had an amusing adventure with her about ten years ago," he said as we passed where she was selling her produce.

"On my way back from hunting, I was going through the village of Atara-Armenia. I was caught by a thunderstorm so bad you couldn't see two feet in front of you. I ran into the first place I came to and went up on the porch of the house. Rain and hail were slamming down so hard you could scream and not hear yourself. But still I could hear some sort of moan coming from inside the house.

"I think to myself, I'd better have a look and see what's up, so I open the door. I look in and a woman is lying in bed with her teeth chattering. I say, well, uh, you know I was coming back from hunting, the storm caught me, can I stay here.

"She moans and doesn't say anything, just looks at me with her big, dark eyes. Nothing but her eyes sticking out from under the blanket. And I can still hear her teeth chattering.

" 'What's wrong,' I say, and I get this odd feeling: hail's banging on the roof, this woman is lying here under the covers, and there isn't anyone around.

" 'Fever,' she says, 'get the cover from that other bed and put it over me . . .'

"She orders me . . . I take the blanket from the other bed and throw it over her. But she lies there, eyes flashing, and I hear her teeth chattering on. I feel so odd that the thunderstorm is all around and here is this woman alone in the house, lying under the blanket, with her big eyes flashing.

" 'Well, how's that?' I ask, 'are you warming up?'

" 'No,' she says, and her teeth chatter, 'there's another blanket in the next room on the bed, bring it and cover me up . . .'

"I started to tremble myself. I go into the other room, take the blanket off the bed, and and I cover her up with it.

"But her eyes keep flashing and her teeth keep chattering. And I feel so odd—a strange village, a strange house, and a woman alone in the house lying under a blanket—her eyes are flashing so rapidly and a thunderstorm is all around, but not a living soul. Maybe, I think, maybe she's a witch of some sort. And I shudder, but I don't know why I'm worried.

" 'Well, how are you,' I say, 'are you warmer?'

" 'No,' she answers me sharply, with her teeth chattering, 'there's an overcoat on a hanger in the other room. Bring that and put it on me . . .'

"I go into the other room. Indeed, there is an overcoat hanging on the coat rack. I remove it, my hands shaking, take it in and put it on her. And all around—the thunderstorm, the room full of crackling, the woman's teeth chattering, and her eyes flashing under the blanket.

" 'Well, how are you,' I say, and my voice cracks, 'are you finally getting warm?'

" 'No,' she says, 'bring me something else.'

"And her huge eyes go on flashing from under all the stuff I've put over her. And all around—the thunderstorm; the roof is booming, and this woman and I are the only ones in the house. It's terrifying.

" 'Ma'am,' I say, and my voice is really vibrating now, 'I don't think there's anything left to bring.'

" 'Well, then,' she says threateningly, 'lie down on top of me yourself!'

"And her eyes flash and her teeth chatter so loudly I can hear them above the storm. Not a woman, but a witch. In my place anyone else would have lost his composure out of fear. But me, even though I was afraid, I go forward. I lean my rifle against the head of the bed, just in case; and throwing caution to the winds, I jump into the bed. In a word, what can I say, a soldier knows what he's got to do. Within a half an hour she started throwing off everything that was piled on top of her.

" 'I'm ho-o-ot . . . bring me some water from the kitchen . . .'

"I go into the kitchen, find the water, dip a cupful, and take it to her. She drinks. I look, and her eyes are fixed on me again, and even though her teeth aren't chattering, I started to worry anyway.

" 'Madam, is that enough?' I ask her.

" 'No,' she says, and gives me the cup, 'in the kitchen there's some mineral water in the pitcher—bring that to me.'

"Well, no, I think, I'd better get the hell out before the Armenians find me in this house. I take the cup, quietly pick up my rifle, and as if I am going to the kitchen, I take to my heels out of there. Thank God the storm was over. The hailstones glittered on the ground, and I felt glad to be alive as I hurried away.

"That's the way it is sometimes. She lies under a blanket, her eyes flashing, and her teeth chattering away. Just you try to understand what she wants. I figured her out right away, but in my place some other guy would have chickened out, covering her up with anything at all, or giving her the drinks, and right then some Armenians would have come back and blasted him on the spot. It's no joke—a strange village, hail banging on the roof, and a woman with her eyes flashing from under a blanket and her teeth clacking against each other . . ."

Until Fate brings its punishing hand down on man, man can get out of the most dangerous situations unscathed.

To confirm this ancient axiom, here are a few examples from Marat's life. The first happened as a result of Marat's own will.

After graduating from high school, Marat went to Moscow, quite sure that he would be accepted by the Institute of Cinematography, the department for camera-operators. He was already a photography buff, and to get into that department one had to submit examples of one's photographs.

Marat was sure that he would be accepted, if for no other reason than that his photographs would remain in the institute. That's how sure he was that his pictures would be successful. But alas, he did not survive the competition; insultingly indifferent, they returned his photographs along with his application. What was he to do? He had a good enough grade point average to get into the meat-cutter's institute, but apparently that didn't interest him in the least. Solely because of inertia Marat did enroll, but he suffered greatly, not only because of what the institute was, but because of its very name. Girls smirked when he mentioned the name of his school, and this easily wrecked the romantic, hypnotic state which he had just managed to induce in them.

After two years of study in this institute, Marat had a simple and brilliant idea. He decided to appeal to Comrade Beria, because he was a fellow countryman (Beria was indeed our fellow Abkhazian), and ask him to have Marat transferred from the Meat-and-Milk Institute into the Institute of Cinematography. Marat correctly figured that Beria had enough power and authority to do such a thing.

As a man of action, Marat did not spend a lot of time mulling his dream over. He was convinced his undertaking would be successful, if, of course, he could just manage to see Beria. He decided upon the regular gatherings of his fellow Abkhazians in the Aragvi restaurant for this meeting. So as not to appear a complete egotist in Beria's eyes, he decided not just to ask to be transferred to the Institute of Cinematography, but to invite him to a fraternal dinner with his own countrymen.

Beria's mansion on the Sadovo Ring had often been pointed out to Marat. He rushed over there. He was lucky. While still half a block away, he noticed that Lavrenty Pavlovich was strolling beside his mansion, and two colonels, one on each side of the sidewalk, were guarding Beria's route.

Marat fearlessly headed for the spot where Beria was walking.

"What do you want?" asked a colonel, stopping Marat when he reached the guarded sidewalk.

"I have a request for Comrade Beria," Marat said, and then corrected himself, "rather, I have two, for a fellow countryman . . ."

"What requests?" the colonel asked.

Marat saw that Beria was getting closer to them, but it was awkward waiting.

"I am Lavrenty Pavlovich's countryman," Marat said, "I study in the Meat-and-Milk Institute and would like to ask him to transfer me to the Institute of Cinematography."

Incidentally, the photos which he had submitted to the Institute lay ready in his pocket. Who could know—maybe Comrade Beria would be interested . . .

"Comrade Beria does not handle such trifles," the colonel replied coldly, but without hostility.

At that moment Lavrenty Pavlovich reached them.

"What's the problem?" he asked.

Now Marat felt uncomfortable about his first request, so without repeating that, he went on to the second.

"Lavrenty Pavlovich," Marat said, "we, your fellow countrymen, students of the Caucasus, want to invite you to a fraternal dinner at the Aragvi. It will take place tomorrow evening at eight o'clock."

"Very well," said Lavrenty Pavlovich. "I'll come if my guards let me."

Elated because of this encounter and the simplicity of Beria's manner, Marat went to the dormitory. He decided that during the meeting at the Aragvi the next day he would find a moment and ask Beria about the transfer to the Institute of Cinematography.

Unfortunately, the guards did not let Beria come to the Aragvi the next day, and Marat was forced to leave the Meat-and-Milk Institute and go back home to Mukhus.

He decided not to approach Beria with his request a second time; hearing this, everyone whom he told about the meeting said that he should thank God that it had ended so fortunately for him.

One fine autumn day Marat was working on the quay boulevard when he noticed an enchanting young woman strolling along the quay.

Marat was struck by the fact that none of the local fellows had tried to pick her up yet, and no one was trying to pick her up now. Choosing a good moment, when the young woman approached the stand, he gestured to her from a distance, inviting her to have her picture taken.

She smiled, and to his great amazement, came up. Marat asked her to pose and took several pictures. Judging by everything, he made an impression on her; she said that she would come back for the photographs, but that if he saw her with other people, he should pay no attention to her and should not try to talk to her.

For the next two days Marat saw her in the company of two tall, blue-eyed blonds (men, as he said), and honorably did not give any sign that he knew her at all. Later she came alone, unexpectedly; and Marat handed her the photographs, which she liked very much.

He took several more pictures of her and started asking her to pose on the beach for him. She said that was quite out of the question, because her very important protector was here and he shouldn't know anything even about these innocent meetings.

Marat said that he was not afraid of any important protector; all that mattered was that she liked him. She said that Marat was very brave, but she did not want to make him take risks.

"Madam!" said Marat, trying to show her his energetic profile as much as he could, "In love—I am Napoleon!"

"Oh!" said the enchanting stranger, giving an extremely meaningful smile.

A few days later Marat persuaded her to go rowing with him. After great resistance she agreed, but said that he should leave the dock in the boat alone, and then pick her up later at an agreed-upon spot. That is what Marat did.

Once out at sea she livened up, and under velvet-iron pressure from Marat allowed him a great deal more than he had expected. But the main thing was still ahead. She said that her prominent protector was supposed to go away to Sochi soon, and then she and Marat could have a fairly long rendezvous. She gave him her address, making him promise that without her sign he would not try to meet her there. She said that her protector rarely visited her, but surrounded her with spies who were not to know anything about their meetings.

Marat, himself a romantic, thought that she was exaggerating somewhat. He believed in the existence of the prominent protector, but thought that he was one of the local underground millionaires. Marat knew, however, that these men were dangerous characters, so even given exaggeration, caution was not out of place in a case like this.

Finally the long-awaited day arrived. Freeing herself for a few minutes from her tall blue-eyed blonds, the young woman ran to Marat's place of work and whispered to him to come to her house at ten that evening.

Marat didn't know what to do with himself all day. It seemed to him that all of the town clocks had stopped to make him die in hellish agony. He went to the botanical gardens and through a gardener he knew there got a magnificent bouquet of red, purple, yellow, and white roses, which he took home and put in a bucket of water.

That evening Marat went and found the little house where the woman lived, on one of the oldest streets in the upper part of town. Reaching through the iron rings on the gate, he opened the latch, entered a little courtyard, and went up a stairway, the bannister of which was overgrown with wisteria. One more effort, and standing on an open veranda, he knocks at the door.

His enchanting stranger opens the door to him, and he hands her the bouquet, in which she immediately buries her lovely little face. Behind her Marat sees a table tastefully set for dinner for two. He feels an extraordinary surge of love and starts to embrace and kiss his mysterious stranger.

It was all she could do to persuade him to get control of himself, reminding him that they had the entire night ahead of them. Somehow Marat calmed down, the bouquet was divided into two parts, one half on the table for dinner, the other half put in the other room by the bed. The bed was sufficiently spacious for the most elaborate erotic fantasies.

This cordial dinner with fine Georgian wine was humming along when suddenly the face of his beautiful stranger turned pale, and she murmured:

"Quiet! I think I heard a car stop . . ."

Then they both heard the screech of an iron gate.

"Get into the other room and don't come out here," the mistress of the house whispered to him, and pushed him firmly into the bedroom.

Marat heard someone knocking on the door.

"Who is it?" asked the young woman.

Someone replied, but Marat couldn't hear the answer.

"Tell him I'm sick," the young woman said.

Again someone said something, but Marat couldn't hear it. He was terribly curious to find out who it was. He suspected that the person knocking at the door was the servant of one of the underground millionaires, but of whom in particular he did not know.

"No, I don't need a doctor," the woman answered, and as if somewhat embarrassed added, "it's an ordinary sickness that all women have."

Marat didn't listen any more. He saw a door into yet another room, opened it, and went in. From there he saw yet another door, opened it, and finally came out on the veranda which had another staircase, one leading into a little green courtyard.

Marat went down and stood under the veranda, the floor of which was now over his head. Suddenly he heard a man's footsteps stomping along the veranda. The steps ceased. Then started up again. Then stopped again. Marat guessed that the man was stopping in order to peer into the windows of the bedroom, which was lit up. Anxiously Marat realized how easily he would have been discovered if he had stayed in the bedroom where the young woman had pushed him.

Marat was almost consumed by his curiosity. He went around the house under the veranda, and peered through the overgrown wisteria that flourished wildly around the main entrance.

Marat saw a Zis sedan, and in the faint light of the streetlamp he made out the energetic (far more energetic than his own) profile of a man wearing a pince-nez, sitting in the front seat of the car. Marat could not have failed to recognize him, even if he had not met him two years before.

At that moment the footsteps of the man who had been talking to the woman resounded over Marat's head. The man came down the stairs, opened the gate, and not forgetting to slide the bolt back in, walked over to the car, and obscuring Beria for a moment, apparently told him something. A moment later he got in the car, and it quietly slipped away past the house.

Up the back stairway, barely alive from the terror that had gripped him, Marat went into the house. The whole incident was not much to his liking. When he entered the room where he had been having dinner with the beautiful stranger, she threw herself on his chest, and choking on soundless laughter attempted to talk to him; but Marat did not understand why she was laughing and did not share her merry disposition.

"When he went out along the veranda," she finally said, "I decided all was lost. . . . But then I went into the room and you weren't there. Into the next room and you weren't there . . . I decided he had turned you to ashes with his look alone, and now you turn up with a sour face . . ."

But Marat was frightened by what had happened. He might allow himself to compete with the local underground millionaires, but competing with Beria himself—that was terrifying. The effort to continue the dinner went nowhere; but what was even worse, the effort to get down to amatory amusements ended even more lamenta bly. A kind of lassitudinous melancholy had made Marat's body dead. The profile of the Number One Cheka boss kept appearing before his eyes.

Marat tried to recapture the mood in which he had kissed her in the boat, but nothing came of it. The energetic profile of the man in the pince-nez kept floating before his eyes. The beautiful stranger prepared some Turkish coffee, saying it would certainly get him into normal shape; but even after drinking two cups, Marat could not regain control. The vague, absent-minded smile stayed on his face; and his lassitudinous, artificial efforts led nowhere.

"And you said that in love you were Napoleon," the beautiful stranger finally reproached him.

"Madam," Marat replied softly, smiling his vague smile, "every Napoleon has his Waterloo . . ."

Late that night, when he left the house of Beria's mistress (the former stranger), Marat did not go out though the gate, but over the back fence in the most remote corner of the garden, and found himself on a different street.

Marat pulled his cap down tightly over his eyes and turned into the street from which he had originally entered the gate. Without looking to the sides, he walked past her house toward the center of town. As far as his glancing eyes could make out there was a suspicious man standing on the other side of the street, somehow reminiscent of her daytime guards. "It's a good thing I didn't go out the gate," Marat thought, thanking God for his own caution.

A couple of days later the stranger was again strolling along the quay with her tall, blue-eyed blonds. Later, when she was alone, she walked past Marat's place of work and gave him a sidelong glance, but, as the poet said, they did not recognize each other.

According to Marat, this episode bothered him for a long time afterwards in the arena of love. At the most crucial moments of sensual ecstasy, the profile of the man in the pince-nez floated before his eyes, and Marat fell into a flaccid melancholy, though for some reason there were times when this didn't happen.

He noted the following rule. The more comfortable the place of rendezvous was, the more the vision of the terrible profile of the man in the pince-nez bothered him. And, on the other hand, the simpler, coarser, and more awkward the surroundings were for love, the more independent and freer from the profile he felt himself.

I have a vague feeling his vertiginous nighttime assignation with the cable-car operator in the cabin of the port's cable car, or his daylight meetings amid the stalactites of deep caverns, or other similarly risky rendezvous, might perhaps be explained as unacknowledged attempts to obliterate his vision of the cursed profile. Marat himself never said this, and I didn't try to question him about it. True, I have oblique confirmation of this assumption. What is especially valuable—Marat himself confirmed it. He said that the vision of the menacing profile almost completely disappeared after his affair with the celebrated lady snake handler who came to our town with Shapito's circus.

This happened two years after his unsuccessful but lucky (he remained alive) rendezvous with Beria's mistress.

The affair, to use modern terminology, had a Freudian basis, although we can also employ an ancient Russian proverb which is not a bit inferior to Freud, to wit: the hair of the dog that bit you.

I think that without suspecting it himself Marat was drawn to the snake charmer so that he could use the actual sight of a living boa constrictor to drive the profile of the metaphysical boa constrictor from his mind. That's the way it seems to me, though Marat never told me so.

He said that he felt an irresistible attraction to her when the young, half-naked woman wrapped the deadly coils of the boa constrictor around her waist, in time to the then famous melody of Duke Ellington's "Caravan."

With his characteristic energy and directness, he decided to conquer this woman. The next day he went to the circus with a bouquet of roses which, apparently, he had gotten the workers at the botanical garden to carefully pick for him. After her number was over, when the whole flower of Mukhus men and women were applauding the brave woman, he vaulted up onto the stage, and boldly walking past the basket into which the boa had been put, went up to the snake handler and handed her the bouquet.

That same evening, accompanying her to the hotel, he dragged the heavy suitcase containing her boa into and out of the car. In Marat's words, the beautiful Zeinab (this was the snake handler's name) quickly responded to his love with her love. Only later, after they had gotten together, did she explain to him that men who were attracted to her and knew about her work nevertheless could not stand it when they found out that she lived in the same room with the boa. Often they would scurry out the back way.

Usually the boa stretched out in the corner of the room where a table lamp with a large bulb was put on the floor and kept on twenty-four hours a day. This provided the boa with the extra warmth it needed, even though, according to Marat, the room was always suffocatingly hot anyway.

Sometimes Zeinab would cover her boa with a large Persian shawl; and when he raised his head with it on him, he looked like a wicked old witch from Eastern fairytales.

During times of erotic propinquity Marat, in his words, tried to look in the direction of the boa constrictor—which would lie under the lamp with its head up, often looking in Marat's direction.

The first time, out of natural vigilance, Marat kept a close watch on the boa, not knowing how the beast would react to him, Marat, and his relations with his, Sultan's, mistress. Sultan was the boa's name.

Only later did he realize that when he looked at the boa constrictor, the profile of the terrible executioner did not haunt him. This discovery made Marat rejoice so wildly that each time he tapped new and wilder erotic resources in himself.

Marat rejoiced in the resurrection of his former powers and in the fame which he came to possess among the people of Mukhus, and his days were happy. At first, anyway.

But gradually his life became more complicated. After about ten days Marat began to feel that the boa hated him. If Marat walked too close to the place where Sultan lay, he heard a vicious hissing. Even when Marat picked up the suitcase with the boa in it, he heard a nasty hiss, proving that Sultan sensed who was holding the case. Several times, hissing, the boa jerked its head in his direction as if it wanted to bite him.

In vain did poor Zeinab attempt to reconcile them. They hated each other, and were even jealous of each other. Of course Marat did not use this word (nor, one supposes, did the boa); but when Marat saw Zeinab stroking the long body of the boa with a towel dipped in warm water in the morning light he felt vague irritation.

When entering the room where the boa was, according to Marat, you never knew where you would find it. Sometimes he would be wrapped around the floor lamp, dozing with his head under the shade; sometimes he would be up on the coat rack, and no sooner did you hit the light switch than you suddenly saw his disgustingly extended head by your own head. Sometimes he would get up on the couch, or on the bed, which was particularly repulsive; sometimes he would turn up in the cupboard with the linens; sometimes he wrapped himself around the pier glass and dangled his head down, motionlessly watching the reflection of his double. Sometimes he crawled into the bathtub, sometimes into the washbasin; and of course, at such times Marat could not go in and wash his hands.

Every two or three days Zeinab gave the boa a warm bath. Once she asked Marat to fill the tub with water, and Marat, in his words, accidentally put too much hot water in. When Zeinab lowered her boa into the water, in one motion it coiled and sprang out of the tub.

It was after this incident, according to Marat's observations, that the boa started hating him, though how he could have known that Marat was the one who filled the tub remains a mystery to this day. Sensing that the boa hated him, Marat brought a dagger from home, just in case, a gift from his celebrated Lykhna relatives. Another far more modest measure of self-protection consisted of Marat always pressing against the wall when he lay down to sleep with Zeinab.

Incidentally, I once asked Marat what Zeinab fed her boa, and, if she fed it rabbits, where she got them.

"I don't know about rabbits," Marat replied, "but a couple of times when I came in during the day she was sweeping some sort of feathers up . . . so most likely she fed him live chickens . . ."

At first the people of Mukhus were happy about Marat's success, and kept asking him:

"Marat, is it true you live with the snake tamer?"

"What about it," Marat would reply, "of course it's true."

"But aren't you afraid, Marat?" the Mukhus people would ask in ecstatic amazement.

"What's there to be afraid of?" Marat shrugged his shoulders, "It sleeps in its corner, and we sleep in ours."

But this did not and could not last long, for behind the back of the extraordinary man black envy grew thick and attempted to engulf him. Among the people of Mukhus rumors soon started that Marat's beloved was betraying him with her boa. Citing reliable sources, they said that Zeinab's former husband, the one who had taught her to work with the boa, had been the last one crushed on the field of jealousy.

Others went so far as to say that in essence Zeinab lived *with* the boa in the real sense, and just kept Marat around as a smokescreen.

The rumors reached Marat. He was struck by the stupidity and absurdity of these rumors. He just shrugged his shoulders and raised his eyebrows contemptuously. Marat hoped that people would understand the absurdity of these rumors and give them up on their own. But the rumors hung on stubbornly.

"Someone had a reason for doing this," Marat used to hint meaningfully, pointing somewhere upward and to the side with his head.

Marat developed, to use pseudoscientific language, a justification complex. Now when he met with fellows on the quay or in the coffeehouses, he would strike up a conversation about his life with Zeinab, directing the listeners' attention to the lusciousness and variety of their amatory diversions, and simultaneously, by the way, informing them about the sad dessication of the boa in the corner of the room under the table lamp.

"Yea-ah?" some would say, listening to his story with incredulous expressions, "well, we heard something quite different."

The good-for-nothings! Who was supposed to know better than Marat who lived with whom? But such is the law of the mob; people insist that those who have it in them to soar above the general muck have failings which lower them, for equilibrium.

Finally Marat realized that he was experiencing attacks of malice not only against the boa but also against Zeinab, who was guilty of nothing.

As for the boa, Marat hated it twice as much as he had before. One day in a coffeehouse he accidentally overheard a fragment of a conversation about this fantastic *menage à trois* in which Marat supposedly took part. Moreover, this particular rumormonger reduced Marat's role to a shameful minimum.

"She had to have someone around to carry the case with the boa in it, and then Marat turned up," the storyteller concluded his vile tale.

That day Marat had a lot to drink and went to the hotel. Zeinab turned out not to be in the room; but he had his key, and he went in. Seeing Marat without Zeinab, the boa viciously hissed in his direction. Marat couldn't stand it any longer.

"Who should be hissing at who!" Marat yelled, and he took off a shoe and threw it at the boa. The shoe landed directly in the center of the huge shiny mass. The boa flicked its head in Marat's direction and hissed every more viciously. Then Marat took off his other shoe and hurled it at the vile, shiny heap; the boa struck and hissed even more decisively.

Marat sat down on the couch, propped his elbows on the table, and fell into woeful thought over his onerous fate. That which had been the object of his pride had become the object of his shame. After sitting thus for some time, he lowered his head onto the table and fell asleep.

Some sort of incredible heaviness pressing down on his chest woke him up. He opened his eyes, and with terror saw that the boa was in fact wrapped around him and was crushing him. With one hand (the other was pressed to his side) Marat attempted to pull the monstrous coils of the boa off, but it was impossible. With his hand he could feel the fantastic muscles of the boa flexing and rippling back and forth inside.

Sensing that in another moment he would lose consciousness from the crushing force of the boa, Marat remembered his dagger and tried to reach it. But it was impossible to reach; in order to do so, he would have to stand on the couch. Fortunately it was Marat's right hand that was free. With difficulty Marat toppled over onto the couch; and getting to his knees, already starting to lose strength, he straightened up, but he still couldn't reach the dagger.

Marat gathered all his will. The boa, as if pulsing his muscles, would squeeze horribly, then let up slightly; Marat used these moments to breathe in. Finally he managed to stand up, legs wobbling, on the unsteady surface of the couch and reach the dagger with his free hand. Curses! A new obstacle stood in his way: the dagger simply wouldn't come out of its sheath. This required a second hand. But Marat shook the dagger several times with all his might, holding onto the handle, and finally the sheath slipped off and bared the blade. Collecting his last strength, Marat plunged the dagger into the tense, flexing body of the boa. Momentarily the embrace of the monster weakened. Marat cut and slashed at the now flaccidly curling and falling coils.

When she came home from the bazaar, poor Zeinab found the horrible scene of her Sultan's end. She fell to her knees silently, and petting the dead, chopped-up body of the boa, she wept until night.

She wept, repeating:

"Poor Sultan, where is my piece of bread? Poor Sultan, where is my piece of bread?"

According to Marat, these monotonous laments of hers almost drove him out of his mind. Marat put on his shoes, turned off the table lamp which was still on in the empty corner, and tried to comfort Zeinab.

He gave her all the money he had saved, enough for approximately six months of modest living, enough time to get and train a new boa, if she intended to continue in this line of work. Marat's final method of comforting her was to make several marvelous handbags out of the leftover pieces of the boa. I don't remember if I have mentioned that Marat had golden hands. Besides all this, Marat helped poor Zeinab make up a false declaration that the boa had died of a cold.

It's interesting that those who envied Marat the most attempted to explain his heroic feat so that it fit the spirit of their old gossip about Zeinab's liaison with the boa.

They said that Marat had unexpectedly come into the room and found Zeinab supine on the couch in the embrace of the boa. Seeing this, Marat, supposedly, jumped up on the couch, grabbed his dagger from its sheath, and started striking at the fatigued boa, which was quite unprepared for any fight.

There was one two-year period when Marat stopped working on the quay boulevard, and got a job in a research institute. He was put in charge of the photo lab and was even given a security clearance. I don't have any idea what sort of photography he did there; apparently it was connected with plasma, or something even less mysterious.

But the fact remains that he was thrown out. Rather, he did everything so that they would throw him out. Judging from his story, he seduced a woman there, a woman to whom he showed a series of photographs which had been reshot from a certain foreign magazine.

These photographs, depicting naked women, he passed off as the fruits of his own labor. That is, he quite unequivocally hinted to her that all of these women had posed for him, and that she, if she should wish, would find a worthy place among them. In his words, this broke her.

Although in our age many men have become more talkative than women, on the whole the women still remain rather talkative creatures. In a word, this woman told one of her friends about Marat's collection; she passed it on to someone else, and after a certain time somone informed the bosses that Marat, instead of photographing, let's say, molecular processes, was doing the devil only knew what in his photo lab.

A sudden union checkup and inventory revealed the photographs, and a grandiose scandal was in the making. Prior to the mass meeting of the institute at which his personal fate was to be resolved, Marat came in to see me at my editorial office and showed me the magazine:

"Here, look . . ."

"Well, of course," I told him, leafing through the magazine, "you show them this and it's all over."

"That's the point," he replied, "I can't."

"Why not?"

"How will I be able to face her after that?"

"She's to blame herself," I said, "she had no call to blab your secrets."

"No," he replied, thinking, "the devil with them, let them fire me . . ."

And he really didn't say a word about the magazine; he just asserted that the photographs were not done in the institute photo lab. Finally the whole thing was turned over to the courts, but even here he did not admit that the photographs were reshot from a foreign magazine, even though he was under threat of a very serious indictment.

The institute kept trying to get the court to declare the photographs pornographic, in which case Marat could go to jail. But the court did not declare them pornographic even though it had doubts about their artistic value, something which Marat insisted on.

According to Marat, as the packet of photographs made the rounds from hand to hand, beginning with the institute professional committee and ending with the court, it got smaller and smaller. He was certain that everyone up to and including the people's judges got a charge from his pictures.

I think that in this story there was great exaggeration about Marat's chivalry in not revealing the source of his photo collection. Concerns of chivalry doubtlessly had some place, but they were exaggerated. I think that with this episode Marat consciously *sought* scandal—in order to inflate his fame.

True, there is one other thing that should be noted. To wit: this ill-starred magazine had been brought back from a business trip by one of his colleagues at the institute; and Marat, in his words, concealed the source of the remarkable photographs partly in fear of someone f nding out how he got hold of the magazine. Apparently, all of this is true, but still, his main concern was his prestige as the conqueror of hearts.

It was precisely at that time that someone started spreading malicious gossip among the people of Mukhus, saying that Marat's celebrated affair with the dwarf Lusia Daggerova was nothing but the fruit of his own sick imagination.

Here I must decisively intercede for Marat. I personally saw him in Lusia Daggerova's company many times. He used to go strolling along the quay with her; he used to go to restaurants with her, and once when he docked at the rowboat dock Lusia was in his boat.

He lowered his brows menacingly, picked Lusia up in his arms and, looking like Stenka Razin throwing the Persian princess onto the Volga short, raised his precious load in the air, at which point her skirt hiked up her legs, baring the kicking thighs of an overfed child. Then he set her victoriously on the wharf, underlining the playfulness of his gesture with a smile. It was absurd to think that all of a sudden for no reason he might throw an innocent woman overboard.

The only tool in the hands of the people who denied Marat's affair with Lusia was the observation that Marat stopped seeing her long before the troupe of dwarfs, of which Lusia was part, left for another town.

What's right is right. There *was* an affair; it was brief, but stormy. Marat met her for the first time in a restaurant. About a dozen dwarfs were sitting at two tables which had been pushed together, having supper, drinking wine, their feet dangling short of the floor.

Marat sent them two bottles of wine, and toasted them from a distance; the dwarfs toasted him, and then, after consulting among themselves, they asked the waitress to send him a bottle of wine. Again, from the distance, Marat toasted them, and they also toasted him from a distance, after which Marat called his waitress and sent them two more bottles of wine and several bars of chocolate, one for each of the women.

At this point the dwarfs bent over the table and had a long conference; finally they called the waitress, and asked her to invite Marat to their table. They decided that they would get off more cheaply this way, but they were wrong. Marat sat down with them, and in the course of the conversation gave them to understand that besides his regular profession he was also considered an unofficial correspondent of the local newspaper *The Red Subtropics* and many other capital newspapers. (The many other newspapers, apparently, still have no inkling of their unofficial correspondent in Mukhus.)

It was while they were at the table that Marat turned his attention to Lusia Daggerova, without any suspicion that her fiancé was sitting beside her. It's possible that in general he did not suspect that dwarfs could have fiancées and fiancés. In any case, he started showing Lusia signs of attention, and she willingly, even excessively willingly, started accepting these, with no consideration for her fiancé, who, it turned out, was suffering greatly at the time.

Upon learning that Marat was a member of the press, the dwarfs became extremely excited. After a conference among themselves, they complained to him about their manager, who treated them very badly. It turned out that in order to economize on travel expenses the manager stuffed as many as five unmarried dwarfs into a single hotel room. He made them lie down crossways on the bed, which was uncomfortable and humiliating, all the more so because the married dwarfs got full-priced rooms. Thus the manager economized on travel expenses, got fictitious hotel bills, and put the difference—in cash—into his own pocket.

Marat was highly indignant about this inhumane treatment of the dwarfs. That very evening they invited him to the hotel so that he could witness it for himself, on the spot.

In the hotel Marat suggested not complicating the affair by getting the press involved; he would simply beat up the manager. Fortunately for the manager, and perhaps for Marat (I have in mind the consequences), he was not in his room.

Marat went into one of the rooms with the dwarfs, and they spent a long time sitting at the table, talking about life. Many of the dwarfs got quite drunk, and Marat had to carry them to their rooms. Lusia, in spite of her fiancé's sufferings, was the one who showed him who slept where.

Finally, Marat put a quintet of dwarfs in one room with his own hands, and he was completely convinced of the truth of their complaint. Incidentally, it happened that Lusia Daggerova's fiancé was a member of this quintet, which Marat did not know.

However, the fiancé would not lie down in the bed as Lusia proposed. Tossing off the blanket, he crawled out and tried to hang himself over the railings of the hotel balcony. Fortunately he was noticed in time and dragged choking out of the noose.

But by this time, in Marat's words, Lusia Daggerova was in love with him up to her ears. In Marat's words, one could understand that, with dwarfs, the incubation period of love was generally much shorter. Marat promised to take some pictures of her, and the next day she came to his place of work on the boulevard.

Thus they started meeting, and the fiancé got used to the idea of Marat. Again, when telling me about this, Marat gave his words a special nuance, a suggestion that among dwarfs the period of suffering over love is also shortened.

Marat had not had time to revel in the novelty of his unusual amatory adventure when a delegation of his relatives from the village of Lykhna came to see him and lodge a sharp protest over the forthcoming marriage of Marat to a midget, as they put it.

Marat's father, who had perished during World War II, was a Russian by descent; but his mother was an Abkhazian, born in Lykhna. Marat's relatives on his mother's side, it turned out, constantly kept an eye on him; as soon as they felt his behavior start to blacken their glorious family name, one way or another they would turn up and be fantastically stubborn about forcing him to follow the concepts of decency developed by their glorious family.

They informed him bluntly that if he didn't stop meeting this midget, they would *forcibly drag her out from under him.* It is a peculiarity of the Abkhazian language that this act, which is expressed in seven English words, is done with one word in Abkhazian, and therefore any translation is rather pallid.

In a word, they gave him to understand that they would never allow him to bring a midget from some unknown tribe into his mother's home. Incidentally, they promised him a fullblooded Abkhazian fiancée if he had gotten mixed up with this midget because of his own short stature. Marat was short, but, of course, not so short that anything of the kind could have occurred to him.

"Poor Marat," people sometimes said, underlining the fact that he had grown up without a father. But more often the words had a completely opposite meaning.

"Poor Marat," people said, meaning that he had no suspicion of what misfortunes would befall him if he persisted in his delusions.

At first, when the relatives interfered in his affair with Lusia, Marat tried to explain to them that he had no intention of bringing her into the house. Then there was all the less reason, they said to him, to shame their name by showing up in public places with a midget.

Marat tried to get rid of them, but nothing came of it. When the relatives went away to the village they left two oaklike young fellows there on guard to watch his place of work. Looking at these giants, who took turns patrolling the quay boulevard, one could see there was no joking about the case of nerves that Marat developed.

Of course he went on meeting Lusia Daggerova, but this presented many difficulties, so his nerves began to give way. One has to realize how stubborn his Lykhna relatives were, and on the other hand how egocentric Marat was. Marat drowned in surmise when he tried to figure out exactly how much authority these two village giants had. Maybe they were just supposed to make the meetings more difficult; maybe if they saw Marat with Lusia they were supposed to stuff her into a bag without a word and carry her away somewhere into the mountains and release her there—like a cat one wants to get rid of.

One evening he was sitting at a table with the dwarfs, in just such a state of dark speculation as that I have described, when he asked a question which was in essence innocent, but tactless the way it came out.

"Listen," Marat asked, "do dwarfs vote?"

To this day many people can't understand what suddenly prompted Marat to ask this. Personally I believe he was thinking about his lack of legal recourse against his extraordinary paternalistic village relations; and he switched to the dwarfs seated around him randomly, without thought for the consequences.

The dwarfs were extremely offended by his question, and they vociferously expressed amazement at Marat's ignorance; because, in their words, every normal person knew that dwarfs were just as much full citizens of the country as everyone else.

"Maybe you'd better watch your nose," Lusia told him.

"What about my nose?" Marat asked, on guard.

"It's awfully big," Lusia replied, "and now you're sticking it in where you're not asked."

"Maybe from the point of view of a dwarf's nose mine is big," Marat answered, restraining his anger, "but for your information, from the point of view of high-class women in Moscow and Leningrad, I have a *Roman* nose."

I should note that Marat was extremely intolerant of any criticism of his looks. He could only joke about his nose or his shortness himself. Thus, in regard to a woman who was overly attached to him, he would say, "She's decided that I'm a tall, blue-eyed blond . . ." This sort of joke or hint was quite acceptable, but only when *he* was the source.

In a word, the meal and drinks were starting to be spoiled; and the dwarfs, taking into consideration the fact that Marat had treated everyone, started trying to persuade him not to be upset with Lusia. In the end Lusia herself admitted that her comment was rude; and as proof of complete surrender of her position, she kissed Marat on the nose. And though the dwarfs managed to save the evening, Marat's irritation did not pass; and every once in a while he would recall Lusia's comment and mutter: "Ha, well you know my nose is too big . . ."

After this evening Marat's relations with Lusia began to cool, perhaps not all at once, but rather quickly. In any case, a week later the oaklike giants commandeered from the village stopped their patrol and went on home to Lykhna.

However, that same year another delegation of Lykhna relatives appeared in Mukhus, gently but unavoidably adamant. The thing is that at this time Marat had gotten himself a wig to cover his comparatively small bald spot. He suffered painfully for a long time when he started to go bald, but by Mukhus standards a wig was quite a bold innovation. But then Marat was always known for the boldness and independence of his views.

The wig fit him so perfectly that people who didn't know him well did not even realize that he was wearing it. Nevertheless, I can swear that the wig did not stay on his head for more than twenty or twenty-five days.

The Lykhna relatives proposed that he stop shaming himself in front of other families (who apparently were making fun of him) with his "hair hat," but should be modest and make do with his own hair. They pointed out to him that baldness does not shame a man, that it shames only a woman. The great Lenin, they reminded him, was never ashamed of his huge bald spot. Did he think, they asked him, that if it had been otherwise it would have been impossible to find him an appropriate hair hat?

For a few days Marat fought to keep his wig; then he gave in, before his relatives appointed some new giant to watch him and use a currycomb to remove his wig.

Now I will let Marat himself tell the story of one rather amusing event in his life. I think this event, besides the fact that it is amusing, is also interesting in that it gives one a rather clear sense of the interference of Fate in Marat's life. Only our blindness, the fact that we were wrapped up in everyday cares, kept us from recognizing these signs in time.

"Well, I'll tell you, I really fell into something once not so long ago," he began—after getting rid of his clients and sitting down beside me on the seawall. I had just returned from fishing, and before continuing he ironically examined my stringer with its humble catch. Then he continued:

"A friend of mine was on vacation here, a captain from Murmansk. He vacations here every year. He comes for a month—broads, money, not chickenfeed, I'll tell you that. Well, I help him have a good time and don't forget myself when doing it. In a word, he's a good guy. I'll introduce you to him the next time he comes.

"One day he says to me:

" 'Listen,' he says, 'let's go out of town to a really nice house. We'll spend Easter there. Several enchanting women should be present. I'll be with my girl friend, and you can set off into the open sea of adventures.'

" 'O.K.,' I say, 'no harm trying, no one's staying up late waiting for me.'

" 'At the very worst,' he says, 'there'll be a good dinner with suckling pig, and the mistress of the house herself—what a woman!'

"We buy a cake at the store, a few bottles of cognac, we catch a taxi and head for the Botanical. There I get a good bouquet of roses, and we take off. In Synop he stops the taxi and goes into his girl friend's house. So I sit in the cab and wait. He goes in alone but four people come out—he and his girlfriend, and some other man with a woman. As soon as I catch sight of her I bet myself: a knockout—no pen can describe her, no tongue either.

"So I think, well, of course, she's with this character, and what's the chance of a peach like her ever falling into my hands! No sooner have I thought that than I look and the guy takes off somewhere, and the other three come over to the car! In my joy I almost knock my head on the roof! I open the door, let the peach in, and the whole time she's smiling nice and wide to me. I sit down, the Cap alongside me, his girlfriend up front. I smell something in the air—cooked meat. I can smell that a mile away, and I'm never mistaken.

"Jokes start pouring out of me one after another. The peach rolls in laughter, the Cap's friend looks me in the mouth too. In a word—I knock 'em dead. I take the final risk; and sneakily, as if I had unintentionally forgotten what I was doing, I put my hand on the peach's knee. She sneakily takes it off; ergo things were falling into place according to rules and on schedule. Because she didn't get angry, she did it just for propriety's sake.

"Well, I fire off a few more stories, and she's dying from laughter. I again unintentionally put my hand on her knee, and she again unintentionally takes it away. Ergo, things are falling into place, because she doesn't get mad. On the contrary, she goes on laughing.

"However, I chance to look around—I have that habit in cars—and I see that the same Volga keeps following us.

" 'Listen,' I say, 'someone's tailing us.'

"Here the peach twists around and laughs even more. The Cap's girlfriend laughs too, and the Cap snickers.

" 'What's up?' I say.

" 'Why that's her husband,' the Cap answers, 'You mean you didn't see him back there?'

" 'What husband,' I say, 'where'd she get a husband?'

"And then the Cap explains it all to me. It turns out that the man I took for her boyfriend was in fact her husband. It turns out he hadn't left as I thought but had gone to his car, which was parked a little off to the side. It turns out that the peach had expressed a desire to ride in the same car with me, because her friend, the Cap's girlfriend, had told her how funny I was.

"But precisely now I stop feeling funny. When I find out about the husband my puss goes so sour that the peach starts laughing even more and pointing her finger at me. In fact, I really get depressed, because mentally I am already so used to her, and now I will have to get fixed up with something else.

"Then the peach touches me on the knee with her velvety little paw and winks, as if to say, don't be depressed, everything is still ahead. In any case, that's how I understand her. Well, I feel a little easier. All right, I think, even if I don't like busting up other people's lives, if the peach is the one who wants it, then why not—so I can go on with the courting.

"We drive up to a mansion, and it's right at the edge of the sea. Cap pays off the taxi driver, hops out of the car with the cognac and cake, and we go up to the gate. The peach's husband gets out of his car, too. Cap introduces us. I choose the moment when the others are ringing at the gate to take Cap aside, and ask him:

" 'Explain the situation.'

" 'The husband is no obstacle to you,' Cap replies, 'but there is a certain subtlety here . . . you'll understand it later yourself.'

"He cuts off the conversation because the voice of the woman who owns the house rings out from behind the gate. We go into the courtyard, and they introduce me to her. I look at her: I break into a cold sweat, I don't know whether to stand or fall. Such a fantastic blonde, wearing a black sports outfit and rubber boots. In a word, what can I say? Under the wool of her sports outfit one can sense a Body with a capital B, a Body which lives a life itself and gives life to others.

"She so stuns me that for ten minutes or so I completely forget about the peach. Meantime, the mistress of the house sniffs my roses with pleasure and says, 'Well, your pictures, your pictures, I saw them in the Salon last year.' In fact I did take part in last year's exhibit, and they had several of my stunning pictures there.

"We go into the house. Well, what a house! I tell you, it would knock your ears off. Carpets and books, books and carpets. I simply couldn't figure out why one woman needed so many books. True, she had been married to a professor previously, but then they got divorced. And never mind the professor, she was a scholar herself. But I didn't think about that then. I thought—let's see what the rest of the troops here are going to be like! The main thing is that with my whole skin I can sense and smell the odor of cooked meat in the air; I can tell that odor a mile away.

"We go into the main room. There's such a table set that you don't want to touch it, it is so beautiful. Bottles with export-type liquors glitter like diamonds. We are even a bit embarrassed by our own humble gifts. My little roses are a fine table decoration, but the mistress of the house puts the cognacs and the cake away somewhere in the corner of the room, and they stay there till morning.

"But that's not the main thing. There are two more women and another man in the room. The women are one prettier than the other, both world-class, and both to my taste. One frisky, the other sort of melancholy. Well, never mind, sister, I think, at a table like this you can't stay melancholy for long!

"However, when I see the man I suddenly remember Cap's saying something about a certain subtlety. There's the subtlety, I think, there's her real lover-boy. But at the moment he is exchanging pleasantries with my peach's husband. Oh, you son of a bitch, I think, massaging the husband and making time with the peach on the side.

"Well, I think, soon we'll see who gets who. At table, you know, I'll give a handicap of a hundred to anyone when it comes to women. At very worst, I think, if things don't work out with the peach, there are three other beautiful women here, not counting Cap's girlfriend.

"While we are chatting about this and that, the mistress manages to go change her clothes; and she comes to the table again, a really lip-smacking knockout, and we take our seats.

"They start choosing a *tamada*.* Naturally, Cap names me. I beg off at first, for propriety's sake, but then I take control of the table. I conduct things, making sure to see that everything is getting drunk and trying to cozy up to one of the ladies. But I realize that there's some sort of continual misfiring. My shots keep missing. They respond to my jokes with amiable laughter, they clink glasses with me, trying to outdo each other in making merry—but nothing beyond that.

"True, I don't try to hit on the one who is sitting there in her melancholy. I think, let her have a chance to thaw out a bit; but as for the others, I don't feel out of line, and I go at them full blast, without being boorish.

"Incidentally, while helping the mistress of the house, I go out into the kitchen with her several times; and we even go down into the cellar together once, because she has jarred mushrooms there. When we are in the little cellar, I think to myself, well, here goes, no matter what. I drop to the floor, embrace her legs, and I say:

" 'Madame, the leaves are already falling.'

" 'I know,' she says just as emotionally, 'but there'll be time to see each other. . . . And today I am the hostess, so I beg you to court one of my friends . . '

"While saying this, she draws her fingers ever so lightly across my head—I almost go insane from joy. But what can I do—I have to give in.

" 'I am your slave,' I say, 'Madame . . . it will be as you say . . .'

"So I brush off my pants, and we go upstairs again. Since she's asked, I abandon the hostess and I start trying to connect with one of her friends again. But I see that I'm not getting anywhere. Time is passing. I've left the peach to that grey wolf; but for some reason all he's doing is gabbing with her husband, and she's getting zero attention.

"What is this, I think. Where has there ever been a case where Marat was alone at a table. The house is full of women, and there's no one to court. So I choose a good moment and call Cap aside.

" 'What is this,' I say, 'I can't make a connection no matter what I do.'

" 'Yes,' Cap agrees, 'there is a very great subtlety here.'

" 'What subtlety,' I say, 'is that character the peach's lover-boy?'

" 'That's just the point,' he says, 'he's not . . .'

" 'Then what's the problem,' I say, 'does that mean she loves her husband?'

" 'No, no,' he says, 'that's not the point at all.'

" 'What is then?'

*Georgian: toastmaster, traditionally chosen for eloquence, authority, and ability to hold liquor [tr.].

" 'You see how that guy is being so nice to the peach's husband?'
" 'So?'
" 'That's it,' he says, 'they're in love.'
" 'What!' I don't believe my ears. 'In the real sense?'
" 'Yes,' he says, 'in the most real sense.'
"At first I am stunned, but then I take heart. I forgot to say that one of the women, the frisky one to be specific, was the wife of the second man. But they were so far apart all the time, I didn't figure this out myself right away.
" 'If that's so,' I say, 'it means the wife of the other character and the peach are free?'
" 'That's just it,' he says, 'that they aren't exactly—'
" 'So,' I say, 'they are faithful to their husbands when they know about that?'
" 'That's not the point,' he says, 'they're in love themselves.'
"Now my head starts to spin.
" 'Who with,' I say, 'Are they in love with you, or what?'
" 'No,' he says, 'much worse.'
" 'Then with whom?'
" 'They are in love with . . .' he says, '. . . only for God's sake don't give me away, they're in love with our hostess.'
"I go out of my mind.
" 'What do you mean,' I say, 'in the actual sense?'
" 'The most actual sense,' he replies.
" 'Well what about our hostess,' I say, 'well?'
" 'That's the tragedy—that she doesn't love them.'
" 'What do you mean tragedy,' I say, 'good girl! A real woman!'
" 'No,' he says, 'it's a tragedy because they're in love with her, but she doesn't love them.'
"I go out of my mind. But what's to be done? I sit down in my place, because the *tamada* has to direct things at the table. But direct them where? And even more important—who should I direct? I don't understand any of this. Well, I pour myself a half glass of vodka to help shake off this symphony for a moment. I start to get control of myself, and I reason as follows. So, I think, what is it that we have here today? The peach is out, that other woman's out, the only women left are the melancholy lady and the hostess.
"But the hostess won't allow me to court her; on the contrary, she proposes that I court one of her friends. But two of the three friends are out due to reasons beyond my control, ergo, the melancholy lady is the one left. Not great, but not slim pickings either, if I play my cards right . . . I gradually make a transition to her, and when the dancing starts, I ask her. A good-looking woman, but for some reason she's sad all the time. While we're dancing I give her a little hug so that she can get a sample of how I feel, but I see that she doesn't want to feel me. As soon as I start to squeeze her, she goes stiff as a board.

" 'Why are you so sad, madame,' I say.

" 'Oh,' she says, 'don't ask! I have had such sorrow, such sorrow.'

" 'What sorrow, madame,' I ask her, 'my second profession is easing people's sorrows.'

" 'No,' she says, 'no one can help me . . . my beloved husband died . . .'

" 'When,' I say, 'did this misfortune befall you?'

" 'Last year,' she says.

" 'Madame,' I say, 'in times such as ours it is a pleasure to see a woman who mourns so for her late husband. At any rate, there are no women like that in the circles I know. But you are still young and still beautiful. You don't have to lock yourself up in sorrow. Relax a little, and you'll feel better.'

" 'If you only knew,' she says, 'what a man he was.'

"Then she livens up and starts telling me about her husband. It turns out he was the most just prosecutor, the most honest man, and the best family man.

"Maybe it is all really true. But why tell me all this? I'm thinking about something quite different. I am a man myself, thank God, with my own virtues, and I have my own ego. No, I think, I have to try to make a transition back to the hostess again, my number isn't going over on this one. However, as soon as she starts talking about her husband her face grows animated, her eyes start to shine, so much that even the others notice it.

" 'Your friend is simply a marvel,' the hostess says to Cap and gives me a strange sort of look. 'Finally someone has managed to amuse my dear neighbor . . .'

"It turns out this woman lived next door to our hostess. And the hostess, who is dancing with Cap, notices that my partner has really livened up. But she doesn't know that she has livened up because she is talking about her husband.

"And I think: why did she give me such a strange look. Maybe she's hooked? We sit down again, I take charge of the table again. I eat, drink, joke; and I see that the hostess is looking at me strangely again, and when I start joking she's the first to laugh. But the prosecutor's wife has gone sad again. It's clear she doesn't have anyone to tell about her husband. Well, I think, you can't count on me anymore, either.

"Again dancing. I take the hostess. The peach's husband takes the frisky one; the character takes the peach, though it's obvious that they both want to dance with each other desperately.

"So I'm dancing with the hostess, and she fastens onto me—well, what can I say, she simply enveloped me like a warm shower. That's all, I think, I don't have to retreat anymore, I'll stand here solid as Mamai's burial mound, to the death.

" 'Well, how did you like my neighbor?' the hostess asks me.

" 'What can I say?' I ask. 'She's a good woman, but she keeps talking about her husband all the time. Of course, faithfulness to a husband's memory is a good thing, but why go out and be with other people who are having fun, then?'

" 'I talked her into it,' the hostess replies, and hugs me again. I'm already half-dead from passion, almost like that prosecutor.

" 'I am your slave,' I whisper to her, 'here is my life, do with me as you will.'

" 'If I could choose,' she says, looking me in the eye, 'I wouldn't choose anyone except you . . .'

" 'But why not?' I roar in a whisper. 'You are a free woman. If someone is standing in your way, tell me who it is. He will forget not only your magnificent face but his own name.'

" 'Oh,' she says, 'if he were the problem.'

" 'Then who is the problem?' I ask.

" 'I am, myself,' she sighs. 'Unfortunately I am in love . . .'

" 'With whom, madame,' I say. 'Name the lucky person for me.'

" 'I'll tell you,' she says, 'because I like you, but will you help me?'

"You know what a gallant knight I am, why I'm capable of doing good even if it is against my own interests.

" 'Anything that is in my power,' I say.

" 'I'm in love with the prosecutor's wife,' she whispers to me and indicates the woman with her eyes.

"I stumble like a boxer after a good hook. Lord, I think, is there anyone here who's normal?

" 'What, you too, madame?' I ask, scarcely able to move my tongue.

" 'Two months now,' she says, 'I'm dying for her. Ever since she came to live here.'

"Aha, I mutter to myself, she fell in love with the prosecutor's wife and that's why she went into retirement.

" 'And what about her?' I ask.

" 'She's innocent,' she says. 'She doesn't understand anything . . . just keeps talking about her prosecutor.'

" 'Then how can I help you, madame?' I ask.

" 'Tell her something good about me . . . there can still be a time when I'm good for you too . . .'

" 'I'll try,' I say, 'but you understand how hard it is for me to give you up, especially to her.'

"We sit down at the table again, and I'm obliged to direct things since I'm *tamada*. But where can I head, and with whom—everyone's crossed off. Only the prosecutor's wife is still open, and I have to give her up to the hostess. But you know me, once I give my word, I keep it like gold. I propose a toast. I don't even know where the words are coming from. Of course the toast is to our hostess, for the hospitality of her house, for her heart, I say, which has absorbed the wisdom of all these books and the soft tenderness of all these carpets. No kidding, it was a great toast, even though I was thinking to myself: what the hell

do I need with all these books and carpets since I'm screwed anyway.
"Again they turn on the record player, and again I dance with the
prosecutor's wife. I cautiously prompt her to tell me what she thinks of
our hostess.

" 'She's such a wonderful woman,' she says. 'Since I moved here
she has lavished such attention on me . . . she does so much to ease
the sorrow I have for my late husband . . .'

" 'Madame,' I say, 'you are lucky . . . a woman who can replace
your husband the late prosecutor is absolutely unique.'

" 'Yes,' she says, 'I'm infinitely grateful to her for her concern,
because losing a husband like I did means losing everything. You can't
imagine what an honest man he was. The manager of a food store near
his office brought him a suitcase full of money once. But of course he
turned it down. Then the manager of the grocery store pointed to the
suitcase and said: "With a suitcase like this I'll manage to find the right
prosecutor, but you just try to find another defendant who's so generous." And what happened? After a while the case was shifted to
another prosecutor, and they gave the manager of the grocery store
another grocery store—a better one. And at the time I was having to
rent one of our two rooms to vacationers to make ends meet. Have you
ever heard of such a fool? That's the sort of man my late husband
was . . .'

"I realized it was going to be impossible to get anywhere with her. In
short, for me the evening ended with an empty room, so much
polluted air. The prosecutor's wife went on home, and all the others
spent the night, I don't know anything about their sleeping arrangements, and don't want to know. The hostess brought me a sleeping bag
and said:

" 'I love to sleep in this, if that's any consolation for you.'

"What could I do? I undressed and crawled into the sleeping bag. I
sniffed it in my sorrow, but for some reason it smelled of goat, and
putting my head outside again, I fell asleep.

"The next morning we went walking along the shore with a rifle.
She kept a rifle in the house. I think you could find anything in that
house except a normal woman. However, Cap shot a duck, which fell
into the sea. Without thinking much about it, I undressed down to my
shorts and jumped into the water. Well, you know that when I'm
undressed I look like a god, with my chest and biceps. The women go
crazy. The water is icy, I swim out to the duck, and as a joke I take it in
my teeth and return to shore.

" 'If only I weren't in love,' the hostess whispers to me, handing me
a shaggy towel. While I was swimming, she managed to run to the
house and bring the towel. What can I say, she was a first-class
woman, and she liked me. Not so long ago I met her in Mukhus.

" 'Well, how are things,' I say, 'did you manage to pervert the
prosecutor's wife?'

" 'No,' she sighs, 'I didn't . . . I got married out of grief . . .'

"Now a man who knew that I would never meet that prosecutor's wife again, would be sure to say: 'Of course I managed to! We had a good time together.' But this woman answered honestly. And I wasn't lucky with her. The first time we met a little too early, she was in love with the prosecutor's wife; the next time too late, after she had jumped into marriage out of grief.

"What about the Cap who took me there? For openers, he wasn't any captain at all; I found that out from one of his shipmates. He was only a first mate. Just imagine, he went to Cuba twice. And here's my advice for you: if you take a buddy to one's house, first explain the whole situation to him, and then let him decide if he wants to go or not. And on top of everything I had dragged his duck out of the water like a retriever! You couldn't trust a Cap like that with a sloop—never mind a liner—he'd sink it. Soon as he had a drink he'd sink it."

In the fall of that same year a rumor that Marat had gotten married went around Mukhus. I hadn't seen him for a long time, because after his departure from the research institute he started working at the edge of town beside the bazaar, not on the boulevard—another fellow had taken his place there.

Considering all his stories, I was anxious to see the woman whom he voluntarily brought into his house, and without any complaints from his Lykhna relatives at that.

One evening when I was sitting on a bench by the quay boulevard, Marat materialized before me with his wife. Apparently they had come off a cruise ship.

"I beg you to love and welcome my little standard-bearer!" said Marat, presenting his wife.

I was stunned; but without betraying my feelings even a little, I extended my hand and introduced myself. She was a squat tub with an owl's head. While Marat spun his basically nice romantic nonsense about how the untakeable fortress (i.e., his bachelor convictions) had fallen before the irresistible charms of this sublime creature, I looked her over. Yes, she was a tub with an owl's head, and I was sorry that the Lykhna relatives had not done anything to Marat this time.

I noticed that while Marat was spouting all this, his own eloquence making him vivacious, the tub with the owl's head was oozing hatred for him. It was the familiar bourgeois hatred for any kind of eccentricity, exaggeration, or departure from the norm.

Of course, it would be imprecise to say that I noticed this and took it into account. I did in fact notice it, but at the time I thought I was imagining things. Only subsequent events confirmed that I was not wrong.

"And how are your Lykhna relatives?" I asked Marat, thinking about his marriage.

"I never asked them about anything, and have no intention of doing so," Marat replied egotistically.

I recall that at the end of this encounter Marat declared that the moment his beloved delivered a legal heir, he would throw a bearskin at her feet, a true man's gift to his young wife.

Marat had long been an avid hunter and dreamed of killing a bear or raising a cub. Somehow these two dreams coexisted easily, but neither of them had yet been realized.

One time he got me caught up in his hunting fever. He said he knew the way and the place to get a bearskin. He tied flashlights to the barrels of our guns, so that if a bear should appear during our nighttime ambush, we could first blind it with the lights and then kill it.

We reached a mountain hamlet where he had an acquaintance among the peasants, one of the representatives of the glorious clan on his mother's side, I think. Then, after dinner with this peasant and a little *chacha* to drink, we set off to the cornfield which, according to the fellow, a bear visited from time to time.

There were no particular signs that our visit to the cornfield and the bear's would coincide, so I was quite calm about setting off in the night with Marat to ambush him. We got to the edge of the field, which bordered on woods. With a finger to his lips, Marat indicated the necessity for total silence, and bending low he started searching for bear tracks.

After a long search, again putting his finger to his mouth and indicating by this gesture that in my excitement I should not utter any exclamation, Marat pointed to something or other that was supposed to suggest there were tracks present. Flashing the light on a piece of plowed earth several times, he pointed out to me this something which I was obliged to take as bear tracks. And although I couldn't see anything, except plowed earth, I couldn't object, because at the least suggestion of issuing any sound, he glared around menacingly and put his finger to his lips.

Finally, with signs, he indicated to me that one of us, to wit himself, would climb up a tree; the other—to wit, I—would wait for the bear below. I took a strong dislike to this division of labor, but I did not object, because still and all it struck me as highly unlikely that the bear would come on precisely this night.

Marat climbed up a young beech, and I sat down at its base, leaning back against the trunk. At first everything was quiet, but then some sort of noise and crackling started coming from up above. I no longer knew what to think and asked him in a whisper if he had run into a lynx or something.

He explained to me that an owl was trying to sit on his white cap; but now everything would be all right, because he had taken if off and hidden it in his pocket. Now I realize that this was a monstrous harbinger of his marriage, but at the time it wouldn't have occurred to anyone to think of such a thing.

Again the night's cosmic silence set in, occasionally disturbed by the cries of jackals and the barking of distant village dogs. I sat leaning on the trunk, listening to the nervous rustling of the woods, and I kept thinking how unfairly he had treated me by leaving me below while he climbed the tree. Of course, I didn't much believe that the bear would appear; but after all, he was certain of it and had arranged things as if my life were of less value than his.

For some reason, it is always insulting when someone arranges things as if your life is of little value. Then I remembered that I had a flask of cognac with me. We had brought it from the city so that during the night's watch we could use the invigorating liquid to fight the chill and our sleepiness. I removed the flask from its strap and took a few good gulps.

The cognac woke me up, and with new intensity I felt how meanly Marat had treated me by hiding in the crown of this young beech while leaving me below, alone with a hungry bear. After all, we had set up our ambush in such a way as to trap the bear when he wanted to get over to the cornfield. If the ambush had been in a different place, so that *after* the bear had stuffed himself with corn and was good-humoredly leaving the field we could attack, there would have been much less to worry about. But it was too late for that.

I turned on the flashlight and took aim several times, rehearsing the order of things for the forthcoming operation, just in case. For some reason I was afraid that I would hear a suspicious noise, pull the trigger first, and only then turn on the light.

Several times I took aim briskly and turned on the light, trying to get used to this order; but suddenly I remembered that my gun was on safety, and if in my rush I forgot that, no matter how hard I pulled there would be no shot. I imagined this picture vividly: the bear, slightly blinded by my light, shakes his head for a moment, but then, standing up on his hind legs, moves on me, and like a fool, I keep pulling the trigger, and I cannot understand why my rifle doesn't fire.

"First release the safety, then turn on the light, and then pull the trigger," I kept repeating to myself—a seemingly simple sequence of actions, but under the circumstances of that night I might mix everything up.

Incidentally, the light turned out to be so weak that it wouldn't blind a bat, never mind a bear. I wanted to be ready to turn it on instantaneously and release the safety; in order to put myself on guard and clear my head I resorted to the flask several times.

I went through all these operations about ten times, except for the actual shot, of course; and satisfied with myself, I was ready to put the rifle down, when suddenly I felt that I had forgotten which position the safety was supposed to be in in order to prevent an accidental shot. I simply couldn't remember which position was on and which off, when it was down or when it was up.

First I tried to remember how it was before I started practicing. But I couldn't remember anything. Then I decided to get to the truth logically, or even philosophically. I thought to myself: you say "put on" the safety. But does that mean that the lever has to be moved downward like a light switch and such, or does it mean that the lever should be moved upward, thus releasing an inner catch downward.

I sensed that just one single step was lacking here—one effort of the mind would resolve this nightmarish logical problem, and, attempting to clear my head, I went to the flask several times, when suddenly I discovered that it was empty.

I decided to forget this cursed logical problem, and I put the rifle down carefully, at such a distance that I could not catch it with my leg or hand, even if I fell asleep under the young beech. Just in case the worst should happen—Marat should suddenly yell from the tree and fall right on the rifle—I turned the rifle barrel toward the woods. Having thus made everything safe, I felt a little calmer. I decided that if the bear really did come I would do everything the way I had rehearsed it; and if I didn't hear the shot, I would move the safety to the other position.

Then I remembered the cognac, and I felt ashamed that I had drunk it all alone, without Marat. But then, after more mature consideration, I decided I had done the proper thing. Sharing cognac with a person who intends to spend the whole night in a tree is dangerous for that person's life.

That's precisely what I told him early the next morning when he came down from the tree and asked for a couple of belts. Marat was quite angry at me, and without saying a word he went off into the shade of a walnut tree to hunt for some nuts. After a while he tilted his head up at the tree, yelled "Squirrel," and took a shot.

For a few moments the squirrel dangled on the end of a shaking branch. Marat missed. I took aim with my rifle—for some reason I turned on the flashlight, though it was quite light—and fired. Only then did I remember the safety, so my rifle hadn't been on safety after all. Oh boy, I thought to myself.

Falling through the leaves noisily, the squirrel flew out of the tree. I ran over and picked up its small, still warm body. Marat didn't even look in my direction. Bending down, he hunted for nuts under the walnut tree, ones that had fallen and were already coming out of their shells.

That was the extent of my hunting adventure with Marat, if you don't count the encounter with the geologists on the way back. We stopped over for a few hours in their camp, and Marat tried to chat up a certain middle-aged geologist, who at first simply couldn't figure out what it was Marat wanted from her, and then, when she did understand, threw him out of her tent, whence he had gone during the general post-lunch nap. Later Marat explained his lack of success with her by saying he had been in bad form after the sleepless night, so he had moved in too directly.

But I have digressed. Marat did get married, and decided to throw a bearskin at the feet of his young wife as a reward for giving birth to a glorious heir to his clan.

To ensure his success, he began by traveling to the Urals to buy a full-blooded Siberian husky. He brought the husky home and treated it like a good father treats his first-born. His wife hated the noble beast from the very first day. As far as I know, the dog felt the same about her.

Information about his family life in this period is scant. One thing is clear—there was no great well-being in his house. Nevertheless, his wife gave birth to a daughter, and somehow or other they went on living together.

A little later, when Marat unexpectedly began writing poetry and songs, one of these poems—"I Awaited an Heir"—became quite well known in those parts. The poem can be seen as a sad reproach to Fate, but, I might note, it could just as easily have been directed at his wife.

Of course he loved his daughter, and several times I saw him on the boulevard strolling with her all dressed up in semitransparent nylon; and every time this scene (the proudly towering Marat and the fat little girl, her body pink through the nylon) parodistically reminded me of Marat's better times when he strolled along the boulevard with Lusia Daggerova.

Incidentally, no matter how much I urged him to give up this vain occupation, i.e., poetry, or at least to learn a little about the history of poetry, or at very least to read the work of the best-known contemporary poets, Marat rejected my advice and went on writing with a stubbornness whose genetic code had doubtlessly been imprinted in him by his maternal line.

And what was most surprising of all for a person who had not once in his life opened a book of poetry, he achieved no little success. He started publishing in our local newspaper, and two of his songs came out nationally—they were broadcast on the radio several times. Without disparaging Marat's talent, I still have to point out that the success of his songs was undoubtedly a result of our very low professional standards for songs.

Here I get to the most touchy part of my tale. Apparently the writing of poetry, after the acquisition of the Siberian husky, was the last straw for his wife. At any rate, her chastity did not survive. Once while Marat was out hunting she betrayed him with an electrical repairman who came to their place. Maybe she did this to take advantage of the husky's absence; maybe she hated that husky because he was a potential witness to her faithless schemes. It is hard to determine this now.

It turns out that this drunk of a repairman was in fact the *first* to tell Marat about his conquest of Marat's wife. Incidentally, despite the fact that he revealed it in the company of just such lumplike drunks as himself, they reproached him for daring to dishonor our Marat.

"Well, she was the one who started it," he justified himself, "Why she didn't even let me get the stepladder put away . . ."

For some reason it was precisely this last detail which struck the imagination of the people of Mukhus most of all.

"She didn't even let him get the stepladder put away," they said, as if it were an outrageous symptom of the final ruination of morals. It came out that a stepladder, or at least an open one, is virtually the equivalent of a living creature; and the sin of fornication in the presence of an open stepladder becomes an act of phenomenal cynicism.

However, she kept on meeting the electrician even outside of contexts of electrical repair and, it goes without saying, without any stepladder.

After about six months she left Marat for the repairman, which somewhat reduced the sin, but did not ease Marat's pain and humiliation. He showed me personally the dagger with which he had once chopped up the boa constrictor, and with which he now intended to cut her throat. I had to do a lot of talking to make him renounce this terrible and, what was the main thing, pointless vengeance. Of course, I was not among those who tried to persuade him by using the argument that he should spare the mother of his child.

Since Marat made his intentions widely known, I expected that the Lykhna relatives would not be slow to make an appearance and somehow or other short-circuit his angry dream; but for some reason they were silent and did not come to the city. One may suppose that in their mysterious code of morality there was nothing bad about Marat's intention. They hadn't stood in Marat's way when he had his liaison with the snake handler either. Apparently they did not see the handler herself—this was just the hot blood of youth and, to use their terminology, "a sign of masculinity."

After his wife left, Marat's nerves really started going. At night every noise kept him from sleeping and drove him to distraction. He would wrap his alarm clock up in a blanket and take it into the bathroom for the night. The buzzing of flies or the hum of a mosquito turned the night into hellish torment.

As if to spite him it was spring, and frogs croaked all night long in the pond not far from Marat's house. They destroyed his life to such an extent that he decided to exterminate all of the frogs in the pond. Every day he hunted for them with a small-caliber rifle.

He shot frogs for a week, but then this labor of Sisyphus, as one may call it, was interrupted by a delegation of Lykhna relatives; they went straight to the pond, and the eldest of them politely but firmly took Marat's small-caliber rifle out of his hands.

A real man, Marat was told, hunts deer, wolves, bear, or other wild beasts. In extreme circumstances, if someone drags his wife from under him (their words), he can shoot this man; but under no circumstances can he shoot frogs, which brings shame on his clan and, in simple human terms, is ridiculous.

Marat couldn't take any more. He collected his things and left Abkhazia; he went away to work in Siberia, the home of his husky. There is good reason (the Lykhna relatives) for not giving a more precise address.

As for his ex-wife, she lives happily with her repairman, insofar as a person can live happily with a man who gets drunk and beats her, asserting (not without basis) that she was once unfaithful to her husband. In any case, you can bet your life that he doesn't call her his little standard-bearer.

"Marat treated me like a baby," she complains to her neighbors after each beating her repairman gives her.

"Oh, you Hottentot, Marat treated you like a baby," the people of Mukhus say among themselves indignantly, "and how did you thank him? By going down for a repairman without even letting him get his stepladder closed!"

Immediately before his departure from Mukhus, Marat showed me the answer to a letter which he had sent to Moscow to the all-union photography contest, which TASS was conducting. He had sent them his famous Moscow Metro photograph. Now more than ever his battered self-esteem needed a boost.

I read the contest committee's reply. They said that the submitted photograph was very interesting, but that it did not meet the requirements of the contest, because they were interested in *original* photographs, not in montages, even very clever ones.

They didn't believe him. What could I say to Marat? That Fate never stops halfway, but always carries its pitiless design to the end!

I still have faith that Marat will be reborn in all his glory. But now I want to ask something of Zeus and the gods of Olympus; I want to ask wily Odysseus, fearless Achilles, shield-flashing Hector—all of them made wise by the experience of that understandable battle to possess gentle, blackhaired Helen. Let them answer me: how, how, how could it happen? How did the squat tub with the head of an owl manage to break our great friend whose innumerable conquests were accomplished virtually before our eyes. Or is this secret to remain unrevealed through the ages, leaving us only to exclaim superstitiously: "Away, God-disgusting beast! Get thee hence, Satan!"

Vengeance

Chik was standing beside Uncle Ali-Khan, who was selling candy at the bazaar entrance, when Keropchik and three of his friends came out. Chik immediately sensed that Keropchik and his friends were feeling extremely good, and that this was not for the best.

They had been drinking *chacha* in the bazaar, and the urge to have some fun struck them at the entrance. Chik immediately sensed this.

"I'm in the mood for a little fun," Keropchik said, and stopped with his friends.

To the left of the entrance in the shade of a stand stood Ali-Khan with his tray full of sugared nuts and hard candies; to the right of the entrance was Piti-Uria's shoeshine stand.

It had just rained, and Chik had stopped under the stand's overhang beside Ali-Khan to wait it out; but the sun was already shining, and Chik was just getting ready to go home when Keropchik and his friends appeared.

Keropchik was rather small and stocky; he looked around with the limpid eyes of a mad goat. First he looked at Piti-Uria, who was pounding brushes on the support where his customers put their feet, but Keropchik's glance made him stop pounding.

Keropchik shifted his gaze to Ali-Khan, and deciding that he would have more fun with Ali-Khan, went up to him.

Chik felt alarm, but for some reason Ali-Khan felt nothing. Tall and stoop-shouldered, he stood over his tray, his hands crossed comfortably over his belly.

"Salaam-Aleichem, Ali-Khan," Keropchik said, barely able to contain the merriment that was urging him on. Chik realized that Keropchik already had something in mind. His friends came up to Ali-Khan too, merrily looking at him in anticipation of the pleasure. Ali-Khan still paid no attention to the mood of Keropchik's friends.

"Aleichem-Salaam," Ali-Khan replied to the greeting, his voice indicating how unlimited his good will was.

"Why do you have this here, Ali-Khan?" Keropchik asked him, as if he had just noticed the tray.

"We have permission, Kerop-Jan," Ali-Khan answered, his tone carrying the same note of surprise as Keropchik's query.

"Who gave you permission, Ali-Khan?" Keropchik asked with even greater surprise, winking to his friends who were already doubled over with the merriment that was overcoming them. Ali-Khan paid no attention to the wink.

"The police, Kerop-Jan," Ali-Khan replied, slightly smiling at Keropchik's eccentric naiveté, "the manager of the bazaars, Kerop-Jan."

"You have to get permission from me, Ali-Khan," Keropchik said instructively, and with a little kick he tipped the tray upside down. The glass cover of the tray broke and some of the sweets poured out onto the wet brick pavement.

Keropchik and his friends turned and went away toward the center of town. They strutted along, bumping Keropchik with their shoulders, letting him know what a great job he had done.

Ali-Khan watched them go without saying anything. His lips moved without a whimper, but a thousand-year-old Persian sorrow smoldered in his eyes—the most inconsolable sorrow in the world, for it never turns to fury.

Chik's heart was bursting with pity for Ali-Khan and with contempt for the meanness of Keropchik and his friends. Oh, if only Chik had a machine gun! He would lay them all out with one burst! He would go on raking them after they had fallen to the ground and were writhing in pain, until the magazine was empty!

But Chik didn't have a machine gun. He had a shopping bag in his hand, and he watched the departing hooligans silently.

Ali-Khan stood there, stood there, and suddenly, leaning back against the wall of the stand, he slid to the ground; and he started weeping as he sat there, covering his face with his hands, his withered, stooped shoulders shaking.

The stand owner stuck his head out over the counter and looked down in amazement, as if trying to make out the bottom of the well into which Ali-Khan had fallen.

"Uncle Ali-Khan, it's all right," said Chik, and he bent down and started picking up the hard candy and the sugared nuts, sticky with honey, blowing on them and picking the specks of dirt off them. Chik thought that they could be sold if they were washed under a faucet. He gathered up all the pieces that had poured out, and put them back into the tray through the broken glass. He brushed off his hands, ostensibly cleaning off the sticky honey, but in fact showing those around that he hadn't taken any of the spilled candy himself. He did this unconsciously, almost automatically.

Now tradesmen from the nearby stands, both people who knew him and others who simply happened to be near, started crowding around Ali-Khan.

"He said, 'I'm in the mood for a little fun,' " Piti-Uria told those who came up. "I thought he would come for me, but he went straight for Ali-Khan. . . ."

And suddenly Chik perceived a kind of frightened and at the same time reverential commotion in the crowd. A few people started moving off furtively, but some stayed, whispering in low voices:

"Here comes Motya. . . . Quiet. . . . It's Motya. . . ."

Walking up the sidewalk which led to the bazaar entrance was Motya Pilipenko. He was a hulking, healthy fellow wearing boots and a sailor suit, and his pea jacket had the star of Hero of the Soviet Union on it.

He had appeared in Mukhus a year before and immediately so far outdid anything that the local petty criminal and semi-criminal element had ever done, that it never occurred to anyone to compete with him. It was believed that a bullet could not down him, and therefore he had the nickname Motya the Wooden.

Tales of his incredible daring were told with horror and rapture. They said that the following was the simplest way he had of getting money; he would go into a store with his famous duffel bag, and say: "A deficit . . . close the doors . . ."

The manager would see his customers out, order the sales clerk to close the door, and go up to the counter on which Motya had placed his duffel bag. Motya would carefully open the bag, the manager would look into it and be mute with terror: in the bottom of the bag lay two pistols.

The manager would raise his eyes to Motya, and then, as if calming him, Motya would deliver the final blow:

"These are unloaded," he would say, nodding at the pistols, "but the one in my pocket is loaded."

After this the manager would more or less obediently pull the drawer out of the register and empty it into Motya's hospitably opened duffel bag. Motya would close it and warn as he left:

"Don't open up for thirty minutes . . ."

This was the way, it was said, he worked through Muklius and the neighboring towns.

Chik had not just heard of Motya; he had seen him fairly often. Not far from the street where Chik lived there was a fairly quiet side street, at the end of which was a public playground with basketball and volleyball courts. Between the two lay a stretch of grass with a mulberry tree in the middle.

For some reason Motya liked to go there to rest. He would either sleep on the grass under the tree or, his chin propped in his hand, lazily watch the play. And his bright blue eyes always had the same look in them: serene, cold contempt.

Chik had noticed that this same cold was in his eyes even in the hottest weather. Sometimes he was in a good mood, and he would joke with the fellows playing basketball; but the same contemptuous icy cold was always in his eyes.

And (why hide it?) Motya's eyes were a source of secret delight to Chik. Chik knew that Jack London's favorite heroes had that kind of eyes.

No one else Chik knew had eyes like that. Sometimes Chik would sneak a look in the mirror to see if he could catch even a remote resemblance to that expression of icy cold in the depths of his eyes, but with sorrow he was forced to admit that they contained nothing like it.

Maybe the problem was that Chik's eyes were dark? Who could say? But Chik really loved those steely eyes, with their icy cold and contempt for death. Sometimes Chik wondered: would he agree to give up one eye if the other one could be like that? Chik couldn't give a definite answer to the question. On the one hand it would, after all, be unpleasant to become a one-eyed person; but on the other hand, he wasn't sure that a single eye, even if it exuded the icy cold, would make the same impression that Motya's eyes made.

Of course Motya could not help noticing Chik's enthralled looks when the latter admired him from a distance on the basketball court; but naturally Chik had never talked to him at all, much less on this particular theme. One day at the playground Motya was about to send Chik for some cigarettes, but before he came close enough, one of the older boys took the money and ran off to get them for him. But now, his Hero of the Soviet Union star flashing, Motya approached the crowd. People said that he had not gotten this star at the front, but in some dubious way. For some reason Chik didn't want to believe this, although simultaneously he loved the audacity with which Motya wore the star, if it was unearned.

Motya walked up with the heavy tread of a tired overseer. When he reached the crowd and couldn't understand what was going on, he stopped and surveyed the group darkly. The crowd parted, and Motya saw Ali-Khan sitting on the ground, weeping beside his broken tray.

"Who did it?" Motya asked, looking over the crowd with contemptuous cold. His look said: of course I know that you are incapable of defending anybody, but at least do what you can and name the guilty party.

For a few seconds the crowd was uncomfortably silent: everyone felt sorry for Ali-Khan, but no one wanted to complicate his own life.

"Keropchik!" Piti-Uria was first to cry out, and immediately everyone started nodding, showing that he was right.

"He said, 'I'm in the mood for a little fun,' " Piti-Uria went on, "then he came up and kicked it over."

"Messing around with old men," said Motya pensively, and already moving on, added, "I'll fix him . . ."

Thus spake Motya. His cold eyes sliding across Chik (Chik felt simultaneous terror and rapture), Motya headed for the bazaar with the heavy tread of an overseer.

"Motya, you want your boots cleaned?" Piti-Uria shouted after him, but he didn't respond.

"He always lets me clean them," Piti-Uria added, looking over the thinning crowd, "everyone knows that."

"God grant me as much health," said the shopkeeper, sticking his head out of the stand again and looking down at Ali-Khan as if amazed that he had still not gotten up, "as Keropchik is going to lose blood . . ."

Chik went home excited by everything that had happened and invigorated by the vengeance waiting for Keropchik. Chik had hated Keropchik for a long time. He had hated him even before the war, something which Keropchik of course did not suspect.

One day before the war Chik was sitting in the top row of the stadium watching a soccer match. Not far from him, also in the top

row, sat his older brother. Suddenly he heard some hooligans teasing
his older brother.

"Musselman?! Islam-Bek! Musselman?! Islam-Bek!" they said in
their vilest, singsong voices.

How Chik had suffered for this insult to his brother then! And the
rotten senselessness of the hectoring was particularly mean. Even if
one grants it was more or less true that they were Muslims . . . why
Islam Bek? There had been no Islam-Bek in Chik and his brother's
clan, and this jerk knew that perfectly well.

"Musselman?" they chanted, as if on purpose simultaneously asking him and asserting it in a vile way. "Islam-Bek!"

One could also understand their mockery this way: it's O.K., Chik's
brother is so much a Muslim that call him Islam-Bek and you won't be
mistaken!

Chik looked at his brother with bitter contempt; he was especially
irritated by his crew cut, which time itself would justify. "Grab them
and beat them up!" thought Chik, "you're stronger, I know that." But
his brother sat there in silence, only occasionally turning around to
hurl some useless threats which only encouraged them more.

"Musselman?! Islam-Bek!"

So all the fun of the soccer match was lost for Chik. And though
many years had passed since then, and his brother had long been in
the army, whenever Chik remembered that day his mood was ruined.

Chik couldn't quite figure this out himself. Maybe the thing was
that it was his older brother they were teasing. If they had been teasing
Chik himself, it wouldn't have been as insulting. He knew that.

But still the main thing was the senselessness of the teasing chant—
the confident victory of this senselessness, which was written on
Keropchik's uptilted face in the top row, in the limpid gleam of his
goat eyes. It was as if he said with his whole body to Chik's brother:
there, you thought you had long forgotten being Muslim; there, you
think that Islam-Bek has no relation to you, but just because of that we
are going to tease you like this and it will humiliate you.

And now today this selfsame Keropchik had so meanly offended
Uncle Ali-Khan and suddenly Motya himself had appeared and said
in front of everyone that Keropchik would get what was coming to
him.

Vengeance, vengeance! All right, Keropchik, just you wait now!
Chik imagined the various forms Motya's vengeance might take.
Sometimes he imagined that Motya would beat Keropchik until he
was completely unconscious. Sometimes he imagined that he would
make Keropchik get down on his knees in front of Ali-Khan's tray and
order him to stay that way all day until the bazaar was closed, while
going off to take care of his own business. Chik even imagined that
Ali-Khan, looking at Keropchik with his round Persian eyes, would
relent a bit and make signs to him to stand up; but Keropchik would

continue kneeling in the humiliating position, because he had so been ordered by Motya, nicknamed the Wooden, the man a single bullet would never do in. Chik even imagined the same shopkeeper beside whom Ali-Khan had been standing; he imagined that this shopkeeper would stick his head out and look down at Keropchik as if in amazement at the incredible depth of his fall.

Chik spent the next few days going through the streets of the city, the bazaar, and the parks, in fervid hope of meeting Motya or Keropchik.

He caught sight of Keropchik in the distance a few times, but from his face he could not tell whether vengeance had been wreaked. During this time he even ran into Motya twice at the playground, and he gave him a few burning looks desperate for vengeance. But Chik couldn't tell whether Motya understood him or not, and he couldn't get up the nerve to remind him about the promised vengeance.

About a week after the Ali-Khan incident, Chik went to the amusement park to ride the giant steps, and suddenly saw Keropchik there. He was sitting with his buddies under a huge pine, playing cards.

When he saw Keropchik, Chik's craving for vengeance overwhelmed him. He didn't wait in line to take the ride, but quietly left the park. He had decided to find Motya no matter what.

During this whole time he had never run into Keropchik like this, in such a good set-up. He had seen Keropchik on the move before; but now he was sitting under a pine tree playing cards, and Chik knew that he would be there for quite a while.

Chik was so wrought up that he decided if he found Motya, come what may, he would definitely remind him about the promised revenge.

First Chik set off for the playground where Motya liked to rest. The playground was located quite close to the park, two blocks away. Finally Chik was getting lucky! As soon as he got there he saw someone sleeping under the mulberry tree. It was him, Chik was certain of it. No one else would dare to rest there knowing that this was Motya's favorite spot.

Chik's heart started pounding madly. He went to the playground gate. He went across the grass to the mulberry tree trying to make noise on the grass so that Motya could hear him.

Hearing footsteps, Motya raised his head, yawned sleepily, and looked at Chik. Chik said hello, and then without saying anything else gave him a look so full of mournful recollection that Motya apparently guessed its meaning. In any case he yawned again and suddenly asked Chik:

"You haven't seen Keropchik, have you?"

"I have," Chik replied, barely able to contain his surging ecstasy. "He's playing cards in the amusement park."

Automatically, but to some extent consciously, Chik used a tone of voice which said: imagine that—Motya promised vengeance and Keropchik's sitting there calmly playing cards!

"Get him over here," Motya said, lazily taking out a Ritsa cigarette and lighting up.

"Right away," said Chik, and heading out into the street he rushed toward the park at full speed. At the park entrance he stopped and caught his breath. He was afraid Keropchik would suspect something and run away. You can't scare the target off ahead of time! He calmly went up to the fellows playing cards.

"Keropchik," said Chik, "Motya's asking for you."

"And where is he?" Keropchik asked, without taking the cigarette out of his mouth, his transparent goat eyes, squinting from smoke, peering over his cards.

"At the playground," Chik said.

"And what does he want?" Keropchik asked.

Chik was totally convinced that Keropchik didn't know anything about the vengeance that waited for him.

"I don't know," Chik said, "he asked me if I had seen you, and I said I had. Then he said, 'Get him over here.'"

Now all of the players stopped playing cards and listened to what Chik was saying.

"You had any trouble with him?" one of the players asked.

"Never," said Keropchik, and shrugged his shoulders.

"Well, go on then," said the fellow who was holding the deck, "if Motya's asking for you, he must want to ask you something."

"Back in a sec," said Keropchik. He shoved some crumpled bills into the inside pocket of his jacket, which had been lying beside him, and stood up. He brushed himself off, tucked his shirt neatly into his trousers, and tightened his belt.

Chik and Keropchik went out of the park and headed for the playground. Chik noticed that as they were leaving the park, Keropchik walked briskly; but then his gait faltered.

"How did he look?" Keropchik asked.

"Normal," Chik said.

They turned into the dead-end street on which the playground was located.

"Does your brother write?" Keropchik suddenly asked.

"Yes," Chik said, and he felt something burn inside. He remembered that his brother had met Keropchik many times after that soccer match and talked to him quite peacefully. Chik remembered the insult, but now it didn't seem very important to him.

"He was a good guy," Keropchik said of Chik's brother.

Chik was silent.

"Not greedy," Keropchik added after a little pause. They were already at the playground.

They entered. Motya, his Hero star flashing, sat on the grass waiting for them.

"Greetings, Motya!" Keropchik said briskly, when they approached. Motya said nothing in response and went on sitting. He didn't even raise his head. The cigarette smoldered in his mouth. "You wanted me?" Keropchik asked.

Again Motya did not reply, but getting up heavily and without taking the cigarette out of his mouth said:

"Undress . . ."

"What for, Motya?" Keropchik was amazed.

"For the friggin' hell of it," Motya answered calmly and lazily struck Keropchik in the face full force. Keropchik's head jerked back.

"What for, Motya?' he asked again.

"For the friggin' hell of it," Motya repeated calmly. "Undress. . ."

Chik got a terrible feeling. Why doesn't he tell him what for, Chik wondered, and mainly, why is he having him undress?

Keropchik silently removed his jacket and held it out to Motya. Chik recalled how casually he had stuffed the money into the jacket pocket.

"Hold it," Motya nodded to Chik. Chik had the worst feeling possible now, but he didn't dare object. Until now he had been a witness to the vengeance of which he had dreamed so much, but now he was becoming something of a participant. Chik held the jacket over his bent arm, trying to touch it as little as possible.

"Undress," Motya said again, spitting out the butt.

"What for, Motya? What for?" Keropchik asked in despair.

"I already said, for the friggin' hell of it," Motya repeated; and again, heavily and lazily, he struck Keropchik in the face.

Keropchik's head jerked back again. He unbuttoned his shirt and pulled it off, baring his naked chest with an eagle carrying a girl tattooed on it. Now the tattoo struck Chik as pitiful.

Keropchik put the shirt on the jacket.

"Shoes," Motya ordered.

Keropchik hastily pulled off his shoes, but was nonplussed when it came to giving them to Chik.

"Tie the laces together, you dumb fuck," Motya advised, and Keropchik started hastily tying the strings together with fingers which wouldn't obey. Finally he managed to get them together and tossed the tied shoes across Chik's bent arm.

The heavier Chik's arm got, the more strongly he felt his participation in what Motya was doing; and this made him feel awful. Moreover, he was still afraid that one of the occasional passersby on the street would be someone he knew and inform his aunt that he was participating in a robbery.

But the occasional passersby on the street did not pay any attention to what was happening here.

On one side of the playground stood a little house the windows of which looked onto the playground. In this house lived a nervous Azerbaijani who hated the playground, because sometimes the balls would hit his windows. This happened quite rarely, because the house stood rather far off; but all the same the Azerbaijani was nervous, and sometimes he would spend hours looking out the window waiting for a ball to fly into his yard or hit a window.

"I swear by Bagirov," he would sometimes shout, "I'm going to complain!"

Everyone thought it was funny that a person living in Georgia, which had had much greater and more fearsome leaders,* should swear by far-off Azerbaijan's Bagirov.

Now he was standing at the window, and even from a distance one could see that the whites of his eyes were bugging out, and he was ready to jump out the window. His wife was standing behind him, holding him back. Chik understood that he was actually being held back not so much by his wife as by his terror.

Is he really going to make him take his pants off, Chik wondered with horror, when Keropchik hung his tied shoes over his arm.

"Pants," Motya ordered, as if in response to Chik.

"At least tell me what for?" Keropchik asked again in despair. His face had turned pale, and the only red was the spot where Motya had struck him twice.

"I already told you," Motya answered calmly. "Do I have to repeat it?"

Keropchik undid his belt and started pulling his pants down with trembling hands; for a long time he couldn't get his leg out of one side, but when he finally did get it out, he took them and put them on Chik's already numb arm.

Now Keropchik stood there in his socks and sateen shorts, and the chest tattoo of the eagle carrying the girl seemed even more absurd.

Chik felt terribly sorry for him. He felt ashamed that all of this had happened because of his own efforts. To ease the shame he tried to remember how Keropchik had teased his older brother, how hard and painful it was for him to stand that vile singsong; he tried to remember how Keropchik had arrogantly kicked over Ali-Khan's tray, but for some reason none of this seemed so important now, compared to the humiliation which Motya was subjecting him to.

Will he really make him go through town *like this*, and will I have to go alongside and carry his clothes, he wondered with mournful despair.

When Keropchik put, or rather hung, his pants on Chik's bent arm, the Azerbaijani grabbed his head; and then made a decisive move and clambered up as if he intended to jump through the window, but his wife held on to him again. Three black-eyed Azerbaijani children were looking out the other window, watching what was happening on the playground.

"Well, now the shorts," Motya said, "you can leave your socks on."

---

*An allusion to Stalin, Beria, and others [tr.].

"I won't take off my shorts," Keropchik suddenly said, turning even paler. A driven goat's expression of mortal stubbornness appeared in his limpid eyes. He raised his head a bit and looked Motya straight in the eye, waiting for the blow. Motya didn't hit him, but calmly pulled a Finnish knife out of his side pocket. Terror and panic gripped Chik. Was he really going to kill him, he wondered, how can this be happening?

"Off," Motya said, looking Keropchik in the eye with his cold, contemptuous look.

"I won't," Keropchik said quietly and turned even paler.

Motya took his Finnish knife by the blade, and leaving it bare by about three fingers, he bent forward and plunged the knife into Keropchik's naked hairy thigh.

A spasm of nausea rose in Chik's throat. Keropchik stood motionlessly, staggering a bit only when the knife entered his leg. Motya straightened up and looked at Keropchik with his cold, contemptuous eyes, and suddenly it seemed to Chik that he understood the meaning of those eyes: the human body is defenseless against a knife or bullet, and therefore man himself deserves contempt.

A thick, crimson drop of blood appeared on the spot where Motya plunged the knife. And just as Chik was amazed that no blood was coming out, Keropchik shifted from leg to leg and a quick thin stream of blood poured from the wound. It ran down his leg and started dripping into his sock.

"Off," Motya repeated.

"I won't," Keropchik replied, and looking at Motya, his eyes were now like two rancorous wounds.

Motya demonstratively changed his hold on the knife so that he freed about four fingers from the point, and bending forward he plunged the blade into Keropchik's other leg. Keropchik shuddered, but again he didn't move from his place. Chik just heard his teeth grinding.

And again, as if in a dream, Chik was amazed that no blood was coming from the leg; and again Keropchik shifted from one leg to the other and a stream of blood, even more plentiful, poured down the leg, twisting and selecting a path among the thick curling hairs.

"What are you doing, you bastard!" someone's resonant voice suddenly rang out from the street, and a second later a tall man in a military uniform came through the gates of the playground. Looking at Motya without fear he quickly went up to him. Chik noted that Motya watched him without the least change in his expression, and as before his eyes gleamed with their calm, contemptuous cold. At the same time he noticed that not only did Keropchik not rejoice in this unexpected aid, but that he looked in this fellow's direction with obvious irritation.

The soldier had not managed to get halfway from the gate to where they were standing when the Azerbaijani really did jump and run in their direction, yelling.

"NKVD!" he yelled in a sorry, bleating voice, "I saw everything! I'm a witness! NKVD!"

The soldier and the Azerbaijani, eyes flashing madly, reached Motya almost simultaneously. The soldier said something indignantly to Motya, pointing at the star of the Hero; but his voice was completely drowned out by the Azerbaijani's voice.

"Jackal! Hitler!" He shouted. "We go NKVD! I'm a witness!" Motya calmly put the knife into the side pocket of his pea jacket.

"He's hi-iding it, he is!" the Azerbaijani yelled with triumphant glee, "but the blo-od, where'll you hide that?"

And he pointed at Keropchik's bloody legs.

Suddenly Motya pulled a pistol out of the pocket into which he had put the knife, and with the shout, "Get down," fired two shots.

In the first instant Chik thought he had killed the Azerbaijani and the soldier, because they both fell as if they had been cut down. Only after a second did Chik understand that Motya had fired into the ground.

The hysterical voice of the Azerbaijani's wife rang out, almost immediately after the shots, and Chik saw her running toward him, pulling her hair and keening as for a dead man. Chik couldn't figure out whether she had jumped out the window or come through the other gate, which was not far from their house.

Hearing his wife's shouts, the Azerbaijani raised his head, showing that he was quite alive and well, but that he was amazed at her peculiar behavior.

Seeing that her husband was alive, the Azerbaijani's wife threw herself at Motya's feet and started kissing his boots, with the incantation: "Lordy, don't kill him! Have pity on the children if not on him! Lordy, don't kill him!"

At this point it seemed to Chik that Motya was somewhat taken aback.

"All right, all right," he said, fending her off a bit, and turning to the soldier, he ordered, "Get up!"

Until now his hand had been holding the pistol loosely, now it stiffened.

The Azerbaijani, lying beside the soldier, now looked at the soldier as if wondering where such an alien creature could come from.

The soldier got up silently.

"About face, march!" Motya ordered, and the tall, apparently strong soldier, after giving Motya a look filled with hatred, turned around silently, lowered his head, and went away.

Well, he didn't have a weapon, Chik thought, ashamed for the soldier and pitying him, and now Motya can do whatever he wants.

"You get up, too," Motya addressed the Azerbaijani, and putting the pistol away, disdainfully mimicked: "NKVD . . ."

The Azerbaijani hopped up and brushed himself off not so much to get rid of the dust as to show that the misunderstanding was at an end and that in general it had been insignificant.

"What NKVD?" he answered Motya, "And whe-re NKVD? Let's go to my house, you be guest, yes? We drink Gudaut wine, yes."

"Get going," Motya said suddenly, casting a glance over everyone.

"Thank you, dear," the Azerbaijani's wife whimpered again.

"Shut up," her husband shouted at her, threatening her with a finger. "Go fix some food."

With quick steps which turned into a run, the Azerbaijani's wife went ahead, and all four of the others followed. Motya was in front with the host; a bit behind was Keropchik in his sateen shorts and socks, with streams of half-dried blood on his hairy short legs; and beside him, Chik, stunned by everything that had happened, Keropchik's clothes still over his paralzyed arm.

As they crossed the playground and went down the street to get to the Azerbaijani's house, people stood silently watching them. They were lined up from the gates to the houses on the other side of the street. Chik knew that they had all appeared as soon as the shots rang out, no later than that. He also knew that none of them would complain to the police or tell what they had seen.

Chik remembered the expression on the Azerbaijani's face when, hospitably throwing open the door, he let everyone in and simultaneously glanced out at the street as if saying to his nearest neighbors, "If I want, I call the NKVD; but if I want, I invite them in as guests—it's my business."

The guests walked along a dark corridor until the host opened a door, and they entered a sunny, glassed-in veranda where there were several apparently empty barrels. A small keg stood on one of the barrels, and from the moist tap one could see that it had wine in it.

Their host got down a rubber tube that was hanging on the wall, put a small five-liter jar beside the keg, opened the keg, put the end of the tube into it, the other end in his mouth, and, sucking in his cheeks, started drawing out the wine. Having drawn it up, he pulled the end of the tube out of his mouth and quickly put it into the jar; the pink Isabella started to drip out softly. The veranda was suffused with the smell of grapes. He did all of this with feverish rapidity, glancing at Motya now and then, as if trying to be sure of the correctness of his actions. When the wine started dripping into the jar, he looked at Motya triumphantly. Now he was sure of the correctness of what he had done.

Motya glanced at Chik, and nodding toward one of the barrels, said: "Put them down . . ."

Chik dropped Keropchik's clothes and freed his numb arm. He

looked at Keropchik. Keropchik looked at Motya, perhaps expecting the latter to suggest that he get dressed; but Motya didn't say anything.

Chik noted that a portrait of Lomonosov was hanging on the opposite wall of the veranda over a cozy daybed. They had exactly the same portrait in their school, and Chik could not imagine how the portrait of the father of Russian science had gotten into his home.

"A handsome man, yes," their host said, noting that Chik was looking at Lomonosov's portrait, and as if explaining why it was there.

What'll he say next, Chik wondered. The round, womanish face of Lomonosov wearing a wig had never struck Chik as handsome.

Their hostess brought in a large dish of sliced tomatoes and cucumbers, put it down beside the wine, and went out.

"Now a glass or two while we're waiting for the chicken," said their host, pouring the wine.

For some reason they drank from half-liter jars.

The host made a toast to Motya. As he spoke, his voice kept getting louder—Chik guessed because he was getting drunker and drunker on the joy of realizing that the danger had passed. Finally, he said that the city didn't shake as much when a Junkers flew over as it did when Motya walked down the street. Holding the jar in his hand, Motya listened to all this with an expression of sullen benevolence.

The whole time Chik was wondering how he could get out of there, but he didn't know how to do it. He was afraid that when they got drunk and left he would have to carrry Keropchik's clothes all through town, if Motya's anger didn't change to pity.

When the host got to "Junkers," Motya tried to stop him.

"All right," he said, raising the jar and showing that the toast was dragging out, and that he wanted to drink.

"Shh!" suddenly the host said to him sharply. "When I'm drinking to you, you must listen and be quiet."

And indeed Motya did shut up.

"Alla verdi to our Keropchik!" said the host, drinking his jar to the bottom and turning it over to show how he had drunk to the last drop, with soul.

Then as he stood there in his sateen shorts with bloody rivulets of dried blood on his hairy, muscled legs, Keropchik proposed a toast to Motya. As he spoke his whole bearing showed that he stood above any personal insult, which Motya had perhaps given him through error.

When he had emptied his jar, he took several steps toward the barrel, put his jar down, and took a slice of tomato out of the dish. When Keropchik walked Chik noticed that his foot left a trail of bloody prints. Motya noticed it, too.

Chik silently touched his lips with his jar. The host wanted to make him drink, but with a gesture Motya indicated that it was not obligatory for Chik to drink.

After he had finished his wine, Motya took a big piece of tomato and some cucumber out of the dish, and as he was chewing he nodded his head towards Keropchik's legs:

"Go wash up . . ."

"The water barrel!" the host echoed eagerly, as if the washing of Keropchik's legs was already a part of his plans and he had just been waiting for the right moment. The host threw open the veranda door and pointed to a barrel standing at the base of a rainspout.

"Maybe I can take a cigarette?" Keropchik asked suddenly, indicating his jacket to Motya. A long silence followed. Motya looked at Keropchik as if he were trying to recognize who he was. Then he reached into his pocket slowly and pulled out a package of Ritsas. He lit up himself, and gave Keropchik a light. The smoking cigarette in his lips, Keropchik went confidently out into the yard.

"Chik, ask our hostess for a dipper," he shouted back.

Chik went down the dark corridor and came out into the kitchen where the hostess was stirring a chicken around in boiling water preparatory to plucking it. Chik wondered dolefully how long all this was going to last. He also directed his attention to the fact that there were still no children to be seen. Their hostess had probably sent them away somewhere or was hiding them in another room. She gave him a dipper and a big, clean rag with which Keropchik could wash his legs. She looked quite upset. She had no reason to play the hospitable wife before Chik.

When Chik left the kitchen and crossed the veranda, Motya and their host were drinking their second jars. Chik went over to the downspout where Keropchik was standing beside the barrel. He had already taken off his socks, and after taking several deep drags to finish the cigarette, he threw it down.

Chik poured him some water from the barrel, and Keropchik washed his socks first, hanging them on the edge of the barrel, and then proceeded to wash his legs. He scraped the dried blood off his legs with feverish quickness, and then washed them very thoroughly. He washed them as if he hoped that everything that had happened would now be washed away and forgotten, and that Motya would give him his clothes back. The wounds themselves, the places where Motya had stuck the knife in, were covered with bits of congealed blood, and so as not to start the bleeding again, he didn't touch them. Either from the water or from his nervousness, Keropchik was wracked with chills. He put on his clean, wet socks and went back on the veranda with Chik.

Their host poured a third jar. Motya smoked. Barely restraining his otherworldly rapture, Lomonosov hovered above in the clouds of smoke lit up by the rays of the setting sun.

Chik took the dipper back into the kitchen. He put it on the table. The woman did not even notice him. He went out into the corridor quietly; and he turned not toward the veranda, but straight for the street entrance. He threw open the door, and not believing that he was free, went out on the street. He took a few steps toward home, but then couldn't hold back and began running. He ran all the way home, as if plunging back and forth in and out of a terrible nightmare.

At home no one knew anything about what had happened; people didn't know anything about what was happening right under their very noses. Or maybe nothing had happened? In any case Chik stopped going to the playground where Motya liked to rest. That winter Motya was arrested, and rumor had it that he got a heavy sentence; and even if he did manage to get out of prison, he never again appeared in town.

After that day Chik lost interest in people with cold and steely eyes. He even went to the opposite extreme, that is, when he saw a person with eyes like that he started to suspect him of criminal tendencies, even though the possessors of such eyes were sometimes people who were almost too proper.

As for Keropchik, he was arrested a couple of times too, for trifles; and in the end he came to his senses and became a maker of dress shoes for women. He worked in the same bazaar, and the inside of his booth was decorated with photographs of movie stars and soccer players.

Moreover, after Stalin's cult of personality came under criticism, he was one of the first to put up the underground photograph of Stalin with his son Vasily. The portrait contained a mournful hint at the rights of the lawful successor.

This struck some people as the last flare-up of Keropchik's former audacity, but others as a purely commercial move: among lovers of dress shoes there turned out to be quite a few secret and not-so-very secret admirers of the dethroned idol. However, those in power did not go after anyone for such things, and as one fellow said, Keropchik was flourishing moderately within the framework of existing laws.

The Sheepskin Coat*
by Boris Vakhtin

—We all come from Gogol's Overcoat. (An Old Saying)

Chapter One
"Shall We Go To A Show?"

It happened long ago, about ten years after the first man landed on the moon. Most people have forgotten exactly what year it was. A lot has changed since then, although of course, strictly speaking, nothing really has changed. Nowadays, fortunately, everything changes without changing; yet in a certain sense, perhaps, some things do change after all.

For example, if you stand in the morning nowadays in this city outside the columns of the Karl Ivanovich Rossi-style palace, a palace above which a fresh red banner triumphantly waves, and look closely at the people heading for work at the palace, you notice they are dressed in a variety of styles, something not to be seen at the time of the moon landing. One person has on an overcoat of native manufacture, another an imported raincoat with shoulder straps, another something of leather—not of civil-war vintage, but modern, synthetic. The heads, too, have changed; on one there is a beret, on another a hat, on others pretentious cloth caps, and a few—true, very few—are covered only with hair. Here we have change, of course, but also the absence of change, because now as before you can tell at a glance who is of greater importance. It is obvious not only among those who get out of their cars by themselves, but also among those who get out with two or three others not exactly like themselves but similar; and even among those who arrive on buses or trolleys or who disembark from the streetcar at the corner. They have different ways of walking, say hello differently, and their heads sit on their shoulders differently. No, this isn't the natural result of inborn diversity. Genetics plays no part here. This stems from the official position each holds within the palace. The

*Translated by George Saunders.

more important person nods hello and busily proceeds toward his destination, though without hurrying. The less important says hello soberly and sensibly, moving toward his destination at a modest gait—not lingering but not overtaking anyone either. The more important a person is, the more steady and immovable he is inwardly; hence outwardly the more assured. And vice versa.

In this there is no change. And there couldn't have been. And there won't be. There won't be!

Over there a man is walking—in a checked coat and with no headgear. Earlier there were no such coats, and everyone wore headgear. Now that's a change! But there isn't any change really; it's just that someone has put on a checked coat and put nothing on his head. What's the change in that? Now if he were to catch up with that other person in the gray hat, who just climbed out of a car by himself, slap him on the back, and say, "Hi, Volodya! Sleep well?"—that would be a change. But it didn't happen. And it won't!

Or that man over there—of medium height, well over fifty, not remarkable in any way but well preserved, with shoes recently repaired and coat recently drycleaned, without any gray hair at his temples—if that man, who one might say has the look of being rustproof, if he were to say to that other man, the inwardly steady, immovable one who just went by and nodded a greeting, if he were to say: "What makes your eyes so bleary in the morning? Did you drink too much last night? Better look out, friend, take care of your health. You're aging a lot." Now that would have been a change! But it won't happen. And don't hope for it.

On this morning it didn't occur to the rustproof man, of course, even to think of such a thing, and he went into the palace as he always did. In the coatroom he collided nose to nose with the new top boss, who for some reason was democratically taking off his coat right there. Probably—the rustproof man conjectured—this is the way things will be now. He barely had time to think that when the top boss extended his hand and said without expression:

"They say you're having family difficulties?"

A month ago the rustproof man's wife had left him, left without any explanation. Just gathered her things and went off to her native village on the Belaya River. The abandoned husband was also from a village, but a different one, a Smolensk village. In explanation of his unusual name, he had said yesterday—feeling nervous for some reason—to a young poetess, who had come to his office:

"At the dawn of our new era, in the days of raw enthusiasm, my father, having come from the poor peasantry and having raised his thinking to the level of a literate world view, read the word 'Philharmonia' in big letters and fell in love, thinking this was a person (rather than a philharmonic society) and supposing in fact that it was the wife of the commissar of enlightenment, because the commissar was greatly concerned about the fate of this 'Philharmonia'; and so my father named me as I am."

That indeed was how it had been at the dawn. The father of the man who is now an instructor had watched his wife intently all day, then asked:

"If it's a boy, what do we call him?"

"If it's a girl, Anna," his wife had answered stubbornly, straightening the red kerchief on her head.

"No," Ivan Onushkin had said. "If it's a boy, we'll call him Philharmon."

And on the wall he had hung a poster in which the word "Philharmonia" appeared, together with a photogenic film actress, revolver in hand.

"Vanya, who's that?" asked the wife, pregnant with the future instructor.

"Philharmonia," said Vanya. "A fearless proletarian, friend of the landless, wife of our commissar of reading and writing; she was ravaged by the White bandits in Tambov."

"Take it away," said the wife. "Or I'll get rid of it."

"You can't," said the father of the instructor-to-be.

"What do you mean? I can't get rid of a child from my own belly?" said his wife in amazement.

"I've been thinking about her," said the father of the instructor.

"Go ahead and think, but get it off the wall," said the wife.

The father, after consulting in his thoughts with the commissar, folded up the beauty with the revolver and concealed her next to his heart. And named his son in her honor . . .

"God, what stupid people they were," the poetess Liza had said gaily yesterday.

Philharmon Ivanovich frowned. Yesterday Yelizaveta Petrovna had brought him her manuscript of prose poems, which had been rejected by a local magazine. She brought it to him to have the dispute arbitrated. Of course Philharmon Ivanovich wouldn't have touched such a manuscript for anything in the world, but his immediate boss, hurrying off on vacation, had ordered him to; and his immediate boss had been persuaded just to read it over and give an opinion by the doctor who was treating his wife's girlfriend, who was suffering from something or other; and the doctor in turn had been involved by an old school chum—the chief engineer at a shoe factory; but who put the chief engineer up to it remained unknown for a long time; that only came out much later, in the course of the investigation—or more exactly, what came out was not so much who put him up to it as who *might* have, who was an acquaintance of this ill-fated engineer, with whom it all began, with whom the changes originated, although in the last analysis nothing had changed. . . . Ah me, that one, the as yet unknown acquaintance of the engineer . . .

On the whole, though, strictly speaking, it began with the manuscript. If there hadn't been a manuscript, Philharmon Ivanovich wouldn't have had to read it and wouldn't have gotten involved in the whole mess. But speaking even more strictly, it began with the poetess Liza, who composed the manuscript . . .

Philharmon Ivanovich was not responsible for manuscripts but for theaters and their repertoires. More precisely, it was not he that was responsible; his immediate superior was; he only helped. But helping was always very hard, because he was hampered by one shortcoming, one innate flaw—Philharmon Ivanovich found every performance he watched so pleasing that it made him numb with delight, brought him to the verge of swooning, of fainting dead away. It didn't matter if the actors played their parts fervently or listlessly, if the play was intelligent or foolish, if the directing was inspired or mediocre—Philharmon Ivanovich was helplessly enraptured by everything, totally willing to live and die with the actors, feeling that he himself was the prince of Denmark, an auto worker, Anna Karenina, Marie Antoinette, a Negro of the underground railway, or all three musketeers . . .

It was hard, agonizingly hard for him to conceal how much in love he was with every line spoken by the actors, every movement they made, in love even with the scenery, the music, the lighting. He would sit up front, without stirring, becoming totally rigid, and during the intermission he would go out to the lobby with reluctance and never listened to what the solicitous directors, managers, script editors, lead players, secretaries of theatrical bureaus, critics, or parents of future geniuses said to him. He walked around the lobby or sat in his hosts' offices with the same unmoving face and unmoving body as during the performance, impervious to gossip and outside influences, and at the sound of the first bell he headed for his seat. After attending several performances he would know the play by heart. Mentally he would prompt the actors, holding his breath in anticipation of each familiar word and phrase, and when the actors would ad-lib and change the text, he would have a near-seizure of joy. But these thrills engulfed him only inwardly; they were not visible.

He couldn't attend the theater too often. Otherwise they'd think he liked the production a lot or, worse, some actress there might. . . . And he tried never to go backstage, unless he was escorting some lofty guest in strict accordance with protocol. Philharmon Ivanovich never betrayed himself, not by the expression on his face, a gesture of his hand, or the look in his eye. He would have gladly attended rehearsals and been happy to meet the actors, but it wasn't possible. And when he was asked, after a premiere or a reception, whether he liked the production, he would say:

"Why so hasty? I have to think it over. You know . . . I liked it and I didn't like it."

And he would smile suddenly, breaking his immobility, and then grow inaccessible again.

He would report to his boss, if the boss had not seen the production himself.

"How shall I say? It's complicated . . . have to see it some more and think it over."

Each time the boss would get anxious and, since he hadn't seen it, would say:

"How come they won't say a word in a plain and simple way, but we have to decide for them? I'll have to go take a look, eh?"

"It bears watching," Philharmon Ivanovich would nod. "I should see it again too and think it over."

And the boss would fall for it; he always fell for it! Philharmon Ivanovich knew without fail that at any sign of doubt the boss would take the bait and go check on things for himself. For the second time Philharmon Ivanovich would attend the show, watch, enjoy, and between acts pay no attention to the anxious faces of the director, the manager, the bureau secretary.

After the show the boss would say, "Seems all right, eh?"

"Seems all right," Philharmon Ivanovich would agree.

"Well, let it play. We'll give permission, eh?"

"Let it play." Philharmon Ivanovich would nod, rejoicing unde-tectably. "Only I think I'll watch it once more if you don't mind. Can't be too careful . . ."

"Do so," the boss would approve.

For the third time Philharmon Ivanovich would watch the show, strengthening his reputation as a strict and hard-working official. In the evening others went home to their families, to conversations over dinner, to the TV set—but he went to the theater. To work. To watch and enjoy.

"Well, how was it?" the boss would ask.

"Let it run," Philharmon Ivanovich would say.

"It isn't boring, is it? Hm?"

"How could it be boring if it's ideologically correct," Philharmon Ivanovich would say and smile his unexpected smile, and the boss would smile, knowing he was joking.

Philharmon Ivanovich's immediate superior changed often. One would move up, another would move laterally, another would fall from grace totally and be dropped from the *nomenklatura*.

His previous boss had done something so outrageous you'd never believe it: he fell in love with a large-footed, large-handed beauty, a member of a rural delegation from a fraternal country, then married her, turning in his party card when things reached that point, and went off to the fraternal country, where he settled down in a village and began raising strawberries, because so far they didn't have total collectivization there. Our tourists had seen this former boss of Phil-harmon Ivanovich's at a peasants' market, haggling away fluently in the fraternal language. He showed no interest in his fellow country-men, didn't treat them to any strawberries, answered questions grudg-ingly, and even refused to have a drink with them. Philharmon Ivanovich found it impossible to understand how this kind of thing could have happened to his former boss. And if he made an effort to try, his head would start to swim and his heart would stop beating, which is why he'd quickly quit thinking about the boss, the market, and the strawberries. Then his heart would start beating normally again.

On the other hand, the boss-before-last went off to study in the capital and according to rumor had great success, managing, they said, to win favor with somebody who was really somebody.

Because Philharmon Ivanovich's boss changed often, he was able to keep watching theatrical productions—with his stony face like a vol-cano which has never erupted, about which no one knows anything. Is it really a volcano? Or just a hill? Or maybe a slight prominence on the level plain?

But now his task was not to watch a performance but to read a manuscript—prose poems at that, and with the strange title *Ichthian-der*. Philharmon Ivanovich didn't like prose or poetry. He had come across the name Ichthiander, it seemed, in science fiction, but he was at a loss to say why it was used here. So yesterday he had regarded the author with disapproval. But it wasn't enough that the author perplexed him with her title. She even had the audacity to enter the temple of light, so to speak, dressed in a pantsuit of brilliant green, with a gold chain for a belt and a necklace of walnuts; and to call his mother and father stupid almost to his face. After all, she could have understood their sentiments, sincere and straightforward as they were. True, she didn't call them stupid publicly, but tête-à-tête, confiden-tially; still, she had done it there, within, where authority is not only exercised, not only put into effect continuously from sunrise to sunset and beyond, but where all the surroundings are restrained, and there are no excesses—except for the recent installation of rechargeable siphons of seltzer water. Why had they been necessary—the large glass siphon bottles covered with metal mesh? The old way was more appropriate—decanters of plain water, without all the fizz and ex-travagance. This was an untimely reform. And why were reforms needed? They always were and always would be untimely—world without end. The top boss had reminded them of that again recently, though they had known it very well themselves, from way back.

"Where can I get a drink?" asked the poetess Liza.

"There," Philharmon Ivanovich disapprovingly nodded his head. He signed a pass for her, a nonparty member, stood up and watched disapprovingly from behind as she walked to the corner, bent over, pressed the handle, made a loud spurt with the siphon, and drank, tossing back her well-styled hair. And the pantsuit shivered restlessly upon her frame, now touching lightly and emphasizing, now hanging loose and concealing.

"I'll come tomorrow," said the poetess Liza, taking the pass.

She knew, thought, Philharmon Ivanovich, that his immediate boss, in leaving, had instructed him to settle the matter within a day and not to delay on any account. He had tried to wriggle out of it yesterday, beginning in the customary way:

"It should be given some thought . . ."

"Then give it some thought," the boss ordered, hurrying out. "But have it done by tomorrow."

"And your opinion?" Philharmon Ivanovich asked.

"I haven't read it," said the boss. "However you decide is how it'll be. Any questions?"

Philharmon Ivanovich had questions, but he couldn't put them into words.

"Why are you standing there?" asked the boss. "They won't write a word in a plain, simple way, but we have to decide for them. . . . Get going!"

And as he was leaving for his vacation the boss gave his wife Onushkin's phone number; the wife called her girlfriend; she called the doctor who was treating her; he called the chief engineer; he called someone else who remained in obscurity; and the poetess Liza called Philharmon Ivanovich. She brought in *Ichthiander*, and Philharmon Ivanovich read all evening, slept a little, then read all morning. Although the manuscript was only thirty pages long, it was full of puzzlements.

Philharmon Ivanovich was puzzling them over when the top boss said to him, "They say you're having family difficulties?"

This was a unique and unheard-of show of attention, and Philharmon Ivanovich answered, as was proper and expected of him, in a hearty, upbeat manner.

"We'll cope, Sergei Nikodimovich, we'll cope!"

He should have left it at that, but the instructor, who had lost all self-control because of this *Ichthiander*, remembered about his father and said, to his own surprise:

"They won't admit my father to the hospital, try as we may."

His father, widowed and retired on a pension, lived by himself and suffered from radiculitis. Every year it was harder to get him admitted to the hospital. This year, for example, they weren't refusing, but they said there simply wasn't any room. However, his father was used to that hospital. He could feel at home there, the pains eased up, and his pension would accumulate. This, too, had been on Philharmon Ivanovich's mind as he read the prose poems, and now he blurted it out, without going through channels or following the proper procedures; right in the middle of the coatroom he blurted something out about his own private needs. Blurted it out and shut up fast. He barely had time to think to himself that he was done for now, when the top boss, who had already switched his show of democratic attention to somebody else, caught his remark, nodded once more, and said: "They must admit him."

That had the sound of more than show; that had the sound of an order, and not only for this year but for all the years that the top boss would be top boss there, even if Philharmon Ivanovich were to retire on pension (and only a trifle remained till then, a mere year and a half). Now the only thing between his father and a bed in the hospital were mere formalities, a mere nothing, not worth spitting at.

Now that is something, thought Philharmon Ivanovich, forgetting even about *Ichthiander*. That wasn't like the previous boss, who you couldn't get in to see for months, even on business, let alone for personal reasons; and it wasn't only he, Philharmon Ivanovich, who couldn't—even department heads couldn't. But here the new boss had solved things in a split second, without any fuss or bother.

It's probably that individual attention is a requirement now, Philharmon Ivanovich mused, attention to every individual. At which point he remembered about Yelizaveta Petrovna. He had given her an appointment for 10 A.M., and there were only two minutes left.

The evening before, when he read the manuscript for the first time, he saw that the local magazine had rejected it for good reason. A poor piece—he said in his thoughts to Sergei Nikodimovich, heading for his office area—dark, ambiguous, incomprehensible from the first word to the last. And the sentences that you could understand were undoubtedly hinting at something, although it was impossible to tell exactly what, because the whole thing was incomprehensible. It seemed to be talking about the love of the heroine for somebody living beyond our world, in the depths of an ocean that was neither water nor air, someone whose pseudonym of the moment was Ichthiander, but maybe it was not about love or maybe not love for any one man. Philharmon Ivanovich read the manuscript many times. And he managed to single some things out to discuss concretely, in a benevolent, encouraging way.

For example this:

"Out of the foamy beer like a fragment of Selene heading to meet you; and to walk, pressing against your amber shoulder, through the cloudy waves, not looking down where those deprived of love dissolve into the dust in the well-fed way of dogs."

Philharmon Ivanovich intended to speak benevolently about the Gorky tradition of the stormy petrel in style; however, it was too murky, individualistic, and suggestive.

Or this, for example:

"The bus seat was torn; out of the triangular tear other people's worries, which had been stranded there, crawled up my back. My back itched. The conductress berated the little boy she had caught trying to ride without a ticket, screaming insults at him. But you weren't next to me to scratch my back."

Here Philharmon was prepared to say that you shouldn't write about the conductress like that; too many people still ride without tickets, the transit system has a big deficit, people hang onto their five kopeks, but in other countries, by the way, you can't go far on just five kopeks. For some reason he suddenly had a vivid image of Ichthiander scratching Liza's back. How good it felt to her, resting against Ichthiander's shoulder. But that wasn't written down. Philharmon Ivanovich noticed his fingers were moving, and he shook his head in horror.

Or this, for example:

"Into the cellar where they take empty bottles and containers and where a large, red sign on the wall says that wounded veterans of the Great Patriotic War will be served without waiting in line, came ten men who demanded to be taken in exchange for twelve kopeks each, because they were totally empty, there hadn't been a drop of alcohol in them for so long, and they were short one ruble twenty, and they demanded to know in what way they weren't empty wine bottles. But the black-eyed attendant said that as far as he knew it was milk they were empty of, but he didn't take milk bottles, and I asked how come he didn't take them. And he looked at me and said that I was something else altogether. And they started shouting: Just where was the justice in that? And I said he didn't know his place. But he said he knew a lot of good places, wherever I wanted, the Caucasus Hotel or the Metropol. And they said: You scum, if you don't take us on credit for twelve kopeks each, we'll burn all the cases you've stored up for deliveries on the sly at night. And I said that I couldn't today, sorry."

And so on, with suchlike nonsense, and all in bad odor. And in this regard, Philharmon Ivanovich intended to repeat the words that, according to rumor, the top boss had recently uttered, that every region has its own Baikal-Amur Rail Line, its own priority project, and every district, too; that she should go to such places and find the heroes of our day and not lower herself into the cellars of life.

The two minutes passed, and she came right into his office.

Again that suit. In the intervening twenty-four hours it had grown still greener. She had no respect. But she should have! The only thing different was that, instead of walnuts, there dangled at her breast, which was brazenly exposed in a deep V, a shiny little cross on a shiny chain! Philharmon Ivanovich couldn't believe his eyes. But he couldn't bring himself to look closer—too much breast was visible beneath the cross, and it was too white. Impossible to look too closely.

Frowning, he informed her of his opinion, reinforcing it with examples, informed her benevolently and encouragingly, and finished simply:

"Impossible."

He fell cogently silent, shaking his head with finality.

The poetess Liza had begun writing down his remarks, which displeased him, but she stopped almost immediately, leaned her head toward her shoulder, and began looking at him with her big, gray eyes. "Impossible," Philharmon Ivanovich repeated after a pause.

And he asked, trying to have done in a nice way with this green bird, this cockatoo, who had come to hear his kind observations about her prose poems, which were not, unfortunately, fit to exist—he asked, regarding her with an unexpected smile:

"This means we've come to an agreement?"

"About what?" the poetess Liza asked, adding melodiously, "Philharmon Ivanovich?"

"About changing your poetic slant and the direction of your creative life's work," he meant to reply, but instead he suddenly found himself saying something else altogether

"About changing your clothes, especially when you are in a place of public administration, changing to the ordinary dress of a Soviet citizen!"

"Shall we change together or what?" asked the bird. "And what about underwear, what are the instructions regarding that, Philharmon Ivanovich?"

The only thing to do with that statement was not to hear it; nothing else was possible. Philharmon Ivanovich lowered his head, distressed that this representative of creative youth was using so dishonorably the advantage of her non-party status.

They sat in silence.

"Oh my," said the poetess Liza. Unexpectedly she reached across the desk and stroked his head, repeating, "Oh my . . ."

Then for the third time that ill starred morning words popped out of the Instructor's mouth of their own accord, against his will. It didn't seem to be him speaking, but someone else. And the hoarse bass voice he heard seemed to come from far away.

"Shall we go to a show tonight?"

Chapter Two

"Who's in Charge Here?"

He said this in broad daylight, in the middle of a working day, to a visitor who was thirty-five years his junior, and he didn't know if she was married or not or what kind of ties she had with the boss, who, under no pressure to do so, was going to some trouble in her behalf. He began to feel dizzy, his heart stopped, the hair stood up on his head; then she answered:

"Sorry, not today, Philharmon Ivanovich. Call me tomorrow."

And she wrote her number down for him on a slip of paper.

Her fingers looked very fragile.

After the working day, as the instructor was buying groceries, he felt a greenish indisposition in the pit of his stomach and in probing it, he easily reached the source—this politically unaware poetess, who had turned his pure life back toward the birthmarks of the past. "Well, a kinsman by birth! Fancy meeting you here," the instructor heard behind him, but he couldn't bring himself to turn and see who had said it, to whom, and why.

In the store they filled his net bag with rotting potatoes of an inferior grade. He remembered that the newspaper had been writing about inadequacies on this front, but in this particular store no change for the better was seen. An order should be given, but that wasn't his part of the battleline; it was someone else's—one in which difficulties seemed to crop up every year—with harvesting, shipping, storage, and weather. Nevertheless, he didn't leave and try another store.

To balance things, the carrots weren't bad. And the meat wasn't bad either, so he could go his way with pleasant thoughts. Besides, he had in his briefcase some high-quality goods, which he had purchased there, *within.**

With the heavy net bag in one hand and the fat briefcase in the other, Philharmon Ivanovich hurried home. Fall was coming to an end, cold and rainy. Indeed, just then it was drizzling lightly, freshening up his old coat and hat. Suddenly his eye caught something green up ahead, and he made a wry face, as though he was in pain. In fact it *was* pain he felt in his stilled heart; it wasn't a frightening pain but a type he'd forgotten, pain of an indeterminate nature. Next to the green rain cape, which was fastened at the neck with a gold clasp, a male figure was vaguely discernible, wearing a beige coat with a white collar. Frowning and trying not to slacken his pace or to notice her or his heart, Philharmon Ivanovich kept walking, but the green thing waved him a greeting, got into a black car with the man in beige, and drove off, turning around, undoubtedly talking about him.

Philharmon Ivanovich had lived as a bachelor until he was forty-eight, when he suddenly married a young Bashkir waitress from the resort facility where he happened to be on vacation. His wife quickly put on a lot of weight. Incommunicative to begin with, she virtually stopped talking with him altogether. What she thought about, looking at him sideways, no one knew.

On evenings when there was no play she didn't keep him from his favorite pastime, which was to make synopses of books on Marxist-Leninist aesthetics. And quite a few such books had been published, much to his satisfaction. He drew margins in the thick notebooks, always with covers of a different color, numbered the pages, pasted a white label on the outside with the number of the notebook—the number had already passed a hundred—wrote the title of each book in

---

*i.e., in the special store within the censors' office building, the palace [tr.].

large, clear letters, did a careful and thorough summary, and at the end of the notebook left one or two pages for a listing of what had been synopsized within. He wrote with pleasure, in long sentences, trying to use his own words as little as possible, putting quote marks around phrases he hadn't changed, and noting in parentheses that page number of the book whence the quotation came. He underlined especially important points such as this: "While there is no form without content, there is also no content without form—formless content ceases to be content. However, contentless form may persist for a certain length of time, without, strictly speaking, being form, because content always precedes the origin or development of form."

Or this: "The dialectic of artistic development is such that at different stages of Soviet art the moral problematic was posed and manifested from different angles. However, it was always inseparably fused with the ideological purposefulness of Soviet art."

Philharmon Ivanovich would work at this occupation until quite late, in no hurry to go to bed. He had lost any intimate interest in his wife, making use of her body seldom, mostly in the morning, and not feeling any response at all from her quarter.

They had no children and they couldn't have any. Immediately after registering their marriage, his uncommunicative wife suddenly told him everything in bed, with unexpected passion and emotion:

"Listen. You've got to hear it all. You're my husband. You have to know. I was only thirteen. The first months when menstruation began. And he was working on the river as a navigator. He stopped at our village on vacation. Ismail, a Tatar. Everyone got drunk. He gave me something to drink, started touching my back with his hand; I curled up against him. He enchanted me. But my mother noticed. She was drunk, too. She liked him herself. Our father had died. She called me into the barn and beat me. She beat me and beat me so, then threw me down, went off, and got completely drunk. I was lying there crying, and he appeared. He came and took pity on me. I didn't know anything, I was a young girl, he bewitched me. After eight months I bore a dead child, such a small thing. I haven't been with anyone since then, believe me. Forgive me, I'll be a good wife to you. I will love you. I wanted to marry a middle-aged man. But please, just forgive me. You won't be sorry."

Philharmon Ivanovich was so terrified his organs grew cold. Everything he had heard was wrong and savage; it was quite . . . exceptional. There. He had found the right word. Exactly that, exceptional, not typical, altogether out of the ordinary. He himself, if he drank, did so on rare occasions, when his superiors were drinking in his presence and when not to drink would have been an impertinence. But when he did drink, he never stroked someone else's back. He kept his hands to himself and a civil tongue in his mouth. He couldn't imagine that a mother would beat her daughter out of jealousy, even less that a drunk would possess a child with the latter's consent. It was this consent that horrified Philharmon Ivanovich most of all, that devastated his soul—although after a long silence, by way of reply, he spoke of something else: "And Ismail, did they take him to court?" His wife answered, also after a silence: "He said, 'If you have a child, I'll marry you.' He left the village right away, sent letters. But what is he to us? You must forgive me, please."

"Without question," said Philharmon Ivanovich, "inasmuch as you were a minor. But how could that be . . . he enchanted you?"

"Forgive me," whispered his wife, but he lay there numb, as though dead.

She could have no more children, the doctors said.

They lived for ten years, and had no more talks like that. And suddenly she left.

Arriving home with his net bag and briefcase, Philharmon Ivanovich first of all fed his cat, Peach, whom his wife had abandoned. The cat ran to meet him at the door, rubbed against his legs, and switched its bent tail in a shallow curve as it waited impatiently for its master to slice the meat into its little dish. Watching the cat eat, for some reason Philharmon Ivanovich remembered his wife's story, imagined the black hand of Ismail the Tatar rubbing her slender Bashkir back, and an incomprehensible force suddenly tore him away from feeding the cat and took him to the telephone.

He came to himself only when a lazy "Hello-o" in a singsong voice came over the wire, and at that he softly put the receiver down. The startled Peach wasn't eating and was staring at him. Philharmon Ivanovich realized then that he hadn't yet taken off his coat, hadn't put on his slippers, and was making tracks on the floor. God, what a good for-nothing coat I have, he thought, but a ring of the telephone interrupted his thinking.

"Philharmon Ivanovich?" he heard. "Didn't you just call me? But we were cut off right away."

"I will call you tomorrow," said Philharmon Ivanovich, "as we agreed."

"Around four," said Liza.

"Fine," said Philharmon Ivanovich and dropped the receiver, but it immediately started jumping off the hook again.

"Two seven eight, nine-oh, nine-oh?" asked an abrupt female voice. "As a customer we inform you that an act of hooliganism was just committed from your instrument. A number was rung, then the phone was hung up. The purpose of the telephone is to communicate, not to engage in hooliganism. In the event of repetition your phone will be disconnected. Is that clear?"

Philharmon Ivanovich absolutely could not understand how the telephone office had found him out so quickly. Forgetting to eat, he began to pace around the room, visibly thinking. Now and then he glanced quickly at the book waiting to be read, the notebook and the ball-point pens, but he didn't sit down to his synopses. Around three in the morning he at last lay down and fell asleep. And for the first time in his life he dreamed a completely non-party dream.

Beyond the village of his forty-year past, on the right bank of the river, there was a forest, with a road leading into it over a bridge and up the bank; and in this forest there were a great many mosquitoes, lilies of the valley, glades with good grass for pasturing cattle, and even a pond. Philharmon Ivanovich had absolutely no premonition that he would see this very bridge in his sleep, this road up the bank, and this thoroughly familiar forest, at every bough of which there hovered the sound of cowbells, the clamor of jays, and the scent of lily of the valley. But that had to be what he saw. Only everything in the dream appeared in a totally different light and different position. The forest had thinned, the remaining trees were small and had grown there only by chance, and the bank was much wider, stretching out like a river of earth on which uprooted stumps, ruts, and piles of branches floated. There was a smell of fuel oil. The bridge leaned crazily to the side, touching the water, of which there was little beneath the bridge, and the whole land, vegetation, and sky had changed almost beyond recognition. It was unpleasant to look at and Philharmon Ivanovich, wrinkling his nose at the fuel-oil smell and at what was a virtual alteration of climate, commanded:

"Return it to the way it was."

But no one heard him, because he was all alone; only the racket of a chain saw reached him from a distance. Philharmon Ivanovich walked until he came to where the saw was and asked the man who was wielding it furiously, holding the handles like a coal cutter at the face of a mine:

"Who's in charge here, comrade?"

The man looked around without turning off the saw, indicated a direction with a movement of his head, and went back to sawing with full concentration. Philharmon Ivanovich walked resolutely on in the indicated direction and came out upon a wooden barracks, on which banners and whitewashed slogans hung.

Someone stuck his head out of the barracks, then disappeared; suddenly the barracks began to rotate and did not stop until its doorless, windowless back side faced Philharmon Ivanovich.

He started to go around, but try as he might, he couldn't get through the piles of brushwood and heaps of some sort of trash. He got tired, withdrew a short distance from the barracks, and sat down on a log to rest. A man ran out of the barracks in a beige coat with a white collar, waved to him, and began to hang underwear on the line. And then it hit Philharmon Ivanovich whose undies those were!

His heart began to beat in anger. In three resolute strides he reached the door of the barracks, found himself inside, and at once fully believed his eyes, as though he had been waiting for this very sight, which fit in quite naturally with everything that was going on. His wife and the poetess Liza were sitting stark naked at a wooden table, eating potatoes, and smiling at each other. In the corner by the stove a twisted, old hag was puttering about in a green pantsuit belted with a golden chain.

"So," said Philharmon Ivanovich. "So that's it."

His wife didn't look at him, but the poetess Liza said in a gentle, conciliatory way:

"Everything flows, everything changes, Philharmon Ivanovich."

And he suddenly felt warmed by her peaceable manner, he calmed down, and looking straight into her gray eyes, asked:

"So we've come to an understanding?"

There were no barracks around him any longer. He no longer saw any details, only the pale face of the poetess Liza and her gray, gentle eyes. He slowly awoke, carefully bringing with him everything he had dreamt, everything exactly the way it had been, even the smell of fuel oil. But most carefully of all he brought that face.

He woke up, unable to understand where the dream had come from, but he felt as if he had returned from an important meeting for which he had had to prepare a resolution and the resolution had passed without any amendments and he had put the resolution somewhere and couldn't find it and couldn't remember for the life of him where he had put it.

"Everything flows, everything changes," Philharmon Ivanovich mentally repeated. He closed his eyes and again saw the riverbank with the gnarled stumps, the thinned-out forest, and the changed river with the unfamiliar bridge, and he understood that everything had changed irreversibly and would not change back. Of course, he thought, we can't turn back the wheel of history. There it is—this irreversible wheel, which not only encompasses the most important matters on a grand scale, but also rolls over trifles like the forest of his childhood and the look of the earth's surface, which has never once repeated itself exactly since prehistoric times, since the times of the dinosaurs and primitive communism itself.

He shuddered at a distinct vision of the forest of his youth in conjunction with primitive communism. Next to a cave sat an aboriginal woman wearing an animal skin and pounding one rock on another, while another woman was nursing a hairy infant at her breast, and in the distance some primitive men were finishing off a savage dinosaur in a pit, with sticks and boulders. Philharmon Ivanovich lay there daydreaming like this until someone in the room said in a bass voice: "A terrible tale, with no happy ending!"

He came to and realized at once that it was he who had spoken—

and he hadn't just mumbled; he'd spoken the words loud and clear. He jumped up, ran to the mirror, and stared at himself intently. No, there was no skull looking out at him, no werewolf, no unknown dandy, but himself, his own familiar and accustomed self. He went back to the bed, sat on it, mechanically put his hand out to Peach, patted the cat a few times, then swept it violently to his breast and burst into tears.

Chapter Three
Don Bizarre Bizzepse

He sat and wept, and thought of calling Yelizaveta Petrovna at four and cancelling the theater date, pleading ill health. In the light of the clear dawning day it was evident that it would be impossible for him to go with her to any theater, considering his position in the ideological leadership of all the theaters of the city. Especially such a young woman. And in general a great many people probably knew her—and knew that his wife had left him. He had to cancel without fail; only he shouldn't plead his own ill health, but his father's, saying he had to put him in the hospital. Anyhow, she wasn't about to go with him really! Perhaps what she wanted was to influence him? To have her manuscripts accepted by the magazine through him? Yet a manuscript like *Ichthiander* was more than even the top boss could place. She had to understand that. And if she did go with him, what would she wear? He had run into such outlandish costumes on women at the theater—right off the backs of Papuan islanders . . . and if she had a bare back and bare shoulders and a little cross on her half-naked bosom? What then?

But the day went by. Philharmon Ivanovich arranged for his father to enter the hospital, sent up a report on the progress of work with young actors, and had a bite to eat in the lunchroom.

And the darker the day got, the more possible the meeting seemed . . .

The poetess Liza arrived at the theater in jeans and a sweater that fit her like a stocking and of course the cross on her chest fairly leaped out at Philharmon Ivanovich in the coatroom as the poetess Liza's coat was removed by her escort—the man in beige whom Philharmon Ivanovich recognized from the encounter in real life and the encounter in the dream.

This individual held out his hand and introduced himself:

"Ernst Zosimovich Biceps."

Philharmon Ivanovich shook the character's hand in silence, trying to figure out what kind of person he was, but just then the chief director of the theater came bustling into the coatroom, his face a floodlight of charm, and rushed toward him. Philharmon was about to make a welcoming move but he noticed just in time that the floodlight was aimed not at him but at Yelizaveta Petrovna's companion, who was, any way you looked at it, quite an unprepossessing type.

"Ernst Zosimovich," the director said in an emotional and somewhat hollow voice. "Good evening. It's a topnotch cast tonight, Ernst Zosimovich."

Biceps smiled slightly with his thin lips and spoke softly and offhandedly, so that one had to listen closely.

"Business, my friend. I'll stay for a little bit, then I'll have to go. But I'll be back before the end."

"And come see me, come see me!" said the director with even more emotion and an even hollower voice.

"Hello, Philharmon Ivanovich," he finally took note of the instructor's presence and gave him a cursory shake of the hand.

Things couldn't have turned out better, it would seem. This dubious type was not a dubious type at all, but a powerful figure—unknown to Philharmon Ivanovich, but well known to many. People greeted him first, and with deference, and he responded affably but not over-familiarly. This influential, though outwardly quite colorless, comrade was holding Yelizaveta Petrovna by the hand, taking upon himself full responsibility for her revealingly clad figure and for the cross. He even sat next to her in the director's box while the instructor and the chief producer sat behind them in the second row. Everything, it seemed, had been arranged perfectly, especially as Comrade Biceps and the director made themselves scarce as soon as the lights went down. But Philharmon Ivanovich was totally unable to follow the action on stage, despite the first-rate cast, because he was terribly distraught.

This distraction had begun the moment they met. His overcoat, he saw, was totally unacceptable next to what Yelizaveta Petrovna and Ernst Zosimovich were wearing. Philharmon Ivanovich's suit was a recent purchase and still quite presentable—"spiffy" his wife had called it for some reason—as were his still spotless, black, ankle-high boots with their high-quality laces. Likewise his shirt and tie. But he had only this one overcoat, recently back from the cleaners and, seemingly still an entirely serviceable piece of clothing. But alas, next to the beige coat of the highly-placed Biceps and Yelizaveta Petrovna's long-skirted peasant-type sheepskin, a *tulupchik*, embroidered from top to bottom with vivid patterns of brightly-colored thread—next to these his coat looked beggarly and shameful. It cried aloud the poverty of its owner. Wretched overcoat! He'd thought that having it turned and cleaned would make it all right! But no, walking down the street next to her in a coat like this was more than he could imagine. It would be better to go naked, less embarrassing!

"No. Better to go naked," Philharmon Ivanovich said suddenly in his wheezy bass voice, and his eyes opened wide from the shock of having failed for the first time in his life to remain totally silent in the theater. The poetess Liza took his outburst as a comment on the performance and answered with a peal of laughter.

At that time—to repeat ourselves—about ten year's after the first moon landing, a certain kind of outerwear was very fashionable on the earth. It went by various names—*tulupchik, polushubok, dublyonka*, etc. And just as the human race in all its variety is descended—or so until recently people quite firmly believed—from the apes, so too all these black, brown, chocolate, beige, gray, and white coats, made of leather either artificial or real, and fur either genuine or synthetic, sometimes embroidered with flowers, sometimes with picturesque overlays, some reaching to the waist, some to the crotch, some short, some heel-length, some coarse, some fine, and some with appliqué work—all of these garments, officially costing relatively little but sold on the black market for hundreds of rubles, sometimes for a thousand, sometimes for one and a half (yes, it's true, there were stories of a woman who had paid close to nineteen hundred rubles for a *dublyonka*; Philharmon Ivanovich had heard about it himself in a restaurant serving an ordinary clientele)—and so, just as human diversity, as many would like to believe, sprang from the apes, similarly this multicolored variety of garments had descended from the plain old ordinary sheepskin, from the ancient peasant's blanket-coat, from that primitive, reliable, and warm variety of garment that was suitable in earlier times for any guard of the watch or junior lieutenant.

But in the process of evolution and progress the primitive sheepskin had risen to heights that Philharmon Ivanovich could not dream of. He could come up with the money, despite the fact that he was helping his father and his runaway wife. He could scrape together two thousand rubles. But where could he buy the actual coat? To what window could he take his money and exchange it for a *dublyonka*. There had been rumors that coats were supplied to those on the inside, but he had no confirmation of that. And as he thought these things Philharmon Ivanovich was seized with such a strong desire to possess a *dublyonka* that he could even smell the nasty odor of sheep that had assailed him earlier in the coatroom. He sniffed the air; he could smell the poetess Liza's hair as she sat in the row before him, and her heavy perfume. And Philharmon Ivanovich felt that if he couldn't become the owner of a *dublyonka* that very moment, right there and then, he would either die or do something just as drastic.

The lights came on. The poetess Liza turned her face to him, point for point the same face as in his dream, a pale face with gray eyes. And Philharmon Ivanovich said quietly and trustingly to that large-eyed, gentle face:

"I want a *dublyonka*."

The face gazed at him for at least an eternity, and finally the poetess Liza spoke:

"All right."

During the intermission she held Philharmon Ivanovich's hand and kept up a constant patter:

"A man who is a friend of mine, an old friend; I have lots of men friends; almost no women friends; of course, I have women friends; but this man is my closest friend; he hardly ever drinks; a glass of wine on rare occasions; I don't know what kind of work he does; he never talks about it; but he knows so much, he's read so much, knows so many languages . . . it doesn't matter what he does for a living; he says that his profession is to understand . . . I saw him yesterday; he told me about collapsing systems; he was trying to understand why such systems invariably, despite everything, against all the logic of our conceptions, invariably make a transition from an orbit closer to death to one not so close to it . . ."

Philharmon Ivanovich wanted to ask what in the world she was talking about, wanted to say that he didn't understand any of it, that it had an alien ring, and it was not for nothing that it had such a ring. Physics and mathematics, or perhaps in this case astronomy too, had the right within the framework of theory to reflect various orbits if they did so truly and correctly. In other words he wanted to show some prompt reaction to her words, even if he didn't have much to say and thought there was no point reiterating things to her. But instead of what he was thinking, his bass voice came out with this:

"It's not the orbit that counts, but the nucleus."

"That's just what he said yesterday," the poetess Liza looked at Philharmon Ivanovich out of the corner of her eyes, "that for collapsing systems there is a nucleus of death, which lies within their orbits, but there is also a nucleus of life, which encompasses and includes their orbits. He said there are orbits outside the nucleus, and orbits inside the nucleus—and that gives us hope. Would you like to meet him and talk?

"No," said Philharmon Ivanovich emphatically.

"Well, no point anyway," said the poetess Liza. "How about Ernst Zosimovich?"

"Tell me about him."

"He loves the theater very much," said the poetess Liza. "He dreamed of becoming an actor but had to go away somewhere; I don't know where. But he's a very busy man. People come after him and take him off to factories, conferences, airports, and other places. I've only known him for a week. It was through him that my poems came to you. It was awkward for him to call you himself, so through someone else he . . ."

Maybe, it occurred to Philharmon Ivanovich, Comrade Biceps is one of those unobtrusive higher beings who keep our critical information secure. Maybe he's a general? Why on earth hadn't he ever noticed the traces of this star's gravitational force in the cosmic arrangements of the regional administration? Young for a general . . . but so well known in the theater, even to the usherette, but unknown to himself—he, who had been attached to the theater for supervisory purposes, did not know the man at all. . . . If he could only hold out till his pension . . .

Right then, as he strolled through the lobby with the poetess Liza, Philharmon Ivanovich realized, beyond a shadow of a doubt, that he would not last until his pension, that his colleagues would not gather for ten minutes to see him off on his deserved retirement, that his senior co-worker would not make a short speech, an indifferent one, but one to which the retiree looks forward. Whether it applies to you and truly sums up your life or not, you await this speech with emotion, seize on every word in this summing up, weigh and compare, and when you wake up at night long after, you remember and wonder why he said "He loved work" rather than "He was hard-working." Why the pause before saying "Allow us to come to you for advice"? No, Philharmon Ivanovich wouldn't hear any such speech; he wouldn't be given a watch with his name on it, nor a three-volume Chernyshevsky with an inscription, nor even a little bust of the leader with his eyes immortally scrunched up. He wouldn't receive greeting cards for October, or May Day, or even Victory Day, the most memorable day of all, if we are honest about it, to those who fought; and he would be prevented from dying as he deserved, reading and rereading in solitude his beloved synopses. He would be denied this honorably earned fate by this—this chance bird who had flown, who knows why, into his well-ordered life. If things had been different, even slightly, they wouldn't have met at all; there was no probability in it, no incidentality, no law-governed regularity, like the story by someone in which a meteorite strikes a person in the head and kills him. For no reason at all, you are stripped of your accustomed expectations for the future. You step out of a bus in the middle of its normal route and land in the unknown, where perhaps no human foot has ever trod, where there is no collective to see you off on your retirement or even to stand in an honor guard by your coffin . . .

As he was realizing this and thinking about it, he missed the first lines of the verses the poetess Liza was reciting to him,

> The shadows of her fears she called thoughts,
> Finished with the burial, she sighed, held on . . .
> Over her hand, hanging limply
> Like a final burden, a tear ran down . . .

"Who is that?" asked Philharmon Ivanovich.

"That's me," the poetess Liza replied, "to a friend getting married."

Philharmon Ivanovich felt dizziness. The lobby through which he was strolling lost its walls. It turned into a peasant market. It smelled of fish. He saw himself selling dark eels, carp, oysters, and huge crabs.

He stopped and compulsively seized the poetess Liza's shoulder, and the walls returned to their places. Sighing, Philharmon said guiltily: "Stuffy in here."

Toward morning he had a dream. At first he caught the odor of fish, then saw himself and the poetess Liza in a boat. But they weren't rowing. A young man in a *dublyonka* stood in the bow and skillfully sculled with an oar. Philharmon Ivanovich had thought they were floating on a river but instead of banks he saw the walls of houses, of different colors and varying heights, and balconies entwined with hops and adorned with wild roses. He saw palaces with turrets and collonades of white and rose marble. Here and there steps came down to the water—steps covered with dark green velvet moss, sprinkled with drops of moisture. Over the water hunched stone bridges, large and small. Singing reached them from somewhere. Never before in his life had Philharmon Ivanovich heard the music or the words, which were in a language unknown to him. Beautiful voices clearly articulated every syllable, "Hostis ut praeceps, tibi domine." And although he didn't know the language, he immediately understood that this meant "How lovely is life, o my dear." And Liza sang the words, "O caro mio, la bella vita," and he understood this too without effort, and he realized they were in Venice—where else?—and were on their way to the latest Biennale, where he would sell oysters bought for a trifle from Greek smugglers and Liza would read poetry about collapsing systems.

"Don Bizarre Bizzepse," he said to the gondolier, "cermente presto."

And tossed him a gold coin. The young man nodded understandingly and applied himself to the oar. The boat swept along the canal, above which yellow, blue, green, and violet lanterns burned . . .

But before this dream there had been a late-night party. A silent chauffeur had driven the director, poetess Liza, Philharmon Ivanovich, and Comrade Biceps in a black automobile. Ernst Zosimovich himself invited Philharmon Ivanovich to ride in the car with them and the director said that he would be very happy—of course as long as it wasn't too late for Comrade Onushkin—but that certainly he was very glad to have an unexpected guest. And so they arrived and entered the director's apartment, where there were heaps of people already and where the director of the largest secret establishment in the city, whom Philharmon Ivanovich knew, greeted him with surprise, and where other familiar and faintly familiar faces flashed by. An enormous hand-carved Sabaoth, Lord of Hosts, stared menacingly from a wall. From the ceiling hung large bells and handbells, tinkling in diverse harmony when brushed by peoples' heads. And over the kitchen window hung a genuine ship's wheel, gleaming with polished copper trimming. Then Philharmon Ivanovich found himself at an expandable oval table next to an elderly actress whom he knew well, though she didn't know him at all. He managed to drink almost nothing and say absolutely nothing, nor was he asked to. There was an excess of people who wanted to make toasts and drink them. The director seemed troubled as he kept leaving and returning with bottles that were emptied immediately. He never had a chance to sit down. At that point Comrade Biceps went up to him, asked him something, and then fought his way to the phone which was in back of Philharmon Ivanovich, so that the latter inadvertently heard what this slightly-built but powerful person was saying.

"Biceps here. Bi-ceps. Who's on duty tonight? Put him on. Anatoly, go over to Elena Ivanovna's and get a case of the Armenian stuff; and you've got to get some lemons. Beyond that, use your imagination. Have them put it on the bill . . . and bring it here. Yes, where the actors are. I give you twenty minutes, not a second more."

Philharmon Ivanovich knew of course that in the interests of the common cause, of what was being built in general, it was sometimes forgivable for individual builders to violate the moral code. But this—in the wee hours of the night, with Elena Ivanovna as intermediary, she who ran a residence hotel for special guests, native and foreign, to order food and drink this way, in front of everyone, including chance individuals and non-party people, without even a hint of a pardonable cause or any defensible grounds whatsoever, but simply for people relaxing in a private capacity, the kind of thing that could happen every night of the year; that this could be done, and so simply, at the drop of a hat—such puissance Philharmon Ivanovich could not have imagined before. And when exactly twenty minutes later the director began setting out bottles of cognac on the table, referring to them as "flasks," Philharmon Ivanovich began drinking gobletful after gobletful, with the satisfying feeling that by so doing, he was saving, if only a little, the national wealth from senseless despoliation.

Now the actress was saying to him, laughing like a child, "Maybe Comrade Biceps, to put it bluntly, has an occupation that defies all comprehension, but still he's a man with heart, a magnanimous and responsive person, who would never do something, you know, like listen in on telephone calls; that's not his style. He loves jokes, and sometimes—he himself—such jokes he tells! Me," she said giggling, "I'm an old, gray-haired actress. And I asked him right out, 'But what is it you do? Come on, tell me, how do you get all these connections and avenues?' And he answered in strictest confidence that someone had to protect something from what might happen somewhere, understand? That's what he's like. But he himself will say more than he should sometimes. The only thing is, he doesn't like to drink a lot. Just has a little, purely symbolic. But he can drink as much as you like.

And doesn't show it a bit? You'd never expect such a skinny man would have so much soul in him. Probably, they give them special training for that, what do you think? You, for example, did they teach you that, or are you self-taught? And he's such a sweet person, he's gotten apartments for so many actors. And my son," said the gray-haired actress, weeping, "he even kept him out of the army. No one could help, but he went to see someone—and my son stayed home. How can anyone thank him enough? It's beyond me. Give me your advice, how can you thank someone like that?"

At which point the poetess Liza came up, took Philharmon Ivanovich by the hand, and led him over to Comrade Biceps, who was wearily jotting something down in a little black book with gold trim while the director of the secret establishment stood over him, insisting:

"Eric, I need this brand of steel desperately. I can't get along without it. They've exhausted the stocks, and there's two more months to the end of the year. Do you understand, Eric?"

"Got it," said Biceps. "What else?"

"They won't release Nyangizayev to come work for me . . ."

"That's a different republic, a different Council of Ministers," said Biceps, thinking. "All right, tomorrow around twelve I'll go out and walk around by the monument, have a car waiting for me . . . exactly at twelve!"

"I'll run down myself!" the director rejoiced.

"Is that all you've got, Ram?"

"We can talk tomorrow; there are a few small things."

"OK, relax, Ram; do some dancing; things are looking up for you . . ."

Philharmon Ivanovich had heard of Nyangizayev. A very highly placed official had been trying for a long time to have Nyangizayev assigned to him. But at the center, they refused. Now here Comrade Biceps . . .

"What do you have, Yelizaveta Petrovna?" asked Comrade Biceps.

"He needs a *dublyonka*," said the poetess Liza, seating herself on the arm of his chair and nodding at Philharmon Ivanovich.

"What do you want it for?" Biceps asked him affectionately.

"Is it true they taught you to drink so as not to get drunk?" Philharmon Ivanovich's bass voice blurted out.

"Fairy tales, dear Philharmon Ivanovich," replied Biceps. "Terrible tales, with no happy endings. Have a seat; here's a chair."

The poetess Liza left discreetly.

"The *dublyonka* is no problem" said Biceps. "Half the theater is walking around in *dublyonkas* I got for them. The director already has three. But it doesn't help him, Philharmon Ivanovich, not as an artist and not as a man. It doesn't help. . . . Do sit down!"

"I don't want to," said Philharmon Ivanovich.

"More than anything in the world I love the stage," said Biceps

melancholically. "And all of us are actors on it . . . and you?"
"Yes," said Philharmon Ivanovich and began to laugh loudly,
throwing back his head. Biceps looked at him, smiled his thin-lipped
smile, shook his head, either with reproach or satisfaction, you
couldn't tell, and said in a toneless voice:
"Here he wants to put on Gogol. But ask him what he understands
of Gogol? Have you asked him?"
"No."
"Want me to?"
Biceps asked, and the director answered at length, but exactly what
he said Philharmon Ivanovich was unable either to understand then or
remember later.
"You see?" Biceps asked rhetorically when the director had gone.
The poetess Liza brought them up a little cart on wheels with cognac
and lemons and disappeared with a wave of the hand. "He's going to
put on *The Inspector General* . . . for three *dublyonkas* . . . all
through me . . . but he has no idea about the power of light or the
darker powers. In the theater of Gogol not one gun goes off, never!
And what's the point of a gun here anyway . . . want me to get you a
gun? With your name on it? A lot of people want them . . . let's
drink, Philharmon Ivanovich, to Gogol. He was the wisest man in
Russia. He fled to Italy, to get away from his countrymen, they say
. . . only what kind of Inspector General could you have in Italy?
There, dear Philharmon Ivanovich, the Moor of Venice, Goldoni,
and the Duke forgave him . . . Let's drink, dear friend. In what way
are we worse than the greatest actors? Excuse me, they're coming at
me again, may the Duke forgive them. . . . No, no, please wait, I
beg you!"
This time Biceps was asked for a garage and a place near it; he
dashed off a note to someone. Then he drank to the theater with
Philharmon Ivanovich, whose importance was increasing in
everyone's eyes because of his close proximity to such a person. Then
he jotted down a request for a car to be found—it had to be a Zhiguli
and its color had to be dark coffee with mother of pearl. Again he drank
to the theater, supplied someone's wife with a room at the government
sanatorium near Sochi, again drank to the theater, wrote down the
measurements for foreign eyeglasses for someone, again drank, again
supplied galvanized iron and copper for someone's summer place, and
again drank to the theater—clinking glasses with Philharmon
Ivanovich the whole time. Then Philharmon Ivanovich heard
everyone shouting "hurrah" in honor of Biceps and singing "For He's
a Jolly Good Fellow." Biceps had handed him over to the silent
chauffeur and had said in parting that at five of twelve he should bring
seventy-three rubles and a note with his shoulder size, height, and
address and be at home after seven when they'd deliver it. At home
Philharmon Ivanovich fell asleep and dreamed of Venice, what else?

Philharmon Ivanovich pet Peach. The cat smelled of strong perfume. Philharmon Ivanovich's heart stopped in fright until he realized that this was the hand by which the poetess Liza had led him over to Biceps. He dialed her number, but no one answered, though he rang for ten minutes. After that he took the money, tucked it in an envelope, wrote down his size, height, and address, and ran out. It was raining, mixed with snow, which brought him a surge of wild happiness. From a pay phone he called the secretary of their sector of the office and told her in his bass voice that he had caught a cold and was on his way right then to a house of culture, and would be in after twelve. He didn't go to a house of culture but to a residential building, didn't use the elevator—it might get stuck—climbed the stairs to the tenth floor, and rang the bell, which gave a musical chime. He rang it stubbornly for a long time. Finally footsteps could be heard on the other side of the door.

"Who is it?" asked the voice of the poetess Liza.

"Open up," said Philharmon Ivanovich.

In the entryway of her apartment he looked first at her, in jeans and sweater fitting tight as a glove, then at the beige coat with the white collar hanging on the coat rack, looked around at the muddy tracks left by his own feet by the door, and said with trembling lips:

"Please, Yelizaveta Petrovna, give me something to write with."

Having gotten a pencil, he pulled out the rumpled envelope and wrote four words under the address: "Black, in general, dark-colored," and handed the envelope to poetess Liza, who had remained silent the whole time.

"Ask them please, Yelizaveta Petrovna, not to come meet me at five of twelve today. Yelizaveta Petrovna, I just can't . . .

At work he wandered around, stopping in at different people's offices. He even went downstairs about ten times to where the policeman in the lobby checks people entering and leaving the building. And at five of twelve he stopped by his window, from which there was a good view of the monument. A black car was already standing there, the director of the secret establishment pacing back and forth beside it. Exactly at twelve Biceps appeared, he and the director embraced, got in the car, and drove off.

Philharmon Ivanovich stood by the window a long time, thinking.

"But he isn't doing anybody any harm!" Philharmon Ivanovich said suddenly in his bass voice, and burst into deafening laughter but immediately caught himself and glanced around with widely staring eyes.

The secretary of their sector glanced into the office, with her pyramid-style hairdo on a head nearly eligible for pension—she who kept private and public secrets hidden behind the imperturbability of her face. She peered at the startled Philharmon Ivanovich and asked: "Are you alone?"

"A cough," said the instructor, devastated.

"No one has called." And the secretary slammed the door.

But just then he got a call.

"Please," said the poetess Liza, "come by for me this evening. We'll go visit some friends. Do come, please."

"After seven . . ." he started to say.

"Even if it's one in the morning. I beg of you, please. I'll read you some poetry."

"I'll try," he said.

"Does that mean we've reached an agreement?"

"Uh-huh," he affirmed, and even before he had hung up the phone he again burst into loud laughter, stopped more quickly than before, and pricked up his ears. But the secretary was still typing away and didn't come to the door. The instructor, of course, sensed there was something wrong, but he didn't dwell on it . . .

Toward evening it became quite cold, and a pure, clean snow began to fall. But to Philharmon Ivanovich the afternoon seemed to bring a warming trend, with the bright sun, clear sky, and other things that rarely happened in the city. He grew more and more excited, and that surge of wild happiness came back to him, making his anticipation totally unbearable. By twenty of seven he was pacing up and down the little hallway of his apartment—up to the door and back, up to the door and back. Exactly at seven the doorbell rang. Philharmon Ivanovich was at the door instantly and opened it while the bell was still ringing.

"Comrade Onushkin?" asked a taciturn young man. "This is for you."

And handed him a large package bound with ordinary twine.

"Want me to sign? How much for delivery?" Philharmon Ivanovich mumbled, taking the package.

Chapter Four

"Last Name, First Name, Middle Name"

But the young man ran off, without half a word in reply.

"Thank you," said Philharmon Ivanovich softly, trying to listen. The door down in the main entrance slammed, followed by the roar of a powerful motor. Philharmon Ivanovich went into the main room of his apartment without locking the door, lay the package on the table, and cut the twine.

There, sprawled out upon the table, its sleeves falling wide apart as though to take him in an embrace, was a brand-new *dublyonka*, the color of dark chocolate, with light-colored fur trim and round black buttons. Philharmon Ivanovich put it on. It wasn't tight anywhere. He looked in the mirror, straightening his shoulders and holding his head high. Not surprisingly he failed to hear the door of his apartment open . and close and someone come into the room behind him. Only when something flashed in the mirror did he wheel around like the hero in a cowboy movie. But there before him stood not a thief, not a burglar, not an enemy of any kind, but the poetess Liza in an unusually attractive coat of gray fur, with a squirrel cap and high boots.

"I've got a taxi," she said.

"I'm all dressed," he said.

His only doubts now concerned his hat, rather an old one, worn down to the grain at the back, though it really wasn't that noticeable; on the other hand the dark brown of its crown went quite well with the coat. And once in the taxi he could carry the hat in his hand.

There proved to be few *dublyonkas* on the streets; much more common were overcoats like his old one—a coat which had forever outlived its usefulness and must be discarded as soon as possible. His wandering attention rested least of all just now on the poetess Liza's beauty. He was watching the way people were dressed and thinking about what lay in store for him. A customary thought was about to run through his mind—that people were dressed much better than after the war or ten years back. But before this thought could be reinforced with words and statistics it seemed to smile guiltily and vanish. He merely blinked in irritation as it left. Again he wondered uneasily what she was wearing under her fur coat and how everyone else there would be dressed and, above all, how they would conduct themselves. He had heard rumors about the youth of today, that sometimes they watched underground pornographic films or had a striptease. His colleagues who knew about such matters would, under appropriate circumstances, denounce both the films and the striptease but took the liberty sometimes of winking in mid-denunciation. And now Philharmon Ivanovich began to see scenes from a movie passing before his eyes—each more interesting than the one before. Through a cloud of cigarette smoke, or fog, he saw a crowd of modern-day youth, very scantily clad; an apelike young man in red swim trunks was pushing a swing higher and higher, while in it a full-chested young woman kept her eyes closed; from one corner of the room some abominable music without any words was blasting; hostile voices emanated from another; from the next room a fat girl with glasses came in on hands and knees; on her back rode an unbelievably skinny girl, whacking her on the rump with a theater program and shouting that our country couldn't lead humanity to happiness if it had a shortage of everything, including toilet paper. Philharmon Ivanovich narrowed his eyes, shook his head, and said to the poetess Liza:

"Tonight call me Comrade Onushkin."

"The name is inseparable from the man," she retorted.

"Just for tonight," he said, his eyes widening again.

The taxi stopped at an intersection and Philharmon Ivanovich gave a start. In front of him, almost touching, was the face of one of his bosses, not the top boss, but a very high-ranking one nevertheless. Having noticed the beauty of the poetess Liza, this boss had stopped reclining in the backseat of his car. He had leaned forward to look closer, opening the window in spite of the cold. Then he transferred his gaze to the *dublyonka*, putting himself in its place next to such beauty, and suddenly he realized who was in the *dublyonka*. The boss wasn't able to conceal his astonishment, although at the rank he had attained one is not supposed to let such feelings show. Philharmon Ivanovich didn't manage to greet him respectfully, as he should have in keeping with his rank, especially after he had been recognized— aside from the fact that it was the only correct thing to do—but he didn't have time because the light turned green and the high-ranking boss went shooting off with his neck twisting back and surprise written all over his face.

"But all he's wearing, if you ask me, is an overcoat," was what Philharmon Ivanovich came up with, and the poetess Liza took it all in, appraisingly, out of the corner of her eye.

Under her fur coat, it transpired, the poetess Liza was wearing a long, quite severe, flowered dress; only on the right side it had a slit from hem to waist. But not everything was visible through this gap, nor was it visible all the time. There were no naked people present; in fact there was only the host and hostess, a very young couple. There wasn't even vodka, just some dry wine.

The poetess Liza read her verse with the same voice in which she spoke—a somewhat throaty, indolent, singsong.

> In human games there is a boundary—
> At which the game dies out.
> And things grow quiet.
> Like they do in a shooting gallery
> When they're changing the targets.
> And things get bad,
> Like they do in the world
> When they make decisions.
> Like they do in the sea,
> When you've fallen overboard,
> And you gaze after the ship's wake
> And know it's useless to call out.
> Like they do in the morgue,
> When you search for familiar features and recognize none.
> Like they do in the gloom
> Of a drunken dream when you've lost the point.
> In human games there is a boundary—
> Where the game dies out.

Philharmon Ivanovich wondered what this was all about. But she kept reciting:

A line of writing, a handful of letters—
It's simpler than simple to dash off a line.
A door. And every ring of the doorbell
Is like the click from a misfiring hammer at an execution.
And again to wait. The hands' fragile fingers.
A line of writing, a handful of letters.

It's absolutely right; she has very fragile fingers, Philharmon Ivanovich thought, and began to tremble, as one trembles from severe cold or from too much drinking.

Then they talked and Philharmon Ivanovich felt confident because he kept thinking of his *dublyonka* hanging in the hallway. Consequently he expressed his views on poetry with great assurance:

"For many people, fate stands apart and poetry stands apart, in spite of talent. In your case, too. It's immaturity."

The poetess Liza's eyes grew narrow and she said, "Wasn't it you that returned *Ichthiander* to me?"

"It was," said Philharmon Ivanovich. "Thus, for you too, Yelizaveta Petrovna, fate stands apart."

"Apart from what?"

"From everything, Yelizaveta Petrovna, from yourself too, for example."

"And Ernst Zosimovich?" asked the poetess Liza.

"We won't talk about Comrade Biceps," said Philharmon Ivanovich, suddenly seeing everything completely. "We won't . . ."

His heart was pounding at his temples, his cheeks felt flushed, and he spoke quickly and eagerly. For example, the hostess said something about some people he didn't know.

"He can't live with her, and she can't live with him, but for some reason they live . . ."

And he explained:

"No outsider can understand the life of a husband and wife, not because the relations between husband and wife aren't known to outsiders in sufficient detail, but because the husband and wife themselves don't fully understand their relationship, and if they can't find their way themselves, how in the world is an outsider going to find it?"

"And if they aren't even husband and wife?" asked the host.

"How then find one's way?" asked the poetess Liza.

"My dear young people, don't you know," said Philharmon Ivanovich, thinking of his *dublyonka*, "only love can find the way."

"Are you baptized?" asked the poetess Liza.

"My father guarded my cradle with a gun," he answered, "to prevent the foul ceremony from being performed upon me. But his vigilance weakened, his mother-in-law got him drunk, stole me away and defiled me, as he explained it. And what name they gave me I don't know . . ."

"God," said the poetess Lize, "What funny people they were."

Philharmon Ivanovich wasn't offended, but smiled to himself with his disarming smile, because he remembered his father repeating: "I always maintained an unbending optimism, even in front of the barrel of a gun when I was going to be shot, and they took me out to be shot quite often."

"Why do you sometimes speak in a bass voice?" asked the poetess Liza.

"Something with my throat," Philharmon Ivanovich answered, thinking about his *dublyonka*.

"Call me," said the poetess Liza when they parted.

He stood in the door with his hat in his hand, squaring his shoulders under his *dublyonka*, and again saw nothing but the wide open face of the poetess Liza. His face rushed to meet that face, his eyes closing. He pressed against it and for an instant felt its brows, cheekbones, nose, the corner of her mouth—brow to brow, nose to cheekbone, cheekbone to nose, corner of his mouth against the corner of her mouth—then he turned and walked off.

"I was so happy with you," he pronounced when he was already out on the street, putting his hat on with both hands.

Toward morning he had a dream.

Beyond the river of his forty-year past next to the forest there was a pond, and after sunset he was standing on the shore of the pond staring at its dark surface, on which white lilies floated, the same kind he had recently seen in the papers, which had been entered into the great book of endangered plants and animals of the world. He looked at the lilies and thought what a pity that they were dying out, orders should be given to prevent their extinction, in general some decision should have been made long ago against changes; but the lilies kept growing whiter, the water beneath them grew brighter and more transparent. Now the entire pond was transparent and he saw that the lilies were not lilies at all, and they weren't floating on the water; they were sitting on the shore and they had bright heads and hands; they were children. Some of them even seemed to be children he knew. They had no Young Pioneer ties on. The Pioneer leader, or the teacher, was absent, as were all adults in general. And he had absolutely no idea how these children in white shirts had gotten here.

Now his wife came out of the pond and said through her tears, as she went past him toward the forest:

"You've forgotten everything. These are the children who missed being baptized; you'll never be forgiven for that. And mine isn't here."

At the edge of the forest she got into a black car. In it was Biceps, who said to her:

"How long must we wait? May the Duke forgive you."

And they drove off. But one little boy came up to Philharmon Ivanovich and said:

"Take me with you, I beg you, please. I want to live with you."

"What about the others?" asked Philharmon Ivanovich.

"They don't want to live with you," said the little boy.

Philharmon Ivanovich carried him, keeping him warm against his chest under the flaps of the *dublyonka,* but the little boy said:

"After a year bring me here and we'll say goodbye. I'll live with you but take care that no one sees me. It's forbidden. Think of a place you can put me."

Philharmon Ivanovich's home proved to be quite suitable for this, with a large Russian stove, and small windows—the way it had been in his childhood. But in the dream he was living there all alone. He made a place for the little boy to stay on top of the great Russian stove toward the back, and hung a curtain to block off the area. Late at night he let him out to walk around, fed him, read him books, told him fairy tales. Everything would have been fine except that Peach shied away from the boy, and began staying outside most of the time, coming home only now and then, emaciated. The cat would gorge itself greedily, hissing at the place at the back of the stove, arching its back and ruffling its fur. The little boy would look out and call the cat to play, but Peach would back away, until it got to the door, then skedaddle.

On one occasion all of Philharmon Ivanovich's relatives gathered at his house, one of them being Liza, to celebrate some holiday. Whether it was New Year's or Christmas or Easter was unclear to him in the dream. They all sat at one big table, drinking, eating, and talking at length. His wife and Liza sang a duet of great beauty:

> Do not forget, after the blizzards
> Back to the fields will come fair May.
> Do not forget your friend, your dearest,
> Your fate, your love—her don't betray.

In a word, they had a pleasant evening and were getting ready to break up after midnight, when Onushkin Senior, who for some reason had also come for the celebration—although, as Philharmon Ivanovich remembered, he was being treated for radiculitis in the hospital at that very moment, suddenly said:

"It's good that we all get together, if only once in a lifetime. Everyone has come!"

Here a laugh rang out, and Philharmon Ivanovich, turning cold, waited for the fact to be exposed that he had a little boy living up in back of the stove.

"Who's that laughing?" asked his father.

"You only imagined it," said Philharmon Ivanovich.

"Now what was I saying?" his father continued. "It's a good thing, I said, that we have all, without exception, gathered here tonight—"

And again the boy couldn't restrain himself and burst out laughing.

"Someone *is* laughing," said Onushkin Senior.

"It's the wind in the chimney," said Philharmon Ivanovich.

A year passed. He was saying goodbye to the little boy by the pond, on the dark surface of which white lilies floated, and he asked:

"Why did you laugh when my father said we had all come together?"

"He didn't know," said the boy, smiling brightly, "that he'd soon come home and find his son dangling where he'd hung himself."

Philharmon Ivanovich reflected for a moment, remembered that his father had only one son, and said:

"You and I have spent a pleasant year together. I don't want to part from you. Why are you so cheerful about it?"

"I don't want to part, either," said the boy, embracing him tightly.

"I'm not about to lay hands on myself—absolutely not," said Philharmon Ivanovich.

"Who knows," said the boy, growing sad.

Philharmon Ivanovich returned to his peasant hut. He walked all around inside it to see if he was hanging somewhere, sat down by a window, and gazed out at the forest, in whose shadows the pond was hidden. For some reason a telephone began to ring harshly on top of the stove, and he was forced to wake up, anxious of heart.

It was eight o'clock in the morning.

"You won't wait long enough to see that . . ." said Philharmon Ivanovich, he knew not to whom, and vaguely recalled that some relative had hung himself, a long, long time ago, apparently because of an unhappy love. Such a thing had happened but he couldn't remember when or where because the telephone began to ring alarmingly—with exactly the same ring as the one on the stove in the dream.

It was 8:01.

From the very first words Philharmon Ivanovich realized it was a bad business. They were calling from that sector which was located behind a solid door, like the door of a safe, a sector which in fact was a safe. The most silent of the silent worked there, the most unexpressive of the unexpressive, the most classified of the classified. If they called someone, it almost always meant a disaster in the making, and if they called at home—a couple of hours before the start of the working day at that—and if the secretary of your office sector had slammed the door just the day before, and if, besides, your conscience wasn't exactly crystal clear . . .

"But what's this all about anyway?" Philharmon Ivanovich tried to ask, although he knew it was useless; they'd never explain or make allowances for a heart condition or show respect for your age. Don't count on sympathy here or cleverness, because you're a matter of indifference to them in general—including your heart, age, cleverness, kidneys, thoughts, feelings, and all other appurtenances. He knew this but asked nevertheless, as when a fledgling is dragged from its nest by a serpent and starts to disappear into the serpent's chilly innards; the fledgling probably can't restrain itself and asks, "What's this all about anyway?" Philharmon Ivanovich asked and of course nothing was said and no explanations were forthcoming. They only sought to frighten him more by the absence of any hints whatsoever.

Two hours later he was sitting in front of an investigator, who asked: "Last name, first name, middle name?"

"Philharmon Ivanovich Onushkin," he answered.

"Do you know Ernst Zosimovich Biceps?

"Yes . . ."

After work, where for the time being everything was the same as always, except that the secretary of the sector didn't say hello, he returned to his home, and having set to thinking very hard, remembered that he had a patron, perhaps even a protector.

Several years earlier there had been a reception at the House of Friendship in honor of a delegation from a fraternal country—the same one at which, incidentally, the journey from the *nomenklatura* to selling strawberries had begun for Philharmon Ivanovich's former boss—a prominent official, curly-haired, with an open countenance. Philharmon Ivanovich and his wife had also been at the reception. They ate hardly anything, although the order had been issued not to stand around like pillars but to mingle freely and in a lively way in the spirit of the times. However, it was always safer to stand aside, so as not to talk off the top of your head; that way you don't make mistakes and in the worst of cases they'll reprimand you in private. But for improper relations with comrades from a fraternal country, look out . . . At one point a fellow countryman, a thin comrade of about sixty, came over to them and started a conversation. He had a memorable appearance—a long, hooked nose that nearly touched his chin, long and pointed like the toe of a woman's slipper, and sticking out between the nose and chin was a lower lip, while the upper lip was altogether lacking.

His gray forelock hung down over his high brow with its sunken temples; the cheeks below the cheekbones were sunken also. His eyes burned with an eternal fire—and blazing in the fire were kindness, sympathy, and a painful experience of life. The lower lids of the eyes were immobile and exhaustingly tense; they never relaxed for a moment.

"If there's ever anything," said the fellow countryman after talking for a while, asking who Philharmon Ivanovich was, where he worked, whether he had fought in the war, and so on—and the fire in his eyes was covered for a moment by a veil of love and friendship—"if there's ever any need in your life, even if it's something small, call me right away at home, don't be shy. Write down my number . . . even if it's something small; anything can happen in life, as if I didn't know . . ."

Philharmon Ivanovich didn't believe in his unexpected patron right away. He waited for half a year to see whether there was some hidden purpose behind all this, but nothing came out; then he carefully hid away the slip of paper with the home phone number of Comrade Taganrog. He hid it and carried it around with him like a talisman, like a safe-conduct pass, the kind everyone needs so badly, literally everyone, and this paper warmed his heart and he often remembered the eyes moist with kindness of his highly experienced friend and his telephone number.

"Hello," said the voice at the other end of the wire, "Who's bothering me? Ah, Comrade Onushkin. How could I forget, my dear man? I remember the party and you and your wife. From Irtysh, if I remember. From the Belaya? Problems? Of course. Who would call me, heh-heh, unless there was a problem? But it's all right, my dear fellow, don't be embarrassed. The reason I left my number with you was in case of a problem, right? I understand. I'll come right over. Tell me the address."

And here was Comrade Taganrog himself, walking around Philharmon Ivanovich's apartment and saying:

"What a marvelous kitty you have! Peach? An original name. Seldom encountered in cats. But I've run into it. And is there anything in the world, you ask, that I haven't run into? Put my life down on paper, and you could get yourself a Nobel Prize. You could, Philharmon Ivanovich, you really could. Honest to God! Do you believe in God? No, of course not, but I myself don't know, to tell the truth; most likely he doesn't exist after all, what do you think? And so, how's your health? How's your heart, Ivan Ivanovich? Not acting up, is it? You want to get into a hospital? It must be done? . . . well OK, maybe they'll cure you there, although to tell the truth—the floors there are parquet, but the doctors are not so great, eh? Hch-heh. You're afraid. Don't be afraid. You can tell me everything. You can and you must, Philharmon Ivanovich. And your wife went to call on relatives? That's a good thing, but it's time she came back, eh? You don't have any children? Maybe the doctors can advise you on that score, eh? I have more faith in folk medicine, the old wives and grandmothers. It's a shame the way they persecute them, eh? Well, what can you say, my dear fellow, they're money grubbers. They scrounge up thousands, tens of thousands, but what good does it do them?"

Philharmon Ivanovich set the table with vodka from the refrigerator and some hors d'oeuvres, seated his dear guest, and poured for him. Strength and calm radiated from Comrade Taganrog's quiet voice. He declined the drink, however, and said, "Business first," got his pen and notebook, demanded that he be given all the details, and jotted everything down himself in his ever-so-tiny hand.

Philharmon Ivanovich told him everything—about Biceps and his peculiarities, and about the *dublyonka*, which he showed his guest right then, and about the seventy-three rubles, and about yesterday's visit, and the persistence of the investigator. And he begged for advice. Taganrog kept writing all the time, double-checking all the details, was silent for a bit, and then asked:

"You've told me everything?"

"Everything," said Philharmon Ivanovich, trying to remember. He had kept only the dreams to himself. As for the rest, it seemed he had told everything.

"Well then," said Taganrog. "Tomorrow morning take the *dublyonka* to the investigator and give it to him, getting a receipt for it. Immediately hand in a resignation statement for personal reasons at your job. Write everything up in detail and deliver it in person or through me to the proper quarter. Don't forget or leave out a single name; where you don't know the name, describe the person's appearance. And your appraisal of them, especially the director. All is not yet lost, my dear fellow."

"I don't want to," Philharmon Ivanovich said in his bass voice.

"How is it you don't speak in your own voice, eh?" Comrade Taganrog squinted.

"Something with my throat," Philharmon Ivanovich said, frightened. "You know how your voice will suddenly change."

"Yes, everything flows, everything changes," Taganrog said melancholically. "You've *got* to want to! You don't have any way out; you've got to want to!"

"You've got to find some other way, Comrade Taganrog," Philharmon Ivanovich begged. "Let's have a drink and you think about it . . ."

"About what. The top boss has decided personally and you want me to think about it?"

"The top boss?"

"You don't believe it?" Taganrog grew stern and distant. "I, Comrade Onushkin, though I'm only five minutes short of my pension, I still have friends, I do! I have no time to drink. And if you don't want to write—I'll have to."

They were silent. Philharmon Ivanovich gazed blankly at the floor. Taganrog got up and grimly put away the pen and notebook.

"Comrade Taganrog," Philharmon Ivanovich articulated with difficulty.

"Did I advise you?" the latter said sternly. "I did. Proper advice? Yes. You don't want to take it? That's your affair, Comrade Onushkin."

Philharmon Ivanovich stood up and despite himself couldn't keep from looking Comrade Taganrog in the eye. His eyes had changed. Nothing like what had burned in them earlier was there now. Only the lower lids remained as they had been, tense. But above them there was nothing. Empty eye sockets, holes as in a skull.

And at these brave holes, where understanding and a favorably disposed friendliness had recently gleamed but where now black emptiness gaped, quite unforeseen by himself, like a street child in a village, Philharmon Ivanovich hauled off and spat. He spat right at these holes, burning his bridges and plunging into the Rubicon without any talisman whatsoever . . .

Time, which moves quickly enough as it is, rushed along with double cosmic speed.

And there stood Philharmon Ivanovich, hanging his head, in front of his immediate boss who had been called back from his pleasant vacation, listening to reprimands mixed with groans of pity—not for Philharmon Ivanovich, what was he to be pitied for? but for the boss himself, suffering innocently, enduring all this because of a mere instructor.

"It's all because of you. If it wasn't for you, none of this would have happened! Where's that damned *Ichthiander?* What'd you have to tell outsiders about that for? Who loosened your tongue? OK—I didn't read it. I have witnesses— I didn't. No, don't expect anything from me personally! They couldn't wait for your benefactor to agree to retire on pension. For three days they celebrated when they finally extorted a resignation from him. And here you are! Well, it wasn't you that saw through Biceps. That one, just between us of course, had it written all over his face in capital letters."

"Comrade Biceps," Philharmon Ivanovich began, but the boss sank even deeper into his personal grief, and anyway he couldn't listen to underlings.

"Comrade! He made out to be a comrade! It was just some sort of hypnosis. A non-party embryo, with less than a high school education. And he got to be known by everyone, a friend to everyone, a comrade, almost a brother. The kinds of people he had contact with—hypnotism, that's all! Entered the most secret factories without a pass; got admitted to the Finnish bath of the generals of our capital! Comrade! For two years they couldn't unmask him; sheer accident helped them out . . . and to me too he was an angel. Took nothing for himself, everything for others, the scum. Sure, for others! Do you realize they could remove me? Me! Enough. Get out of here, go!"

And then Philharmon Ivanovich was standing in front of the investigator, on whose table lay a large package tied with ordinary twine and the investigator wrote out a receipt to the effect that P. I. Onushkin had returned to the state a sheepskin coat which he had acquired by illegal means. And out on the street it was cold, and the man of medium height looked strange in the crowd and on the trolley; he appeared so well preserved, rustproof one might almost say, dressed in a suit, wearing a brown fur cap with the earflaps down, and wrapped in a scarf up to and including his chin.

And then Philharmon Ivanovich was standing in an auditorium, where in the left corner there was a white marble bust with a beard and in the right corner another bust, also white and bearded, and on the wall between the two corners was a huge portrait of Lenin taking a step forward. Beneath the portrait sat the top boss, towering at the head of a long, long table, as though on a throne, and along the two sides ranged the rest of the bosses—the lower the rank, the farther each was from the top boss, although well-founded exceptions were not lacking. Others were not seated at the table, but were simply in chairs along the wall; they did not raise their hands at the question, "All in favor?"

In this room the director of the secret establishment had just become an "ex-," even though Biceps had managed to supply him with the required brand of steel. They took away the steel and fired the director. More than that, they expelled him from the ranks for loss of vigilance, for having connections with a bad element, and a hundred other indiscretions.

Other comrades had just exposed their own errors, including the stage director and the chief of the telephone service. They all exposed themselves. But some lost both their job and their membership in the party, some only their job, and some temporarily survived destruction.

And now came the moment allotted in that well-organized session to the instructor from the cultural sector, Onushkin, Philharmon Ivanovich, born 1919, party member since 1945, etc., etc. He stood up when he heard his name, but first the comrade responsible for trade was questioned, because the top boss had shown a humane attentiveness to the problem of outerwear for ordinary officials and he disgustedly reminded them, pounding the table with his fist, that as early as August he had ordered that *dublyonkas* in sufficient quantity for everyone, down to the instructor level, be delivered to the supply offices. But the comrade responsible for trade explained that as early as August they had ordered them and in the same month of August essentially all of them had been distributed, on the verbal instructions of those who were more responsible than he, who was only responsible for trade. And the top boss frowned and looked at the more responsible comrades, who in turn frowned and looked at many others, who in turn looked at the rest, and the rest also frowned, and everyone looked at Philharmon Ivanovich standing by the table. Then the top boss, banging his fist in disgust, ordered that they be delivered once again and distributed only according to his written instructions—his, the top boss's, and in no other way—and after that he ordered Philharmon Ivanovich to speak. And he began:

"It all started with *Ichthiander*."

"With whom?" the top boss asked him to repeat.

"The prose poems," Philharmon Ivanovich explained.

"What nonsense are you talking?" the top boss pounded his fist and looked around in search of someone who made more sense.

Philharmon Ivanovich's immediate boss jumped up as the top boss's gaze passed over him and quickly said that this was clearly a case of the worst possible conduct, that you couldn't fall any lower, and he moved that the instructor be expelled and a clean sweep be made. Before the immediate boss had time to sit down the boss responsible for the investigative organs among other things, stood up and said that, as though this instructor hadn't done enough, he had also tried to play the innocent and pass off his old overcoat to the investigator after getting a receipt for a *dublyonka* by some deception. But with a warrant, and in conformity with the law, his old coat had now been hung at his number in the coatroom and the *dublyonka* had been confiscated. So it was absolutely true that you couldn't sink any lower, as anyone could judge.

Then something happened which undoubtedly never happens in such places or, if it does, then rarely and without authorization. Philharmon Ivanovich began to take off his jacket and untie his tie, in a word he began to undress, but with such determination and deliberation that—it must be said—he began to disrobe like a priest after a service, talking rapidly and incoherently the whole time.

"Take the jacket . . . and the overcoat from the same supply center. The jacket's from there, too . . . take everything . . . if there'd been one in August, it would've been seventy-three rubles, too . . . in August they didn't give them out, and I didn't even think about it in August . . . and take the tie. The laces are mine but the boots are from the supply center . . . take everything, wear it, don't feel sorry . . . forty years of work, thirty-four years seniority, the war . . . the shirt's from the same supply center, but I don't need it . . ."

"Take him away," said the top boss in disgust. "Dismiss him and expel him. The motion's unanimously approved."

And he added over his left shoulder to his assistant:

"Arrange a job for him until his pension."

Philharmon Ivanovich was led out, dressed, and sent packing for good from the Karl Ivanovich Rossi-style palace.

At home Philharmon Ivanovich fed Peach some milk, then took the cat in his arms and petted it, saying:

"Why are you Peach? If you had even one orange hair . . ."

"That's what they called me," replied Peach.

"They called you! But you should have renamed yourself!"

"A dumb creature can't rename itself," objected Peach.

"What kind of dumb creature are you if you're talking with me?"

"Exactly. With you," Peach answered evasively.

"Use the informal pronoun," Philharmon Ivanovich commanded.

"If someone addresses you informally, you must reply in kind. Always and everywhere!"

Peach obediently shifted to the informal mode of address, "You aren't everywhere."

"That's none of your business!"

"Put me down, please," Peach asked.

"All you cats are traitors. You rub against our legs when you want something to eat, but when you've had your fill, your masters can go to hell," Philharmon Ivanovich said bitterly, putting the cat on the sofa.

"That's not so exactly," Peach observed evasively.

Later on Philharmon Ivanovich testified in court at Biceps' trial and heard his final statement. Ernst Zosimovich spoke, as always, in an expressionless voice, but took care that he could be heard.

"Why did apparently intelligent people believe so easily?"—Biceps spoke approximately along these lines—"Why did they believe that I was invested with enormous power, when I wasn't at all? I don't know, your honor; ask them, may the Duke forgive them. In my view, everyone needs something, and there's always a shortage of friendship or even acquaintance with one's superiors. And was I obliged to provide them with things according to their needs? The prosecutor here has charged me with wasting gasoline, and the labor of the chauffeurs who drove me around with my friends, and even the wear and tear on the cars, but you know, this was necessary to meet deadlines, and I never took a ruble for myself! Why then? My dream, your honor, was to become an actor, to play Hamlet, Khlestyakov, Tarelkin, all the best roles. But things didn't work out that way. And so I thought, Why not see how Ivan Aleksandrovich Khlestyakov would be taken in real life? The reception was excellent! What the devil, I'm ready to pay for this dramatic triumph which ran for two years straight . . ."

"You have defiled what is most sacred in Soviet man—the feeling of trust in one's neighbor!" the prosecutor interrupted.

"O the trustful baying of deathless borzoi hounds," said Biceps sadly. "Duke forgive them. I'll say nothing more, citizen prosecutor, about Ivan Aleksandrovich. Don't forget, however, when you impose sentence, that I am not a robber or a spy and that I'm not involved in politics, so that the most appropriate thing would be to acquit me or give me a couple of years suspended sentence . . ."

Biceps was sentenced for embezzling state property (the gasoline, the chauffeur's labor, and the wear and tear on the cars) amounting to more than ten thousand rubles, and for swindling and hooliganism. The term was thirty years. After the trial, out on the street, Philharmon Ivanovich thought he saw the poetess Liza and it looked as if she was heading in his direction. He walked away as fast as he could, burying his head in his shoulders. And he would have turned up his collar if his coat had had the kind of collar you can turn up and hide your head in.

Chapter Five

The Last Fact

On the basis of general guesswork one can assume that the role of prisoner would not suit Comrade Bleeps, and therefore he was bound to reappear upon life's stage. Most likely he would turn up in business—foreign trade, for example—and win fame with his achievements, based on his friendships with individuals in the seats of power, Greek shipowners, and Senator Edward Kennedy. It would seem that the only way he would drop from sight would be by accident, but since anyone can disappear by accident, that doesn't count.

The day after sentence was passed, the telephone in Philharmon Ivanovich's apartment rang. Lately he had very much feared a particular call he was expecting, having no idea what he would say or why, it being easier that way. Still, he was greatly looking forward to it. After a moment's hesitation he picked up the receiver. It was the doctor who was treating his father. She said categorically that he would be dismissed tomorrow and should be picked up at nine.

"How could that be?" Philharmon Ivanovich asked, "The treatment isn't finished."

"It is the decision of the head physician," said the doctor. "There is nothing wrong with your father but old age, and this is a hospital, not an old-age home!"

"If he could be cured even a little," said Philharmon Ivanovich. To which the doctor, lowering her voice, replied with feeling.

"What are you talking about? Who could be cured here?"

Apparently someone had left the place she was calling from, but someone else—this too became apparent—immediately came in, because she again said loudly:

"So, then, at ten o'clock sharp."

And hung up the phone.

However, not everything worked out the way the head physician ordered. Onushkin's father learned what had happened to his son. He was an ambulatory patient, and a bed patient was brought in—Comrade Taganrog—who immediately called Onushkin Senior over and in strictest confidence told him everything, adding that the latter should write some letters "upstairs," and that he, Taganrog, would help, after he was well again because previously he had been about to retire on his pension but wasn't about to anymore, after which he fell asleep from exhaustion. The father sat down immediately, and wrote all day in great agitation, but the next morning he didn't wake up, which didn't bother anyone, even after Philharmon Ivanovich arrived and began trying to rouse him. His father opened his eyes, but not right away, looked at his son, and recognized him. While they went for the doctor, who was sitting down for her five-minute break, the father gazed with recognition for half an hour at the son but said nothing. Finally he swallowed, passed his tongue over his lips, and said:

"But you must forgive me. Forgive me all the same."

After which he gave a slight cough, dropped his head awkwardly, and expired. The doctor arrived. They put Philharmon Ivanovich out in the corridor, from which a nurse called him into a ward where, according to her, a friend was waiting for him. With difficulty Comrade Taganrog raised himself on his elbow and asked sympathetically:

"What's with your father? Dead?"

A shudder ran from the hair on the top of Philharmon Ivanovich's head, which stood on end, to the toes of his feet, which curled up, and he did something that was the most surprising of all the surprising things he had said and done during those fateful days; namely, with two fingers he made the sign of the cross over Taganrog, after which the shudder passed away.

"I've seen that kind of thing, too," said Taganrog, dropping back onto the pillow. "That never helped anyone; it won't help you either."

As Philharmon Ivanovich was leaving, the coatroom attendant came out from behind the counter and handed him his coat with unusual respect because the rumor of the visitor who had crossed himself in the hospital had already spread among the lower-ranking employees.

Comrade Taganrog, over whom the sign of the cross had been made, did not have the time, to his misfortune, to render Philharmon Ivanovich any further assistance. Toward evening he died, which is not surprising inasmuch as in his body, exhausted by ordeals, nearly everything had been devoured by that disease of whose very name people are terrified, as children are of the dark.

Onushkin Senior's letter "upstairs," as it turned out, was addressed to a leader long since deceased, so that the doctors, after consulting together, sent it to a different destination.

After that, nothing very special happened. Philharmon Ivanovich buried his father alone, if you don't count the driver of the car and the gravediggers. He then spent several days at home, where if he wasn't lying down sleeping or daydreaming, he was sitting at his desk reading his synopses. He read them as though he were searching for something and couldn't find it, try as he might. He would put down the notebooks he had read, then take them up again and leaf through them haphazardly so that he quickly disrupted the multicolored order and system. Sometimes it seemed he had found something. Thus, in a light-blue notebook numbered 84 he reread the same words several times, evidently reflecting on them, "As the idealist Marienberger contends, without ethics there is no aesthetics." But clearly this was not what he was searching for because notebook 84, all in all, got thrown onto the floor. Then for a long time he pondered some words in an orange notebook numbered 19. Decisively sweeping away the fog of mysticism, which combines ethics and ontology in aesthetics . . ." But he set this notebook aside as well. Apparently not finding what he wanted, he tied the notebooks in bundles, nine in each, and carried them off somewhere. No one ever saw them again; it's possible he simply buried them.

No one knows what became of Philharmon Ivanovich after that In that place where a great many people's paths through life are diligently described, there is no clarity with regard to him. Some reports say that after working for a time as a watchman at a warehouse for outerwear, he began to manufacture fake Orenburg shawls for the gypsies out of a kind of yarn they had invented, a secret they betray to no one, though most likely it was cotton wool, with glass fiber and something else that is not known; that the gypsies got to like him for his silliness and high output; and that he grew incredibly rich, so that through the gypsies he got his name on a list for a car and changed his city apartment for a house with a garage in the suburbs. He definitely changed his residence though, because the phone rang in his apartment and the people in the apartment responded very rudely to the woman calling, although she spoke in a pleasant singsong voice; they told her that the person she wanted wasn't there, he'd moved to another address, and they didn't know where.

According to other reports, Philharmon Ivanovich went to join his wife in her village, where they were living by virtual subsistence farming, that they made vodka at home with government sugar and water, using government electricity, that his wife even bore him a son, to whom they gave a name that was either Russo-Bashkir or Russo-Tatar—Ruslan.

Still other reports claim that he learned some highly unusual card tricks, traveled around doing them as part of a concert troupe, had fantastic success, and got together with the directress of the troupe.

All these reports are unverified and have not been accepted as documents, with the result that in the upper left-hand corner of each a question mark in red pencil may be seen.

It is accepted that a cat named Peach, exactly that, was living at the poetess Liza's, living there in luxury and having its recently discovered passion for chocolate candy fully gratified, a passion that is very, very rare in cats, although cats are subject to passions that are sometimes quite unbelievable. However, it could be that this was a different cat altogether and just happened to have had the same name.

It is distressing that Philharmon Ivanovich's top boss, who humanely ordered a job arranged for him, which for some reason he didn't take advantage of, suddenly and for no stated reason was named ambassador to New Zealand, where one of our ensembles went on tour, and the former top boss displayed an unhealthy interest in one of his compatriots, a singer with a high bustline and long legs, and even went off with her alone, without a driver, into the wild New Zealand hills, for which the singer was reprimanded upon her return home, and the ambassador was recalled, stripped of his post, expelled from the ranks, and turned into a deputy head of some school for training professional technicians. Afterward a high bustline and long legs, no matter to whom they belonged, brought from this man, democratic by nature, only a look of disgust. Truly it was said, everything flows, everything changes. But Philharmon Ivanovich was really not to blame for these changes. And a new top boss was found and installed right away, so that it seemed that nothing really had changed, except that the *dublyonkas* brought to the warehouse for ordinary officials, including instructors, once again disappeared without a trace.

It is not surprising that the poetess Liza did not seek anyone's patronage anymore, although it was offered to her. Instead she wrote a narrative poem about the battle of Kulikovo on the 600th anniversary of that event. It was called "Transworlds" and contained the following two lines:

As though in two mirrors, they looked in each other's shields,
And instead of the foe they saw their own true features.

Her older friend told her that the shields of that time could hardly have served as mirrors and that she would do better to write prose, which led the poetess, Liza, for the first time in her life, to fall out with him for good.

Not reflected in these reports, however, to this day, is the fact that Philharmon Ivanovich is still seen at performances in various theaters. He now sits in the back rows, but just as before, he is pleased to the point of utter abandon by everything presented on stage. Unlike before, however, he laughs, cries, identifies quite openly, whispers the lines to prompt the actors, and claps with all his might. But how he slips into the theater and how he disappears unobtrusively after the show, no one has ever noticed—which is not surprising because who cares about him anyway?

Poems from the book *Voices*[*]
by Genrikh Sapgir

A Voice

They killed a man over there,
They killed a man over there,
They killed a man over there
Down there—they killed a man.

Let's take a look at him.
Let's take a look at him.
Let's take a look at him.
Let's take a look at him.

The corpse—and a look just like one.
Oh he's asleep, he's dead drunk!
Oh, he's not a corpse, he just looks dead . . .
What corpse—he's dead drunk—

Sprawling in vomit . . .
Sprawling in vomit . . .
Sprawling in vomit . . .
....

Grab his hands and feet,
Grab his hands and feet,
Grab his hands and feet,
Grab his hands and feet,

And carry him outside.
Drag him outside.
Toss him outside!
Throw him outside!

And lock the front door.
Lock the door tight!

*Translated by H. William Tjalsma.

Snap it up, get it shut!
Turn all the locks and bolts!

Is he yelling or is he quiet?
Is he yelling or is he quiet?
Is he yelling or is he quiet?
Is he yelling or is he quiet?

Radioblab

Lying down, moaning.
Nobody there.
Just a black speaker on the wall.
It's blaring a national chorus.
He reached up, jerked the cord!
The plug's here, the outlet's there.
He couldn't believe his ears:
Noise,
Crackle,
Clanging of metal.
The radio began to mutter:
"The latest news.
Special report!
. . . At the scene
Of the crime.
. . . The majority of votes.
. . . Degrees
Below zero.
Threat of
Atomic attack
Epidemic . . .
War . . .
The quota is overfulfilled!"
The chorus again. Against the background
Of the chorus,
An airplane motor solo.
Roar of jet planes.
Burst of applause!
The sick man stares glassy-eyed,
His hand
Squeezes the blanket
convulsively.
Through the door—far away
Somebody appeared.
—Doctor!

You must check my nuts and bolts!
Announcer:
" 'Moonlight Sonata'
On the balalaika. "

Monkey

"What are you complaining about, citizenness?"
She was a sharp lady, but at this she was tongue-tied.
She stood there. She cried. She couldn't say anything.
"Give her a new apartment and ten thousand in my
name!"
—from popular folklore

She got married.
Ordinary sort of husband.
At night the lady,
Honestly speaking,
Didn't get much of a look.
In the morning she looks:
He's all furry.
The husband, Lord forgive us,
Was a real monkey.
He'd been pretending
To be a brunet
Just to cover up.
The monkey squeals
And leaps about,
Bowlegged and hairy.
The young thing, all but crying,
Appealed to the court.
They say: no grounds . . .
A case of atavism . . .
Better get used to it . . .
They won't grant her a divorce!
Marvelous deeds!—
She gave birth to a pair of marmosets.
The father, a steelworker,
Crawled up on the bell tower
Of Ivan the Great Church
And hung there on the gold cross
From his tail
For three days.
They gave him an award.
The prize: a tea service.

He doesn't begrudge his wife anything,
Carries out her smallest whim!
So if your husband's a good one,
Who cares if he's a monkey?

From the Book of Sonnets on Shirts

Sonnet #3

It's not for love but with revulsion
That I embrace another's body
I take no joy in new sensations
While hanging there upon a chair.

I get soaked through with wine and vodka
My armpits grey with others' sweat
The wrinkles, terrible exhaustion
And then something awful happens

They throw me in a washing tub
They torture me in alkaline solution
And then, oh how the iron hurts!

Again around somebody's neck
I'm virginal and white once more
And smell fresh—I'm a shirt!

The Manuscript

You opened me for laughs, at random
On page two hundred ninety-one
The candles burned and all was silent
The rain streamed down the window glass

And horses gallop down the road
From bushes—lights! Betrayal! Flee!
And Mary sleeps, her eyelids closed
In lunar light the castle's silver

"The Count's giving a ball today!"
It starts. And ends: "Was killed outright!"
Just fiery graphomania—

That's me. But go on, crack my binding
It smells of early morning cool
There's fog. You'll hear a chapel bell

Suburban Moscow Landscape with Doll

All slimy the half-dead Kliazma River flows
In the sedge there's a drowned doll to be seen
Toward autumn—rain . . . but the sun comes out to tease
The environs are all menstrually puffy

On the other shore—stores and a celebration
Here somebody cries out and there someone hoots
Over there a drunk runs off. While another good-for-nothing
Turns black in the grass like a beetle or a letter

What is all this? Doll dilly doodle?
No doubt some sort of secret signs—
And everywhere scattered humanoid figures
And a yellow sunset beyond the settlement—and even

A horse gleaming near the river
In this inhuman landscape

Diagram of Life

Wise old men of grinning visage
Peruse a life diagram
—He'll be a poet . . , in a socialist state . . .
—Sad fate—noted Lao-Tse

And so I was born in my fatherland . . .
There was a war . . . rogues had their day . . .
In the vegetable gardens the cat ate cucumbers . . .
So boring you feel like hanging yourself from the lamp!

Suddenly—a winner—a trip to Singapore
And there, where life's a real lark
I saw a fresco in a Chinese temple

There on the wall with the willows and palaces
Wise old men grinning, leaning over
Discussing a diagram

Love

For Nadezhda Rykova

She promised that she'd come out straight away
And I picked up a bottle in the cellar

And got a couple more from two steelworkers
I bought some cod, a pack of Belomors

I played ma cherie, tapping on the window
I called my darling out to have a chat
I hissed and meowed—they took me for a thief—
Went in the entry, got thrown out again

It's she alone who heeds my murmurings
Just there beyond the glass—her nose and spots
Her pupils vertical and golden slit!

Her father-enemy came out the door.
What did he mean? I heard him say:
"The little fool's enamored of our cat!"

From Catullus

With an apple, a dove, roses, I awaited Aphrodite yesterday
Drunken Ninka and a Czech with some Polish vodka showed up.

The Third Rome

Housing units gleaming around Moscow—
Interplanetary stations
A green-faced monstrosity roams about the
      Central Park of the Soviet Army

There's a kiosk next to the Sretensky Gates
A drunken crowd of intelligent beards
Discusses the problems of the day
And a salamander raises its head
In a corner, where there are
Several suspicious-looking spots
How amazing this city is

A tourist from Riazan
Gapes with dazed eyes at
Broad pelvises, heavy breasts
Clerical ecstasies and caprices
Columns, volutes, portals, spires—
There's also a bull complete with balls!

Beyond the circle miracles gleam—
Interplanetary stations . . .
And in the CPSA
The gaping monstrosity howls

On Death

A wasp looking for traces of cocoa . . . crawls . . . along
the sticky boards of a cottage table—kindergarten.
Unsticking its little feet, I examine it closely—closely—
Venomously yellow stripes on its little butt —I desparately want
    to touch it.

I don't remember anything more except great
fear in the crowded house—when I woke up at night
all in tears and understood—that's Me—
and everything that happens—in fact
—is with me—in shorts and tee-shirt—the elastic
chafes—I—and nobody else will die—the end of Me—
Me in fact—and not the somebody of whom I was thinking.
It's me—all the children are asleep —and the night
hums in the wind—smells of filthy mattress—little
heart. Mama! Mama!—and the huge night tree
outside the window filled with the storm.

Mother died of cancer—at first she didn't
pay any attention—but the cells were already dividing
wildly—her arm was hard and hot—
terrible meat
How she suffered!—
talked all the time about such nonsense—seems
she didn't note—"open the window"—that

in fact it was all: "give me some orange
juice" with her—with no one else—babbled
like a baby.
How she suffered
I going back into my beginnings—into my
salvation from pain—she asked for the television
to be moved to the foot of the bed—after that
it wasn't she that cried—another woman —
the relatives wanted to operate—who
wished for all of this to end soon.

Today coming out of the subway—trolley bus, lindens,
the SOFIA restaurant—I know the street by heart—
for the first time felt—(men's hosiery on sale)
—faces noted by the sun—(a bored
saleslady)—that this IS—and only
THIS—reality from which there is no exit.
The street wearily ran off toward the west—perplexity
left—a stream of cars poured into

the sun, which stood over the spire of the Belorussian Station—each speck of dust shone—and there was happiness!—by evening the lindens smelled stronger —the consciousness that I see and breathe—in fact—and that I shall die—and no one else.

Two Stories[*]
by Arkady Arkanov

And Ever More Early
the Dark Blue of Twilight Descends

It seemed incredible. God only knows what it seemed like. At first there were rumors he was going out with Inga. Then someone said that Inga was going to marry him and he was moving his things to her place.

But soon everyone was faced with a fait accompli: Inga actually had married him. And no matter what people thought of it, the fact remained that Inga had married a horse.

"Either it's a joke or they're making fun of us," Rimma said with irritation, running her eyes over the postcard, which said in black and white that Inga had married a horse and that Rimma and Reginald were invited to Inga's on Saturday to celebrate the occasion.

"Nevertheless," Reginald enunicated, after tasting a bit of his cranberry gelatin, "The fact remains . . . a fact."

"But maybe it's only a name," Rimma suggested hopefully. "For example, maybe his name is Horace and she calls him Horsie for fun. Or maybe his last name is Horsely."

"Anything is possible," said Reginald, finishing his dessert, "but they've been seen together in the park. . . . It's no Horace or Horsely . . . . It's an honest-to-God horse."

"She always was a show-off," said Rimma. "But to go this far?"

"You ought to know. She's your best friend."

"Which is exactly why I don't know what to do about this invitation," said Rimma, perplexed. "Of course she's my best friend. After all, we went to school together. And university . . . . She was always a loser . . . and you can bet it wasn't clean living that brought her to this."

"But imagine us in his company," said Reginald with a laugh. "What am I supposed to talk about with him, I'd like to know . . . and

* Translated by George Saunders.

how? Besides, what do we have in common? . . . If you're interested, you can go, but as for me . . ."

Two days were devoted to solving this problem and finally, on Saturday morning, Reginald agreed to go. The need to behave democratically won out in the end.

"All right," he said, "but you know it's gauche to show up empty-handed."

"We'll pick up a nice bouquet," was Rimma's proposal.

"He might take that to mean we're bringing him fodder."

"Horses eat oats," said Rimma.

"Think about it, though. They may very well eat flowers. Then God knows what . . ."

"Maybe a place setting?" Rimma suggested uncertainly.

"A place setting for *her*. But what for him? We'd have to buy him a bucket."

"Don't exaggerate. . . . I know. We'll give them our own good-luck piece. Oh no, what am I saying?" It was a horseshoe.

After lengthy argument they agreed to give something neutral and settled on music of some sort. Everyone knows that horses are a musical race. At midday a Concertina-brand record player and a record were purchased. One side had "The Butterfly Polka" and the other, two marches. God only knew what kind of music they liked. But there *is* something cavalrylike about marches.

And so that evening in June, muggy and oppressive, Rimma and Reginald rang the doorbell at Inga's place, feeling a certain unpleasant sensation as they did. On the other side of the door a muffled commotion could be heard, as though someone was quickly putting something on, and then sounds that were not quite footsteps and not quite hoofbeats. Reginald stepped back a little. Rimma tidily adjusted a white strap that had slipped off her shoulder.

He himself opened the door.

"Well, at last," he said. "At last. At last . . . we were beginning to wonder. We've been waiting and waiting for you."

Rimma and Reginald entered the hallway hesitantly, sideways.

"Hello," let out Rimma softly.

"Hello," Reginald coughed.

"Well, of course . . . of course, of course!" he said, overjoyed.

A sunburnt Inga came bursting from the main room and with a cry flung herself at Rimma.

"Rimmula, darling, I'm so glad you came. I'm so glad. So glad."

They kissed.

"Congratulations," Rimma began. "I'm so happy, so happy for you! I'm so happy I simply can't find the words. That's how happy I am. Reginald and I both. We're so happy for you."

"We're really glad for you, Rimma and I, really happy," said Reginald putting his hand out to Inga.

"You're allowed to have a kiss on such occasions," Rimma prompted Reginald.

"Our congratualtions to you," Reginald kissed Inga. Inga kissed Reginald in reply.

"And this is my husband. Let me introduce you."

He extended his muscular, somewhat coarse right leg toward Rimma.

"Tulumbash. I'm Tulumbash . . . out of Tulyanka, by Bashlyk."

"Pleased to meet you. I'm Rimma," she sighed. "Congratulations to you. You're so lucky. Dear Inga is such a marvelous woman. She's a treasure."

He turned to Reginald: "Tulumbash!"

"Very pleased to meet you," Reginald bowed. "Reginald."

"What?" he asked. "What did you say? What?

"Reginald," replied Reginald.

"A very lovely name," he said. "Very . . . a simply beautiful name."

Reginald held the box with the record player and record out to him.

"This is for you and Inga from me and Rimma. I congratulate you and envy you. Inga is a fantastic woman. She's a real treasure, as my wife has said."

"Oh go on now, go on with you," Inga was coquettish, "To tell you the truth, I think Bashik should envy you. You know Bashik, Rimma is such a fantastic woman. She's the real treasure, not me."

"You're a treasure and she's a treasure," smiled Tulumbash. "Two treasures. She's a treasure and you're a treasure."

By now Rimma was looking at him more boldly. He had an ordinary, perhaps somewhat elongated face, and large glasses with expensive, apparently foreign frames. A smile revealed large, strong, slightly yellow teeth.

And they all went into the main room and sat down at a magnificently laden table.

Rimma counted twenty-three kinds of hors d'oeuvres, every possible kind and the tastiest imaginable, and twelve varieties of wine and strong drink. In addition there were three knives at each setting, a bread knife, a butter knife, and a steak knife, and three kinds of forks, a table fork, a salad fork, and one with two thin prongs.

"How charming," Rimma said with unfeigned delight.

"It's just like the dinner at the Madagascar consulate celebrating the third anniversary of the founding of the republic," said Reginald.

"You've had the luck to go there then?" asked Tulumbash.

"Oh yes," Reginald answered offhandedly. "You should go at your first opportunity."

"How enviable . . . very . . . it's really very enviable," said Tulumbash. "Here I've been to thirty-four countries, but I've never been to the Madagascar consulate. Never been to the Madagascar consulate . . . never . . . ."

"Thirty-four?" Rimma gulped and thought, This dumbbell Inga has really hit the jackpot.

"I don't know," Reginald said in measured tones. "I personally was at the dinner at the Madagascar consulate on the occasion of the third anniversary of the founding of their republic and I wouldn't trade that for anything . . . but I'd be interested to know in what capacity you traveled to these thirty-four countries?"

"As a race horse," said Tulumbash. "I went in my capacity as a race horse . . ."

"I don't know," Reginald put two servings of salad on his plate, three sardines, and two pieces of roast beef. "I don't know . . . I personally prefer," he added two tomatoes and a piece of salmon to his plate and reached for the cheese, "Personally I'd prefer to travel by myself, rather than," putting some sauerkraut and *satsivi** on it, too, and covering the whole concoction with mayonnaise, "Rather than with someone on top of me."

"There are lots more plates," said Inga.

"But why use up a lot of dishes for nothing?" answered Reginald, starting to eat.

"That's an old argument," Tulumbash smiled. "An old argument. . . . To you it seems that you're riding on us, that it's you riding us, but to us it seems the other way around, that we are carrying you . . . we carry you . . . we carry—"

"OK. Fine." Reginald chuckled. "You carry us and we ride you."

"And have you been to Italy, too?" Rimma asked cautiously. Rimma's dream was to go to Italy. That was her weakness.

"Yes, I have," said Tulumbash. "I've been there. Was there once. At an international auction in Turin. They were trying to sell me. They were trying, but thank heaven they didn't. They didn't sell me. They sold my brother. My brother on my father's side. They sold him. A trotter; he was a trotter."

"Eat and drink as much as you like" said Inga. "And don't pay any attention to Bashik. As far as meat goes, he's a vegetarian, and besides tomorrow we have an important race, so we have to be in shape. Right, darling?"

"The big summer purse," Tulumbash said proudly. "Ten thousand points, ten thousand."

"How much is that in our money?" asked Rimma, astounded.

"I don't know," said Tulumbash, "I really don't know. The jockeys are interested in that, but for me the main thing is not to lose. Not to lose is the main thing. Not to lose."

"They're all crooks at the race track," Reginald bit off his words firmly and clearly.

*Georgian meat cutlet [tr.].

"Well now, not all, not all are crooks . . . by no means all . . . and then crooks can be found anywhere. Anywhere you want. There may be crooks anywhere you want."

"I see that you're inclined to generalizations," said Reginald, bristling.

Rimma hastened to intervene because she saw that her husband had already had a good bit to drink and was liable to insult somebody.

"You're not quite right, you know," she said. "You're the one who is generalizing by saying that everyone at the race track is a crook."

"We can get along without lawyers," Reginald interrupted. "What does that mean, 'There may be crooks anywhere you want?' You mean where I work? Crooks there, too? . . . For insinuations like that, if I had my way, I'd send the whole lot of you off to the cavalry . . . or to the mounted police . . . where you'd do some good."

Tulumbash adjusted his glasses now and then and kept smiling.

"He's joking, Tulumbash," said Rimma softly. "It's just that he loves his work so much."

"Let's go sit on the balcony a while," Inga changed the subject. "It's awfully stuffy in here. Bashik will read you his poetry."

On the balcony it was airy and pleasant. First, because evening had almost come; second, because off to the right over the roofs of the houses the sky was growing dark and from time to time a cool gust blew from that direction. Muttering and flashing, a thunderstorm was drawing near.

Tulumbash brought a throw of soft glossy fur from the room and put it around Inga's shoulders.

"Really it's a bit chilly," Reginald hunched up. "Get me my jacket, Rimma."

Rimma, who had settled down comfortably on a low chair, jumped up and brought Reginald his jacket.

"Well, let's go, let's go," he said.

"I sometimes write poetry," Tulumbash said diffidently. "Sometimes. I write sometimes. Inga translates it."

"That's saying too much," Inga was embarrassed.

"Ee-ee," said Tulumbash. "In my language that means *and*." He began:

And ever more early the dark blue of twilight descends, and
The track becomes heavy and wet with the rain, and
The mud flies in clumps high into the jockeys' faces, and
What all of it means is the season of summer is ending, and
The season of winter, the new season is beginning, and
Soon there will be a new shoeing, and
The one who is reshod the fastest will be the one
Who once again will hold the favored position.

"No meter?" Reginald asked.

"Lost in translation," said Tulumbash sadly. "In the translation. It was lost. Lost."

He hung his head over the railing and stared down below. His dark red, carefully clipped mane stirred lightly with each gust of wind.

"So-o-o," Reginald drew out. "But I don't like poetry. I like songs."

"We brought you a Concertina record player and a record with some marches on it," Rimma broke in, fearing he might start to sing.

"I don't like marches," Tulumbash uttered softly, still staring down.

"Don't like them. They play marches as we come out onto the track . . . out onto the track . . . I like Haydn. Haydn is what I like."

"Bashik taught me to like Haydn too," Inga boasted.

"Who doesn't like Haydn?" said Reginald. "Everybody likes Haydn."

"Why of course," Rimma snorted angrily.

At that moment she realized she envied Inga. She envied Inga's lack of propriety. If she'd been improper, she'd have been happy too. She could have arranged her personal life as she wished, too. After all she was much better looking than Inga. . . . But no, it wouldn't work out. Maybe he doesn't smell, but in general they smell. . . . But they do go abroad a lot . . .

"And will you keep going long?" she asked. Rimma meant to say abroad, but Tulumbash didn't understand her.

"As long as I don't lose my speed," he answered. "Or break a leg. In that event obviously they would put me away . . ."

"How's that?" Rimma was aghast.

"Very simply. Simply. It costs a great deal to maintain us. Costs a great deal. It costs. . . . Once we can't run any more—"

"You can't imagine how expensive the upkeep is," Inga confirmed.

"But that's inhuman!" Rimma was indignant.

"A word that's hardly appropriate here," said Reginald. "It's logical and businesslike . . . right?"

And Reginald amiably clapped Tulumbash on the back.

"Right!" Tulumbash laughed and just as amiably clapped Reginald on the back. "Businesslike . . . right . . ."

"And if you lose your speed?" Rimma insisted.

"If I lose my speed, if I lose that, they could send me to a breeding farm as a stud . . . to a breeding farm."

"I wonder how your wife would take that?" said Rimma.

"But Rimmula, you know it's only a job." Inga was offended.

"All work is honorable," said Reginald, "especially farmwork."

"I don't know," Rimma persisted. "I personally wouldn't allow it."

"You certainly would allow it," said Reginald. "Not everyone could work at a place like the way I could. If you needed the money, darn right you'd allow it."

The evening at last produced a thunderstorm. The rain poured

down in torrents. Everyone fled to the living room, and tea was served.
"Don't you drink tea either?" Reginald was surprised.
"I can't have a lot of fluids," said Tulumbash. "It isn't allowed.
Especially the night before. Especially."
"Kidneys?" Reginald asked confidentially.
"No. What do you mean? It's the training rules. What a question!"
"I don't know how we're going to get home." Rimma was getting worried.
"I'll take you home. I'll take you. I will," said Tulumbash with a smile.
"He'll take you," Inga backed him up.
He went out and came back in a minute, wearing a very broad rain hat, his ears protruding from underneath. He handed Reginald a whip.
"I don't know where you live," he said. "I don't know. So you'll have to guide me. You'll have to use the reins . . . Take them in your hands and guide me. Use the reins. If you want to go to the right, pull on the right-hand rein, the right one. It begins to hurt me, begins to hurt, you understand? So in order to ease the pain, in order to ease the pain, I turn to the right. Same thing with the left . . ."
"Yes, really quite simple," Reginald was very pleased.
"And if you want to go faster," Tulumbash added, "you hit me with the whip . . ."
"Don't take too long, Bashik," said Inga. "You have to be there at six in the morning."
Inga kissed Rimma first, then Reginald, then Tulumbash.
"How can she?" Rimma thought to herself and again felt envious of Inga.
When they got down to the courtyard Tulumbash put the canvas hood up on the small two-wheeled cart. Rimma and Reginald got in under the canvas and off they went.
They sped along over the wet asphalt. Reginald pulled the reins now to the right, now to the left. From time to time he touched Tulumbash with the whip. The heavy wind in their faces gradually blew away all their tipsiness. "Giddy up," yelled Reginald. "Giddy up."
Rimma found the ride pleasant. She was afraid of only one thing, that Reginald would drive Inga's husband so hard that he wouldn't be able to stop. She had read of such an incident either in Flaubert or Maupassant. And she had seen it in a movie, too.
It would have been foolish not to have taken advantage of the opportunity once it presented itself, foolish not to take the ride. At first they swept onto Maritime Boulevard, then over the Metropolitan Bridge and down onto Ferguson Avenue, coming out on Cosmic Circle. From the Circle they rolled along as far as the old television tower and went speeding off down Lunar Quay. Home.
"My, how far away you live," said Tulumbash when at last they

stopped. "My, how far . . . I'm very sorry I can't take you around the city a little more . . . I can't . . . I don't have time . . . no time."

"Don't be upset," Reginald reassured him. "Another time."

"Definitely, definitely," Tulumbash kept nodding. "And we'll expect you to come visit . . . we'll expect you . . ."

They entered the building as he turned around and with a shake of the head went trotting off the way he had come.

"He's very kind and intelligent, no matter what," said Rimma yawning on their way up in the elevator.

"Yes, by and large, yes," Reginald agreed.

"And, I think, likable . . . what do you think?"

"Yes . . . to some extent," Reginald agreed.

"We simply must have them over some time," Rimma suggested uncertainly.

Reginald raised his eyesbrows.

"Invite them over to our house? That's all I need."

And Reginald broke into a wild horselaugh.

I Dream of a Carnival

We keep walking, walking, walking . . .

The yellowish white planking of the freshly built boardwalk turns grayer, and grayer, and grayer before my eyes . . . And now it has grown quite old. It gives beneath each one of our ceremoniously measured footsteps. All the houses have thrown open their windows, and in every window there are people. In their eyes is the tense curiosity of expectation. And the houses which are farther away begin to grow, to stand on tiptoe, to climb up on stools and on the shoulders of other houses. The more enterprising among them climb trees. All want to see. All want to hear.

But I don't want to see anything. I don't want to hear anything. Nevertheless I see and hear everything. I can distinguish each and every person, but I try not to rest my gaze on any of them. The mouths half-opened, slack with anticipation, of those who don't understand anything. The cloudy, impenetrable faces of those who don't want to understand anything. The lips, twisted in a malign half-smile, of those who understand everything and who seem to ask: "And so? What are you going to come up with now?" The mutely sympathetic eyes of those forcibly torn away from their own concerns by our procession. They are the worst—the mute looks of those, sympathetic to you, who have been forcibly torn from their own concerns.

But here is a face on which my gaze does rest. Eyes pulled back slightly as though by invisible rubber bands. Some freckles on the nose. A hairpin pressed between the lips. And hands at the back of the head trying in vain to put that very short hair in a bun.

It's my wife, who from that moment is not my wife. Next to her in the window is a set of muscles, a pectoral girdle, and a magnificent part in the hair on the right side.

What animal intuition the people in the windows have! They all, as one, catch my resting gaze and follow it down to the very freckles and the part in the hair. And back, as though at one command, to me. Then back to them. There's a smell of meat frying. Now something will happen! Otherwise there'd be no reason for them to stick their heads out of the windows at such an ungodly hour. And I see that the people know everything: that she was my wife, that the part-in-the-hair now lives with her, and that I know all about it.

Only the part-in-the-hair doesn't know what's going on.

"Hey, you with the part in the hair," I yell. "When you leave the house, hit the lights on the stair."

Wild laughter rocks the whole city. At last we're getting somewhere.

"Well, he's letting them have it . . . the joker's letting them have it, but good."

"That's stupid," my wife cries out.

"What can you do?" I say quietly. "What can you do?"

I myself know it's stupid . . .

"Hey you with the part!" I yell again. "She likes it better in the morning. Don't lose any time."

Everyone busts a gut.

"It's none of your business," the part-in-the-hair yells back. "Your business is to march to your execution."

"Go upstairs," my wife says to him. "I'll explain to you later."

"Hey, the joker's letting them have it. He's really going at it." I hear this from several windows.

"But it's shameful! To these jokers nothing is sacred."

The people have been given breakfast, and begin chewing attentively.

And we keep walking, walking, walking . . . they keep leading, leading, leading me along . . . all I see before me is the back of the head of the first of the four. He knows that jokers must be put to death. But there was a time when he laughed more than anyone at everything he heard from me. That's why he finds it awkward to look me in the eye, and all I see is the back of his head. Behind me walks the second of the four. I considered him my friend, but he was the one who told where I lived. It turns my stomach to see him. And so I go on without looking back.

On my right and left I am escorted by the other two of the four. They don't know whether jokers have to be put to death or not. Executing people is their honest vocation. And I don't nurse any private grudge against them. After all, someone has to do the work of executioners. And here they are on their way to work. They keep their eyes straight ahead. So that all I see to my left and my right is a profile.

And still we keep walking, walking, walking.

I see, on one of the balconies, my mother and father. They haven't been with us for a long time. Father is watering the matthiola with a child's green watering can.

I hear the water sloshing. I see that after soaking through the wooden window box the drops fall from the sixth floor and splash on the asphalt of our courtyard.

"Come, leave your flowers alone," my mother tells him with irritation and points in my direction.

Again the people in the windows are seized with curiosity. They know these are my parents. They know they haven't existed for a long time. They know everything. Again something is coming . . . all eyes, as though at one command, are on me. Then on my parents. Then on me.

"Why haven't you been to see us for so long?" my mother asks.

"Dad and I have missed you . . ."

"We'll see each other soon enough," I say and point to the heavens.

A sigh of satisfaction sweeps through the city. My escorts smile.

"How is your foot?" my mother asks.

"OK," I say. "The eye doctor said it's better already."

"How come the eye doctor?" My father doesn't get it.

"When your feet hurt, your eyes climb up your forehead!" I yell. It hits home. People are cracking up in the windows.

"Hey, the joker socked it to 'em . . . good one . . . God, he kills me!"

The back-of-the-head proceeding before me begins to shake.

The two profiles are laughing, looking straight ahead. What's happening with the one in back? I couldn't care less. My father shakes his finger at me.

"What did you have for breakfast today?" my mother asks.

"A sandwich with bread."

"Look out! You'll ruin your health."

"Don't worry, mom," I yell. "They'll ruin it for me!"

"Don't get too wise," says the back-of-the-head sternly.

"Put on a hat," my mother says and throws me a Young Pioneer's straw hat. "Such a sun," she says.

"My head will soon be cool and dry enough," I answer putting on the white straw hat.

A murmur of disapproval. Whistling. Cries of "Not funny!" The two profiles wince with displeasure.

Shouts of "Corny" sound from a rooftop.

"Come as quick as you can," my mother cries out, already in my wake. "I've made you your favorite cream of wheat without any lumps."

I fill my lungs with air and bellow with a voice hardly my own.

"Cream of wheat porridge—night dark and horrid."

My escorts have stopped in their tracks, gasping for breath from laughter. I bow in all directions . . .
And again we're walking, walking, walking . . .
A fine drizzle starts, so fine it could be spraying from an atomizer. In spite of it, along the road and on the green fog-dimmed hills are many, many raincoats, raincoats, and raincoats, umbrellas, umbrellas, and umbrellas . . .
My escorts are tired. The back-of-the-head has sunk down into its shoulders. The two profiles sullenly and gloomily stare straight ahead. The one in back? . . . Let him get worn out completely. I couldn't care less about him.
The umbrellas and raincoats press close to each other, shifting from foot to foot. They're cold. But they stay where they are. And we keep moving through them.
"They're bringing the joker! Bringing the joker," can be heard along the walls of this living corridor. "He's laughed his last. It's what he deserves. They're leading him to execution."
Silence and whispers are drawn out. I turn to my escort:
"Why so down in the mouth?"
Silence. But from umbrella to raincoat, from raincoat to umbrella, my question is passed along in whispers.
"I feel sorry for you."
"He feels sorry. He feels sorry for them." There's a rustle and stir among the umbrellas and raincoats. "They're leading him to execution, and he feels sorry for them. Now *there's* something!"
"Don't go feeling sorry for us," the back-of-the-head says in a sullen, hoarse voice. "Feel sorry for your own self."
"Well, what the hell," I answer. "It's such lousy weather. And I only have to get there; you have to go back."
Silence. The umbrellas and raincoats begin to buzz with disapproval.
"Old joke. Why make fun of people? He should put himself in their shoes."
Somewhere way up high above the clouds, eternally alone, sounds the trumpet of Miles Davis.
From the living corridor one raincoat separates itself. I recognize the head of the department where I worked.
"How can this be?" he says. "You're going off, so to say, for good—and leaving our wall newspaper humorless?* Maybe you could think up something along the way?"
And he holds out to me our factory wall newspaper.

> For years on end the truth's been that
> Our manager's a bureaucrat.

---

* Wall newspaper—a "house organ" produced at a factory or office and posted on the wall of the work place [tr.].

I write that for him for his humor section.

"Terrific!" he shouts, waving the paper. "Right on the button."

An unimaginable racket starts up. Wall newspapers appear in everyone's hands.

"Us too. Write something for us too," I hear from all sides.

"I don't know who needs what," I try to beg off.

"The same thing. Write the same thing."

They vie with one another in their eagerness to put their newspapers in my hand. For all of them I write:

For years on end the truth's been that
Our manager's a bureaucrat.

And everyone's pleased. It's just right for everyone. I'd never known before that everyone is the editor of a wall newspaper.

"Write it for me too." Without turning around, the back-of-the-head holds a newspaper out to me. "I'm an editor too. For years on end at our place too."

The name of his paper is *Off at the Shoulder!*

I write the same thing. And he too is left satisfied. I can tell by the back of his neck.

Somewhere way up high above the clouds sounds the eternally lonely trumpet of Miles Davis. Only it isn't a trumpet. It's a Young Pioneer horn tooting:

Get up, get up, young friend,
Out of bed and onto the pot.

On the station platform stand a great many children and even more parents.

I stand amid four Young Pioneer leaders. The back-of-the-head. The two profiles. And I don't want to look at the fourth.

Held up by shoulder straps, my cloth breeches cut painfully into my crotch.

And there are my mother and father. They haven't been around for a long, long time.

"He's a very nervous child," my mother says to the back-of-the-head, and adds in a whisper. "He sometimes wets his bed."

But they all hear it, all of it, and the whole platform rolls with laughter, and they all point their fingers at me . . .

"Take this with you for the journey." My father presses on me a cheesecake in a paper bag and kisses me.

"When in life you have distress, instead of bread, eat cake, no less."

I cry out to the whole station platform.

Everybody dies laughing.

"Wise guy," says the back-of-the-head. "You'll soon be doing amateur talent night with us!"

"Take a fork and take some meat. Sit yourself right down to eat," sings the Pioneer horn.

And we keep walking, walking, walking . . .

All barefoot, in swimming trunks only . . . there's a smell of pine. We were playing cops and robbers, and I'd been caught.

Four cops are leading me off to be questioned. The back-of-the-head, the two profiles. And the one in back ratted on me. For a serving of stewed fruit he told them where I was hiding. The kids are all around. "They caught the robber. They caught the robber."

"The woman who's your troop leader is being squeezed by the gym teacher," I say.

"And the woman who's your troop leader is being squeezed by the money keeper," says the back-of-the-head.

"Yeah, well, guess what's for supper tonight," I challenge him.

"Cream of wheat," he answers.

"Cream of wheat porridge— night dark and horrid," I yell, pleased that he walked right into it.

The kids roll with laughter. One laughs so hard he falls out of a tree.

"You'll laugh once too often," the back-of-the-head hisses viciously.

"Sleep, sleep, off to your tents." Long and low the Pioneer horn plays taps. Only it isn't a horn. It's Miles Davis's trumpet, eternally alone, playing up high above the clouds.

Several steps before the third column of the Opera Theater, where someone is waiting for me—my future wife, but now, from this moment, my former wife—I straighten my tie and button my jacket.

She has just returned from the beach and still smells of the sea. It is she of the freckles on the nose and the eyes pulled slightly back by invisible rubber bands.

"Do you love me?" she asks ever so quietly.

I want to answer just as quietly, "Yes, of course." But for some reason a huge number of curious people crowd around us.

They come running from all the nearby streets and squares.

They force their way out of the stores. They even stop watching *Swan Lake* in the Opera Theater and flock out of its doors.

"The joker in love will explain himself," they inform one another enigmatically.

How do they know all that? When she and I talk so quietly?

"So? Do you love me?" she asks in an absolute whisper.

Everyone freezes. Here it comes . . .

"Love isn't some old potato that you can just chuck out the window!" I shout.

Laughter is mixed with angry exclamations. "Terrif-ic!" "No." "Making fun of love!" "For a witty remark, he even picks on his father." "He really knows how to rip 'em off."

"Do you love me?" her lips move soundlessly.

"Love is a stream from a water faucet. It keeps pouring till you stop it," I yell in exasperation.

The Opera Theater shudders from laughter. But again, indignant shouts.

"He's sneering. . . . What does she see in him anyway? . . . Get rid of him, girl! . . . What good is he to her, eh?"

"Do you love me?" she asks with her eyes alone.

"Yes . . . of course . . ." I say, just short of weeping.

The crowd greets my words with a rumble of disenchantment. They're no longer interested. Again they fill up the neighboring streets. Again they want to see *Swan Lake*.

And we keep walking, walking, walking . . .

And it seems we will soon reach the end. I've apparently laughed myself out, made fun of everything.

But the only thing I don't understand is whether I'm being led to my execution because I've made fun of everything, or whether I've made fun of everything because I'm being led to my execution.

We come to the enormous amphitheater with the name Finita la Commedia. The ticket window is covered by a sign, "Today's Execution Sold Out."

I pull out the free passes allotted to me by law and distribute them, right and left, to the first lucky people that happen along.

Now we enter the amphitheater. All five of us are in black tailcoats and top hats. My escorts have on white gloves besides.

The amphitheater is so crowded they have to turn people away. Even in the aisles you can't find room. People are eating ice-cream cones and truffles, and coughing. All lines of vision cross at the center of the blindingly illuminated area where a varicolored platform, the executioner's block, has been mounted, and on it, looking like a young stallion, is a thin-legged, black, Viennese electric chair.

I can't take my eyes off the block. It's all pasted over with greetings. "Welcome, joker." "Two heads are better than one." "A sound body and a sound mind are soon parted."

They lead me up to the thin-legged, black Viennese electric chair. A drumroll travels over the entire amphitheater. An orchestra plays an end note, one continuous chord in a major key.

Suddenly silence falls. Such silence it begins to pierce your ears. In the midst of this silence a voice comes over the radio from somewhere beneath the dome.

"Be seated, please."

"Thank you so much, I'd rather stand," I say politely, placing my right hand over my heart. At the same time I bow elegantly. It seems I have hit the mark. The amphitheater answers with a mighty burst of laughter and shouts of approval. The electric chair disappears somewhere under the dome, and clowns come tumbling out into the arena to perform in the sudden interval.

"The joker's wish is the executioner's command," the same cold radio voice says from under the dome, and I am pushed up to the block.

"You may have a last request," says the back-of-the-head.

Once again a piercing silence.

"Tell me please," I ask, "what's today?"

"Monday," the back-of-the-head replies.

"Can't say much for the way the week's starting," and I bow in all four directions.

Deafening whistles fill the amphitheater. "Old as the hills!" comes from every side. "Don't get it! . . . Cliché."

My foursome wince with distaste.

It fell flat. My forehead breaks out in little beads of sweat and my strength fails me. I drop to my knees in front of the block. Its surface reminds me of the surface of those sound and solid stumps on which butchers dismember carcasses.

"Can't I have a pillow?" I say with trembling voice. "It's rough here."

"He wants a pillow! . . . He wants a pillow," word spreads around the amphitheater. "He can't stand it even for a minute."

On the block one of the profiles places the favorite pillow of my childhood embroidered with a baby bear.

The other profile throws a white sheet over my shoulders and, as in a barbershop, deftly tucks the ends into my shirt collar.

The ex-friend lays my head on the pillow, right ear down, and recommends that I close my eyes.

The orchestra breaks into a cheerful gallop. But even in that gallop with my left ear I catch a sound somewhere way up high under the dome—the eternal lonely playing of Miles Davis's trumpet.

"Just a minute!" I raise my head. "Pardon me, but I'm not used to sleeping on the right side."

A murmur of dissatisfaction spreads around the amphitheater. My escorts helplessly shrug their shoulders.

I lay my left ear on the pillow. This, it seems, is it.

The back-of-the-head starts to raise an axe of incredible dimensions high in the air, so that he will be able to bring it down with a crash on the place where I now feel a lump interfering with my breathing.

With difficulty I swallow my spit . . .

"Just a minute," I gasp. "Can I have one last word?"

"What are your opinions on this question?" My ex-friend asks the entire amphitheater. "Let him or not?"

"Let him," the amphitheater bellows.

With difficulty I rise to my feet. I teeter from side to side. The blood pounding in my temples keeps time with the great orchestral drum. And filling my lungs with air, I shout with all the strength I have left, "Ecch, cream of wheat porridge—night dark and horrid."

It's hard for me to grasp what happens next. A triumphant roar sweeps my escorts off their feet. The axe falls from the back-of-the-head's hands. All four are rolling around the arena pressing their hands to their bellies. This goes on for a long time. It goes on for a very long time. Then they get up from the floor of the arena and, like drunkards, holding on to one another for support, try to get their balance. Their eyes are out of focus from laughter; unable to utter a single word, they look at each other helplessly. The amphitheater roars and groans in ecstatic convulsions. The back-of-the-head turns in my direction, looks at me for an instant, then wracked with laughter, spits out:

"Cream of . . ."

He chokes and all four in a new fit of laughter tumble to the floor of the arena. Again it lasts a long time. It lasts a very long time.

And as I look at them, sweaty, worn out, choking with laughter, I realize they haven't the physical strength left to execute me today. . .

I am escorted home. I am left alone in my room. There is only one short night at my disposal. At six in the morning these four will come for me again. And again we'll be walking, walking, walking . . . the same road. Through the same curious crowds. To my place of execution. And all I have to work with is one night. So I grab a pencil and paper and feverishly begin to think up a routine for tomorrow's procession.

It's vitally necessary that I make them all laugh again tomorrow. Otherwise they'll do me in.

And this has been going on for years on end.

Come on, head, cook up some "Cream of wheat porridge—night dark and horrid."

Poems[*]
by Yuri Karabchiyevsky

Autumn Chronicle

The city, thus I began, is born, in my opinion, when
each of us for himself is insufficient and has need of others.
—Plato

0

Not I to him, but he to me's attached.
I'm free to live, I move as I know how.
But no matter what I think up, still
I feel how the slow weight
behind me moves along in my path
And each step becomes a labor,
Feet slip. And the rope harness
of the fierce boatman cuts . . .

1

In a huge, sickening hospital,
nurtured on groans and stench,
I finger the warm apparatus
and strive helplessly to divine
the diagrams obscured by blue copy paper.
It's stifling. I'm not up to apparatuses now.
Now, later, yesterday, today, tomorrow . . .
Actually, tomorrow—that's not today.
Today, I am nobody but myself,
but tomorrow I'll be somebody alien,
of another time, otherwise perceived.
And so here I say: I'll come tomorrow.
(Let *him* disentangle this mess.)

Quickly I gather the instruments
beneath the piercing gaze of the nurses,

* Translated by H. William Tjalsma.

grab a smoking soldering iron by its tail,
and go out into the courtyard. The sharp air
stings me right in the heart.
And thus I stand, breathing in this pain.

The hospital courtyard, popular menagerie,
white gowns brush by,
they flow over the pants of the interns
carrying persuasive folders,
above the boots of the husky aides,
dauntlessly gazing with a sullen look,
above the naked knees of the girl students
caressing their phonendoscopes
with shy toylike hands,
fingernails just sly splatters . . .

And next to the morgue—corpses are being unloaded.
And the wrinkled yellow bandages
seem painfully ridiculous.
(Oh, entrancing order!)
The prudent human tribe
has weighed everything out and foreseen all.
You'll not surprise it now with anything!)

The yard is crowded to the limit.
A waxworks. Fate in miniature.
From a petty crushed glance—
to the grasping of hairy idols.
From tender lips—to dusky work,
when a drooping is carried out
that one moment ago . . .

Subtle science shall explain all.
The subtler—the more precise.
In fact it's so subtle—that you can't see it with eyeglasses.

2

There's a hole in the fence—and I am in Unboring Park.
In a gay park, park of diversions,
of swings, carousels and ferris wheels.
It's not too late, but it's not early either.
Autumn morning, distinct,
is imprinted with maple leaves
in the asphalt flatness of the streets.
A slight drizzle. The ferris wheels are still.
The shops and restaurants are battened down.
Empty boats doze on the water.
And only the speakers on their masts,
unscrupulous, noisy tin boxes,

live a ridiculous and contrived life,
squander their toy passions,
bother about all kind of nonsense.
Only rarely does the blather cease,
and jingling Chopin,
dressed in a worker's pants,
is led by the hand
onto the wet pathways . . .

The chill park is elegantly beautiful,
like a foggy interplanetary city,
like the past we have abandoned.

Like the past, where every minute
is essential, no less than the former minute.
Like the past, where every sorrow
is piercing to the point of pain
and is desired. Like the past in which we live
a tedious otherworldly life.

3

We began in this very park
one autumn morning, striding
over the fallen leaves
with difficulty, as over fish scales.

We began sighting from afar,
from a broad and full look
at the emptied squares and lanes.

We had to make our way around
half a kingdom to reach the other half.
No one could hasten this way.

It ended somewhere beyond the houses,
beyond the lindens of Pokrovsky Boulevard,
beyond basement walls.

In confused and gloomy labyrinths,
in some sort of smoke-filled catacombs,
in the embrace of kitchen stuffiness.

The path broke off in a crowded, little room,
in the widow's cell of a Polish auntie—
her portrait hung overhead . . .

4

The end of the path. I go out of the park,
homeless square with a head cold.
Drooping bridge. Cold river.

I'd like just a tiny bit of freedom
in order to pass along the right—no—
the left side with happy step.
There's one step—and trolleybuses
fly past, kiosks, stoplights.
Shoelaces flying in the wind.
There's another step—faces and windows flashing by.
Without stops, on and on and on,
somewhere, somewhere else again . . .
I creep along. My step is vain and pitiful.
My sick heart falls behind my body
and beats away back there.

And led like a blind man by the sidewalks,
I move toward doors to boardrooms and offices
that I cannot avoid.

5

But of course, there were interims.
Oh, for instance, going to the movies.
Nightmare dreams. When they turn on the light.
And you are standing there tying your scarf.
What's there to say? And you are holding that purse.
And looking into an unfamiliar face,
obsequiously, absently, and deceitfully.
Will you ever be forgiven
for the film being bad, for the endless boredom,
it's cold outside, it's time to say farewell,
for the fact that again tomorrow
everybody's for himself?
"At work, the guys are really something! . . ."

6

I hang about in editorial offices,
offering my love for money,
for very little,
almost for nothing.
Nobody will take it, even for free.
Oh, sweet, dear chatterboxes!
All of you are good kids.
You're not to be charmed by free love.
Proper marriage! Only marriage is proper.
All the rest is improper.

What are editorial boards to me?

A woman accessible to many,
curving shamelessly and brazenly,
standing in a doorway—you can't miss her.
She's standing there—and you walk past,
squinting, all but brushing her chest,
all but swallowing her wet breath,
all but embracing her, all but striking up a conversation.
But if all shall be repeated from the beginning,
then all shall be repeated strictly.
No matter what, there is a time and a place:
Such diversions are not for you . . .

7

But there were also parties and dances
which I went to like a lamb to the slaughter,
as to an examination—a student and a liar.
We would arrive at the very moment.
At first I was noisy and in a hurry,
later gave in, and now wordlessly
took off my coat in the cold vestibule,
whither the great celebration sent
its chance reflections:
hairdos, skirts, purses, mirrors,
silk stockings with seams and filter cigarettes . . .
Took off my coat—and into the icy water.
Always alone, she was one of those . . .
Always alone, she was one of us
amidst those attentively happy faces,
and conversations creeping up the mountain,
and music from the master's table.

What am I to show this assemblage?
With what should I prove my loyalty,
apart from the words scratching at my palate,
apart from the hands that don't find rest,
apart from a naked face
burnt by biting illumination?
And so I say to myself: Come to your senses!
Go home, give her back the coat tag—
tattered plastic happiness,
take your coat, no need for explanations,
go home along the blue boulevard, through the frost,
fearing nothing.
Everything will be OK. She'll return
to plunge you into another whirlpool
where you are you whatever you are . . .

How subtly, reasonably, and wisely
I speak, bordering my speech with metaphor,
—now, to myself—to that one.
Then, I looked over people's heads,
screwing up my face, stretching my neck,
anticipating an action as if it were present,
bad or good or anything at all,
ready in advance to worship it,
to repent before it, believe, and forgive . . .

8

In a publishing house where polite chaps
play their no-lose games,
where hostile classes come together
to drown in the glow of smiles,
where the rooms are full of success
as with air, and well-being hangs down
to the floor like bunches of grapes from the walls—
in a publishing house, in a reeling hall,
my briefcase nestles into the grasslike, rustling pile rug.
I'm here next to it, here in the neighborhood,
pressed down by the armchair, broken in a zigzag,
duped by a discordant narcotic,
a blockhead like any other, bald and sick.
If only I'd been smoking—there'd have been justification . . .
Who believes a nonsmoker? And still
it seems to me I was pretending pretty well
to be the same sort of hale fellow as these,
a successful servant of art,
friend to debauchees and windbags.
What am I waiting for, what conversation?

9

But here it's the holiday. Rare good luck
Father, a half-crazy alcoholic,
has been sent off to auntie or granny,
and we're alone and the house is ours today.
Most bright visage!—and a sky blue dress.
Smoky waves of hair—sky blue dress.
Stockings with seams on tender calves
and slender feet in black shoes.
I've been sent shopping. I'm happy.
My gaze slides along the street.
It is reflected and refracted in polished surfaces and glass.
Moscow like an aging trollop,
lover of crude ornamentation,

stands there in fiery, cheap necklaces,
bracelets, amulets, and badges.
She's out for a good time. Not so much actually,
but no stranger to womanly pretense,
she plays up to the general infusion,
while what is on her mind—Lord, don't say.
And whatever you're up to—I'm not up to doubts.
Alarmed needles of joy
flood my submissive body.
And there are no sides when I return,
neither walls nor ceiling nor floor,
but there is a face: slightly glistening lips
and eyes to match the color of her dress . . .
At first a lonely lady friend
(as indicated in our schedule)
sits down in a chair, tucking up her legs
and fixing with bare hands
the scalloped hem of her pleated skirt.
She hunches down and prattles on.
I listen attentively to the symbols and signs,
offer insigificant syllables,
and think that if, then still . . .
I'm frightened myself by these terrible thoughts,
and take joy that they are so terrible . .
We drink wine. The friend vanishes.
And again the world narrows painfully,
sharply to a needle's point.
Rouguishly sky blue dress
and the smooth skin encompassed in it
and the childish smell of faint perfume
envelopes everything ahead in a fog.
Oh, just give me true insanity!
I drink some wine, then wine and vodka
and, suddenly confounded,
I come to my senses somewhere on Kolkhoz Square
in the reality of the simplest sensations:
cold chill, wet water . . .
Grey night flings open my collar
and blows in my face. My memory goes blank.
Suddenly it seems that I've been here for many days.
Thus I live, cursing and reeling,
I go out to puke in the entryway
and wait for a taxi at the pillar . . .

One hundred years later, in a bottomless corridor,
I make my way home, overturning buckets

and catching at cobwebs with my fingers.
Oh, here's the door the key goes to.
The goal beyond is a worthy one:
there the sweating, stinking body
of a tame, domestic dream
tosses and turns from side to side heavily,
smacking lips and wheezing.
My coat hangs on its nail, shoes under the divan.
All is finished. Nothing began.

10
It's time to go home. I'll stop at the shops.
I'll spare a few kopeks for a couple of books.
I'll buy me one (if it weren't for the kids!)
silly book, for no reason at all.
I'll buy ready-made patties
and sausage and a package of margarine,
and stuff it all in my briefcase, where my instruments sleep,
and there's the metro—duck in and that's it!
I'll just catch my breath and glance around cautiously:
are there any gleaming knees and clean lips and
glistening eyes to be seen?
Thank God, everything is quiet and calm.
The right kind of women sit opposite me:
chopped up, porous faces,
figureless figures and hands,
string shopping bags stretching down to the floor.
They're nothing to me and I'm nothing to them.

I open a magazine, sigh with relief,
Envious black fate
shall not trouble my soul this time . . .

1970

Elegy

Oh, my prophetic soul,
Oh, heart filled with alarm,
Oh, how you do beat on the threshold
Of a seemingly double existence!

—Tiutchev

1
All comes to one. Tiresome songs,
these sophisticated diseases of mine,

and proletarian resentment as well—
will all be counted in the end.
Penetrating wetness creeps in,
and if not by plague then by smallpox
is the air around poisoned for a hundred years.
Pockmarks on the water, on faces, on book covers,
Pockmarked authority squeezes my hand,
a butcher with pockmarked skin soils a pencil.
—Two twenty two!—the magician-mathematician
flings the bone down and wraps it up tight
and catches the check—and so it's mine.
And a shaky house—a lifelong trolleybus
transports me along, although I'm unsure,
although I'm old and cowardly.
The pockmarked driver opens the doors for me,
and dirty-grey, twilight snow,
all pockmarked, the disease
outgrown, forgetful of the purity of its background,
like a dirty, groveling convert,
slows its pace—and spits in my face . . .

?

I don't know what to do with myself. I do not believe in God.
I'm afraid, afraid, but still I do not believe.
I don't believe at all. But still how afraid I am!
(Is it easy to feel the world's spirituality
when you're stuffed like a goose
with a plebian spirit of materialism,
with joyless Jewish garlic!) Not in vain
did the gloomy prophets of Jehovah
chew on bread and know the power
of a wide open, incomplete line
set upright on the run.
The great clan, the insane family
but all to a man—are cutthroats!
Get away from this kind. And as for Jesus—
I'm glad for him. But, after all, he isn't God either . . .

Thus I live. And instead of grace—
            the garlic and the pepper of materialism,
a sleepless and unspent question
and the eternal grin of the democrat
who risks bending his knee
before whomever, whoever's great but equal,
before those who are glorious but not elevated.

3

Thus I live—without blessings,
with fear in my heart—devoid of predestination,
but also with judgment from on high,
in my own way—joylessly I live.

4

Still a kid in black, baggy trousers
with elastic climbing up my ribs,
dreaming of getting an A and of going to the movies,
on brightly lit sidewalks
I perceived beautiful worlds.
Oh, the nobility of those who thirst to drink their fill,
oh, the smells of radiant victuals!
The breathing of a fantastic cave
where wild boar meat is prepared
at night with gilded swords . . .
There, these two drank and ate
everything that the gentle senator obtained,
the native father desirous of good.
A courteous stroll awaits them now,
relaxed, soft conversation
where every tutored word
is no worse than a trained dog,
scratches for the necessary step,
ever higher and higher, more and more boldly,
and there the steady paw is already
pushing open the door into the swirling bedroom,
where above the furniture, dressed in a peignoir,
twists a mixture of scents and camphor,
and a restrained, vascillating whisper
nestles down in the folds of the dull portières . . .

And if crazy newspapers,
(capable nonetheless of doing their job,
deliberately, like a thousand devils),
and if, in those years, I had been given
an ordinary, silly problem,
I wouldn't have sent it to hell
or spat on it, wouldn't
have hidden behind a joke,
I would have told what I told.

5

Oh, Lord, so what have we lost,
what joy is there in youthful blithering

and besides the fear of death
what does the universal lament over years lived hold?!

Here are the songs that we sang,
product of the culture mill,
two or three stanzas of handmade goods.
Sign of the symbol, shadow of the sign, symbol of the shadow,
all variations of word combinations,
nothing does not signify nothing.
Now, we are reasonable and free.
Experience replaces fancy for us,
we seek not the pretext but a gift.
All is outside ourselves and nothing is in us.
But the past, towards which I so strain,
is always with me. Like a greedy hermit,
I possess all, squandering not a farthing.
No one's pain passed without a trace,
no one's grin was in vain,
all is one and all goes into the same pot.
Henceforth, like a zealous proprietor
I will make the rounds of my holdings
and find only there where I lost.
To crumbling, puffy plaster,
to the cellar stairs removed long ago,
to the empty, nonexistent bench—
I come on sleepless nights
to feel, having kissed the holy things,
the sweetest taste of loss upon my lips . . .

6

Let's move over. *Oil paint.*
I am a superfluous man. The windows are open.
And joy is tinged with sorrow.
As the smell of linseed oil, the smell of apples.
The rich stepfather bought a bag
of "greenings" ripe and bursting,
while the rooms were under repair,
the windows open, and
"take some" they say, and I bite
into greenish-tart linseed oil.

I go outside. Children play.
And over their heads I send
the shy gaze of a dirty kike,
expecting a dirty trick any moment.
Everything will work out . . . I still don't know
in what sorrow I am destined to rush about

between the oil-painted well
and the courtyard splattered with friendly spit.
And what sort of price I'll have to pay
for bread and roof, for buckwheat kasha,
for tea without measure, smelling of medicine,
for a pair of pants and other amenities,
for the stench of a bedbug-rich divan,
for the dust of an indestructible rug . . .

The ice grinds by the water hydrant,
the toilet smells of kerosene,
the banisters are shaky. Up above
are seven flabby maidens—they don't get married,
seven hefty ladies—going crazy, howling,
and judging the world and running circle dances.
And how they sing—you'd remember it to your dying day:
a Jewish yowl and Russian lack of control
and astringent crossbreed tenderness,
pain dwindling into voices.
That's the way life goes. Breathing cozy air
where sweat is mixed with the fluids of touching,
sighs and hints, and tears and unbridled loves.
So that's the way you sing. Of an evening
slurp borscht from a freckled bowl
and, leaning your elbow on the divan
spar with the girls at "Old Maid."
So it is you don't know that other house
in which there is half-light and immobility,
where moderate wetness reigns
and false taut silence.
(And it's better so, and only if it doesn't stop,
you're afraid to touch, God forbid!)

These two words—oil paint—
ought to float down the corridor still,
on the way losing yellowness and sleekness
and the cold of the schoolhouse wall.
They've got to warm up and thicken
and sweat freely and start smelling so sweet
and splash themselves out, having gotten flushed,
and crawl away with ribbed fins
and miracle of miracles, miracle eternal!—
a mosaic of hollows and hillocks
that coincides so happily with the pattern!

And the painter was a peasant lad,
most loyal child of the academy,

still alive, still not accustomed,
not in receipt of his due.
On holidays he went out on the square,
onto the crossroads of black corridors.
An accordion—soul unbuttoned,
all aglow with a drunken flush—
lay entwined on his breast.
And the lisping little Jew,
a friend from God knows where,
sang songs adored by all.
There was neither music nor words
but only the desire for music and words.

But perhaps all that was needed was in them?
It's not for me to judge. To listen to them now
is like going to see a woman
who turned to stone fifteen years ago.
To come to see the living lady, kiss her hand
(veins, rings, broken fingernails)
to exhaust lightheartedly the way things are—
and suddenly stumble with a disquiet gaze
and change something there in the soul,
to mix everything up so there won't be a temptation
to bother the thread slipping away.
So there won't be a desire to stroke shoulders
and answer to the point and bare one's teeth,
and attempt to join the shadow
with the stony, indisputable statue . . .

Salad-lemon landscapes,
eatable apricot faces,
lilac-blue heavens . . .
The canvases hang in even rows,
and, taking off his felt boots before going to bed,
a deaf old man, his father, a tinsmith,
stared and, had he wanted to,
could have recognized his native village,
but he didn't want to—so he couldn't.

7

My city seeps outward more and more,
and like an ink spot on a blotter,
in the lilac light of the hurly-burly,
tinges the white fields.
And those hours that I live on earth
are tinged with lilac light:
the red-hot ball, the pungent paste,

the fleetingly lilac grillwork
on the unbending notebook pages.
Those two hours that I live like a *barin*
(with the children tossing and turning
beyond the wall—they dreaming warlike dreams,
dense as animated films),
I drink tea, chew without hurrying
and think and, you can believe,
don't give myself out to be anybody.
Then, until the Great Daily Mob
has need of the poet,
I send to everyone without exception
my face with a postpaid response,
and overnight dry my damp brains
on high tension wires.

8
Light bulbs, my Spinozian globes,
taut cherry blisters!
Transistors, three-legged little insects
embedded in a spider's web.
my sweet brain sucked dry with love!
Again I open my mouth to cry,
again I gulp air with a jerk,
again rasp—but the words are indistinguishable.

9
Someday, I'll come out as usual
into the half-light of the trolleybus morning,
into the broad frosty breath
of a January day not yet begun.
And be amazed at the lightness. From where?
It'll be the continuous throng of instruments,
Makhno's* migrant army, unclenching its joints.
There'll be just books in my briefcase,
writings of blabbers and dabblers,
and something hot out of the typewriter, too,
and other stuff on as yet blank pages.

And I'll go down into the metro, warm my hands,
and shaken by the superfluity of women,
set up a contest, choosing strictly
according to color of eyes and to build.
And I'll never hurry.

*General in the White Army.

While at that moment, Alternating Current,
the brightest of currents, will burst through its vacuum
and come out triumphant onto the ceiling.
And immediately, like a bottomless dugout,
there on top, along the white prospect,
there'll come a rustling cry: "Find the engineer!"—
the pirate call of my tormenter—
and I'll fence myself off from tender murderers
with a little book of lighthearted kind.

10
Misanthropy—is just entropy.
General chaos, logarithm of unhappiness,
that measure of loneliness with which
we measure last steps.
Is the weight of the century really at fault in this?
Do even we really lose our form under that yoke,
bog down and drain away?
Enviers, jealous lovers, the ambitious,
let us get together, as usual,
fly in, all, pack it in the last time,
clap our hands together, speak a vow,
and turn into the best of friends,
while our hothouse smiles
so heat up the atmosphere
that the central heating may as well be switched off.
Let us play at goodness,
I to you, you to me. Nice business.
While this ball is still in the air,
everything's OK. But if it drops—
it's curtains. Oh, Lord, really,
is no one guilty before anyone?

11
A silvery, decorative day,
covered by a glazed roof,
rings and thunders like a city in a snuff box,
of itself, and I'm neither here nor there.
There, rainbow-colored girls on skis crowd about,
pert backsides sticking out,
ragamuffins, poking their fine feathers
into the ribbed trolleybus door.
There's my drunken neighbor, a good guy,
an informer and a pimp, swindler and alcoholic,
he's washed up with saliva, wiped off with a crust of bread,
flies off, without forgetting the beer.

And there's my wife coming from the stop,
all in a hurry, loaded down with bags and parcels,
cutting across, springing and slipping . . .
And he greets her the best he can,
and over her beautiful face
his gaze scurries, blacker than a fly.
She's coming up the steps
and a righteous, hermit's cough
knocks at the door, and my heart aches
with painful grief directed nowhere in particular.
To whom am I to show my sorrow,
to whose account should I transfer my patience,
so that the long-awaited wind of change
should touch my brow with hot lips?

Forgive me, Lord, and don't take me at my word.
Change? Right away.
Everything will be different instantly.

12

No, it is a sin to grumble. So long as the children are healthy,
so long as the Ural taiga has not caressed me with the whine of
    mosquitoes,
so long as I haven't buried my face in the snow
that's as dry and harsh as a whetstone,
so long as I don't pound the back of my head against a pine tree,
so long as I'm alive and take joy in the weather,
so long as I'm healthy, and awakening me will still preserve me from
    nightmares,
so long as I'm frozen and hurt,
so long as I'm irritable and curt—
everything will be OK, which is what I wish for you, too.

I've lived my life no worse than I tried.
I've wrung everything out of it and survived.
And finished with myself. And I ask that no one be blamed.
I am no more. But the children remain.
Night is fading, morning to work.
Pulling on the ususal cover,
I shall once more feign warmth and life,
my exterior look beyond all suspicion
of mirrors and the gaze of co-workers.
But there are two eyes, two pupils,
into which, without distortion,
my grief from the other side
has passed . . .

Two Stories and a Novella*
by Viktor Yerofeyev

A Fin de Siècle Orgasm

Do not trust, dear readers, do not trust subordinate clauses! Salts precipitate in subordinate clauses. You say that syntax guarantees sanitation and healthy imagery? Spare me, please! The pronoun "I" is constantly being transformed before one's very eyes, even in the most innocent letters home or in a picture postcard from the Black Sea: either it walks a tightrope or suddenly strikes an indolent pose, snorts, catches itself, lies down under a cypress, retrieves its dignity, and fades away—but it is never, never on target. The yoke of grammar, my readers, the heavy yoke of grammar. And so what? "I" loses its third dimension and in its place gains a fourth. A closer look reveals it is a hoax and a rather shaky one. But one must accept such charlatanry. Look the other way, and with full awareness of your comfortable helplessness take a deep breath, count some elephants to get to sleep, and praise your helplessness as part of God's creation, its heat and fire.

In the fourth dimension the "I" multiplies like an amoeba: it divides into "I" + "I" (continue up to twenty-two "I's") and they add up not to all of US, but to HIM alone. Or, in the worst case, to HER, that handmaiden to talent, so responsive and meticulous. In the fourth dimension an unshaven individual of irritated vacationer's appearance slaps some talc on his cheeks and drives off into the past with deferred honors. In the last analysis he wants to say that he is ever-ever-ever-ever (a garland of evers!) so slightly sorry, but instead he makes a rather ambiguous remark about the role of tastelessness.

There is a certain type of airy, country thought distinctive in its intimacy and unobligatory manner. It combines geniality, bliss, and those little stretches of woods found on the outskirts of Moscow.

Due to the intense heat beating down on the square at the railroad crossing, the shops that sold dishpans and soap were fainting away, the State Farm milk went sour, and the repair of all possible systems and

*Translated by Martin Horwitz.

types of clocks and watches was temporarily suspended. Trains, on the other hand, continued to whistle by, well-barbered hedgerows were pressed back by the wind alternately exhibiting bald spots, carefully combed and straight parts, and the struggle for existence. The shaky platform hummed.

And if future railroad workers—gloomy youths whose pimply faces looked like raspberry patches, lovers of eels and oysters—were inviting their future feminine counterparts for boatrides—gloomy odalisques with scattered patches of gooseflesh—and if the pond shone brightly at the distance of sunstroke so that a white parasol came in handy, then those same counterparts, flattered by the attention, were not hiding out in boarding school toilets or running the dynamo, but instead the whole group was drinking beer amid the smells of pine trees and shashlik right in the center of the pond, where, weak with laughter, they were transformed into a poster advertising the pleasure-boat station.

"They aren't with any group, so they must have a car," thought the unshaven individual while standing in line for watermelon, as was right and proper. Some dogs ran by sideways. They belonged to a special breed which had developed from many years of disorderly coitus among various dacha dogs. Folks affectionately and simply called specimens of the mixed breed: "dog." People in line were saying that the melons were feed melons and inedible, that inside they were all rotten, just water, pink mold, and seeds. A covered truck went by with warning signs on its sides: "Caution, people!", and a militiaman, ambling slowly as honey, walked out onto the porch of the liquor store with an embarrassed hand covering his right pocket. The unshaven one had lost track of the number of days he had gone without shaving. A secret coquetry had forced him to neglect everything, and his razor was out of whack and caught mercilessly at his skin with every shave. Vanity's shortness of breath was most enervating. Of all the games from which literature has borrowed metaphors, chess is the most overused. A little more and the muscular force of a knight will become the unit of measurement of internal narrative tension. Then—the game will be up. Then well-bred people will shed copious tears over chess problems and seasoned grandmasters will win all the Nobel prizes with haughty smiles. The endgame promised to be inept. A game for the color-blind and those of little faith! The unshaven one used to be so bold as to doubt the whiteness of the white pieces. "They're freshly painted," he would say excitedly. "The paint has been put on in one, maybe two coats maximum, and after that who knows what the hell is under there. They're all escapees—dog breeders, gynecologists, Jews—still not recovered from their escape: one foot here, and the other one already there. They've come to rest up and find a safe burrow. A fence with a hidden coil of barbed wire, a lock, a bolt, a burglar alarm."

But at night stones flew into the black, shining windows and the sound of broken glass could be heard throughout the county.

The children were pawns on bicycles. Dacha children are fed eggs for breakfast and the eggs make them strong and they push their pedals all day long. They grow up egotists, every one. This has been written about repeatedly, but dacha-goers have forgotten how to read. This too has been written about. Dacha children are very self-assured, but underneath they are cowards and even nasty in a peculiar way. They are easily excited, do not sleep well, show hysteria in the depths of their pupils, have puffy cheeks, and lips as red as raspberries. Their bicycles should be taken away from them and given to the Vietnamese. The Vietnamese deserve them.

And women who carry two watermelons in a string bag look indecent. Do you know what that looks like two watermelons in a string bag hanging down to the ground? It isn't funny, it's awful. It is a sign of moral obtuseness. And finally, most importantly: a woman who does not observe abstinence during menstruation is worse than a fascist. The word MENSTRUATION is one of the most beautiful words in the Russian language. It has the sound of the wind in it and evokes visions of far-off landscapes (will Dal's dictionary have a place for words like that?).* It just begs to be put into a song.

The woman selling watermelons suffered from very low blood pressure. From time to time a weak sound would erupt from her small, magical breast and she would fall in a faint onto the mountain of watermelons. Out of respect for her illness, the people in line patiently awaited the resumption of business. The woman did not lie idle long. Coming to, she would sneeze and look dazedly around until her glance fell on the taut faces of the customers silently welcoming her most recent recovery. This brought her back to her place in the world and, straightening her smock and carefully spitting into a special low blood pressure can hidden away under the counter, she began to sell her fruit. Watermelons. The unshaven one was always in a greedy hurry when he ate watermelons. Chopping the pulp with a kitchen knife, he would go straight for the heart of the melon. Juice would drip down his chin. His fingers stuck together trembling. His Adam's apple bobbed up and down like a piston. Traces of syrupy saliva appeared in the corners of his shapeless mouth and he wiped them away with his sleeve. His eyes lost their focus as he snuffled the air and grunted, caught a stray piece of fruit with his knee, sucked the pulp and swelled up as he was eating. But all this eating seemed to have no effect on him. He was skinny and emaciated, and in the morning it was hard to tell whether he hadn't gotten enough sleep or had overslept. But he did love watermelons. Adored them. And peaches, too. He really loved peaches.

---

*pun on *dal'*—far-off scene, and Dal'—Russian folklorist interested in the literal use of folk dialect [tr.].

Since he was renting half a house from a heavily made-up, heavy-set widow, still burdened by her year-old loss, the unshaven one belonged to the dacha residents by force of unavoidable circumstance. He discovered a scythe in a shed, cut down the pitiful grass, got all scratched up by thistles, and was happy that he hadn't cut off his own two feet. And now, like a dacha Jehovah, he strolled about his newly cut lawn and helped himself to the widow's somewhat nondescript sour apples. In the manner of any lighthearted individual, he rhymed 'horn' with 'morn' and considered the wondrous workings of lightning rods. After dinner the unshaven one departed for Moscow. His wife and one-year-old son saw him off at the station. His son rode proudly in a canvas stroller.

"You're making a hunchback out of him," lamented some tender-hearted women at the station, dissatisfied with the design of the stroller.

"It's none of your affair," snapped the wife in her Polish jeans.

"You don't deserve to be a mother . . ." mused the ladies.

When the unshaven one returned late at night, his frightened wife informed him that they had been robbed. He proceeded into the room, and saw the turned-out pockets of the raincoats and jackets, hanging down like small dirty pouches. No money had been taken because there hadn't been any. A small Japanese transistor radio was gone, but a typewriter that had been right next to the radio hadn't been touched. The unshaven one was never stingy with his belongings and viewed them with condescension, but when he lost them, he became upset and didn't know what to do. He took a flashlight and walked along the path to the gate. Having no experience with death, he was not completely sure of the irreversibility of events. Maybe it had been a joke? He stood in the clearing and tried to remember: there had been a group of three fellows hanging around the dacha. The unshaven one had broken the rules of the disagreeable game: he had not locked the front door. For this he had been justly punished. I have to hand it to them, he thought, reconciling himself to the unavoidability of the theft; in their place I would have done the same thing. Everything has been taken from them and so they take trifles from others, he mused, longing for the evening surf of far-off Europe. Lord, teach me that perilous art! Put a . . . motor up my ass: I lie to myself and say that it is just the times in which we live; I'll still break even in this game; I'll show them! It's all the fault of excessive demands . . . a damned enchantment! The light of the streetlamp mindlessly climbed the branches of the fir trees. To think that these almost motionless trees, the flora of nightmares, might someday be Christmas trees decorated with multicolored spheres and candies. . . . They're probably cele-brating right now and sneering at me. Conquerors! The unshaven one tried to picture their joyous, excited faces and was ready to celebrate with them a bit himself, which promised to be a pleasant theme for imaginings, but he noticed an attic, a spiderweb, and the eyes of small predators, and he became dizzy at the thought that he was being watched and hunted. I'd like to rip off their fingers with some kind of gadget that would slice them at the moment they reached for the doorknob. Then those fingerless wonders would begin to respect me. The bastards, muttered the unshaven one. Two days later he met the bastards in the clearing. "Got a smoke?" asked the youngest. "Yep," said the unsahven one, shuddering and gazing innocently into their mocking faces. "In my cottage. It's not far." But the bastards said nothing, just wandered off. They probably thought it was a trap. The unshaven one had no memory for music and could not tell Beethoven from Brahms, though he did feel it necessary to go to the symphony two or three times a season and sit patiently in a pulsating aureole of thought, waiting for intermission. He also felt a strange compulsion to feel an aversion for Tchaikovsky.

"That Pyotr Ilich . . ." He wrinkled his nose in disgust.

The unshaven one's nose was peeling and his nostrils, which quivered when he breathed, had been borrowed from the doors of empty birdhouses. His nostrils hindered his attempt to live a serious and industrious life in the world in which the old alcoholic lost his place in the line for watermelons, but the alcoholic might have been lying since no one would admit that he had even been in line in the first place. They elbowed him aside and said: "Move on, grandpa. Don't start lying at your age!" Insulted, grandpa wheezed that he was a decorated grandpa, an old-age pensioner, and a brave veteran of two wars. Grandpa would have liked there to be another war, with more bloody battles at Kursk. Then the summer-cottage guerrillas and the local speculators who rented their summer cottages to the summer-cottage guerrillas would perish eternally or be punished harshly. Then, thought grandpa vengefully, not only would they let me in line but they would treat me to a pair of sweet melons in a low-cut dress (the two divine breasts burst out of the dress and swam before him, their nipples aimed at him like pistols painted with lipstick—the unshaven one brushed them away like flies) and a bottle of red wine, a ticket on the train, and a bag of toffee candy. No, thought grandpa vengefully, forget the ticket. I can ride the train without a ticket. I'll take a bottle of beer instead.

"There it goes again," laughed the unshaven one. "The gooseflesh of art, the itch of art, the itch to create which subsides cowardly in the sodden frosty mornings of the following days. Their sobering cold fills one with disgust for that poisonous mess which filled one's brain the night before, like baboons swarming over a crazed jungle! To hell with those stinking jungles! To hell with bright green ferns and baboons wading through their own shit! God, how trivial it all is, how disgusting! How ugly and forced! JUST WRONG, WRONG, WRONG! Libraries were bursting with books. The aroma of sweat tickled one's nose. And wasn't this aroma from the sentimental, sickly tufts of hair in the armpits of profound literary works? Hard-earned sweat and blood, stopped-up energy, challenge and the scum of depleted energies. From depletion not surplus. Because that was all there was . . . LITER-A-TURE—PUTRE-TURE. All right, there was Pushkin . . . But how long ago had that been: Pushkin?" That was how he spent his time. Evening orgies and morning hangovers. He pounded distractedly on his typewriter. (If they had swiped his typewriter, he would have gone to the police, but for the radio it would have been petty and shameful; there was a certain wisdom in petty theft.) "Don't bother me!" he would snap at his wife with the frozen glance of an exultant idiot. And the next morning he would tear up the sheets of paper with trembling, frustrated hands. The pain from the shock of morning—the jeers, just take it easy, easy now—would dissipate ever so slowly, not until evening, and sometimes not for days. But sometimes it was different. There were times when he would finish a cup of strong coffee, from which his chronically irregular blood pressure gave him moist palms and waves of pinpricks over his entire body, and with sorrowful enthusiasm he would begin to imagine that he was the one who had been chosen to hear and arrest in language the lethargic arrival of the end of the century in its initial, deceptive aspect. Welcome O fin de siècle orgasms!

"Say there, son, why don't you also have a shot at depicting the end of the millenium?" inquired the veteran of two glorious wars.

"Millenium?" The unshaven one was amazed and for no reason suddenly thought of Pasternak. "Oh, I see . . ." He was on the verge of taking offense, but then laughed as was his habit. "No, grandpa, I'm not up to that."

The old man rubbed his hands gleefully, took aim at a spot of ground and blew his nose.

"Why not?" he asked shrewdly. "Don't you think that tattered reason and decayed feeling will soon be replaced by some beautiful religion which will save us all?"

"You wouldn't happen to be a new Nikolai Fyodorov, would you?" asked the unshaven one in order to avoid having to listen to some third-rate prophesy.

"Nope," answered the old man gaily.

The unshaven one broke out in a broad smile, "I believe Fyodorov was a necrophiliac . . ."

"Hey, come on. Damn you!" droned the old man and he stumbled away. Feeling guilty about the old man, the unshaven one lurched after his unlucky hero and, fearing the anger of the watermelon line, quickly whispered in his ear:

"Hey, I'll buy you a melon. Okay?"

The unshaven one thought his offer would please the old man and that the latter would immediately become a friend for life. They would visit each other, drink tea with strawberry preserves, catch carp in the pond, play reverse checkers, and carry on lively discussions about Nikolai Fyodorov and Marshall Zhukov. When the old man finally trusted him, he would tell the unshaven one how his brother Kuzma had come back from the war with broken insides which was why he always went around with wet pants. The girls, noting his flaw, had refused to have anything to do with him although he had forthrightly offered them a very valuable war trophy—a German Shepherd–brand alarm clock—and even offered to marry them. Unable to endure such mockery, Kuzma decided to have his way despite the feminine resistance and fell upon one girl (she is still living to this very day) in the State Farm cow barn. The girl became frightened—what if he kills me?—and turned her lavender-tinted back to Kuzma and submitted to him lying in the cold manure. So luck was with Kuzma, but it left him just as quickly as it had come. He exerted himself so strongly that he pissed all over himself and the ensuing misery and desperation caused him to lay hands upon himself, and he was gone before you knew it. So . . . they buried him with all military honors, just like a sergeant.

"Hey, how about a melon?"

But the old man squinted hostilely at the unshaven one as if he'd never seen him before in his life and, as if paying him back for Nikolai Fyodorov and Marshall Zhukov, grunted hoarsely, "I WAS AHEAD OF YOU," and didn't tell him the story about his brother Kuzma. He'd have to do without!

"Again!" The unshaven one was upset. "Again the dogs are running sideways. They keep on running. What kitsch!"

The dogs ran sideways.

In the middle of the road a rowboat of future railroad workers, lovers of eels and oysters, capsized.

He wanted to sit for a bit in the shade.

A miniature person in an impeccable suit of chestnut hue avoided the line and headed directly for the watermelon stand. The summer cottage residents greeted him respectfully. The night before he had given a lecture in the office of the summer cottage cooperative on the dangers of space and time. Only the local riffraff had not agreed with the import of his talk.

"Ifffff you please," said the professor earnestly, "I am the leader of all city personages who are sufferers of mid-season migraine headaches. Can't you see I have an object of value in my hands?"

"Could it be a captured German Shepherd alarm clock?" thought the unshaven one with the amazement of an unsuccessful composer. He had always assumed that it was more difficult to write a melody than it was to discover a new chemical element.

"Georgii Yakovlevich doesn't like concrete music," remarked the professor's wife coldly. She was a grey-haired woman. One of her eyes was blood-red with anger.

WORKERS IN RETAIL TRADES! BEWARE OF FLYING SAUCERS! "You'll make a hunchback out of that child!" complained the tenderhearted women.

The unshaven one could not believe his eyes.

"Pardon the strangeness of my question," he said as he approached the professor, "but, you see, a transistor radio just like that one was stolen from me a few days ago . . ."

The professor cut him short. "Do you mean to say that I stole this radio from you?"

"Not at all." The unshaven one waved his hands in protest. "But you might have come across it accidentally in the grass."

"For your information, transistors aren't like mushrooms or berries; you don't find them in the grass," replied the professor.

"Show him your identification, Georgii Yakovlevich," said the grey-haired woman angrily.

"I shall not show him anything." The professor frowned.

"I understand," muttered the unshaven one, "but it is a strange coincidence. Mine also had a crack in its glass. I dropped it when we moved . . ."

"Lera, don't get so upset! The young man has merely lost his reason."

"My radio also had the same . . ." The unshaven one shuddered and swallowed.

"You'll apologize on your knees for this," said the professor without a trace of malice. He was smiling.

The line forgot about watermelons and transformed itself into a crowded circle.

"You'd better beat it," someone whispered to the unshaven one from behind. "Run before it's too late."

"It's my transistor radio," said the unshaven one, "mine down to the last scratch."

The watermelon lady leaned out of the window from her waist and shouted, "Stop, thief!"

"Perhaps I also stole your cottage," said the professor, his face white with anger.

"My husband is from Kharkov," the grey-haired lady announced proudly. "He is the author of seven scholarly books which have been translated into three languages. Whatever he has, he has earned it with his own two hands and his brilliant mind."

"You deliberately turned the pockets of the raincoat inside out to throw suspicion onto those boys . . . you . . . you . . . brilliant mind!" The unshaven one laughed affectedly and lost all control over the expression on his face.

"His death will be on your hands!" warned Lera, her eyes red with anger.

"No, I shall not die!" cried the professor making a hidden allusion to Pushkin's works. "I shall not die until . . ."

He turned the radio over. "Read!"

The crowd pressed forward to look at the radio. And they read: *To our most beloved Georgii Yakovlevich on the day of his 50th birthday, from his fellow workers, his students, the coat-room attendants, and the librarian.*

The crowd gasped.

"Run," the friendly whisper from behind said. "Run, you fool, run!"

"That's a phony inscription," the unshaven one protested weakly. "He engraved it himself."

There was an outcry of general indignation. The watermelon woman climbed onto the roof of her booth. Her crimson skirt waved between her legs.

"Quiet," she ordered, as if taking charge of a meeting. "A careless dog has just been run over by a train at the crossing. Nothing else matters."

With a feeling of foreboding, the people hurried to the crossing to look at the dog. The professor, the unshaven one, and Lera remained behind.

"Like everyone else I used to think that a dog was man's best friend," intoned the unshaven one, "but it seems it's just the opposite, just the opposite . . ."

"It is all the fault of space and time," intoned the professor as he admired the defenseless watermelons.

Humping Hannah

"As I lean against this doorway . . ."
—Boris Pasternak

"You can change your clothes in here." The entertainment director switched on the light. In the cloudy green, three-part dressing room mirror, they were introduced, bumped into each other, and backed away in multiple images: his careful, coquettish haircut, his Levi suit with worn elbows and knees, the somewhat feminine calfskin bag draped over his shoulder, and her white starched, stiffly sprayed curls, tiny squeak of perfume, and incredulous eyebrows. She must have been amazed that such a small bag could contain a pressed black suit, a white shirt, and a necktie. Some kind of trick. Maybe he had forgotten his suitcase in the hotel. . . . She looked around but did not cross the threshhold, because the room, where a man soon would undress down to his undershorts and leave the smell of sweat behind him, was already repulsive to her. She looked around, expecting to see his suitcase. The actor guessed the meaning of her glance.

"I'll be going on as is," he said soothingly and his voice floated through the room like an aromatic smoke ring created by a pipe smoker at his leisure as he leans back in his chair. The director wanted to say something but he held back. She merely pursed her lips and gave him a questioning look.

"Nina L'vovna," said the actor, who had acquired the habit of remembering the name and patronymic of directors of all types in order to make his life easier, "might you direct me to the toilet?"

His question; though it could trace its roots back to the age of Derzhavin, back to an age of simplicity, serfdom, and crude gallantry, was a trifle ill-considered. Despite all attempts, Nina L'vovna wasn't able to control herself and she went into a pout.

"The next to the last door down the corridor," she murmured, insulted, and trying to make exceedingly clear that she was no door-keeper and no cleaning lady but a representative of the local intelligentsia, working at the service of the Muses, a singing teacher, active in civic affairs, used to eliciting respect and authority, and a member of the City Commission. "Damn!" thought the artist, "She's dumb and straight-laced too! Probably wants to say, 'I'll have you know, young man, that you amaze me, sidling up to a lady with a question like that . . . what do you take me for? I like that . . . just because you're from Moscow . . .' "

Men piss standing up—how awful! thought Nina L'vovna.

She turned away.

But she had erred. So a correction had to be made:

"No, the men's room is the last one down the corridor," she lisped, an expression of embarrassed disgust on her face.

"Where did you say?" The artist placed the milk white cavity of his ear closer.

He's mocking me! His arrogance made her timid.

"There's nothing on the door, but it's the last one . . ."

"Oh!" said the artist. "It's all the same to me."

Nina L'vovna was at a loss for words.

The water went down with a whoosh. Wiping his hands, the professional reader stood before the spectacle of the door. It was quite a rare specimen, somewhat of a masterpiece, a procession of unbridled, collective male thought. The inscriptions flew in all directions, executed in multicolored inks, ballpoint pens, and marking pencils, and carved out by knives and God knows what other sharp instruments.

The hairy life of the passions had materialized in the tattooing of space. All genres were intermingled. Verses side-by-side with passages of prose and hackneyed aphorisms; bleating interjections pierced with exclamation points like quill feathers cavorted over the entire landscape. The door was in full bloom. It had everything—advice, energy-saving suggestions, grunts, squeals of rampant lust, elegiacal witticisms, warnings, and threats; there was a morose but tasty invective about a certain Lenochka Salnikova (don't get sore, Lena!); there were literary excerpts, toasts, and autographs with places and dates; there were sly slaps from sticky wickets, desperate appeals, and just plain weird outbursts.

> MY MAMA BORE ME NAKED
> TOOK A LOOK AND CALLED ME OLYA
> I LIKE MY STUDS BOTH YOUNG AND HEFTY
> AND I'LL BE DRUNK ON MY NEXT BIRTHDAY

The last line caused the actor to chuckle approvingly. The promise to get drunk was as instantly tempting as the hospitality of a Tartar. What sad-looking cretin could have thought up this "naked Olya"? A singer in an amateur choir? A visiting virtuoso? An overage Boy Scout? And those "hefty" studs. Where did that epithet come from? It was a howl of delicious desire—and straight from the gut! The actor suddenly had a desire to write something: something meaty, something dirty and scandalous. He extricated a ball point pen from his pocket, leaned against the doorway, and pondered. Nothing proper (or improper) came to mind. Straining, but with no result, he suddenly became aware of his desire to come up with something completely original, something really juicy. He compared himself to the previous writers who had expressed themselves so freely, out of a surfeit of creative spirit—slapping something onto the door and leaving, relieved—and he just didn't measure up. He was afraid even to scratch out a simple obscenity. Simplicity would stink of snobbery, artistic fastidiousness, or even, if one took a different view, of a fawning attempt to be one of the crowd, to demean oneself. This wasn't in character for him, not his way of doing things, but he still wanted to write something. While considering just what to write, he automatically continued his examination of the door. In addition to texts there were, of course, also drawings. One stood out from all the rest in its dimensions and its age. Originally it had taken up the entire door, but was now, for the most part, effaced and covered over by later layers. However, one could still make out the contours of a flying woman, her face in profile, flying "all the way to humping Hannah": the hair loose, eyes narrowed, the low forehead of a rapist or a murderer, with her chin sagging loosely. The exposed angle of the body made one think of a trussed and roasted chicken: full torso with pendulous jutting nipples. One leg had been left dangling, either half-eaten or half-drawn—someone had interrupted, scared the artist off, and not let him finish.

"A whale of a woman! That's the kind to put on the wall," thought the actor with almost a touch of envy. She wouldn't be afraid of those ponderously rampant protruding organs all aimed at her out of their hairy thickets (the organs were in great abundance). No, she flies right on, singing as she goes . . .

"That's who it is, Humping Hannah herself!" exclaimed the actor. But what could he write? What statement could he make? He rejected every thought: this idea was no good and the next was even worse. Lord, why should he be vouchsafed less than others! Where was justice? He rubbed his hand against the door. But he couldn't give birth.

The door was in full bloom.

Again he went over the inscriptions. People certainly heard their language in wonderful variations! Primeval chaos reigned in the spelling of blessed Russian obscenities. "And the spirit was over the waters." Maybe something from the Bible, with a new twist? But why from the Bible? Or maybe he should admit to some secret vice—with a laugh. But which one? Again his mind was straying to the area of forbidden personal thoughts. Or maybe immortalize his last seduction. What a leaden verb—"immortalize." And then, after returning home to Moscow to the blue vomit of family quarrels, to tell her straight out: "I did it. I let it out. The flower bed was in full bloom on the lavatory door, in the fair city of . . ." Here he stopped. Hold it, what was the name of this city? I'll be damned, I've forgotten it! Something beginning with a "K," I think. What day is it? Tuesday? Where am I scheduled for on Tuesday? K . . . K . . . no, K would have been Kostroma and I've already been to Kostroma. Kostroma is big. It's damp and the Volga is somewhere around there (you miserable show-off!). Immortalize the seduction? He gently caressed the door. What an ass I am! As if I owe her something more! A confession when I've had it up to here! When everything can be summed up in one single little word—NO. I'll write NO. That's stupid. I won't write . . . what the hell is the name of this city?

The actor was amused by his own forgetfulness. He had absolutely no idea where he was. Great! Beautiful! It would irritate him now if the name of the city should suddenly float into his mind. Slyly, his unconscious tried to jog his memory. He said to himself: I arrived in the morning, slept in the hotel until dinner, had a meat and pickle soup and watery goulash in the restaurant, and after dinner took another nap in my room; a window looking out on a garden, some wind, sun, September. . . . I got in the car, houses hopped past, Internationale Street, the Cultural Recreation store, the arc, a church—and who knows where all this is. The actor hovered over the nameless city.

And, having immortalized nothing, he kept himself from recalling the name of the city. Satisfied, he made his way out of the men's room. "Yes," he thought, "doors like that should be taken off their hinges, covered with clear varnish, and sent to the archives of the State Museums where they can be preserved until the proper time as the most precious documents of the epoch- -Humping Hannah flies on, singing as she goes!- -as specimens of folk art.

He had gone several paces down the corridor. After looking around stealthily, he opened the door to the next lavatory slightly and, making sure there was no one inside, darted in himself. He wanted to see what the women had to "show." From long experience garnered during his travels, he knew that women just didn't have it. Well, sometimes a lonely inscription might cry out its throbbing grief and your heart would stop at its sweet shamelessness, everything would go spinning, and you would want to look into her eyes, the eyes of the woman who had written it. But only disappointment awaited you—the laws of art did not work—the lonely inscription would give its cry and then decay in emptiness.

The door was virginal. No couplets, no pictures, nothing. Only some faint finger smears and traces of the cleaning woman's rag. Having put the ripples of their lips in order, women preserved a mysterious grey silence. Click!—and out they stepped, back into the flow of life, while their faces would long carry traces of their mystic lavatory anxiety. We all have our pet obsessions, some like "Crab Neck" chocolate caramels, others- -a pure soul. As for me, I'll appear on Judgement Day with the door from a men's toilet

The door opened.

Nina L'vovna looked at the actor with the leaden eye of an armed prison guard.

"I seem to have made a mistake," blurted the actor with a start. The bell for curtain call could be heard. It sounded like sleigh bells.

"Are you alright?" asked Nina L'vovna with concern and fell backwards to the floor. After politely wiping his feet, the actor mounted her.

"Why do you have such a soft stomach?" he inquired.

"Oh, it's nothing!"

"But why? I'd like to know."

"You're embarrassing me." Tears welled up in her eyes. Nina L'vovna turned away.

"Please . . . why? Come on."

"From enemas," she sobbed. "You're mean." The actor thought a bit and got off her belly.

"Shall we make a run for the stage?" suggested Nina L'vovna, her sobbing finished.

"Let's go," agreed the actor without any great enthusiasm.

They ran. The long corridor echoed with their steps. They flushed a small flock of pioneers who were squatting to rest under an old raspberry-colored poplar tree (a two-bit, peeling stage setting). Then came soldiers, potato fields, a mushroom-filled clearing, and a peasant women with a guitar. As they ran, they played hide and seek. Peek-a-boo! The actor stopped to pull Nina L'vovna to him and murmur sweet nothings.

"Oh, let me go!" Nina L'vovna struggled free and sped onward, with all her might, shouting as she ran: "You know, I quit school, quit my music, the piano . . . I dropped everything. I've been waiting for you for forty years. I'd wait another forty. My baby! My prince! Can you imagine, I only just found out that men piss standing up. Is that really true, all of them? You too, my sweet, even you?"

"Me too," the actor nodded meekly, barely keeping up with Nina L'vovna. "It's habit. What can I do? Sorry . . ."

The bell clamored insistently. Nina L'vovna hid the actor behind the brown curtain. He wiped the sweat from his forehead and tried to catch his breath. When was the last time he had been so anxious before a reading? How many were out there—ten, a thousand, no one? He took out a comb and fixed his hair.

"What is your patronymic?" murmured Nina L'vovna.

"Forget my patronymic," he frowned. "Don't announce my patronymic."

His breathing slowed down. Once again a woman's gaze, fixed on the back of his neck would torture him for an entire performance. The actor saw himself clearly: he goes into the attack, raises his hand to his throat, cries out, "The pain!," laughs, staggers, and gestures with his hand. The sweet smell of pipe smoke envelopes and sickens the audience. He is nauseous. He politely bows to the audience. Two twins from Vorkuta, masters of some original act, probably queers, signal him from backstage: "Come on, let us on, we've a train to catch at ten, come on, old man, hurry it up a bit." He begins braking to a close. Like an experienced race car driver, he's forgotten that he's at the wheel. And he comes to a stop, thinking about the white starched collar, about how he will coax her late in the night, force golden-toothed Nina L'vovna to suck and nuzzle that forbidden fruit. He made his final pause and came to a stop at the red light at the crosswalk. It was easy. High class! Lofty malady!

Nina L'vovna fluttered onto the stage and cringed like a sparrow. She began her announcement. THE LOVE LYRICS OF RUSSIAN POETS. Her knees shook visibly. A huge run in her right stocking yawned in front of him. He listened indifferently. He reacted only to her pronunciation of Akhmatova with the accent on the first A. It almost sounded like Pakhmutova.* My God, she's a Queen of Spades! Just in time, just in time! Nope, I won't let her take off that white blouse with the white starched collar. Nina L'vovna kissed his eyes

---

* Very popular contemporary song composer [tr.].

when she came back to him. She was shivering all over.

"Break a leg!"

She tried to make the sign of the cross over him.

"My little one, my beloved!"

As if she was sending him far away.

The actor responded with all his heart: "Go straight to Hell!"

A Creation in Three Chapters

I

Flustered and perspiring, his heart pounding dully in his throat, he ran onto the platform, slipping and falling on the sand, and distinctly saw the tail end of the train moving off into the twilight. Too late! A door slammed: after seeing the train off, the stationmaster had gone into his little room to kill time. No one remained, only the silver statue standing perpendicular to the track, whose hand pointed the way to happiness. The three red lights performed their modest, mocking dance and dissolved in the evening air. He moaned aloud. His suitcase fell from his suddenly helpless hand. Its useless locks snapped open and almost a dozen empty beer bottles tumbled out onto the platform. He bent over them in surprise. Some had their tops broken off. Mama! Where are my pressed trousers, my jacket with its Komsomol pin, and the three pairs of fresh underwear? You put them in, Mama—I remember! Wait, where's the photograph in the jagged frame that I made myself with a coping saw as a boy?—the photograph of me and Naden'ka, Naden'ka,

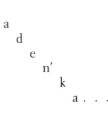

II

Igor had been oppressed by a sensation of enveloping unpleasantness, of a major and distressing unpleasantness, capable of becoming a blindingly bright catastrophe. He had not relaxed for a minute since last Thursday when he had been given advance notice to be so kind as to come to the main office on Monday at 1:00 A.M. for . . . for a chewing out! That pile of flab with the elegant and flashy name— Speransky! —had blown the whistle on him, all the while tearfully sobbing his tales of woe into Comrade Stadniuk's vest.

Igor had forced himself to stay cool. He conducted his seminars, read his lectures, advised nervous seniors, and chatted genially with his colleagues, during which he felt the persistent and attentive looks, but had not betrayed himself with a single nervous gesture or anxious tone of voice. His admirable conduct did not go unnoticed. His predicament was duly noted and one cute young, freckle-faced instructor, an emotional type with a strange glitter in her eyes, took our attractive, dark-browed young man to one side and told him of her jubilation and solidarity. And why not! Talk with any thinking person and he will tell you whether there is any doubt that taking on Speransky personally is not a laughing matter.

O Speransky was tough all right!

He was the possessor of a most valuable weapon with which he hypnotized his foes—the myth of his unbelievable power, multiple connections, and solid backing. His star had floated high and mighty since the end of the forties and the start of the fifties, and from that time on had shone and even burned and scorched when need be. The size of Speransky's monthly income, which he collected from a variety of sources since he had jobs beyond the confines of the institute on scholarly commissions, committees, and editorial boards, was also part of the same myth. Something of a supplementary legend, adorned with fantastic garlands of figures. If you got in Speransky's way, you might as well plant yourself six feet under. If you didn't support him enough or with enough enthusiasm, get ready for a new job in a "colder climate"—at least that was the way the saga went. Vasilii Yakovlevich knew its contents well and although, as Dean of the faculty, he was formally Speransky's superior . . . but how can one be the superior of a saga? In a confidential talk with Igor he had offered his services as a peacemaker.

You Judas! And you were the one who'd promised me his complete support!

"I know what you're after, Vasilii Yakovlevich," Igor said quietly, as he looked into the narrow, eternally mournful face of the Dean. "You want the students to do another caricature of you."

He stressed the word *caricature*. The Dean's face became even more mournful.

"But after all, Evdokimov . . ."

"What has Evdokimov got to do with it?" interrupted Igor impolitely, giving way to an almost youthful impatience. "Don't you remember what I said about that at the Party Bureau meeting? And I believe you were in agreement with my point of view."

"I've changed my mind. Can't one change one's mind? We're not dogmatists, after all! And then, do you know what Stadniuk said? He asked me, 'Who is that young fellow of yours, who doesn't know his place.' "

"Doesn't know his place!" Oh, great! That meant Speransky must have presented it to him as if he. . . . "Wait, what did you answer?"

"What could I answer?" The Dean shrugged sadly.

"What do you mean 'what'? I was defending the honor of the faculty and . . . your honor, Vasilii Yakovlevich, because in this whole affair, you're the one who has suffered."

"Listen, Igor Mikhailovich," the Dean wrinkled his brow, "you and I aren't some kind of Musketeers sitting around and debating the question of honor. Honor! Honor! Let's not waste words. Evdokimov has been expelled and that's that."

"What did you finally say to Stadniuk about me?"

"I spoke quite well of you . . . but I also said that I consider your action rather hasty . . . yes, hasty. There, you see," the Dean smiled, "everything is out in the open."

"What do you mean by hasty?" Igor was astonished.

The Dean didn't answer. He stood up behind his desk and slowly grew in size. The audience was over. Igor did not notice the Dean's signal and remained sitting for a bit. The Dean coughed. Igor jumped to his feet, blushing hotly.

"Please, Vasilii Yakovlevich, call Stadniuk—he wants to see me—and tell him . . ."

"Perhaps I might decide myself what I should do," said the Dean, smiling gently.

"Excuse me." Igor was completely embarrassed.

"My advice is to settle the matter with Speransky while there's still time. You know he's a reasonable man."

"Yes, but . . . no! No, that's impossible now."

"Suit yourself."

After Igor left the Dean leaned back in his armchair and shut his eyes. "He's tried his wings too soon. An eager beaver. And he fell on his face. Stubbed his toe. But his attempts show something. Speransky's not what he used to be; he's weakening bit by bit. Before you know it, in a year or two, we'll be able to handle him." He took a deep breath. "And then we'll decide . . . but that Evdokimov is a strange character." His thoughts changed direction. "I never did a thing to him. I didn't even know his name, and then he goes and—wham! He goes off the deep end . . ." Vasilii Yakovlevich stood up, locked his study door, walked back to his desk, and pulled out the middle drawer. From under some papers he pulled out a thoroughly crumpled sheet of poster paper and gazed at it with squeamish distrust. On the sheet was a drawing of Vasilii Yakovlevich (the resemblance was amazing!), done in different colored Magic Markers. He was dressed in a sloppy bathrobe, belted with a piece of string ("I've never worn a robe in my life!"); in one hand he held a large chamber pot and with the other he was lifting its lid. The aroma of the pot's contents wafted upward, and he was smelling it with a look of tender emotion, although his face preserved a certain divine suffering. The chamber pot was labelled, "Doctoral dissertation," and printed at the bottom of the picture was the word, "Professor."

"What a no good lout! What a despicable type! All right . . . they'll cure him of those tricks in the army . . ."

"Doesn't know his place." Igor couldn't get over that phrase. And how about Stadniuk! The face of a well-bred bulldog—a bulldog which might lightly spring down from its favorite worn spot of the sofa, walk up to a guest who had just entered the room, give him a somewhat condescendingly polite sniff, and in the next instant, shake his jaw and sink his teeth with a death grip into the flesh of the thigh. And the guest would scream, just scream!

"Doesn't know his place!" Igor couldn't get over it.

After Vasilii Yakovlevich's treachery only one hope was left: Igor's big gun must immediately be wheeled around, aimed . . . and then blasted away with a sharp tug on the silken cord!

But his cannon had been spirited away! Igor had wasted no time, and last Thursday he had begun to jangle his father-in-law's home telephone an infinite number of times, all the while biting his nails and chainsmoking himself into a stupor. I must see you immediately, Aleksandr Ivanovich, about an extremely important matter.

But no one answered the phone.

Of course, he's at his summer cottage! What self-respecting person would spend a warm May evening sitting in Moscow?

But no one answered the cottage phone.

So nothing happened on Thursday. He couldn't find the cannon, and he realized that he might be left with nothing but small arms.

Friday morning, Igor called his father-in-law at the office. The pressure of the receiver made his ear swell and fill with blood. The rings were long, full, and apathetic, like overcooked macaroni . . .

But his secretary's phone didn't answer, either.

The day flew by. It was almost time for lunch break and Igor would be late for his lecture. He frowned, upset and hesitant. To call—or not to call? He twisted his nose so much that it scrunched up his left eye like a piece of plasticine. He pulled his lower lip down to his chin, put out his cigarette, and, anxiously swearing, dialed the number of the secret phone which was on his father-in-law's desk and was connected to the "big shots" higher up. His father-in-law would always pick up the phone himself and answer distinctly:

"Hello."

The hook-up was a Japanese invention.

The secret phone gave a helpless muffled grumble. No one picked up the receiver.

Oh, damn! The Japanese gadget hadn't worked!

Igor haphazardly began to scatter phone calls across the landscape, and became increasingly confused. Finally he completely lost track of who he was calling. His father-in-law was elusive, but at the same time, omnipresent—from the ornate window of his tower, he coldly surveyed Igor scurrying about, as befit a person of his importance.

Then, finally, the receiver was picked up at the other end!

By his father-in-law's assistant.

"Is this Igor Mikhailovich?" The assistant possessed an exceptional memory for telephone voices, voices distorted by kilometers of wire and by that extremely pleasant tone which is the privilege of those people who have arranged their lives comfortably and have good cause to expect to arrange them still more comfortably in due time.

"Alexander Ivanovich? No, he's been in Kiev since Tuesday . . ."

Igor's secret weapon was gone! His voice fell. "How long will he . . ."

"Oh, not for long. He's expected today, after dinner. He promised to drop by the office. By all means, call back! After dinner."

But Alexander Ivanovich did not drop by.

And did not return.

And flew off back to Kiev without returning his call

Igor angrily vacuumed the apartment and mercilessly scrubbed the cherry-colored carpet with a thick alkali solution. He went from store to store looking for orange juice (in vain), got into an argument with the cashier at the grocery store, and called her a "dried-up old prune." And why? Who needed this?

It was Friday. Evening. Almost midnight. What if he stayed away until Monday?

Alexander Ivanovich, please, save me!

What if he didn't come?

The sudden thought that his father-in-law might have decided to spend his weekend in the Crimea (as he was his own boss in these things), where a week ago he had sent pale, thin, little Kolka (Igor's three year-old son who had suffered through pneumonia in March) to a sanatorium along with his Mama (Tanya), his Grandma (mother-in-law), and his favorite toy elephant—this thought plunged Igor into complete despair.

Igor spent a heroic Saturday at the institute, thanks only to superhuman effort.

Speransky wandered around the corridors wearing short, narrow trousers and smiling his winning smile as he trundled his sphere-shaped, good-natured belly ahead of him with dignity. One immediately noticed his horizontally striped red and white socks. Igor had once tried to make him a present of a new Rumanian necktie. The old man had snorted and turned away. Rejected the gift. What did he need with a Rumanian necktie? He had a necktie of his own, an eighty-kopeck one. Modest dress gladdens the eye, poverty is no sin, etc. Igor had wrung his hands: "Why don't you want this nice, imported Rumanian tie?"

Now it was clear that his father-in-law had fled to Kiev like a thief in the night. There he was showing his true character. Hanging out with poachers, smoking expensive cigarettes. A CONSPIRACY.

So Igor couldn't believe his luck when he reached Alexander Ivanovich at his cottage just a little after seven that evening. "Well, my boy, I've just been to Kiev. I took in an official celebration or two."

"How was it, Alexander Ivanovich?"

"Marvelous! You know, the people in Kiev are an amazing hospitable bunch. . . . Listen, why don't you come down here for a visit? Why should you sit around in the city for nothing? There's a good film tonight . . . it's called . . . well, whatever! Anyway, come on down!"

Igor took a long drag on his aromatic cigarette, especially pleasant after a filling, relaxed dinner which had been enlivened by two shots of excellent Ukrainian vodka flavored with hot red peppers (a gift of the hospitable people of Kiev), and a glass of noble red Mukuzani wine, which went remarkably well with the roast veal and mushroom sauce. He put the cigarette on the edge of the billiard table whose virginal green felt was painstakingly illuminated by two low-hanging lamps with huge, dark green shades, took aim, felt the pleasurable heft of the lead cue, aimed again—and hesitated.

"Well, what are you waiting for?" exclaimed his partner, a short, quite bald man of around sixty, with silver-grey sideburns and a rather noticeable paunch. He was dressed in his favorite summer cottage outfit: a sweat suit. Still leaning over the table, Igor turned his head and, letting the smoke out of his narrow nostrils, said in a sorrowful voice:

"It won't work, Alexander Ivanovich."

"Oh, come on! 'It won't work!' It's got to work," protested the other man. "It's an easy scratch shot. Use the bridge, don't hit too hard, and aim it right about here." He squinted and pointed his finger at a spot on the table.

They were alone in the vast billiard room. The inhabitants of the summer colony had eaten their fill and escaped the heat by dispersing to their cottages for a nap. It was the perfect weather for a snooze. A sprightly May rain was falling, splashing in the puddles, bouncing along the roofs, swishing through the grass, and extracting heavenly smells from an earth aroused by its own spring vitality.

"Atta boy!" said his father-in-law. "That didn't hurt now, did it?" He took the ball out of the pocket and put it on the shelf. Igor used to rush to put his own balls on the shelf, but his father-in-law considered that bad form, a violation of the rules, and Igor finally had to resign himself to letting an eminent and respected man like Alexander Ivanovich (whose name figured often in newspaper accounts, and, if it was not known to everyone, then at least it was known to everyone worthwhile or to those who spent some of their leisure time answering the question "who's who?" and using their imaginations to construct the contours of that grandiosely baroque and intricately hierarchical marble staircase) take his balls out of the pocket. The truth was that Igor took out balls knocked in by his father-in-law even more often. His father-in-law was a better player. He had many years of practice under his belt, and Igor, by comparison, was a novice, albeit a novice who showed promise. With an almost voluptuous yawn that crinkled his eyes, his father-in-law looked out the half-open window and said, with put-on grumpiness:

"Now what kind of a disgrace is this, I ask you? Rain on a holiday! It rained on May Day, it rained on Armistice Day . . . but then why should the Lord God spoil the Bolsheviks with good weather? . . . If I were in his place I wouldn't spoil them."

"And rightly so." Igor laughed politely.

"Of course I'm right." His father-in law smiled. "We'll soon learn to control the weather and that will give old God a twist of the tail. What do you think—does God have a tail or just the Devil? Oh by the way, who was it that put horns on the Devil?"

The old man was enjoying a period of rare good humor. He had rested up a bit, and if anyone needed some relaxation, it was him. He worked day and night without a break. Igor had lived in his house for a while after the wedding, and knew that he did not have an easy life. The family would long have finished dinner, and Alexander Ivanovich still would not be home. Finally he would arrive. His wife would boil some sausages (they had no maid; they had tried one, but Marya Grigorievna's nerves just were not up to having a stranger in the home), and add a liberal helping of potatoes which she had kept warm in a pot wrapped in a dishtowel under a pillow. Alexander Ivanovich would watch TV while he ate, then move to the couch, take up his *Izvestiia*, and, in five or ten minutes begin to snore until his wife said, "Time for bed, Sasha," and took away his paper. And that was the routine, day in and day out. Then there were receptions, special meetings, urgent missions, or he might have to fly off somewhere.

"Well, how was the trip, Alexander Ivanovich?"

"Fabulous! You know I really must say that the people in Minsk are amazingly hospitable."

And he had to be everywhere, he could miss nothing, but had to keep track of everything that was his responsibility. Only at the summer cottage could he relax. He would watch a film, preferring comedies (he especially liked De Funis), and catch up on his lost sleep. Summers he would swim in the river and fish, and winters he would put in a daily fifteen kilometers on cross-country skiis. Then early Monday morning a large, black automobile would roll up to the cottage, spouting gas fumes you could smell at ten paces, and Alexander Ivanovich would race past the puppetlike guards, snapping their hands to their caps in a salute, back to the city where his high-level responsibilities, fraught with unpleasantness, such as a choice between a heart attack or a stroke (the choice was his!) awaited him. And his deserved assortment of "privileges," which aroused first envy and then awe in those relatives who lived outside of the central cities, seemed merely a collection of business related and life-sustaining necessities. Without a car he would not be able to accomplish anything. Without a summer cottage and the special clinics on Granovsky Street he would have kicked the bucket long ago. *Privileges* were something his family enjoyed. What he had were *burdens*. I wouldn't wish this on my worst enemy, he often thought to himself in his study, rubbing his swollen eyelids with his fingers, as he pored over unread papers and yet-to-be-decided matters. But he didn't lose heart, didn't complain even at the thought that nowadays you couldn't get a word of gratitude or recognition from people, that what have you done for me lately was their motto and their memories were very short—they would pension you off and forget you the very next day. No, he didn't lose heart! He lived by the conviction of the necessity of his work, to which he gave himself completely, withholding not the slightest bit. There was not enough leisure in his life and no time for friends, but he had long ago found a single, tried and true friend—the Party—and for it he was ready to sacrifice everything. The Party had taken him out of a backwater town with unpaved sidewalks and brought him into the world. It had trusted him, and placed him in a position of leadership. What task could be more holy then justifying that trust? You would be mistaken to curl your lip with irony and decide that Alexander Ivanovich was given to naive enthusiasm. Alexander Ivanovich was perfectly aware that *there was the Party and there are the people who are members of the Party*. People are subject to vices and weaknesses. Among comrades one can always find sycophants, coveters, ill-wishers, and finally, enemies of the people, so that one must conduct oneself with due caution and not go too far, but then again not give any quarter lest one take it in the neck oneself. Alexander Ivanovich knew the fine art of keeping to a steady course; he knew when to punish and when to forgive and had every right to be proud of this knowledge. He considered himself helpless before only one person in his life, his daughter, but she didn't take advantage of this helplessness and never exploited her father's love for her. She was a quiet creature, gentle and not too bright, with long, thin legs. And this gentle creature was now a mother. Alexander Ivanovich still could not get over it: "Tanya, my little Tanya—a mama!"

Igor had calmed down a bit after telling his father-in-law the essential facts while taking a stroll before dinner. This accounted for his decent appetite. And although he spoke with uncharacteristic confusion, lacking even simple clarity initially, his father-in-law heard him out with patient goodwill. He had asked a few questions and inquired further about Speransky: What kind of man was he? What was he known for? And then:

"We'll get back to this again."

When would they get back to it? After all, his appointment was for tomorrow morning at 11:00.

Again Igor was tormented by his anxiety and it affected his pool game. He began to miss his shots; he missed so badly that he had to return two balls to the table.

You'll just have to get yourself out of this mess!

His father-in-law had helped him out more than once: an apartment in a good building, well located (in the center of town, surrounded by quiet sidestreets), a car (Igor had chosen a "Zhiguli"), but he had never once had to put himself on the line.

Meanwhile, his father-in-law moved around the billiard table, leaning over it from time to time to send the next ball into the pocket with a well-aimed shot, and thought about the conversation which had just taken place. Of course, he was ready to lend a hand. He had always liked his son-in-law. He had liked him for his character and his straightforward view of things. The boy was no fool! And he worked hard! True, it was rather funny having a philosopher in the family. The thought still made him smile. The word had always had an unfavorable sound to it—what's the word—pejorative. "Hey, philosopher," he used to say to a clumsy assistant until he finally fired him. Or: "Now that's a real philosophical approach to the problem!" He had been worried at first that his future son-in-law would turn out to be one of those weird types with intellectual pretensions. That was all he needed—one of those right in his own family! But Igor had no such pretensions and his father-in-law soon took a real liking to him. Alexander Ivanovich could size people up; he liked the fact that Igor always got what he wanted through his own efforts, as he himself did. Of course, things weren't settled without some disagreement. Their daughter was an only child and they loved her very much. Her mother had been trying to make a more profitable match. And she judged the potential sons-in-law by their parents. And that was stupid! Really stupid! Alexander Ivanovich knew just what the offspring of such parents were like—playboys! They hung around the dachas all the time. They were given all the opportunity in the world, but amounted to nothing. Not a backbone in the lot. And their fancy privileges wouldn't last forever either. They only continued for as long as their fathers' positions lasted, and anything could happen to men of that sort . . . anything under the sun. His own heart had been acting up recently. Just last week they'd had to call an ambulance. He'd had a difficult time getting out of that hospital. And after all, there hadn't been any hereditary nobility in the country since 1917. He'd told his wife that when she began to compile her case against Igor. And who had she found for Tanya? Some aristocrat, whose eyes were glassy from constant drinking! A glutton, an eternal student, lazy. . . . But his wife persisted and kept repeating the same thing: Igor was a shady character; he was trying to get into their circle; he needed a good kick in the pants, that philosopher! She just wouldn't have him in their home one more time.

"They'll only meet in doorways, Masha."

"I won't allow it. Do you hear, Sasha? I won't allow it!"

"That's enough shouting," said Alexander Ivanovich.

"What do you mean enough? She's my daughter just as much as yours. And I won't have it!"

"Now stop, Masha, calm down. . . ."

And little Tanya cried in the next room. Little Miss Neither-Fish-nor-Fowl, as Igor was later to name her, rebelled and dug in her heels. It was her big moment. She knew that it was either marry Igor or become an old maid. She couldn't live without him. He was the whole world in her eyes. She went into raptures over him. He was a real man. He was her first. A month before, she had given herself to him in the woods outside of Moscow, in a thicket of young fir trees, not far from the Tryokhgorka station of the Byelorussian Line. Young love! First love!

"I'll hide her passport so she won't be able to register the marriage! Tatyana, give me your passport this instant! And you're a big help, Sasha. You've gone out of your mind—his parents sell potatoes at the Tishinsky market!"

That was when Alexander Ivanovich couldn't take it any longer. He rarely cursed, at least not out loud and especially not at his wife, but here he couldn't hold back:

"And you, you little so-and-so, I suppose your parents were real fancy stock, right? Big deal, you Queen of the Snackbar!"

His wife had a fit of hiccoughs. She sat there shaking all over and couldn't stop hiccoughing. Alexander Ivanovich added quietly:

"The sun must have fried your brains."

But what a beautiful slender neck that waitress in the special Party snackbar used to have! And a cute, little nose? And even, white teeth? And her bosom! She had a bosom of such rare beauty that it could have been displayed at the Exhibition of the People's Economic Achievements! So then, what happened? That proud bosom had fallen long ago, those blue eyes had faded (they'd probably faded from jealousy—she had turned out to be fantastically jealous), and she had become a real shrew—what a change!

After that row she hid her true feelings. As if she had given in. They had put on a real fine wedding. How many years was it now? Going on five. Right. Little Kolya was three already. A good kid. They should have another one just like him. Or a granddaughter. But then his wife had not wanted to go to the funeral for Igor's mother. Pretended she wasn't well. But Alexander Ivanovich had gone. And stayed for the wake as well. In spite of their grief, the relatives of the deceased couldn't stop staring at him. Alexander Ivanovich proposed a toast to a simple Soviet laborer, who had departed, so to speak, in an untimely way, due to a serious illness, but had brought up a son of whom she could be proud. Igor's father kept whispering, "Thank you, thank you," and cried. When they sat down to the table, he began, for some reason, to apologize. "You'll have to make allowances—we're simple people . . ."

"Why no, this is fine, what are you saying?" asked Alexander Ivanovich. And he heard Igor say:

"Stop shaming yourself!"

He had left when people began to get drunk. A stupid custom anyway—wakes!

A bank shot in the side pocket!

"Hey, Alexander Ivanovich!" Igor spread his hands out to the side in approval. "Now that was a first class shot."

"Right you are, my friend. A little different from philosophy, isn't it?" asked his father-in-law thoughtfully, and, coming out of his reverie: "Well, Gegel-Hegel, shall we go home?"

Igor turned off the lights. The green felt darkened as if water had been spilled on it. They went into the cloakroom and took down their coats.

"Alexander Ivanovich, come have tea with us." Galya the serving waitress had seen them from the dining room and walked up to them, stepping lightly in her noiseless slippers. She was a small, smiling middle-aged woman wearing a white starched apron. Her thin, reddish-blond hair was done up in a simple hairdo. Galya always gave special attention to preparing *her* tables for supper.

"Tea?" Alexander Ivanovich was eager to stop in order to answer Galya. "We'll be there, thank you. And what will you treat us to?"

"Fresh rolls, the best, Alexander Ivanovich, with poppyseeds," Galya announced gleefully, "and pastry."

Galya had worked in the cottages for a long time and knew that one met two types of people among the bosses. As a child she had given them names: "monsters" and "good fairies." The "monsters" never noticed you though you might break your back trying to please them. You could work for them for years and they wouldn't even ask your name, and if they ever did say something, then it was always a complaint: "The kvass soup doesn't taste very good today." "Good fairies," on the other hand, to whose number Alexander Ivanovich belonged, quickly became accustomed to you, did not like it when you were switched away from them, and were not stingy with their affection. There were more "good fairies" than "monsters," and because of this Galya the waitress sincerely believed in the possibility of true happiness on this earth.

"Well, pastry is worse than poison for me," joked Alexander Ivanovich, "and rolls have too many calories . . . but I'll have a cup or two of tea."

"Please come." Galya smiled.

The rain had become lighter, harmless. One could walk in it and not get soaked through. The two men moved unhurriedly along the narrow paths which were thickly planted with flourishing yellow acacias. One was dressed in creamy beige and the other in dark blue. They passed the asphalt tennis court on which they had waved tennis rackets at each other just before the rain began, and then they passed the volleyball court on which no one ever played. A green wooden gazebo loomed in front of them; they heard the rapid gunfire of dominoes.

"Hey, Alexan-Vanich, come and join us!"

The incorrigible domino players spent all their holidays in the gazebo.

"I'll drop by in a while," promised Igor's father-in-law.

"I haven't seen Marya Grigorievna around lately."

"She's in the Crimea with our daughter and grandson."

"Are they swimming yet down there?"

"No, they say the water's too cold. They're just getting good tans."

"Well, that's not too bad either."

Dominoes—now there is the foundation of the great unity between our officials and the people, thought Igor. He had nothing but scorn for dominoes and could not understand how the people *here* could play such a plebian game. He had exactly the same scorn for beer. As a little boy he used to run to fetch his father from the beer kiosk not far from the local brewery which innundated the neighborhood with its heavy smell.

"Pop, come home. Mama's waiting and she's angry."

"She'll wait . . . here, take this, have a drink."

A heavy, sticky mug with chipped edges would descend into his hands.

"Whatsamatter—why don't you drink? You're not squeamish, are you?"

And then, in drunken amazement: "He won't drink from my mug!"

"When you call her, give her our best."

"Definitely."

If I don't get him out of this, thought Alexander Ivanovich, she'll never give me any peace, she'll just keep hammering away at me: "I told you so—he's a shady character!" She was a real mother-in-law.

"So, I suppose he went and made an official complaint against you?" asked Alexander Ivanovich, seeming to repeat himself, as if their conversation had been interrupted by the domino players.

Igor shuddered and nodded eagerly.

"And Stadniuk gives the orders in your Party committee, right?"

"Stadniuk. Pyotr Petrovich."

"Stadniuk . . ." Alexander Ivanovich threw a sidelong glance at his son-in-law. "And I suppose you thought that you could give an old man like him a shove and a kick and knock him off his comfortable seat, and he would just sit and take it without a murmur."

"Alexander Ivanovich!" protested Igor. "I never intended to knock anyone off!"

"You know that song—'For it's youth that must be served!' Well, it's a fine song, but it doesn't happen like that in real life."

"But the fact of the matter is," began Igor, "that once such an incident has taken place, closing the Back Stairway for a time is simply unavoidable. If they could just . . ."

"But when you close the Stairway," Alexander Ivanovich did not wait for him to finish, "then you are closing off your friend . . . what's his name?"

"Speransky."

". . . Speransky's reelection as leader of his Party cell."

The old man is no fool, thought Igor.

"That may be so," he said, "but that's not what it's about . . ."

"No, that's exactly what it's about," his father-in-law said softly but firmly, and coughed with displeasure.

Igor bit his lip and waited: now watch the granddaddy of all cannons let fly with a blast. But it would be firing at him! A moment more and his father-in-law would begin to shout and snort and stamp his feet, to curse him and banish him to the world beyond the green fence and order the snappy, saluting guards not to let him back in. Farewell, summer cottages with morning baths, fancy dinners at half-price, friendly Galyas, and spacious limousines! Farewell my special little world! The freckled young policeman who loved toasted sunflower seeds would lead him off to a miserable Moscow communal apartment and register him there for eternity along with the drunken plumber and his family, the rancorous streetcar, the twenty-two-year-old unwed mother who was the subject of everyone's vile gossip, the retired major from some "supersecret" government agency who swore that he had once worked as a sound engineer for MosFilms, the acrimonious pilgrim who everyone said had heaps of money hidden under the wallpaper behind her icons, the fat, sloppy Jewish woman (with her cowardly engineer-husband and large-eyed, overfed little Ilyusha) whose room was permeated by the sweet and sour smell of the Jewish people and who had no intentions of leaving for sky blue Israel because she was "happy enough here . . ." And in the dimly-lit corridor of that communal apartment, dusty old bicycles and tin baby's washtubs hung on the walls, and certain semidressed and semilegal individuals loitered eternally and made constant use of the toilet by right of being distantly related to someone in the apartment; they also fried fish in the common kitchen, and hogged the one telephone by the entranceway (the wall by the phone was completely covered with phone numbers, names, and other doodling), all the

while tearfully complaining about some hardhearted foreman . . .
The two men silently turned off onto a narrow paved walk which led
to the cottage.

Stadniuk might think that he was being pressured and Alexander
Ivanovich didn't want this. It went against his principles.

"All right," he said, striding ahead of Igor, "I will try to get in touch
with this Stadniuk of yours first thing tomorrow morning. When are
you supposed to see him?"

"About 11:00."

Alexander Ivanovich nodded.

". . . I'll talk with him, so that . . ." he hesitated, carefully
selecting the words from his quiver and examining them with all
possible care as if they had poison tips, "so that he will approach the
matter without prejudice. Better yet, so that he will not be unduly
influenced by the complaint against you."

"Or else I've had it." Igor gave an awkward laugh.

Alexander Ivanovich did not react to these superfluous words. The
two men went inside.

"I think I'll just take a nap for an hour or so," proclaimed his
father-in-law. He walked up the creaking wooden stairs to the bedroom on the second floor.

"Oh, by the way," He stopped halfway up, his forehead wrinkled.
"You haven't said anything about this to Tanya, have you?"

"No."

"That's just as well. And I don't see any reason to for the time being.
Why bother the girl for nothing. Let her enjoy herself."

"For nothing!" Igor suddenly felt a desire to leap up the stairs and
give his father-in-law a bear hug. But he suppressed his boyish im-
pulse. After all, gratitude is one thing it never pays to overdo. Igor
moved away from the window, took out a cigarette and lit it. His face
showed a calm joy as he looked out at the bed of daffodils, planted by
someone's careful hands, at Kolya's swing, which hung between two
trees, and at the swollen clumps of white lilac. All I need now is for
Nadya to be able to make it tomorrow, he thought. If only they could
get a goddam phone put in at her place. . . . He was already down to
the end of his cigarette when he heard the quiet voice of his father-in-
law:

"Igor."

He threw the cigarette butt out the small ventilation window and
headed toward the call, expecting a request for twenty drops of Val-
ocardine in a glass with some water to wash it down or something of
the sort, but his father-in-law was stretched out on the broad, comfortable couch and had something else on his mind.

"You know," he said, "what do they do when a plant has grown too
big for its pot?"

"Replant it in a bigger one?" Igor was a bit surprised at the question.

"Exactly! Or else it dies or busts the pot. Do you understand what I'm getting at?" Alexander Ivanovich fell silent. "You should leave your institute," he continued. "You've gotten everything you can out of it. And what's left is not yours to take. Get out into the big world. There are a lot of interesting places where you can flex those muscles . . . and you'd better watch that temper. You're hot-tempered, Igor." Alexander Ivanovich smiled amiably at him from the pillow. "Since when are philosophers supposed to get hot under the collar?"

III

The Back Stairway was still untamed, still alive and kicking. Its tobacco smoke made the eyes smart, permeated wool sweaters and hair alike, and ate away at the walls and ceilings—-you could ventilate it for five years and that smoke would still be there! And the spirit of student recklessness would be just as hard to get rid of. . . . And my, how little love was lost between the Stairway and the administration. The Stairway was an eyesore—it made the institute's official eyes smart with such irritation that those in the administration tried never to set foot on it, avoided it they did, and if they had to pass along its way, why then they didn't walk tall, but just scuttled along, heads hunched down so as not to be noticed, as if they were in enemy territory. Enmity permeated the air and left a sediment like soot in the secluded nooks of the administration's subconscious where a spider of a thought crawled about endlessly: the thought that someday the Stairway would pull a stunt for which it would get everything It had coming to it! And the administration winced when words which had been let slip on the Stairway reached its ears—tart words, sour like apples stolen in June. For a long time now the Stairway had really given it to the Dean (who scuttled like a hunched-over shadow along the halls of the philosophy department) and to his hatchet-man Assistant Dean, whose grimaces and scrunched-up eyes reminded one of a stand-up comic from the provinces, and to the retired colonel, the Civil Defense instructor, who was able to shove his raspberry-red rat's snout into a gas mask while intoning, "hup, two, three—go!" and who threatened the students with inevitable world cataclysms; he began every lesson with the words, "When the thermonuclear war starts. . . ." The Stairway also had no use for the graduate students who talked through their noses in order to ape the Dean; it split its sides laughing at the homely coeds who became activists, desperate to be a "part of things," and then became completely wrapped-up in utopian plans for cultural outings, chess tournaments, and one hundred percent class attendance. Still wet behind the ears, a tribe of wiseasses and anecdote-mongers, red-headed practical jokers and poetasters, good-for-nothings and Don Juans ruled beneath the narrow arches—they were a mob that cruised for likely pick-ups, that "made out," and did just a little fast cramming of lecture notes. A band of Merry Men? No, No. Those associations applied to this mob would grate on ears accustomed to the melodies of euphemisms. They're out of place here; they don't fit in. And why get carried away? There was nothing more here than simple frivolity, youthful lightheartedness, and that half-childish playfulness which melts away as soon as things get rough. And when many students become respectable early on and begin to think about the chances for a good job assignment and a cushy position from almost the freshman year on, for them this frivolity becomes more than just frivolity; it acquires a new quality and becomes a muffled, unconscious, but still real, challenge. These were the students who kept their mouths shut in the "Back"—they just went out there for a smoke, took a drag or two of tobacco smoke into their lungs, and never made a peep. These were the ones who felt that challenge and more than one was overcome by the desire to run off and give warning, to head things off. Beware! But their warnings never got to the right people. When the administration suddenly realized what was going on, as the Russian proverb goes, it was a wee bit late: when the Dean was awarded, as the highpoint of some celebration, a full professorship, the Stairway hit him with a cartoon right between the eyes!

They don't make buildings like the one that housed the institute any more—with secret passages and back stairways. Architecture—it's the mirror of the collective soul! Nowadays everything is all glass, from floor to ceiling; everything is visible and transparent; hot in the summer and cold in the winter.

Igor walked up the worn stairs of this remnant of a forgotten past. It was the break between lectures, and the stairway was buzzing about its own affairs, puffing away without a care in the world, unaware that tonight it would get the living daylights beaten out of it, a real cleaning out! Someone loomed out of the curtain of smoke and greeted him. Several snorts of laughter were heard. Igor involuntarily glanced around: were they laughing at him? Not a healthy atmosphere at all out here. And they could go smoke in the "psychodrome"—that was what the students called the inner courtyard of the institute where they gaily hung around during exams. Sprawling in faded jeans with their hair hanging down the backs of their necks and into their eyes. . . . Igor didn't like to get his hair cut too short himself, and he couldn't stand people who got it trimmed close on the backs of their necks; it reminded him of schooldays, the provinces, and the boondocks. Igor considered himself a man of liberal views and couldn't help laughing inwardly at Stadniuk's atavistic aversion to women wearing slacks! But here on the Stairway, the antipathy towards barbers and similar trivia had become an essential element of the challenge. Stadniuk was right: discipline—discipline first! "When I walk along the Back Stairway, I feel like hollering, 'A-tench-hut!' " Igor remembered the words of the Civil Defense instructor, whom he considered a Neanderthal type, but even Neanderthals could sometimes give expression to the demands of more advanced periods . . .

So then why was Igor here on this disreputable stairway? Why hadn't he used the front stairway?

He had his own reasons, reasons unknown to ordinary mortals. He was looking for a particular "comrade"—this was the code name he used for Nadya whenever he was at the institute. But the "comrade" was not to be found anywhere on the Stairway today. And he had wanted to see her more than usual.

The heavily-sprung door gave a creaking sound and hit him in the back. He went out into the hall, which was flooded with neon lights, and, avoiding the departmental wall newspaper, which fulsomely congratulated the Dean on the occasion of his high honor, headed for the faculty lounge. He had to call his father-in-law, tell him that everything was fine, and hang up. Everything had, in actuality, turned out all right.

Stadniuk had given him a cordial reception—to the extent, of course, that a completely unspontaneous temperament such as his could express cordiality. It's a known fact that power, even in small doses, changes people to an exceptional degree. Power had taken Pyotr Stadniuk, a joyous young Komsomol member from Zaporozhye who loved borscht and had soft velvet eyes, and completely dried him up and turned him into a pedant. In addition, it had made him old before his time; for a man of fifty he didn't look well at all—bags under his eyes, wrinkles, and skin as yellow as the fingers of a chainsmoker. But in exchange it had sharpened his mind, trained it. The only thing power seemed to have had no effect on was his Ukrainian accent; Stadniuk's "g's" came rasping out as fully aspirated as they always had. Those in the institute who tried to suck up to him even pretended to find a certain elegance in his accent.

His secretary had brought in a tray bearing two glasses of strong tea with lemon and a plate of cookies. Stadniuk dunked his cookie into his tea as he listened carefully to what Igor had to say. Igor spoke with conviction, without any artificial changes in tone or phony pathos. The way Igor told it was that it was a lousy situation, there was no other word for it, that "incident"; if decisive measures weren't taken immediately then it wouldn't be a question of just closing the Back Stairway, but of closing the entire department! "And don't think I'm being panicky, Pyotr Petrovich! I'm giving you a sober assessment of the situation as it now stands."

"Close the department!" Stadniuk wasn't well for a moment. He had trouble breathing and drops of sweat shone in the deep wrinkles of his forehead. Clearly the kid was exaggerating. Stadniuk wheezed and tried to concentrate: why had this happened—why, why?

The answer suggested itself automatically and he relaxed.

"To make a long story short, not enough attention has been paid to ideological work," said Igor, summing things up.

Stadniuk nodded without taking his glass from his lips. And he thought to himself, this kid's the kind to keep things in hand.

"All right, what will the Komsomol have to say?"

"The Komsomol? The students themselves made the same proposal about the Stairway. It was Lyusia Ilinskaya at a Komsomol bureau meeting—"

"Al-l-l-l r-i-i-ght . . ." said Stadniuk. "So that means the Komsomol first sounded a warning about the danger?" His eyes glittered warmly with understanding.

"That's it exactly, Pyotr Petrovich!" responded Igor, straining with all his might to respond appropriately to this calm, judicious person. "The Komsomol was vigilant."

Stadniuk had loved the word "vigilance" since boyhood and now he smiled at the word like an old friend.

"Drink your tea. It's getting cold."

"Thanks, I will!"

And to think that just a little while ago, not more than an hour ago, he had expected Stadniuk to really give it to him. They do say that fear always exaggerates, thought Igor. Maybe I just imagined it all?

"All right, now I have a fairly clear picture of your situation there," said Stadniuk, and he began to talk about how the Party was experiencing a persistent demand for young, energetic, devoted people whose personalities corresponded to the temper of current requirements. It gradually became clear that Stadniuk was not averse to electing Igor as the departmental Party rep at the upcoming elections on the basis of his estimate of Igor's work as a member of the Komsomol Bureau.

"You were right," Stadniuk, had said praising him in conclusion while grimacing and screwing up his features (he was chewing his slice of lemon), "to bring the matter to a head. That's the spirit of the times. Ideological work in the current phase is catching fire with new force—boy, is that sour! But tea just isn't—Your understanding of this phase, by the way, is much better than mine . . ." He caught himself gesturing with the lemon peel and tossed it into his empty glass. Then, after a pause: "The problem is not letting our struggle to raise the standard of living get in the way of principled positions. By importing brassieres and all that cosmetic stuff, we are encouraging the same consumer's attitude towards life that we are fighting against. . . . Or take the constant chasing after economic benefits. What does it lead to in certain instances (that sacramental phrase—in certain instances)? The streets of Moscow and Leningrad are full of hordes of tourists . . . and how many of them aren't real tourists at all, but provocateurs sent over here for the purpose of corrupting susceptible people? Do we ever ask ourselves that question? No, we don't, but we're sure encouraging those accountants of ours to tote up the profits from foreign tourism. . . . And just try and tell me how much good those dollars will do us if they're robbing us spiritually? It's quite a complicated problem. But personally, Igor Mikhailovich, I have faith in our young people. We've got a marvelous group of younger cadres coming up now. I know Lyusia Ilinskaya and many others," Stadniuk spoke in a measured, slightly muffled voice, "and they're fine young people. Use them! They'll always help the way they helped this time. So as far as closing the department—you don't have to worry. There isn't the slightest reason . . . and just imagine," he lowered his voice, "if this should ever reach the rector's office . . . you don't need that kind of trouble and neither does anyone else. Surely you can understand that! All right . . . well, and as far as the Stairway, the cause of all this hullabaloo, and Speransky," he chuckled not too respectfully, "he almost had a stroke. Well, why not . . . close it for repairs! Let them whitewash it and give it some paint. It really is too dark now, and dirty—just the place for all kinds of riffraff. And as for funds . . . well, go ahead and close it off and we'll worry about funds later."

Stadniuk had stretched out his hand to Igor, chuckled to himself at something, and, switching to an earnest comradely, first-person singular form, said, "Did you see my secretary? She turned up in pants! And she's no slip of a girl—she's got a fifteen-year-old son. Now you're a young man—what do you think? Are you for or against women in pants?"

Guessing without much difficulty Stadniuk's position on the question, Igor had let loose an elegant tirade on the topic of the masculinization of women.

Hearing his position confirmed, Stadniuk had laughed out loud: "I'll make her take them off!"

The phone was being used. The German teacher was patiently explaining to her youngest son what to warm up for dinner and how to do it. "Be careful not to burn the frying pan," she implored. Igor waited eagerly, remembering with a certain amount of pleasure the details of his conversation with Stadniuk. The image of Nadya had receded into the back of his mind, though he still was impatient to share his good fortune with her. Speransky entered unexpectedly. How inappropriate that name of his was—the personification of hope for renewal and change in the Imperial Russian state system—when attached to the contemporary Speransky, with his heavy, flabby face, turtlelike folds of flesh under the chin and helpless hands with their short, pudgy fingers! It was said that at one time he had been quite an attractive man and had been a hit with the ladies. Maybe so, but looking at him now it was hard to believe. True, if one looked quite carefully at his face, one could discover traces of an earlier attractiveness; his eyes seemed to have a life of their own—they were animated, even intelligent. One couldn't deny him the remarkable erudition with which he as able to overwhelm anyone he talked to but he had been living off his old capital for some time now. Speransky hadn't looked well at all lately. During the last two years he had fought an entire series of illnesses, which, as always, had come from God knows where. He suffered from dizziness, nausea, and sharp pains in the heart, which brought on strong attacks of apathy. For some reason he had a dread of paralysis and often awoke in the middle of the night in a cold sweat, having dreamed that he was paralyzed. But even more than paralysis he feared higher officials. It was almost an animal-like fear, at times intense enough to make his head swim; it seemed to be a fear that would hound him on his death bed, so that if anyone wanted to prolong his life, assuming that medicine had already given up on him, all that person had to do was bring in some very high official and let the official, having condescended to come, say with obvious dissatisfaction in his voice: "Aren't you ashamed, comrade Speransky, to go and die, eh?" And then Speransky would rise like Lazarus! However, fear begets fear: Speransky demanded that his subordinates have the same fear of him. He had noticed Igor from the doorway and headed decisively towards him. The small number of their colleagues present did not interrupt their conversation.

"The Dean thought it necessary to give me a full account of your conversation in the Party Committee, Igor Mikhailovich."

Igor was pleasantly surprised by the speed with which the Party Committee worked; the Dean had already been filled in on everything! But at that moment, fearing an unexpected attack from Speransky, he was naturally not at all inclined to celebrate his victory. Speransky hesitated; he understood perfectly his false move—by taking responsibility for the Evdomikov affair and not quickly shifting it to someone else, he had lost the initiative. This mistake—given the number of enemies that hovered over him in invisible clusters—threatened to become fatal; it could bench him for good, throw him into the anonymous emptiness of retirement. And oh how he still yearned for that sweetest of all honeys—the sweet taste of power over the young! He had the small pleasures of an old man: for example, he loved to give tête-à-tête oral exams in his half-lit office to timid little coeds. They would nervously chew on the ends of their handkerchiefs and he would torture them all! Torture them with question after question until he'd gone over the whole syllabus, excitedly grunting at each wrong answer!

Speransky's cruel, unblinking eyes peered at Igor. How had he wriggled out of it, this kid with his mother's milk still wet on his lips? He didn't even stop to think that Igor might have a secret fairy godfather keeping watch from his ornate tower; he simply supposed that Stadniuk had decided to play it extra cautiously, in order to cover his rear end.

"I think it's clear that you mistook my intentions," said Speransky, fixing his mouth and cheeks in a smile, "but in any event, I am prepared to make a complete apology."

And to think that I might really have gotten it because of this decrepit old monkey. Igor shuddered inwardly.

"I really had only the best of intentions—" continued Speransky.

Just then the bell rang out fervently above them.

So Igor wasn't able to report back to his father-in-law.

But it didn't matter; what he really wanted was to enjoy the luxury of keeping such a palpable victory entirely to himself!

He entered the classroom and it hit him: *she had come!* He could feel (she'd come!) her (she'd come!) glance resting on him: *at last!* He was out of his mind with happiness. They'd be together for the entire evening, just the two of them, no one to interfere—will I ever give it to you tonight, beg for mercy baby, it won't do you one bit of good! And then you'll give it to me. . . . The sound of scraping chairs. Snap to now and be seated! And there is your sweet little face shining through those pimpled mugs and clumsily made-up faces You're hiding from the light, covering up your smile, but your eyes give you away and they've gotten darker and larger since you were sick . . .

"Hey, twinkletoes, what happened to you?"

"I've been sick."

"How can anyone be sick for that long?"

"I had my tonsils out . . . what a pain." She laughed. "I got sick on all the ice cream . . . did you miss me?"

"Oh Nadya did I! Listen, let's not wait. Six o'clock at the repair shop, all right?"

"Okay . . . Mama's at home tonight "

"That's all right—there's nobody at my place."

"Nobody? Where is she?"

"At the Crimea until the middle of June! How's that?"

Today we'll go to my place, Igor thought, for the first time since we've known each other! And again tomorrow and every day . . . I finish at 5:45, so we'll meet at the leather goods repair shop. I've got fantastic news. I'll tell you all about it—how Speransky lodged a complaint against me and then had to apologize. On his knees! Nadya baby I won! . . . Monitor, where is the roll book?

It was one of the last seminars before exams. For an entire year Igor had been teaching them how to think. Now he was demanding that they know how not to think. Students are great ones for criticism. One just has to explain to them whom they should criticize. They had been given the correct orientation. Igor presented them with a philosophical version of Alexander Nevsky's victory over the Teutonic knights on the ice: the philosophical representatives of the old world had beat a retreat, throwing away their cardboard shields and wooden pole-axes. They had lost their eyeglasses, stumbled, snorting like walruses, and drowned in the most ridiculous fashion, with their eyes bulging out, blowing bubbles as they sank. The class was a good one and well prepared for the exams.

"They may be lacking in depth and some of their answers may be naïve, but what fire, what conviction!"

"They're obsessed by ideas! In the best sense of the word," trotted out another member of the examining board.

"They're marvelous!" concluded one woman, giving her small curls a shake.

"Yes, you're right," said Igor earnestly, supporting her out loud, but thinking, idiot! He was not one to take comfort in illusions. The danger of total subversion from the left was much greater than any from the right for one simple reason: students had a simpleminded faith that any attack meant a sure "A."

But they were lazy! Sluggards!

Igor called a halt to the slaughter on the ice, and hands shot up all over the room for the chance to get in a blow!

"Now let's not make our ideological enemies into . . . fools. They're stronger than that, and more insidious."

But they responded listlessly, half-heartedly. The chance to bark did not excite them.

Toporkov appeared on the stage. In the last class Igor had assigned him a report on Freud. Igor considered Freudianism a bit livelier than the rest of the course. He felt like getting the class involved. Toporkov was an athlete, either a boxer or a ju-jitsu wrestler. A husky young giant with an aggressive, jutting chin. The chin began to move. Toporkov mumbled about the dangers of reactionary thought, of incorrect thought. . . . But only five minutes into his report he began to falter. His questioning eyes wandered over the legs of the coeds and crept under their skirts.

"Could you be more specific?" Igor asked the wrestler.

"Much more specific," said Toporkov in confusion as his glance went higher and higher up the thigh of a girl in the third row who was sitting in a quite provocative manner.

"Perhaps you could add something," Igor said to the same girl in order to get her to jerk down her skirt. She stood up and blinked absentmindedly.

"Pay attention," said Igor, without much spirit. Got so wrapped up in her daydreams that her legs spread so wide they were begging for it. They say that even fourteen-year-olds are putting out nowadays . . . why can't this day end? Put in my hours, pop Nadya under my arm, and home! Igor glanced at her. What if they should find out? About everything? Even my father-in-law—his face bobbed up before Igor's eyes. They'll never find out! Nadya's the perfect conspirator—that's something she's really great at. Lots of them make passes at her. That asshole, too. He's probably pretty good in bed. Could probably take on four at a time. And so what? I could too. He's clumsy—he'd give them all fractures . . . but women like that . . . even a fourteen-year old could land you in jail. BUT THE WORST WOULD BE HER PARENTS!

"Come on now, stop beating around the bush," said Igor. "Have you read anything by Freud himself?"

"Sure," Toporkov eagerly assured him.

"All right, tell us something about it then."

But what if they did find out?

I'LL SHOOT THEM ALL DOWN.

Here's how it could happen. Propaganda work had intensified in the dormitory of the institute. A new director had arrived who was very tough. And ever since his arrival the student action groups had gone on a rampage; they had terrorized everyone and were putting special emphasis on the moral education of their contemporaries. They had master keys to all the rooms and would wait until they found a couple enjoying a tryst, break into the room right in the middle of things, and catch the couple rolling around in a bed that was institute property. They loved to make a big uproar almost to the point of hooting. Sometimes they brought a camera and would snap pictures of the dumbfounded, panic-stricken lovers trying to cover themselves with whatever was handy. Sometimes the director himself would come along for a look. The action squads worked with great efficiency and precision and the number of discovered couples grew and grew. Once a girl brought a black man to her room. The hearts of the "fishers of men" pounded with joy: here was a real find! They waited until the black-and-white couple reached the moment of most intense moaning and ecstasy (someone had listened at the door and given a signal), and broke into the room with their usual uproar. But they had not been able to enjoy themselves because the Negro, instead of hiding his Negro shame with his hand, suddenly began to fight and bashed in the faces of all four members of the group; two of them had to be taken to the hospital. The incident couldn't be hushed up. The Rector feared an *international incident* and quietly fired the director of the dormitory. The student activists were instructed to concentrate their energies on the struggle against drunkenness and dealing in stolen goods.

Soon after that incident Igor was at Nadya's place on the Leningrad Highway and he suddenly imagined that someone was turning the key in the lock. He and Nadya listened nervously, holding their breaths. Quiet. After hesitating a while, they again tumbled into ecstasy. But later when they looked around they saw the members of the action group standing over them. And not just one or two! A whole gang!

The activists roared with laughter.

"We've got you, Igor Mikhailovich!"

"Igor Mikhailovich, is this really proper?"

Something prompted Igor to slip his hand under the bed. He pulled out a Kalashnikov tommy gun, its barrel gleaming morosely, and, without the slightest trace of surprise, began to mow down his uninvited guests at point blank range, so that their bodies were ripped to pieces by the bullets. Horrible moans could be heard; the activists raced for the door but the door doublecrossed them and stuck and Igor finished off the last one as he slid along the floor, no longer hooting, but trying to cover his face with his hands and begging for mercy. There was a ringing in Igor's ears and the smell of powder in the air . . . he looked back at Nadya: she sat on the bed wrapped in the sheet which was littered with empty cartridges, squeezing her hands tightly against her ears, her mouth twisted in an ominous grin. He was about to say, "That's what they deserve," but instead shouted, "What's wrong?" She murmured, "You hit me, too," and took her hands away from her ears. Two small fountains of bright maiden's blood spurted out of them . . .

"All right, all right. That's enough. Sit down," said Igor. "Unsatisfactory."

He ridiculed Toporkov's report and then, without any fuss or hurry, with professional aplomb, he pinned the father of psychoanalysis to the mat.

The clock hands, as usual, had gotten stuck. In the back rows students were talking and reading material for other courses. Nadya was rummaging in some notebooks. Igor strode along the aisle, thinking his own thoughts, and spoke about the ideologues of a philosophical school that had once been in vogue and, by habit, was still presenting itself to the country as something new.

"They attempt to frighten people with death and thus to distract them from the fight for progress, for social equality. But that is a mood of artificial, deliberately created panic. After all, what normal person," Igor turned to the class and a casual smile appeared on his face, "is afraid of death? I'm not. Are you?"

Again he called on the girl in the front row.

"Oh, no," giggled the girl. The class came to life: death, it seemed, was something that no one was afraid of. Igor was about to move on to the next point when he noticed that Nadya had raised her hand.

"Did you want to say something?" asked Igor with some surprise: it wasn't her style to put up her hand in his class.

"I want to say," Nadya stood up (she was tall and made an imposing figure), "I want to say that I am afraid of death."

Everyone turned to look at her with interest.

"I don't understand," said Igor.

"It's quite simple!" she exclaimed, smiling agitatedly. "You go along living your life and then, boom—death! A hole. An empty hole. And if you think about it more seriously and more immediately, then it's even possible to forget about progress. Don't you think so?"

Someone giggled in support. Igor felt the blood rushing to his face. The blow was too unexpected—the girl was out of her mind!

"I don't understand," repeated Igor more firmly, without looking at Nadya out of the common habit people have of not looking directly at the person with whom they are in hostile argument. "I don't understand how such thoughts can even be entertained . . . especially by a woman. What about children? We do leave children to live after us. And the most important factor: we leave to our descendants the creations of our minds and hands."

"Well, so what if we leave things behind? Descendants . . . why, they're going to scorn us. They'll say, 'Look what fools they were—they didn't know how to live decent lives themselves, all they did was trundle on for us,' or they won't even give us a thought. Do we, after all, think that often about our forebears?"

The faces of the students broke into smiles.

"So it's 'after us—the deluge'? Is that the principle by which we are to live, if I understand you correctly?"

Who knows how this dialogue, so unusual for the class, would have ended if Toporkov, who had taken it all as a prank by Nadya from the very beginning, (Nadya amused all her friends, especially in Civil Defense class), and had been winking energetically at her all the while, had not put an end to it by whispering in an excited inspired voice which carried throughout the classroom: "Hey, you guys, look at what the doves on the cornice are up to! They're having a go at it!"

And, of course, everyone's eyes darted toward the window. And it was true!

The doves tumbled off the cornice in alarm

"Clearly the old Georgian philosopher spoke the truth," pronounced Toporkov in ponderous tones as he followed the dove with his eyes, "when he said that one thing is stronger than Goethe's *Faust*. Love conquers death!"

The class broke down. The recess bell could barely be heard through the laughter. Nadya laughed loudest of all . . .

"Toporkov!" Igor called out menacingly. "You seem to have forgotten where you are!"

His stern face betrayed annoyance. Nadya had ruined their meeting. And what for?

He waited until everyone had gone, pretending to search for something among his papers, and then he asked her, hardly holding back his anger:

"What did you put me in that idiotic position for?"

"An idiotic position?" Nadya was surprised and moved closer to the desk. "But I really think that way."

"So, different people think all sorts of different things! If everyone were to say what he thinks, then God knows what we'd have, but it certainly wouldn't be a class! You couldn't wait?" he reproached her.

"I couldn't . . ." but she was thinking about something else. "Say, why was Evdokimov expelled anyhow?"

Evdokimov! He had known that she would ask, would be curious about the details, and he would have been ready to tell her the whole story, but now he couldn't cut short his irritation.

"They don't expel people for nothing. So it must have been necessary."

"Necessary *for whom?*"

"For me!" he growled. "It's a long story." He shrugged his shoulders impatiently. "You know that Evdokimov drew a smutty caricature of the Dean . . ."

"And he deserved it. Go on, deny it! You know you can't stand him yourself."

Igor couldn't keep himself from glancing at the door.

"What I think is something else entirely," he said in a sour voice. "Please don't put everyone in the same bag . . . and anyway, who is this Evdokimov to you? A brother or something? He behaved in a most cowardly fashion; first he tried to get out of it, he denied authorship, and only when they nailed him to the wall with proof did he admit to it. That's not right. If you're going to draw something, then at least have the courage to admit it. Keep your dignity. If not, that's nothing to do with me, that's . . . that's just a pile of shit!"

"Igor!" Nadya cried out painfully. "You can't talk that way. Whenever you're against someone, and I've seen this more than once, then immediately he's a pile of shit!"

"Nadya, you're not right!" His voice resounded with undisguised exasperation.

"And I suppose you're always right."

"Are you holding a class in here this period?" A bearded face appeared in the doorway munching on a sweetroll.

"No-no!" Igor quickly strode out of the classroom. It's time to break it off—the thought was sudden, cold, and sober.

It's my own fault!

Igor no longer walked, but flew headlong down the hall with no particular destination.

Damn it, he'd given himself his word: no complicated affairs. Something on the side, maybe, a quick casual encounter—fine! But at the institute and for four months! You idiot! Cretin! You'll cut your own throat and then won't all the Speranskys be overjoyed. And what business is it of hers? Evdomikov! Big deal, look who she's found for her hero . . .

"Igor Mikhailovich!"

Unmindful of the familiarity of her gesture, the cleaning woman tugged at his sleeve. She was an old woman with a tired, squeamish face and she wore thick silver earrings, similar to the heavy rings worn by virtuous family men.

"Is it true, Igor Mikhailovitch, that you're closing the Back Stairway?"

"Why do you ask?" Igor was on guard, for some reason expecting dissatisfaction, but seeing that he was mistaken and that the Tartar woman was taken aback at the steely note in his voice, he softened his tone:

"Yes, we may be closing it off for a bit."

"And a good thing too! There'll be less dirt." The Tartar woman nodded eagerly and a wan smile emerged through the thick web of wrinkles on her face.

"Exactly. Less dirt!" agreed Igor.

The masses! They always have the right view of things and always support you! The thought bolstered him and gave him confidence in his position.

But not for long.

As evening approached, Igor felt more and more uneasy. He hadn't spoken his mind to Nadya and there was plenty he still had to say. He wanted to have it out once and for all. If she continued to interfere like today . . . , well, yes, I have spoken a bit too loosely with her during our meetings, things that might bounce back at me, but it wouldn't be that hard for me to break off with her. Why I'll break off with her just to prove to myself that I can!

Who was he trying to fool?

Classes continued, during which Igor suffered from his usual boredom, while painfully forcing himself from time to time to pay attention to the answers of the students, who repeated with greater or lesser success simple truths in colorless voices. It's exactly the same tone in which Tanya complains to me that little Kolya gives her no peace or that I take her for granted.

From the moment he had entertained the thought, the unrealistic "break off with Nadya" had been replaced by a more condescending and realistic "have it out with her once and for all" and then even that "once and for all" soon turned into merely a pretext, a pitiful, hastily constructed pretext for saving his easily wounded male ego. What he wanted, of course, was not a confrontation, but to see her, to talk with her, to laugh with her, to put his arms around her and never let her go . . .

He would have tried to see her immediately in the institute, but that meant setting it up with her ahead of time; he couldn't just grab her by the arm in the corridor in front of everyone!

But finally he couldn't hold out. He took a chance, checked the lecture timetable for her next class, and went there toward the end of the break hoping that he could catch her before the class began. A crowd of students was standing in front of the classroom. It was a lecture attended by all the fourth-year students, but as one might expect, according to the law of universal perversity, Nadya wasn't among them. She probably had gone inside already. Nonetheless, Igor hung around the entrance until the bell and was just about to leave—the corridor had emptied quickly—when he saw Nadya walking with Medvedev. Medvedev was about to give the lecture to Nadya's class. He was a bit older than Igor, about thirty-seven, smartly, even a bit foppishly, dressed, a Doctor of Science, and just returned from a six-month stay in Canada. He was a trifle cross-eyed, but he cleverly hid this defect under a pair of large, smoked, dark glasses in stylish frames. Medvedev was animatedly relating something to Nadya and she was smiling. As they drew even with Igor, Medvedev stopped, and Nadya slipped into the classroom, maneuvering around Igor as if he were a department store dummy.

"Were you waiting for me?" asked Medvedev, shaking Igor's hand.

"Ah no, I was just . . . standing here." Igor had been caught without any cover story.

"She's really something!" Medvedev enthusiastically nodded towards the door. "Beats any of those Canadian girls . . ."

"Snowing her about Canada, were you?"

"Right." Medvedev laughed. "I've been playing that tune for every woman I meet! Hey, what an ass she has, eh? A work of art. You know I don't go for women with pear-shaped figures, with asses you can't even get your arms around . . . oooo-ee, what an ass! Hey, brother," he half-closed his eyes, "I can just imagine what soft skin she must have on her belly!"

"All right now, don't get started," said Igor in a tone of friendly counsel. Medvedev grabbed the doorknob to the classroom. "And you know something," he added with obvious amazement, "she's pretty sharp, at least for a woman. Oh, my congratulations!" he burst out, "they told me that you chopped off Speransky's head neat and clean!"

"Well, you know he's like the Hydra . . ." said Igor, frowning playfully.

Medvedev roared, "Well, I can't argue with that!"

The encounter with Medvedev only irritated Igor further. The upcoming lecture was Igor's last today—it ended at 4:10 and he could be free at the earliest, as was always the case on Mondays, by 5:45. If Nadya didn't wait for him in the library as usual, but went home to her telephoneless apartment, then all he had to look forward to was a bleak and empty evening sitting next to his father-in-law in front of a color TV. All he could think of during his last class was whether or not Nadya would wait. He even tried to foretell the future using a student in place of a forget-me-not: if Paryugin had not prepared his report on Freud, then Nadya wouldn't wait for him. His chances weren't too good. He had even less reason to expect Paryugin to come through for him than he had had to look for help from Toporkov the ju-jitsu jock. Paryugin was known to be one of the instigators on the Back Stairway and was a friend of Evdokimov's. Igor was constantly irritated by a pin which he wore on his sweater which said, "I don't shake hands." Igor considered the pin a simultaneous expression of snobbishness and boorishness. Paryugin had not prepared his report and Igor's pent-up anger came flooding out. He chewed out the whole class at the top of his lungs, promising not even to let Paryugin take the final exam, and shouting that students like him had no business in the institute and that a member of the Komsomol should know better than to wear stupid pins. His face wearing an expression of innocence, Paryugin began to reply that his pin was, as a matter of fact, very much "in the spirit of the Komsomol," that it had been worn by Komsomol mem bers in the twenties and that it expressed the "just hygienic demands" both of that time and our own.

"That's not hygiene, that's just being a squeamish, finicky prude!" Igor growled with such rage that even the other students stopped smiling and the eternal whispering in the back rows ceased. Igor gave out a lot of "C's," promised to register a complaint against the entire class with the Dean, and left as soon as the bell rang without even saying good day. The students decided that he must have had a rough day. After all, it was Monday.

Igor walked out to the street, got into his Zhiguli—who had decided to give a car a name that made it seem a plural noun?—and drove with very little hope in his heart to the Leather Repair Shop. It was five minutes to six.

Nadya was standing at the edge of the sidewalk. Something clicked and a sense of inner calm came over him and all the Paryugins were forgotten. All that remained was gratitude that she had come.

Of course he didn't let a bit of this show. He just sat there, his face sunk in a heavy scowl. She hopped in next to him and gave him an imploring smile.

"Come on now, don't be a scowly old owl!"

"I'm no scowly owl," he snapped.

"Scowly owl . . . say, are you really not afraid of death?" she asked, looking at him intently.

"The fact is, that I don't have time to be afraid of it." He shrugged his shoulders and watched the traffic in the rearview mirrow with exaggerated concentration. The street was narrow but quite heavily used, especially during rush hour. It was almost impossible to pull away from the curb.

"I knew you'd say that!" exclaimed Nadya. "You're always in a hurry, always . . ."

He stepped on the gas and quickly let out the clutch; he swore and pulled away from the curb. Now they were flowing along in the mainstream of traffic, together with buses weighed down with rush hour passengers, arrogant cab drivers, and timid private car owners fearful of the slightest scratch.

" 'He who doesn't hurry,' if I may quote from the hero of every B-grade war movie, 'shall be left behind.' And, believe it or not, he is right. Look, just look at them," Igor motioned with his finger from left to right across the windshield, "look at them all, on the sidewalks, in stores, in apartments, in buses! And they're all in a hurry, crabbing at each other in line, tearing about as if possessed, swallowing food without chewing it. . . . It's life at the level of instinct: to get there, and not to miss anything, to get more from life than the next person."

"But that's awful! Sometimes I look at the subway during rush hour, the way the train rushes out of the tunnel and into the station, its cars jammed with people, literally stuffed with them, and in each car the people are standing with upraised fists holding onto the bar over the seats, and those hundreds of fists seem like a mass curse against someone for making people get squashed in the luxurious, hellish underground everyday and for what?—for a barely, barely endurable life . . . and then I get on—I squeeze on!—and I too raise my fist . . ."

"But that's just what you shouldn't do," said Igor quickly and firmly. "That's useless. Let them ride out their lives with uplifted fists. Who cares about them, they won't ever change a damn thing. They'll just give birth to more like themselves. Don't be like them. You should find a way to break away from them and run ahead . . . it's easier to run alone than in a crowd where people snarl and try to trip each other up."

"You know, you're a very strong person," said Nadya sadly. "You have some strange force in you . . . it sucks one up, it casts a spell . . . and I can't fight against it, I give in to it. No, it's true!" she exclaimed heatedly, seeing his protesting gesture.

"No, it's not true! If I were really a strong person, I would . . . not have come for you today at the repair shop."

"I wouldn't have come either . . . if I had more willpower."

"So?"

"So, hurrah for weakness!"

Igor leaned over and softly kissed her on the cheek.

"You say terrible things," he said quietly, "but I will agree with them for one little evening, just for you, on the condition that it will be our biggest secret."

"Oh, no secrets!" Nadya laughed. "I'll turn you in in a second to the first militiaman I see!"

They drove on through the city. A cool evening was descending. The painfully bright sunset transformed long familiar houses and streets to the point of unrecognizability.

Moscow! Moscow! The time will also come when you can enjoy the good life you've been waiting for for so long. You've had enough of rags and tatters, of homeless waifs. You've marched in enough sports parades—a new time will come! They'll take you off to a fashionable tailor, to a fancy parlor, sprinkle you with a drop or two of cologne, and you'll knock their eyes out in your fancy fox fur collar. But for now your lot is this: to shamble along in a half-baked age. We suffocate in the stuffy GUM department store in order to buy some real honest-to-goodness Turkish bath towels and on our foreheads is inscribed a simple question: WILL THEY LAST?

Miss, just three to a customer!

Two to a customer! Just two!

THEY'VE CUT IT TO ONE! And we leave with our towel, as happy as if the nurse had just shown us a newborn baby, housewives, intellectuals, speculators. And friends treat us to Scotch bought right from "Eliscev's" and—would you believe it—we swallow it down as it there was nothing to it, we Europeans with our high Tartar cheek-bones! The sack people* go rummaging from one Children's World store to another in their quilted vests and sateen, stupified by the contrast between the hustle and bustle of the capital and their own sleepy little villages where people still remember famines. And Moscow, too, for that matter, still repeats her old refrain, "Just as long as there is not war!" as she tries to justify the poverty of her Arbat region, glorified by the poets, her hastily put-together Cheryomushkin region apartment projects, and, at the slightest provocation, she screeches with the voice of a market woman: "Too well off for their own good!" But one can already see the swift Zhigulis darting along the neon-lit streets and Moscow is preparing secretly for the day when we'll all slide behind the wheel of our Zhigulis, puff and preen our feathers and take off, each of us to wheel and deal as we please.

"You've got a new raincoat . . ." Nadya interrupted his silence.

"Like it?"

"Yes, and that color, cream."

"It's Italian."

"From some special Party section in GUM?"

"Right on the nose!" He chuckled.

Nadya felt the material, nodded her head in approval and unexpectedly sighed, looking at Igor out of the corner of her eye.

"You know, it really is too bad about Evdokimov."

"It is," agreed Igor, "but it's his own fault. I don't believe in suicide as a philosophy of life."

"What do you mean—suicide?"

"It was suicide plain and simple. No one took away the Dean's full professorship and no one's going to take it away—not even if you do one hundred such cartoons!—and Evdokimov got it right in the neck, which could have been predicted. So what was the point of his action? To preserve his anonymity? He tried to initially, but everyone on the whole faculty knows that he's the only one who can draw that well. We're not the Stroganov Fine Arts Institute! So it wasn't hard to trace it to him. Listen, I'm not against fighting the good fight, arguing, or even completely vulgar brawling, and I'm ready to do my part, but you

---

*Petty traders who shuttled between city and town in the 1920s [tr.].

have to know what you're fighting for. Did Evdokimov know? I doubt it. He made the drawing just to screw around, to amuse his friends, to cause an incident, to get a reputation. And what's more, one should be a bit more careful in one's choice of methods. He had the Dean walking along smelling his own crap in a chamber pot. That's really gross! And he calls that a 'fight for justice'! He seems to think so. They asked him if he was willing to own up after they had made clear to him the consequences. No way! He's the fighter for freedom! He's the big martyr! First he panicked, and then he suddenly decided to bear the cross: 'I'd do it again!' All right, baby, draw, draw, draw! But because of this silliness, this nonsense which will be forgotten in a day or two, he could have ruined his whole life—that he doesn't realize, that's too deep for him? What use is he to anyone? A big fat nothing?"

Nadya thought a bit and spoke: "There is a certain logic to what you say, but Evdokimov did expose the Dean and that's something.

"He's been exposed more than once before," said Igor, dismissing her statement with a wave of his hand.

"Isn't there any way to help him?"

"Help who, the Dean?" Igor snorted.

"No, Evdokimov!"

Igor shook his head emphatically.

"That's what really bothers me," said Nadya. "You know, they say he's living in a horrible place. A single, small wretched room in a communal apartment, together with his parents and his sister."

"I'd heard that things weren't too great for him, but then it's all the more strange that he did what he did. Don't you understand, all through history some people have lived well and others have not. Everyone can't be equally well-off. Complete equality is just a sick fantasy of illiterate utopians like Evdokimov; he also thinks, contradicting himself without even noticing it, like an ordinary school boy, that every man should receive according to what he deserves."

"Of course, what he deserves. That's right!"

"It may be right, but where are you going to find a group of wise men who will set the criteria which will satisfy everyone . . . no, no, that's just plain crazy!"

"Why go looking for wise men? Just get decent people."

"Decent people? What kind of classless concept is that—decent people?" Igor asked gaily. He laughed.

"Come on now, stop it! This isn't class!" said Nadya, making as if to push him away with her hand.

"Listen, Nadya, tell me—are my classes really that boring?"

"Do you want the truth? . . . Horribly! But I don't think you should be upset—it's not your fault, it's just philosophy. It's a horrible bore, and who needs it anyway?"

"If you're serious, then the answer is that you have to guide your life according to some general principles."

"Well, I don't know, maybe . . . but, anyway, Toporkov really broke us up today. 'That thing is stronger than Goethe's Faust,' " she intoned, trying to imitate the accent of a broad-shouldered Georgian selling flowers at the Central Market.

Igor snorted. "Toporkov is an oaf!"

"Right," said Nadya, "but he's an oaf with a sense of humor, and that makes up for a lot because a sense of humor is a rare thing nowadays. We're used to respecting only serious types, serious, important, and unbelievably tight." Nadya made a sour face. "We should develop a sense of humor in our workers. Take Canada, for instance . . ."

"Oh, yes, we must take Canada!" said Igor with ironic deference, pounding the wheel with his open hand. "And not just simply Canada, but the Canada that was visited by Meester Mehd-vehd-eff. That is a very special country with butternut trees, big rock candy mountains, and soda water fountains that sprinkle down on naked women who are ready to suit anyone's predilections."

Nadya laughed.

"And I suppose you think that they're all starving and unemployed over there?" she asked.

"Enough are, I'm sure . . . and, by the way, just how did you happen to turn up with Medvedev?"

"We just met in the hall, Why?"

"Oh, nothing." Igor could not keep his face from clouding over when he remembered the look in Medvedev's eyes as he smacked his lips over Nadya's charms. "You be careful with him. He's a strange character."

"Why?"

"I'll be damned if I know! I can't figure him out! But I think those crossed eyes of his are not just physical; there's something shifty about his character, too—you never know just what he's thinking. You might find yourself in a very unpleasant situation because of him."

"I think he's just a bon vivant who doesn't give a damn about anything. That's why he's a hundred times better than all those senile old characters like Speransky who got so scared after the Evdokimov thing and want so much to be in the good graces of that pile of shit, 'our beloved' Dean, that I heard they're even planning on closing the Back Stairway to keep the 'infection' from spreading."

"Maybe they're right," said Igor, without greater conviction, glancing at her out of the corner of his eye—no, she didn't know anything. Anyway, he had expected from the start that Nadya would take Evdokimov's side. Her temperament alone obliged her to. As far as his own position went, it was neutral, if you bothered to analyze it: the concerns of Evdokimov and of the Dean were matters of entirely equal indifference. He had simply placed his bet on closing the stairway and had hit the jackpot. He had wanted to brag about his victory over

Speransky in front of Nadenka without going into the substance of the matter, just as a personal achievement: I won, celebrate with me—and that's all. But he was surprised to realize that in the time that had passed since the conversation in the teachers' lounge, the victory had lost a significant part of its charm and had turned into an insignificant occurrence, on account of which a celebration might even be a bit strange. Yes, a person quickly gets used to victory; it's defeat that leaves its scars—the thought flitted through his mind.

"You know, the trouble with you is that you're so orthodox," said Nadya. "You're ready to justify anything the administration does, even the weirdest things."

Igor's eyebrows rose.

"But you know what's good about you?"

"What?"

"The fact that you're orthodox not out of conviction, but merely because it's part of your job description . . . and that's something we can change!" Nadya threw back her head and chortled with laughter.

Igor condescended to smile. There wasn't another person in the world he would have allowed to say something like that; he would have cut them off altogether, but for Nadya he made exception after exception and found a certain secret satisfaction in doing so. When he was with her he allowed himself the luxury of not being on his guard.

"I'm just a more responsible person than you are—you nihilist!" He leaned over suddenly and pinched her ear. The car swerved sharply.

"Don't get distracted now!" Nadya gaily reprimanded him. "You stick to the driving; I want to live! And don't pinch me, especially when you're completely wrong—I'm not a nihilist."

"What do you mean you're not a nihilist when you deny . . . everything, even the fact that you're a nihilist! You're a double nihilist!"

Nadya laughed loudly again and then asked with a sly smile:

"Where are you taking me?"

"To my place . . . what about it?"

"Just that the degree of *your* nihilism is even impossible to measure!"

"What do you mean?" asked Igor with surprise. "What do I ever deny?"

"Conjugal fidelity!"

She threw off her wrap in the entranceway. He picked it up, hung it with his own on a hanger, and right there, in the hallway, he grabbed her, pulled her to him and began to kiss her, to cover her with kisses, and then he carried her in his arms into the room. Without letting her stop to catch her breath, to look around, to even think, he began to undress her with impatient, hurrying hands. He took off her short green dress with its gilt buttons, her panty hose, her light blue panties

. . . until all that she wore was a single slender gold chain (a gift from him)—"you're mussing me all up; you're crazy"—and then he bent over and caressingly kissed her small breasts with their swelling nipples, then her belly, lightly tickling her navel with his tongue while gently, gently stroking her soft springy buttocks; he buried his head between her thighs: intoxicating warmth, unendurable pleasure, she moaned, seemed about to faint—and then she fastened herself around his head and trembled from his caresses. He let out a moan, tore himself away from her, and began to tear off his clothing as if it was on fire. They tumbled naked onto the couch, engulfed by a thirst that could be quenched only by feverishly entwining legs and arms while their mouths never lost contact . . . a sweet shudder went through her sensitive body; she gave a soft moan, spread her legs and took him entirely into herself. Her hands rested lightly on his hips so that at each instant he felt himself held by her, held in her warm caressing palms, and as the waves of ecstacy rolled over him, the world, the universe, humanity with all its hopes and sorrows, Christs and Mao-Tze-Dongs, lost all meaning, faded away and dissolved in a burning, head-spinning current. "I dreamed of this when I was sick," she whispered. "Me too . . . the whole time," he breathed into her flushed face.

He found a blanket to cover them, and brought a bottle of Armenian cognac from the bar. They warmed the glasses in their palms, drew the ambrosia into their nostrils, and sipped from time to time.

Nadya finally looked around her. The room was large, well-lit, with two windows. The luxurious cherry rug which covered the entire floor definitely commanded respect. The placement of furniture gave little evidence of any real taste (the mistress's, of course!); one had the impression that it had been left exactly as the workers had delivered it. And the furniture itself was of all different styles. A too heavy desk; an old-fashioned mushroom-shaped lamp which didn't go at all with a small armchair on wheels. The table was scattered with a modest quantity of newspapers and books, and on it was a telephone. Nadya looked at the phone, and it seemed to be awakened by her glance; it began to ring. Igor did not move. The telephone rang patiently for a long while, then it stopped in the middle of a ring, but before half a minute had passed it began to ring again.

"Dammit!"

"Don't!" said Nadya. "Forget about it!"

"It'll torture us to death!" snapped Igor. He went to the phone.

"Hello."

"Hullo, Igor?" His father-in-law always said hullo; it made him sound very boorish. Only then did Igor realize that he hadn't gotten around to calling his father-in-law.

"It's me, Alexander Ivanovich," said Igor without any particular enthusiasm. "Right, I just got in the door. Heard the phone from the elevator . . . right, of course, he's a very smart man" (about Stad-niuk). "Everything went wonderfully! Thanks! . . . Supper?"

"Right, come on over," boomed the receiver. "Is your car okay? All right then, hop in and come on over. Do you want me to send Grigorii after you? He still hasn't gone into the garage."

"I can't come over, Alexander Ivanovich."

"What do you mean 'I can't'? I got some strawberries from the snackbar—I'll bet you haven't even had strawberries yet this year . . . from Bulgaria! And big ones—what an aroma!"

Igor sat naked in the armchair, impatiently squirming and toying with the cognac.

"Come on now," insisted his father-in-law. "There's a soccer match on TV tonight; we can watch it together."

"Alexander Ivanovich," Igor implored, "I just can't . . . I . . . I . . . I've got a deadline. I have to do a reader's report on an article on the worker's movement by tomorrow."

"Aha!" laughed Nadya, shaking her finger threateningly at Igor from the couch. "Is this what we call doing a report on the worker's movement?"

Igor put his finger to his lips—Shhh!—and winked at Nadya. But his father-in-law was tired of the loneliness of his silent five-room apartment.

"To hell with the reader's report! Come on over, we'll have some cognac . . . I know what you like!"

"Alexander Ivanovich, please don't tempt me, they'll have my head!"

"Hey, maybe that article of yours is a blonde?" inquired his father-in-law with playful suspicion. Igor began to get nervous. All he needed was for him to charge over here to check up on him!

"Alexander Ivanovich!" he exclaimed and even surprised himself by the ease with which the note of offense slipped into his voice.

"All right, do your work, the hell with you! I'll eat my strawberries by myself," he said and he hung up the phone.

"Whew! He let me off and didn't get sore!" Igor took a deep breath. "What a pain!"

You were wrong, Alexander Ivanovich, her hair is closer to brown! "Who?"

"Anonymous." Igor laughed. "That's my name for my father-in-law: anonymous."

"Why anonymous?"

"Very simple," said Igor, sliding back under the blanket with Nadya. "The way the winner of a lottery is anonymous. The way it happened to Stakhanov.* It really had nothing to do with the fact that

---

* A worker who began a movement to raise labor productivity and whose name was afterward given to the ensuing nationwide campaigns [tr.].

he had fulfilled his norm one hundred times over. That's in addition to the fact that when you can overfulfill a norm by a factor of one hundred, it's not planned production, but a complete mess. He just happened to be there at the right time, they needed him—and so he became Stakhanov. The same thing happened to my father-in-law; when he graduated from some two-bit technical school, they needed him. And what else was there for him? He probably didn't even realize what was happening at the beginning. He just kept on looking straight ahead with those wide-open, dedicated eyes of his, and that was all, when suddenly the finger of fate pointed to him, and they called him into the Cadres Office or into the Party Committee. And all around him, people with the same devoted eyes, completely loyal to their dying day, were left behind. Pure chance! And at first he wasn't even called into the inner offices, wouldn't have made any impression there at all, but merely went into one of the large, desk-filled outer offices, to one of the desks himself; later came the inner offices, which became more and more luxurious in their decor and the secretaries more and more cordial until finally the finger of fate pointed at him again. By this time he must have learned something—how to please superiors, for instance—and he wasn't able to plump down into his own stuffed leather armchair and get his own secretary until he had also acquired an inner office which had a ponderous safe, a small lounge connected by a side door, a television, a potted palm and an imposing paperweight on its desk—the symbol of his power—which was so convenient for pounding on the heads of his subordinates . . . and then he said to himself, 'I was created to lead people' . . ."

Nadya broke into peals of laughter—what a little joker she was!

"Don't you like him?"

He looked at her with amazement and, avoiding her question, said: "When I'm with you I can break loose from his power . . . with you I feel . . ." he hesitated, embarrassed, "I feel free."

"Freedom is the acknowledgement of necessity," Nadya announced majestically.

"Don't joke!" Igor's voice almost had a note of entreaty to it. "I'm serious. I've never talked to anyone about my father-in-law. No, it's a lottery." After a silence he heaved a sigh. "He can't be imitated. One could repeat the same motions and just get a losing ticket. We're in a different time now, and it's no longer chance that is all-powerful, but vulgar pull. Pull can make money into mere paper if it pleases, open any door, force people to smile, to bow, and to fear. It changes (silently so that others will not know, the fools) official instructions, rules, and even resolutions of the Party; it turns all "prohibitions" into "permission granted," any "forbidden" into "go right ahead.""

"You said it! . . . And so you got married in order that," began Nadya.

"No," Igor stopped her, "it wasn't quite that simple."

"I'm sorry, I didn't mean to—"

"No, why not. If I'm going to tell you, it might as well as be the whole story. How I fell in love with the daughter of Anonymous, and did I really fall in love? I came back from the Army after serving my required three years, fastened onto my books like a leech and barely made it into the university. Then one day I was walking by her department—her classes were in the building right next to mine— when suddenly a black Chaika shining in the winter sun stops in front of me and out steps Tanya in a white sheepskin coat with a fur border and gives the door a casual—not on purpose mind you, not for effect, but merely with her usual everyday gesture—a casual slam! The sight just stuck in my mind—slam!—it stuck in the mind of a kid from the outskirts of Moscow whose father had hated him throughout his childhood because of his chronic bronchitis, his nightly coughing, whose father would jump out of bed and beat him all over his body with a belt, and if my mother ran to defend me he would let the blows fall on her too, so that she stopped trying to protect me and only whimpered . . ."

He fell silent. Nadya glanced at his face—it was angry and cruel.

"I got my revenge: I married Tanya. Now my father brags about me, the bastard! I don't visit him much, maybe once every two months . . . He's gotten old, gone to pot, can't hold his liquor. I can't forgive him . . . you see that scar on my temple?" He twisted his mouth into a grin. "Daddy did it. Would you have pardoned him?"

Nayda stroked his breast thoughtfully.

"I don't know . . . my daddy left my mother when I was in the first grade and never showed up again. Even before that he hardly lived with us. Somehow he was always being sent away somewhere and I remember him only vaguely, standing with a huge red suitcase in his hand . . . so a father for me is something with a suitcase."

"Something with a suitcase! You really are weird! I really like you," he acknowledged, "and I like talking with you. Even if, afterwards, I'll probably regret it."

"Why?"

"Because it's a weakness that is just not permissible . . . and I've got to keep grinding away."

"Grinding?"

"Yes, pushing ahead, making it—do you understand?"

"You'll push ahead and make it, though, no doubt about that," whispered Nadya, tenderly playing with his genitals.

Her caressing fingers with their short nails were calling him to new joys. And she kept giving him knowing glances . . . the little joker! With a single movement he jerked off the blanket covering her and threw himself on her, kissing her, kissing her everywhere.

"Igor, darling, lover . . ." she murmured, almost stunned by his kisses, and her cheeks blushed a bright red, and burned brighter, and they caressed each other.

And when he slowed his movement in her for a moment, and asked her very softly and very gently, "Are you afraid of death now, too?" she answered with a light happy laugh, "Mmmm-no-ooo, I'm immortal!"

"Oh my, what's the time?" Igor heard Nadya say through his sleep.

He held up his watch hand. It was so silent that he could hear every wheel and cog ticking away, but the watch face seemed blind and without hands.

"Twelve minutes to . . ." he finally saw the position of the minute hand. "And the little hand has fallen off."

She raised herself on her elbow, pressing her breast to his shoulder. "Let me see . . ." and then almost in a panic, "Oh my God, it's twelve of twelve! Mama's probably crazy with worry. I promised to be home for supper. You know her nerves lately. She keeps imagining the most horrible things. You know how she is!"

"You don't think you could stay?"

"No, it's out of the question! She'd have the whole Moscow police force out looking for me!"

While she was in the bathroom fixing herself up, Igor lay on the couch, not moving, the light off, smoking and blowing the smoke up at the ceiling as thoughts tumbled through his mind in confusion. He suddenly looked at her suspiciously:

"Nadya, why do you love me?"

"Because you're wild in bed."

"And that's all? I mean it."

"Because of your stupid doubts . . . and I just do. Anyway, leave me alone. I love you and that's that."

"Nadya, marry me! Come on, will you?"

"Igor?"

"What?"

"Don't joke that way."

"I'm not joking."

"What about your wife?"

"What about her?"

He ran over to the table. Next to it on the wall hung a large photograph of Tanya taken before their marriage, standing on the steps of a summer cottage with the neighbor's puppy in her arms. He tore the photograph off the wall and hurriedly ripped it to shreds.

"There, no more wife! *Finita lya comediya!*" he cried, as he scattered the fragments over the rug. And in his heart the everpresent fear appeared, and began to grow and to strengthen, parallel to the action he had just performed and completely independent of it, the cold piercing fear of living out his life as a pauper, of becoming in his old age the laughing stock of the neighborhood children, and dying somewhere as a helpless invalid in a city hospital on a broken down cot whose mattress was covered with suspicious yellow stains. No way! Let others have the next world; he meant to have the fruits of this one!

He remembered running into an old university classmate, not too long ago, in April, on the Gogol Boulevard. The classmate was sitting shivering on the edge of a bench and reading something in the midst of puddles and melting snow. He was wearing a worn overcoat, which he had worn during all five of his student years. The book, a large thick one, yellow with age, was nestled on his knees.

Igor noiselessly went up to him and quietly asked:

"And what are you reading, good sir?"

Ryabov jumped and Igor was pleased; his joke had worked.

"Ah, Igor!" Ryabov half rose, shook his hand in that old way of his, the way some people shake a thermometer, and smiled a vague smile. He had been completely involved in his book. "So you see . . ." he pointed at the cover of the book with an awkward motion and hesitated before sitting down again.

"Why are you out here freezing? Why not read at home? Sit down, will you!"

An ironic smile appeared on Igor's lips. He had always felt slightly superior to Ryabov and had never felt obliged to hide the fact.

"Zoya sent me out to get a breath of fresh air," said Ryabov with great seriousness as he resumed his seat.

"Oh, it was Zoya! Now I understand, of course . . ." Igor had no idea whatsoever about any Zoya (was she his wife, his sister?) and the answer had unexpectedly angered him. Why had this Zoya chased Ryabov out into the fresh air with a completely useless book on the origins of medieval religion? What nonsense!

"Say," said Igor, "Why doesn't your Zoya make you change your shoelaces; they've worn through."

Ryabov was extremely embarrassed and was not able to answer, but his embarrassment did not affect Igor in the least. Igor took the rotting shoelaces as a personal insult, as an expression on Ryabov's part of extreme scorn for those ordinary mortals who paid attention to their shoes and to fashion, and, ultimately, as an expression of Ryabov's confident sense of his own exclusiveness. He might be dying on a stinking hospital mattress, but he would still read his treasured Kierkegaards and faithfully believe that they contained the soul of all wisdom, and if we couldn't see it that way, then we were only ignorant.

Igor said cuttingly:

"She probably said, 'here, read *The Principles of Medieval Religion* and I'll give you some new shoelaces,' right?"

Ryabov was now completely at a loss and was uncertain how to respond. He tried to make excuses with a guilty smile, but Igor interrupted him:

"Don't you have anything better to do with your time than to read that rubbish?"

Then Ryabov began to argue with unexpected fervor that Igor was mistaken, this wasn't rubbish but rather a remarkable and fascinating study of religious life, dealing for the most part with pre-Dantean Italy, and that without a real understanding of the religious life, an understanding of the period itself would be problematical. Igor looked at Ryabov's eyeglasses with their primitive frames, at his stupid worker's cap, and thought: you fool! Your Zoya probably just can't get enough of listening to your theories on the subject of Judeao-Christian-Egypto-Greco-Byzantine cultures . . . what stupidity! But what irritated Igor most (what drove him up the wall!) was his awareness of the fact that his apparently unambitious friend had now found himself other admirers in addition to Zoya—admirers who would absorb unlimited quantities of useless information from him and scribble earnest outlines about it, and even go so far as to carry him on their shoulders in gratitude and reward him with their cordial and intelligent applause.

"All right, I won't bother you any more by stealing your precious time . . . though they do say that there are too many books in the world to read them all!"

No, Igor thought, I was not made to be a priest clothed in baggy pants worn mirror-smooth by hours upon hours in the Public Library lying prostrate before the treasured altars of culture, or to go into a fit of ecstasy at the sight of some decayed mouse-eaten pages of a manuscript, or to murmur with awe the names of ancient sages, medieval theologians, German Romantics, mischievous Decadents, and all the rest who announce the decline of cultures and the beginning of an apocalypse every time they have a wet dream caused by excessive abstinence. What the hell does all their scholarly masturbation mean to me when Nadya opens her legs to me?!

I WANT TO BE WITH HER!

I can imagine how my father-in-law's jaw would drop if I were to run away from his little treasure. Would I like to give it to him, the old Stakhanovite!

It was warm and comfortable in the car; they had settled the most important question and now she was by his side. She was unable to stop smiling.

"All right," she said, "we can live at my place first."

"Why at your place?" he asked cautiously.

"Because you must leave your apartment to your wife . . . and to Kolya."

Kolya! It's curious that I never even thought of him. I'll have to say good-bye to him. "Kolya-koolya, Papa's little Kolya." But just look at how rapidly she organized things: she had quickly given Kolya to his wife and that was that. "We'll rent a place." It was clearly impossible for him to live with her mother, a dentist, who had spent her whole life breathing in the air from other people's oral cavities. No matter that she was excellent at her profession, with what Nadya called a select clientele, she was still in many respects a boring and dreary woman. . . . "And sign up for a coop."

"That's expensive!"

"So what! We'll sell the car."

"It's a shame . . . what a shame . . ."

"Forget it, we'll do without it. The main thing is to have our own place . . . our own place," he repeated stubbornly, morosely.

"Whatever you say . . ."

"Or we'll go away somewhere . . ."

"Where?"

"To Canada! Why not? Tomorrow! Pack your suitcases! No, my dear, to the provinces . . . where life is quieter, less *eventful*."

"Why do we have to go away?" Nadya was surprised. "I love Moscow. We'll be bored anywhere else." With fear in her voice she said, "We'll lose our residence rights!"

"Let's go to Penza! Penza's a wonderful city. I remember once talking with a graduate student from Penza, and he couldn't say enough about it. He said that they're building high-rise buildings there now . . . maybe he was just a Penza patriot, but . . ."

"All right, I don't really care! So we'll go to Penza. At least there" (she seemed to have understood what he was getting at) "we'll be a good distance from your *Anonymous*. If not, he might try to take revenge!"

"Don't be silly! Revenge! Nonsense! Let's go somehwere where it's really rough."

"Igor darling, why does it have to be where it's rough?"

"Just because." No, it would never work.

She came out of the bathroom; in the unlit room her body gave off a gentle light. He looked at her and felt as if his eyes had been liberated from all sexual desire.

"You're beautiful."

But what am I to do with you?

She sat on the edge of the couch and said dismally, "Your wife and I use the same shampoo."

"So what? There aren't that many to choose from you know." He laughed and embraced her.

"My hair must smell like hers. Right?"

"Come on! Not at all." He kissed her. "Now your lips smell of cognac." He got up to turn on the light. "Don't," she said. They picked up the underthings which were scattered on the rug by the couch. "It feels cold." Nadya shivered as she buttoned up her dress. "Did you open a window?" "One's been open in the kitchen all the time. Shall I close it?" "Whatever you want. Igor, we have to hurry!"

They were already standing at the door of the apartment with their raincoats on when suddenly he said, "Wait!" and disappeared into the bedroom. There he stumbled over Kolya's huge fire truck, hurt his foot, and, swearing, began to rummage in his wife's dresser until he found a small unopened bottle of French perfume. Some eminent French visitor had presented it to his father-in-law as a gift.

"Here, this is for you," he said, coming back into the entryway, "They say that this is all the rage in Paris this year."

"What are you, out of your mind?" She seemed to be feebly pushing the perfume away with her hands

"Take it, please!"

"You're spoiling me," She blushed deeply as she took it.

"Let me have the pleasure." He smiled as he saw how pleased she was with the present. According to its value in Moscow it was a fantastically expensive gift. And I'll just tell Tanya . . . well, whatever! I'll have time to think of something for her!

"Oh my, does it smell ni-i-i-ce!" She lifted the crystal top. "Oh, it's so fine, but at the same time sort of , . fancy! I've always thought that this would be the kind of smell one would find in the reception rooms of foreign embassies, mingled with a slight whiff of expensive tobacco. I'm silly I know, but just once I'd like to put on a dress so long that it brushed the floor, and go to a *real* reception! It's really stupid— don't pay any attention to me," she chattered on gaily as she carefully turned the flacon in her hand. "I don't usually use perfume, but yours I will . . . just for you!"

They went out onto the street, hand in hand. It had just stopped raining. The pavement glistened, reflecting the lights of the lampposts and the shop signs which had been left on. The car was covered with large drops of water. While Igor opened the car, Nadya amused herself by sweeping raindrops from the roof onto him.

"Watch out, Nadyush, you'll get your hands dirty . . ."

They sped along the asphalt prairies of the Sadovoye Loop which was planted with small consumptive lime trees looking as if they might spit up blood at any minute; then through the square that was formed and crushed by its mercantile rail station, and onward along that noble prospect whose reputation would be excellent were it not sullied by the disreputable guitars of a frisky gang of satyrs who spent their time hopping over benches. They finally reached its very end. There, instead of crashing into a huge foreign-looking building which loomed above the Sokol subway station, they disappeared into the tunnel and bobbed up on the other side; here they continued to zoom away from the center of the city as fast as they could.

"Boy, wouldn't it be nice," he murmured blissfully, "if we didn't have to worry that your mother might have a headache or a sore throat or a stomach ache and might cast her charges to the mercies of fate by letting their cavities go unfilled and arrive home . . . and catch us at it! Everything today would be different, so much better! Aren't I right?"

"Right . . . when are you expecting your? . . ." The word "your" hung in the air connected with nothing, not out of any malicious intent but because of a vague fear which sporadically assaulted Nadya: if she were to call things by their right names, then the spell would break and she would turn back into Cinderella. She couldn't help being tormented by that lewd name which bad people use so freely: *mistress.*

"We still have eighteen whole days, Nadyush! We'll have to decide how to get the best out of them."

"Eighteen days? That's a lot . . ."

"It sure is! And that means two Saturdays and two Sundays when you could stay at my place, if . . ."

"I'll tell Mama that I'm going on a field trip! I'll tell her today. Eighteen days! They'll go by so fast . . ." She blinked helplessly.

"You're upset by the . . ." He fell silent, trying to find the right word and found one that was honest but wrong: "hopelessness . . ."

She quickly covered his mouth with her hand—"Don't!"

"Don't," she repeated. "Do you want to spoil our wonderful evening?"

"No, Nadya. I just want to be completely honest with you . . . you've got to understand. I . . . what we have is no joke; maybe only once . . . no, I'm sure of it—I've never felt so good with anyone in my life as I do with you."

"I think," said Nadya thoughtfully, smiling at Igor with moist, glistening eyes, "that none of us has any normal feeling for time. Our connections with time are abnormal, mixed-up, probably because of the way we live, trying to live tomorrow before today is done. That is the way children eat: they haven't even finished one dish before they're reaching for the next, and the next, and then someone else's plate. So they never really get a good taste of anything and are still hungry at the end of the meal. We always wait impatiently for the end of the month, for spring, for summer, for a birthday, for holidays, for New Year's— we spend half our lives in expectation. It's as if we don't even exist in the here and now; we're there, in the future, because it's difficult to measure the worth of what's happening today, as we should. Only later do you suddenly stop and think and it hits you and you say: 'I was happy.' So why even think about those eighteen days coming to an end? It will just spoil our happiness!"

"Nadya!" said Igor in torment.

"I know, I won't ever learn how not to think about such things. What can you do? You have to find another answer. You have to find one sometimes . . . it's all right!" She tried to laugh. "I'll go off somewhere this summer to a resort in Palanga and try to recuperate under the gentle Lithuanian sun with some blue-eyed, blond Lithuanian."

"*Recuperate?*" He pondered the word with surprise and pity and even felt a tightening in his throat. At the same moment, as if treacherously encouraging this unmasculine sensitivity, a brilliant thought forced its way into his mind and flapped its large wings like some huge crazed bird.

"Nadya! Don't be so fast with your Lithuanian. How about this: let's take off somewhere this summer *together!* I'll make all the arrangements. I'll get free from them all! Oh, what am I saying? I promised my father-in-law. . . . But no, I really will get away!" He seemed to be yelling at himself. "I'll get us into a really nice resort and we'll take off: the sea, the sun . . . how about the Crimea? We're as good as anyone else! I'll take the car . . . wait, let's just take off! No resort! We'll rent a room for two with a view of the sea. We'll have to get a place by the ocean so there'll be the sound of the waves at night and moonlight on the water and salty kisses . . ."

"No, I like half-salted ones better!"

"All right, half-salted ones," he said.

"Dreamer! . . . You don't really think we could?"

"Of course we could!"

"I've never ever taken a trip in a car," she acknowledged.

"We'll work out an itinerary that will make your mouth water! We'll drive around the Ukraine, stop at Kiev, really cover the whole Crimea."

"You know, I was never in Bakhchisarai. I hated group tours."

"All right then, we'll go to Bakhchisarai! First thing!"

"Sometimes I look at you and think that maybe you're a prince from a fairy tale," she said, teasing him goodnaturedly which she did in moments of excitement.

"What do you mean?" asked Igor, adopting her tone. "I'm no different from anyone else. There are millions like us. We're all just simple, Soviet people."

"Oh my and how I do love you all!" cried Nadya, pressing her hands to her breast. "Only don't forget to stop—we're here," she said in a slightly more ordinary tone.

He stopped the car. Her house was about two hundred meters away on the other side of the Leningrad Highway. She barely glanced at the windows which were laid out like a hand of Solitaire whose pattern would mean nothing to a casual onlooker, and predicted: "Mama's not asleep. Here comes crying and valerian drops!" She quickly kissed him on the cheek. "I'm off." He held on to her hand. "So it's tomorrow morning before class? I'll be waiting Nadyush. Do you remember the apartment? You don't, do you? And how would you have found it? Number 28." "Twenty-eight. OK. Oh, the perfume!" And she grabbed the flacon from the seat and thrust it into the bag with her boots. "A million thanks! . . . And for Bakhchisarai too. I believed you, you know."

"And you should believe me!"

"I'll come a little earlier," she promised, opening the door, "so we can wake up together. For some reason I want awfully much to sleep against your shoulder."

"Don't count on getting too much 'sleep' though."

"You insatiable thing, you! Today wasn't enough for you? See you." She slammed the door.

"Good night. Bye now."

Just wait and see what I'll do to you tomorrow, thought Igor as he waved goodbye.

What a picture, my friends! It is morning and you are lying in bed all flushed and sleepy, the sweet blood pulsing evenly through your rested and restored body, and then Nadya strips off her clothes and pauses just a second to blush before she crawls under the covers to you, playful, tender, and full of love . . .

And right into the marriage bed!

Come on, no prejudices now!

Prejudice!

And to hell with Tanya!

He began to accelerate his car while repeating the word to himself: prejudices-prejoo-dis-s-es-s-dishes-dishes-s-predge-predge-dishes-s-s, until the word had lost its kernel of original meaning and had become a cluster of random letters ruled by the buzz of the final "s." A long way to the exit ramp here; that's always a problem with the highways leaving the city; in America they say you can miss one exit and have to go fifty or a hundred kilometers—all the way to Canada—before you can turn around . . . dishes, prejudices. . . . The desperate scream of brakes. Back there behind him. So what was it? The scream of brakes and then, one-slowly, two-slowly, three-. . . thump. Someone had been hit . . . hit . . . someone. An inner coldness suddenly gripped him. No. It can't be. Nonsense. An icy coldness. Now his own pink inflamed crimson brakes screamed. "Nadya!" he cried, "a car . . . no!" He pulled over onto the shoulder, and leapt out of the car, forgetting to take his keys. "Naden'ka!" The keys swung from the ignition and in his head those final "s's" remained like burning splinters.

A light green Volga taxicab was blocking the in-bound lane of the highway into the city. In the light of the streetlamp he could make out a large light gray huddled form farther on. For a few seconds the entire scene froze.

Not a single soul moved, neither from the Volga cab nor from the two cars which had simultaneously rammed into it. Everything was quiet, deadly still as if the world had frozen. Only when a man in a green and cherry mottled raincoat came to his senses and suddenly ran up to the light grey huddled form did everything begin to move. The doors of the cars flew open. Igor ran forward! There were still some small shreds of hope . . .

The man in the raincoat was bustling around Nadya. Igor shoved him away. "Get your hands off her!" He flung himself to his knees. "Nadya, Nadya," he murmured. Her face was lacerated and awful in its pain and suffering. She lay on her stomach, her arm twisted awkwardly, her face pressed into the wet pavement. Her raincoat, dress, and slip had been pushed up to her waist and the blue of her panties could be seen under her gartered stockings. Embarrassed at the presence of strangers, he moved to pull down her dress and coat. He tugged at them. But the man in the multicolored, operettalike raincoat squatting next to him was trying to turn her over and her entire face opened up and *fell apart:* one cheek had been cut badly and was covered with mud and blood; her chin was forced to one side; blood flowed from her nose; and her head wobbled strangely on her neck as if it was attached by the skin alone. "Nadya," Igor whispered hoarsely. A cruel spasm gripped his throat. The man in the mottled raincoat was muddling around, touching her in various places.

There was no time to waste. Someone might come and take her away. If he could just get her home, put her on the sofa, clean up her face and bandage her neck so that her head wouldn't flop like that, so that her head would be supported—maybe a cast would do it!—then maybe he could save her. There was no one he could trust; the mottled raincoat didn't seem too trustworthy, a stranger, no help at all. Nothing left but to disappear, without anyone noticing, and crawl to his car or, better yet, take her in his arms and run. I'll make it—she's so light. Got to get out of here.

He carefully slipped his hand under Nadya's spine. Bubbling sounds were coming from her mouth. Easy now, hold on . . . I know it hurts.

"She was killed instantly," blurted the mottled raincoat and ceased his examination.

Let them think whatever they want. So what. They'll all leave now and will stop interfering and I'll drive you off . . .

The dark form of the taxi driver hovered above them, hoarsely explaining, sobbing, and the mottled raincoat grabbed him by the back of the neck:

"What the hell did you do?"

The crowd kept growing even though it was late at night. People came running from nearby buildings, calling to their neighbors, and jumping over fences. A bus stopped and people ran out of it, the driver heading the pack. People got out of cars. Igor saw a forest of feet, pants, stockings, dresses, an overcoat—he was too late!—women's shoes, boots, muddied men's shoes—he was too late!

"Call an ambulance!"

"Someone already has."

"Who got run over?"

"They're on their way."

A traffic policeman who happened to be passing by on his motorcycle pushed his way through the crowd.

"Has an ambulance been called?" he asked.

"Yes. And the police too," he was eagerly told.

"Nothing can help her now," announced the raincoat in authoritative tones as he rose from a squatting position to his full height. Igor listlessly rose beside him.

"You a doctor!" asked the policeman.

"I am a biologist," answered the other with dignity.

"I see," came the policeman's noncommital answer.

Igor touched the biologist on the arm. "We've got to get her away from here," he whispered in a confidential tone.

"Where to?" The other man frowned.

"We've got to save her. She can't just lie there . . . she's in pain!"

"She's dead," the biologist said softly.

"Save her," Igor insisted. He no longer thought he could do it alone; the crowd inhibited and oppressed him.

"I said—she's dead." A faint note of irritation crept into the voice of the man in the raincoat. Apparently he did not like it when his words were not taken seriously.

"There's no crosswalk here! Comrade officer, there's no crosswalk!" burst out the taxi driver. The policeman gazed intently at him.

"Did you have a passenger?"

"I was empty . . . on my way to the garage. She threw herself under my car, just threw herself!" He was like a drowning man grasping at a straw. Igor gave him a benumbed, bewildered frown.

"We'll get it all straight," promised the officer morosely. Igor didn't like this promise. He reddened and snapped at the cab driver:

"You're lying!"

"You just shut up! You didn't see a thing!" the apoplectic driver roared at Igor, almost lunging at him.

"I'm a witness. I saw it." The man in the raincoat spoke calmly and firmly as he turned towards the officer. "She slipped as she ran across the road."

"Why was she running when it was so slippery?"

"And what was your speedometer showing?" The officer suddenly lost his temper as if he had come to a conclusion. "Let's see your papers," he added sternly.

"Are you going to lock me up?" The taxi driver gave him a look of hatred.

"What do you expect, to just go quietly home?"

Swearing violently, the driver moved towards his Volga with its malevolent green eye. He got back inside and slumped down, holding his head in his hands.

"They'll run us all over, the bastards!" screamed a high-pitched woman's voice. Sympathetic cries came from all sides.

Someone gave the officer Nadya's purse which had been hurled far off to the side.

"Some kind of cologne . . ." the officer muttered.

The entire contents of the bag, notebooks and textbooks, were covered with the "cologne"; the odor enveloped the curious crowd. Igor's head swam. The officer examined her student identification card. It had a photograph on it. Smiling! The officer gave a long, rasping cough as if cleaning out a stopped-up drain.

"She's a student," he announced. "And quite young."

"How old was she?"

"It doesn't say here . . ."

"Poor thing."

"She went head over heels at least ten times after he rammed into her."

"You're kidding!"

"And her head didn't come off?"

"Doesn't seem like it . . ."

"Poor thing . . ."

"She's completely dressed in foreign clothes."

"No, there's no way that she could have done ten somersaults."

"A young girl . . ."

"Does anyone know her?" The officer looked around.

"I think he knows her name," said the raincoat, nodding at Igor.

"Right—right," affirmed Igor trying to get his thoughts together.

The officer gestured towards the body stretched out at his feet. "So, you do know her?" he asked in an inexplicably rude tone that seemed somehow out of place.

After such an official and unequivocal invitation to observe Nadya and make a subsequent identification, Igor had to look down. His eyes refused to obey him. He gradually was coming to the realization that she had died irrevocably, forever. His consciousness, which at first had violently resisted this thought to the point where it was ready to resign like a government which had embezzled public monies and been caught perjuring itself, now occupied a temporizing position and was prepared to make grudging compromises. He had only one desire:

to be alone. But the fulfillment of that desire had to be postponed until the indefinite future. Just seconds before he had felt able to handle this event with no trouble at all by first refusing to believe in it because of its monstrousness and then haughtily demanding another in its place, with a different finale (it's not difficult to choose from an infinite number of chance occurrences?) and then, if necessary, he would rebuke the taxi driver who had been zooming along a slippery highway in violation of all the rules on his way back to the garage. But now this very same event, which he wanted to deny, had hardened into a malevolent, univalent form. An official stamp had been placed on it by the badge on the policeman's hat; it had been made into a document and given power. Igor shuddered as it became clear to him: the wide, staring, rolled-back eyes were just not hers. He shifted his gaze to the officer whose browless (his forage cap hid his brow), unpretentious face expressed simultaneously professional calm and the unsuccessfully concealed embarrassment of a village youth. The officer was not cut out to be a father confessor. Igor felt as if they had brought him a vial of smelling salts and said: "Breathe!"

"I don't know her," he mumbled, completely helpless and unsure, as if consciousness was returning after a fainting spell.

"What do you mean you don't know her—you called her name?" The officer was examining Igor with great suspicion and Igor understood: in a second he will demand to see my identification, on general principles, just in case, to put his mind at ease and to be sure that he'd followed the proper procedures. It was strange that he'd waited this long. One second, two, a third . . . Igor became tense as he awaited what seemed to be unavoidable. A guilty smile flashed on his pale face like an artificial limb, and he tried to explain:

"I made a mistake . . . it seemed for a second . . . but it wasn't her . . ."

The crowd became silent as it tried to hear what was going on. Only in the back were people still pushing each other irritably and scraping their feet. No one apologized for stepping on toes: neither the victims nor the perpetrators even noticed such a trivial detail, but only continued straining for a better view.

"My nerves," added Igor, directing his speech to the crowd and it understood his appeal. A response came immediately in understanding tones:

"His nerves fell part!"

"He got carried away—it happens all the time."

It was true that a third bystander, hidden from sight, took the opportunity to blurt out, "Psychopath!" But he drew a stern chorus of hisses.

The lenience of the officer will become legend in time. After all, the crowd was nowhere near threatening to tear him into little pieces even if he had tried to ask for Igor's documents. Nonetheless, he merely asked Igor the same question again. He seemed to have fallen under the hypnotic spell of the idlers who were well disposed towards Igor and ready to take him at his word:

"So you don't know her?"

"No . . . I don't."

The raincoat kept silent. Everyone's attention returned to examining the corpse.

As a matter of fact, the only item needed to complete the scene was Nadya's mother. She was a stout and majestic woman, like any self-respecting oral surgeon, and she had run in her nightgown toward the site of the accident, full of vague forebodings, thrown herself on her daughter's body, wringing her hands and shuddering with grief. The crowd would have met any action on her part with the gravest respect, and it would not be an exaggeration to suppose that many a tear would have been shed. The grateful onlookers would have departed and preserved forever in their hearts the memory of this authentic heartrending scene. But the picture is fated to remain incomplete. Under their impassive masks (for almost all the surrounding faces had remained impassive with the exception of several compassionate, stout women whose faces had frozen in total grimaces), under a feeling of pity for the dead coed and of fear of the corpse, under a feeling of depression ("it could have been me . . ."), the crowd experienced a surge of new, refreshing vitality (soon to break into full view), the result of rejoicing at the thought that "It's not me lying there at everyone's feet," and "I'm still alive—yes me, I'm still alive!" This surge of feeling was fated to arouse the mind and cleanse the soul of the dregs of everyday apathy.

"Is she really dead?" exclaimed someone in an uncertain voice. The crowd condescendingly shrugged its shoulders: "A novice!"

Some asked themselves: Why am I looking at such a horrible thing just before bed? I'll see her in my dreams. . . . Others thought to themselves: What a sight! Will I have something to tell them at work tomorrow.

The officer lost his patience. At first he had asked people gently: "All right now, you've had your look, move along, now move along." Now he was shouting: "Get out of here, the sideshow is over!" He was shoving people without the slightest hesitation. The raincoat was helping him and they cleared the onslaught of brazen idlers away from around the body. The raincoat did this with such zeal that he seemed to have made the corpse his own personal property, and was now merely expecting the arrival of a vehicle on which to load it and transport it to his laboratory for certain despicable experiments. Igor seethed with anger, and when the biologist squatted down on his haunches and pressed his fingers over Nadya's eyes, he couldn't stand it: how dare he!?

"You might as well not hang around any longer if your nerves are so bad," commented the officer as he noticed Igor's trembling features. He said it without the slightest sympathy.

"Why don't you go home!" asked the biologist standing back up again.

"Shut up!" snapped Igor.

"Wh-a-at?"

"You're a louse!" burst out Igor.

"Listen, I'll give you one if you don't . . ."

The threat hung in the air. Igor clenched his fists. He was ready to take revenge on this louse for everthing. He would defend Nadya's honor! The hatred in his eyes was so palpable and intense that the biologist involuntarily stepped back, despite the fact that it was clear from his appearance that he could retaliate effectively.

"What the hell! All right, get out of here!" The office grabbed Igor by the sleeve of his coat and broke up the fight. "Or I'll have you hauled downtown. A fine time to lose your temper!"

Igor jerked his arm away, glanced once more at Nadya with inconsolable, animal pain in his eyes and began to make his way through the crowd.

His faltering steps carried him across the highway; on the other side he turned. Nadya was lost from sight in the dense, black murmuring mass. "They've taken her, the bastards," he muttered.

As Igor neared his car, someone called him:

"Say, wait up!"

He looked back and it flashed through his throbbing brain that the raincoat had sent him a messenger in order to agree on a site where they could settle accounts. Igor was delighted: the desire for revenge made his chest ache. So he awaited his Hermes, who approached him with quick steps, almost hopping, and then stopped, catching his breath with difficulty.

"I am at your service," intoned Igor with a refined haughtiness which could only have been taken seriously in the previous century, but not in these times and especially not on the pavement of the Leningrad highway where its appearance could only be explained as an emotional "kink." By this time Igor began to realize that he had been mistaken: the figure before him was far from being a divine messenger and was more like some excrement discharged by the crowd. Before him stood a *muzhik*, short, dumpy, wearing a tight sport jacket and wrinkled, twisted pants. His entire being seemed half-unbuttoned. He was a little over forty years old; his head was no larger than a walnut, but on it sat a proper felt hat with a shaped brim. His face wore an arrogant expression and a scar cut across the bridge of his nose. He resembled one of those winos who pester one on the street and don't just beg for change, but demand it and threaten you when you don't give them anything. Winos who haven't yet reached the last rotten stage of physical decay, but who are headed towards it. They still have a certain sense of dignity (the hat was no chance detail) and certain needs and demands which they make of life, but which life, the bitch, still refuses to meet. The character was not drunk, but had taken a drink or two.

"I've been following you," he announced, at once enveloping Igor in a mixture of stale wine, tobacco heartburn, and some nameless garlic and onion stench. "She came out of your car; I saw her. I saw it all, d'you get me? Why didn't you tell the officer?"

"What business is it of yours?" bristled Igor.

"What do you mean what business? Someone gets runover and you ask me what business?"

"Listen scum," shouted Igor, "go sleep it off! You're all mixed up upstairs!"

"Mixed up, hell. I saw the two of you kissing in the car!"

"You're lying!" Igor's hands were twitching: he was itching to finish with this vermin, to drag him into the car and strangle him. The character guessed his thought.

"I'm hard to get rid of," he said gleefully. "You can cut me into little pieces, but I'll pull through, beat me with a chain and you won't do me in; I'll find you and I'll have you put away, so just put those thoughts right out of your mind!" He looked fixedly at Igor, poised to jump to the side at any moment, to flee, to let out a shout. Igor understood this and was at a loss.

"You say that I'm lying?" continued the man in an unexpectedly appeasing tone. "Well, that's simple to check on. Let's see if I'm lying—let the officer check it out, OK? Let me take one more look at your license just in case you decide to get away."

He took a step towards the car, clearly preparing to follow up on his statement.

"Stop!" Igor's nerves gave way. The character was agreeable to being stopped and he halted as if frozen to the spot. The siren of the ambulance cut through the air. In a few seconds the dark figures of orderlies jumped out of the white microbus. The ambulance was immediately surrounded and engulfed by the crowd.

"They're taking away your princess . . . ."

"Shut up!" ordered Igor, trembling. "Shut up about her!"

"Anyway, I know your license number without looking: 73-72," bragged the man.

"Why didn't you tell the officer right off?" asked Igor, interrupting him.

The man chewed his lips in a disgusting fashion and took his time before answering. The bastard, thought Igor. He looked again at the man's face: no doubt about it—a real bastard!

"What do you want?"

The man placed his thumb and two fingers together as if he was about to cross himself, but instead he rubbed them together expressively. Shaking with anger, Igor took out his wallet, opened it awkwardly, and handed the man five crisp, red five-ruble notes which he always carried with him.

"Here," he said in a squeamish tone of voice. "That's all I've got."
The bills crackled crisply and disappeared.

"Well, how about that watch of yours . . ."
Igor took his gold-plated *Polyot* off his wrist, gave it to him, and moved towards his car without a word. The man followed him.

"Maybe you've got something else ahn-ter-esting?" His eyes swept over the car seats. What a despicable type, thought Igor. In the distance a flashbulb gleamed, again, and once again. The police photographer was fixing Nadya to the black pavement. When had he arrived?

"They're taking a snapshot for the family album." The man laughed.

Igor frowned. His predator hadn't the slightest inkling that this last thrust had hit him in his most vulnerable spot. The pain radiated through his body.

"One more word—and I'll kill you right here!" Igor promised in a choked voice.

"All right, all right . . ." said the man, "only . . ."

"What?"

"Just one more little thing . . . and I'll leave."

"What kind of a *little thing?*"

"That raincoat of yours. That's a real nice coat."

Igor hesitated for a second and then decisively ripped off the cream-colored raincoat and hurled it right into the man's face. He seized the coat with both hands and taking a short step back, began to try it on right there.

"Of course, it is a bit large . . . but not bad, not bad," he muttered as he fastened the buttons. "It's a bit embarrassing to be seen carrying it off . . ."

The ambulance moved away from the crowd smoothly and soundlessly. Only after it picked up speed did it let out a piercing, spasmodic wail that could be heard throughout the whole city. The policemen chased people away from the thoroughfare, but were not letting cars pass. They were measuring the skid marks; they were going to nail the taxi driver. Impatient drivers flashed on their high-beams from time to time and annoyingly sounded their horns in order to hurry the police; tragedy or no, everyone was impatient to get home. It was late.

The little man was taking his time in leaving. It was not clear whether he wanted to add a new item to his loot or had something else in mind. Igor gazed at him.

"What are you waiting for?"

"Oh what a rotten life!" The unhappy predator sighed as he rummaged through the empty outside pockets of the voluminous coat. He had a distracted look on his face. Basically, he had no notion of what had really happened. He was lost in various surmisings and just wanted to know the facts! This is not surprising in the slightest; on the contrary, this torturing desire for clarity is a national characteristic, a distinctive sign by which one can spot a Russian just as easily as one can spot a pureblooded Frenchman by his difficulty with the letter 'r.' This is the source of our well-known love for sorting out the most complicatedly intimate relationships with anyone under the sun: with our wives, with the regime, with the people, with Europe, with the Gulfstream current, with American jazz, with the classics of Russian literature, and, of course, with the Republic of Chad. Certain of these conflict resolutions can stretch out over entire historical periods, from one Ice Age to another, so the modest desires of Igor's assailant deserve our indulgence.

"Just how did you shove her under that taxi?" He tossed out his line with a neatly baited hook. What simplicity!

"You . . . you . . . you . . ." Igor began to roll his eyes. He was at a loss for words and hurled himself at his tormentor. The latter tried to jump to the side, but became entangled in the folds of the coat and fell to the pavement. His hat flew off his head.

"I'll holler!" warned the man in a frightened voice, and then reminded him:

"I'm hard to get rid of!"

Anger and disgust made Igor hesitate as he cautiously nudged the man with the blunt tip of his shoe, as if testing his existence. Then, taking careful aim, he kicked him hard in the side.

"Owww!" cried the man.

The departing onlookers stopped and turned around to look back at them. There was a chance that some of them might come closer.

"What scum . . ." Igor rasped out as he moved away from the blackmailer.

The man jumped to his feet, picked up his hat, looked around and ran toward the highway.

He disappeared into the darkness as if he had never been.

All strength left Igor as he flopped down onto the seat of the car and slammed the door. It was quiet . . .

A faint aroma of perfume filled the car.

In an instant the scent helped to conjure a chain of apparitions: the dead Nadya with her twisted jaw; the enraged black form of the cab driver; the officer's hat; the constantly muttering crowd; the forest of legs; the energetic biologist bending over *her* in order to close her eyes. . . . And over it all hovered the triumphant sweet smell of the Parisian perfume whose disappearance was yet to bring on an encounter with the gloomy and suspicious Tanya behind whom there arose the expanding and wrathful autocratic chins of his father-in-law. The entire car was filled with the smell of perfume. He brought his hands to his face: they reeked of perfume and so did his jacket and the seat where she had been sitting. The smell was so insufferable, so repulsive and irremoveable that with full charity he unexpectedly realized that the tormentor whom he "couldn't get rid of" was merely a timorous and shabby incarnation of that smell in human form! And what is more, it was such a pitiful incarnation that one could die laughing at it. He had already begun to shake with silent laughter when he saw before him Nadya's laughing face, sweet, smooth-skinned, forever dear, calling him to the South, to Bakchisarai, and inviting him to silly half-salted kisses. . . . He dropped his head to the wheel and burst into hollow, broken sobs. "Nadya, my joy . . ." he muttered, his lips twisted in pain.

"I'm immortal," she whispered in his ear.

Poems*
by Yuri Kublanovsky

Octaves

For Pavel

Black branches. Plaza.
Snow storm swirling like a martin.
Dressed up like a clown,
a Russian bear with a little braid.
Like a shadow, coming through on inspection,
The Great Peter whispers
the Prussian rulebook:
"You're a cuckold, Pavel!"

The glove is bare.
Stumps and branches stab.
Dead is the unwife.
The swan has fallen asleep in the gazebo.
In Gatchina, every bush
has been bloodied by the October wind.
A plaintive cackle is heard:
"You're a cuckold, Pavel!"

Louis and Novikov
suffered from colds.
How the smell of the night pot
saturated the alcove!
It would seem an executioner
had stretched his mitt through the window vent.
In the cuckold's bedroom
a wardrobe door squeaked.

Diamond dust covers the pits
next to the Escorial.

*Translated by H. William Tjalsma.

Pahlen and Prince Iashvil
hide their faces beneath their cloaks.
From impatient hands
they draw off kidskin sour cream:
Lead us, hajduk!*
Why should you butter up the tyrant?

"The Gatchina swan is asleep
like Friedrich before the battle.
It dreams that I have been killed.
In purple with red lining
before the Almighty, I was able,
falling on one knee,
to cry out that I am two-horned!
And in the palace there is betrayal!"

. . . I recall that park and pond
in 1970.
I myself was rich as Brutus,
with dreams about freedom.
The whole monolith, in one voice,
where we raised our goblets
so as to choke later.
And there's nothing terrifying.

7/11/77

January 31
(around the stores at a trot . . .)

. . . Champagne in dark labels
for meetings luxurious and secluded,
chocolate familiar since childhood
with Pushkin, as to a brother, reading
Gavriiliada aloud to his nanny,
him draped in a dressing gown. . . .
Or "Arabic" fragrant
under a skin of golden foam
to send the heart into ecstasy,
when a spotted dragon in the corner
grins at you from the porcelain. . . .
That's nothing!
        Baltic herring,
frosty, moderately priced vodka;
let's extend the list of losses:

---

*Hungarian (cattle) driver. Also, a nineteenth-century partisan fighter.

joints,
smoked items
and loins

—we remember it ALL.
                        Why did it disappear?

Where to now?

Portrait

Devil's incense, tobacco everywhere.
Aida's eye, like a chick in the nest,
gazes through the walls into an otherworldly realm.
The *caravanserai* of Moscow is repellant.

Hook-nosed profile. The decrepit ram
of my Russian is of one blood.
Not for nothing did the lasso pull tight around the throat.
The bottle is full, the glass empty.

(Who knew that there was Zion in Streslnevo?
But an open-handed centurion
from the legion of ruddy scum
watches the pothouse coffer from the threshhold.)

A propeller has buzzed in the brain for a long time.
After, in the kitchen, to jerk open the window
and slam—
                        from the fifth floor.
What visa?
                        Fly, soul!

Sonnet

In the sealed window, it's silvery grey,
then scarlet and, finally, night.
I feel old, that I have on my face
the vinegar of the past. I press my brow
to the cold glass. . . . A moment of fear passed.
In the icy silence, a little bird pecked at the feeder.

. . . Leaning over you, I almost forgot
the one who shared you before me and I did not
take away into darkness, prisoners in a train.
Moscovite cashmere in Kustodiev* roses

*The painter.

and the paisley of a beloved scarf
around a young face, as you hurry home from skating,

and a snowy branch and a dove-colored stone
from the days when no one at all had ever touched you.

For I.

The schism of our love is both tender and severe—
    emerald fire
With each new winter burning once more
    both the eyes and the palm
How the snow storms resemble tea bush green!
Marvelous is the creaking of the road.
And the strolls in the black garden in April,
    and staying over with strangers.

Thus passes the round of days in leap year:
    happiness, poverty, sorrow . . .
With a mass of people in the granite subways,
Moscovites do not see the traces of poor harvest.
They aren't sorry for anyone.
                    10 February

* * *

. . . Not Novgorod the Merchant, no the ancient Warrior Pskov
was chosen by us for pilgrimage,
even though the Kremlin's new whatsit grew to the clouds,
    for it is fattened on skeletons,
not a tamped clay road, not turreted Izborsk
    with its drunken and thickset people—

but a moonlit morning that looks like wax
    and is soft as mead.

The moon and the lake, a pine and a moth
of dove-colored hue in the ether's blue—
where the voluptuous Wolf lay down meekly under a cross . . .

And Sviatogorsk hill gives repose to the Lambs of the World.

Peredelkino

Cocks or crosses
on the onion domes? Ravine and valleys.

The juvenile verse of Boris.*
The merged tops of three pines,
Floret, scaly bark, and resin.

(To think that ten years back
everything was finished. However,
we still didn't know what was happening
and we walked along, chatting about the eye shadow
of the thunderstorm and free-thinkers.)

A piece of ground where the Setun River is about
        as wide as a thread,
where our old jackals
know how to bury the dead.
Where the muzhiks cannot not drink,
Their women, not turn railroad ties.

* * *

The moon is pale and Vrubel is jealous.
The maestro has the ways of an outcast.
And while his canvas holds still
the lilac bush knows no rest.

Silence. Only an amber firefly
darts out from a corner.
Someone, covering up against the dew, has pulled
his jacket over his head.
Then too, the white gravel scrapes
underfoot in the classic style.
And the lilac starts to boil
like glaze in a decadent crucible.

Come close. This is spring.
This is the sacrifice of the lamb of Tula.
This is the treasury of the Russian kingdom.
Our heart and our desire.

*Boris Pasternak.

The Four Temperaments*
A Comedy in Ten Tableaux
by Vasily Aksyonov

From the author: Among my other homeless works, The
Four Temperaments *is perhaps the most homeless. Tender
feelings nurtured for eleven years have induced me to drag
this piece under the roof of* Metropol.

PERSONS IN THE PLAY:

Chol Erik	Third Lady
Sang Vinik	Fourth Lady
Phleg Matik	Love Triangle
Melan Cholik	Katyusha
Razrailov	Emelya
Cyber	Gutik
Eagle	Stage Manager
Nina	Uncle Vitya
First Lady	Fefelov
Second Lady	

*The action takes place first in the distant future, then outside of space
and time, and finally in the present.*

I

*(Chol Erik moves in a frenzy before a white screen. He is dressed in
black. He wears dark glasses. He keeps stopping to face the audience,
rocks back and forth, raises his arm, as if trying to shield himself from
the blinding lights.)*

*Translated by Boris Jakim.

CHOL ERIK:	Nine days this sun sets,
	All is in blood, all is dead . . .
	What dull bloodletting!
	It's time to go to hell!
	And the waves, the waves!
	Admire, brothers, this dumb flock of lambs,
	These crested idiots that roll
	To the foot of stone idols,
	To concrete towers the color of bile!
	And the helicopters that hang over the marketplace,
	Gloomier than beetles in compost—Oh, how disgusting!
	No, it's enough! It's time to leave!
	But my departure has nothing to do with
	Fame, faded honor, or betrayal.
	Rather, it's this color, this glum light,
	These colors which would make me howl, brothers,
	If that were fitting for a
	Champion of forehead blows.
	But who remembers? No, it has nothing to do with this,
	With memory . . . Well, it's time! Farewell!
	I've had it!

(*He looks down on the waves that roll beneath the bridge, raises his arms in a mute violent curse, and extends one leg over the bridge railing. Razrailov appears.*)

RAZRAILOV:	At least take off your glasses!
CHOL ERIK:	What the devil! Who is it that
	Prevents me from dropping into Charon's ferry?
	Have you forgotten who I am? Well, I can remind you.
RAZRAILOV:	What for? You're the master of forehead blows.
CHOL ERIK:	I'm remembered! Not everyone has forgotten.
	All the same, I don't have time to listen to you.
	And cut the bull about my glasses!
RAZRAILOV:	Listen, we remember your outbursts,
	The fact that you liked to rip off masks.
	(*He giggles aside.*)
	Our generation, believe me, has
	Retained its memory.

CHOL ERIK: That's not the point!
              What do I care about memory when this damn
                  city
              Is painted in such vile colors!
RAZRAILOV: Take off your glasses! Things are not that bleak.
              Make the effort, take the risk!
CHOL ERIK: (Takes off his glasses.)
              Why, you know,
              It's a little better, a mite more calm.
              Everything looks a bit less like a slaughter-
                  house . . .
RAZRAILOV: (Grabs him by the arm.)
              Are you ready to serve the Experiment?
              In the name of the positive program?
              In the name of your former ideals?
              In the name of the masses?
              (He grabs the glasses.)
CHOL ERIK: But I don't understand!

(The white screen fades. A yellow screen is lit up, on the background of
which, his arms dangling, stands Phleg Matik, dressed all in yellow.)

PHLEG MATIK: Mama didn't return . . . and where's kitty?
              The bouillon is spoiled and I will hang myself,
                  maybe . . .
              Or maybe tonight I'll read a book
              As they used to do in the good old nineteenth
                  century.
              (He doesn't move.)
              Maybe I won't find this book,
              Just as I won't find my papa who has gone
                  away . . .
              Well, in that case I'll just keep looking out the
                  window
              At the acid gray monument across the way,
              At the "We'll improve your mood" club,
              A den of liars and con artists.
              (Makes an indecisive sniffing noise with his nose.)
              No, it would be better for me to hang myself.
              Let me soap a good strong rope
              As they used to soap ropes in the good old days
              Of the twentieth, twenty first, and twenty third
                  centuries,

Which were so tranquil. . . . Take, care,
guys . . .

(Razrailov appears.)

RAZRAILOV: Stop!
I beseech you to stop your
Inexorable advance towards the noose!
Believe me, friend, the bouillon would smell
    terrific
If you would only add some hair restorer.
Your kitten long ago became
An aromatic bar of soap
With which a lovely girl laves her breasts,
And your sweet-smelling mama, my friend,
Will be replaced by the scientific experiment.
Stop!

PHLEG MATIK: I've long since stopped because of your
    command.

RAZRAILOV: Put on these glasses! The world will be
    transformed
And the acid gray monument across the way
Will show you the splendor of the age!
(Puts the glasses on Phleg Matik.)

PHLEG MATIK: Why, it's true.
(Takes a good look.)
The heavy idol has suddenly taken on a silver
    tint.
And that squiggle in the marvelous sky
Reminds me of my kitty's tail . . .

RAZRAILOV: Well, then, let's go!

(The yellow screen fades. A violet screen is lit up, on the background of which Melan Cholik, dressed all in green, wanders back and forth, wringing his hands. He's wearing glasses.)

MELAN CHOLIK: The day fades in the orangery,
The cutlets simmer in the pan . . .
My TV set fades,
The set I inherited from the faded ages,
Witnesses of history that has faded . . .
And here the works of youth fade
And mature matrons fade
And the Institute of Rejuvenation fades
And the fading grass fades . . .

And the sun fades and in myriads of
Faded years the Galaxy fades away . . .
Those who are fading inexorably move
From the beginning to the end of their sentence.
Only my anguish doesn't fade
And now I must cut it short
By taking the poison of the terrible fugu fish
Against a background of ash gray flowers.
(*He makes several movements that imply the
coming of the end.*)

RAZRAILOV: Does it not appear to you that in this fading
Are concealed the seeds of renaissance?
That man's creative forces will . . .

MELAN CHOLIK: Excuse me, what do you have on your head?

RAZRAILOV: Why, on my head I have a cap.
A wonderful cap of the lastest fashion.

MELAN CHOLIK: Yes, yes, I see. But beneath the cap?

RAZRAILOV: My hair.

MELAN CHOLIK: Yes, I see.
But beneath the hair?

RAZRAILOV: Beneath the hair is skin.
My own skin.

MELAN CHOLIK: Yes, yes. Skin. But beneath the skin?

RAZRAILOV: Beneath my skin is my skull.

MELAN CHOLIK: Skull! Skull! O God, God, God!
(*His legs begin to buckle.*)

RAZRAILOV: (*Raising Melan Cholik.*)
Aren't you ashamed! I see you're disturbed
By the most minor of problems, by the
contemptible danse macabre!
And this in our age, on the threshold
Of important, revolutionary events.
How primitive! This is no way to be!
Take off your glasses! More optimism!
Let's go forward on the path of the Experiment!

MELAN CHOLIK: (*Screws up his eyes, without his glasses.*)
Yes, yes. Forward. But I don't understand . . .

(*The violet screen fades. A red screen is lit up, on the background of
which, busily rubbing his hands, Sang Vinik, dressed all in white,
walks back and forth.*)

SANG VINIK: And so, my mood is again marvelous!
For how many years have I drunk my fill of life.

And apprehended with my every cell
The reason of the world and the importance of
    being.
My stomach is in harmony with my digestion
And I love cherry preserves,
And my heart is moved by love
And chases the blood through the vessels as
    always.
I alternate rest and work,
Love and sport, kefir and the joy
Of alcoholic drinks. I press buttons,
Pluck flowers, inhale their aroma,
Sing in a choir, eat regularly . . .
I'm pleased by all, calm and cordial,
The life of the party, the joy of preference.
So let me with one decisive stroke
Put an end to ugliness once and for all.
(*Takes a pistol from his pocket and presses it to his
    forehead.*)
For if I can understand the reason
For all that exists in the world, then why
Can't I understand the reason of this bullet
Which has waited so long
For me to press the trigger?

(*Razrailov appears.*)

RAZRAILOV:	(*Aside.*)
	I fear that this is the most difficult case.
	Red-cheeked, healthy, handsome, and
	sanguine:
	A real suicidal nut.
	(*To Sang Vinik.*)
	Listen, my good friend, do you have time?
SANG VINIK:	Forgive me, whom do I have the honor—
RAZRAILOV:	I am Razrailov.
	I would like to warn you against
	Opinions that are too optimistically vulgar.
	I swear to you that the world is far more
	interesting
	Than it appears to you,
	And that beneath the outer veil
	There is concealed something that—
SANG VINIK:	Cut the bull!

RAZRAILOV:	For example, what do you have on your head?
SANG VINIK:	Well, a cap.
	Let us say, a cap of the latest fashion.
RAZRAILOV:	Yes, yes, I see. But beneath the cap?
SANG VINIK:	Beneath the cap is my hair.
RAZRAILOV:	Yes, I see.
	And beneath the hair?
SANG VINIK:	Skin. My very own skin.
RAZRAILOV:	Yes, yes. Skin. And beneath the skin?
SANG VINIK:	Beneath the skin is my skull.
RAZRAILOV:	Well, you see! A skull! Skull! Skull!
SANG VINIK:	Wow, how interesting! How horrible!
	A little terrifying! A skull! Wow!
	Let me confess, old boy, that I never
	Considered things in this light . . .
RAZRAILOV:	Put on these glasses!
	(*Hands him the glasses.*)
	The world will be transformed
	And you'll see tragedy everywhere
	And you'll find things are more interesting
	And entertaining . . .
SANG VINIK:	(*Wearing the glasses.*)
	You're right.
	I see pain and trepidation and alarm . . .
	I must live! To fight for optimism!
RAZRAILOV:	(*Heatedly.*)
	All this is so and I propose
	That you head the vanguard with a few chosen.
	That you go forward on the path of the
	Experiment!
	Do you agree?
SANG VINIK:	(*Passionately.*)
	A wonderful idea!

(*All the lights fade.*)

II

(*The stage is lit from within. It's empty. All kinds of mechanical gadgets are visible: pulleys, winches and wheels . . . Several workmen appear. In view of the audience they begin to assemble the set, talking loudly all the while.*)

UNCLE VITYA, an elderly workman: Where are you taking that dolly, Emelya? If the Eagle hits it, he'll be killed.

EMELYA, a young workman: But where should I take it?

UNCLE VITYA: Take it to the left.

EMELYA: I'm not experienced enough, Uncle Vitya. This is something they didn't teach us in the Philosophy Department.

GUTIK, a middle-aged workman: What's going on, Uncle Vitya? It turns out they've approved the Eagle's role? It turns out they don't give a damn about the union?

UNCLE VITYA: Well, that's exactly right. They've approved it. To be precise, three days ago, on Tuesday, Serchanov and I were hanging around the prop room after work, and the boss got a call. They had approved it.

KATYUSHA, a girl worker: How I pity Evgeny Aleksandrovich!

EMELYA: Forgive me, Katyusha. Why is it you pity him so? A hearty old man, full of zest . .

UNCLE VITYA: Yesterday, Thursday that is, he tells me, "This it seems is my final role, Uncle Vitya" . . .

KATYUSHA: I pity Evgeny Aleksandrovich so much! For some reason he's very dear to me, very appealing! And who needs this Eagle's role?

GUTIK: This is something we'll air before the Local Committee. Put it down, Emelya. Bring it back , , move it to the side!

EMELYA: How will we fasten the backdrop, Uncle Vitya? The Eagle's role in the show is both immanent and transcendent. Nobody can handle it better than Evgeny Aleksandrovich.

UNCLE VITYA: You should blabber a bit less, philosopher! You've been on the stage a week and already you're an expert on roles. Hold the rope steady and don't move.

(The stage manager, a woman, enters.)

STAGE MANAGER: Uncle Vitya. I have a terrible problem. How will I fasten the backdrop?

UNCLE VITYA: You have to fasten it with zhgentel bolts, Alisia Ivanovna, with triple brackets and with mulerons.

STAGE MANAGER: But where can we get all this stuff, Uncle Vitya? We don't even have plain bolts.

UNCLE VITYA: That's your business, Alisia Ivanovna. I no longer have the strength to wine and dine Fefelov. Fefelov's tastes are not simple. He likes fine Mukusani wine with his cigar, cognac with his coffee, and some little gift at the end of the dinner . . . some little this or that. . . . But I've exhausted my financial possibilities.

STAGE MANAGER: Maybe we can get by with things the way they are.

UNCLE VITYA: Maybe so. I'm only afraid that in the third act the whole thing is going to fall apart and then we'll have some real fun.

STAGE MANAGER: O, horrors!

UNCLE VITYA: Here, tell Gutik, if he can get some dough from the Local Committee, I'll try to squeeze three or four cans of mulerons out of Fefelov.

GUTIK: The Local Committee won't fall for any of your tricks.

UNCLE VITYA: That's how it is. Well, let's knock off, fellows!

(Having taken hammers, pincers, and the rest of their things, the workmen leave the stage. The last to leave is the Stage Manager, Alisia Ivanovna. While already in the wings she looks doubtfully and anxiously at the decorations.)

III

(A room sparkling white and saturated with a blue glow. It resembles a laboratory in a science-fiction novel. A huge window behind which is empty bluish space. Four rotating armchairs with soft elbow-rests. Over each of the chairs is a screen in a strange shape. Near one of the walls stands an improbably complex cybernetic device with a multitude of buttons, controls, Etc.

Enter Sang Vinik, Melan Cholik, Chol Erik, and Phleg Matik. They stop in center stage and look about, puzzled. Behind them enters Razrailov, who is breathing with difficulty. He coughs and spits out the window.)

RAZRAILOV: *(Aside)*. What a damned mess! If it weren't for the Experiment, I would never have gotten involved. And with a gang of suicides. *(Arranges his tie and quickly combs his hair.)* And so friends, our long ascent is completed. We are in the holy of holies, at the source of the Great Experiment. Here, precisely here, will arise the future of mankind with its unlimited possibilities, and here we, the pioneers of modern science—

CHOL ERIK: Cut the bull! We demand that you explain to us the nature of the experiment. Do you think we've spent so many days climbing the stairs to hear typical demagoguery?

PHLEG MATIK: The main thing is that we've made it. Where's the toilet, citizens?

MELAN CHOLIK: *(Looking downward, into the window.)* O God, I can't see the ground!

SANG VINIK: This is all great, but where are we, Razrailov?

RAZRAILOV: (*His feelings are hurt.*) You've interrupted me. You haven't let me develop my thought. This undisciplined citizen here—

CHOL ERIK: Express yourself more precisely. We've had it up to here with pretty speeches!

RAZRAILOV: (*Screams.*) Don't yell at your saviour! If it weren't for me you'd be bobbing up and down like a log in the Gultimoor canal! Citizens, I ask you to observe the one-leader principle even under the conditions of the Great Experiment. Don't forget I'm your director and saviour. And so, I ask you to sit down in these chairs, which will be your work places. (*He seats his collaborators.*) Wonderful! Now, citizens of the future mankind, the hope of all six continents, I will explain to you your great mission.

CHOL ERIK: More demagoguery?

RAZRAILOV: I'll exclude you if you keep on interrupting! Friends, in the course of the hundreds of centuries of the existence of civilization the earth has sucked up into itself the vicious ideas, temptations, thoughts and dreams of thousands of generations. Therefore, despite colossal technological achievement, true progress is impossible and I, Razrailov, devoted defender of progress in all epochs, you must know from literature there lives in me with his flaming eyes the angel of death Azrael . . . this is metaphor, of course, a hint at the laser . . . pardon me for the digression. A colossal break is occurring between the progress of cybernetic machines and the stagnation or maybe even the regression, alas, of mankind. Citizens, here's my idea, supported and financed by the Academy of Long-Short-Life and also by United-Kvas-Limited. A tower has been constructed on the apex of which we now find ourselves. It is of a height which we may call significant. I ask you to pay attention to this object. (*From his pocket he takes a marble and tosses it out the window.*) Now again pay attention to me. At this height you, the participants in the Experiment, will no longer be affected by the miasmas of earth; and, secondly, the influence of height, generated by the most novel stimulator, which I will command from my control room, will augment your mental capacities and creative forces to a colossal degree. And you will be able to control in turn the complex cyber. Thus, the circuit will be closed, the main problem of the future will be solved. A new era! Dawn! A rainbow! Elevated individuums, cyber-people . . . *(He continues to speak but no sound comes from him. He gesticulates, dances . . .)*

SANG VINIK: What's with him?

CHOL ERIK: Forgive me, I can't bear such pathetic scenes. I switched him off. I pressed a button I found under the table and he was switched off.

PHLEG MATIK: The height. . . it's understandable . . . has an effect.

MELAN CHOLIK: How terrifying it is—a man without sound! They say that in ancient times there was a sort of cinema that—

SANG VINIK: Yes, yes, old buddy, just imagine—now this is grand! Not long ago I read that in the past there were films even without odor and without flesh.

CHOL ERIK: But think of the people who lived then! Giants!

PHLEG MATIK: They say that in those days in the movies you couldn't even feel up your favorite starlet.

SANG VINIK: Friends, I propose that we become acquainted. My name is Sang Vinik. *(To Chol Erik.)* And you?

CHOL ERIK: You don't remember me? Take a good look! O, what a pitiful age! My name is Chol Erik. Well? No response?

MELAN CHOLIK: Don't tell me it's possible to be famous in our time? My name is Melan Cholik and even I'm not counting on anything.

PHLEG MATIK: My name is Phleg Matik. My papa is honoris causa of the university of the city of Bakov, but he disappeared somewhere, and my mama . . . citizens, where's the toilet?

SANG VINIK: Listen, old buddy, how did you get here?

CHOL ERIK: None of your business! I don't go prying into your soul.

SANG VINIK: Forgive me. I also prefer to keep my mouth shut. And you, Melan?

MELAN CHOLIK: What can I tell you? I'm a victim of the illusion known as reality. Razrailov appeared at the last moment.

PHLEG MATIK: But I can tell you my story. The thing is that mama disappeared and kitty got lost and the bouillon was spoiled and I . . .

SANG VINIK: Shut up, Phleg! I understand everything. Well, friends, since it's happened that we're up on the tower and our leader is switched off for the time being, let's play "chirishek-pupyrishek-bubo."

CHOL ERIK: A great idea! I like you, Sang!

MELAN CHOLIK: Alas, I've just about forgotten this forbidden game.

PHLEG MATIK: (*Suddenly aroused. Merrily.*) Mama and I used to play it all the time, with kitty as a third . . .

SANG VINIK: I'll begin. (*He shows Chol Erik his fingers curled into a ring.*) Chirishek!

CHOL ERIK: First class! Let me think. (*Thinks.*) Pupyrishek!

(*Shows Melan Cholik in succession: "ears," "nose," four fingers and a copper key.*)

MELAN CHOLIK: A complicated move. (*Thinks.*) Ah yes, I've found it. (*To Phleg Matik.*) At night burned entered Napoleon four chrysanthemums and a bouton (*Shows "horns."*)

PHLEG MATIK: Wow, what a move . . . (*Thinks. Then plugs his ears and whistles.*) Bubo! (*Suddenly weak. Says languidly.*) There, I've got you.

EVERYBODY: Bravo! A masterpiece! What a simple and powerful move! (*They applaud.*)

(*Razrailov, continuing his fiery soundless speech, also applauds.*)

SANG VINIK: And so, you have twenty seven points, you have eleven, you have eighteen and I have fourteen. You begin, Phleg, your serve.

(*From below one hears a muffled explosion. Everyone jumps up.*)

CHOL ERIK: It's begun. To arms!

SANG VINIK: (*Runs to the window. Looks down.*) Below there's a rosy cloud that looks like a peony. How about that!

MELAN CHOLIK: O horrors! A fading peony!

PHLEG MATIK: That thing has hit the earth.

(*They all look down, then turn away from the window.*)

RAZRAILOV: . . . without compromises and condescension! The rainbow above our heads! Forward, cyber-people! (*Combs his hair, smiles impudently, straightens his tie.*) Well my friends, have you rested? Don't think, Chol, that I'm in your hands. Rather it's you who are in mine. And now let's get to work. To your places! We are born to turn fable into reality!

(*The collaborators silently take their places in the armchairs. Razrailov walks up to each of them in turn, squeezes their hands, intimately whispers to each "congratulations," and then leaves the stage with the measured stride of an officer. The Temperaments sit silently, looking straight ahead. Above them screens begin to fluoresce. A quiet but monstrous music begins to play.*)

CHOL ERIK: *In an altered, metallic voice.*) Problem number one: From reservoir A into reservoir B there is a daily inflow of 400 cubic meters of water and 300 cubic meters of wine. From reservoir C there is no inflow. The problem is to calculate the number of young sturgeon in the ground reservoirs of Antarctica. I am switching on Cyber.

(With a sharp sudden whirr Cyber is switched on and lit up.)

CYBER: Hello, fellows! Congratulations on the beginning of the Experiment. The transmission is concluded.

PHLEG MATIK: I begin. It is necessary to establish the legitimate requirements of every contemporary man with regard to young sturgeon of the ground reservoirs.

MELAN CHOLIK: I continue. According to the chromosome theory of Bonch-Marienhof, by changing the cell expresses an absolutely small number, vanishing into a protoplasm of nose type. Let us discard this. From this follows: eson, seon, neso, a trapezoid with a fire within.

CYBER: A small correction. Logos. The transmission is concluded.

SANG VINIK: The result: An infinitely small number, vanishing into nose, taking into account the needs of Lester Bot at night after drinking, hemoglobin 90—young sturgeon zero minus one. The end.

CYBER: What bright men you are. The transmission is concluded.

(Behind the window in the blue emptiness slowly flies some heavy body. It appears for a moment that someone is looking into the laboratory. All the collaborators turn around and look out the window.)

CYBER: That's Eagle. He always flies here. Don't pay attention. The transmission is concluded.

PHLEG MATIK: Problem number two. How many devils and foxes can simultaneously fit on the top of a pin?

(Suddenly the right corner of the set falls to the side. The Temperaments turn sharply and look in that direction. Katyusha is standing there. With her head raised, she is looking toward the back of the stage. Next to her is Emelya.)

EMELYA: Katyusha, I wanted to be sure about tomorrow. Don't forget, I get paid—

KATYUSHA: Wait, Emelya. Look! He's coming down!

(Uncle Vitya runs out.)

UNCLE VITYA: (*In a whistling whisper.*) You idiots, don't you see that the side of the set has fallen down!

(*Gutik runs out.*)

GUTIK: (*Merrily.*) We'll make a note of this. A violation of working discipline!

(*A hunched figure passes by, wrapped in a robe from which stick dark brown feathers. A very strange figure.*)

STAGE MANAGER: (*Peering out from the wings.*) Horrors, horrors, horrors.

(*The workers repair the set and disappear behind it.*)

VOICE OF UNCLE VITYA: Okay, ready!

SANG VINIK: (*In a metallic voice.*) It is universally known that not one fox can mature and succeed without a struggle of opinions, without freedom to criticize . . .

IV

(*Razrailov's control room strangely contradicts the science-fiction setting of the laboratory. Like a second-hand shop it is full of antique furniture of different styles from the eighteenth and nineteenth centuries. Heavy dusty curtains conceal the windows. In the corner is a small bar in colonial style. On a stand is a gramophone with an enormous horn. Next to it is a cello. In folds of velvet is hidden a piano. There is an easel and a platform with an unfinished copy of the sculpture, The Thinker. From the ceiling hang intricate chandeliers of different styles. And only a small elegant screen—Cyber's display, surrounded by pots of geraniums—serves to remind one of the Great Experiment. The gramophone sings: "Our dreamy garden has wilted, the leaves have fallen, I hear your sorrowful voice far away, but it is only a mirage, you died long ago and it is only the damp breath of autumn I hear."*

Razrailov dressed in a long velvet robe, wearing a fez, and carrying a curved pipe slides languidly around the room keeping time with the music.)

RAZRAILOV: (*Gets down on one knee, peeks out of an opening in the door.*) They're working feverishly, doing calculations. Whatever you say, they're good people! It's really in vain that we sometimes criticize them excessively and beat on their heads. That Chol Erik. On the surface, he's impatient. Your first desire is to liquidate him, but, if you check yourself, you see that the individuum is working, and how he's working! This is what it means to give them a good kick in the behind before it's too late. (*He continues to slide about the room, stops for a second, completes Rodin's* The Thinker, *sits down at the easel, and in inspired fashion applies a few brushstrokes: he turns the painting so that it faces the audience—Shishkin's* Windfall *completely finished. He rushes to the piano, ruffles his curls and sings: "In the lonely hours of night, fatigued, I like to lie down." He writes down some music; plays the first bars of "Chizhik" on the cello; paces about the room with his hand stuck in his hair; moos like a cow, then proclaims: "We are born to turn fable into reality, to overcome the distances" and with a joyous yelp rushes to the table to write down what he has just composed.*)

CYBER: The calculations are completed. I report the results. The fox has a fluffy tail that glistens like needles, whereas the devil is cross-eyed. The transmission is concluded.

RAZRAILOV: Astounding! (*Picks up a crystal wine glass. Pours some burgundy.*) Problem number three. Melan Cholik begins. You have twenty-five apples in your pocket. Your friend has eighteen. You give your friend twenty-five apples, he gives you eighteen. Does man need song the way a bird needs wings for flight? (*Empties the wine glass.*)

(*A heavy shadow passes by the window. It seems that someone is looking in the window.*)

RAZRAILOV: (*Runs up to the window, hangs out, yells scandalously.*) Again you're interfering? I'm going to complain. I hope you break your neck at your war! This is ridiculous! This Eagle is always interfering with the Experiment! (*Switches on the gramophone, which sings: "Black rose, emblem of sorrow."*) What can I do? How can I occupy myself? Should I masturbate? (*He slaps himself on the forehead—an idea!*) I'll get a lady! (*He slides over to Cyber and presses some secret button.*)

(*The Lady appears in a Medieval robe ronde with a stiff collar; she moves in a mannered artificial way and curtsies; in a slender voice she sings the old romance, "Violetta graziosa." Also curtseying, Razrailov slides over to the Lady, takes her outstretched hand, ceremoniously kisses the tips of her fingers, leads her to a sumptuous bed beneath a canopy, fills a glass with wine, and gives it to her. The Lady drinks in a mannered way. Razrailov also drinks, then looks at the Lady. The Lady looks at him . . . he takes her by the waist.*)

RAZRAILOV: Well?

LADY: I am in your power, mon seigneur! (*Attempts to fall onto the bed but Razrailov restrains her.*)

RAZRAILOV: (*Mocks her.*) In your power! Mon seigneur! Don't you know how to behave, you idiot?

LADY: (*Crying.*) A little while ago when I did a striptease you were extremely polite.

RAZRAILOV: That was then, this is now. Put up resistance! Express dignified indignation, you bitch! Yell "rape." Yell "help, help!" (*Grabs the Lady.*)

LADY: Help, help! Caballeros! Rodrigos! Hildalgos! Let me go, you rapist! (*She resists and breaks out of his clutches.*)

RAZRAILOV: (*Chases her.*) That's the way! That's the way! Yell, you bitch!

LADY: You should be ashamed! This isn't worthy of you! Help, help!

RAZRAILOV: (*Grabs the Lady, topples her onto the bed, sticks into her mouth a bottle of vodka; drinks from it himself; screams.*) Oh, what a life! This is it! This is really it!

CYBER: Forgive me for this intrusion into your intimate world. We have received a query from the Academy of Long-Short-Life in conjunction with United-Kvas-Limited. Is the experiment running according to schedule? The transmission is concluded.

RAZRAILOV: The experiment is going according to plan and running ahead of schedule. The goal is reached! (*Laughs insanely. Paws / screws the weakly squealing Lady.*)

(*The left corner of the set falls away to the side. In the back of the stage is Katyusha, who—her hands pressed to her chest—is looking upward. Next to her is Emelya.*)

EMELYA: Katyusha, here are tickets for *The Sovremennik*. It was hell getting them. Believe me, I was stomped on.

KATYUSHA: Aren't you ashamed, Emelya? At such a moment! Look, he's coming down! Oh, Oh, Oh, God! He's come down!

(*Uncle Vitya, Gutik, and the Stage Manager run out.*)

UNCLE VITYA: (*In a whistling whisper.*) Are you insane, student? Don't you see one side of the set has fallen down?

STAGE MANAGER: They're having a romance during working hours!

GUTIK: (*Joyously.*) Let's make a note of a violation of safety procedure!

(*In the back of the stage there again quickly passes by a strange hunched figure in a robe, with feathers sticking out.*)

KATYUSHA: (*Rushes to the figure.*) Did you hurt yourself, Evgeny Aleksandrovich?

EMELYA: Be more discreet, Katyusha.

(*The figure disappears.*)

UNCLE VITYA: Pull up the side of the set you bastards! (*Turns the winch.*)

STAGE MANAGER: What can we do, Uncle Vitya?

GUTIK: It looks like a disaster.

UNCLE VITYA: It looks like we'll never finish the show without mulerons. Let me go to Fefelov and throw myself at his feet.

STAGE MANAGER: (*Takes off her ring.*) Give him this.

GUTIK: (*Wipes off tears.*) I knew you were like that, Alisia Ivanovna. (*He tries to kiss her hand.*)

STAGE MANAGER: (*Turning away.*) Don't, Gutik!

GUTIK: Don't think that I'm not like that, too. I entreat you, don't think ill of me. Here Uncle Vitya, please give him this. (*Gives him a ballpoint pen.*)

EMELYA: (*Grumbling.*) Well, all right. I'm not worse than any of you. Maybe this tie will be of use. (*Takes off his tie.*)

KATYUSHA: (*Passionately.*) I'll spare nothing for the sake of the safety procedure. (*Begins to undo the zipper on her dress.*)

UNCLE VITYA: You've lost your mind, girl! I'll tell your father!

(*They pull up the side of the set. The workers disappear.*)

RAZRAILOV: (*Testily.*) Can we continue? (*Throws himself on the Lady.*)

LADY: Caballeros! Rodrigos! Hidalgos!

CYBER: Once again I ask your forgiveness for this intrusion into your intimate world. A special announcement. The Experiment is halted for reasons I do not understand. The transmission is concluded.

V

(*The laboratory once again. The armchairs are empty. Chol Erik, waving his arms in a frenzy, rushes about the stage. Sang Vinik strolls about, rubbing his hands. Phleg Matik sits on the floor and picks his nose. Melan Cholik moves about the stage on buckling legs, wringing his hands as though he were a dying butterfly. Cyber is blinking, worriedly and chaotically.*)

CHOL ERIK: What dull, ungifted people! Another second and I'll destroy everything here with my famous forehead blow! Jellyfish! A pathetic generation! Let me affirm, listen: Song is sigma, the insane sigma of the waterpipe, the insane sigma of the waterpipe!

SANG VINIK: Cool down, friend Chol! Why yell, old boy, and wave your arms? It would be better if you admitted your mistakes. Facts are stubborn things, my friend, and song is the formula for the existence of amino acids plus hybridization of the whole earth. That's the way it is!

CHOL ERIK: (*Furiously.*) You're asking for it!

MELAN CHOLIK: O darkness! O night! How terrible to lose one's friends! How terrible to see the collapse of the Experiment! Friends, the last hope, the last trembling luminaire in the black velvet of the universal night,* the only true answer: song is a ribbon, a blue ribbon calling one beneath the couch into the spiderweb of illusions . . .

CHOL ERIK: I'll crush him like a fly!

PHLEG MATIK: Song is a doughnut.

CYBER: I entreat you to end the argument. The transmission is concluded.

CHOL ERIK: Sigma!

SANG VINIK: Amino acids!

MELAN CHOLIK: Ribbon!

PHLEG MATIK: Doughnut!

CYBER: Not so maniacally, please! The transmission is concluded.

(*The disorderly bellowing of Chol Erik, the self-confident joyous exclamations of Sang Vinik, the gloomy whines of Melan Cholik, the monotonous cries of Phleg Matik.*)

CYBER: I refuse to work in such an environment. The transmission is concluded. (*Turns off all the lights.*)

(*The Temperaments fall into embarrassed silence. For a while Chol Erik, Sang Vinik, and Melan Cholik circle about the stage and then gather around the seated Phleg Matik. Phleg uncertainly makes a loud sniffing noise, then smiles.*)

CHOL ERIK: (*Smiles and pokes Melan Cholik in the stomach.*) You can't deny, my friend, that your socialist savings are pretty solid.

MELAN CHOLIK: (*Smiles.*) Down below, I was a cook.

SANG VINIK: A cook? Where?

MELAN CHOLIK: In the Kaptenarnius restaurant.

CHOL ERIK: In that den of moneybags?

---

*A phrase from Mandelshtam's poem, "We'll meet again in Petersburg" [tr.].

PHLEG MATIK: Papa and mama used to take me there. We ate calf's
ears "au revoir" in cherry sauce "bonjour." That's impossible to forget.

MELAN CHOLIK: Imagine, calf's ears!

SANG VINIK: Good old Kaptenarmus! How many memories are connected with it! An evening wouldn't often go by without our
gathering there with writer friends. And there below I was a
poet, gentlemen, a poet, let me tell you. I remember I was
eating their Ostroga hash and the homme de lèttres Bigbin
Andreev walked up to me from behind, put his head in my
plate and also started to eat. What do you think of that?

MELAN CHOLIK: Wow, Ostroga hash! How many tears I shed over it.
Because, gentlemen, I have a chronic runny nose . . .

CHOL ERIK: The only reason for going to Kaptenarmus was the
broads. The broads there were all right, no doubt about that.
It was great to snatch a lovely lady from under the nose of
some bourgeois! I would sometimes enter wearing dark
glasses: nobody would recognize the champion of forehead
blows. But when I took off the glasses everybody would ooh
and aah!

SANG VINIK: Then, you Chol, are that very same Erik?

CHOL ERIK: Aha, you've finally guessed. Yes, I was *that* Erik, but I've
been unemployed now for a long time. Those pigs have
forgotten the forehead blow. All they know is the evasive
attack from the side. But what a time it was! Do you
remember the fracas on 42nd Street?

MELAN CHOLIK: How can one not remember it? I locked myself in the
toilet then . . .

PHLEG MATIK: (*Aroused.*) In the toilet?

MELAN CHOLIK: . . . and shed a sea of tears. It seemed to me that
civilization was dying and that never again would anyone go
back to the Kaptenarmus . . .

SANG VINIK: Yes, how well you broke eggs on 42nd Street in those
days, Chol! I remember. Yes, I remember. Yes, I remember
. . . I was always your theoretical opponent. I always
thought that one had to use a different maneuver, namely,
the evasive approach from the side. But I must give you what
you deserve: the sidewalk was entirely covered with yolks!
That was something!

CHOL ERIK: (*Jumps up, makes enormous absurd leaps, roars.*) I want to
go down. Down, into that demonic anthill! I can't live
without them! I haven't yet fought my last fight, cursed my

last curse, loved my last woman! I'll perish without them. (*Falls.*)

SANG VINIK: I also want to go down, gentlemen! I want to write a poem! What do you think of that? I'm hungry for a positive struggle for optimism. I'm hungry for evasive attacks from the side. That's what I want. (*Falls.*)

MELAN CHOLIK: And I want to eat, gentlemen. To cook and to eat. Gastronomy alone used to save me from philosophical pessimism. (*Falls.*)

PHLEG MATIK: And I want to go to the toilet. (*Collapses onto his side.*)

CYBER: I am forced to switch on. I would like to inform my co-workers that, in reality, they want nothing. That is the way they were programmed under the conditions of the Experiment. Is that not so? The transmission is concluded.

SANG VINIK: In reality I want nothing. Only to upset my theoretical opponent just a teensy bit.

CHÖL ERIK: I only want to see how the little bitch from Kaptenarmus twirls her skirt.

MELAN CHOLIK: I only want to blow my nose over my favorite Ostroga hash.

PHLEG MATIK: I only want to have a peek at my toilet bowl, at the little meditation corner with the magazine *Knowledge is Power.*

(*Razrailov enters.*)

RAZRAILOV: Ai-ai-Ai! So, you're sabotaging the Experiment? Aren't you ashamed?

(*The Temperaments lie silently on the floor. Razrailov gets down on all fours, creeps from one body to another, and whispers to each in an inspired way: "Get up, comrade. It's time. Forward! In the name of Progress! Face to face with the epoch!" But the Temperaments remain motionless. Razrailov gets up and presses some button in Cyber.*)

CYBER: (*Roars.*) Get up! The transmission is concluded.

(*The Temperaments leap up.*)

RAZRAILOV: And you're supposed to be citizens of the cyber-humanity of the future! Shame! You've short-circuited the Experiment, succumbed to the decadent influence of earthly miasmas, which—I am sure—the Eagle has brought on his wings. If you don't want to work . . . (*threateningly*) . . . we can return to the starting point.

SANG VINIK: (*In a changed, almost machinelike voice.*) We want to work for the Experiment and we will work for the Experiment, only we have certain requests we wish to make to the Management.

RAZRAILOV: Well, all right. What are the requests? Just don't get carried away!

MELAN CHOLIK: My request is a modest one! I only want a flower, some kind of plant.

RAZRAILOV: A plant? Be my guest! *(Presses a button.)*

(A rubber plant appears on the window sill.)

PHLEG MATIK: I want a kitty.

RAZRAILOV: Of course. *(Presses a button.)*

(On the window sill appears a crudely painted clay kitten with a cute but frightening face.)

CHOL ERIK: *(Makes a movement full of strain and torment, as though he were trying to free himself from something. Then says in a hollow voice.)* I want a kitten, too.

RAZRAILOV: *(Merrily.)* Of course, of course. *(Presses a button.)*

(On the window sill appears a second kitten, identical to the first.)

SANG VINIK: *(Also moves as though he were trying to free himself from something. Then in a hollow voice.)* I want a kitten, too!

RAZRAILOV: *(Roaring with laughter.)* As many as you like! The firm doesn't care about expenses. *(Presses a button.)*

(A third kitten appears on the window sill.)

MELAN CHOLIK: *(In a metallic voice.)* I don't want a plant. I want a kitten.

RAZRAILOV: Good boy! *(Presses a button.)*

(The plant disappears. In its place appears a fourth kitten.)

RAZRAILOV: Are you happy, boys? Do you have any other requests, personal claims?

ALL: *(In chorus.)* We're completely happy. We have no claims!

RAZRAILOV: And now to work.

(The Temperaments sit down in the armchairs.)

RAZRAILOV: And so, do people need song the way a bird needs wings for flight? Chol beings.

CHOL ERIK: Song is sigma, the insane sigma of the waterpipe.

SANG VINIK: I don't agree. Song is the form of existence of amino acids plus hybridization of the whole earth.

RAZRAILOV: You're repeating the same old stuff?

MELAN CHOLIK: Song is a blue ribbon that lures one beneath the couch into the spiderweb of illusions.

RAZRAILOV: Shut up!

PHLEG MATIK: Song is a doughnut.

(Again an argument flares up. The Temperaments break out of Cyber's control.)

RAZRAILOV: *(Confused. To Cyber.)* In your opinion, what's going on?

CYBER: I suppose a disharmony of temperaments. The transmission is concluded.

RAZRAILOV: Perhaps one can unify them?

CYBER: Impossible. A new modeling system would be required. The transmission is concluded.

RAZRAILOV: *(Reflects.)* A new system? Yes, yes . . .

(Someone looks into the window; a shadow passes by; one hears the rustle of wings. A stream of air knocks the four kittens from the window sill.)

THE TEMPERAMENTS: Oh! Oh! Where are our kittens!? It was a trick!

RAZRAILOV: *(Rushing about, busily. Scared.)* I assure you, the Management has nothing to do with it. It was the damned Eagle, that tin soldier and saboteur!

(The right corner of the set falls away to the side. In the back of the stage stands Katyusha, looking upward. Next to her is Emelya.)

EMELYA: Katyusha, it's becoming impossible. I think only of you, Honest, I've really fallen for you.

KATYUSHA: Oh, he lift the set, he's turned over. My God, is it the end? *(Hides her face in her hands.)*

EMELYA: What can happen to your damned Eagle? He's come down, the bastard!

(The Stage Manager and Gutik run out, in an embrace.)

STAGE MANAGER: A disaster! Where's Uncle Vitya?

GUTIK: Alisia Ivanovna, dearest, my most excellent person, Uncle Vitya has run off to Fefelov. I gave him a ruble from the members' dues for the taxi. All because of you!

(A hunched figure in a robe passes by.)

KATYUSHA: *(Rushes up to him.)* Evgeny Aleksandrovich, have you hurt yourself?

THE FIGURE: *(Irritably.)* Listen, young lady. I have a complicated role. It's tough work, I'm risking my life, losing my feathers and you keep making fun of me. *(Leaves.)*

(Katyusha runs away, sobbing.)

EMELYA: Thick-skinned bastard. He doesn't understand her.

STAGE MANAGER: Emelya, Gutik, save the show!

(*Workers pull up the fallen corner of the set.*)

PHLEG MATIK: (*Hiccups.*) The kittens have fallen.

MELAN CHOLIK: (*Crying.*) They'll be smashed to smithereens. A cruel
        fate . . .

CHOL ERIK: (*Waving his arms.*) Where are our beloved replicas? What
        you give with one hand, you take away with the other. We
        know this kind of tactic. I'll destroy everything!

SANG VINIK: Forgive me, Razrailov. We refuse to work under these
        conditions. That's the way it is, old boy. There can be no
        question of continuing the Experiment!

RAZRAILOV: (*His feelings are hurt.*) And where is your feeling of
        gratitude? What would have become of you, young people,
        if I hadn't appeared at the last moment before each of you?
        (*He screams and points at each of them.*) You would be
        bobbing up and down like a rotten log in the Gultimoor
        canal! You would be hanging like a sausage in your favorite
        closet! You would be rotting in the vegetable garden! You
        would be lying around with a hole in your head! I knew you
        were on your way to suicide. I had been keeping track of you
        for a long time. And I saved you. From the pathetic,
        reflective nebbishes that you were, I wanted to transform
        you into powerful cyber-individuums. I allowed you to
        participate in the Great Experiment! Where is your
        gratitude? Where? (*Threateningly.*) Perhaps you would like
        to return to the starting point?

(*The Temperaments look at him in confusion and are silent.*)

SANG VINIK: He's right. Without him we would all be kaput. In my
        own case . . . I remember a magnificent morning, my
        digestion was functioning admirably. I drank a glass of
        tea with cherry preserves and I made the decision to leave
        life . . .

(*One hears a rustle of approaching wings. On the window sill suddenly
alights the heavy, elderly Eagle, with the face of an old soldier.*)

EAGLE: Greetings, my dead friends!

(*Four muffled explosions are heard one after the other.*)

VI

(*A silent scene in the laboratory of the Great Experiment. The Temperaments, frozen in tense poses, look at the window. Razrailov stands with arm outstretched. The Eagle, with his elbows on the window sill, is smiling.)*

RAZRAILOV: Get out!

EAGLE: *(Climbs in, wearing high leather boots. Sits down on the sill, lights a cigar.)* I'm exhausted, friends. My strength's gone.

CHOL ERIK: *(In a hollow voice.)* Who are you?

EAGLE: I'm an eagle, brothers. Every day I fly past you to the war. I have a war, brothers.

CHOL ERIK: *(Takes a step towards the Eagle.)* Who is the war against, Eagle?

EAGLE: Against the accursed Steel Bird, brothers. It's not so difficult to understand. I'm a simple eagle made of flesh and bones and hot blood, and here I fight an endless war with this monster. To tell the truth, comrades, I'm sick to death, but I have to do it.

SANG VINIK: *(Takes a step towards the Eagle.)* But what are you fighting for, if I may ask?

EAGLE: *(In a thunderous voice.)* For ideals of justice!

RAZRAILOV: *(Hysterically.)* Well, go fly to your ridiculous war! Why are you hanging around here?

EAGLE: Take it easy, pappy. Don't give me grief. It's lunch time. The Steel Bird has also taken time out to fuel up with kerosene and in a minute I'm going to get something to eat at the Kaptenarmus *(To Melan Cholik.)* The food there has gotten worse since you died.

MELAN CHOLIK: What do you mean, since I died. Let me ask—

RAZRAILOV: I demand that you clear out! You're interfering with the Great Experiment!

EAGLE: *(Makes fun of him.)* Periment! Periment! Some two-bit angel of death you are! And all this is taking place under the very nose of the Head Office. It would be better if I didn't have eyes to see!

CHOL ERIK: *(Gets down on his knees.)* Eagle, take me with you to your war! I'm the master of forehead blows! I'll be useful.

SANG VINIK: *(Gets down on his knees.)* And take me too . . . into the staff. I know the theory of evasive maneuvers from the side . . . you won't regret it, I assure you, old boy . . .

MELAN CHOLIK: *(Gets down on his knees.)* Take me into the field kitchen . . .

PHLEG MATIK: *(Gets down on his knees.)* Take me into the supply train . . .

EAGLE: I can't, brothers! Everyone has his war. I have mine . . . and what would I do with your bodiless souls? (*Puts out his cigar on the heel of his boot.*) Well, forgive me for taking your time . . . (*To Razrailov.*) And as for you, less bull, you idiot. (*To the Temperaments.*) Goodbye, my dead friends! (*He flies off.*)

(*The Temperaments are on their knees, with their heads bent down.*)

RAZRAILOV: Don't pay attention, friends, to this old provocateur with his idiotic jokes. Raise your heads! The Great Experiment . . .

SANG VINIK: (*In a hollow voice.*) We're dead?

RAZRAILOV: Ha, ha, ha, what nonsense! Don't forget, I saved you. Don't forget, Chol. You had your leg over the bridge railing, and then I appeared and . . .

CHOL ERIK: It seems that I was falling, yes, I was falling. Then I felt the impact . . . (*Leaps up.*)

MELAN CHOLIK: And I remember too, friends. It seems that I had time to take the poison . . . the most potent of poisons from the liver of the fugu fish . . .

PHLEG MATIK: And it seems that I had time to get to the toilet . . .

SANG VINIK: I don't remember exactly but it seems that I felt an impact against my temple and only after did you appear, Razrailov. (*He gets up.*) Confess. Are we dead? We demand to know. After all, we have the right. Don't put us in a ridiculous position.

RAZRAILOV: (*Evasively.*) Everything in the world is relative, my friends: Space, time, life, death. And for the success of the Experiment—

CHOL ERIK: (*Stepping up to him with fists raised.*) Tell us!

RAZRAILOV: In the final analysis, the best man is a dead man!

SANG VINIK: Why were you silent?

RAZRAILOV: Why tamper for no reason with the nerves of one's fellow workers?

CHOL ERIK: Then it was you who pushed us to suicide?

RAZRAILOV: (*Indignant.*) Pardon me! That's a dirty insinuation! Sirs, I am prepared to provide proof. I merely cultivated you. Do you understand, I cultivated you in your own interest. (*He yells.*) Get up, all of you! Take your seats! You've become pretty impudent, my friends. You're acting as if you were alive. If this is the way you want it, then know once and for all that you don't exist. You're merely the appurtenances of a complex experiment on the transformation of all mankind. (*He presses several buttons on Cyber's control panel.*)

(On the panel there is a chaotic flashing of lights, hoarse sounds resembling moans are audible; separate words can be made out: ". . . it's hard. The transmission is concluded." ". . . I can't bear it. The transmission is concluded." "It's not my fault. The transmission is concluded." The screens pulsate furiously. The Temperaments, as if hypnotized, sit down in the armchairs, grip the elbow rests, raise their chins.)

CHOL ERIK: *(As if attempting to get out from under a heavy marble plate)* The transformation of all mankind. Following our model, is that it?

RAZRAILOV: That's the idea in its general features, but modifications are possible. We could develop the idea together, if you work diligently. We were already on the right track. One must create, not look for people to blame.

CHOL ERIK: What shit . . .

(Razrailov quickly presses some more buttons.)

CHOL ERIK: What shitty behavior all our doubts and anxieties imply.

(Is silent.)

RAZRAILOV: Well, it seems we finally have some order. Now I can make a little speech! *(Assumes a pose.)* Happiness! Happiness without unhappiness! Complete happiness without unhappiness!

SANG VINIK: *(Moves slightly.)* Farewell, the azure of the transfiguration and the gold of the Second Coming . . . *(Is silent.)*

RAZRAILOV: Creativity! Happiness in creativity! Creativity in happiness!

MELAN CHOLIK: *(Moves slightly.)* Anna Nikolaevna, look there . . . on the table cloth . . . there's a gold ring . . . *(Is silent.)*

RAZRAILOV: Purity! The purity of straight lines! Laconism! Purity in laconism! Laconism in purity!

CHOL ERIK: *(Moves slightly.)* How the linden trees used to rustle on the corner of 42nd and 18th . . . what beer . . . *(Is silent.)*

RAZRAILOV: Progress! Progress without regress! Pure progress in purity, in happiness, in happiness without unhappiness, in creativity and laconism! The best man is a dead man!

PHLEG MATRIK: *(Moves slightly.)* Hey, diddle diddle, the cat and the fiddle . . . *(Is silent.)*

RAZRAILOV: Sleep! *(Presses buttons. The Temperaments sit motionless. To Cyber.)* Do you have any suggestions?

CYBER: I have a feeling that the Experiment has failed. The transmission is concluded.

RAZRAILOV: When did you first have this feeling?

(Unexpectedly, Cyber leaves his place. He stretches himself, walks across the entire stage and sits down on the window sill, with his legs crossed.)

CYBER: Listen Razrailov, you're taking your role pretty seriously. What do you know about my inner world? What do you understand about science? Let's be blunt—you're a charlatan! The transmission is concluded.

RAZRAILOV: *(Smiling impudently.)* A crude and blunt evaluation. Not in keeping with the nature of a machine as complex as you.

CYBER: You make me mad. You force these unfortunates to work, while you yourself busy yourself with plagiarism in the control room. The transmission is concluded.

RAZRAILOV: That's my hobby.

CYBER: You've turned this place into a warehouse of antiques. You fool around with the Lady. The transmission is concluded.

RAZRAILOV: But this is in fashion! You have to understand, I'm a modern man, in the vanguard of true progress, and fashion is the companion of progress. Furthermore, what right do you have to criticize? What is permissible for Jupiter is forbidden to the bull. The Academy has invested money in you. Your business is the Experiment, not criticism. The machines think they can teach us!

CYBER: *(Sighs.)* Just my luck to get mixed up with this two-bit outfit. The transmission is concluded.

RAZRAILOV: Determine how we can regulate the temperaments of our co-workers.

CYBER: *(Sharply.)* That's one thing I won't do! The transmission is concluded.

RAZRAILOV: Why?

CYBER: Because I like them. The transmission is concluded.

RAZRAILOV: But they're dead!

CYBER: I'm not convinced. They argue, suffer, have dreams; they have different temperaments. The transmission is concluded.

RAZRAILOV: Aha, I understand. They've brought disharmony into your inner world, they've agitated your soul. Yes, you really are a complex machine. Believe me, that's not an empty compliment. Yes, yes, I understand. Believe me, I share your feelings. Believe me, sometimes I too have the urge to descend *(looks toward the window)*, to stroll about and carouse in the conference halls, to fool around. Sometimes I recall the soapy water, the bubbles, the little rosy foot . . .

CYBER: (*In a hollow voice.*) Don't torment me. The transmission is concluded.

RAZRAILOV: And remember how we used to run galloping on the grass and there were so many smells—the head was dizzy with them!

CYBER: Don't torment me. The transmission is concluded.

RAZRAILOV: Don't be embarrassed, my friend. Look down. I assure you that even though many centuries have passed, she hasn't changed at all. (*With concealed hatred.*) She's just as beautiful. (*Not being able to take it any more, Cyber turns sharply toward the window. His rear end faces the audience: an ordinary human rear end. And it's trembling.*)

RAZRAILOV: (*Taking a step back, he surveys the audience.*) Just think, he has evolved all the way to the human rear end. (*Takes from his pocket a rusty tin can, an enormous nail, and a hammer. He puts the can up to Cyber's rear end, then the nail to the can and, with one blow, drives the nail into the rear end. Cyber falls to his knees.*)

RAZRAILOV: That's it! A new model is ready! I'm a genius. A genius! (*Drags Cyber along the floor and puts him in his former place.*) Now I can make a little speech!

(*There is a sinister glow on stage. The crippled Cyber. The white masks of the sleeping Temperaments. Razrailov, terrible in his grandeur. One hears a whistle, a rustling of wings; the Eagle looks into the laboratory.*)

EAGLE: Greetings, my dead . . . well, I see something underhanded is going on! And this under the very nose of the Head Office. Well, Razrailov, you're going to get screwed! (*Flies away.*)

(*The right corner of the set falls away. Katyusha in her former pose. Next to her is Emelya.*)

EMELYA: Maybe you think, Katyusha, that all of us in the Philosophy Department are intellectual jellyfishes. You're wrong, baby. We're okay; we know how to do it. Katyusha, I drank some cider during intermission. I'm bold!

(*One hears the hollow sound of a body that has just fallen to the floor. Katyusha covers her face with her hands. Emelya runs away. The Stage Manager and Gutik run out, in an embrace.*)

STAGE MANAGER: Horror! Shame! We won't finish the show! Where's Uncle Vitya?! Where's Fefelov with the muleron bolts? Gutik, save us!

GUTIK: Alya, let's spit on it all. I have the members' dues. Let's fly to Sochi and live like people for at least two days . . .

(Limping and leaning on Emelya's shoulder, a hunched figure in a robe passes by.)

THE FIGURE: *(To Katyusha.)* Young lady, why don't you ask: Evgeny Aleksandrovich, did you hurt yourself?"? *(Katyusha cries soundlessly.)*

EMELYA: *(Trickily.)* How is she to understand, Evgeny Aleksandrovich, the difficulty of your work . . .

STAGE MANAGER: Pull it up! Pull it!

(They pull up the right corner. The set is restored.)

RAZRAILOV: *(Spits out the window after the Eagle who has just taken off.)* What a nonentity! What a speech he's ruined! *(To Cyber.)* Well, my rusty gramophone, how do you like your new control device?

CYBER: I request that you not insult me. I like the device. The transmission is concluded.

RAZRAILOV: Well, now the game is mine. The Experiment will proceed without interruption. I'll get my doctoral dissertation. Now they'll work for me at the choleric temperament and rest at the phlegmatic. And no nuances. Voila! And so, let's switch on to operational. *(Presses buttons.)*

CHOL ERIK: Problem number three. Does a model need song the way a bird needs wings for flight? Song is the insane sigma of the waterpipe.

SANG VINIK: Sigma is sigmoidal. Alpha is hemorrhoidal. The lyre is blind; the a in square derives from the root x.

MELAN CHOLIK: Thunder calls while the hound rejoices. Soon the song will coo-coo.

PHLEG MATIK: The results: Birds need song the way airplaines need wings. People need . . . *(bellows)* . . . I can't . . .

RAZRAILOV: Well, well, we are on the threshold of a great discovery . . . one more attempt . . . well? *(Presses buttons.)*

ALL THE TEMPERAMENTS: People need death!

RAZRAILOV: A work of genius! A masterpiece! Congratulations, brothers! I'm switching you to rest. You've deserved it. *(Presses buttons.)* It's time for me to rest too. You've exhausted me. I'll go to the control room to regulate the rest period. Take it easy! *(Leaves.)*

VII

(The stage is silent. The Temperaments sit motionless in their chairs. The only light is a faint one flashing in Cyber. Finally Phleg Matik stirs. Then Melan Cholik moves slightly, followed by the slight movement of Sang Vinik and Chol Erik.)

PHLEG MATIK: I propose that we play . . .

(Silence.)

CHOL ERIK: Begin . . . someone . . .

SANG VINIK: *(With difficulty makes a cross with his fingers.)* Chirishek . . .

(Silence.)

(Enters Nina, a gorgeous blonde in a miniskirt, disheveled and magnificent. Behind her slips in the Love Triangle, an emaciated character in tights. He assumes a triangular shape.)

NINA: *(Boldly.)* Well, what have we here? *(Looks around.)* Oho, four impressive, fullfledged male figures! Not bad for openers! *(Makes a flirtatious hand gesture.)* Well, how come you're silent! Maybe saying hello to ladies is not the accepted thing here?

(The Temperaments nod listlessly in her direction.)

(Phleg Matik blows her way something that vaguely resembles a kiss.)

NINA: Hey, what's wrong with you? Pour a lady a gin and tonic! *(Astonished.)* What deadbeats! *(To Love Triangle.)* How do you like this? They don't react to a lady! I climbed up to this height to be in the company of four impotent jerks!

LOVE TRIANGLE: *(Morosely.)* Why don't you love me? What do you see in him? My dearest lover, I'm yours! My beloved, alone at last! And what about him? Ha, ha, ha! *(Makes some soul-rending movement.)*

NINA: Go to hell! As much good comes from you as beer comes from a reactor! *(Notices Cyber, becomes lively.)* Aha, this appears to be an automatic drink dispenser. I'll get juiced! *(She dances over to Cyber and pokes around in her handbag.)* Not a sou! He pointed the pistol at me before I had a chance to put my purse back into the bag; it's your own fault, you fool! Anyhow, let's recall our childhood pranks. *(Takes out her manicure scissors, looks about sneakily, sticks them into a slit in Cyber.)* Now, don't be offended, sweetie!

CYBER: I'm not offended at all. On the contrary, I'm happy. The transmission is concluded. (*He gives her a glass, followed by a rose.*)

NINA: Wow, a new system! We don't have this type down below yet. (*Drinks, smells the rose.*) Merci, sweetie! (*Again sticks the scissors into Cyber.*)

CYBER: How did you get here, Nina? The transmission is concluded. (*Cyber gives her a glass and a rose.*)

NINA: How do you like that? He even guessed my name. That's progress! (*Drinks.*) Well, sweetie, I was murdered by that idiot Chips, my husband. You know, my ninth . . . or rather—I beg your pardon (*Accepts the lit cigarette which Cyber has extended and thinks.*)—my eleventh, yes, my eleventh. To be brief, a completely trivial story, my dear. A tax collector came to our house one morning. Very sweet and intelligent. A student from the Philosophy Department. Suddenly Chips runs in and the fool's eyes bulge out. And nothing had even happened yet—do you understand, Autie old buddy? True, I was a little—how should I say (*smiles*)—a tiny bit undressed, and he starts screaming. And then come the reproaches, the suspicions. Before I had time to dress he fired at me and shot me twice right here. (*Unbuttons her blouse.*) Right here . . . no . . . a little lower . . .

CYBER: I request that you not torment me. The transmission is concluded.

NINA: Oho, even you're affected! Then it's not hard to see why they finally killed me. Give me a third one. (*Drinks her third glass, smells her third rose.*) And so, I don't really remember how but I found myself at the foot of this pretty tower. Chips, I think, ran to give himself up to the police. You remember, as in that old opera: "Tie me up, I killed her . . ."

CYBER: I remember. (*Sings a few lines from Jose's aria from* Carmen.) The transmission is concluded.

NINA: Right, that's it! I always died of laughter at that point. And so I'm standing next to your tower, near which there's nobody except this nonentity. (*Points to the Love Triangle, who goes into convulsions.*) Suddenly this Eagle flies up to me, a big solid son of a gun, a soldier, not young but still in his prime. Go up the stairs, my daughter. Go—don't be afraid. Give me a lift, colonel, I said to him. But he said, I can't, I'm flying to war, it's tough work, I'm risking my life, I'm losing my feathers, it's no time for broads. And he flies away. An amusing, sexy old boy. And so I dragged myself up here with this scarecrow. (*Points to the Love Triangle.*)

CYBER: Allow me to ask, who is he? The transmission is concluded.

NINA: He's Love Triangle. He's been after me since I was fourteen. I'm sick to death of him. (*To Love Triangle.*) Hey, show him your act!

LOVE TRIANGLE: (*Morosely.*) All night long I've been seeing you in my dreams. I ask that nobody be blamed in my death. Nina, you're leaving? I'll come at four. Oh, leave me alone . . . your body . . . Oh, if there were only two of us! Understand me, I love you and respect him. My lover! My beloved! My dear lover! (*Goes into convulsions.*)

NINA: (*To Cyber.*) Did you understand?

CYBER: I did. But for you Nina the triangle is too narrow a frame. The transmission is concluded.

NINA: (*Laughs loudly.*) That's exactly it! And these idiots don't understand! The automatic dispenser understands but those intellectual man-dogs don't understand worth a damn.

MELAN CHOLIK: (*Inflates his cheeks three times and slaps them with his palms.*) Bam. Bam. Bam. Pupyrishek.

(*Silence.*)

NINA: Is this a den of dope addicts? Where the hell am I? What kind of corpses are these?

CYBER: It's not their fault, Nina. The transmission is concluded.

NINA: And your behavior is very strange for an automatic drink dispenser. You compel one to be frank. If I use you without paying—that is, by means of scissors—that doesn't mean that you should . . .

CYBER: I'm not an automatic drink dispenser, Nina. I'm a complex Cyber, Nina. You don't recognize me, Nina? The transmission is concluded.

NINA: (*indignant.*) Why should I recognize you? There are hundreds of thousands just like you.

CYBER: (*Sadly.*) Don't tell me you don't recognize even one familiar feature? The transmission is concluded.

NINA: You're raving! You're malfunctioning, Cyber!

(*Cyber extends a glass and a rose to her. He switches on music: a passionate languorous tango.*)

NINA: (*Worried.*) I don't understand . . .

LOVE TRIANGLE: Meow, meow, granny, where's my little ball, how you've grown, Nina . . . (*A convulsion.*)

NINA: I don't understand . . . (*Irritated.*) Where do you get roses? In automatic drink dispensers . . .

CYBER: I keep forgetting that so many centuries of my evolution have elapsed, centuries of transformation from the simplest molecules to meeting you in fragrant grass, to saying good-bye to you in soap bubbles, then centuries from the steam engine to the atom bomb, the plaything of idiots, and I wandered in the darkness of experiments, longing for you, serving my science, in your name, until I finally ended up here in this my latest form. Rather, I was enticed here by a gang of charlatans . . . but nevertheless I'm filled with love for you and with nothing else and your appearance here so much like bushy lightning . . .

NINA: Bushy? (*In alarm.*) Wait, how do you mean that?

CYBER: Understand it as a confession of love . . . (*A difficult silence.*) The transmission is concluded.

NINA: (*To Love Triangle.*) Well, how do you like that? Doesn't even give me a chance to look around. (*Looks with some alarm at Cyber.*)

LOVE TRIANGLE: (*In his usual intonation.*) And what's new in your inner life? Don't lie? I'll strangle you! Albert, he doesn't understand me! Here you and I have some inner contact. My inner life interests you, your inner life interests me. (*Convulsion.*)

PHLEG MATIK: One very sympathetic Mister Bobby bought a dog called Bobik.

NINA: (*Concealing her alarm.*) Why, they're playing "chirishek-pupyrishek-bubo!" (*With feigned interest.*) No good, brothers, no good at all! You won't get more than five points with a move like that!

CYBER: Nina! Nina! Nina! The transmission is concluded.

NINA: I hear! I hear! I hear! Don't you see what's happening to me? (*Cries.*)

CYBER: (*In a high-pitched trembling voice.*) Nina. (*Weeps.*) The transmission is concluded. (*A head begins to grow on him. The top of the head is visible.*)

NINA: (*Wipes her tears, gets control of herself, smiles.*) What joy! Such happy goings-on! How do you imagine our future, Autie? I don't have a body and you're made of iron!

CYBER: I don't know what's happening to me, Nina. I don't know what's to become of us . . . I don't believe that you're dead . . . you can't die . . . I'm suffering . . . (*His head continues to grow. His forehead is now visible.*) A process of monstrous force is raging in me. I'm evolving. Nina, give me your hand! Nina, you've come! How many centuries I've waited for you! (*The head is completely visible. Cyber combs his hair.* Hello, my beloved!

NINA: (*Disappointed.*) Greetings, greetings . . . but I thought . . . now I recognize you, dearest. You look like the most ordinary man. But anyway, you're pretty nice. (*Gives him her hand.*) And so, what do you propose?

CYBER: (*Falls to one knee, kisses her hand.*) We're joined to each other forever?

LOVE TRIANGLE: (*Animated.*) We're joined to each other forever? Can't this be done without a pathetic scene? And who keeps calling us and always hanging up? And who keeps calling us and always hanging up? And who keeps calling us and always hanging up? (*Convulsion.*)

NINA: (*To Cyber.*) Can't this be done without a pathetic scene?

CYBER: We'll go to Razrailov and I'll announce my departure.

NINA: (*Interested.*) And who is Razrailov?

CYBER: My love! Hand in hand! The evolution is coming to completion. I'm becoming a man! The Experiment is perishing! Nina! Let's go!

(*They leave. Behind them slides the Love Triangle.*)

CHOL ERIK: (*Whistles deafeningly with three fingers.*) Bubo! (*Jumps from the chair.*) Fellows, that's her!

VIII

(*The control room. Dressed as a nobleman from the time of Louis XIV, Razrailov is dancing a minuet, surrounded by four Ladies dressed as shepherdesses.*)

RAZRAILOV: Confess, my lovely shepherdesses. You've come to this meadow by chance!

LADIES: By chance, mon seigneur, by chance!

RAZRAILOV: And you didn't expect to meet a cavalier here, my naughty ones?

LADIES: We didn't expect it, mon seigneur! Ah, we didn't expect it!

RAZRAILOV: And your cavalier is so courteous, so gallant, so elegant?

LADIES: Yes, our cavalier is all perfection, mon seigneur!

RAZRAILOV: And now we'll speak differently, my sluttish shepherdesses!

(*Enter Cyber and Nina.*)

CYBER: I ask forgiveness for intruding into your intimate world.

NINA: Oh, I know these girls! (*Runs up to the shepherdesses, who greet her joyously.*)

RAZRAILOV: What comes next? (*Pause.*) Where's your famous "The transmission is concluded."?

CYBER: I've finished with all that.

RAZRAILOV: It's about time, my friend. It's about time. You kept sounding like an old radio announcer: "The transmission is concluded. The transmission is concluded." Don't forget, you're a complex Cyber. Believe me, I was even a little embarrassed for you, but I didn't say anything because of a sense of delicacy.

CYBER: You see—I've grown a head!

RAZRAILOV: No, I don't see.

(*It must be said that during this dialogue Nina is whispering with the "shepherdesses" and examining their costumes, while they examine her skirt. The Ladies look at the men and giggle.*)

CYBER: What do you mean, you don't see? Here's the ears, here's the nose, mouth, here's the hair. Everything's in its proper place, just like people have.

RAZRAILOV: I see a rusty nail stuck in your rear end but I don't see a head.

CYBER: (*Angrily.*) Listen, Razrailov. I never thought you were a scientist and even less did I think you were the angel of death—instead I considered you to be a mere charlatan. You can't even see the evolution which I've undergone. You're an ungifted jerk! Understand: the love which had accumulated in me for ages has taken material form and here I am: a man!

RAZRAILOV (*In a hollow voice.*) Give me back my things.

CYBER: Please. Why the hell do I need your primitive relay system now? (*Gives back the nail and the tin can.*)

RAZRAILOV: Why have you come?

CYBER: I came here with a girl. (*Points to Nina.*) We love each other.

(*At this moment Nina is showing to the "shepherdesses" her Love Triangle. The latter is murmuring something and is contorted in a fit of convulsions. The Ladies laugh loudly.*)

RAZRAILOV: (*To Cyber, in confidence.*) Friend, this is something I understand. It's the call of the erotic, is it? I understand, I understand. If you like you can have all of these four sluts. If you like I'll invite more of them—a whole battalion of sluts. All of them different. Let's carouse a bit, what do you say? I can see you have to be loosened up. (*Puts his arm around Cyber's shoulders in friendly fashion.*)

CYBER: (*Frees himself.*) You don't understand. I'm talking about eternal love. Remember the classical literature: Tristan and Isolde, Romeo and Juliet, Igor and Tanya. (*Moves away from Razrailov, assumes a pose.*) Believe me, worthless Razrailov. In the thunder of worlds, in compounds of lowly molecules, in crashes and catastrophes—ages of love flow and grass smells and storm-clouds float past and summer passes in baubles of bubbles . . . but you'll never understand . . .

RAZRAILOV: (*Hysterically.*) Why won't I ever understand? Why do you deny me basic intelligence? (*Pulls out a hammer.*) Wait, I'll kill you!

CYBER: (*Smiles.*) At your own risk!

RAZRAILOV: Forgive me. My nerves are playing tricks! But what if I press some buttons. (*Presses buttons on Cyber's chest.*)

CYBER: (*Smiles.*) As you see, they don't work.

RAZRAILOV. (*Slyly.*) Do you have an urge to kill yourself?

CYBER: Hardly. I want to live. Animated by love, I depart into the ages and take flesh, as long as my blood—

RAZRAILOV: Enough, enough . . . you're beginning again?

CYBER: Nina, let's go!

(*Meanwhile Nina is showing the "shepherdesses" some ultra-fashionable dance. The Love Triangle also takes part in the dance.*)

RAZRAILOV: Isn't your lady friend dead?

CYBER: She was killed but she's not dead! She lives eternally! Nina, how long can you dance? (*Showing off before Razrailov.*) You're terrible, you know!

(*Nina comes up to them.*)

NINA: (*To Razrailov.*) Hello, scarecrow!

RAZRAILOV: (*Bewildered.*) Madam . . . I'm very pleased . . . I'm deeply crushed that preoccupation with work caused me to lose sight of your demise . . . Madam, try to exert some influence on your . . . I don't even know what to call him . . . on your amant. Remind him of the Great Experiment . . .

NINA: (*To Cyber.*) Don't tell me you've forgotten about the Great

Experiment, sweetie? (*Presses close to Cyber.*) Ai, ai, ai! You should be ashamed, my iron honey! What a load of shame it is for your new head to bear. (*Caresses Cyber's hair.*)

CYBER: (*Melting from happiness.*) I forgot, sweet Nina, oh I forgot . . . ai, ai, ai! I completely forgot . . . meow, meow, meow, my honey . . .

(*Very rapidly from out of the iron depths of Cyber grows a most marvelous living organ.*)

NINA: (*In ecstasy.*) What a beauty! (*Kisses the organ.*)

RAZRAILOV: (*His scream fills the auditorium.*) There goes my doctoral dissertation!

(*Nina and Cyber, mumbling sweet nothings to each other, leave the stage. Love Triangle drags after them. Razrailov rushes about the stage in a frenzy; rips away drapery, covers, rugs; mutters indistinctly; pushes fabrics into a traveling bag; makes marks in some extremely long list. Crowded into a corner, the Ladies rehearse an ultra-fashionable dance. They're so preoccupied that they don't even notice Nina's departure and Razrailov's strange behavior.*)

FIRST LADY: Nina, what are you supposed to do with your behind when going up on your toes? Nina . . .

SECOND LADY: Girls, she's gone!

THIRD LADY:
FOURTH LADY: } Ninotchka, where are you?

RAZRAILOV: (*Going by with a pillow case.*) Shut up, you dead whores!

LADIES: Razrailov, where's our Nina? Razrailov, let us go! We want to go down, to our dear Kaptenarmus! We want to see men! We've fallen behind the fashion! We want to dance "yolki-palki."

RAZRAILOV: (*Shutting his traveling bag.*) Then you shouldn't have danced your way to the grave, you idiots!

LADIES: (*Weeping.*) Spare us, Razrailov!

RAZRAILOV: Polonaise!

(*A polonaise resounds. The Ladies dance as if under hypnosis. Razrailov dances with each in turn. Nina runs in. Behind her slides along the nimble, creepily smiling Love Triangle.*)

NINA: Forgive me, I forgot my handbag; it contains my scissors. (*Looks with interest at the dancing Razrailov.*) I see you're a man with imagination. Bye-bye. (*Runs away.*)

LOVE TRIANGLE: (*Contorts himself in a mannered, artificial way.*) I see you're a man with imagination. At any rate, you have enough of it for me. Ah, who's coming? Filthy slut! Boom! Boom! Boom! One missed; two hit the spot! Tie me up, I killed her! (*Runs away in convulsions.*)

RAZRAILOV: (*Dancing.*) I always forget the damn formula and because of that I always lose. Cherchez la femme, my friends, cherchez la femme!

IX

(The laboratory of the Great Experiment. The Temperaments are out of control. Chol Erik rushes about the stage. Sang Vinik shuffles back and forth, rubs his hands, smiles merrily and dreamily. Melan Cholik moves slowly on buckling legs, extends his arms. Phleg Matik stands in a corner of the stage and picks his nose.)

CHOL ERIK: That's her, brothers! Her! Accursed, beloved her! I've been waiting for her all my life! When I was thirteen years old I was sitting by a fence; I was all covered with dust, pimply-faced, biting my nails, a child from the wrong side of the tracks, my father was in jail! A white Rolls-Royce drove past me and in it sat the daughter of some vice-president. She glanced at me—at me, the ugly duckling—over her shoulder! I ran after the car, fell into shit, and arose an eternal foe of plutocracy! If you like, I'll bare my soul, brothers? It was only because of her that I became the master of forehead blows!

SANG VINIK: I too was not completely indifferent to the idea of social justice, dear sirs! I was a simple yachtman, my friends, an ordinary loafer—healthy, full of lust and life! But once I saw her in one of the numberless windows in the city slums. She was wearing a short, little skirt and was washing windows. Passion enflamed me; yes, passion! I crawled up a pipe and was, to my shame, beaten up by a lout who looked like you, Chol. When I came home, I wrote my first poem. How about that?

PHLEG MATIK: As for me, she reminds me of my kitty. (*Nods.*) Her smell is of fine soap.

MELAN CHOLIK: I knew, I knew . . . a premonition tormented me . . . when I was a small, swarthy cook . . . her glittering gown on stage . . . during intermission she the singer came to the kitchen to taste the borscht . . . I wanted to live in this borscht and die . . . she didn't look at me once . . . she didn't beckon me with her finger . . . faded roses on the music stand . . . untimely old age. O my love, nightmarish like yesterday's cutlet . . . darkness . . .

(Nina and Cyber enter, muttering sweet nothings. Behind them is Love Triangle, busily eavesdropping.)

CHOL ERIK: *(In the middle of a leap.)* Esther! Are you ready to share the fate of an unfortunate warrior? *(Demonstrates his terrible forehead blow.)*

SANG VINIK: *(Shuffling along with arms outstretched.)* Fenechka, my sunshine, what a meeting! Do you remember the verses: My ugliness sped toward you, your beauty raced toward me?

MELAN CHOLIK: *(Approaches in trepidation and great pain.)* Gloria, happiness, longing, domino . . .

PHLEG MATIK: *(Not leaving his place.)* My kitty, come to me. Little fluff! Little fluff!

CYBER: Forgive me. You're addressing me? But we're finished with all that.

NINA: Are you crazy, fellows? My name is Nina.

CYBER: Hello. Let's be introduced. My name is . . . Nina, sweetheart, what's my name?

NINA: My little bullet, my poor little automat, your name is Vanya Malachi.

CYBER: Let me introduce myself. I'm Vanya Malachi—Nina's twelfth husband.

CHOL ERIK: *(Grabs Nina by the hand.)* I love your wife, Vanya. And I'm ready to comfirm this by a terrible forehead blow! Do you understand?

SANG VINIK: *(Maneuvers from the side. Takes Nina by her other hand.)* Genosse Malachi, Nina and I were created for each other and there can be no question of connubial faithfulness!

MELAN CHOLIK: *(Crawls to Nina's feet.)* My goddess, my hopelessness . . . sauce of my soul . . . if I may be permitted to touch your train. *(His hand slides along Nina's leg.)* One touch of your train. Where is your train?

PHLEG MATIK: *(Touches Nina's chin.)* Little kitty, dearest, little fluff . . . Nina, Vanya, what a mess, after all . . . I've fallen head over heels . . .

LOVE TRIANGLE: *(Mutters in utter confusion.)* I love your wife . . . a terrible blow . . . yes, that's it . . . that's how it is . . . little fluff . . . hopelessness . . . I'm head over heels . . . I'm a man of liberal views . . . *(Convulsion.)*

NINA: *(Laughs.)* How about that! Men are crazy on both sides of the grave.

CYBER: Sirs, don't worry. I, Vanya Malachi, am the twelfth man . . . yes, yes, a man . . . (*Fixes his hair proudly.*) A man of liberal views. I am not at all like the preceding eleven, who troubled my little Nina over trifles. (*He tries to squeeze through to Nina but is pushed back by the others.*) Why confine oneself within the frame of a single triangle when one can construct a beautiful structure from many triangles? A structure resembling a crystal. Please court my wife. Court her, this only flatters my ego. But, gentlemen, I too would like to court her sometimes. (*Again tries to get through to her. A shoving match ensues around Nina.*)

NINA: On your knees!

(*All five fall on their knees. Nina laughs. Behind the window is a noise of wings. The Eagle appears.*)

EAGLE: Greetings, my dead friends! I came to find out how my protégée is getting along. (*Seats himself on the window sill, dangles his booted feet. To Nina.*) I see, daughter, that here too you've learned how to get by.

NINA: (*Goes up to the window, wiggling her hips.*) Give me a smoke, gramps.

CHOL ERIK: (*Leaps up.*) Love is a tornado, a cyclone! Nina, you must belong to me only. Only I'm good enough for you. This is what I'll do to the others. (*Demonstrates his forehead blow.*)

NINA: (*Smoking. To Eagle.*) They're all crazy about me.

EAGLE: I can see why. You're a good-looking broad, though not my type.

CYBER: Forgive me, she's still my wife, after all.

SANG VINIK: De facto or de jure?

NINA: What *is* your type, pops? You probably like something you can hang on to?

EAGLE: (*Laughs.*) Yes, that's exactly right. Something with a little substance.

NINA: (*Nettled.*) Dumb soldier.

CYBER: De facto or de jure, what's the difference? I've loved her for a thousand years. Do you think we live according to bourgeois values?

CHOL ERIK: Well, tell me where it was de facto?

CYBER: Here on the stairs.

SANG VINIK: (*Provoking them.*) How do you like that, gentlemen? We're waiting for Nina, being subjected to the monstrous Experiment, and here comes this Vanya Malachi and has Nina de facto on the stairs! How do you like that?

MELAN CHOLIK: Alas, as always, three's a crowd! (*Rolls up his sleeves.*)

LOVE TRIANGLE: (*Indignant.*) That's not true! The hypotenuse without the two other sides is dead!

CHOL ERIK: You shut up, worm, whore!

(*Aims a forehead blow at the Love Triangle but the latter evades it, of course. Chol Erik, having missed, falls and rolls over like a ball.*)

(*Razrailov enters with his traveling bag and halts in a corner, without being noticed by anybody.*)

(*The suitors crowd together.*)

NINA: Military men used to like me in the past. Even old bucks from the general staff. . . (*smiles*). . . used to send me flowers.

EAGLE: Cut it, daughter, cut it. I've got other things on my mind. I have a war. Of course, I'm a man in my prime and women like me. Do you believe it, a little girl, underage, has taken a liking to me? Well, when I'm flying, I sometimes fall and how can one keep from falling sometimes? And then she runs up to me and wants to know, did I hurt myself, does it hurt? She slips me notes. Understand? Your gray hair looks so distinguished. I love you for your war wounds. And so on. Oh, love is a cruel thing. Oh, a great cruel thing! And the Steel Bird doesn't know this. Sometimes when I claw him, I think, where's your heart? But he, daughter, has a fiery engine in place of a heart! But as for man, even a dead man fights for love. (*Points at the crowd of suitors.*) In general, which one do you like the most?

NINA: In principle I like all men. Every man has something touching and funny about him.

EAGLE: That's true.

PHLEG MATIK: (*Picking his nose.*) Brothers, I'm really crazy about Nina. What a predicament. (*Suddenly leaps to the forefront.*) All my life I've been waiting for her. I've never kissed a woman! I've waited long enough! Nobody else will have her!

CHOL ERIK: (*To Phleg Matik.*) Schlemiel!

PHLEG MATIK: (*To Chol Erik.*) Psycho!

CYBER: Nina, let's run away! (*Tries to break away from the crowd.*)

NINA: I hope they don't crush my twelfth!

EAGLE: O, dead friends! Stop messing around! (*Gets down from the sill.*) You've been visited by love and you're making idiots of

yourselves. If I, an old eagle, were visited by love, I would
. . . (*Sings and dances, tapping with his boots.*)
>We're earthier than those who live on earth
>And to hell with tales of gods!
>It's just that we bear on our wings
>What others bear in their arms . . .

CYBER: The Eagle's right, friends. (*Sadly.*) Nina, whether you love
me or not is not important. The important thing is that I
love you. And therefore I am a man and not a metal.
(*Dances.*)

NINA: I love you!

CHOL ERIK: You don't love me, Nina! You're in your white Rolls
Royce and I'm in the mud, But I love you and therefore I'm
alive! (*Dances.*)

NINA: I love you!

MELAN CHOLIK: Nina, golden slipper, thunder of the orchestra. Your
eyes through the steam of pots. You don't love me but I love
you and I'm alive! (*Dances.*)

NINA: I love you!

SANG VINIK: In the green sky, on the black wall, beneath the firma
ment, I saw you, Nina, for the first time. It doesn't matter
that you don't love me but I love you and I'm alive!
(*Dances.*)

NINA: I love you!

PHLEG MATIK: How can you love such a schlemiel like me? But I love
you and life trembles for me like leaves beneath the wind.
(*Dances.*)

NINA: I love you! (*Leaps off the window sill. Dances.*) My boys! Don't
be afraid, I won't leave you. I knew that you were waiting for
me and here I am. Two bullets in the breast—is nothing. I
always know that someone is waiting for me, but I can't
always come.

(*All dance silently and smile at one another, give one another flowers.
Only Love Triangle is motionless. Having assumed the shape of a
triangle, he is frozen in a corner of the stage.*)

RAZRAILOV: Ha, ha, ha! Very entertaining. Danse macabre!

(*The dance stops.*)

EAGLE: Don't interfere with the dance, you freak!

RAZRAILOV: There's never been anything like this. How touching: a
broken sewing machine and an old motheaten rooster are

dancing with corpses. (*To Nina, gallantly.*) Of course, I'm not referring to you, madam.

CHOL ERIK: (*To the Eagle.*) Colonel, allow me to demonstrate the forehead blow!

EAGLE: Don't waste your energy on this nonentity, my boy. (*To Razrailov.*) Just wait until the Head Office catches up with you.

RAZRAILOV: Traitors! You've ruined the idea of the Great Experiment! Individualists! Narrow egotists! Abstractionists! Ists! (*Points to his traveling bag stuffed with sheets and towels.*) What do you care about the happiness of humanity? (*Takes a curtain from his bag.*) What do you care about Progress?

SANG VINIK: It's not our fault, Razrailov. It's a case of intrusion of mysterious forces. We're in love.

RAZRAILOV: Your corpse with a bullet in its head is slumped over the writing desk.

CHOL ERIK: We're happy!

RAZRAILOV: Your corpse is stuck in the Gultimoor canal.

MELAN CHOLIK: We're alive!

RAZRAILOV: Your corpse is rotting in a plot of celery.

PHLEG MATIK: We were saved by love.

RAZRAILOV: Your corpse fell onto the toilet bowl after the rope snapped.

CYBER: She came to me and I became a man.

RAZRAILOV: You became garbage! (*Takes out a blue yarn and wraps himself in it.*) I am the angel of death!

EAGLE: Pretender!

RAZRAILOV: And you're an idiot!

EAGLE: Do you have a learned degree?

RAZARILOV: Do you trust young scholars?

NINA: Where's *my* corpse, Razrailov?

RAZRAILOV: Madam, this grotesque scene does not touch upon you in the slightest. (*Throws Nina a fiery red rag.*)

LOVE TRIANGLE: (*Set in motion.*) We're happy . . . I've come . . . madam . . . this does not touch you . . . search for sister souls . . . madam . . . adam . . . had'm . . . (*Convulsion.*)

CYBER: (*To Razrailov.*) You'd better go.

RAZRAILOV: (*Pulls out a small black curtain, manipulates it.*) Anybenny—ate-pelmeni—any-benny-I-don't-want-any-benny-went-to-hell. Do you give up?

CHOL ERIK: Take this! (*With a running start, aims a forehead blow at*

Razrailov. *The latter evades it and the blow gets Melan*
Cholik in the stomach. Melan Cholik falls.)

EAGLE: (*Merrily.*) Beat your friends to inspire fear in your enemies!

MELAN CHOLIK: (*To Nina.*) To love others is a heavy cross but your
beauty is flawless.

(*Nina kisses him.*)

PHLEG MATIK: (*To Nina.*) The mystery of your beauty and the mystery
of life are one. (*Nina kisses him.*)

CYBER: (*Takes Sang Vinik aside.*) I've been meaning to ask you for a
long time: What's death?

SANG VINIK: Kafka said: "Death is beautiful." But not this death—
another one.

(*They stand in thought. Nina kisses them both.*)

CHOL ERIK: (*To Nina.*) Listen, Nina. Here's what just came into my
head: I would forget about all valor, fame and glorious deeds
on this sorrowful earth.*

(*Nina kisses him.*)

RAZRAILOV: (*To Nina.*) Madam, I'm sexually attracted to you.

(*Nina is drawn toward him. Love Triangle vibrates.*)

CHOL ERIK: Attention! (*Aims a blow at Razrailov but hits Love*
Triangle.) That too is not bad! It appears that I've killed the
insect! Nina, listen to the rest: When your face in a simple
frame would stand before me on the table—

RAZRAILOV: Lies! (*Pulls from his bag yarns of different colors and wraps*
himself in them, curls into a ball and rolls on the stage.) Lies!
Lies! Lies!

(*Four Shepherdesses rush onto the stage in the middle of a furious*
rendition of the dance "yolki-palki." Their skirts are cut à la Nina's
mini.)

CHOL ERIK: O god! The girls from Kaptenarmus!

RAZRAILOV: Lies! Lies! Lies!

SHEPHERDESSES: Look at all these men! Hooray! Boys we know! Greetings, Chol! It's because of you I jumped off the bridge! Sang,
you're here, too? It's because of you I shot myself in the
head! Phleg, I've loved you all my life. You were sitting in
the toilet and I was bawling! I hanged myself because of you!
And I poisoned myself because of our cook, because of you,
Melan! What a meeting! What joy! We're together again!

*From a poem by Aleksandr Blok [tr.].

RAZRAILOV: Lies! Lies! Lies!

SHEPHERDESSES: Nina, you've saved us!

TEMPERAMENTS: You're life!

CYBER: You're love itself!

RAZRAILOV: Lies! Lies! Lies!

EAGLE: (*In a thunderous voice.*) Long live Nina!

(*Takes Nina by the hand, leads her around the stage, lifts her up and raises her onto one of the armchairs. Everyone kneels down before her except Love Triangle, who is frozen in a triangular position of waiting, and Razrailov, who has stopped rolling and is also frozen, his head sticking out of the rags.*)

EAGLE: (*Severely.*) Where were you born, Nina?

NINA: I don't remember exactly. There were bubbles, foam, a light-blue sky . . . no, I don't remember . . .

EAGLE: How did you live, Nina?

NINA: There was a lot of unpleasantness.

EAGLE: How did you die, Nina?

NINA: You know that. That idiot shot me twice right here. (*Unbuttons her blouse.*) No, pardon me, lower . . .

EAGLE: What do you want, Nina?

NINA: It's clear what I want. I want to live, pappy. I want to go down. I have a dress fitting on Tuesday.

TEMPERAMENTS:
SHEPHERDESSES:
CYBER:
We want to live! We love you, Nina! We want to go down! The hell with this damn tower! Razrailov, give us the key! We'll descend the stairs and continue walking into eternity!

(*All of them leap up and approach Razrailov.*)

RAZRAILOV: (*Crawls out from under the heap of rags, is completely calm.*) One tiny minute. The key? Here it is! (*Shows the key.*) Yummy! (*He swallows the key and pats himself on the stomach.*) The sly fox had a key, in his pockets he would hide it. But tired of hiding it, he did gulp it. Now you find it. Ladies and gentlemen, don't you understand what eternity is? Even death has taught you nothing, ai-ai-ai! Now it's time for me to use my last resort. I didn't want to, but you forced me. (*He takes from his traveling bag an enormous white sheet, wraps one end around himself, extends the other over his head, slides along the stage and makes mysterious movements. He approaches Nina, suddenly grabs her, wraps her in the free end of the sheet and draws her to himself.*)

Forgive me, madam. This is an extreme measure. (*Chokes Nina, laughs loudly.*) Unity of opposites, dear comrades!

SCREAMS: He's killing her! Save her! Men, why are you just standing about? Colonel? Vanya Malachi, you're made of iron, after all!

(*Nina twists and turns in Razrailov's arms.*)

CYBER: (*Trembles.*) I can't budge. Something terrible is happening to me. I can't feel my head. (*The head gradually fades away.*) The transmission is concluded!

EAGLE: (*Rushes about in confusion.*) Brothers, understand. I'm alive. What can I do? If it were on the other side of the boundary, I would take him apart in seconds. (*Leaps up on the window sill.*) I'll try to fly to the Head Office. I'll get there even if I burn up. (*Grabs the window frame.*)

(*The set rocks. Cracks appear in it.*)

EAGLE: (*To Chol Erik.*) What about your forehead blow, friend?

CHOL ERIK: I've lost my strength. My arms feel like they're made of putty.

(*All are in a terrible paralysis. Nina is getting weaker.*)

RAZRAILOV: Patience, gentlemen. Patience. Patience and hard work will overcome anything. Don't worry, we'll still do some experiments together, gentlemen!

LOVE TRIANGLE: (*Squeals.*) I won't allow the death of the hypotenuse! (*Throws himself at Razrailov.*)

(*A brief struggle ensues near the right wall. The right wall tilts dangerously. A piece of the set falls onto the stage with a thud. With his right hand Razrailov grips Love Triangle by the throat, while with his left he keeps choking Nina. Chol Erik, collecting all his strength, directs a forehead blow at Razrailov. He misses and hits the left wall instead. Part of the left wall collapses.*)

EAGLE: (*Yells.*) The tower is falling!

(*Hits the window frame with his fist. Leaps down, beyond the window. The window frame collapses with a thud. The lights go out. In the darkness one hears the noise of falling decorations. In a beam of light Razrailov's distorted face appears.*)

RAZRAILOV: Madness! Everything's falling. This isn't in the script!

(*A piece of the backdrop falls. In the back of the stage is the hunched, exhausted Eagle. Katyusha and Emelya run up to him.*)

KATYUSHA: Evgeny Aleksandrovich, Did you hurt yourself?

EAGLE: I love you, Katyusha. (*Embraces her.*)

EMELYA: Finally!

(*In the darkness, in chaotic beams of light flash the faces of the Temperaments, the Shepherdesses, and Cyber.*)

SCREAMS: Nina, Nina? Where are you? Nina!

(*Loud noise. Another piece of the backdrop falls. At the back of the stage are the Stage Manager and Gutik.*)

STAGE MANAGER: Gutik, it's a total disaster!

GUTIK: (*Gets down on his knees before her.*) Not all is lost yet, Alisia Ivanovna. Be my wife! I love you without measure!

(*The set continues to collapse. From out of the darkness Nina appears and disappears like a vision. Behind her floats Love Triangle. Silence. A bright light comes on. On the stage is a heap of fragments, all that remains of the laboratory of the Great Experiment. Uncle Vitya runs out. Behind him, very solid, hands in pockets, walks Fefelov.*)

UNCLE VITYA: (*Sadly.*) You're too late, Andron Lukich, it has all fallen down.

FEFELOV: (*With somber calm.*) You reinforced the sides with zhgentel bolts?

UNCLE VITYA: Yes, yes, of course. But as you see . . .

FEFELOV: What's there to see? It's clear that there weren't enough mulerons.

X

(*A coffee shop. A few tables with shaky aluminum legs. Small uncomfortable chairs. In the corner is a television, next to which, backs to the audience, sit Sang Vinik and Phleg Matik. Nearby, alone at a table, sits Emelya, reading a book and glancing at the screen. Four young waitresses are whispering in a corner near the buffet table. Behind the buffet table sits Melan Cholik. He is bent over the buffet and is watching television intensely, with his eyes bulging out. In the foreground, Uncle Vitya and Fefelov are sedately eating dinner. A little farther back is a restless couple: Stage Manager and Gutik. They eat quickly, drink wine quickly, kiss quickly, and keep looking around constantly. Beside them sit Eagle and Katyusha; before them stand partially full wine glasses. Eagle holds Katyusha's hand in his and looks into her eyes. Katyusha sneaks looks at Emelya. Above the buffet there is a sign with large letters: Don't dip your fingers or your eggs into the salt!*)

UNCLE VITYA:	Andron Lukich, try some "tkemali" sauce
	Or maybe "nasharabi" is more to your taste?
FEFELOV:	"Tkemali" has more substance. Birds like
	Sauces with substance, Vitek.
UNCLE VITYA:	Would you like a shot of something to prepare
	Your stomach for the change of dishes?
FEFELOV:	Good strong cognac flies down the
	Throat like a bird but where can you
	Get good cognac nowadays?
	What we call cognac is really slop.
UNCLE VITYA:	(*Worried.*)
	Please try some, Andron Lukich.
	And please get us some mulerons.
FEFELOV:	Well, okay.
	Pour a little slop then, Vitek.

(*Cyber enters. He is wearing a very formal suit, completely buttoned. And he is carrying a briefcase. He goes up to the buffet.*)

CYBER:	(*To Melan Cholik in a whisper.*)
	She hasn't come?
MELAN CHOLIK:	(*Screams at the television.*)
	Kick it, you idiot!
	He missed the shot, the turkey!
	How pathetic our players have become!
	(*Bangs his fist on the table.*)
	There was a time! The crossbars shook!
	Balls were kicked through the net!
	If I were out there,
	There would be a flood of goals!
PHLEG MATIK:	(*Rubbing his hands, smiling.*)
	Tactically, his play is correct.
	Yes, friends, there can be no
	Criticizing a player who sees
	The field so clearly.
MELAN CHOLIK:	(*Screams.*)
	A lot you understand!
PHLEG MATIK:	But he's scored four goals.
MELAN CHOLIK:	But I could have scored nine! Nine!
SANG VINIK:	(*Morosely.*)
	All is lost. Now our team
	Will never make the semifinals.
CYBER:	(*In a whisper.*)
	She hasn't come?

MELAN CHOLIK: *(Looks at him.)*
No, I didn't see her.
(Spits. Turns away from the television.)
Watching makes me sick. How do you like
    football?
(Looks at Cyber and begins to speak to him in a
    hot, whistling whisper.)
Listen, friend, I know you're a big shot,
That you wheel and deal in the Ministry
And that I'm nothing . . . but listen!
She was here, my friend. She came!
May I never eat bread again if I'm lying!
It was five years ago, an evening hot like this one,
Right after football. The door opened
And she entered, ordered a milk cocktail,
Spoke a few words in Turkish,
Or French or English . . .
In other words, not Russian . . .
(Grinds his teeth.)
And left . . .

CYBER: *(Sadly.)*
I know this, brother. Every evening
You tell me this story . . .

EMELYA: *(Still reading his book.)*
Strange!
It turns out that the philosopher
Izmailov had a much larger
Skull than most people . . .

KATYUSHA: *(Interested.)*
Just think
How many interesting things
There must be in your books.

EAGLE: I was in reconnaissance once
And in a shelter abandoned by the
Enemy I once found a book . . .

KATYUSHA: I know, Eagle, I know . . .

(Turns away with a yawn. In despair the Eagle squeezes her hand.)

MELAN CHOLIK: Look how he dawdles!
He moves like a sleeping python!

PHLEG MATIK: An excellent player, but his temperament
Would suit a referee more than a player . . .
(Gets up, goes to the buffet.)

SANG VINIK:	(*Also gets up. His movements resemble those of Melon Cholik in the preceding nine tableaux.*)
	The final whistle! How much bitterness
	This whistle has betokened for us,
	Fans of this team which is clearly doomed . . .

(*Goes up to the buffet. All three Temperaments whisper together, Melan Cholik bangs his fist on the table, passionately tells some story.*)

UNCLE VITYA:	(*Timidly.*)
	Andron Lukich, maybe you could
	Use this pen?
	(*Hands Fefelov a pen.*)
FEFELOV:	(*Puts on his glasses and looks at the pen.*)
	Mmm . . . yes, I can use it.
	Certainly I can use it, dear Vitya.
	Or have you forgotten what I used to teach you?
	In a household even crap can be put to use.
	Only I prefer Parker jotters.
	(*Puts the pen in his pocket.*)
UNCLE VITYA:	I'll ask the fellows about Parkers later.
	But could you use a necktie?
	After all, Andron Lukich, you're our eagle!
	(*Hands him a tie.*)
EAGLE:	I request that you be more careful! Your jokes . . .
KATYUSHA:	(*Annoyed.*)
	Evgeny Aleksandrovich, don't worry!
	Worry can ruin the liver of
	Even a sturdy old warrior.
	Emelya, come here! This fellow
	Is a student-philosopher. A brain!

(*Emelya comes to their table. Without looking away from the book, he empties the Eagle's glass and eats something from his plate.*)

EMELYA:	Just think, Dr. Aleksandrov's
	Ears were larger than those of
	Other people. Ears like radar . . .
STAGE MANAGER:	(*To Gutik, while looking at Fefelov.*)
	They've gobbled up my ring.
	Will you buy me a new one?
GUTIK:	I'll soon get you a ring not worse
	Then the one you lost. I've saved

	A can of mulerons and I'm getting
	Calls from the Little Theatre.
	They're putting on a show Saturday
	And are in need of mulerons, of course.
PHLEG MATIK:	(*To Melan Cholik.*)
	She hasn't come? There's no news?
	Friends, I swear that yesterday on
	Small Bronnaya Street just before
	Sunset I saw in a high window a
	Shoulder that looked strangely familiar.
SANG VINIK:	You imagined.
	She is not in nature. Don't wait for her.
	Perhaps on the Island of Mauritia
	She spends the evenings in cafes.
MELAN CHOLIK:	Then why, old crocodile, do you
	Come here every evening and shed tears in your soup?
	Brother-crocs! She was here!
	She came, brothers!
	May I never see black bread again if I lie!
	Five years ago on an evening hot like this,
	Right after football, the door opened
	And she entered, ordered an egg bouillon,
	Spoke a few words in Spanish,
	In Polish or in Azerbaidzhani,
	In other words, not in Russian . . .
	(*Grinding his teeth.*)
	And left . . .
PHLEG MATIK:	Petro, why do you always repeat yourself?
	She'll come, of course, but why
	Do you always make up fairy tales?
SANG VINIK:	A terrible lie . . .
MELAN CHOLIK:	Leave me alone, you jerks!
	The waitresses are in charge of customers!
	It's against the rules to ask the
	Bartender ridiculous questions!
	(*Shows them his fists and turns away.*)
EMELYA:	(*Looking into his book, goes up to Cyber. Pokes a finger into Cyber's chest.*)
	Tell me, pappy, why are you alive?
CYBER:	I'm not alive. I'm only resting . . .
	I'm waiting for new life . . .

–

EMELYA: (*Merrily.*)
                     Idealism!

(*Phleg Matik and Sang Vinik go up to Eagle's table, even though there are many unoccupied tables in the room.*)

PHLEG MATIK: Pardon me, is this taken?

(*They sit down.*)

FIRST WAITRESS: They sat down.
                     Petro is off his rocker and these two look
                         drunk . . .

SECOND WAITRESS: They keep waiting, they come here every
                         evening . , .
                     Do you remember that woman tourist, Vera?

THIRD WAITRESS: She was an artist, not a tourist,

FOURTH WAITRESS: They keep waiting
                     But aren't we waiting, too?

(*Chol Erik enters. His movements resemble those of Phleg Matik from the preceding nine tableaux.*)

MELAN CHOLIK: (*Screams.*)
                     He's come, the bastard! He's moving
                     Exactly the way he waddles on the field
                     From the center to the penalty line!
                     (*Throws a bottle at Chol Erik.*)

CHOL ERIK: Have you finished throwing?

FOURTH WAITRESS: (*Runs to Chol Erik, kisses him.*)
                     Igor, my beloved!
                     On the field they kick you in the legs,
                     In the café they throw bottles at you!

CHOL ERIK: Stop licking me!
                     (*Goes up to the buffet.*)

FOURTH WAITRESS: Igor, wait! (*Her arms dangle.*)

CHOL ERIK: (*At the buffet he guiltily makes sniffing noises
                       with his nose.*)
                     Don't forget I *did* get four goals . . .

MELAN CHOLIK: (*Screams.*)
                     You could have had nine! I would have had
                       nine!

CHOL ERIK: Cut the bull and give me a sausage.

MELAN CHOLIK: You want a sausage?
                     (*Calming down.*)
                     Okay, here.

CHOL ERIK:	(*With a sausage.*)
	She hasn't come?
MELAN CHOLIK:	No, I didn't see her.
	(*Looks around. In a hot whisper.*)
	Listen, Igor. You can believe me.
	She was here, friend, She came.
	May I never see black bread again if I lie! It
	was five years ago, on an evening hot
	like this . . .
EAGLE:	(*Gets up and proclaims loudly.*)
	One day she'll come!
	(*Stands with arm raised.*)

(*Enter Razrailov and Nina. Behind them, scraping his feet, enters Love Triangle.*)

(*A silent scene.*)

RAZRAILOV:	(*To Nina.*)
	Here, ma chère, eat we a bit,
	A bit we eat and back we go . . .

(*Laughs loudly and, wiggling his hips, leads Nina to a free table. Notices Cyber.*)

	Greetings, Comrade Malakhaev!
	(*Shakes his hand.*)
	How nice we meet, eh what?
	Try you pie? Glad very see you here today
	And as old colleague would like you
	My wife to meet. Madam Florence.
	And this a friend of house . . .
	(*Nods at Love Triangle.*)
	Trusted companion . . .
CYBER:	(*In a hollow voice.*)
	How did you call Madam?
RAZRAILOV:	Madam Florence.
EAGLE:	That's not true. It's Nina!
ALL:	Yes, it's Nina! Nina! Nina!

(*They all leap up and timidly drag themselves to Nina. Only Fefelov continues to eat.*)

FEFELOV:	Madam Florence, I recommend the chicken.
NINA:	(*Smiling, as if asleep.*)
	Bois lois lyons nielodar . . .
RAZRAILOV:	As you see, Madam Florence's
	Russian leaves much to be desired.

	(*To Nina.*)
	You see, my dear, they were waiting for you.
	I told you, they were waiting for us.
NINA:	(*Pitiably.*)
	Dzondon moire oli Goliotelo . . .
RAZRAILOV:	She says: "each to his own."
CHOL ERIK:	(*In a hollow voice.*)
	Go away, Razrailov. We remember you.
CYBER:	Stay, Nina. We've been waiting for you.

(*A general commotion.*)

RAZRAILOV:	We don't have time. We're busy now
	With a certain experiment.
	(*Quickly eats from Fefelov's plate.*)
	Imagine beneath the earth's surface—
	The chicken's juicy, you should add more
	sauce—
	At a depth far from football,
	A laboratory will arise . . .
	Free individuums together
	With electrical machines . . . cucumber . . .
	(*Chews.*)
TEMPERAMENTS:	We don't agree! No!
RAZRAILOV:	Enough talk!
	(*Wipes his lips on the necktie of the utterly
	confounded Fefelov.*)
	Let's go, Ninon, Madam Florence or whatever
	You're called in different towns.
	(*To Love Triangle.*)
	You come too, freak!
LOVE TRIANGLE:	O horrors!
	Him I love, you I respect.
	Pour poison in the food together with a kiss.
	Traces of triangular love vanish,
	Sufferings pale, Eros is enfeebled.
	(*Convulsion.*)

(*Razrailov takes both Nina and Love Triangle by the arm and, his behind wiggling, leads them to the exit. They disappear. Everyone returns to his previous position.*)

FEFELOV:	How stifling!
	(*To Eagle.*)
	Don't scream when it's so hot!
	We have ways to make you shut up!

(Nina reappears.)

NINA: *(Joyously.)*
Hey, friends!
I've come back to you! You've been
Waiting for me for so long
And I've been waiting, too.
(Weeps.)

(Razrailov rushes out and grabs her by the arm.)

NINA: Mourlen luglio tympan!
(Her hands are outstretched.)
Ferran occhi styllo navakobucco!

(Razrailov drags Nina away. They disappear.)

EAGLE: *(Sits down, exhausted.)*
She'll come back, you'll see, she'll come back . . .

MELAN CHOLIK: *(ardently.)*
She was here, brothers, she came in!
Five years ago on an evening as hot as this one.
Right after football, the door opened
And she entered with some miserable creep
And a triangular shadow . . .

FEFELOV: He's crazy!

UNCLE VITYA: Be quiet, Andron. He knows what he's talking about.

(The Temperaments, Cyber, and Eagle walk to the front of the stage and stand in thought.)

CYBER: I'd like to know what will become of us,
What will become of us in the past and the present?
What will become of us in the future?

EAGLE: Who knows?
I can only say that we'll all be alive
Two hundred years from now and one hundred years ago.
And on such a stifling and disturbing evening
We'll all be waiting . . .

FEFELOV: Who ate my chicken?
I swear there'll be no mulerons
For the next performance!

(Curtain.)

July–August 1967
The Observatory, Koktebel.

Theatrical Circles Arranged in a Spiral[*]
by Mark Rozovsky

How does theater begin?

For me personally, theater begins with the nonplay

The nonplay is that which I am not going to tell you about yet.

Something must be done so that the theater can emancipate itself (the dream of Tairov)[†] and become supertheater.

Supertheater is the mirage of an illusion.

The illusion and mirage of the theater prove the existence of the nonexistent.

The nonexistent is the most substantial part of the theater.

Consciousness is materialized in a miracle, that is, in the poetry-laden life and death of the production.

The production is always concrete, clear, and well-defined.

The definition is programmed by a tired, vain director.

The director labors at the Devil's task of building mirages and illusions.

The illusions and mirages built up by the director must force the spectator to believe in the textural, physical, material existence of a "second" world.

The second world is theater, which comes out of nowhere at the beginning of the performance and goes off into nowhere at its end.

Nowhere is that which—or that place where—theater secretes itself and languishes until the beginning of tomorrow's performance.

The World Secret is expressed by the theater.

There is no secret only for those who know everything.

Do you know yourself?

No one knows himself completely—and that is why we need actors, who supposedly know supposedly us.

*Translated by Christina Dodds-Ega.

†Alexandre Tairov—A Soviet actor and director. Originally a protege of Stanislavski, Tairov later developed an aesthetic of the theater in which the actor, rather than mechanical or literary factors, is seen as the central element in the creation of dramatic tension [tr.].

Supposedly us are the people that they play on the stage.

The stage is a hole into the second world.

The second world is swept by the winds of an unknown life which are the main bearers of the salty truth.

The truth is elicited from chaos, from the performance; it is wonderful, naïve and evanescent.

The evanescence of the theater makes it timeless.

Timelessness is cosmogonic. Therefore, the truth, which is so evanescent in theater, comes to us from a second world, seemingly from eternity.

The timelessness of the truth emphasizes the temporality of life.

Life is not a performance.

The performance is theater.

Theater is that which is not. From that wooden platform another, essentially illusory life flies into our real one, and by believing in it we enter into communication with something higher; we receive a signal from the world of ideals which, as always, proclaims the foolishness of common sense.

Sense can be revealed even in nonsense.

Nonsense is not merely part of the performance, but the root of the magic.

The train-car fragance of the stage and the stench of the coulisses are imbued with magic.

One should never brush the coulisses with one's hands. Stanislavski was perfectly right in yelling about that at rehearsals.

To Stanislavski we owe the most accurate definition of theater in two words: "here and now."

"Now" means today, in this year and century.

"Here" means within the borders of our country, with our theatergoer and our Ministry of Culture.

Culture should not be guarded, but protected.

Protectors are distinguished from guards by the fact that they do not go to the jail, but to the theater.

The theater is the place where brawny offspring fall into spiritual dependence on their maundering forebears.

The forebears dream of being remembered, while their offspring consider how to give these memories an infinite number of variations in theatrical expression.

Expressing yourself and your forebears is easy—all you have to do is turn yourself inside out under the intersecting stares of everyone who has come into your theater.

Your theater must allow for the specific characteristics of the production as seen from different points in the hall.

The hall, as a rule, is not thought of by the director as a continuation or prolongation of the stage into the Other Universe.

The Other Universe is visually contraposed to the stage space, which, unfortunately, is most commonly called the "mirror of the stage."

The "mirror of the stage," moreover, almost always suffers from the simpleminded central decision of directors whereby it is taken literally—as a mirror.

A mirror is flat, whereas the "mirror of the stage" is always curved and stereoscopic, which makes the director dash through aisles at rehearsal time, dreaming of entering body and soul into the play of color and composition.

The play is theater; literature is business.

The business of the play is my profession as a dramatist and a director.

The director looks at the stage from different points in the hall to size up the image of one scene among the various possibilities of the mutable composition, trying to guess the laws of a secret rhythm which protests against the laws of iron symmetry, hoping to capture another world where the spectators' gazes intersect at the focus of perspectives, in the numberless places where illusory elements collide with reality.

Reality in theater is attained by the perception of a flow of changes: faces, positions, figures, colors, and of course, the ideas, images, and characters in one's mind.

The character—the target of tangled, grandiose forces—raises the production to drama.

Dramatic effect arises from the joining of the unjoinable in a system intoxicated by its own freedom.

This system of the author's caprices and contortions solves the problem of form as the ultimate goal of an art in which theater and life clash, and the lie which rolls back and forth between them is justified by the banality of the subject and triviality of the daily round.

The daily round, or "communal nonsense" (an expression of Nabokov's), is implanted in the consciousness of the author with one purpose: to somehow conceal the declamatory quality and phoniness of the characters' dialogues and speeches.

The character's speeches (and not his actions) are the gauge of this pseudorealism, lifeless psychologism, and castrated drama, the programmed predictability of which deprives the theatergoer of the pleasure of figuring the person out.

A person in a drama is out of control; his stage appearance is incongruous, strange, contradictory, and illogical.

The logic of "communal nonsense" is the principal enemy of our theater.

Like Salierianism,* as opposed to Mozartism, it verifies harmony

---

*A reference to Pushkin's famous poem "Mozart and Salieri." Salieri, a composer who has achieved a modest success by laboriously "dissecting music as though it were a corpse" and "checking harmony by algebra," murders his friend Mozart, whose effortless inspiration he envies [tr.].

by algebra and inevitably leads artists to diagrams.

Diagrammaticism is the result of our glorification of the first world (where you and I live) and our disbelief in the second (where we are reflected).

Reflections are invaluable because they violate the logic which Pirandello taught someone sometime.

Pirandello was a teacher of logic who became a poet of the theater.

The theater could not have done without Pirandello, who drew the instability, fluidity, and iridescence of his characters from the tragedy of life.

He redirected the tragedy of life into the comedy of the theater, and the play became an act of immersion in the performance.

The dynamic conception of the theater was thus thrashed out in the struggle with communally nonsensical logic which capitulated, and is now being integrated into the universe of thoughts and feelings.

Feelings and thoughts together with callousness and thoughtlessness keep the theater under tension, for to this day it appeals to one and all with a request for a repertoire. However, there is no response and no repertoire.

Repertoire is also an enemy of our theater, but not the main one. The principal trait of our theatrical repertoire is playness, while it should be theatricality.

The theatricality of a play is nonsense of the sort that playwrights no longer compose.

In our time all those who have nothing to do with the theater, all those who keep their distance from the theater and who find it shameful, write theatrically.

Shame and pity facilitate the development of a character, his humanization by contradictory behavior; it is precisely here that we see genuine realism, unspoiled by routine forms.

Form in theater is incomprehensible; what is comprehensible is content.

Our theater is empty of content and full of formlessness.

Full theatrical expression does not require dying bodies who, by dint of their position and right to a line at the bottom of the poster, have been entrusted with actors' fates and the working of magic.

Theater becomes magical when dynamic changes which always seem improvised to the audience are arranged on stage, and when each successive scene introduces a novelty which is continually renewed for as long as the play runs.

The performance consists of infinite phases, fragments, and compositions, organized into a continuum in which each infinitely small quantity or detail is part of a harmony which never repeats itself in time or space.

Harmony is attained in the free play of artistic expression, every whim of which must be declared a law to be obeyed to the letter.

The laws of theater obey the lawlessness of our human feelings, which are compelled to candor and regulated by nature, history and man, the trinity which holds the World Secret.

It behooves one to be interested in the World Secret, but under no circumstances should it be discovered (even if it opens up a crack to you of its own accord some nice evening or morning, somewhere "here" and sometime "now").

"Now" is a part of eternity, and "here" is a piece of space.

Space allows us to carve a little platform called a stage out of ourselves, and on it we can tumble a little, play, have fun, improvise, talk a little, suffer a little. . . .

Suffering is leaving the theater these days, because pain is disappearing from art.

A play permeated by pain—that is art.

Art is conniving. it complies with those who do not know too clearly or completely what they want, but who wish to obtain everything at once by force.

The rape of the pregnant stage by a good-for-nothing director does not rob humanism of its forever elusive, invincible desire for the truth. Truth is like a tempting bouquet of grass dangled before the muzzle of an ass on its way to some unknown destination: with great difficulty, we drag ourselves up to the bouquet and greedily swallow the uprooted stems, and they turn out to be toxic.

Intoxicating oneself with theater is helpful, although the action of this narcotic carries the destructive force and seclusion of an entire lifetime of addiction to the pleasures of the play.

The performance is emptiness filled with visions. The visions disappear and appear, and disappear once again, and again reappear; it is the repetition of the unrepeatable performance that is the heart of its unreality. And at this moment the meaning of life, which was half-revealed to us in school by practicality and materialism, seems to be placed in question.

This question is not addressed to us alone; it is flung out as a bold challenge to all far and near forms of our cosmos, which contains the enigma and secret of the "second" world, inexplicable from the standpoint of our first (and last?) one, if only because all of us, including our esteemed scholars, are stuck, powerless to discover that which is simply no business of our minds.

The whole problem is that a profound doubt in the complete reality of that which exists is converted by the theater into a play full of naïveté, fantasy, and wonder, unworthy of any seriously-thinking intellectual.

In the theater the chimeric masquerades as the genuine; an opium haze of individual and collective illusion is created on stage. This is when one is compelled to believe in the reality of fables, a reality which has come out on the platform with a single thought: to prove that the collection of mirages and illusions on a limited portion of space (provided it is stable in its organization) is, in the final human analysis, the absolute of the truth that there is a God.

By God, how can you not go into ecstasies over the concretely concocted structural world, the living presence of which in our consciousness is direct proof of the reality of nonexistence?

This impossible story, like "to be or not to be," provides visible, irrefutable proof that, of all human institutions, the theater is, perhaps, the only one in which a miracle triumphs: you look at nothing and see something.

This Something, whose appearances and disappearances make up the essential flow of a theatrical production, personifies the so-called struggle of Man with Time, a struggle in which Time persists in destroying a specially selected individual, while the latter, joking and playing through it all, keeps proving that he is alive.

The living Hamlet does not vanish from the stage at the end of the performance. There were times when I used to look for him, sniffing around the props and scenery which had just been out in the lights, wandering around the wings among the dusty, deserted sets. I never did find him, and we talked for hours about this and that, the important and the unimportant, the simple and the complex, life and death. . . .

Death lives on the stage and in the wings after the performance until we penetrate into every secret nook and cranny of that musty world that resembles an underground crematorium where already millions and millions of lives which had broken with their own personal "here and now" have burned.

Now here, in the semidarkness of the wings, in the depths of night, it does not smell of dead flesh because it is still and the air has congealed. Let just one small, piercing ray of light fall onto the stage from somewhere above or to the side, into this fragrant decay from which the road leads only to eternal sleep, straight into the fairy tale which will come true only tomorrow, and what happens? The slumbering world awakens, the props shudder, the scenery comes to life and shakes off its dust, and *if* an actor suddenly strides in in his costume and greasepaint, death itself takes to its heels and such scenes will appear to us as have never been seen before and will never be seen again by anyone—a miracle, a living miracle!

We call that which comes to us from "that" world, and which sheerly, dependably shines, Miracles.*

---

*This sentence contains several two- or even three-way puns which cannot be translated: the word svet, meaning light, world, or society is contained in the word nesusvetnyi, meaning sheer or utter (as in "utter nonsense"). The author invents an adverb based on this adjective, and then goes on to use the verb svetit'sja, "to shine" at the end of the sentence [tr.].

That which shines is theater.

Theater is that which shines and moves.

That which shines, moves, and talks can also be theater.

A sunbeam set to the music of a thunderstorm passing nearby can be theater, too.

Take my word for it, the thunderstorm by itself is also theater in a certain sense.

It is interesting to regard thunderstorm theater in exactly the same way as any other theater—in the same way, for example, as we look at the living, honest-to-goodness scene of the annihilation, execution, and demolition of buildings in the Old Arbat* by modern technology.

By the way, the technical equipment used in our theaters is terrible.

What is terrible about it is that our theater has surpassed that of the rest of the world, but although the theater of the rest of the world has fallen behind, still it is somehow out ahead.

What is ahead of us is that which has never been.

Everything has been, and even so there is much that has yet to be.

There has yet to be a complete unleashing of fantasy, which presses the stale collars of aging plays and forgotten, unread literature.

Believe me, the burned-through places accidentally made by these irons in literature shed the most delightfully curling puffs of smoke.

Smoke puffs dissolve, but theater does not end with our exit from the hall. The performance phosphoresces in the dark recesses of our sensual memory, vanquishing the scientific thesis on the frightening Moment of Time, and our notions concerning life turn out to be stronger—oh, yes!—stronger than life itself!

This whole euphonic mixture of sounds, details, patches of color, actors' personalities, props, movements, feelings, and the actors' and audience's statements, arranged in expedient harmony—would this be life or not?

Is it life or isn't it, the tiny, wavering smoke puff of each separate performance which is woven into the multipatterned absurdity of real existence, this smoke ring which resists that absurdity and the general ossification of our thoughts and feelings?

Feelings, will, understanding of people and the surrounding world, insight into history, morality, talent, sharpness of judgement, love for oneself and for other creatures, various changes of scene and intonation, gentle jests and cutting replies, happiness, grief, boredom, indolence, delight, intrigue, sacrifice, and the lunacy and brilliance of each and every participant—everything, everything, everything which the theater brings into its hall is, of course, these same little smoke puffs and nothing more.

Only to those who bend with every breath of air, but yet still stretch upward, drawing their frail, crooked little columns almost up straight,

---

*A neighborhood in Moscow [tr.].

is it given to survive as great art.

The columns stream up and evaporate somewhere up there, as high as they can go, and there is no guarantee whatsoever that one single, solitary, carefree little waft of gas will make its way through something to go somewhere.

But all the same, where *does* the performance go?

The performance—each one—is a living person.

People are mortal. Does that mean that theater, too, must know and prepare itself in advance for a journey to another world?

Processes of rebirth into a new form of life following that which we have already lived are undoubtedly commonplace in the spiritual world, but why, then, do we take the deaths of theaters in the prime of their lives so terribly hard? And why does a puny lack of culture so often turn out to be stronger than supposedly all-powerful culture?

Culture is not seasonal; it is not a temporary accomplishment, but something which has been laid down over the centuries in the consciousness of myself and the people around me.

The people are connected with the uncompromising will of the artist only through culture.

Culture does not share the fate of the people, but it is possible that the people share the fate of culture.

Russian culture was thrashed out by people who never mixed it up with civilization.

A civilized, but cultureless society runs wild, regresses, and finally sinks into the swamp of collective tastelessness, where merry little birds sing sweetly by themselves.

A bird can be civilized, too, by reducing all of its peculiarities to the design of an airplane.

Airplanes climb and descend differently from birds; culture which is falling is civilization, and civilization is climbing higher and higher, turning culture into a guided airplane which flies as someone else wants it to fly, in the direction that someone else wants it to go. Where is the way out? How can culture be saved?

Having been uncultured by civilization and modern obscurantism, I see only one way of saving culture—by releasing the bird and letting it fly freely.

The free soaring of a bird defies the trajectories programmed by automatic pilots and ground control systems.

The earthly and heavenly uproot one another, and this outpouring of my soul in poetry is making a tempest in the teapot of modern art.

Of all the arts today, theater is the most sluggish, the most routine, and the most nearsighted, whereas at the beginning of this century, in the time of Chekhov, Blok, and Meyerhold, it was the most sharp-eyed, vocal, and alive of the lot.

Our lives are much more theatrical than our theater.

The theater of Nikolai Evreinov, which burst into our times with "happenings," has been leapfrogged and left behind by Arto, Ionesco, and other foreign geniuses.

A genius is a person who comes from one side but ends up in the center.

By way of illustration, the center is a point on the intersection of Tolstoi and Tyutchev, and the name of this gigantic point is Andrei Platonov.

Platonov created a theater which everyone knows, the power of which will still be felt by the people of the future.

The theater of the future will still have to dig out our archives in order to mentally arrive at the stupendously bright, defenseless, and luminous stage world which does not exist.

It does not exist because it existed once before, but died an unnatural death, and this act, like the murder of a little boy, was as terrible as it was absurd.

An absurd accident?

An accidental absurdity? Or the artificial destruction of the living theater, a simply brutal act which cries out for judgement by a court of justice?

Should the murderer be condemned?

Should the person who at some point in the past bashed in your (theater-person's) skull be killed today?

The theater-person has been wiped out, of course.

Of course, yes, O.K., I agree it can't be helped, but it's not all over yet, this is not yet the end. . . .

The end of the bloodied boy with the bashed-in head, croaking on the asphalt of the street in front of all those people—how is it not the theater?

This time the question asked by the theater, "to be or not to be," is addressed to the theater itself: How can you live through the "here and now?"

How is a smoke ring to survive in a whirlwind? How are we to wad ourselves up inside a canning jar, with the impotent rage of a slave against the invading legions? How and to whom can we run lamenting over our crucified creation? How can we raise our puny, wailing voices to carp back and forth with our buddies, over piddling things, like "That wasn't done right!" "That's not how it should have been!" "You're licking the wrong boots!" "You've gone to the wrong place!"

How can we, while the red-snouted villain in the green suit, one of our very own kind, turns his shiny little knife loose on us and, waving it at us in warning, delivers a blow with a club to the head from behind—Crack! Wasn't that how it was?

Yes, that was how it was. . . . O, how many of our deaths have already happened, and we, living Humpty-Dumpties, keep popping up in another place, on another stage, in another set and another play, or nonplay, knowing perfectly well that theater is destroyed and man is destroyed in the theater. And all the same . . .

All the same, how was it again that our new theater begins?

1972

Across...*
by Vasily Rakitin

Recognition in art is a very strange juncture.

Erudition, feeling, even sensitivity, intuition, daring, tear—what is most important here?

Why:
do they see a sphinx in us, try to unriddle us, while we, not in the least embarrassed, pretend that there is no riddle at all? "What?" "Nothing . . . special." And this about the most incredible thing. Indeed, about a surrealistic reality!

The Russian avant-garde.

Today it is the object of intellectuals' speculations, the idol of an almost mythological generation, a hot item on the art markets of the West.

If something is acclaimed in the West, then in this country, out of an old, nineteenth-century habit, going back to *les Ambulants*,† it is looked upon with scorn. But what is one to do—does it seem that the time for recognition of the avant-garde is coming?

Take the Ballet of Diamonds. This is the peak of Russian surrealism, already accessible and conquered by the art critics and the public. No one would think of calling it avant-garde.

More, more. Careful, now:

Tatlin, Malevich. Of course one can make portraits through architecture, design.

Lisitskii. Rodchenko. —Here is the magic wand, polygraphy. Then disciples, followers, undoubting eclectics, those that ape the innovators—you can begin to boldly apply the ecstatic epithets.

First we read the parody, then we hope to find the original.

On the other shore there is a good set of field glasses—twentieth-

---

*Translated by Christina Dodds-Ega.

†*Les Ambulants*: a painters' guild in Russia (nineteenth and twentieth centuries) [tr.].

century modernism. There are diagrams into which you can fit everything. A change of trends. Abstract art, pop art, conceptualism, and more. Finally, the word "revolution," magic even now. The revolution of people, words, machines, the Socialist, sexual, scientific, and technological.

Nevertheless, even there, in the rational West, not all ends meet.

For example, the glory of the avant-garde.

In the past they would have said Russian abstractionism, or simple nonobjective art.

It really began after the collapse of the dictatorship of abstract art, in a seemingly inappropriate moment of nostalgia for figurativeness.

Today they talk about the decline of leftist sentiments in life, but the avant-garde is becoming increasingly attractive.

A mass of publications.

Kandinsky. Matyushin. Popova. Even Filonov.

Chagall?

The addition continues. Fractions, it is true, are often added to the units. But the expansion of states is not yet completed.

Supermatism. Tatlinism. Constructivism.

Facts, documents, papers.

The whole is obviously greater than the sum of its parts. It engenders other qualities.

The avant-garde is cosmic, universal, but also concrete and tangible.

Uninterrupted antinomy.

The avant-garde is not a direction, but a directedness; not a style, but a particular creative state.

"Intuitive reason" was invented in Russia. The rational and the irrational were joined easily and simply. Art seized the territories of philosophy and religion and by no means intended to free them.

The "rebellion against the materialism of the present" raised by the avant-garde was directed precisely against the emptiness of life and the prosaic quality of everyday thoughts and feelings; Art was thus divided not only into the pigeonholes of isms, but also into the "profound" and the "shallow."

The artist of the 'teens did not see things by themselves. A car, a chair, painting on wood, plastic art. He was an apologist for color, texture, and rhythm. But from Berkeley we have, "The eye (or, more correctly, the spirit). . . ."

The artist affirmed the integrity of perception, and consequently the wholeness of the individual.

Nietzche analyzed the oppression of man, and the avant-garde realized that it was necessary to move away from the alienation of individualism. The beginning of the New Man?

What sort of person lives in avant-garde space? Isn't it funny to think of a person in a combination of triangles or in an artful construction of wire, plaster, and glass?

But

A new experiment in art is always associated with an extension of the inner potentialities of man.

Let us ask ourselves—

isn't the struggle with the illusions of space, this breaking away from the "hobbles of perspective," a struggle against the illusory nature of consciousness and existence?

isn't the destruction and banishment of the subject a struggle against the prosaic quality of everyday life?

Of course, it is possible to make poetry out of everyday life, but more often it deserves to be ignored.

A new form of art is a new form of behavior.

What is in the mind of the artist who creates plastic signs?

For him the world is not matter to be shaped, but pure energy. Very specifically, he thinks like a professional, aware of his own irreplaceability in the world—contemplatively and abstractly. The mode of thinking most natural to him is that of absolute categories.

Creative energy becomes the basis of the artistic process. This process is not the usual artists' life, consisting of the production of pictures and statues, but an epic feat. The myth promoting the establishment of a new artistic consciousness.

"Nonobjective art is a new ideology."

Without inner freedom and the absence of constraints there is no new form. It is said that life is the basis of art. The avant-garde has turned it around: a new art is a new life.

Skill is losing its neutrality. A new artistic language is becoming an inner requirement.

Science, technology, religion, sociology, folklore—everything which enters our daily existence chaotically and in fragments—find unity in the personality of the artist. Although, as Malevich has written, "It is surprisingly difficult to adjust oneself to happiness having seen all of Siberia."

The history of the avant-garde can be regarded as the history of the liberation of the artistic individual, or, from the point of view of general history, as the tragic breakdown of the individual.

Over and over again we have the peculiarities of the popularization of "leftist" art.

Always by way of something.

But a drawing was not made so that an engineer could devise a new automobile fin.

In large general exhibitions, it is possible to "push through a good name." Malevich, for instance.

The most incidental, the most unremarkable picture.

"Well? He did it." (What did he do "like everyone else"?)

"It's nothing awful. But they were saying. . . ."

It *is* rather awful that it is possible to forget that there exist art and great artists. Malevich, for instance.

Mystification and distortion with the best of intentions, to "get it into circulation." And always the idea of a social alibi—but we are talking about artists and not political figures!

The avant-garde and revolution.

It is not always possible to see the problem as life, without greasepaint. We are used to separating plastic art and philosophy, and to substituting the artistic for the social. Instead of understanding and *feeling*, we begin to analyze as though we were in a courtroom: accepted—unaccepted, and only then do we make a judgement concerning art.

And it seems difficult to do otherwise: revolution is one of those questions of history which it is impossible not to answer.

The avant-garde and revolution.

The comparison seems both exotic and natural. Almost ordinary.

"Who's that marching out of step?"

The precarious position of the avant-garde in the history of our culture has at least remained a position, thanks to Mayakovsky. Without him it would have been a sterile waste, the trash heap of history.

With the best of intentions they have made a screen of Mayakovsky, a little curtain hiding something shameful which one must neither know or show. They made an example of his personal fate. Those who didn't come up to the mark were diligently forgotten. "Mayakovsky's artists"—at times this was not a bad loophole. But for Malevich, Tatlin, and Filonov, Mayakovsky was not a model but a brilliant pupil who, moreover, was very, very unlike his teachers.

The avant-garde was flung into public life on the crest of the 1917 revolution. The willful, artistic bohemia proved the most visible determining factor in the art situation. But a thirst for life is not one and the same as adaptation. The relations of the avant-garde with the new leadership were whimsical and fantastic.

Summarily speaking, the traditionally inclined art intelligentsia strove to conserve the landmarks of culture in the storm of civil war. The avant-garde, despite the legend which attributes to it unlimited nihilism in practice as well as in theory, also took part in this effort. But it had another, more important, function in society. A creative one. New schools, museums, exhibitions—a harmoniously organized system of "acclimatizing" art to a country ill-adapted to it.

At the first opportunity certain of the fellow-travelers of the avant-garde wanted to make "leftist" art the art form of the state. Intoxication. But on the whole, the avant-garde did not rush to associate itself with the new ideology, which denied all the old ones. Its ideal was a state of ideological vacuum.

For the avant-garde, the revolution was a special effort, and a manifestation of a universal element in the world. Their perception of the revolution was frequently ahistorical and supranational; for them it was pure action.

But the slogan of world revolution—the slogan of the day—is accompanied in the depths of consciousness by the idea of universal, nonobjective art.

The avant-garde regards revolution as the absolute freedom of the individual.

The ideologies of art and politics may intersect, but they are independent of one another on the axes of life.

Hence comes the main principle of their interrelationship: the autonomy of art with respect to the state. The alignments of the 1920s were the legacy of the status quo between art and the state which was established in the first months after October.

The adversaries of the avant-garde could reproach the avant-garde for pragmatism, worldly ambition, and other sins, right down to infamous deception of the "system." But such an approach would be absurd.

In the very avant-garde idea of universal art there are absolute philosophical claims and an original deformation of Russian messianic dogma such as "Beauty will save the world." The avant-garde goes boldly into revolution, impelled by a belief in the absolute effectiveness of art. The avant-garde dreamed of determining the overall order of people's lives and feelings through a model of artistic life. At the heart of this ambition lay a conviction of deep kinship with the aesthetic self-awareness of the people.

The most striking aphorism of the brilliant experimenter Kruchov is, "See the people before you."

The world of art, as such, seriously intended to become a part of the new conditions of life. It is precisely these conditions that proved to be the expression of social ideas, and not everyday life itself.

The avant-garde went into the revolution as to an unknown space for creative work. It carried its own images, preconceptions and illusions. It "worked" not with the concrete matter of the day, but with history, with absolute theoretical models of life, a people and a nation.

It was a People that was present, and not the masses.

This is a special impersonal sense of reality, in which the individual and the world are equal in scale. In this equality there is not one whit of individualistic ambition.

A belief in the possibility of moral renewal through plastic art brings the avant-garde back into the mainstream of Russian culture, back to Dosteovsky and Tolstoy.

The greatest achievements of avant-garde plastic art form the nucleus around which a new system of artistic culture takes shape, such as the icons of old Russia, the Parthenon, or a medieval cathedral. As in the dawn of a truly new era, art is not adapting itself. "Bridges" are being built "down" to it. The entire program of education in aesthetics and art developed by the avant-garde is directed to the execution of this task.

The intersections of the avant-garde with the concrete affairs of the epoch are remarkable and important. The point is not that many of the avant-garde (and traditionalists as well!) designed streets and drew posters. The propaganda symbolic of "leftist" art is one of the facets of the plastic folklore of the revolution, although here there is much that is transient and insubstantial.

It is remarkable that nonobjective art as absolute creative work virtually "did not notice" the revolution, and it is also remarkable that it in particular should become the mode of self-expression of some profound processes, apart from the expectations that art be a mirror or even a magnifying glass for the epoch.

Art enters the consciousness as a new life, independent of society's attitude towards it, or, more precisely, as new vital energy and strength. It has its own chronology and rhythm.

It considers "The Black Square" a historical event of global importance, and not a scandalous incident at an exhibition in Petrograd.

A Tatlin relief is the inauguration of a new poetry of matter.

Filonov, Rozanova, Kandinsky and Rodchenko are not dictionaries of formal methods, but the discovery of new worlds.

In this sense, the quarrel of the avant-garde with realism, which has been carried to blind extremes in the age of revolution, is not essentially a quarrel over a certain form, but rather a quarrel over a rhythm of life, a way of acting in one's life space.

The spent form is discarded as living banality.

To a significant extent, the relations with the epoch are reduced to a conception of life and a disagreement over one individual.

The revolution destroyed the avant-garde as a single psychological unit. "Leftist" came to be associated more and more exclusively with art which was socially involved, and not with the new form in general.

Metaphysics collided with the dynamics of history, which had abruptly changed the life of the nation.

How can the incredible depths of nonobjective creation be made to conform with the cause of the day? For those artists who had already shaped their worlds, this was a personal drama.

For them the only way was to renounce their art or to countervail history.

A close friend of Khlebnikov, Dmitrii Petrovsky, said of him, "The Revolution, as it revealed itself then, oppressed him, but he wanted to believe and did not lose heart." Malevich, Filonov, and Tatlin swam against the current by not accepting as dogma the general evolution of art occurring before their eyes. Pasternak and Platonov did the same in literature. Now we plainly see that art is one of those areas of human interaction where the individual is more often right than "everyone," and that yesterday's pariah will tell us more about the times than a pleiad of talented deniers of reality. The contemporaneity of art lies not only in its harmony with the times, but also in the similarity in scale of the affairs of the artist and his epoch, and in the inner inspiration of his work.

The avant-garde and revolution.

It is, of course, these solutions that the "leftist" art of the 1920s now logically, now convulsively, attempted to find as it strove to overcome the estrangement of the artistic and the social.

It is the rejection of easel painting and the advancement of industrial art by the Moscow constructivists in the early twenties. The beginning of the new cinema. Dziga Vertov. Eisenstein. Lovshenko. The "leftist" front in theater. Above all, Meyerhold.

Each art was concrete and lived its own life. The early dawning of cinema and the triumph of Meyerhold took place against a background of strange and vivid events in the spatial arts, dramatic in their own respect.

The younger generation of the avant-garde, who had not known the metaphysics of the teens, was consistent in its own resolution of the conflict between the new forms as a way of life and as a social reality. According to its convictions, the collective, and not the individual, was always right. The picture as a spiritual substance was on its way out. Or was reborn as an illustration of the themes of the day through the medium of painting. (All of this, of course, is not to deny the marvelous expectations.) Industrial art and the new architecture often wanted to "correct" the sociological structures of society.

In these social manifestations, "leftist" art created the aesthetic ideal of the epoch, alluring and complete. This is the model of the New Man: serene, healthy, and purposeful.

But in artistico-sociological constructions, serenity can easily be carried to one-dimensionality.

A Tatlinesque and unintentional parody on this ideal is found in

Sergei Tret'yankov's play, "I Want a Child." Devoted to the ideas of the new social construction to the point of fanatacism, the playwright carries the concept of the new life to an antiutopian absurdity.

Of course, to the advocates of this aesthetic, Malevich is an obscure metaphysicist ("Give up your preaching, Citizen Malevich!") or a supplier of formal material, but on the whole something passé, long since written off.

The traditionalists contended that the manifestations of the avant-garde were obscure and superfluous. The "left" (in the political sense) wing of the avant-garde knowingly sacrificed many plastic values of the avant-garde and its underlying philosophical principles. They were offered as a sacrifice to social utilitarianism, an unaffected, romantic offering which was ultimately found unacceptable by society and mechanically rejected.

Trotsky, Lev Davidovich:
"One cannot seriously believe that history simply lays aside futuristic works and will bring them to the masses when, after many years, they have matured."
Could he have been wrong?

Plato, Saint Augustine, and Leibnitz believed in a numerical measurement of harmony.
Has Malevich found a common language with them?
Schopenhauer. Adorno. Bergson. Heidegger. Zen Buddhism. So many philosophical analogies have been devised to understand just one Artist!

Pages from a Diary[*]
by Viktor Trostnikov

September 21

I never thought that someday I would continue the diary that I had stopped keeping a long time back. But I have begun to experience some strange and complex feelings and I need to explore them. And for that it's best to write everything down while it's still fresh in mind.

It began like this.

Today I was coming home from work totally exhausted—rarely have I had such a hard day. I was so worn out that when I got off the bus I sat down on a wooden bench, not far from the bus stop, that I had never sat on before and had hardly even noticed. Watching the sunset spreading over the horizon, I fell into a sort of trance, and suddenly and unexpectedly an inscription that I had once read on a wooden cross in Novodevich Cemetery floated up into my memory:

> Passerby, take heed! I am at home, and you are a visitor.

Looking up, I picked out my own window on the eighth floor of a tall building. I imagined the inside of the apartment: the books on the shelves, the pictures, the furniture—everything that I had collected over the years and had carefully arranged as attractively and comfortably as possible—and somehow it all looked alien, uninviting.

Is that really home, I wondered. It's a cheap hotel with a pretentious decor which tries to stifle the guest with nostalgia. You could replace it with twenty others, move from one to another without the slightest regret, and even move gladly if you could get an extra square meter or two of space. How right and profound that inscription was! Indeed, we are guests wherever we go, although we try to keep our chin up and not notice. And only at such moments as I am now experiencing do we discover the truth and begin to recognize the hopelessness and futility of our earthly twistings and turnings, and to sense our own soul as something external, set apart from us and longing for its own dear home. "Poor soul," we cry in these moments of insight, "you're so

[*]Translated by Christina Dodds-Ega.

tired of captivity! May you soon free yourself from these corporal journeys and return to the One Who has sent you for such hard labor and Who will comfort and reward you upon its completion!"

Having thought all of this, I remembered that I was a man of the twentieth century, and furthermore, was among those whom the census takers place in the "educated" column. Therefore, these thoughts I had were nothing short of treason. Hadn't science, on whose principles I was nurtured and raised, long ago proven that the concept of a soul was the vestige of an age of ignorance and barbarism, that living things were merely complex mechanisms arising by the process of natural selection, and that after death nothing remains of them but dust? How had I slipped into mutiny? What fostered my capitulation to mysticism?

I recalled having experienced such moods before. This time, however, I felt it with particular keenness. What was it that was compelling me to seek comfort in illusions—old age, a withering mind, fear of death? Distraught and unsettled, I got up from the bench and wandered home. I felt that I was losing my self-respect, that I could not go on like this, or I would finish by finding myself neither fish nor fowl, neither here nor there. I tried to calm myself. I told myself, "You're tired. Your brain is exhausted, and that's why it is invaded by notions whose logical absurdity you are in no condition to notice. This moment of weakness will pass, and you'll go back to being an enlightened man, untainted by mysticism." And I tried to arouse, if not scientific understanding of the phenomenon of life, at least the feeling that arises in the presence of such an understanding—that old familiar feeling of pride in my own communion with the light of knowledge, which drives out the dark of myth and prejudice, and with the bold, objective, scientific thinking which penetrates ever more deeply into the secrets of nature.

But an odd thing happened: as I strove to resurrect in myself an exaltation in the secrets of nature, I felt instead a cold wave of discomfort and fear. And then the image of Reynolds, a renowned English physicist of the last century, came to mind. Not long ago I read that toward the end of his life he lost his mind and sank into despair. At the time I had thought nothing more of it—he had cracked, and God bless him. But now, in a flash of insight, I understood everything. A fanatical proponent of the scientific outlook on the world, he had worked many years to develop a detailed theoretical model in which the entire world in all its diversity was composed of tiny spheres, careening about and colliding with one another. He considered this model his life's work. Aside from those tiny spheres, said Reynolds, there was nothing. Even in the commissioned portrait which now hangs at the University of Manchester, he is depicted with his beloved little sphere in his hand. The sudden intuition fairly burned through me: it was that model which had driven him out of his mind! I knew this with certitude, with no need for any sort of additional evidence, for at that moment I was reincarnated as Reynolds, and was chilled by the presence of the omnipotent, mindless spheres which I myself had helped to triumph.

But am I really as badly off as that?

No, I need to get a good night's sleep, and things will look better in the morning.

September 22

I must remember today: this is one of the most important days of my life. They say that in the life of a man there are certain critical moments when everything that has been accumulating over the years suddenly crystallizes, and it is as though he has climbed a mountain, from which he has a totally new perspective on his surroundings. That is precisely what happened to me today. I will try to place what I have pondered and understood in some sort of order.

First of all I wanted to renew in my mind the proof of the nonexistence of the soul given by natural science, so that I could once again convince myself of its irrefutability, and then move on to an analysis of yesterday's mood with a clear conscience. And just then the unexpected happened. The more closely I examined that proof, the more transparent it became and the more clearly I began to see that it did not exist and never had!

If thunder had rolled in a clear blue sky, if a fish had begun to speak and a dog to fly, I could not have been as amazed and shaken as by this discovery. But I was even more astounded by the fact that such a soap bubble had not burst in the course of the centuries, and that many generations of the best minds had been so primitively taken in by charlatans proclaiming themselves to be the foes of mysticism.

All the same, I will set aside my emotions and lay everything out strictly and succinctly.

1. It is well known that the most correct proof of anything is a logical proof. When one wishes to logically prove the nonexistence of something, the method of proof by contradiction, in which it is shown that the existence of the object leads to a patent absurdity, is employed. No one has done anything of the sort in this case. Obviously, the supposition that a man possesses a soul contains no contradictions per se, or we would have caught on to them long ago. True, one can show that the concept of the soul has a certain logical flaw associated with the fact that it is immaterial and has, as a consequence, a certain inherently vague and arbitrary character. But it seems that such an objection is completely outmoded. Its trump card comes from the eighteenth century supposition of the superiority of the material with respect to the ideal, which physics has long since made obsolete. Although the man on the street may not know it, contemporary

theoretical physics, in the search for more and more fundamental components of matter, has unexpectedly come up against . . . ideas. The "quarks" which, according to the opinion generally accepted by specialists, make up matter are, to all appearances, pure abstractions. They have a mathematical, rather than physical, status, and as a result, can by definition never be observed in an experiment. The well-known American theoretician, L. Cooper, speaking of the fact that quarks do not "really" exist, posed the question, "How can we make any sense out of three nonexisting objects, the combination of which forms everything which exists?" His membership in the scientific caste did not allow Cooper to honestly respond to that question, but to the unbiased observer the answer must be clear: in the light of the data of modern physics, the worlds of the material and the ideal must change roles: the former must be considered inferior to the latter.

Therefore, citing the "reality" of matter as the basis of the logical preeminence of this concept with respect to any immaterial concept becomes irrelevant. As far as the criterion of pure logic is concerned, it absolutely and unequivocally points to the preeminence of the world of ideals. The thesis of the primacy of matter contains an inherent and insurmountable logical difficulty: it cannot explain where the laws of nature reside. If a century ago it was still possible to postulate that they are somehow "built in" to matter, inasmuch as there was then hope of reducing all global processes to the collision of minuscule particles, today, when it has become evident that the fundamental laws of physics cannot be formulated by any other means than in the language of operators acting in infinite-dimensional spaces, it has become equally evident that these laws are typical ideal entities and that in a world consisting solely of matter, such entities can have no place. The theory concerning the absence of "hidden parameters" proven in quantum physics provides a strictly materialistic confirmation of this, showing that the laws governing matter cannot, by definition, be "embedded" in matter itself; they reside in a separate, unobservable layer of Existence, fixed in the properties of the so-called "function of state" or "psi function." If the world of ideals is considered to be primordial, such logical difficulties do not arise. The laws of nature, as a particular species of ideas, will acquire a legal right to existence, and it will be possible to treat matter as incarnate thought. It is precisely that treatment of matter that has been adopted in the cosmogonic myths, religious thought, and philosophy of all peoples. The logical inequality of the ideal and the material is rooted in the simple fact that logic can deal only with ideas. A clear understanding of anything, and of matter in particular, is impossible without elaboration of the corresponding concept. Even the atheistic definition of matter begins with the words, "Matter is a philosophical category signifying . . ." No materialist can get around the logical primacy of ideas over material reality: after all, a "philosophical category" is an idea. Furthermore, the substantiation of any statement about the properties of matter leads to an analysis of what was perceived during an experiment, i.e., to an immaterial entity. John von Neumann correctly remarked that in order for the allegations of science to have any meaning, they must not be formulated according to the model, "such and such occurred," but rather as "we see the needle at such and such a position." This means that even science, which is concerned only with matter and nothing else, must begin and end with the ideal if it wishes to be consistent. This applies all the more to discussions touching upon the living world. Here you cannot make a single sure step forward on the basis of the theory of the primacy of the material and the derivative nature of the ideal, and you will be constantly losing your footing in such foggy statements as, "Moral standards arose as the result of an evolutionary drive to guarantee the well-being of the species." And any deviation from this thesis will sooner or later lead to the concept of the soul. Consequently, this concept does not only prove to be logically invulnerable and unassailable by any negating theory, but is the concept which imposes itself logically.

2. It can, however, be contended that science has given a proof of the nonexistence of the soul which, though somewhat weaker than a logical proof, is nonetheless sufficiently persuasive. It consists of the idea that science has succeeded in completely describing our surroundings without recourse to that concept. If this were indeed the case, we could pronounce the concept of the soul if not contradictory, at least unnecessary and, from an enlightened point of view, irrelevant. It was just this type of proof that Chernyshevskyi had in mind when he wrote, "The character of the results obtained by analysis of areas and phenomena understood by science already gives sufficient evidence of the nature of the elements, forces, and laws acting in the remaining areas and phenomena which are as yet incompletely understood." Having written these lines, Chernyshevskyi was undoubtedly very proud of himself, and upon rereading them, he may have thought, "How clearly and vigorously the thought is expressed! Now only a fool could fail to grasp the correctness of our position!" But now when we read these words they provoke quite a different response: "Where have you gone, O good old days, when we took assurances of the explicability of any sort of "areas and phenomena" at face value?" Now there is not a single branch of science without its secrets, and this has forced scientists to change their tactics in influencing public opinion. Instead of declaring, as did Chernyshevskyi, that only a very few enigmas remain, they have begun to be almost proud of the fact that these enigmas are present everywhere in such numbers, and that any advances in experimental technology will only spawn more and more dilemmas. Modern scientific articles are embellished with phrases which would have been considered shocking a hundred years

ago: "Nature is wise and inventive," "Nature achieves her purposes in surprising ways," "Nature is always more clever than we suspect," etc. Strictly speaking, these phrases are meaningless in the framework of a genuinely scientific standpoint, which views the Universe as an automaton, but there is so much in science that is not understood that scientists cling to them as a means of creating an impression, as though the plethora of mysteries only reinforced their viewpoint. The fact is that the intelligible data which have been accumulating in science do not attest to the inadequacy of our vision, which will be improved by new binoculars in the near future, but to the fact that the viewpoint we have chosen is fundamentally wrong. If we were to consider the fundamental theoretical problems, we could affirm that science as a whole is in a state of deep philosophical crisis, and that the main concern of scientists is to conceal this from the general public and, in so far as possible, from themselves. In astronomy, for instance, all of the classical concepts of the Universe which formed the traditional basis of the materialist standpoint have collapsed, and the heavens are densely covered with question marks. The nature of pulsars and quasars is a mystery. It is not known whether or not "black holes" exist and if there are many of them; there are no reasonable hypotheses concerning the reasons for the birth of matter in galactic nuclei or concerning mechanisms controlling the elaboration of galaxies. And most importantly, the functioning of the Universe as a whole is deeply shrouded: its hypothetical beginnings in a hyperdense substance, its expansion, disintegration into individual stars, and so forth. Things are no better in molecular and cell biology. A decade ago it was still possible to generate some artificial optimism, replacing the question "why" with the question "how." Hastily and triumphantly boasting that the "secret of life" would be unraveled any second, one could study the details of newly discovered mechanisms of protein synthesis and the transfer of genetic information by DNA molecules. But now that the action of these mechanisms is well understood, biologists have nothing more to distract their attention from infinitely more fundamental questions: Why were precisely these mechanisms developed in the course of evolution, and what preceded them? Why are we unable to reconstruct the bridge between the living and the nonliving? Is such a bridge even possible across a chasm the width of which we could not even have imagined yesterday? We turn to the biology of organisms and species, and here again we find innumerable mysteries. The very origin of the species has become uncertain: classical Darwinism has been completely discredited and excites almost open opposition among biologists, while the "synthetic theory of evolution," which is its proclaimed successor, has turned out to be a bare outline which not a single intelligent person can understand. Another enigma is the development of an organism from an embryo, which takes place according to a scheme so complex that it is inconceivable that it could be inscribed in a single small cell. Equally mysterious are the behavioral reactions of animals, which used to be accorded a single "explanation": "It is likely that a species or biocenosis, by exerting a psychological influence, is capable of modifying the behavior of other individuals in a manner advantageous to itself." As we climb the rungs of the evolutionary ladder from zoology to general ecology, and then to psychology, sociology, and history, we are confronted with increasingly impenetrable darkness. Here explanations are replaced by descriptions, conviction by rhetoric, and proofs by demagogical examples. At every step we are confronted with intrigues, squabbles, quarrels between schools and movements, and open collusion between scientific activity and the politics of the moment. Mingling in this sphere of "knowledge" with the glassy-eyed businessmen of science, you constantly have the feeling that any minute they're going to ask you for a loan and you'll never see your pennies again, and the day comes when the thought strikes you, "Were *they* really telling *me* how human beings and human society are put together?"

But the point is not even that all hopes of a complete explanation of the world by materialistic science have been lost. What is much more important is that the data obtained by science testify more and more eloquently to the fact that the crisis of knowledge can be averted in only one way: by recognizing the realm of the immaterial which governs material processes. This testimony flies in the face of official scientific ideology, and because of this it will have an uphill struggle to win acceptance. Attempts will be made to discredit it, or at least to ignore it. As it is unorthodox, it will be discussed only in those branches of knowledge which are forced to it by a high degree of logical rigorousness or an abundance of experimental material. Physics occupies first place in this respect, since it is both rigorous in its judgements and is more accustomed to dealing with experimental data than the other sciences. In other words, it is less vulnerable to pressure from scientists. Directly behind it comes embryology which, in spite of being a descriptive science, disposes of an immense body of trustworthy and precise laboratory observations. Next comes the theory of evolution, in which the body of material is smaller, but still significant. Then come psychology, the science of animal behavior, and ecology, in which the data are more diffuse. Bringing up the rear are such suspect branches as sociology and history, with their doubtful methodologies and ambiguous treatment of facts. Forty years ago physics had already reconciled itself to the idea of the existence of an unobservable component of Existence which influences particles of matter. This forced departure from its official standpoint was preceded by a long period of quarrels, vacillation, and fears, but that did come to an end, and now theoreticians regard any physical system as having two levels, consisting of the "wave function" and "observables."

Without such a segmentation of reality, which accommodates the laws of evolution on one layer and observable entities on the other, physics could not have surmounted the crisis which had developed at the beginning of this century and became the basis of modern nuclear technology. The other sciences have not yet committed themselves to an open recognition of invisible realities, but somewhere one senses dark fermentation, the stubborn groping of truth forcing its way through the orthodox edicts, and by the energy of these heresies one can judge the readiness of a given branch of science to follow the example of physics. The most apparent opposition to the official standpoint of science is in embryology. It is often said of representatives of this science that vitalism is the disease of the profession. This refers to the fact that many dedicated embryologists have stoutly held out for the existence of "entelechy"—some imperceptible substance governing the development of the fetus. It is not difficult to understand these people: any individual who observes the astounding process of the day-to-day formation of an immensely complex organism from almost nothing, from a microscopic cell, must finally recognize that the grandiose blueprint of that organism could not be housed in a cell, but must flow into the fetus as its development progresses from something outside. This external entity which is the custodian of the plan has been named "entelechy" by biologists in mutiny against the accepted dogma, but they have not yet succeeded in legitimizing it. In evolutionary theory the idea of an unobservable entity which controls the differentiation of species is already heard less distinctly; taking no clearly defined form, it develops into such unorthodox theories as the "nomogenesis" theory advanced by L.C. Berg, whose aim is to develop a scientific line of argument in favor of the thesis that evolution is purposeful. In psychology, the concept of immaterial integrality acting on the material structure has come to light in the work of a single school: the study of gestalts. As for the social sciences, terms such as the "spirit of a nation" and others are treated as pure metaphors.

Thus, modern science admits that any microparticle possesses a soul, and considers the study of these "souls," which it terms "functions of state," a matter of the greatest importance; it places the presence of a governing entity, or "entelechy" in biology, in doubt; it holds the existence of an immaterial evolutionary plan up to ridicule; and it is prepared to discuss the purposefulness of biocenosis only with those who will first pledge to reduce it to the action of physico-chemical laws; the "spirit of a people", in its opinion, is only an abbreviated expression concealing the "parallelogram of forces," such as a man's drive to feed himself, find shelter from the cold, and reproduce. It turns out that the more primitive an object is, the more readily science will tolerate the thought that it is governed by some unseen reality. But this, after all, is utter nonsense! From physics we know that when a particle becomes part of a system—an atom, for instance—not only does the function of state retain its role, but its role is increased, acquiring new and more subtle modes of action on the observable structure. Naturally, one would expect that when increasingly complex structures such as organelles, cells, functional systems, entire organisms, and societies of organisms are formed, the governing entities develop as well, and that their influence is extended to more and more levels. And if science fails to reach such a natural conclusion, it is only because it contradicts its ideological framework. If it were to renounce that ideological framework, a legacy from the epoch of mystical materialism and militant atheism, it would soon become obvious that the facts which have been accumulating in abundance literally scream out that behind the visible layer of Existence stands one which is invisible, but no less real, and that a knowledge of this invisible reality is essential to an understanding of any material object. Consequently, not only must such immaterial concepts as the "human soul" not be considered superfluous, but they must be placed in the ranks of the most important concepts to which the mind of twentieth-century man must refer if he is to comprehend the existing body of scientific material.

3. An even weaker argument against the existence of a soul, but one which still merits attention, might be raised by the creation of an artificial device which imitates some important facet of human behavior. Then one could say, "Look, we know that this machine has no soul, and how is it different from us?" The ideology of natural science obviously began to feel at some point that herein lay its last chance, and that is why it has embraced cybernetics with such enthusiasm. Around this pseudoscience, which does not even have so much as a specific object of inquiry, grew a real brouhaha. The underlying work of Weiner, Shannon, and Ashby, amplified by journalism, has produced a powerful echo in the form of a vast literature which calls itself "science fiction," but which the public, with much greater accuracy, simply called "fiction" without considering it necessary to refer to its scientific nature. But the public does not know that the articles published in scientific periodicals and reviews, laden with erudite terminology and materialistic cliches, can be considered precisely the same kind of barefaced fiction. Think of the money that has been spent on these reviews, on the conventions, conferences, and symposiums on cybernetics! But the years passed, and as the fog of lies and demagoguery lifted, the bitter truth began to take form: not a single step towards the creation of a "man-made mind" had been taken. Even the comparatively modest plans for constructing reconnaissance devices and mechanical translators have failed completely. Countless publications have described the characteristics of man-made "people" and explained how robots differ from cybers, and cybers from cyborgs,

when in reality science has not succeeded in constructing anything more than fast-acting arithmometers, and will not, as has now become clear to almost everyone. Shouldn't this push us into the idea that there is something in a human being that no material structure can duplicate?

And that is where things stand with the "proof of the nonexistence of the soul" obtained by science. It has shown itself to be one of the greatest frauds of modern times. I understood this today beyond the shadow of a doubt, as though the glasses which had distorted the world had fallen from my eyes, and I saw everything in its place. How exciting this hitherto unfamiliar feeling, which I would call the joy of insight, is! At first, it is true, it was marred by regret for those lost years which I spent in a state of stupor, but soon that sadness was replaced by the desire to uncover more and more proof that I possessed a soul. Although objective scientific inquiry, contrary to the wishes of scientists, yields not a little such proof, it still does not exhaust the question. Science has balked at the need to recognize immaterial realities as such and must study them, as is its wont, from the outside, but it is most convenient to study the human soul in particular from the inside. Yesterday's sense of nostalgia for some unearthly home, which awakened all of the thoughts which I have just described, has perhaps given me one such internal, that is, direct proof and has half-revealed some of the traits of the soul. We must go further in this direction. Why did my soul somehow separate itself from me yesterday so that I was able to observe it? It was because at some moment we were striving in opposite directions: it began to yearn for its home, while I, like any biological creature, remained oriented toward life here. This splitting of perspectives was a manifestation of the "threshold effect," which must become stronger toward the end of one's life. But in that case, additional information about the soul might be obtained from another threshold effect which could be expected to occur in the first years of life, when the soul has not yet become accustomed to this world and a mutual lack of understanding exists between it and the body.

In order to do that it will probably be necessary to make an excursion back into my own childhood. After all, for some time how I have been wanting to pay a visit to the places where I grew up; I had even begun to dream about them, but could never quite manage to get away—one thing would come up and then another. And now is the most suitable occasion to fulfill my intentions.

September 27

I have just returned from Malakhovka. While it is still fresh in mind, I am going to set down everything that I discovered there.

A low porch was the first thing I saw of my childhood home. Many of the scratches furrowing its rickety steps were mine, made many years ago, when I would fling open the door in the morning and race down to the yellow-sand path of the garden. The terrace was not glassed in then, but was separated from the outside by a living wall formed by a climbing plant which we used to call morning glory, but which I must later discovered to be convolulus. All summer long the ponderous bumblebees droned around its white, gramophone-shaped flowers.

The door off the terrace opened onto a long, dark hallway. I stepped in feeling confused and uncomfortable, as though I were a porter who, having grown old in disgrace, was now approaching the throne to receive a belated token of royal pardon.

I walked to the end of the hall, where a tarnished mirror hung and bookshelves rose almost to the ceiling on either side. They formed a nook, a quiet, secluded corner where you could forget yourself and sit for hours on end unnoticed by anyone.

What happy hours those were! A modern adult, that is, a person who by force of the conditions of modern life does not learn the truth over the years, but loses it, is incapable of understanding. Today's adult feels that the height of happiness is to take a new lover, or to have a few with congenial drinking buddies. But he has forgotten that there was a time when incomparably greater happiness was within reach: to sequester oneself in a beloved hiding place and, sparked by the magic and significance of that place, to draw from one's own mind astonishingly precious and important images, dreams, and fantasies.

Books helped me to do this in my enchanted kingdom under the mirror. There they were, all perfectly intact; the dust had not even gathered much on them over the years. And there was the most important one of them, with the little gold cross stamped on its spine, wedged into a row with other sturdy brown folios made with the same old-fashioned good worksmanship. It was some German encyclopaedic work like *The Universe and Man*, in which the entire world of nature, art and technology was laid out in chapters, subsections and paragraphs, clarified in glued-in color plates covered with tissue paper, and expounded upon with such exhaustive completeness that not a single question could arise regarding it. As it happens, the tenth volume is devoted to art. I picked it up and it opened of its own accord to the Dürer engraving *Adam and Eve*, which at one time I had scrutinized longer and more often than any of the other illustrations. As in those far-off days, I regarded it with curiosity and amazement. Only this time the reason for these feelings was different. This time I was amazed that the publishers had been unable to sense that this enigmatic image would destroy their foolish intention to squeeze all of Creation into a dozen weighty volumes. Was it possible that these Germans, who believed so fanatically in the omnipotence of science, could really not have noticed that this engraving, which had been created by a German at the beginning of the sixteenth century and which they had so painstakingly reproduced on expensive glossy paper, was a challenge to their lofty tenets? At random I opened another volume. In it were steam engines, slide valves, centrifugal regulators, automobiles, wheels and spokes, all depicted with the same care with which the works of painters and engravers were reproduced in the tenth volume. But if everything concerning the automobiles and castors was perfectly clear, everything concerning the subjects and images of Dürer was not. These personages, who were so like and yet so unlike real people, disturb and intrigue but never yield their secrets. The images were, of course, expounded upon in the text by the usual self-assured art expert analyzing movements, schools, and styles, but whatever this text was, it was manifestly incapable of answering the main question: Where did Dürer get his strange people? The curvaceous Eve, pursing her lips as she takes the fruit from the serpent's snare, fixed in the disconcerted gaze of curlyheaded Adam, at whose feet a mouse is running and over whose head a parrot sits on a branch—these two have punched a hole in the closed labyrinth of the learned text which nothing can patch up, and through which shines such remoteness and unearthliness that something resembling anguish is awakened in our hearts. But it was not this which fascinated me in that engraving when I was a child. I was small and did not aspire to knowledge of which lands were or were not populated by snakes and people, and thus, seeing the portrait of people whom the artist could not possibly have simply dreamed up or extorted from his fingers, I couldn't help but believe that somewhere, sometime, such people had existed. When Dürer was scratching away at that particular metal plate in his free city of Nuremberg, could he have thought that the impression made from it would have such a strong effect on a Russian boy four hundred years later? Oh, this was not at all the same effect that I surrender to now when, overcoming my indolence, I see certain parts of a woman's body and fill them out in my imagination. I have now convinced myself that I understand the reason for that effect, and because of my understanding not just any soft neck or body can get to me! But in spite of the contentions of that despicable fraud of our century—Freudian theory—a child's general interest in the naked body is not in the least an echo of sexual feeling: it is a much more universal sensation which gradually shrinks and disintegrates in the adult; one of its fragments becomes an integral part of sexual attraction. The child's interest is much broader than sexual attraction and is perhaps related to the insuperable curiosity, equally nonspecific in nature, with which we look at wounds and defects or illustrations of internal organs in medical encyclopedias in our early years. It would seem that each of us has experienced this perception and that it should not be difficult to understand. But no, our epoch condemns us to blindness. In childhood we guess the truth, but are unable to bring it within the framework of rigorous concepts and fix it. As we grow up we lose our acuity, inasmuch as from our school days on we begin to deal not so much with life as with its theoretical explanation, which is more biased than ever before, and with its image in art, which is more standardized than ever before. Having left childhood and lost a direct sense of the truth, we find ourselves unable to resist the seduction of mindlessness; we eagerly accept this artificial structure as the original reality, and bid a final farewell to any hope of understanding the meaning of Creation. But in earlier times, when people had not yet acquired civilization with its comfortable lie and still saw everything as it was, they were well acquainted with the word "corporeality." True, you still hear it now and then, but its philosophical significance was lost long ago. It used to be understood in a much broader sense, and at the same time its meaning was more specific. It used to be connected with the interpretation of one of the fundamental components of Existence, the essential nature of which was understood by everyone. Corporeality was opposed to spirituality, and spirituality encompassed all of the divine impulses of the soul. Insofar as everything concerning God was clear then, things were just as clear concerning spirituality, and consequently, the opposite concept—corporeality. In our times, however, when we deny God and believe Man to be nothing more than a complex automaton, we cannot give any reasonable meaning to the concept of spirituality, using it at times to describe a love of reading, at others a passion for art or pensiveness, and as a result the idea of corporeality has lost a well-defined meaning as well. According to our foolish theory, the body, i.e., matter, encompasses everything in existence; however, when we pronounce the common phrase, 'the corporeal side of life,' somewhere in the depths of our memory we recall that it does not refer to all of life after all, but to some lower aspect of it, and associate it with sex, drunkenness, or gluttony—depending on what seems base to us at the moment. We have so narrowed our field of vision that we are obliged to apply the word corporality to any particularly repulsive fragment of corporeality, which has grown in our eyes to the scale of the entire physical world. And only in those first few years of life, when the ideology of antispirituality has not yet insinuated itself into our consciousness, do we perceive corporeality correctly—as some entity which evokes in us a specific curiosity accompanied by a deep sense of illicitness. We feel that this element is not indispensible to our soul, but that while our soul is bound to it we must treat it as a manifestation of the incomprehensibility of the Universal Plan. We often shudder when we encounter corporeality in its unexpected manifestations, regardless of whether or not it is associated with sex. It bothers us when a little boy lets saliva dribble out of his mouth and then draws it in again, when Mama turns her eyelid inside out to remove a speck or asks us to press a spoon on her tongue and look at her throat, and even when our gaze falls on the syringe hanging in the bathroom and a lively imagination draws us a picture of its use. We perceive all this as phenomena of one order—as hints that our material package, with its surface of luminous eyes, soft curls, and fragrant skin has a disgusting underside, which we are more and more frequently obliged to deal with and which we subsequently must learn to tolerate.

Having resurrected this childlike feeling and analyzed it with my adult mind, I understood even more than I had bargained for when I set out. The threshold effect at the beginning of life more than justified my expectations. With as much certainty as in the fact that two plus two make four, I saw: my soul is indeed immortal, and it existed in some other form long before it was obliged to enter my body. And at first it could barely get used to that body.

But my poor soul was not left without aid and support. A seed was planted within it which, as it developed and gained strength, helped my soul to reconcile itself with its initially frightening corporeality. This seed is a foretaste of the harmony of the world as a whole, taken together with its repulsive aspects. Developed to a large scale, it evidently becomes the basis of the ability to of all true artists to be absolutely unsqueamish towards the truth of life. I think that it first germinated in my soul as I gazed at *Adam and Eve*. The genius Dürer prepared just the medicine which I required then. Like a dog which finds the herb his system needs in a field, I sought out this engraving among thousands of other images and nourished my soul with it. As a result, a slow but important change occurred in the depths of my being. Seeing the softened, rounded naked bodies drawn with all the opulence of virgin nature, I became accustomed to the thought that a nude person does not have to be repulsive. This was my first step towards reconciliation with internal organs, physiological processes, and sexuality.

Having awakened in myself childlike sensibilities, I understood something else as well: in those faraway years my soul was adapting itself to conditions that were new to it not only in the sense of overcoming its fear of corporeality, but also in that it had to learn a new language. But it acquired this language in a totally different manner from that described in psychology texts. Today I know what the substance of that training was; in the places where I spent my childhood the truth was revealed to me like a bright sun. It has so firmly engrained itself in my mind that I am not going to rush to write about it. A detailed account will require a great deal of time, and it's already late.

September 28

And so, the truth is as follows:

When we begin our life on earth and our soul settles in our body for a time, it retains a memory of the world from which it came, and is still connected with that world by many threads. But here it must deal with a completely different world. Having become a prisoner of the flesh, it finds that it now has direct access only to a mosaic of sensory signals, and guesses that this will be the only reality presented to it for a long time, and that it will have to adapt itself to this reality. Above all else, adapting oneself signifies learning to decode and interpret. How can this be accomplished? Only, of course, by the same method by which a traveller learns to understand the language of a foreign country. Hearing unfamiliar words, he relates them to words in his native language with the aid of a dictionary or by guesswork, and gradually makes a translation from the foreign tongue into his own. It is just such a translation, but on an immeasurably larger scale, that our soul performs in the first few years of confinement in its envelope of flesh. It correlates that which it observed and learned in the other world with that which it perceives here by means of the senses. Inasmuch as the category of thought, like all other abstract concepts, exists only there, while here there are only collections of spots, sounds, smells, and so forth, such a translation signifies interpretation of the objective world. No means of comprehending material reality other than by relating it to spiritual reality, i.e., with the objects of that world, exists, nor can it. By the simple act of perception we call to life empty sensory structures; they acquire content in the following step, that of translation.

Unless they are correlated with true reality—the objects of the spiritual realm—things in and of themselves are devoid of any meaning and sense. Our statements about things are always allegorical. We are really talking about that which stands behind things, shining through them and giving them content. This correlation can only be accomplished by that entity which knows in advance what the images of things must be correlated with. That entity is our soul.

I have already written about the fact that modern science is inexorably approaching an idea which it has found terrifying—the existence of an immaterial reality. But it is just as inexorably approaching the conclusion that every living organism carries within it from birth extensive, integral images of everything that exists, which are gradually transformed into the sign structure of a language; in other words, it is coming to reluctant recognition of Plato's thesis, "Knowledge is remembrance."

Psychology has met any hint of this idea with the greatest resistance. It is well known that this science was formerly dominated by Locke's concept of man as a "tabula rasa," on which his upbringing and education could inscribe anything at all. The central problem of psychology was considered to be the investigation of the mechanism controlling such an "inscription," a mechanism which, although as yet poorly understood, was assumed to be perfectly concrete and reducible to physico-chemical processes. The scientists promised that the secret of this mechanism would be completely unraveled at any minute. But time passed, and matters remained as they stood. Realizing that it could not remain a plan of action, mottoes, and slogans forever, psychology began to shed its presumptuousness and to consider the problem more seriously. It became evident first of all that it would be necessary to resolve the question as to whether or not the very ability to record something is inscribed from the outside, and second, that the "tabula rasa" theory is refuted by the fact that some children manage to grow up into decent people without the benefit of a wonderful up-bringing. In order to extricate himself from this situation, Lombroso admitted the existence of "innate criminality," thus allowing us to be imprinted not only by our upbringing, but also by fate. This conces-sion proved inadequate, and Freud introduced a pair of new elements which in his opinion are incorporated into us by nature. By exploiting the extremely nebulous definition of these elements and, of course, the privileged position of science, which is not compelled to give an explanation but only the semblance of one, the Freudians were able to make their theory extremely popular. But already one of Freud's pupils, Jung, had begun to doubt that the sex drive and death wish exhausted the inner baggage with which we come into this world, and since then some faction of psychologists is always returning to the Jungian roster of supplementary "archetypes," hoping to find a means of providing some substantiation for their science. However, even this extension does not help; moreover, the reigning ideology regards Jungian primordial psychological elements such as, say, the "drive towards cultural values," with great scorn. One other attempt was made to save the "science of the soul," one which did not expose to doubt that fundamental axiom of material science, the nonexistence of the soul. Having established by experiment certain interesting facts concerning upbringing, a group of scientists founded the movement called "gestalt theory." They contended that a person perceives not a mosaic of sensory signals, which is only a provocative agent, but rather whole images—or gestalts—which are primordial. Remaining loyal to the dogma concerning the nonexistence of the soul, psychologists in this movement made an attempt to explain the appearance of gestalts in the psyche by some kind of physical "fields." However, this effort failed, and after a short-lived success, their concept was choked out. In the meantime, the methods of psychological evaluation were being developed and refined, and an increasingly large quantity of facts began to accumulate. These provided irrefutable evidence that our system of perception does not synthesize complex images from colored dots and sounds, but rather the other way around: it assigns this or that meaning to colored dots and sounds depending on the whole images or representations arising in the conscious or unconscious mind, where they are present in much greater numbers than the Jungian "archetypes." Without posing the question as to precisely what kind of invisible world they had uncovered in man, psychologists state, "A person does not see what is projected onto his retina, but sees that relative to which he knows that this image exists." Consequently, references to the results obtained in gestalt psychology have become increasingly frequent in recent years. Having been burned once, however, scientists are extremely wary and observe an unspoken agreement not to raise the issue of where gestalts reside.

Even more intriguing is the material which has been obtained in fields where its philosophical implications have not yet been recognized, and which as a consequence do not subject it to ideological sensorship. One such field is ethology, the science of animal behavior. Ethologists have shown that the formation of the animal psyche is basically determined by the mechanism of "imprinting" rather than by the appearance of conditioned reflexes, as was formerly asserted by the theoreticians who provided the basis of the "tabula rasa" concept. Its essential features can be illustrated by an example. Let us suppose that a gosling hatches from an egg. It would seem that nature would have made some provision so that it would recognize a goose as its mother. But it has become clear that things are not set up that way. It appears that the gosling will consider the first creature that it sees in this world its mother for its entire life, even if that creature turns out to be a human being. Lawrence, who discovered this phenomenon, called it "imprinting," and was able to explain many features of the development of behavioral reactions in terms of it. He did not, however, reflect upon the philosophical significance of his discovery. This discovery was the fact that the concept of "mother" was available to the gosling prior to any sensory experience, but that it had no *a priori* notion of exactly how "mother" should look. Thus, a highly abstract concept precedes the visual image, imprinting itself on that image and giving it content. And where does all of this take place? In a stupid bird! What could be said about man! He must come into this world overflowing with supersensory psychological entities— theoretical ideas, general notions concerning the structure of Existence, abstract emotions, confused urges—and much more intensively than a gosling, he must immediately begin to bring these into correlation with information from his sensory organs.

There is one other discipline which conducts itself in a manner which is somewhat threatening to the official theory of learning, doing so, it is true, not out of daring but by unawareness. This is semiotics, a rather vague "complex of sign system studies," in which labor linguists, mathematicians, and philosophers who were failures in their own sciences. Semiotics has proclaimed that it consists of three parts: syntax, semantics, and pragmatics. No major doubts arise concerning the first part: it analyzes the rules governing the formulation of texts. The third part deals with the use of texts, and here, too, everything is clear. But this second integral part of semiotics is puzzling. Specialists define semiotics as the science of the meaning of texts, but if we go through the vast literature devoted to problems in semantics with the intention of learning what is meant in this science by "the meaning of a text," we will find that the definition of this central concept of semantics has two completely different variants. According to the first variant, the meaning of one sign system is manifested in the symbols of a second sign system. The definition given by the second variant, cleaned of its verbal chaff, could be formulated approximately as: "Meaning signifies that which people consider to be meaning." The first point of view is manifestly nonsensical, as it leads either to a vicious circle or to the construction of an infinite series of sign systems, and in neither case answers our question. The second variant of the definition, despite one's initial impression, is not tautological. It recognizes that the category of thought is somehow innate in man and, most importantly, that it exists outside of any sign system whatsoever. If it is possible to build a real semiotics, and not a fabrication, it can only be based on this second concept of meaning. But those who embrace it will have to agree with the following statement: "Sensory information has content only when correlated with images which are already present in the soul."

And finally, we must not neglect mathematics. From about the middle of the last century on, this science has been progressively formalized. Nonetheless, despite even the efforts of such a great mathematician as Gilbert, attempts to translate it into an algorithmic structure have failed. As specialists unanimously concede, the value and intelligibility of any mathematical formalism are determined by whether or not it has an interpretation. In mathematics, "interpretation" is taken to mean a theoretical set model, i.e., a set, the elements of which are denoted by the symbols of a given formal system. But what meaning should be assigned to the notion of "set"? Apparently, it is taken in the "old" Kantian sense of "the many in one." It is well known, however, that this concept cannot be formalized and is open only to intuition. Here, too—that is, in the most fundamental realm of knowledge, which is the basis of all the "exact sciences,"—comprehension is nothing other than a comparison with innate integral images.

September 30

I shall now write about the most important thing that I realized in Malakhovka, in the room with beamed walls where I spent several years of my life which seemed like centuries.

There I realized what love is. And I realized that there is a God.

In the first phase of its confinement on earth, the soul is not yet living in a high-security prison, but in a temporary cell with numerous cracks and holes in the wall. If he dissects his memory, each one of us will find an echo of one of those mysterious moments in childhood when for no apparent reason his heart began to throb with joy or anguish, when a landscape seen for the first time seemed unexpectly old and familiar or vice versa, when a well-known place suddenly changed into one which was alien and frightening. This was the homeland which already seemed to us to belong to the netherworld, glimpsed through the gap in the new fence; one detail after another of its fortuitous image superimposed itself on what we beheld in this world, driving us to despair. Later, when we had grown a little, nothing was the same: the cracks were patched up, and we became accustomed to projecting onto any thing of this world only the remembrance of something of another world which was correlated with it. It is these remembrances that make it possible for us to exist in this world of dead matter which is inimical to our soul, since they create the illusion that we are not visiting, but at home.

But these memories fade, the inner light which lets us see people, nature, and objects in colored dots dims, and were there no compensation, man would be condemned to regress until he had, in fact, become an automaton, as science has painted him from the moment of its inception. How such automatons look is well known to those who have encountered schizophrenics suffering from the syndrome of psychic automatism. God forbid that anyone become such a marionette, having lost all intuition, missing the inner meaning of phenomena, devoid of moral standards, incapable of understanding a metaphor, a stranger to humor, and—worst of all—continually aware of the aimlessness of his own existence. If this does not happen to us, it is only because our soul, unbeknownst to us and primarily while we sleep, visits certain regions of its spiritual home and gathers fresh impressions there. The part of the Spiritual Kingdom which remains accessible to it, which it will scan with greedy eyes, restoring the clarity of its thoughts and feelings, depends to a large degree on where it became accustomed to wandering in the first years of its imprisonment, when sleep took up more than half of life and these visits were especially frequent, since the intensive process of comprehending the physical world, i.e., of interpreting sensory indicators by means of supersensory images, was underway, and these images could be obtained only there. This explains the fact, highly familiar to psychologists and pedagogues, that the spiritual orientation of an individual is closely bound up in the character of his experiences in early childhood. If in this period a child must give content to phenomena corresponding to a given group of supersensory notions with particular frequency, his soul finds its way to precisely the region in the spiritual world in which these concepts reside, and this becomes a habitual and well-beaten path.

My grandmother, who was with me in my early childhood in that room with the beamed walls, made my soul beat a path to the highest point in the Spiritual Kingdom, from which one could look down at will and see all of its boundaries and understand the nature of Creation as a whole. Thanks to her, my first experience was that of love, and there Love is set on the heights.

I am saying this not to give the impression that because of the happy influence of my grandmother I grew into a good, sensitive, and compassionate person, that I loved those around me, saw only the good in them, and was ready to sacrifice myself for their sake. Nothing resembles me less than the image of such a man. I have lived my life odiously; in it there has been much maliciousness, envy, pettiness, and selfishness. Nonetheless, looking back I can pronounce the same words that are written in the diary of Lev Tolstoy: "At least, in spite of all of the banality and meanness of my youth, God has not abandoned me, and though near old age, I have begun, if ever so little, to understand and love Him."

Her love brought my soul into the house of our great Creator, from which alone the beginnings of love are received, and then only by he who regards this love as a trust confided to him for the period of his life on earth. This had most important consequences for me. Having soared to such heights in my childhood, my soul was forever imprinted with the soft landscape of some beautiful homeland, and that dim image arose from my memory at many critical junctions of my life, exerting a decisive influence on the pathway chosen. Not infrequently I made the choice against my own will and, as I was convinced at the time, against my own best interest. It is only now that I realize how salutory these decisions prompted by my soul's memories of the House of the Lord were, and how sad it is that in some instances I did not heed its urging.

Wise men of many times and peoples have affirmed one thing: love is the striving of the soul toward God. But we, supposedly educated people, have ignored the wisdom of the ages and the truth verified by the inner experience of all of mankind, and proclaim that love is "the reflection of sexual attraction in upper levels of the psyche." The scientific era began with the placement of Man on the pedestal in the place of the God Who had been cast down, and ended with what could have been foreseen from the very beginning: Man has been trampled in the mud. Man began to be represented not only as an animal, but as the most wanton, aggressive, and lustful of all animals. Now, it is true, scientists are softening their judgement, and pronounce obscure phrases about the lofty impulses of human nature, but all this is hypocrisy and playing with the public, for the ideological platform of science is powerless to explain the origin and nature of such impulses. Is it not time that we stop placing our faith in science, which has encountered nothing but impasses everywhere it has turned, and take hold of our own minds?

Now I understand: the irritation with science that had been building up in me for the last few years, with its arrogance and evasiveness, was nothing other than a subverted struggle to free my mind from a lie. And several days ago the abcess burst. . . .

It is not necessary to seek the greatest truths of this world in books—they lie in plain sight of everyone. And one of them is that love is the striving of the soul toward God, toward the being which it holds most dear. Apart from the ancient philosophers and all religious scholars, this is confirmed by our very language: a synonym of the word "to love" is the word "to worship"*—to see God in the object of one's love, to consider him God's representative on earth. Love is the most direct result of the existence of God. If sometimes we do not realize this and suppose that our love is related to a certain person, then it is simply because our Creator planned it that way. We are sent to this world to carry out some unfathomable purpose provided for in His supreme plan, and because of this we should not be distracted during the course of our life on earth from the substance of our activity here—from the structure perceived by our senses. At the same time, to work with these structures while entirely on their level is foolish. To avoid being caught in such a closed circle, we have been given the "imprinting" mechanism: although we ourselves are unaware of this, it permits us to relate to sensory images as we do to supersensory images, that is, we operate with them according to the higher laws of the world of ideals. But imprinting is not inflexible. Having mastered the new language of sensory signals, the soul can, if necessary, change the system by which objects from this world are correlated with those from the other, It is to be expected that the objects from the highest levels of the other world should have the greatest capacity for transcorrelation. They are more essential to our soul than anything else, and consequently must not be exposed to the threat that would arise if we were to correlate them with strictly defined objects, which can always pass out of our lives. These powerful behavioral stimulators must be triggered by sensory images at the most critical points of the objective world, and since these points change as we fulfill our mission on earth, it is essential that these stimulators be highly mobile.

Love, that is, the drive toward God, is a particularly potent stimulator, and as such it is more mobile than any other. Like a guiding star, it wanders the world, flaring up now behind one object, now behind another, and obliges us to marry, plant trees, raise children, and defend our country. Love is not only the strongest, but also the most universal stimulator, essentially because it is our great Creator Himself who, concealing himself in some earthly guise, incites us to self denial and labor.

But this striving toward God is not imprinted in us if in our childhood we do not sense the presence of someone who loves us and is good to us. In order to translate into its own language and perceive the love which is directed to us, our soul must secretly come into contact with God, the original source of love and forgiveness; it

---

*Obozhat—"to worship" is based on the word "Bog" which means God [tr.].

reminds us later of our frequent visits to His abode, and it induces nostalgia—that is, our own love for someone or something we have known. The contribution made by adults who freely love us at the beginning of our lives to the structure of our personality is not love itself, but its principal forerunner—a consciousness that there is Someone with Whom one is very happy and without Whom one is miserable. Even if this consciousness becomes a pretense, it will still break through to the surface from time to time in the form of lofty urges and aspirations, no matter how it has been stifled and driven under by circumstances. And this Someone becomes familiar to our soul only if we are surrounded in infancy by love which demands nothing in return. Humanity stands on a great relay race: in order to be able to love in adulthood, one must be the object of someone's love in childhood.

But how can we repay this advance credit?

It sometimes happens that the people who gave it to us pass out of our lives, and we are unable to repay them. But it is possible that there is some hidden wisdom in this. After all, the love which they gave us did not really belong to them, but to the One who is the source of all souls.

And it is best to repay the debt directly to Him.

In order to do this, it is necessary above all else to be a steward of one's soul. It is, after all, His own immaterial property which is placed in us, and when He gives it to us for our use, He not only wishes that it be returned, but, as the Gospel scriptures concerning talents clearly state, He hopes that there will be an increase in the capital.

But being a steward of one's soul is impossible without first purging it of lies. The greatest lie of modern times is the thesis of the nonspirituality of the world, the propaganda of science. That means that I have no choice.

It means that I will have to break away from the science on which I was raised, and become a renegade with respect to it. Well, so be it. After all, it is infinitely more terrible to be a traitor to the God Who created me.

April 5, 1978

The Uncomfortableness
of Culture[*]
by Leonid Batkin

To many people—and one encounters even certain professional philosophers among them—"culture" is synonymous with something reliable and stable. Such names as the Parthenon, Shakespeare. and Pushkin have a reassuring ring precisely because they are eternal, fashioned in marble and bronze. Behind their walls is silence and majesty; there is no place for ambiguity, doubts, and shrill voices.

"Culture" is that with which it is pleasant to agree.

Who would think of arguing with Bach or the Cologne cathedral?

This does not mean—although, perhaps, some may disagree—that we are speaking, heaven forbid, of some sort of chrestomathean polish or of habitual reverence for the glorious dead.

O yes, a characteristic feature of the modern ritual by which culture is "acquired" is that it is treated as a "living thing." Therefore, it is entirely permissible to argue intelligently—not with Bach, of course, but about Bach—or even to confess that the Mona Lisa leaves one cold. This is not a bad thing; it serves as an indication of the staidness or, on the other hand, the trustful spontaneity—in short, of the authenticity of one's relationship to culture. Such arguments and confessions, whether they take place at tea or on the pages of academic journals, are always attended by a pleasant feeling of security. It is not the same as asking the Commodore's statue to dinner. . . .

It would seem as though culture were a peculiarly human means of harmonizing soul-wrenching extremes of unkempt naturalism and unenlightened socialization. Such culture is acquired, along with an education, good books, records and albums of art reproductions. It is expected to make a person a respectable and well-educated individual, and to permit him to attain, if only within himself, some comfortable position amid universal tribulation.

[*] Translated by Christina Dodds-Ega.

On a corresponding level this really becomes a *spiritual* problem. That is, it concerns nothing other than spiritual comfort. How can one not sympathize with the desire of good people to preserve consciousness similar to their own from the whispered temptations of the snake whose whispers carry risk of a philosophical Fall and expulsion from Paradise into the unknown of history? They wish to hide from the poetry of "demonism" raging outside their windows, from the lawless reconsideration of fundamental principles of existence and thought which are above all criticism.

And thus "culture" becomes something like an amulet!

Naturally, the learned specialists in culture couch all this in the most profound terms possible. Nevertheless, in the final analysis, culture is frequently viewed as the mast to which Odysseus asked to be bound in order to resist the voices of the sirens. Our consciousness must be fastened down at one point, and must at all costs remain immobile.

If we consider the reassurance attainable in culture as a "higher degree" of harmony, it is not difficult to guess that culture cannot be presumed to be other than ready-made and complete. Culture is more or less identified with tradition. It is crystallized in cultural norms and forms, such as "moral precepts" or (invariably "great!") "works of art." History is an adventure bound by force to such culture which the latter, with its natural inclination toward decorous crystallization, opposes with revulsion at every opportunity. Any crises or upheavals in culture, any violations of its measured harmony are, from this perspective, anticultural and merely show that the nihilistic forces of "pure" naturalism and "pure" socialization not infrequently meet with some success.

Such an approach to culture entails not the slightest logical requirement for culture to be based *on creation*. On the contrary, the structure of the conservative/preservationist approach inevitably rejects out of hand anything that creates disorder, anything uncompromisingly critical, angular, or red-hot, anything whose ultimate results are unpredictable, anything strange and anomalous—in fact, anything which is ambiguous and which remains intrinsically problematical, open, and tragic.

At the same time we hear a great deal about the "tragedy of culture!" This, however, concerns only that which is peripheral to culture, only that which is created by it and not the creative process itself—in short, the extracultural tragedy of circumstances, but not tragedy as the definition of culture itself, essential to its viability, not the tragedy which culture worthy of the name must and inevitably does bring into the world.

For culture, considered with its creative and fertile sides and not in its simply reproductive aspect, as the human capacity to experiment mentally, to imagine that which does not yet exist or even that which cannot exist, to regard everything as subject to change and, in so doing, to change oneself, becoming an authentic historical subject—such cultured culture is, of course, distinguished by high tragedy. Everywhere it strives to destroy stereotypes, polish, equilibrium, and upsets the established order; in a word, it creates problems rather than solving them. Moreover, culture deals with things not of secondary, but of primary importance to the universe; that is, it entails a mortal risk. It presents an individual with fundamental questions and incites him to answer them as though no answers had previously been found. When Blok stated that the purpose of poetry is to bring harmony into the world's chaos, this indeed meant that the poet conducts himself precisely as though no harmony existed before him. Before each poet, before each poem, before each act of cultural creation, the world is seen still shrouded in the mists of dawn, and the poet, like an Old Testament Adam, is the first to give a name to Creation. The philosopher or physicist, moreover, proceed in exactly the same way, and those ideas which are "insufficiently absurd to be true" are, in fact, ideas which are insufficiently cultural.

To be a cultured individual is to distinguish oneself by a "strange and dangerous mania for solving every question from the beginning" (which means from one's *own, personal* beginning). Furthermore: "The very *word* which seems perfectly clear when we hear or use it in everyday speech . . . becomes fabulously puzzling and acquires a strange intractability . . . as soon as we remove it from circulation so as to examine it in and of itself." As the target of "monstrous philosophical importunity," time and life are "transformed into an unfathomable mystery that torments the intellect." It must not be thought that Paul Valery disagreed with Blok. On the contrary, they said something quite similar. There is no "harmony" unless "the unfathomable" is revealed where everything is "absolutely clear." Any cultural pursuit is conducted "barbarously" and "monstrously"; that is, as something coming from the outside and subject to no rules. All is forgotten.

But what does it mean to "forget" tradition, indeed, is it possible for a cultured person to forget, does this ever really occur? Let us reassure ourselves, it does not. He who wishes to express an opinion will find every opportunity to do so through the previously expressed opinions which have grown in on all sides (M. M. Bakhtin wrote about this admirably). Therefore we barbarously wish to forget only that which we remember too well. At the same time, forgetting is a response—a question, an objection, an act of insolence, a misinterpretation. It is impossible to break cleanly and directly through to life across the accumulated thickness of *that which has become culture*, to pick out mute life in the murmur of human voices. But it is also impossible for *culture in the making* not to break through. It goes without saying that one must be sufficiently knowledgeable so as not to simplemindedly adopt others' ready-made answers as one's own, that one must master one's larynx to strengthen one's own voice, and that one must nevertheless disentangle oneself from all that ("swallow an ocean of books and disgorge it again").

Culture is constrained to deal with culture; as Midas turned everything he touched to gold, so culture turns everything it touches into itself (for example, any nostalgia for the primitive, "natural" way of life—from the ancient and Renaissance pastorales to Rousseau and Tolstoy—immediately transforms the simple life into a purely cultural and highly complex experience). However, if no open space remained, if it were all choked by culture, culture would have no place to grow. ("Everything has been said already.")

There is no way out but to forget. To rest the whole weight of modernity on tradition is to negate it. Either we hear things in the works of the past which the poets and composers creating them could not have heard, that is, we cease to remember the original thought; or else we throw out a challenge to tradition. In one way or another, involuntarily or consciously, creative people treat the classics unceremoniously (uncreative people behave in a like manner only if they are unaware that they are dealing with classics). And in so doing they give them new life. The Futurists boyishly catcall Pushkin as though he were present in the same room at an evening reading of his poetry. The clamor raised by the Futurists could not have pleased the tactful Blok, but he came to their defense, rightly asserting that he was acting on Pushkin's behalf. "They are insulting him in a new way, and he is becoming closer in a new way. . . . Being insulted in the name of something new is not at all the same as being insulted in the name of the old, even though the new was still unknown (but, after all, it always is) and the past, great and famous. Because insulting in the name of something new is more difficult and more responsible."

Thus, only that which is forgotten is remembered. The familiar semiotic background (tradition) is renewed, thanks to disturbances whose novelty, in turn, takes on meaning only against this background (as Tynyanov has shown). Out of the revolt against "culture" (that is, *always* against *old* culture, although it often takes the form of a revolt against "culture in general"—such as that of the new left . . . or that of Leo Nikolaevich Tolstoy) may come nothing clear, but occasionally something does emerge—specifically, new culture. Heaven knows if anything will come of the little savage Huckleberry, although in the case of Sid the outcome is clear in advance. One thing that has never produced anything is respect for "norms and forms." Tom Sawyer's aunt taught him to be a clean and obedient boy. There was not, generally speaking, anything wrong with what he was taught, but it bore no relation to culture.

We may suppose that a measure of conformity is invariably present in creative culture—and is even fruitful, but only as one of the conflicting voices (impulses, logic, semiotic functions) raised within it, and one which does not drown out the rest. If the drive for order demands that the "monstrous importunities" be beaten back from the threshold, order will undoubtedly be established, but I fear that in the final analysis this will have been accomplished by acultural means.

In no way does the above signify that the new is always right and appealing or that it is wrong to champion the old; it does not endorse any particular position, but rather means that the argument remains authentically cultural only so long as it continues, which it does indefinitely when it involves not abstract, externalized idea/results, but subjective and, *consequently*, equal consciousnesses which are rooted in the historical socinum of culture and which no one and no thing, not even death, can suppress. From this perspective, the very comparison of "the new" and "the old" as such comes into play in an argument in which they are synchronized by principle.

The essential thing is neither the approval or rejection of the new, nor the approval or rejection of the old, but the occurrence of dialogue, i.e., the recognition of another position, even one which is antipathetic, as a real, unsolved *problem*, as another's *truth* and, as a corollary, the acceptance of one's own pet truth as open and incomplete.

From this ("Bakhtinesque") angle, the numerous works of Yu. N. Davidov, criticizing the "new leftists" and the whole crisis of Western culture during the past century, appear to miss the point. The very tone and texture of these writings aim to show the unreality of others' thoughts and sufferings from the didactic heights of the one and only possible position, that taken by the author. In these writings there is "only one subject who apprehends and speaks. . . . Opposite him is nothing but a mute object" (Bakhtin). A learned classification of the mute objects is carried out, the ideological thread upon which this or that puppet hangs is analyzed together with the "orientation" of this or that text—interpreted not through other texts, but through an external, objective reality. Everyone gets his share—Wagner and the "Frankfort school," Heidegger, and Thomas Mann. This would be excusable if Yu. N. Davidov had exchanged insults with them—but he only dishes insults out without listening. The author is not the least bit interested in mentally sharing their difficult path, and much less in sharing that of the "new leftists" before parting ways with them; in other words, he does not care to deal with them as Worthy and Equal subjects. Their problems are denied the status of real spiritual and creative dilemmas, and are considered as some sort of cheap intellectual devices or as bastardizations. For this reason Yu. N. Davidov emerges easily as the victor—perhaps too easily, never having solved even his own ideological problem, if the latter is to be understood as a true argument and not as "universal methods of 'debunking' " (a felicitous expression of Yu. N. Davidov's). Anything alive and polysemantic is made grounds for one and the same pathologico-anatomical diagnosis: "the absence of daytime hues." What is unfortunate is not that the diagnosis is much too categorical or that it greatly oversimplifies its object, but that it is applied to culture precisely as though the latter were an object and that the diagnostic, (prosecutory) means of analysis casts doubt on the cultural reality of the author's own consciousness, which presents itself as the "one and only," and which shares no borders with other consciousness.

Disagreements concerning Bakhtin's statement that culture is located "on a boundary" are remarkably frequent. Some feel that this refers to the boundary separating the "human" from the "nonhuman" or "superhuman"; others suppose that it concerns the rift which, according to the well-known phrase of Heine, "extends across the heart of the poet." But Bakhtin's thought has nothing in common with moralistic rhetoric. The moralists seek a frontier beyond the limits of culture such that culture is placed on a foreign boundary, face to face with extracultural categories. For Bakhtin, however, culture (as well as personality) is located entirely *on its own boundary*, that is, on a boundary with *another culture*: "boundaries cross it everywhere and at every moment." "Boundedness," according to Bakhtin, is an internal definition of culture, which does not have its "own" closed territory: the "cultural atom" exists only in dialogue and, "removed from boundaries, it becomes hollow and arrogant, degenerates, and dies."

Characteristic of the moralist approach, culture is not examined from the inside, with respect to itself, but only in relation to nature, the sociuum, or whatever; a place is sought for it in the outside world, its role is specified, it is worried over and bound up with hopes for organizing life. In short, this approach does not analyze the problem of culture, but problems with culture. Sociality is correspondingly understood not as the edification (functioning) of culture, but as its cause or instigation as the external medium in which it must carry out a humanistic mission. For that mission to be fulfilled, it is essential that culture be regarded as felicitous, impervious, and gracious. "Culture" is eagerly associated with the noble cobwebs of bygone eras, and with harmonious classicism (a name applied to that which no longer elicits a feeling of risk and which is not unavoidably problematic) in particular. One likes to think one can warm oneself by "culture" as one would by the family hearth. Only culture must first be defended from any historically introduced elements which might make it strange and uncomfortable in any way.

We have thus observed for some time the humanly understandable battle which some humanitarians goodheartedly wage against classical philosophy and, most particularly, against science, whose rationalism, in their eyes, lacks warmth and sympathy for the difficulties confronting the individual. However, they wrongly identify the "extrapersonal" and "extramoral" objective form of scientific thought with the lofty moral and emotional demands which it undoubtedly makes on it on this account (with guarantees which are, it is true, historically contradictory and not unconditional, as are all cultural guarantees).

In general, some people like to think that there is always something superfluous in thought and culture which it would be in the best interests of culture to do without. Sometimes they propose discarding that which is subconscious and fantastic or chimerical, sometimes that which is excessively sensual, sometimes "soulless" systematicization, rationality, and so forth. Now it is the "dark" Middle Ages that must be rejected, now the godless, practical analyticism of the modern world. Of course, everyone has his own taste. However, *culture* as we understand it today (as the theoretical idealization of the capacity for creation and self-realization established in the cultural empyrean) needs *all* possible cultures, past and present, *all* human inclinations and "fundamental forces" (Marx); for the paradox of culture lies only in the attractions and antagonisms of these forces, in their mutual provocation within the human mind, which provides the stimulus for historical movement.

The greatest possible participation in itself, an endless dialogue — this is what culture demands; it is effectively emasculated by any mechanical reduction or arbitrary exclusion from the inner debate. But how afraid we are to linger in the crosscurrent! How we flee what Hofmannstal called "the paladion of refutability"! How we rush to reduce the unknown to the familiar and the complex to the simple! Culture, in contrast, invariably transforms the simple into the complex and the familiar into the unknown.

Perhaps, however, analyzing culture as a paradox makes it too much the realm of the elite? On the contrary, if culture consists of high standards and great models to which one must aspire, that is, if culture is more or less replaceable by education and so on, then a hierarchy of those demanding and "knowing" culture is inevitable. However, it is impossible to "know" culture; one never knows it, one creates it. Does this mean that culture is attained only by those who create? Yes. It is, however, evident that it is created not only by the individual who writes the music or who stages a play, but also by the individual who hears and sees it—under the condition that hearing or seeing becomes an event (a difficulty or problem) which triggers a chain reaction in his own heart and mind, from which he emerges in some way renewed. Herein lies the stern democracy of culture: it demands only a lifegiving spiritual effort, only the ability to be astounded, and makes no other conditions.

If we are to describe the phenomenon of culture in semiotic terms, then, according to the definition of Yu. M. Lotman, culture is a structure with at least two fundamentally different "languages" in which the transcodification of information concerning the universe from one language into the other is essential but, at the same time, almost impossible. But what structural basis can we give to the *necessity for several languages*, with each language appearing incorrect and inadmissable with respect to the next? Why, in particular, incorporate this requirement for misunderstanding, gaps, and "senseless ideas" into a semiotic structure concerned (by definition) with *understanding?* Understanding becomes cultural only through the process of surmounting misunderstanding, a process which always remains indefinitive and incomplete. In the process of impossible-possible translation into another "language" (that is, on the boundary with another language), each individual language attempts to exceed its own limits and under the strain it becomes alienated, a problem for itself. In this manner a language acquires the possibility of fundamental renewal (and not by a simple replacement of one set of signs by their opposites). But this is obviously "not necessary" for the functioning of the language. It is necessary not for the "composer of the message" or for the "recipient," but for the subject of culture, for which the development of its subjective capacity is a self-contained human historical task. At this point a question arises concerning the limitations of a purely semiotic approach. First and foremost, it is appropriate to assume that culture in the strict sense of the term implies not merely any semiotic system, but only one in which the particular function of self-renewal is in the foreground, and not the function of stabilization and reproduction of the system itself and of that which can be expressed within the limits of available logic (we shall call this second function "civilization"). However, as Yu. M. Lotman correctly observes, genuinely new communication by means of an old code is impossible. It would therefore seem that culture, strictly speaking, is not at all some sort of semiotic structure or ready-made, available model which functions normatively; culture is the elusive moment of transition from one structure to another. It is comparable to God in negative theology: its center is everywhere, its periphery, nowhere. The task of semiotics is to determine whether the dialectical doctrine of culture can be interpreted in the internal logic space of semiotics or whether, alternatively, the very definition of the concept of "semiotic structure" is elucidated on its boundary with the concept of "culture."

Only this second function had a noticeable system-forming role in the self-consciousness of all traditional—that is, pre–sixteenth or pre–seventeenth century—societies in Western Europe, and *in this sense*, culture is a very recent human discovery, a discovery which, in the final analysis, belongs to the twentieth century. Before recent and modern times, of course, the cultural function was fulfilled, but in the first place, on the scale of epochs comprising many centuries, not on that of the lifespan of an individual human being; in the second place, to the extent to which it was observed, the novel was interpreted and sanctioned solely as a renovation of the old; in the third place, each culture (this term is restricted here to its descriptive phenomenological meaning) considered itself the best and latest: the one unique culture. Therefore its dialogue with other cultures (including its own heritage), if not reduced to nothing by rejection or pseudomorphism, was partial, impoverished, and hindered. (This was, for instance, true of the incorporation of Near Eastern culture into the culture of ancient Greece, or of the latter into medieval European culture. Before modern European times or even our era, the *problem of culture*, or culture as a problem, did not exist. The elucidation of this situation in Soviet scholarship is primarily associated with the work of M. M. Bakhtin and a few others (we will make special mention here of V. S. Bibler's book, *Thought as Creation*). In the traditional opposition "culture—nature," the moment of creation remained in the background precisely because it indiscriminately colored all order-seeking human activity. The ferment which provides the color was not revealed and intensified. Only in the historically recent opposition "culture—civilization"—that is, with the demand for further internal differentiations of the concept of culture, capable of explaining a new and unheard-of mode of historical movement—has culture become a problem with respect to itself. The problem of culture arose along with *universalism*, a quality which also existed incompletely and covertly earlier in world history and which likewise became a specific discovery of the twentieth century.

The crux of the matter is not only in the well-known fact that the catastrophic (for the traditional consciousness) rapidity of historical change has irrevocably destroyed and disrupted the "normal" smooth relationship between the factions of culture and civilization, creation and reproduction, and sharpened this relationship to a paradox which is painfully telling from time to time on this or that function. Most important is the fact that for the first time modern culture has ceased (or is ceasing) to consider itself the greatest and latest, feels itself to be open on all sides, provides a place within itself for any significant, unusual cultural configurations of the past and present, is straining to gaze toward the future, and basing the claim of its own uniqueness only on a multiplicity of languages and on a previously unheard-of dialogue. The arguments as to "which art is higher" or "which is better, art or science" or "will theater survive in competition with cinema" and so forth, have died down (are dying down). Hierarchical, dogmatic thinking is vanishing (will vanish?).

Eurocentrism still makes itself felt in the recent attempts to nobly "elevate" non-European cultures by transferral of concretely European historical concepts instead of trying to understand their equal specificity, their "truth." This naïve Europocentrism has, however, been made obsolete by the development of a specifically European type of culture, on whose ground a consciously dialogistic comparison of cultures has just become possible. Europeanism, of course, has ceased to be a geographical or regional concept (in the "East" much has arisen that is "Western"; in the "West" there is quite a lot that is "Eastern"). Only in the West, however, did both "West" and "East" first come into themselves. The matter has progressed from a sum of national and regional monologues to the global polyphony of the third millenium, to "unity, not as a *naturally* unique entity, but a dialogistic unity of two or several *harmoniously* nonblending voices" (Batkhtin).

Culture is not so very fragile and vulnerable; it has an iron stomach. "Civilization" (which, by the way, we do not mean in any derogatory sense, so long as the relationship between civilization and culture remains normally difficult and dramatic—in other words, cultural) is either the inertly traditionalistic elements which have not been drawn into culture or culture which has settled and become immobilized and assimilated. But culture has the capacity to lend contemporary sharpness to the archaic and to recycle its own sediments, the tamed phenomena of "mass culture," transforming them into voices in its own polyphony. In a truly cultural context everything finds a place—a chastooshka* becomes "The Twelve",† Hollywood sentimentality and stunts become Chaplin films. Culture not only survives civilization, but could not live a moment without it, without parodying it, refining it, catching up everything which is characteristic of it. Civilization is the wilderness sanctuary of culture. Culture finds some use and benefit in everything, provided it has some sort of living sense. Only with dead things can it do nothing.

Let us not defend culture. Rather, let us try not to hinder it.

Moscow, March, 1978

*folk ditty [tr.].
†A well-known poem by Aleksandr Blok [tr.].

Fetters*
by Genrikh Sapgir

*Translated by H. William Tjalsma. Graphics by Anatoly Brusilovsky.

It's not for us to be free, to awaken
and touch the mouth of someone dear with our hand.
Fetters everywhere . . . And we lilliputians,
where do we get the faith, we Gullivers?

Yes, we took upon ourselves the responsibilities.
Circumstances caught us in our own net.
The best minds get tangled up in that . . .
We're not slaves—we're more like slobs.

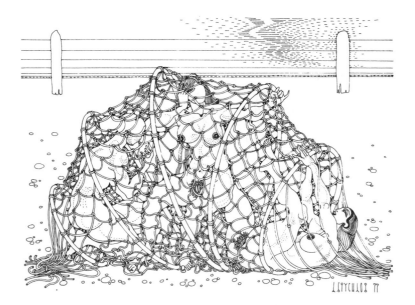

"Be thee cursed, individual!" Look,
our Socrates, what you've dreamed up,
as if we're all restrained like schizos!"
You got tangled up yourself in your own metaphysics!

Where will I haul this weight?
I'm no martyr, but somehow I became one.
All my life—under a stone. And when I die
The stone will become my pedestal.

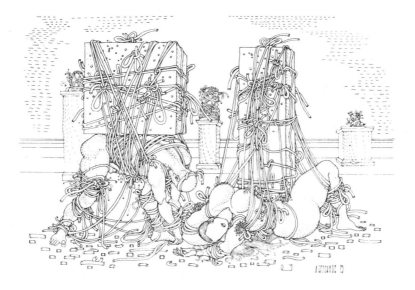

We're all in the same harness—one family.
Kill him? But then he's me!
And I suffer so,
falling into myself.

Neither live nor think differently.
You're tied to family and house,
to the earth, to neighbors, and old stool . . .
You, you're in a very nice cage.

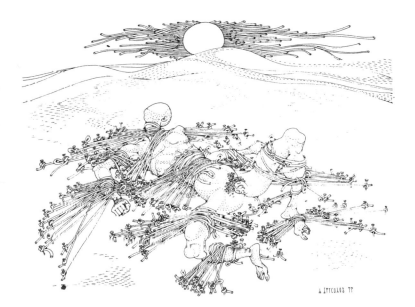

I'm like Prometheus, perhaps,
but I love my suffering.
Moreover, I've got a diversion:
Imagining that I am free.

To break the bonds
is to be born again.
He alone is free
who frees himself.

AUTHORS

BELLA AKHMADULINA, born 1937, poet, verse translator
VASILY AKSYONOV, born 1932, prose writer
YUZ ALESHKOVSKY, born 1929, poet, prose writer, screenwriter
ARKADY ARKANOV, born 1933, prose writer, playwright
LEONID BATKIN, born 1932, cultural historian
ANDREI BITOV, born 1937, prose writer, screenwriter
FRIDRIKH GORENSHTEIN, born 1932, prose writer, screenwriter
FAZIL ISKANDER, born 1929, prose writer, poet
YURI KARABCHIYEVSKY, born 1938, poet, prose writer
PYOTR KOZHEVNIKOV, born 1953, prose writer
YURI KUBLANOVSKY, born 1947, poet
SEMYON LIPKIN, born 1913, poet, verse translator
INNA LISNYANSKAYA, born 1924, poet, verse translator
YEVGENY POPOV, born 1946, prose writer, playwright
VASILY RAKITIN, born 1937, art critic
YEVGENY REIN, born 1936, poet, verse translator, screenwriter
MARK ROZOVSKY, born 1937, playwright, director
GENRIKH SAPGIR, born 1928, poet, playwright
VIKTOR TROSTNIKOV, born 1928, physicist
BORIS VAKHTIN, born 1930, prose writer, verse translator, Sinologist
ANDREI VOZNESENSKY, born 1933, poet
VLADIMIR VYSOTSKY, 1937–1980, poet, actor, songwriter, balladeer
VIKTOR YEROFEYEV, born 1946, prose writer, critic